THE CONFESSIONS OF
Jean-Jacques Rousseau

THE CONFESSIONS OF
Jean-Jacques
Rousseau

THE ANONYMOUS TRANSLATION INTO ENGLISH
OF 1783 & 1790 REVISED AND COMPLETED
BY A. S. B. GLOVER, WITH
A NEW INTRODUCTION BY MR. GLOVER

Illustrations by William Sharp

New York THE HERITAGE PRESS

CONTENTS

INTRODUCTION

Two of the world's outstandingly great books have as their title *The Confessions*. One, the work of an African, was written in Latin; the other, that of a Swiss, in French.

At the moment of crisis which marked the collapse of the Classical world, as the material culture and moral assurances of Mediterranean civilization were crumbling before the twofold onslaught of barbarian arms and Christian ideals, a Christian bishop, Augustine of Hippo, wrote what, for all we know, was the first of autobiographies: the first, at any rate, to be concerned rather with inner emotion than with outward achievement. For over a thousand years it stood alone. Perhaps the Christian believer of the ages of faith felt little need or desire to attempt self-justification before his fellows and posterity; for justification to his God his confession was not a matter to be committed to parchment or paper. The *Life of Herself* by Teresa of Avila, Augustine's fellow-saint; George Fox's *Journals;* Bunyan's *Grace Abounding*, are, save for Montaigne, whose secular introspection stands apart, almost the only autobiographical accounts of inward experience written between the fifth and the eighteenth centuries to retain a place in literary memory; and all these are less records of self-searchings than of what their authors felt to be God's work done in and through their means. But, with the advent of humanism, romanticism was round the corner; men were coming to find an interest in themselves and in each other less as pilgrims of eternity than as partakers in a human society whose prime concern was no longer with supernatural values, but with natural virtue — or vice — and with reason rather than faith. The change is reflected and summarized in a comparison between the second sentence of Rousseau's book and the second of Augustine's. "I mean to lay open to my fellow-mortals," says Jean-Jacques, "a man just as nature wrought him; and this man is myself." "Man," says the Bishop of Hippo, "who is a part of what Thou hast created, desireth to praise Thee; yes, man, who carrieth his mortality about with him, the proof of his sin, and the testimony of this, that Thou, O God, dost resist the proud."

Jean-Jacques Rousseau, who describes in the *Confessions* the first fifty-three years of his own life, was the son of a watchmaker whose family, coming originally from Paris, had settled in Geneva in the middle of the sixteenth century. When Jean-Jacques was ten years old his father, in consequence of a quarrel, left the city, and an uncle placed the boy at Bossey with a M. Lambercier, a Protestant clergyman, to be educated. Here he remained for over two years, but then, on being unjustly accused of breaking a comb, he returned to Geneva, and for a few months lived with his uncle till his future should be decided on. He was apprenticed first to an attorney, who soon dismissed him for stupidity, and after that to an engraver, with whom he remained for three years, until one evening, on returning from a walk beyond the city gates, he found them shut on him. Fearing punishment if he went back to his master, he wandered about for several days until, through an introduction given him by a priest with an eye for a possible convert, he met Mme. de Warens at her house at Annecy. The story of his relations with his "Mamma" is one of the main threads of the *Confessions*.

At the suggestion of an acquaintance of his patroness, he was sent to an institution for catechumens at Turin, where he abjured the Protestant faith. After being admitted to the Catholic Church, he was given a small sum of money and turned loose to shift for himself. He became personal servant in succession to the Comtesse de Vercellis and the Comte de Gouvon; but he soon found such an occupation uncongenial, and ran away with a young fellow-Genevese, one Bâcle, intending to lead a vagabond life. The slender resources of the happy-go-lucky pair were soon exhausted; Rousseau returned to "Mamma" and, at her wish and at the expense of the Bishop of Geneva, entered a seminary to study for the priesthood. His teachers found little use for him, and his career as seminarian was very short; but at this time he developed an interest in music, which was encouraged by Mme. de Warens. After a visit to Lyons he returned to find that "Mamma" had left for Paris; and, though he could neither play nor read music, he attempted to teach it, first at Lausanne and then at Neuchâtel. At the latter place he met a Greek archimandrite of doubtful credentials, who had come to the West to collect alms for the Holy Sepulchre; and to this queer companion he attached himself. Warned of the *mala fides* of his new friend by the French representative at Soleure, he abandoned him and went to Paris, provided by the charitable diplomat with a letter of introduction to a prospective employer. But the proffered employment turned out to be another valetship: Jean-Jacques refused it, and returned to Savoy, to become once more the protégé of Mme. de Warens, now at Chambéry.

"Mamma" secured for her difficult "Little Dear" a post in the Land Registry at Chambéry; but this was soon abandoned, and in 1738 began that period of residence with his patroness at Les Charmettes of which he writes so touchingly in the Sixth Book of the *Confessions*. After a couple of years, he left her to become tutor to the children of the provost of Lyons, M. de Mably. When this new venture failed, he set off for Paris, intending to put before the Academy a new system of musical notation which he had invented, and armed with a couple of indifferent plays that had been written in his leisure moments. He obtained introductions to certain fashionable and literary personages, among them Diderot, Marivaux, Fontenelle, and Réaumur, the last of whom secured for him an opportunity of reading an account of his music-notation proposals to the Academy, whose preliminary approval was afterwards changed to condemnation.

Soon a friend secured him the appointment of secretary to M. de Montaigu, French Ambassador to Venice, and in that city he arrived in August 1743. Dismissed a year later, he returned to Paris, and shortly after met Thérèse le Vasseur, the simple and almost imbecile sewing-maid who became his companion for the rest of his days, and was the mother of the five children whom, according to his own story, he abandoned to the Foundling Hospital, and who outlived him by twenty-three years.

This second sojourn in Paris marks the turning-point of Jean-Jacques' career. To the friends whom he had already made there before his year at Venice, he added new ones, among them Grimm, the Baron d'Holbach, and Mmes. d'Epinay and d'Houdetot, who were to play so important a part in his life in the succeeding years.

An opera-ballet which he had composed, *Les Muses Galantes*, was performed in 1745; but his real fame came to him suddenly in 1749, when his essay on the Arts and Sciences won the prize offered by the Dijon Academy. Meanwhile he earned a livelihood by music-copying. In 1752 his only musical work to display any real aptitude for the art, the opera-ballet *Le Devin du Village*, was performed before Louis XV at Fontainebleau. His Majesty was charmed with the piece, and commanded the composer to appear before the regal presence the next day; but Rousseau preferred losing a probable pension to betraying that principle of social levelling which was to be the subject of his next public appearance, the *Discourse on the Origin of Inequality*, written in 1753, and published two years later. Jean-Jacques, now a famous man, paid a last visit to Mme. de Warens, now in greatly reduced circumstances, and went to Geneva, where, after he had returned to Protestantism, his citizenship was restored to him in July 1754.

In April 1756 Mme. d'Epinay offered Rousseau shelter at the Hermitage, near Montmorency, and he there began to write *Julie, ou La Nouvelle Héloïse*, which was finished in 1759, and published two years later. After some eighteen months, a quarrel with Diderot and Grimm led to his leaving the Hermitage and establishing himself at Mont Louis, a small house near by. There he wrote his famous attack on the theatre, the *Letter to d'Alembert on Stage Plays*, published in 1758, and his two major works, *The Social Contract* and *Emile*, both issued in 1762. The publication of Rousseau's full exposition of his new social philosophy caused a storm of opposition not only on the part of the government, but also from the Church and the *philosophes; Emile* was condemned by the Paris Parlement, and publicly burnt by order of the Council of Geneva. Warned that his arrest might be expected, Jean-Jacques took flight to Yverdon, and, finding that return to Geneva was forbidden him, rented a house at Motiers, in Neuchâtel, then Prussian territory under the government of Frederick the Great's friend, Marshal Keith. It was about this time that he adopted "Armenian dress." The sensation caused by the publication of *Letters from the Mountain* at the end of 1764, and the attacks of Voltaire, drove Rousseau from Neuchâtel to the Island of St. Pierre on the Lake of Bienne; his life at this lonely refuge is the subject of some of the most beautiful pages of the *Confessions*. Expelled from the island in October 1765 by the order of the Council of Berne, he made his way, via Strasbourg and Paris, to England, whither David Hume had invited him. Here he met Johnson and other famous figures of the day, and settled for a time at Wootton, Staffs, in the country house of Mr. Davenport. It was here that he made a serious start with the writing of the *Confessions*. A quarrel with Hume, resultant upon a letter attacking Rousseau which Jean-Jacques assumed Hume to have written (the real author was Horace Walpole), led to his return to France, where he settled at the Prince de Conti's Château de Trye, and resumed the writing of the *Confessions*. In 1768 he married Thérèse; after residing in Grenoble, Bourgoin, Monquin, and Lyons, he returned to Paris in 1770, and lived there for some years, gaining a sufficient income by music-copying, and mixing with many of the great men of the day. In 1778 he moved to Ermenonville, where on 3 July he died suddenly — almost certainly from natural causes, though a belief in his suicide was long held by many. Buried on an island in the lake in the park there, his body was in 1794 removed to Paris and interred in the Panthéon.

A letter from Rousseau to Malesherbes written in 1770 records that at the time of his departure from Mont Louis in 1762 he had already formed the project of some day writing his memoirs. In 1764 his friend Duclos and his publisher Rey urged him to do so, and the composition seems to have been begun almost immediately, to be quickly abandoned. When staying in England at Mr. Davenport's he resumed the task, the first six books being written in 1766 and the following year. Books Seven to Twelve were composed during 1769 and 1770, at the Château de Trye and at Monquin. The first few pages of the seventh book record the change of mind that had come to Rousseau in the intervening years.

As the author records at the very end of his work, readings from the MS. were given in Paris to a group of friends in the winter of 1770-1; the section chosen being that which relates his quarrel with Mme. d'Epinay, who, by complaint to the authorities, succeeded in having the readings stopped. Rousseau made no attempt to secure publication of the *Confessions* during his lifetime, and it was not until three years after his death that the first six books were issued, the remainder following seven years later.

It is not without interest that in December, 1764, when the *Confessions* had probably just been begun, Rousseau received a visit from Boswell, then twenty-four years old. Boswell seems to have been more impressed by the "genteel black man in the dress of an Armenian," the "great Judge of Human Nature," than Rousseau was with him, for the autobiographer's references to the biographer in his published correspondence are remarkably scanty. It was then only eighteen months since Boswell had first met his hero Johnson, whose comment on Rousseau he was later to record: "Rousseau, Sir, is a very bad man. I would sooner sign a sentence for his transportation than that of any felon who has gone from the Old Bailey these many years."

Judgements on the *Confessions* have covered a wide range. To Rousseau's rather unsympathetic biographer, Mr. C. E. Vulliamy, "with all its passages of beauty, even of unsurpassed beauty, the book remains a sad memorial of decaying reason and of moral disaster."[1] For George Eliot it was the one book she liked best in the world. Ruskin found that great parts of it were so true to himself that he felt as if Jean-Jacques must have transmigrated into his body.[2] Perhaps one of the most understanding verdicts is that of Lytton Strachey: "To strict moralists, and to purists in good taste, the *Confessions* will always be unpalatable. More indulgent readers will find in these pages the traces of a spirit which, with all its faults, its errors, its diseases, deserves something more than pity — deserves almost love. At any rate, it is a spirit singularly akin to our own. Out of the far-off, sharp, eager, unpoetical, un-psychological eighteenth century, it speaks to us in the familiar accents of inward contemplation, of brooding reminiscence, of subtly-shifting temperament, of quiet melancholy, of visionary joy . . . [Rousseau] understood simplicity: the charm of little happinesses, the sweetness of ordinary affections, the beauty of country faces. The paradox is strange; how was it that it should have been left to the morbid, tortured, half-crazy egoist of the *Confessions* to lead the way to such spiritual delicacies, such innocent delights?"[3]

---

[1] *Rousseau* (London, 1931), p.254.

[2] *Letters of John Ruskin to C. E. Norton* (Boston), II, p.298.

[3] *Landmarks in French Literature* (London, 1912), pp.194-5.

The version of Rousseau's *Confessions* here reprinted was the first to appear in English; the translator is now, unhappily, unknown. In its first printing (Books One to Six, 1783; the remainder in 1790), a number of the personal names were represented by initials and dashes (a key being provided at the end of the last volume of the Second Part); and certain passages were omitted. In the present edition the names and omissions have been supplied, the spelling modernized, a few of the translator's more striking infelicities of phrasing smoothed, and some errors corrected. A few notes have been added where this seemed especially necessary. The translation follows the MS. on which the first French edition was based; this was given by Rousseau in 1778 to his friend Moultou with a view to its posthumous publication. The actual first publication took place in 1782 (the first six books) and 1789 (the remaining six). The Moultou MS. is still preserved at Geneva. A second MS. of the *Confessions*, retained in the author's hands until his death, was in 1794 presented by Thérèse le Vasseur to the National Convention at Paris, and is now in the Library of the Chambre des Députés. A few variant readings from that MS. are recorded in the notes to the present text.

A. S. B. GLOVER

Principal Dates in Rousseau's Life

1712	June 28	Rousseau born at Geneva.
	July 4	Baptised.
1722		Education under M. Lambercier.
1724	end	Returns to Geneva to live with his uncle.
1725		Apprenticed as attorney.
	April	Apprenticed as engraver.
1728	March 3	Leaves Geneva.
		First meeting with Mme. de Warens at Annecy.
	March 24	Leaves Annecy for Turin.
	April 12	Enters Hospice for Catechumens at Turin.
	April 23	Baptised as a Catholic.
	June	Leaves the Hospice.
		Servant to Comtesse de Vercellis.
1729		Escapade with Bâcle; returns to Mme. de Warens; teaches music at Lausanne.
1730-31		Teaches music at Neuchâtel; journey to Soleure with the Archimandrite.
1731	end	Goes to Paris.
1732		Returns to Mme. de Warens at Chambéry and enters Land Registry.
1737	end	Visit to Montpellier.
1738	June 24	Begins residence at les Charmettes.
1740	April	Leaves Mme. de Warens and becomes tutor to M. de Mably's children at Lyons.
1741		To Paris with new system of musical notation.
1743	August	Secretary to M. de Montaigu, French Ambassador at Venice.
1744	August 22	Leaves Venice for Paris.
		Meets Thérèse le Vasseur (born 22 Sept. 1721)
		Clerk in office of M. Dupin.
1747		Rousseau's father dies.
1748		Meets Mme. d'Epinay, Diderot, d'Alembert.
1749		Wins Dijon Academy prize with *Essay on Arts and Sciences* (published 1750).
1750		Music copying.

1752   *Devin du Village* played at Fontainebleau (published 1753).

1753   *Discourse on Origin of Inequality* (published 1755). Revisits Mme. de Warens. Returns to Protestantism.

1754 June 1 Leaves Paris for Geneva.

   July 29 Citizenship restored at Geneva.

1756 April Begins residence at the Hermitage.

      Begins *Julie* (finished 1759).

1757 December Leaves the Hermitage for Mont Louis.

1761   *Julie, ou La Nouvelle Héloïse* published.

1762   *Emile; Le Contrat Social.*

   June 11 *Emile* condemned by Parlement of Paris (and on June 19 by the Council of Geneva).

   July 29 Death of Mme. de Warens.

   July Goes to Motiers, Neuchâtel; writes *Lettres de la Montagne*. Adopts Armenian dress.

1765 September 8 Leaves Motiers for Ile de Saint Pierre.

   October 29 Leaves Bienne; goes to Strasbourg and Paris.

1766 January Arrives in England on Hume's invitation.

   March To Wootton, Staffs; first six books of *Confessions* begun.

1767 May Returns to France; goes to Prince de Conti's Château de Trye; continues *Confessions*. *Dictionary of Music.*

1768   Marries Thérèse le Vasseur.

1769   To Monquin; writes tenth book of *Confessions*.

1770   To Paris; gives readings from *Confessions*.

1778 May To Ermenonville.

   July 3 Dies there, possibly by his own hand.

1782   *Confessions*, Books 1-6 and *Rêveries du Promeneur Solitaire* published at Geneva.

1789   *Confessions*, Books 7-12 published at Geneva.

1794   Rousseau's body translated to the Panthéon. Thérèse le Vasseur gives MS. of *Confessions* to the National Convention.

1801 July 12 Thérèse le Vasseur dies.

THE CONFESSIONS OF
Jean-Jacques Rousseau

Foreword

HERE *is the only portrait of man, painted justly according to nature and with complete truth, which is in existence, or, probably, ever will be. You, whosoever you be, whom my destiny or my confidence has made umpire of these pages, I conjure you, by my misfortunes, your own kindness, and in the name of all mankind, not to wipe out of existence an useful and unique work, capable of serving as a first sketch for that study of men, which certainly has yet to begin; and not to deprive the honour of my memory of the only assured monument of my character which my enemies have not defaced. Even were you yourself one of my implacable enemies, be so no longer towards my ashes; let not your cruel injustice endure till the day when neither you nor I longer live, so that you may for once at least bear to yourself the noble testimony of having been good and generous when you might have been evil and revengeful; if indeed evil done to a man who himself has never done or sought to do evil can bear the name of revenge.*

J.-J. ROUSSEAU

BIRTHPLACE: GENEVA

BOOK ONE

I AM undertaking a work which has no example, and whose execution will have no imitator. I mean to lay open to my fellow-mortals a man just as nature wrought him; and this man is myself.

I alone. I know my heart, and am acquainted with mankind. I am not made like anyone I have seen; I dare believe I am not made like anyone existing. If I am not better, at least I am quite different. Whether Nature has done well or ill in breaking the mould she cast me in, can be determined only after having read me.

Let the trumpet of the day of judgement sound when it will, I shall appear with this book in my hand before the Sovereign Judge, and cry with a loud voice, This is my work, these were my thoughts, and thus was I. I have freely told both the good and the bad, have hid nothing wicked, added nothing good; and if I have happened to make use of an insignificant ornament, it was only to fill a void occasioned by a short memory: I may have supposed true what I knew might be so, never what I knew was false.

3

I have exposed myself as I was, contemptible and vile some times; at others, good, generous, and sublime. I have revealed my heart as thou sawest it thyself. Eternal Being! assemble around me the numberless throng of my fellow-mortals; let them listen to my Confessions, let them lament at my unworthiness, let them blush at my misery. Let each of them, in his turn, lay open his heart with the same sincerity at the foot of thy throne, and then say, if he dare, *I was better than that man.*

I was born at Geneva in 1712, of Isaac Rousseau and Susan Bernard, citizens. A very moderate estate, which was divided amongst fifteen children, having reduced almost to nothing my father's share, he had no other subsistence than his trade, which was that of a watchmaker, in which he was undoubtedly very clever. My mother, a daughter[1] of the minister Bernard, was richer; she had prudence and beauty: it was with some trouble my father obtained her. Their affection began almost at their birth: from the age of eight or nine they took a walk together every evening on the banks of the Treille; at the age of ten they could never leave each other. Sympathy and resemblance of soul strengthened in them the sentiments habit had produced. Each born for tenderness and sensibility, only waited for the moment to find another of the same disposition, or rather that moment waited for them, and each of them gave their heart to the first expanded to receive it. Fate, which seemed to oppose their passion, animated it still more. The young lover, not able to obtain his beloved, wasted away with sorrow; she advised him to travel and forget her. He travelled in vain, and returned more fond than ever. He found her again whom he loved, tender and faithful. After this proof nothing remained but to love each other for life; they vowed it, and Heaven blessed their vow.

Gabriel Bernard, my mother's brother, fell in love with one of the sisters of my father; but she would not consent to marry the brother on any condition but that of her brother's marrying the sister. Love arranged all, and the two marriages were celebrated the same day. Thus my uncle married my aunt, and their children were doubly my cousin-germans. Each of them had a child at the end of a year; and once more they were obliged to separate.

My uncle Bernard was an engineer: he served in the Empire and in Hungary under Prince Eugene. He distinguished himself at the siege and battle of Belgrade. My father, after the birth of

---

[1] She was actually his niece.

my only brother, set off for Constantinople, by desire, and became watchmaker to the Seraglio. During his absence, the beauty of my mother, her wit and talents,[1] drew admirers. M. de la Closure, resident of France, was the forwardest in his offers. His passion must have been intense; for thirty years afterwards I have seen him melt at her name. My mother had more than common virtue for her defence: she tenderly loved her husband; she pressed him to return. He left all and came. I was the unhappy fruit of this return. Ten months after, I came into the world infirm and ill; I cost my mother her life, and my birth was the first of my misfortunes.

I know not how my father supported this loss; but I know he was never happy afterwards. He thought he saw her in me, without being able to forget I had taken her from him: never did he clasp me in his arms, but I felt, by his sighs, by his convulsive embraces, that a bitter regret was mixed with his caresses, though they were the tenderer for it. Whenever he said to me, Jean Jacques, let us talk of thy mother, I said, Well, father, we shall cry then; and this word alone immediately drew tears from him. Ah! said he with a groan, give her back to me again; comfort me for her; fill up the space she has left in my soul. Could I love thee thus, if thou wast only my son? Forty years after her death, he died in the arms of a second wife; but the name of the first was on his tongue, and her image in his heart.

Such were the authors of my being. Of all the gifts heaven had bestowed on them, a feeling heart was the only one they left me; but that which was their happiness, caused all the misfortunes of my life.

I came into the world almost dead; they had little hopes of preserving me. I brought with me the seeds of a disorder which years have strengthened, and which now I am sometimes relieved from, only to suffer otherwise in a more cruel manner. A sister of my father, an amiable and prudent young woman, took so much

---

[1] They were too brilliant for her situation; the minister her father, who adored her, having taken great care of her education. She was taught drawing and singing; she accompanied the theorbo, had learning, and composed tolerable verse. Here is an extemporary piece of hers, in the absence of her brother and husband, while walking with her sister-in-law and their two children, on a conversation with some one about them.

> Ces deux Messieurs, qui sont absens,
> Nous sont chers de bien des manières;
> Ce sont nos amis, nos amans;
> Ce sont nos maris & nos frères,
> Et les pères de ces enfans.

[*Note by Rousseau.*]

care of me that she saved me. At the time I write this, she is still living, nursing at eighty a husband younger than herself, but worn out by excess in drinking. Dear aunt, I excuse you for having saved my life, and am sorry I cannot return you, at the decline of your days, those tender cares you heaped on me at the beginning of mine. I have likewise my governess Jaqueline still alive, healthy and robust. The hands, which opened my eyes at my birth, may close them at my death.

I felt before I thought; it is the common fate of humanity: I have proved it more than anyone. I am ignorant of what passed till I was five or six years old: I know not how I learnt to read; I remember my first studies only, and their effect on me: this is

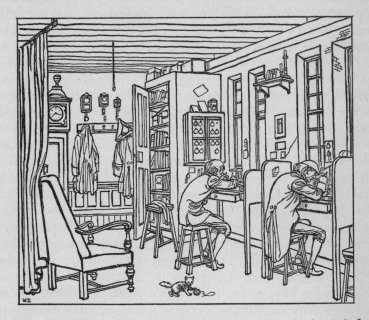

the time from whence I date, without interruption, the knowledge of myself. My mother left some romances. My father and I read them after supper. At that time the point was to exercise me in reading entertaining books only; but very soon the interest in them became so strong, that we read by turns without ceasing, and passed whole nights at this employment. We never could leave off but at the end of the volume. Sometimes my father, on hearing the swallows in the morning, would say, quite ashamed, Come, let us go to bed; I am more a child than thou art.

In a short time I acquired, by this dangerous method, not only an extreme facility in reading and comprehending, but also a knowledge of the passions peculiar at my age. I had not the least idea of things, but the sentiments were known to me. I conceived nothing; I had felt the whole.[1] These confused emotions, which I found come one on the other, did not hurt the reason I was not yet possessed of; but they formed one of another sort, and gave me a romantic extravagant notion of human life, which experience and reflection have never been able entirely to eradicate.

The romances ended with the summer of 1719. The winter following produced other things. My mother's library being exhausted, recourse was had to that part of her father's which had fallen to our share. Happily we found some good books among them: it could not well be otherwise, this library having been collected by a minister in the true sense of the word, and not only learned (for it was then the fashion), but also a man of taste and sense. The *History of the Church and the Empire*, by Le Sueur, the *Discourse* of Bossuet *on Universal History*, Plutarch's *Illustrious Men*, the *History of Venice* by Nani, Ovid's *Metamorphoses*, La Bruyère, Fontenelle's *Worlds*, his *Dialogues of the Dead*, and a few volumes of Molière, were carried to my father's closet, and I read them to him every day during his employment. My taste for them was uncommon, and perhaps not to be equalled at that age. Plutarch, particularly, became my favourite author. The pleasure I took in reading him over again and again cured me a little of romances, and I soon preferred Agesilaus, Brutus, and Aristides, to Orondates, Artamenes, and Juba. From these engaging studies, from the conversations they occasioned between my father and me, was formed that liberal republican spirit, that proud invincible character, impatient of restraint or servitude, which has tortured me through the whole course of my life, in situations the least proper for giving it action. Incessantly occupied with Rome or Athens, living in a manner with their great men, myself born citizen of a republic, and son to a father whose love of his country was his ruling passion, I glowed at his example; I thought myself Greek or Roman; I was transformed into the person whose life I read: the recital of an act of constancy and intrepidity which struck me, rendered my eyes fiery, and my voice strong. One day at table, reciting the story of Scævola, they were affrighted to see me go forward, and hold my hand over a chafing-dish, to represent his action.

---

[1] The Paris MS. adds: "and the imaginary maladies of our heroes have drawn from me a hundred times more tears in my childhood, than my own have ever made me shed."

I had a brother seven years older than I. He learned the profession of my father. The extreme affection for me caused him to be a little neglected, and this is not what I approve of. His education felt this negligence. He gave into libertinism, even before the age of a real libertine. He was sent to another master, where he played the same pranks as at home. I seldom saw him; I can scarcely say I was acquainted with him; but I nevertheless loved him tenderly, and he loved me as much as a rake can love anybody. I recollect once, when my father chastised him severely and in anger, I threw myself impetuously between them, and closely embraced him. I covered him thus with my body, receiving the strokes aimed at him. I persisted so much in this attitude, that my father was at last obliged to pardon him, either softened by my cries and tears, or being unwilling to beat me more than him. In fine, my brother grew so bad, he went off, and entirely disappeared. Some time after we heard he was in Germany. He never once wrote. He has never since been heard of, and thus I became the only son.

Though the poor boy was neglected, it was not so with his brother; the sons of kings could not be better taken care of than I was during my tender years, idolized by all around me, and always, which is very rare, treated as a beloved, not as a spoiled child: not once, whilst under parental inspection, was I permitted to run about the streets with other children; never required reprimand or gratification in any fantastical humour, imputed to nature, but which springs from education only. I had the faults of my age; I was a prattler, a glutton, and sometimes a liar. I sometimes stole fruit, sweetmeats, and victuals; but I never took pleasure in mischief, waste, accusing others, or torturing poor animals. I remember, however, making water once in the kettle of one of our neighbours, whose name was Madame Clot, while she was at church. I own too the recollection still makes me laugh, because Madame Clot, a good creature if you please, was, however, the most grumbling old woman I ever knew. Thus you have the short and true history of all my childish misdeeds.

How could I become wicked, when I had nothing before my eyes but examples of mildness, and around me the best people in the world? My father, my aunt, my governess, my relations, my acquaintance, my neighbours, all who surrounded me, did not obey me indeed, but loved me, and I on my part loved them. My wishes were so little excited and so little contradicted, I never thought of any. I can make oath that until my subjection to a master, I never knew what a caprice was. Except the time I spent

in reading or writing with my father, or that my governess took
me out a walking, I was always with my aunt, observing her
embroider, hearing her sing, sitting or standing by her side, and
I was happy. Her sprightliness, her mildness, her agreeable
countenance, are so strongly imprinted on me, that I yet see her
manner, her looks, her attitude; I remember her little caressing
questions; I could tell her clothing and head-dress, without forgetting the two locks her black hair formed on her temples,
according to the fashion of those times.

I am persuaded I am indebted to her for a taste, or rather passion, for music, which did not show itself till long afterwards.
She knew a prodigious number of tunes and songs, which she
sung with a soft and melodious voice. The serenity of soul of this
excellent girl drove from her, and those who surrounded her, sadness and melancholy. The charms of her voice so allured me, that
not only several of her songs remain in my memory, but some of
them come to my recollection, now I have lost her, though totally
forgot since my infancy, and present themselves still as I grow
old, with a charm I am not able to express. Would one think that
I, an old dotard, worn out with care and trouble, surprise myself
sometimes in tears like a child, in muttering these little tunes with
a voice already broke and trembling? One of them in particular
I have recollected entirely again, as to the tune; but the second
moiety of the words constantly refuses every effort to recall it,
though I catch the rimes in a confused manner of some of them.
Here is the beginning, and what I have been able to recollect of
the remainder.

> *Tircis, je n'ose*
> *Ecouter ton chalumeau*
> *Sous l'ormeau;*
> *Car on en cause*
> *Déjà dans notre hameau.*
>
> . . . .
> . . . . *un berger*
> . . . . *s'engager*
> . . . . *sans danger;*
> *Et toujours l'épine est sous la rose.*[1]

---

[1] The conclusion is:

> *Un cœur s'expose*
> *A trop s'engager*
> *Avec un berger;*
> *Et toujours l'épine est sous la rose.*

I have sought for the moving charm my heart feels at this song: it is a caprice I cannot comprehend; but there is an impossibility of my singing it to the end without being suffocated by tears. I have a hundred times intended to write to Paris, to get the remaining words, if it should happen that anyone still knows them. But I am almost sure the pleasure I take in recalling them to my mind would vanish in part, if I had a proof that any other than my poor aunt Suzon sung them.

Such were the first affections of my entrance into life; thus was formed and began to show itself that heart of mine at once so proud and so tender, that character so effeminate, but nevertheless invincible, which, always floating between weakness and courage, between ease and virtue, has even to the last set me in contradiction with myself, and has caused abstinence and enjoyment, pleasure and prudence, equally to shun me.

This course of education was interrupted by an accident whose consequences influenced the rest of my life. My father had a dispute with a M. Gautier, a captain in France, and related to some of the council. This Gautier, an insolent and ungenerous man, bled at the nose, and to revenge himself accused my father of having drawn his sword against him in the city. My father, whom they wanted to send to prison, insisted that, according to law, the accuser should be sent there likewise. Not being able to obtain it, he chose rather to leave Geneva and quit this country for the rest of his life, than to give up a point where honour and liberty seemed in danger.

I remained under the tuition of my uncle Bernard, at that time employed in the fortifications of Geneva. His eldest daughter was dead, but he had a son about my age. We were both sent to board at Bossey with the minister Lambercier, to learn, with Latin, all the insignificant stuff which accompanies it, under the name of education.

Two years spent in a village softened a little my Roman fierceness, and brought me back to my state of childhood. At Geneva, where nothing was forced on me, I was fond of application and study; it was almost my whole amusement. At Bossey application made me fond of play as a relaxation. The country was so new to me, it was impossible to tire myself with its enjoyment. My taste for it was a passion I never could extinguish. The remembrance of the happy days I have passed in it, makes me regret its abode and its pleasures at every age, quite to that which has brought me there again. M. Lambercier was a very sensible man, who, without neglecting our instruction, never loaded us with extreme tasks. The proof his method was a good one is, that, in spite of my aversion to constraint, I never recollect with disgust my hours of study; and though I did not learn much of him, what I learnt was without trouble, and I still retain it.

The simplicity of that rural life was an advantage inestimable, as it opened my heart to friendship. Till then I had been acquainted with elevated, but imaginary sentiments only. The habit of living in a peaceable state together tenderly united me to my cousin Bernard. In a little time I had more affectionate sentiments for him, than those I had had for my brother, and which have never worn away. He was a tall, long-shanked, weakly boy, with a mind as mild as his body was feeble, and did not much abuse the partiality shown him in the house as son of my guardian. Our labour, our amusements, our tastes, were the same; we were alone, of the same age; each of us wanted a playmate: to separate us was in some measure to annihilate us. Though we had not many opportunities of showing our attachment to each other, it was extreme; and not only we could not live an instant separated, but we even thought we never could endure it. Each of a humour to yield to kindness, complaisant if not constrained, we always agreed on every point. If, favoured by those who governed us, he had the ascendant over me while in their sight; when we were alone I had it over him, which established the equilibrium. At our studies, I prompted him if he hesitated; when my exercise was done I helped him in doing his, and at our amusements my more active taste always guided him. In fine, our two characters were so alike, and the friendship which united us so real, that for more than five years that we were nearly inseparable, both at Bossey and Geneva, we often fought, I allow, but it was never necessary to separate us; no one of our disputes lasted more than a quarter of an hour, and we never once accused each other. These remarks are, if you will, puerile; but the result is, perhaps, a singular example since children have existed.

The manner I lived in at Bossey was so agreeable, that nothing but its continuance was necessary absolutely to fix my character. Tender, affectionate, peaceable sentiments were its basis. I believe an individual of our species never had naturally less vanity than I. I raised myself by transports to sublime emotions, but as suddenly I returned to my languor. To be loved by all who saw me was my greatest wish. I was mild, so was my cousin; those who governed us were the same. During two years I was neither witness nor victim of a violent sentiment. Everything nourished in my heart the dispositions it received from nature: I knew nothing so charming as to see everyone contented with me and everything else. I shall for ever remember that, at church, answering our catechism, nothing so much troubled me, when I happened to hesitate, as to see, in the countenance of Mlle. Lambercier, marks of uneasiness and trouble. That alone afflicted me more than the shame of faltering in public, which, however, extremely affected me: for, though not very sensible to praise, I always was very much to shame; and I can now say, that the expectation of a reprimand from Mlle. Lambercier alarmed me less than the dread of making her uneasy.

However, she did not, on occasion, want severity, any more than her brother; but as this severity, almost always just, was never in anger, it afflicted me, but without complaining. I was more sorry to displease than to be punished, and the sign of discontent was more cruel to me than afflictive correction. It is painful to me, but I must speak plainer. The method taken with youth would be changed, if the distant effects were better seen, from what is always indiscriminately, and often indiscreetly, made use of. The great lesson to be learnt from an example as common as fatal, makes me resolve to give it.

As Mlle. Lambercier had a mother's affection for us, she had also the authority, and sometimes carried it so far as to inflict on us the punishment of infants, when we deserved it. She confined herself long enough to menaces, and menaces were so new to me as to seem very dreadful; but after their execution, I found them less terrible in the proof than in the expectation; and, what is more extraordinary, the chastisement drew my affection still more towards her who gave it. Nothing less than the reality of this affection, and all my natural mildness, could have prevented me from seeking a return of the same treatment by deserving it; for I felt in my pain, and even in my shame, a mixture of sensuality which left more desire than fear to experience it again from the same hand. It is certain that, as there was, without doubt, a forward instinct of sex in it, the same chastisement from her brother would not have appeared in the least pleasing. But from a man of his humour this substitution was not much to be feared, and if I did abstain from meriting correction, it was only for fear of vexing Mlle. Lambercier; for such an empire has benevolence established in me, and even that the senses have given birth to, that it always gave law to my heart.

This relapse, which I retarded without dreading, happened without my fault, that is my will, and I benefited by it, I may say, with a safe conscience. But this second time was also the last: for Mlle. Lambercier, perceiving, doubtless, by some sign that the chastisement did not answer the intention, declared she renounced it, and that it wearied her too much. Until then we had lain in her chamber, and in the winter sometimes even in her bed. Two days after we were removed to another room, and I had in future the honour, which I could very well have done without, of being treated by her as a grown-up boy.

Who would believe it, that this childish chastisement, received at eight years old [1] from the hand of a girl of thirty, should decide my tastes, my desires, my passions, for the rest of my days, and that precisely in a contrary sense to what might have been expected naturally to follow it? At the very time my senses were fired, my desires took so opposite a turn, that, confined to what they had experienced, they sought no farther. With blood boiling with sensuality almost from my birth, I preserved my purity from every blemish, even until the age when the coldest and backwardest constitutions discover themselves. Long tormented without knowing by what, I devoured with an ardent eye every fine woman; my imagination recalled them incessantly to my memory, solely to submit them to my manner, and transform them into so many Mlles. Lambercier.

Even after the marriageable age, this odd taste, always increasing, carried even to depravity, even to folly, preserved my morals good, the very reverse of which might have been expected. If ever an education was modest and chaste, it was certainly that I received. My three aunts were not only people of an exemplary prudence, but of a reserve women have long since forgot. My father, a man of pleasure, but gallant after the old fashion, never advanced to the women he loved most a word which could make a virgin blush, and never, than in our family and before me, was shown more of that respect we owe children. The same attention was found at M. Lambercier's on that article; a very good maid-servant was discharged for a word a little waggish she pronounced in our presence. Not only I had no distinct idea of the union of the sexes at the age of adolescence; but the confused idea never presented itself to me but as odious and disgustful. I had an aversion for public women, which has never worn away; I could not

[1] He was in fact ten.

THE SWISS

see a debauched fellow without disdain, nor even without terror;
for my abhorrence of debauchery was carried to this point, since,
in going one day to the little Sacconex through a hollow way, I
saw on each side cavities in the earth, where I was told these
people copulated. What I had seen of the coupling of dogs always
struck me in thinking of others, and my stomach turned at this
sole remembrance.

These prejudices of education, proper in themselves to retard
the first explosions of a combustible constitution, were aided, as
I have already said, by the diversion caused in me by the first
motions of sensuality. Imagining no more than I felt, in spite of
the troublesome effervescence of blood, I knew not how to carry
my desires but towards that species of voluptuousness I was acquainted with, without ever reaching that which had been rendered hateful to me, and which drew so near the other without
my ever suspecting it. In my stupid fancies, in my erotic fury, in
the extravagant acts to which they sometimes carried me, I borrowed, in imagination, the assistance of the other sex, without
supposing it fit for any other use than that I burned to make of it.

I not only therefore thus passed my whole age of puberty with
a constitution extremely ardent, extremely lascivious, and extremely forward, without desiring, without the knowledge of any
other satisfaction of the senses than those Mlle. Lambercier inno-

cently gave me the idea of; but when at last the progress of years had made me a man, it was likewise what might have destroyed me that saved me. My old childish taste, instead of vanishing, so associated with the other, I could never remove it from those desires my senses enkindled; and this folly, joined to my natural timidity, has always rendered me very little enterprising with women, since I cannot dare to say nor am able to do all; since that sort of enjoyment whereof the other was to me but the last stage, may not be usurped by him who desires, or guessed at by her who can grant it. I have thus passed my days in coveting and in silence with those I most loved. Never daring to declare my taste, I at least amused it by relations which preserved its idea. To fall at the feet of an imperious mistress, obey her orders, have pardons to ask her, were for me the sweetest enjoyments, and the more my lively imagination inflamed my blood, the more I had the air of a bashful lover. It may be conceived this manner of making love is not attended by a rapid progress, nor is very dangerous to the virtue of its object. I have therefore possessed little, but have not been without much enjoyment, in my manner; that is imaginary. Thus have the senses, agreeing with my timid humour and romantic mind, preserved my feelings pure and my morals chaste, by the same inclinations which, perhaps, with a little more effrontery, might have plunged me into the most brutal pleasures.

I have made the first step and the most painful in the obscure and dirty maze of my Confessions. It is not criminality we are most unwilling to divulge; it is what is ridiculous and shameful. Henceforward I am sure of myself; after what I have dared to disclose, nothing can be able to stop me. You may judge how much such acknowledgements cost me, since, during the whole course of my life, carried sometimes away, with those I loved, by the fury of a passion which deprived me of the faculty of sight, of hearing, out of my senses, and seized with a convulsive trembling all over my body, I could never take upon me to declare my folly, and to implore, during the most intimate familiarity, the only favour lacking to the rest. It never happened but once, in my childhood, with a child of my age: besides, she it was who first proposed it.

In thus remounting to the first traces of my sensible being, I find elements, which, seeming sometimes incompatible, have yet united to produce with force an uniform and simple effect; and I find others which, the same in appearance, have formed, by the concurrence of certain circumstances, so different combinations, that one would never imagine they had the least resemblance to each other. Who would believe, for instance, that one of the most vigorous springs of my soul was tempered in the same source from which luxury and ease were communicated to my blood? Without abandoning the subject I have just spoken of, I will show you a very different impression it made.

I was one day studying alone in a chamber contiguous to the kitchen; the maid had put some of Mlle. Lambercier's combs to dry by the fire. When she came to fetch them, she found the teeth of one of them broken: whom suspect of this havoc? None besides myself had entered the room. They question me; I deny having touched the comb. M. and Mlle. Lambercier consult, exhort, press, threaten; I persist obstinately; but conviction was too strong, and carried it against all my protestations, though this was the first time they caught me in so audacious lies. The affair was thought serious; it deserved it. The wickedness, the lie, the obstinacy, were thought equally worthy of punishment; but this time it was not Mlle. Lambercier that inflicted it. My uncle Bernard was written to; he came. My poor cousin was charged with another crime not less serious; we were taken to the same execution. It was terrible. If, seeking the remedy even in the evil, they had intended for ever to allay my depraved senses, they could not have taken a shorter method. I assure you, they left me a long time at peace.

They could not force from me the acknowledgement they sought. Accused several times, and thrown into the most dreadful situation, I was immovable. I would have suffered death, and was resolved on it. Force itself was obliged to yield to the diabolical stubbornness of a child; for no other name was given to my constancy. In fine, I came out of this cruel trial in pieces, but triumphant.

It is now near fifty years since this adventure, and I am not afraid now of being punished again for the same fact. Well, I declare in the face of heaven, I was innocent; that I neither broke nor touched the comb; that I never came near the fire, nor even thought of it. Let me not be asked how it happened; I know not, nor can comprehend it; all that I know of it is that I was innocent.

Figure to yourself a timid and docile character in common life, but ardent, haughty, invincible in his passions; a child always governed by the voice of reason, always treated with mildness, equity, and complaisance; who had not even the idea of injustice, and who, for the first time, experiences so terrible a one, from those, precisely, he most cherishes and respects. What a perverting of ideas! what a disorder in the sentiments! what confusion in the heart, in the brain, in all one's little being, intelligent and moral! I say, let anyone imagine to themselves all this, if possible; for as to myself, I am not capable of discovering or following the least trace of what passed in me at the time.

I had not yet reason enough to feel how much appearances condemned me, and to put myself in the place of others; I kept to my own, and all I felt was the rigour of a dreadful chastisement for a crime I had not committed. The soreness of my body, though violent, I scarcely felt; I only felt indignation, rage, and despair. My cousin, in almost a like case, who had been punished for an involuntary fault as a premeditated act, grew furious by my example, and excited, so to speak, in unison with me. Both in the same bed embraced each other with convulsive transports; we were suffocated; and when our young hearts, a little eased, could breathe out their indignation, we sat up in our bed, and began both of us crying out a hundred times, with all our force, *Carnifex! Carnifex! Carnifex!*

I feel in writing this my pulse still rise; those moments would be continually present, were I to live a hundred thousand years. This first sentiment of violence and of injustice is so deeply graven on my soul, that every resembling idea brings back my first emotion; and this sentiment relative to me in its origin, has taken such a consistence, and is so far from personal interest, that my heart is inflamed at the sight or recital of any unjust action, whatever may be its object, or wheresoever it may be committed, as if the effect fell on me. When I read the history of a cruel tyrant, the subtle black actions of a knavish priest, I could set off heartily to stab these miscreants, though I should perish a hundred times in the attempt. I have often sweated in pursuing or stoning a cock, a cow, a dog, an animal I saw torment another, only because he knew himself to be the strongest. This emotion may be natural to me, and I believe it is; but the profound remembrance of the first injustice I suffered was too long and too strongly annexed to it not to have greatly strengthened it.

This was the end of my childish serenity. From this moment I ceased to enjoy pure happiness; and I feel even at this instant the remembrance of the charms of childhood stops there. We remained at Bossey a few months afterwards. We were there, as the first man is represented in the terrestrial paradise, but having ceased to enjoy it. It was in appearance the same situation, but in effect quite another sort of being. Attachment, respect, intimacy, confidence, no longer bound the pupils to their guides; we no longer thought them gods who could read our hearts; we were less ashamed to do wrong, and more fearful of being accused; we began to be sly, to rebel, and to lie. All the vices of our age corrupted our innocence and clouded our diversions; even the country lost in our eyes its alluring sweetness and simplicity which reach the heart: it seemed to us desert and gloomy; it was, as it were, covered with a veil which hid its beauties. We ceased to cultivate our little gardens, our herbs, and our flowers. We no more went to scrape up the earth, and cry out with joy on discovering a shoot of the grain we had sown. We grew dissatisfied with this life; they grew tired of us, my uncle took us home, and we separated from M. and Mlle. Lambercier, cloyed with each other, and little regretting our separation.

BOSSEY: THE PRESBYTERY

Near thirty years passed away after I left Bossey, without having recollected my abode there in an agreeable manner, by remembrances a little intimate: but since I have passed the prime of life, and am declining towards old age, I feel the same remembrance of things spring up again, while others wear away, and imprint themselves in my memory with a charm and a force which daily increases; as if, finding already life flying from me,

I seek to catch hold of it again by its commencement. The least facts of those times please me, for no other reason than that they were of those times. I recollect every circumstance of places, persons, and hours. I see the maid or the footman busy in the chamber, a swallow coming in at the window, a fly settling on my hand while I was saying my lesson: I see the whole arrangement of the room we were in; M. Lambercier's closet on the right, a print representing all the popes, a barometer, a large calendar; raspberry-trees which, from a very elevated garden, in which the back of the house was buried, shaded the window, and sometimes came quite in. I know the reader has no occasion to be acquainted with all this; but I have occasion myself to tell it him. Why may I not relate equally every little anecdote of those happy years, which yet make me leap with joy when I recollect them? Five or six particularly — Let us compound. I will leave out five, but I will have one, only one; provided you let me relate it as fully as possible, to prolong my pleasure.

If I sought yours only, I might choose that of Mlle. Lambercier's backside, which, by an unlucky fall at the bottom of the meadow, was exposed quite bare to the King of Sardinia, as he was passing: but that of the walnut-tree on the terrace is more amusing to me, who was the actor, whereas at the fall I was only a spectator; and I own I could not find the least cause for laughing at an accident which, though odd in itself, alarmed me for a person I loved as my mother, and perhaps more.

O you, curious readers of the grand history of the walnut-tree on the terrace, listen to the horrible tragedy, and abstain from trembling if you can.

There was on the outside of the court-door a terrace on the left hand on coming in, on which they often sat after dinner, but it had no shade. That it might have some, M. Lambercier had a walnut-tree planted there. The planting it was attended with solemnity: the two boarders were the godfathers, and whilst they were filling the hole, we each of us held the tree with one hand, singing songs of triumph. It was watered by a sort of basin round its foot. Every day, ardent spectators of this watering, we confirmed each other, my cousin and I, in the very natural idea that it was nobler to plant trees on the terrace than colours on a breach, and we resolved to procure ourselves this glory, without dividing it with anyone.

To do this, we went and cut a slip of a willow, and planted it on the terrace, at eight or ten feet from the august walnut-tree. We did not forget to make likewise a hollow round our tree; the difficulty lay in getting wherewithal to fill it, for water was brought from a considerable distance, and we were not permitted to go out to fetch it. However, it was absolutely needful for our willow. We made use of every wile to let it have some for a few days, and we so well succeeded, we saw it bud and throw out small leaves, whose growth we measured from hour to hour; persuaded, though it was not a foot high, it would not be long before it shaded us.

As our tree, taking up our whole time, rendered us incapable of any other application, of all study, we were as in a delirium, and the cause not being known, we were kept closer than before; we saw the fatal moment wherein our water would fall short, and were afflicted with the expectation of seeing our tree perish with drought. At last, necessity, the mother of industry, suggested an invention to save our tree and ourselves from certain death; it was to make under ground a furrow which would privately conduct to the willow a part of the water they brought the walnut-tree. This undertaking, executed with ardour, did not succeed immediately. We took our descent so badly, the water did not run; the earth fell in and stopped up the furrow; the entrance was filled with filth; all went cross. Nothing dispirited us: *Omnia vincit labor improbus.* We cut our earth and our basin deeper, to let the water run; we cut the bottoms of boxes into little narrow planks, whereof some laid flat in a row, and others forming an angle from each side of them, made us a triangular channel for our conduit. At the entrance we placed small ends of thin wood, not close, which, forming a kind of grate, kept back the mud and stones without stopping the water. We carefully covered our work over with well-trodden earth, and the day it was finished, we waited, in agonies of hope and fear, the hour of watering. After ages of expectation, this hour at last came: M. Lambercier came also as usual to assist at the performance, during which we got both of us behind him to hide our tree, to which happily he turned his back.

They had scarcely finished pouring the first pail of water, but we began to perceive it run to our basin. At this sight prudence abandoned us; we set up shouts of joy, which caused M. Lambercier to turn round; it was a pity, for he was pleasing himself greatly to see how greedily the earth of his walnut-tree swallowed the water. Struck at seeing it divide itself between two basins, he shouts in his turn; sees; perceives the roguery; orders, in haste, a pick-axe, gives a stroke, makes two or three of our planks fly,

and hallooing with all his strength, *An aqueduct! an aqueduct!* he
strikes on every side unmerciful strokes, every one of which
reached the bottom of our hearts. In one moment the planking,
the conduit, the basin, the willow, all were destroyed, all plowed
up; without there having been pronounced, during this terrible
expedition, any other word than the exclamation he incessantly
repeated. *An aqueduct!* cried he, at the same time breaking up all,
an aqueduct! an aqueduct!

You would think the adventure ended badly for the young
architects. You mistake: the whole ended there. M. Lambercier
never reproached us for it; did not show us a different countenance, and said no more of it to us; we even heard him soon after
laugh with his sister with all his might, for the laugh of M. Lambercier was heard afar; and, what is more astonishing, after the
first sensation, we ourselves were not very afflicted. We planted
in another place another tree, and often called to mind the catastrophe of the first, repeating with emphasis to each other, *An
aqueduct! an aqueduct!* Till then I had had fits of pride, at intervals, when I was Aristides or Brutus. This was my first movement
of well-marked vanity. To have constructed an aqueduct with
our own hands, having put a slip of wood in competition with a
large tree, appeared to me the supreme degree of glory. At ten
I thought more of it than Caesar at thirty.

The idea of this walnut-tree, and the little history that relates
to it, was so well retained in my memory, that one of my most
agreeable projects in my journey to Geneva in 1754 was to go to
Bossey, and review my childish amusements, and particularly
the beloved walnut-tree, which must at that time have been the
third of a century old. I was so continually beset, and so little my
own master, I could not obtain a moment to satisfy myself. There
is little appearance of the occasion ever being renewed. I have not,
however, lost the desire with the hope; and I am almost certain,
if ever I return to these charming spots, and should find my beloved walnut-tree still existing, I should water it with my tears.

Returned to Geneva, I passed two or three years[1] at my uncle's,
waiting till they should resolve what to do with me. As he intended his son for engineering, he was instructed in a little drawing, and he taught him himself the Elements of Euclid. I learnt
all this as his companion, and it took my taste, particularly drawing. However, it was debated whether I was to be watchmaker,

---

[1] Actually a few months only.

lawyer, or minister. I liked best to be a minister, for I thought it very clever to preach; but the little income left by my mother, which was to be divided between my brother and me, was not sufficient to support my studies. As my age did not render the choice very pressing, I remained in the meanwhile with my uncle, losing, nearly, my time, not without paying, very justly, pretty dear for my board.

My uncle, a man of pleasure as well as my father, knew not like him how to submit to his duties, and took very little care of us. My aunt was devout, even a pietist, who preferred singing psalms to overseeing our education: they left us almost at an entire liberty, which we never abused. Always inseparable, we sufficed to each other, and not being inclined to frequent the rakes of our age, we learned none of those habits of libertinism our idle life might have prompted us to. I am to blame even to suppose us idle, for in our lives we were never less so; and the greatest happiness was, that every amusement which we successively pursued, kept us together employed in the house, without being inclined ever to go into the street. We made cages, pipes, kites, drums, houses, blowpipes, and bows. We spoiled the tools of my good old grandfather, to make watches in imitation of him. We had particularly a taste of preference to daubing paper, drawing, wash-drawing, illuminating, and splashing colours. There came an Italian mountebank to Geneva, called Gamba-Corta; we went once to see him, but would go no more: but he had puppets, so we

set ourselves to making puppets; his puppets played a kind of
comedy, and we made comedies for ours. For lack of practice, we
counterfeited in our throat Punch's voice, to act these charming
comedies our good relatives had the patience to see and hear. But
my uncle Bernard having one day read to the family a fine sermon of his, we left our comedies, and began to compose sermons.
These details are not very interesting, I allow; but they show how
much our first education must have been well directed, as that,
masters almost of our time and of ourselves at an age so tender,
we were so little tempted to abuse it. We had so little need of play-
fellows, we even neglected the occasion of seeking for them. When
we were taking our walk, we regarded their play as we passed
without coveting it, without even thinking of taking part in it.
Friendship so much filled our hearts, it sufficed to be together for
the simplest tastes to be our delight.

From being continually together, we were remarked; the more
so as, my cousin being very tall and I very little, we made a couple
pleasantly sorted. His long slender carcase, his small visage like
a baked apple, his heavy air, his careless walk, excited the children to ridicule him. In the gibberish of the country, they gave
him the nickname of *Barnâ Bredanna*[1]; and the moment we were
out we heard nothing but *Barnâ Bredanna* all around us. He suffered it easier than I. I was vexed; I wanted to fight; it was what
the young rogues wanted. I fought; I was beat. My poor cousin
gave me all the assistance in his power; but he was weak, at one
stroke they knocked him down. It was then I became furious.
However, though I received some smart blows, it was not at me
they were aimed, it was at *Barnâ Bredanna;* but I so far increased
the evil by my mutinous passion, we could stir out no more but
when they were at school, for fear of being hooted and followed
by the scholars.

I am already become a redresser of grievances. To be a knight-
errant in form, I only wanted a lady. I had two. I went from time
to time to see my father at Nyon, a small city in the Vaudois
country, where he was settled. My father was much esteemed,
and kindness was extended to his son on that account. During the
short stay I made with him, it was who could receive me best.
A Madame de Vulson particularly showed me a thousand kind-
nesses, and, to fill up the measure, her daughter made me her
gallant. Anyone can tell what a gallant of eleven is to a girl of

---

[1] Bridled ass.

two-and-twenty. But these rogues are so glad to put their little puppets in the front to hide the great ones, or to tempt them by the show of a pastime they so well know how to render alluring! For my part, who saw between her and me no inequality, I took it up seriously; I gave into it with my whole heart, or rather with my whole head; for I was very little amorous elsewhere, though I was so even to madness, and my transports, my agitations, and my fury raised scenes that would make you die of laughing.

I am acquainted with two sorts of love, very distinct, very real, but not in the least allied, though each is extremely violent, and both differ from tender friendship. The whole course of my life has been divided between these two loves of so different a nature, and I have even experienced them both at the same time; for instance, at the time I speak of, whilst I claimed Mlle. de Vulson so publicly and so tyrannically that I could suffer no man to approach her, I had with a little Mlle. Goton meetings that were short enough, but pretty passionate, in which she thought proper to act the schoolmistress, and that was everything; but this everything, which was in fact everything to me, appeared to me supreme happiness; and already perceiving the value of the mystery, though I knew how to use it only as a child, I restored back to Mlle. de Vulson, who did not much suspect it, the trouble she took in employing me to hide other amours. But, to my great mortification, my secret was discovered, or not so well kept by my little schoolmistress as by me; for we were soon separated, and some time after, returning to Geneva and passing Coutance, I heard some little girls calling to me in a low voice, *Goton tic tac Rousseau.*

This Mlle. Goton was in truth a singular person. Though not handsome, she had a face difficult to be forgot, and that I too often, for an old fool, call yet to mind. Her eyes, in particular, were not of her age, or stature, or carriage. She had a little imposing and lofty air, extremely well adapted to her part, and which occasioned the first idea of anything between us. But that most extraordinary in her was a mixture of impudence and reserve difficult to conceive. She permitted herself the greatest familiarities with me, but never permitted me any with her; she treated me exactly as a child. This makes me think, she had either ceased to be one, or, on the contrary, she herself was still sufficiently so, as to perceive no more than play in the danger to which she exposed herself.

I belonged in a manner to each of these people, and so entirely, that with either of them I never thought of the other. But as to the rest, no resemblance in what they made me feel for them. I could have passed all my days with Mlle. de Vulson without a thought of leaving her; but on seeing her, my joy was calm, and did not reach emotion. I was particularly fond of her in a great company; her pleasantries, her ogling, even jealousy attached me to her: I triumphed with pride at a preference to great rivals she seemed to me to use ill. I was tortured, but I liked the torture. Applause, encouragement, smiles, heated me, animated me. I was passionate and furious; I was transported with love in a circle. Tête-à-tête I should have been constrained, dull, and perhaps sorrowful. However, I felt tenderly for her; I suffered if she was ill; I would have given my health to establish hers; and observe that I knew by experience what good and bad health was. Absent, I thought of her, she was wanting; present, her caresses came soft to my heart, not to my sense. I was familiar to her with impunity; my imagination asked nothing but she granted: I could, however, not have supported seeing her do as much for others. I loved her as a brother; but was jealous as a lover.

I should have been so of Mlle. Goton as a Turk, a fury, or a tiger, had I only imagined she could grant others the same favours she did me; for these were a boon I had to ask on my knees. I approached Mlle. de Vulson with an active pleasure, but without uneasiness; but at the mere sight of Mlle. Goton I was bewildered; every sense was overturned. I was familiar with the former, without taking liberties; on the contrary, trembling and agitated before the latter, even in the height of familiarity. I believe, had I remained too long with her, I could not have been able to live; my palpitations would have smothered me. I equally dreaded displeasing them; but was more complaisant to one, and more submissive to the other. I would not have angered Mlle. de Vulson for the world; but if Mlle. Goton had commanded me to throw myself in the flames, I think I should instantly have obeyed her.

My amours, or rather my rendezvous with her, did not continue long, happily for her and me. Though my connections with Mlle. de Vulson were not so dangerous, they also were not without their catastrophe, after having lasted a little longer. The end of these affairs ought always to have an air a little romantic, and cause exclamation. Though my correspondence with Mlle. de Vulson was less active, it was perhaps more endearing. We never separated without tears; and it is singular in what a burdensome void I found myself, whenever I left her. I could talk of nothing but her, or think of anything but her; my sorrows were real and lively: but I believe, at bottom, these heroic sorrows were not all for her, and that, without perceiving it, the amusements of which she was the centre, bore a good share in them. To soften the rigour of absence, we wrote each other letters, pathetical enough to split rocks. In fine, I had the glory of her not being able longer to hold out, and she came to see me at Geneva. This once my head was quite gone; I was intoxicated and mad the two days she stayed. When she departed, I would have thrown myself into the water after her, and long did the air resound with my cries. The following week she sent me sweetmeats and gloves, which would have appeared gallant, had I not at the same time learnt her marriage, and that this journey, whereby she had been pleased to honour me, was to buy her wedding-suit. I shall not describe my fury; it may be conceived. I swore in my noble rage never more to see the perfidious girl; thinking she could not suffer a greater punishment. However, it did not occasion her death; for twenty years afterwards, on a visit to my father, being with him on the lake, I asked who were those ladies we saw in a boat not far from ours. How, says my father, smiling, does not your heart tell you? These are thy ancient amours; it is Madame Cristin, it is Mlle. de Vulson. I started at the almost forgotten name; but I told the watermen to turn off, not judging it worth while, though I had a fine opportunity of revenging myself, to be perjured, and to renew a dispute twenty years past with a woman of forty.

Thus did I lose in foolery the most precious time of my child-hood, before my destination was determined. After great delibera-tion on my natural dispositions, they determined on what was the most repugnant to me: I was sent to a M. Masseron, registrar of the city, to learn under him, as M. Bernard said, the useful science of a scraper.[1] This nickname displeased me sovereignly; the hopes of heaping money by ignoble means flattered but little my lofty temper; the employment appeared to me tiresome and insupport-able; the assiduity and subjection completed my disgust, and I never went into the place where the registers are kept, but with a horror that increased from day to day. M. Masseron, on his part, little satisfied with me, treated me with disdain, incessantly up-braiding me as a fool and a blockhead; repeating daily that my uncle had assured him I was *knowing, knowing,* whilst in fact I knew nothing; that he had promised him a sprightly boy, and had sent him an ass. In fine, I was turned out of the Rolls igno-

---

[1] *Grapignan;* slang term for a lawyer.

miniously as a fool, and the clerks of M. Masseron pronounced me fit for nothing but to handle the file.

My vocation thus determined, I was bound apprentice; not however to a watchmaker, but to an engraver. The contempt of the registrar humbled me extremely, and I obeyed without murmur. My master, named M. Ducommun, was a boorish, violent young man, who made a shift, in a very little time, to tarnish all the splendour of my childhood, to stupefy my amiable and sprightly disposition, and to reduce my wits as well as my fortune to the true state of an apprentice. My Latin, my antiquities, history, all was for a long time forgotten: I did not even remember the world had ever produced Romans. My father, when I went to see him, saw no longer his idol; the ladies found nothing of the gallant Jean-Jacques; and I was myself so well convinced that M. and Mlle. Lambercier would no longer recognise me as their pupil, that I was ashamed to be seen by them; and since that time I have never seen them. The vilest inclinations, the basest tricks, succeeded my amiable amusements, without leaving me the least idea of them. I must have had, in spite of my good education, a great inclination to degenerate; for I did so in the most rapid

manner, and without the least trouble, and never did so forward a Caesar so quickly become a Laridon.[1]

The art itself did not displease me; I had a lively taste for draw-

---

[1] The names of two dogs in a fable of La Fontaine (Book VIII, fable 24).

ing; the exercise of the graver pleased me well enough, and as the talent of a watch-case engraver is very confined, I hoped to attain perfection. I should have reached it, perhaps, if the brutality of my master, and excessive constraint, had not disgusted me with labour. I wasted my time, to employ it in occupations of the same sort, but which had in my eyes the charms of liberty. I engraved a kind of medals to serve me and my companions as an order of chivalry. My master surprised me at this contraband labour, and broke my bones, telling me I exercised myself in coining money, because our medals bore the arms of the republic. I can safely swear I had not the least idea of counterfeit, and very little of real money. I knew better how to make a Roman As, than one of our threepenny pieces.

My master's tyranny rendered the labour I should otherwise have loved insupportable, and drove me to vices I should have despised, such as falsehood, laziness, and theft. Nothing has so well taught me the difference between filial dependence and servile slavery, as the remembrance of the change this period produced in me. Naturally timid and bashful, no one fault was so distant from me as effrontery. But I had enjoyed a decent liberty, which had only been restrained till then by degrees, and at last entirely vanished. I was bold at my father's, free at M. Lambercier's, discreet at my uncle's; I became fearful at my master's, and from that time was a lost child. Accustomed to a perfect equality with my superiors in their method of living, never to know a pleasure I could not command, to see no dish of which I did not partake, to have no wish but was made known, to bring, in fine, every motion of my heart to my lips; judge what I must be reduced to in a house where I dare not open my mouth, where I must leave the table without half filling my belly, and quit the room when I had nothing to do there, incessantly chained to my work, seeing nothing but objects of enjoyment for others, and none for me; where the prospect of the liberty of my master and his journeymen increased the weight of my subjection; where, in disputes on what I was best acquainted with, I dare not speak; where, in fine, everything I saw became for my heart an object I coveted, for no other reason than because I was deprived of it. Farewell ease, gaiety, happy expressions which before often caused my faults to escape chastisement. I cannot recollect without laughing, that one evening, at my father's, being ordered to bed for some prank without my supper, and passing through the kitchen with my sorry bit of bread, I saw and smelt the roast meat turning on the spit. People were round the fire; I must bow to every one as I passed. When I had been all round, eyeing the roast meat, which looked so nice, and smelt so well, I could not abstain from making that likewise a bow, and telling it, in a pitiful tone, Good-bye, roast meat! This sally of ingenuity appeared so pleasant, it procured my stay to supper. Perhaps, it might have had the same effect at my master's; but it is certain it would not have come to my mind, or that I had not dared to deliver it.

It was by this method I learnt to covet in silence, to be sly, dissimulate, lie, and at last to steal; a thought which till then never struck me, and of which since that time I cannot entirely cure myself. Covetousness and inability to attain always lead there. This is the reason all footmen are thieves, and why all apprentices ought to be; but in an even and tranquil situation, when everything they see is at command, they lose, as they grow up, this shameful propensity. Not having had the same advantage, I could not gain from it the same benefit.

It is almost always good sentiments badly directed which turn children's first steps to ill. In spite of the continual wants and temptations, I had been over[1] a year with my master without being able to resolve on taking any thing, not even eatables. My first theft was an affair of complaisance; but it opened the door to others, which had not so commendable an end.

There was a journeyman at my master's, named M. Verrat, whose house, in the neighbourhood, had a garden at a considerable distance, which produced exceeding fine asparagus. M. Verrat, who had not much money, took in his head to rob his mother of her forward asparagus, and sell them for a few hearty breakfasts. As he did not choose to expose himself, and was not very nimble, he chose me for this expedition. After a little preliminary flattery, which won me so much the readier as I did not perceive its end, he proposed it as an idea which that moment struck him. I opposed it greatly; he insisted. I never could resist flattery; I submitted. I went every morning and gathered the finest asparagus; I carried them to the Molard, where some good old woman, perceiving I had just stolen them, told me so to get them cheaper. In my fright I took what they would give me; I carried it to M. Verrat. It was soon metamorphosed into a breakfast, whereof I was the purveyor, and which he divided with another companion; for as to me, happy in a trifling morsel, I did not even touch their wine.

[1] Paris MS.: "nearly a year."

This game went on several days before it came into my mind to rob the robber, and to tithe M. Verrat's harvest of asparagus. I executed my roguery with the greatest fidelity; my only motive was to please him who set me to work. If, however, I had been taken, what a drubbing, what abuse, what cruel treatment should not I have undergone, while the miscreant, in belying me, would have been believed on his word, and I doubly punished for having dared to accuse him, because he was a journeyman, and I an apprentice only. Thus, in every state, the great rogue saves himself at the expense of the feeble innocent.

I thus learnt that it was not so terrible to thieve as I imagined, and I made so good a use of my science, that nothing I wished for within my reach was in safety. I was not absolutely badly fed at my master's, and sobriety was no otherwise painful to me, than because I saw him keep so little within its bounds. The custom of sending young people from table when those things are served up which tempt them most, appeared to me well adapted to render them as lickerish as knavish. I became, in a short time, the one and the other, and found it answer pretty well in general; sometimes very ill, when I was found out.

A recollection which makes me even now shudder and smile at the same time, is of an apple hunt which cost me dear. These apples were at the bottom of a pantry, which by an high lattice received light from the kitchen. One day, being alone in the house, I climbed on the oil-barrel to see in the garden of the Hesperides the precious fruit I could not approach. I fetched the spit to see if it would reach so far: it was too short. I lengthened it with another little spit which was used for small game; for my master loved hunting. I pricked at them several times without success; at last I felt with transport I was bringing an apple. I drew it very gently; the apple already touched the lattice; I was going to seize it. Who can express my grief? The apple was too big; it would not pass through the hole. What invention did I not make use of to pull it through? I was obliged to seek supports to keep the spit right, a knife long enough to split the apple, a lath to hold it up. At length by schemes and time I attained its division, hoping afterwards to draw the pieces one after the other. But they were scarcely divided when they both fell into the pantry. Compassionate reader, partake of my affliction!

I did not lose courage; but I lost a deal of time. I dreaded being surprised; I put off till the morrow a happier trial; I return to my work as if nothing had happened, without thinking of the two

indiscreet witnesses of my transaction, which I had left in the
pantry.

The next day, seeing a fine opportunity, I make the other trial.
I get up on my stool, I lengthen the spit, I aim, am just going to
prick. . . . Unfortunately the dragon did not sleep; all at once the
pantry door opens; my master comes out, crosses his arms, looks
at me, and says: Bravo! . . .The pen drops out of my hand.

Very soon, by continual bad treatment, I grew less feeling: it
seemed to me a sort of compensation for theft, which gave me a
right to continue it. Instead of looking back at the punishment,
I looked forward on the revenge. I judged that to beat me like a
scoundrel, gave me a right to be so. I saw that to rob and to be
beaten went together, and constituted a sort of trade, and that by
fulfilling that part of it which depended on me, I might leave the
care of the other to my master. On this idea, I set to thieving with
more tranquillity than before. I said to myself, What will be the
consequence? I shall be beaten. So be it; I am made for it.

I love to eat, without avidity; I am sensual, but not greedy. Too
many other tastes take that away from me. I never employed my
thoughts on my appetite but when my heart was unoccupied; and
this has so rarely happened, I have seldom had time to think of
good eating. This was the reason I did not long confine myself to
thieving eatables; I soon extended it to everything I liked; and if
I did not become a robber in form, it was because money never
much tempted me. In the common room my master had a private
closet locked; I found means to open the door, and shut it again,
without its appearing. There I laid under contribution his best
tools, his fine drawings, his impressions, all I had any mind to,
and that he affected to keep from me. These thefts were innocent
at the bottom, as they were employed only in his service; but I was
transported with joy at having these trifles in my power; I thought
I stole the talent with its productions. Besides, he had in his boxes
the filings of gold and silver, small jewels, pieces of value, and
money. If I had four or five sous in my pocket, it was a great deal:
however, far from touching, I do not recollect having glanced a
wistful look at any of those things. I saw them with more terror
than pleasure. I verily believe this dread of taking money and
what produces it, was caused in a great measure by education.
There were mixed with it secret ideas of infamy, prison, punishment, gallows, which would have made me tremble, had I been
tempted; whereas my tricks appeared to me no more than wag-
gery, and in fact were nothing else. The whole could occasion but

a good trimming from my master, and I was prepared for that beforehand.

But once more, I say, I did not covet sufficiently to have to abstain; I saw nothing to fight down. A sheet only of fine drawing-paper tempted me more than the money which would purchase a ream. This humour is the effect of one of the singularities of my character; and has had so much influence on my conduct as to merit an explanation.

I have passions extremely violent, and, whilst they agitate me, nothing can equal my impetuosity: I am a total stranger to discretion, respect, fear, or decorum; I am rude, saucy, violent, and intrepid; no shame can stop me, no danger can affright me. Beyond the sole object that employs my mind, the whole world is nothing to me: but all this lasts but for a moment, and the moment following I am a worm. Take me in my calm moments, I am indolence and timidity itself: the least thing startles and disheartens me; the humming of a fly makes me afraid; a word spoken, a shrug of the shoulders, alarms my laziness; fear and shame subdue me to such a degree, that I should be glad to hide myself from mortal eyes. When I am forced to act, I know not what to do; when forced to speak, I have nothing to say; if I am looked at, I am put out of countenance. When I am in a passion, I find sometimes enough to say; but in ordinary conversation I can find nothing, nothing at all: this is the sole reason I find it insupportable, because I am obliged to talk.

Add to this, none of my most favourite tastes consists in things to be purchased. I want none but pure pleasures, and money poisons them all. I love, for instance, those of the table; but not being able to suffer the constraint of good company, or the intemperance of taverns, I enjoy them only with a friend; for alone it is impossible; my imagination being busied on other things, I have no pleasure in eating. If my heated blood demands women, my beating heart still more demands love. Women who are to be bought have no charms for me; I doubt even whether my money would not be paid in vain. It is thus with every pleasure within my reach: when they are not gratis, I find them insipid. I am fond only of things which are for none but the first who knows how to enjoy them.

Money never seemed to me so precious a thing as people think it: and more, it never appeared to me a very convenient thing; it is good for nothing of itself; to enjoy it, you must transform it; you must buy, bargain, often be duped, pay dear, and be badly served. I want a thing good in quality; with my money I am sure to have it bad. I buy a new-laid egg dear, it is stale; the best fruit, it is green; a girl, she is tainted. I love good wine, but where shall I get it? At a wine-merchant's? Do what I will, he will poison me. Would I be perfectly well served? What attention, what trouble! Make friends, correspondents, send messages, write, go, come, wait, and often at last be deceived again. What trouble with my money! I fear it more than I love good wine.

A thousand times, during my apprenticeship and since, I have gone out to buy something nice. I go near the pastry-cook's, I perceive women at the counter; I think I already see them laugh, and make a jest among themselves of the little greedy-gut. I pass by a fruit-shop; I leer sideways at the fine pears, their savour is tempting; two or three young people close by watch me; I see at a distance a girl coming; is it not our maid? My near sight presents a thousand illusions. I take all who pass for persons of my acquaintance: everywhere I am intimidated, restrained by some obstacle: my wishes increase with my shame, and I return at last like a fool, devoured with lust, having in my pocket wherewithal to satisfy it, without having dared to buy anything.

I should enter into the most insipid particulars, were I to follow up in the use of my money, whether by myself, whether by others, the trouble, the shame, the repugnance, the inconvenience, the disgusts of all sorts I have always experienced. As I go on with my life, the reader, getting acquainted with my humour, will perceive all this without my fatiguing him with the recital.

This understood, one of my pretended contradictions will be easily comprehended, of reconciling an almost sordid avarice with the greatest contempt of money. It is a movable of so little use to me, I never think of desiring that I have not; and when I have any, I keep it a long time without spending it, for want of knowing how to employ it to my fancy: but does an agreeable and convenient occasion offer? I make so good use of it as to empty my purse without perceiving it. However, do not imagine that I have the miser's trick of spending through ostentation; quite the reverse; I lay it out privately and for my pleasure: instead of glorying in expense, I hide it. I so well perceive that money is not for my use, I am almost ashamed to have any, much more to make use of it. If I had ever possessed an income sufficient to live commodiously, I should never, I am certain, have been tempted to be avaricious. I should spend my whole income without seeking to increase it: but my precarious situation keeps me in fear. I adore liberty; I abhor constraint, trouble, or subjection. As long as the money lasts which I have in my purse, it ensures my independence, it frees me from contriving to get more; a necessity I always detested: but for fear of seeing it end, I make much of it. The money we possess is the instrument of liberty; that we pursue is the instrument of slavery. This is the reason I hold fast and covet nothing.

My disinterestedness is therefore nothing but laziness; the pleasure of having is not worth the trouble of acquiring; and my dissipation is likewise nothing but laziness: when the occasion of an agreeable expense offers, we cannot too readily lay hold of it. I am less tempted with money than things; for between money and the desired possession there is always an intermediary, but between the thing and its enjoyment there is none. I see the thing, it tempts me; if I see only the means of acquiring it, it does not tempt me.

I have therefore been a pilferer, and am yet sometimes, of trifles which tempt me, and that I had rather take than ask for. But little or big, I never recollect having in my life taken a farthing from anyone; except once, not fifteen years ago, I stole seven livres ten sous. The story is worth telling; for there is seen in it a priceless concurrence of impudence and stupidity I should find some difficulty to give credit to, had it regarded anyone but myself.

It was at Paris. I was walking with M. de Francueil, at the Palais Royal, about five o'clock. He pulls out his watch, looks at it, and says to me, Let us go to the Opera. With all my heart. We go. He takes two box tickets, gives me one, and goes in first with the other; I follow. In going in after him, I find the door crowded. I look; I see everybody up; I judge I might be lost in the crowd, or at least give reason to M. de Francueil to suppose me lost. I go out, ask for my check again, afterwards my money, and away I go, without thinking that I had scarcely reached the door when everyone was seated, and that M. de Francueil saw plainly I was not there.

As nothing was ever so distant from my humour as this behaviour, I note it, to show there are moments of a sort of delirium, when men are not to be judged by their actions. It was not precisely stealing the money; it was stealing the use of it: the less it was a robbery, the more infamous it was.

I should never end these accounts, were I to follow every track through which, during my apprenticeship, I passed from the sublimity of a hero to the baseness of a villain. However, in taking the vices of my condition, it was not possible entirely to take its tastes. I grew tired of the amusements of my companions, and when too great restraint had likewise disgusted me of work, everything hung heavy. This renewed my inclination for study, which had been long lost. Those studies, taking me off my work, became another crime, which brought on other punishments. This inclina-

STREET IN GENEVA

tion became by constraint a passion, and very soon a furious one. La Tribu, famous for letting out books, supplied me with every kind of them. Good or bad, all went down; I never picked them: I read them all with the same earnestness. I read at my work, I read in going to do a message, I read in the necessary, and forgot myself there for hours successively; my brain was turned with reading; I did nothing but read. My master watched me, surprised me, beat me, took my books. How many volumes were there not torn, burned, and thrown out at window! What sets remained imperfect at La Tribu's! When I had no money, I gave her my shirts, my cravats, my clothes, and my allowance of threepence a week was regularly carried there.

Thus, therefore, I might be told, money is become necessary. True; but it was when reading had deprived me of all activity. Entirely given up to this new taste, I did nothing but read, I robbed no longer. This is another of my characteristic differences. In the heat of a certain habit of being, a nothing calls me off, changes me, fixes me, at last becomes passion, and then all is forgot. I think of nothing but the new object which employs me. My heart beat with desire to dip into the new book in my pocket; I pulled it out the instant I was alone, and thought no more of pilfering my master's closet. I do not think I should have robbed even if my passions had been more expensive. Confined to the present moment, it did not reach my turn of mind to provide for futurity. La Tribu gave me credit; it was but a trifle, and when once I had pocketed my book, I looked no farther. Money that came to me naturally passed to this woman; and when she became pressing, nothing was at hand but my own things. To rob beforehand was too much foresight, and to rob to pay was no temptation.

By repeated quarrels, beatings, private and ill-chosen studies, my humour became reserved and wild, my head began to be impaired, and I led the life of an owl. However, though my taste did not preserve me from flat, unmeaning books, my good fortune preserved me from obscene and licentious ones; not that La Tribu, a woman in every respect very complaisant, would have made the least scruple at supplying me with them. But to raise their price, she named them with an air of mystery, which precisely forced me to refuse them, as much from disgust as shame; and chance so well seconded my modest humour, I was more than thirty years old before I first saw any one of those dangerous books which a fine lady of high society finds inconvenient, for, as she says, they can be read only with one hand.

In less than a year I ran through the thin shop of La Tribu, and then found my leisure hours cruelly unoccupied. Cured of my childish, rakish fancies by my taste for reading, and likewise by reading, which, though without choice, and often bad, brought back my heart, however, to nobler sentiments than my condition inspired; disgusted of all within my reach, and finding all that could tempt me, out of it; I saw nothing possible to flatter my heart. My senses, having beat high for some time, demanded an enjoyment of which I could not even imagine the object. I was as far from the proper one, as if I had been of no sex; and already at puberty and tender, I sometimes thought of my follies, but I saw no farther. In this strange situation, my uneasy imagination took a resolution which tore me from myself, and calmed my growing sensuality. It was to contemplate those situations which had attracted me in my studies, to recall them, to vary them, to combine them, to apply them so much to myself as to become one of the personages I imagined; to see myself continually in the most agreeable situations according to my taste; in fine, to let the fictitious situation in which I contrived to place myself, make me forget my real one, of which I was so discontented. This fondness of imaginary objects, and the facility of using them, filled up the measure of disgust for everything around me, and determined the inclination for solitude which has never left me since that time. We shall see more than once, in its place, the wild effects of this disposition, so unsociable and dull in appearance, but which proceeds in fact from a heart too affectionate, too amorous, and too tender, which, for want of other beings which resemble it, is forced to feed on fictions. It suffices, for the present, to have traced the origin and first cause of an inclination which has modified all my passions, and which, containing them in themselves, has always rendered me too lazy to act, by desiring with too much ardour.

Thus I reached sixteen, uneasy, discontented with everything and with myself, without relish for my trade, without the pleasures of my age, gnawed by desires whose object I was ignorant of, weeping without a subject of tears, sighing without knowing for what; in fine, caressing tenderly my chimeras, for want of seeing something around me that equalled them. On Sunday my companions came to fetch me after sermon to take a part in their pastime. I would have gladly escaped them if I could; but once beginning to play, I was more eager and went farther than the best of them; difficult to be led on or off. This was at all times my constant disposition. In our walks out of the city I went always forward without dreaming of returning, unless someone thought for me. I was caught twice; the gates were shut before I could reach them. The next day I was treated as you may imagine, and the second time I was promised such a reception for the third, that I resolved never to expose myself to the danger of it. This third time so much dreaded happened nevertheless. My vigilance was rendered useless by a cursed captain called M. Minutoli, who always shut the gate, where he was on guard, half an hour before the others. I was returning with two companions. At half a league from the city I hear them sound the retreat; I redouble my pace; I hear the drum beat; I run with all my might: I come up out of breath, all in a sweat: my heart beats; I see at a distance the soldiers at their post; I hasten; I cry with a suffocated voice. It was too late. At twenty steps from the advanced guard, I see the first bridge drawn up. I tremble to see in the air those terrible horns, the sinister and fatal augur of the inevitable fate this moment began for me.

In the first transport of rage I threw myself on the glacis, and bit the earth. My companions, laughing at their accident, immediately decided on what to do. So did I, but in a quite different manner. On the very spot I swore I would never more return to my master's; and the next morning, when, at the hour of opening, they went into the city, I bid them farewell for ever, begging them only to acquaint privately my cousin Bernard of the resolution I had taken, and of the place where he might see me once more.

On my becoming an apprentice, being more separated from him, I saw him less. For some time, however, we met together on Sundays; but insensibly each of us took other habits, and we saw each other but seldom. I am persuaded his mother contributed much to this change. He was, for his part, a boy of consequence; I, a pitiful apprentice; I was nothing better than a boy from St. Gervais. Equality was no longer to be found between us in spite of our birth; it was degrading himself to frequent me. However, connections did not entirely cease between us; and as he was a boy naturally good, he sometimes followed his heart in spite of his mother's lessons. Having learnt my resolution, he hastens, not to dissuade me from it, or partake of it; but to throw in by trifling presents something agreeable in my flight; for my own resources would not carry me far. He gave me, among other things, a little sword, which greatly pleased me, and which I took as far as Turin, where want caused me to sell it; and I passed it, as they say, through my body. The more I have reflected since on the manner he behaved in this critical moment, the more I am persuaded he followed the instructions of his mother, and perhaps of his father; for it is not possible but of himself he would have made some effort to retain me, or have been tempted to follow me: but no. He encouraged me in my design rather than dissuaded me from it; and when he saw me quite resolved, he quitted me without many tears. We never more saw or wrote to each other; it was pity. He was of a character essentially good: we were made for each other's friendship.

Before I abandon myself to the fatality of my destiny, let me be permitted to turn my eyes one moment on that which naturally awaited me, had I fallen into the hands of a better master. Nothing agreed so well with my humour, or was more likely to make me happy, than the quiet and obscure condition of a good mechanic, in certain classes particularly, such as is at Geneva that of the engravers. This art, lucrative enough for an easy subsistence, but not sufficient to lead to a fortune, would have bounded my ambition for the remainder of my days, and, leaving me a decent leisure for cultivating my moderate tastes, it had kept me in my sphere without presenting me any means of going beyond it. Having an imagination rich enough to ornament with its chimeras any art, powerful enough to transport me, in a manner, as I chose from one to another, it signified little which in fact I fell into. It could not be so far from the place I was in, to the greatest castle in Spain, but it would have been easy for me to have established myself there. From whence only it followed, that the most simple condition, that which caused the least bustle or care, that which left the mind most at liberty, was best adapted to me; and this was absolutely mine. I should have passed, in the bosom of my religion, of my native country, of my family and my friends, a calm and peaceable life, such as my character wanted, in the uniformity of a labour suited to my taste, and in a society according to my heart. I should have been a good Christian, a good citizen, a good father, a kind friend, a good artist, a good man. I should have liked my condition, perhaps been an honour to it; and after having passed an obscure and simple life, but even and calm, I should have died peaceably on the breast of my own family. Soon forgot, doubtless, I had been regretted at least whenever I was remembered.

Instead of that . . . what a picture am I going to draw? Ah! we will not anticipate the miseries of my life; my readers will hear but too much of the doleful subject.

BOOK TWO

As MUCH as the moment, when terror suggested the project of flight, had appeared afflicting, so much did that of executing it appear charming. Still a child, leaving my country, my parents, my support, my resources; an apprenticeship half finished, without knowing enough of the trade to subsist by it; to be given up to the horrors of misery, without perceiving the least means of getting out of it; in the age of weakness and innocence, to expose myself to every temptation of vice and despair; seek afar off misfortune, error, snares, slavery, and death, under a yoke more inflexible than that I had not been able to bear — all this I was going to do; this was the perspective I ought to have held up. How different was that I painted to myself! The independence I thought I had acquired was the only sentiment which struck me. Free and my own master, I thought I could do everything, attain all: I had but to launch, and I thought I could raise myself to fly in the air. I entered with security into the vast space of the world; my merit was to fill it: at each step I expected to find feasting, treasures, and adventures, friends ready to serve me, mistresses eager to please me: I expected, on my appearance, the eyes of the universe to be fixed on me; not however the whole universe; I dispensed with that in some sort, I did not want so much; a pleasing society was sufficient without troubling my head about the rest. My moderation inscribed me in a narrow sphere, but deliciously chosen, where I was sure to carry the sway. One castle only satisfied my ambition. A favourite of the lord and lady, the young lady's gallant, her brother's friend, and the neighbours' protector, I was satisfied; I desired nothing more.

Awaiting this modest future, I sauntered a few days round the city, lodging with country-folks of my acquaintance, who all received me with more kindness than I should have found from inhabitants in the city. They welcomed me, lodged me, and fed me too well to claim the merit. This could not be called receiving alms; it was not attended by a sufficient air of superiority.

By great travelling and running about, I went as far as Confignon, a country of Savoy two leagues from Geneva. The parson's name was M. de Pontverre. This name, famous in the history of the republic, struck me greatly. I was curious to see how the de-

scendants of the gentlemen of the Spoon[1] were formed. I went
to see M. de Pontverre. He received me well, talked of the heresy
of Geneva, of the authority of our sacred mother the church, and
gave me a dinner. I found very little to answer to arguments which
finished in that manner; and judged that parsons who gave so
good a dinner, were at least as good as our ministers. I was most
certainly more learned than M. de Pontverre, gentleman that he
was; but I was too knowing a guest to be so good a theologian; and
his Frangy wine, which seemed to me excellent, argued so vic-
toriously in his favour, I should have blushed to have stopped the
mouth of so kind a host. I therefore yielded, or at least I did not
openly resist. To have seen all the discretion I made use of, one
would have thought me false; it is an error. I was only courteous,
that is certain. Flattery, or rather condescension, is not always a
vice; it is oftener a virtue, especially in young people. The kindness we receive from a man, attaches us to him; it is not to impose
on him we submit; it is not to vex him, not return evil for good.
What interest had M. de Pontverre in entertaining me, treating
me kindly, and wanting to convince me? None but mine. My
young heart told me so. I was touched with gratitude and respect
for the good-natured priest. I was sensible of my superiority; I
would not let it trouble him in return for his hospitality. There
was no hypocritical motive in this conduct: I never thought of
changing my religion, and so far from contracting a familiarity
with the idea, I thought of it with a horror that should have long
driven it from my mind: I only meant not to vex those who flattered me with this view; I meant to cultivate their benevolence,
and leave them the hopes of success in seeming less armed than
I really was. My fault in that respect resembled the coquetry of
honest women, who sometimes, in order to gain their point, know,
without permitting or promising anything, how to cause more to
be hoped than they ever intend to perform.

Reason, pity, and the love of order, certainly demanded, instead
of giving into my folly, that I should be dissuaded from the ruin
I was running into, by sending me back to my friends. This is
what any man, truly virtuous, would have done or tried to do.
But although M. de Pontverre was a good man, he was not a virtuous one. He was, on the contrary, a devotee, who knew no other

---

[1] The "gentlemen of the spoon" were a league of Catholic knights formed
against the Genevese at the Reformation; they were subjects of the Duke of
Savoy, and had sworn to "eat the Genevese with a spoon." They were led by
a de Pontverre, and wore a spoon hung round their necks as a party badge.

virtue than worshipping images, and telling his beads; a sort of missionary, who imagined nothing better, for the good of the faith, than writing libels against the ministers of Geneva. So far from thinking of sending me home again, he took the advantage of the desire I showed to leave it, by putting it out of my power to return, even though I wished for it. It was a thousand to one but he was sending me to perish with hunger, or become a villain. He did not see this. He saw a soul taken from heresy, and restored to the faith. An honest man or a villain, what did that import, provided I went to mass? You must not imagine, however, this manner of thinking is peculiar to Catholics; it is that of every dogmatical religion whose essence is not to do, but to believe.

God has called you, says M. de Pontverre. Go to Annecy; you will find there a good and charitable lady, that the King's goodness enables to turn souls from the errors she herself has quitted. He meant Madame de Warens, lately converted, whom the priests forced, in reality, to divide, with the blackguards who had sold them their faith, a pension of two thousand livres the King of Sardinia allowed her. I felt myself extremely mortified at having occasion to apply to a good and charitable lady. I had no objection to their supplying me with what I wanted, but not to their bestowing charity on me, and a devotee did not much please me. But being urged by M. de Pontverre, and by hunger at my heels; glad likewise to make a journey and to have a prospect in view, I determined, though with some trouble, and set off for Annecy. I could easily get there in a day; but I did not hurry, I took three. I saw no country-seat to the right or the left, without going to seek the adventure I was sure awaited me there. I dared not enter, or knock; for I was very timid: but I sung under those windows which had the best appearance; much surprised, after having tired my lungs, to find neither ladies nor their daughters appear, as I knew some charming songs my companions had taught me, and which I sung most admirably.

I at last arrive; I see Madame de Warens. This period of my life has determined my character; I cannot resolve to pass it lightly over. I was in the middle of my sixteenth year. Without being what is called a handsome fellow, I was well made for my small size: I had a smart foot, good leg, an easy air, sprightly physiognomy, delicate mouth, hair and eyebrows black, small eyes rather sunk, but which threw out forcibly the fire which heated my blood. Unfortunately I knew nothing of all this; for in my life I never thought my person worth a thought, but when it was too late to make anything of it. Thus I had, with the timidity of my age, a natural one very amiable, always uneasy for fear of displeasing. Besides, though my mind was pretty well furnished, not having seen the world, I totally failed in its manners; and my judgement, far from assisting, served only to intimidate me more, in making me sensible how little I had.

Fearing therefore my presence might prejudice me, I took a different advantage; I wrote a fine letter in the style of an orator,

MME. DE WARENS

where tacking the phrases of books to the expression of an apprentice, I displayed all my eloquence to captivate the benevolence of Madame de Warens. I put M. de Pontverre's letter into mine, and set out for this terrible audience. I did not find Madame de Warens; I was told she was just gone to church. It was on Palm-Sunday, in the year 1728. I ran after her: I see her, I come up with her, I speak to her. . . . I ought to remember the place; I have often since that watered it with my tears, and covered it with kisses. Why cannot I surround with pillars of gold this happy spot? Why cannot I persuade the whole earth to worship it? Whoever is fond of honouring monuments of the salvation of the human species, ought not to approach it but on his knees.

It was in a passage behind the house, between a rivulet on the right hand, which separated it from the garden, and the wall of the yard on the left, leading by a private door to the church of the Cordeliers. Just going in at this door, Madame de Warens turns round on hearing my voice. How did I change at this sight! I expected to see a devout grim old woman: M. de Pontverre's good woman could be nothing else in my opinion. I see a face loaded with beauty, fine blue eyes full of sweetness, a complexion that dazzled the sight, the contour of an enchanting neck. Nothing escaped the rapid glance of the young proselyte; for I instantly became hers, certain that a religion preached by such missionaries must lead to heaven. She takes, smiling, the letter I present with a trembling hand, opens it, runs over M. de Pontverre's, returns to mine, which she reads through, and which she would have read again, had not the servant told her the service was begun. So! child, says she with a voice which startled me, you are running about the country very young; it is pity, indeed. And without waiting my answer, she added: Go to my house; tell them to give you some breakfast: after mass I will come and speak to you.

Louise-Eléonore de Warens was a young lady of La Tour de Pil, a noble and ancient family of Vevey, a city in the country of Vaud. She was married very young to M. de Warens, of the house of Loys, eldest son of M. de Villardin, of Lausanne. This marriage, which produced no children, not turning out well, Mme. de Warens, driven by some domestic uneasiness, took the opportunity of King Victor Amédée's presence at Evian of passing the lake, and throwing herself at the feet of this prince; thus abandoning her husband, her family, and her country, by a giddiness nearly resembling mine, which she likewise lamented at her leisure hours. The King, who loved to affect the zealous Catholic, took her under his protection, gave her a pension of fifteen hundred livres of Piedmont, which was a great deal for a prince so little profuse; but perceiving, that, from this reception, he was thought amorous, he sent her to Annecy, escorted by a detachment of his guards, where, under the direction of Michel Gabriel de Bernex, titular Bishop of Geneva, she made her abjuration at the convent of the Visitation.

She had been there six[1] years when I came, and was then eight-and-twenty, being born with the century. She possessed those beauties which remain, because they are more in the physiognomy than in the features: hers was therefore in its first splendour. Her air was caressing and tender, her look extremely mild, the smile of an angel, a mouth the size of mine, her hair of an ash colour, of uncommon beauty, to which she gave a neglected turn which rendered it very smart. She was of a small stature, short, and thick in the waist, though without deformity. But it was impossible to see a finer face, a finer neck, more beautiful hands, or well-turned arms.

Her education was a mixture. She had, like me, lost her mother at her birth, and indifferently receiving instruction as it came, she learnt a little of her governess, a little of her father, a little of her masters, and a great deal from her lovers; particularly a M. de Tavel, who, having taste and knowledge, adorned with them the person he loved. But so many different sort of knowledge hurt each other, and the little regularity she bestowed on them prevented these several studies from extending the natural clearness of her mind. Thus, though she had some of the principles of moral and natural philosophy, she still retained the taste of her father for empirical medicine and chemistry; she prepared elixirs, tinctures, balsams, remedies, and pretended she possessed secrets. Quacks and cheats, seeing her weakness, beset her, ruined her, and consumed, amidst furnaces and drugs, her mind, her talents, and her charms, which might have been the delight of the noblest society.

But although these vile knaves abused her ill-directed education to darken the lights of her reason, her excellent heart was proof, and remained always the same: her amiable and mild character, her feelings for misfortunes, her unbounded goodness, her sprightly humour, open and free, never changed; and even at the approach of age, plunged into indigence, ills and divers calamities, the serenity of her noble soul preserved, to the last, all the cheerfulness of her happy days.

Her errors proceeded from a fund of inexhaustible activity, which incessantly demanded employment. It was not the intrigues of women she wanted, it was planning and directing new undertakings. She was born for great affairs. Madame de Longueville, in her place, would have been a mere pretender; she, in

---

[1] Actually two; she had arrived in October 1726, and was now 29.

Madame de Longueville's place, had governed the State. Her talents were misplaced, and that which would have raised her to honour in a more exalted station, ruined her in that wherein she lived. In things within her reach, she always drew her plan in her mind, and always comprehended her object. This was the cause that, by employing means proportioned to her view more than to her strength, she miscarried by others' faults; and, her plan failing, she was ruined, where others would hardly have lost anything. This inclination for business, which brought on her so many evils, was at least of great service to her in her monastic asylum, in preventing her from passing the remainder of her days there as she had intended. The uniform and simple life of a nun, the silly gossiping of their parlour, could never flatter a mind always in motion, which, forming each day new systems, wanted liberty to expand itself. The good Bishop de Bernex, with less wit than Francis of Sales, resembled him in many points; and Madame de Warens, whom he called his child, and who resembled Madame de Chantal[1] in many others, might have resembled her in her retirement, had not her taste diverted her from the laziness of a convent. It was not want of zeal that prevented this amiable woman from giving herself up to the trifling formalities of devotion which seemed necessary to a new convert under the direction of a prelate. Whatever was her motive for changing her religion, she was sincere in that she had embraced. She might repent for having committed the fault, but she did not desire to return to her former profession. She not only died a good Catholic, she lived one in good earnest; and I dare affirm, I who think I have read the bottom of her soul, that it was solely aversion to grimace that she did not act the devotee in public. She had a piety too solid to affect devotion. But this is not the place to enlarge on her principles; I shall find other occasions to speak of them.

Let those who deny the sympathy of hearts explain, if they can, how, on the first interview, the first word, the first look, Madame de Warens inspired me, not only with the liveliest passion, but a perfect confidence, which was always retained. Suppose what I felt for her was really love; which would, however, appear very doubtful to those who will follow the history of our amity; why was this passion accompanied from its birth with sentiments it least inspires; the tranquillity of the heart, calmness,

---

[1] St. Jane Frances de Chantal (1572-1641), Foundress of the Visitation Nuns, and spiritual daughter of St. Francis de Sales, Bishop of Geneva.

serenity, security, assurance? How in approaching, for the first
time, an amiable, polite, and dazzling woman; a lady in a superior
situation to mine, and such as I had never access to before; her
on whom depended my destiny, in some measure, by the interest,
more or less, she might take in it; how, I say, with all this, did I at
once find myself as free, as easy, as if perfectly sure of pleasing
her? Why had not I a moment's perplexity, timidity, or constraint? Naturally bashful and discountenanced, having seen
nothing, why did I take the first day, the first instant, the freedom
of manner, the tender language, the familiar style, I had ten years
afterwards, when the closest intimacy had rendered them natural
to me? Do we feel love, I don't say without desires, for I had
them; but without uneasiness, without jealousy? Would we not,
at least, know from the object we love, whether we are loved?
That is a question which no more came into my mind ever once
to ask her, than to ask whether I was loved by myself; nor was
she ever more curious with me. There certainly was something
very singular in my feelings for this charming woman, and you
will find, by the sequel, extravagances you do not expect.

The question was what was to be done with me, and to talk of
it more at leisure she kept me to dinner. This was the first meal
of my life where I wanted appetite; and her woman, who waited
at table, said too, I was the first traveller of my age and of my
sort she had seen wanting it. This remark, which did not hurt me
in the mind of her mistress, fell a little hard on a great fellow who
dined with us, and devoured to his own share a meal sufficient for
six people.

As to me, I was in an ecstasy that did not permit me to eat. My
heart was fed by a feeling quite new, which engrossed my whole
being; it left me no spirit for other functions.

Madame de Warens wanted to know the particulars of my
little history: I once more found, in telling it her all the heat[1]
I had lost at my master's. The more I engaged this excellent soul
in my favour, the more she complained of the fate to which I was
going to expose myself. Her tender compassion appeared in her
mien, in her looks, and in her gesture. She dared not exhort me to
return to Geneva. In her situation it would be a crime of high
treason against Catholicism, and she was not ignorant how much
she was watched, and how her conversation was weighed. But she
spoke in so touching a tone of my father's affliction, you might

---

[1] Paris MS.: "all the heat with which Mlle. de Vulson had inspired me, and
which I had lost at my master's."

plainly see she would have approved of my going to console him. She did not know how much, without thinking on it, she pleaded against herself. Besides, my resolution was taken, as I think I told her: the more I found her eloquent and persuasive, and the more her discourse reached my heart, the less I could resolve to separate from her. I saw that to return to Geneva was raising an almost insurmountable barrier between her and me, without returning in the steps I had taken, and to which it was as well to keep at once. I therefore kept to them. Madame de Warens, seeing her endeavours fruitless, did not proceed so as to expose herself: but, says she, with a look of compassion, Poor little fellow, thou must go where God calls thee; but when thou art grown up, thou wilt remember me. I fancy she did not think this prediction would be so cruelly accomplished.

The whole difficulty still remained: How subsist so young from my own country? Scarcely reached half my apprenticeship, I was far from knowing my trade. Had I known it, I could not live by it at Savoy, a country too poor for arts. The great fellow who dined for us, obliged to make a pause to relieve his jaws, gave an advice which he said came from heaven, but which, to judge by its effects, came rather from the contrary place. It was that I should go to Turin, where, in an hospital founded for the instruction of the catechumens, I should have, said he, temporal and spiritual food, until, belonging to the Church, I should find, by the charity of good people, a place that would suit me. As to the expenses of the journey, his Highness my Lord Bishop will not be backward, when Madame proposes this holy work, in providing in a charitable manner for it; and Madame the Baroness, who is so charitable, said he, leaning over his plate, will with earnestness, certainly, contribute likewise.

I thought all these charities very afflicting: my heart was full; I said nothing; and Madame de Warens, without catching at this project with the ardour it was offered, contented herself with saying everyone ought to contribute to good according to their abilities, and that she would speak of it to his Lordship: but this devil of a man, who dreaded she would not speak to his wishes, and who had a trifling interest in the business, ran and acquainted the almoners, and so well instructed these good-natured priests, that when Madame de Warens, who dreaded the journey for me, would have spoken of it to the Bishop, she found it was an affair settled, and he instantly gave her the money destined for my little viaticum. She dared not ask my stay; I was approaching the age when a woman like her could not decently want to keep a young man with her.

My journey being thus regulated by those who were so careful of me, I was obliged to submit, and I did it even without much repugnance. Although Turin was farther than Geneva, I imagined that, being the capital, it had more relation with Annecy than with a city which was foreign to its state and religion: besides, departing to obey Madame de Warens, I looked on myself as still living under her direction; it was more than living in her neighbourhood. In fine, the idea of a great journey flattered my wandering fancy, which already began to show itself. It seemed a fine thing to me to pass the mountains at my age, and to raise myself above my companions by the whole height of the Alps. To see the world is an allurement a Genevan rarely resists; I therefore gave my consent. My great fellow was to set off within two days with his wife; I was entrusted and recommended to them, as was likewise my purse, which was increased by Madame de Warens: she likewise secretly gave me a little stock, to which she added ample instructions; and we set off on Wednesday in Holy Week.

The day after I left Annecy, my father, who had traced me, arrived, with a M. Rival, his friend, a watchmaker like himself, a man of sense, of wit even, who wrote verse better than La Motte, and spoke almost as well as he; nay more, he was a perfectly honest man, but whose misplaced learning only served to make his son an actor.

These gentlemen saw Madame de Warens, and contented themselves with lamenting my fate with her, instead of following and overtaking me, which they might have done with ease, being on horseback and I on foot. The same thing happened with my uncle Bernard. He came as far as Confignon, and from thence, knowing I was at Annecy, he returned to Geneva. It seemed my relations conspired with my stars to give me up to the destiny which awaited me. My brother was lost by a like negligence, and so thoroughly lost they never knew what became of him.

My father was not only a man of honour; he was a man of great probity, and had one of those generous souls which produce shining virtues. Besides, he was a good father, particularly to me. He loved me very tenderly, but he also loved pleasure, and other inclinations had a little cooled paternal affection since I lived a great distance from him. He married again at Nyon; and although his wife was not of an age to give me brothers, she had relations: that made another family; he had other objects, other connections, which did not often recall me to his memory. My father was growing old without any support for old age. My brother and I had a trifling legacy by my mother, the interest of which was for my father during our absence. The idea did not strike him directly, or prevent him from doing his duty; but it acted sullenly without his perceiving it, and sometimes slackened his zeal, which he had carried farther without it. This is, I think, the reason that, once traced as far as Annecy, he did not follow me to Chambery, where he was morally sure to come up with me. This is also the reason that, going often to see him since my flight, he always showed me the caresses of a father, but without great efforts to detain me.

This conduct of a father, whose tenderness and virtue I was so well acquainted with, has caused me to make reflections on myself, which have not a little contributed to keep my heart sound. I drew from them this great maxim of morality, the only one perhaps in practical use, to shun those situations which put our duty in opposition with our interests, and which show us our good in the misfortunes of others; and that in such situations, however sincere a love for virtue we bear, we weaken sooner or later without perceiving it, and become unjust and wicked in fact, without ceasing to be just and innocent at the heart.

This maxim, strongly imprinted on my heart, and put in practice in all my conduct, though a little late, is one of those which have given me the most whimsical and foolish appearance, not only among the public, but more particularly among my acquaintance. I have been charged with being original, and not doing like others. In fact, I thought little of doing either like others or otherwise than they did. I sincerely desired to do what was right. I avoided, as much as possible, those situations which procured me an interest contrary to that of another man, and consequently a secret, though involuntary, desire of hurting that man.

Two years ago,[1] my Lord Maréchal would have put me down in his will. I opposed it with all my power. I wrote him word I would not for the world know I was in any man's will, and much less in his. He complied; at present he offers me an annuity. I do not oppose it. They will say I find my account in this change: that may be. But, oh! my benefactor, my father, if I have the misfortune to survive you, I know that in losing you I lose everything, and that I shall not get by it.

---

[1] Paris MS. adds note: "In 1763."

This is, according to me, sound philosophy, the only one that truly suits the human heart. I am every day more penetrated with its great solidity, and have resumed it in different manners in my late works: but the public, who are frivolous, have not been able to remark it. If I survive the completion of this undertaking long enough to begin another, I propose giving, in a continuation of *Emile*, an example so charming and so striking of this same maxim, that my readers shall be forced to observe it. But here are reflections enough for a traveller; it is time to go on my journey.

I made it more agreeable than might be expected, and my clown was not so morose as he appeared. He was a man of a middle age, wore his grisly black hair cued; a grenadier's air, strong voice, gay enough, a good walker, a better eater, and who was of all trades, for want of knowing any one. He proposed, I think, to establish at Annecy some manufacture or other. Madame de Warens did not fail to give in to the project, and it was to get it approved by the minister, he undertook, his expenses well repaid him, the journey to Turin. This man had the talent of intrigue in pushing himself always amongst the priests, and affecting a readiness to serve them; he had learnt at their school a certain devout jargon which he incessantly made use of, setting himself up as a great preacher. He also knew a Latin passage of the Bible, and it was as if he had known a thousand, for he repeated it a thousand times a day; rarely in want of money, when he knew of any in others' purses; more cunning, however, than knavish; and dealing out, in the tone of a mountebank, his paltry sermon, he resembled the hermit Peter preaching his crusade, with his sword by his side.

As to Madame Sabran, his wife, she was a good-natured woman enough, quieter by day than by night. As I always lay in their chamber, her noisy watchings often awoke me, and would have awakened me much more, had I known their subject. But I did not even suspect it; I was in this regard of a dulness, which left to nature only the whole care of my instruction.

I got on gaily with my pious guide and his buxom companion. No accident troubled our journey; I was in the most happy situation of body and mind I ever was in my days. Young, vigorous, full of health, security, and confidence in myself and others, I was in that short but precious moment of life, when its expansive plenitude extends in a manner our being over all our sensations, and embellishes, in our eyes, all nature with the charms of our existence. My sweet uneasiness had an object which rendered it less wandering, and fixed my imaginations. I looked on myself

as the work, the pupil, the friend, almost the lover of Madame de
Warens. The obliging things she said to me, the little caresses she
gave me, the tender concern she seemed to have for me, her charming looks, which appeared to me full of love, because they inspired
me with love; all this fed my ideas during the way, and made me
dream deliciously. No fear, no doubt of my fate, troubled these
dreams. To send me to Turin was, in my opinion, to settle me
there, to place me agreeably. I had no apprehension about myself;
others had taken those cares on them. Thus I walked on lightly,
eased of that weight: youthful desires, enchanting hopes, brilliant
projects, filled my thoughts. Every object I saw seemed to warrant
my approaching felicity. In the houses I imagined rural feastings,
in the meadows wanton games, along the river baths, walks, and
fish, on the trees delicious fruit, under their shade voluptuous
meetings, on the mountains tubs of milk and cream, a charming
laziness, peace, simplicity, and the pleasure of going wheresoever
I chose. In fine, nothing struck my sight without carrying to my
heart some enticement to enjoyment. The grandeur, the variety,
the real beauty of the prospect, rendered these delights worthy of
my reason. Vanity too threw in its mite. So young and to go to
Italy, already to have seen so much country, to follow Hannibal
across the mountains, seemed a glory beyond my age. Add to all
this frequent and good repose, a good appetite and plenty to satisfy
it; for, faith, it was not worth while to let me want, and at the
table of M. Sabran what I ate could not be missed.

I do not recollect to have had, in the whole course of my life, an
interval more perfectly exempt from cares and trouble, than the
seven or eight days[1] we took to make this journey; for the pace
of Madame Sabran, by which ours was regulated, made it no more
than a long walk. This remembrance has left me a lively relish
for everything which resembles it, particularly for mountains and
journeys on foot. I have journeyed on foot in my best days only,
and always with delight. Very soon business, luggage to carry,
forced me to act the gentleman and take a carriage: care, embarrassment, and constraint, got in with me; and from that time,
instead of feeling, as I used to do in my former journeys, nothing
but the pleasure of going, I felt nothing so much as the desire of
getting to the end. I long sought at Paris for two companions of
the same turn as myself, who would each devote fifty guineas
from their pockets, and a twelvemonth's time, to make together,

---

[1] Actually nineteen days (March 24-April 12).

and on foot, the tour of Italy, without any other encumbrance than a young fellow to carry a bag for our nightshirts. Many offered, much pleased in appearance with the project; but at bottom, taking the whole as a mere castle in the air, which we talk over in conversation without intending to execute it in fact. I remember that, speaking with delight of this project to Diderot and Grimm, I at last gave them a fancy to it. I once thought it a thing done; but the whole ended in making a journey on paper, in which Grimm found nothing so pleasing as to make Diderot do a great many impious actions, and to thrust me in the Inquisition in his place.

My regret at arriving so soon at Turin was alleviated by the pleasure of seeing a great city, and by the hope of soon figuring there in a manner worthy of me; for the fumes of ambition had already reached my head: I already regarded myself as much above the condition of an apprentice; I was far from foreseeing that in a short time I should be much below it.

Before I proceed farther, I ought to make to the reader my excuse or justification, as well for the trifling narrations I have just entered into, as for those I may enter into afterwards, and which have nothing engaging in his eyes. In the work I have undertaken of exposing myself entirely to the public, nothing of myself must remain obscure or hidden; I must keep myself incessantly under their eye, that they may follow me, through all the wanderings of my heart, into every recess of my life; they must not lose sight of me for a moment, for fear lest, finding in my relation the least void, the least gap, it should be said, What was he doing all that time? and I should be accused of not having told all. I give scope enough to the malignity of men by my relation, without giving still more by my silence.

My little stock was gone; I had been babbling, and my indiscretion was not to my conductors an entire loss. Madame Sabran found means to get from me even a little riband, embroidered with silver, which Madame de Warens had given me for my little sword, which I regretted more than all the rest: the sword had also remained with them, had I been less obstinate. They faithfully defrayed my expenses on the journey, but had left me nothing. I arrive at Turin without clothes, without money, and without linen; and leaving wholly to my sole merit all the honour of the fortune I was going to make.

I had letters; I carried them, and was immediately led to the Hospital of the Catechumens, to be instructed in the religion for

which they sold me my subsistence. In going in I saw a large door
with iron bars, which when I had passed was double-locked on my
heels. This beginning appeared to me more imposing than agreeable, and began to set me thinking, when I was conducted to a
pretty large room. All the furniture that was there was a wooden
altar, with a large crucifix on it, at the bottom of the room, and
around it, four or five chairs, also of wood, which appeared to
have been rubbed with wax, but which shone only from continual
use and rubbing. In this assembly-hall were four or five frightful
banditti, my companions of instruction, but who seemed rather

the devil's bodyguard than candidates for the kingdom of God.
Two of these villains were Slavonians, who called themselves
Jews and Moors, and who, as they owned to me, passed their time
in running over Spain and Italy embracing Christianity, and
being baptized wherever the produce was worth the labour. Another door of iron was opened, which divided in two a large balcony that gave on to the court. By this door entered our sisters the
catechumens, who like me were going to be regenerated, not by
baptism, but by a solemn abjuration. They were the greatest sluts
and the nastiest street-walkers that ever bestunk the flock of our
Lord. One only seemed pretty and engaging enough. She was
nearly of my age, perhaps a year or two older. She had roguish
eyes, which now and then met mine. That gave me some desire

to be acquainted with her; but during almost two months she remained in this house, where she had already been three, it was impossible to accost her, so much was she recommended to our old jailor's wife, and watched by the holy missionary, who laboured for her conversion with more zeal than diligence. She must have been extremely stupid, though she did not appear so; for never was so long an instruction. The holy man never found her in a state to abjure; but she grew weary of her cloister, and said she would go out, Christian or not. They were obliged to take her at the word, while she still consented to become one, for fear she should grow refractory, and hear no more of it.

The little community was assembled in honour of the new-comer. They made us a short exhortation; to me, to engage me to correspond with the grace of God bestowed on me; to the others, to invite them to grant me their prayers, and edify me by their example. This done, our virgins being returned to their cloister, I had time to contemplate, quite at my ease, that wherein I found myself.

The next morning we were again assembled for instruction: it was then I began to reflect, for the first time, on the step I was about to take, and on the events which had brought me there.

I have said, I repeat, and shall repeat, perhaps, a thing whereof I am every day more persuaded; which is, that if a child ever received an education reasonable and sound, it was I. Born of a family whose morals distinguished it from the vulgar, I received none but lessons of prudence, and examples of honour from all my relations. My father, though a man of pleasure, had not only great honour, but a deal of religion. Gallant in the world, and a Christian in the interior, he early suggested to me those sentiments with which he was penetrated. Of my three aunts, all prudent and virtuous, the two elder were devotees; the third, a girl at the same time full of grace, wit, and sense, was perhaps more so than they, though with less ostentation. From the bosom of this estimable family, I went to M. Lambercier's, who, though of the Church and a preacher, believed inwardly, and acted almost as well as he said. His sister and himself cultivated, by gentle and judicious instruction, the principles of piety they found in my heart. These worthy people employed, to that end, means so apt, so discreet, and so reasonable, that, far from wearying me with their sermon, I never left it without being internally touched, and making resolutions to live well, in which, by seriously thinking on it, I rarely failed. At my aunt Bernard's, devotion was a little

more tiresome, because she made a science of it. At my master's,
I thought but little of it, without, however, thinking differently. I
found no young people to pervert me. I became a scamp, but not
a libertine.

I had then as much religion as a child of the age I was of could
have: I had even more, for why should I now disguise my
thoughts? My childhood was not that of a child. I felt, I thought
always as a man. It was only in growing up I returned to the
ordinary class; at my birth I left it. I shall be laughed at thus to
give myself out for a prodigy. Be it so; but when they have laughed
heartily, let them find a child that at six years old a romance
affects, moves, and transports, to a degree of weeping showers of
tears; I shall then see my ridiculous vanity, and will agree I am
wrong.

Thus, when I said we should not converse with children on
religion, if we wish they may one day have any, and that they
were incapable of knowing God, even after our manner; I drew
my sentiment from my observations, not from my own experience: I knew it was not conclusive for others. Find J. J. Rousseaus
at six years old, and talk to them of God at seven, I will be answer-
able you run no hazard.

It is understood, I suppose, that for a child, or even a man, to
have religion, is to follow that he was born in. Sometimes you
take from it; rarely add to it: dogmatical faith is the fruit of education. Besides this common principle which tied me to the religion of my forefathers, I had the peculiar aversion of our city for
Catholicism, which we were taught was dreadful idolatry, and
whose clergy were painted in the blackest colours. This sentiment
was carried so far in me, that, at the beginning, I never glanced
towards the inside of a church, never met a priest in his surplice,
never heard the bell of a procession, without shaking with terror
and affright, which soon left me in cities, but has often returned
in the country parishes that had more resemblance to those where
I first experienced it. It is true, this impression was singularly
contrasted by the remembrance of the caresses which the priests
of the environs of Geneva bestow on the children of the city. At
the same time the hand-bell for the viaticum made me afraid, the
bells for mass or vespers reminded me of a breakfast, a collation,
fresh butter, fruits, or milk. The good dinner at M. de Pontverre's
still produced a great effect. Thus was I easily turned from those
thoughts. Considering popery only as it related to amusement or
guzzling, I accommodated myself, without trouble, to the idea of

living in it: but that of solemnly entering into it, never presented itself to me but in a passing manner, and in a very distant futurity. At this time there was no means of changing: I saw, with the most violent horror, the sort of engagement I had made, and its inevitable consequence. The future neophytes I had around me were not adapted to support my courage by their example; I could not dissimulate that the holy deed I was going to perform was, at the bottom, but the action of a cut-throat. Though still young, I saw that, whatever religion was the true one, I was going to sell mine; and that, though I should even choose well, I was going, from the bottom of my heart, to lie to the Holy Ghost, and merit the contempt of mankind. The more I thought on it, the more I despised myself; I groaned at the fate that had led me there, as if this fate was not my own doing. Sometimes these reflections were so powerful, that, if I had seen the door open one instant, I should certainly have gone out of it; but it was not possible, and this resolution did not hold, neither, very strong.

Too many secret desires combatted it not to vanquish. Besides, the obstinacy of the design formed not to return to Geneva, shame, and even the difficulty of repassing the mountains, the trouble at seeing myself far from my country, and without a friend, without resources; all these things concurred to make me regard as a late repentance the remorse of conscience: I affected to reproach myself of what I had done, to excuse that I was going to do. In aggravating the faults of the past, I looked on the future as their necessary effect. I did not say to myself, Nothing is yet done, and you can be innocent if you will; but I said, Lament the crime of which you have rendered yourself culpable, and of which you have made it necessary to fill up the measure.

In fact, what rare magnanimity of soul must I not have had, at my age, to revoke all that, till that moment, I had promised or let myself hope, to break the chains I had given myself, to declare with intrepidity that I would remain in the religion of my fore-fathers, at the risk of all that might happen! This vigour was not of my age, and there is little probability of its having had a happy issue. Things were too far advanced to be recalled, and the more my resistance had been great, the more, by some manner or other, they had made it a merit to surmount it.

The sophism which ruined me is that of the greater part of mankind, who complain of want of power when it is too late to make use of it. Virtue is dearly bought only by our own fault; if we were always prudent, we should seldom have occasion of virtue.

But inclinations which might be easily surmounted, drag us without resistance; we yield to light temptations whose danger we despise. Insensibly we fall into perilous situations from which we might easily have preserved ourselves, but from which we cannot extricate ourselves without heroic efforts which affright us; so we fall at last into the abyss, in saying to God, Why hast thou made us so weak? But, in spite of us, he replies by our conscience, I made you too weak to get out of the gulf, because I made you strong enough not to fall into it.

I did not precisely take the resolution of becoming a Catholic; but seeing the time was not very nigh, I took time to accustom myself to the idea, and thought that in the meanwhile some unforeseen event might deliver me from my embarrassment. In order to gain time, I resolved to make the best defence possible. Very soon my vanity dispensed me from thinking of my resolution; and whenever I perceived I sometimes puzzled those who would instruct me, nothing more was wanting than to try entirely to overthrow them. I even applied in this undertaking a zeal very ridiculous; for while they were at work on me, I wanted to work on them. I honestly thought they wanted no more than conviction to become Protestants.

They did not, therefore, find in me that facility they expected, neither on the side of knowledge nor will. Protestants are, in general, better instructed than Catholics. It cannot be otherwise: the doctrine of the one exacts discussion, that of the other submission. A Catholic must adopt the decision they give him; a Protestant must learn to decide for himself. They knew that; but they did not expect, either from my condition or my age, much difficulty to people exercised as they were. Besides, I had not yet received my first communion, nor received those instructions which relate to it: they knew that too, but they did not know that, in its stead, I had been well instructed at M. Lambercier's; and that, moreover, I had by me a little magazine, very troublesome to these gentlemen, in the *History of the Church and of the Empire*,[1] which I had learnt almost by heart at my father's, and since that almost forgot, but which returned again to my memory, as the dispute grew warmer.

An old little priest, but pretty venerable, held with us, in common, the first conference. This conference was, to my companions,

---

[1] By Jean Lesueur, Amsterdam, 1730. It seems somewhat strange that Rousseau should have drawn his verbal artillery from a work which was first published two years later than the date (1728) of this encounter!

a catechism rather than a controversy; he had more trouble in instructing, than resolving their objections. It was not the same with me.

When my turn came, I stopped him at every point; I did not spare him one difficulty I could give him. This rendered the conference very long, and very tiresome to the assistants. My old priest talked much, exerted himself, ran to his books, and got out of the hobble by saying he did not understand French enough. The next day, for fear my indiscreet objections should hurt my companions, they put me in a separate room with another priest, much younger, a good talker, that is to say, dealing out long phrases, and proud of himself, if ever doctor was. I did not, however, suffer myself to be too much brought under by his imposing countenance; and finding, after all, that I made my way, I began to answer him with a tolerable assurance, and to maul him, on right and left, as well as I could. He thought to knock me down with Saint Augustine, Saint Gregory, and the rest of the Fathers; but he found, with an incredible surprise, I could handle all these Fathers almost as nimbly as he could: not that I ever read them, or he either perhaps; but I retained many passages taken from my Le Sueur; and whenever he cited one, without disputing on the citation, I parried it by another from the same Father, and which, often, greatly puzzled him. He got the better, however, at last, for two reasons: one was, he was above me; and seeing myself, in a manner, at his mercy, being so young, I rightly judged I should not drive him to a non-plus; for I plainly saw the little old priest was not well satisfied with my erudition or me. The other reason was, the young one had studied, and I had not. That gave him, in his manner of argument, a method I could not follow; and whenever he found himself unable to answer an unexpected objection, he put it off till the next day, pretending I left the present subject. Sometimes he rejected even all my citations, maintaining they were false, and, offering to fetch the book, defied me to find them. He knew he ran no great hazard, and that, with all my borrowed learning, I was too little exercised in the handling books, and not Latinist enough, to find a passage in a large volume, even though I was assured it was there. I suspect him likewise of having made use of the perfidy of which he accused the ministers, and having sometimes forged passages to extricate himself from an objection which troubled him.

While these little cavillings lasted, and the days were spent in argument, mumbling prayers and wasting time, there happened a nasty and unpleasant little adventure, which all but turned out very badly for me.

No man is so vile, no heart so savage, as not to be open to an attachment of some kind. One of the two bandits who called themselves Moors took me into his affections. He took up with me eagerly, talked to me in his gibberish jargon, did me small services, sometimes made me share his portion at meals, and often specially kissed me with very unwelcome ardour. Though I naturally experienced some dismay at his gingerbread face, adorned with a long scar, and his fiery look which seemed furious rather than tender, I put up with his kisses, saying to myself: The poor fellow has conceived a strong friendship for me; I should do wrong to rebuff him. He came gradually to adopt freer manners, and held such strange talk with me that sometimes I thought his head was turned. One evening he desired to come and sleep with me; I opposed it, saying my bed was too small. He urged me to enter his; I again refused; for the wretch was so dirty and stank so strong of chewed tobacco, that he made me sick.

Next day, in early morning, we were together in the assembly room; he began to caress me again, but with movements so violent that it was terrifying. In fine, he sought to pass by degrees to the most dirty familiarities, and to force me, by taking hold of my hand, to do the same. I freed myself impetuously, uttering a cry and making a jump backwards, and, while showing neither indignation nor anger, for I had not the least idea what he was engaged in, I expressed my astonishment and dislike so strongly that he let me go; but as he was finishing the struggle, I saw issue towards the fireplace and fall to the ground something sticky and whitish that made my stomach turn. I rushed on to the balcony, more moved, disturbed, frightened even, than ever in my life, and ready to faint.

I could not understand what the villain was doing; I supposed him seized with a fit, or some frenzy yet more dreadful, and in faith I know of nothing more hideous to the sight of an equable person than this obscene and dirty behaviour, this frightful visage aflame with the most bestial lust. I had never seen another man in such a state; but if we are truly like that in our transports with women, they must indeed be fascinated by us not to hold us in horror.

I was in a hurry to tell everyone what had happened to me. Our old preceptor told me to be silent, but I could see that the story had moved him strongly, and I heard him mutter between his

teeth: *Can maledet! Brutta bestia!*[1] Since I understood not why
I must be silent, I still went on talking, spite of the prohibition,
and chattered so much that on the morrow one of the administrators came early to administer a pretty lively reprimand, accusing
me of making overmuch noise about a small matter, and of com-
promising the honour of a holy house.

He went on with his censure by explaining to me many things
of which I was ignorant, but which he would not believe he was
teaching me, supposing that I had defended myself knowing what
was wanted of me, and being unwilling to consent to it. He told
me gravely that this was a forbidden act, like lechery, but yet that
its intention was not to offend the person who was its object, and
that I had no reason to be so vexed at having been found lovable.
He told me straightforwardly that in his own youth he had had
the same honour, and, having been surprised in a state where he
could make no resistance, he had found nothing so dreadful about
it. He pushed his impudence so far as to use plain language, and,
imagining that the cause of my resistance had been fear of pain,
assured me that such fear was vain, and that there was nothing
to be alarmed at.

I listened to this infamy with an astonishment all the greater
that he was not speaking for himself; he seemed to instruct me
only for my good. His discourse seemed to him such a simple matter that he had not even sought the privacy of a tête-à-tête; and we
had for third party an ecclesiastic who was no more offended by
all this than was he himself. This natural air imposed on me to
such a degree that I came to believe it was no doubt a practice
admitted by the world, but one in which I had so far had no occasion to receive instruction. This made me listen to him without
anger, if not without disgust. The image of what had happened
to me, but particularly of what I had seen, remained imprinted
so firmly on my memory, that in thinking of it I once more felt
sick. Though I had no more of it, the aversion for the act extended
to its apologist, and I could not hold myself back enough for him
not to see the bad effect of his lessons. He threw at me a look of
dislike, and thenceforward he spared nothing to make my stay
in the hospital disagreeable to me. He succeeded so well that, seeing but one way by which to leave it, I hastened to take it, as much
as I had until then sought to set it aside.

This adventure sheltered me for the future from the enterprises

---

[1] "Cursed dog! Brute beast!"

of the knights of the cuff,[1] and the sight of those who seemed to be of their number, recalling to me the air and gestures of my frightful Moor, has always inspired me with so much horror that I have found it hard to hide it. On the other hand, women gained much in my mind by this comparison; it seemed to me that I owed them, in tender feeling, in personal homage, reparation for the offences of my sex, and at the remembrance of this false African the ugliest little she-dwarf became in my eyes an object of adoration.

As for him, I do not know what was said to him; it did not seem that, save for dame Lorenza, anyone looked on him with a less kindly eye than before. But he did not accost or speak to me again. A week later, he was baptised with great ceremony, robed in white from head to foot, to mark the candour of his regenerated soul. The following day he left the hospital, and I have never seen him more.

My turn came a month afterwards; for all that time was necessary, that my directors might have the honour of a difficult conversion, and all their tenets were called over before me, to triumph over my new docility.

In fine, sufficiently instructed and sufficiently disposed to the will of my new masters, I was led processionally to the metropolitan church of St. John, to make a solemn abjuration, and receive the ceremonies of baptism, though they did not re-baptize me in reality: but as the ceremony is nearly the same, it serves to persuade the people Protestants are not Christians. I was clothed in a kind of grey gown, with white frogs, devoted to these occasions. Two men carried before and behind copper basins, on which they struck a key, where everyone put alms according to his devotion, or the concern he had for the welfare of the new convert. In fact, nothing of Catholic pageantry was omitted to render the solemnity more edifying to the public, and more humiliating to me. The white coat only might have been useful to me, which they did not give me as to the Moor, since I had not the honour of being a Jew.

This was not all. I must afterwards go to the Inquisition, to receive absolution for the crime of heresy, and return to the bosom of the church, with the same ceremony to which Henry IV. was subjected by its Ambassador. The countenance and manner of the right reverend father Inquisitor was not of the sort to diminish the secret terror which had seized me on entering this house.

---

[1] Pederasts; *cf.* d'Argenson, *Mémoires*, III, 88.

After several questions on my faith, on my condition, and on my family, he asked me bluntly if my mother was damned. My consternation repressed the first motions of my indignation; I contented myself with replying, I would hope she was not, and that God might have enlightened her at her last hour. The monk was silent; but his sour look did not appear to me a sign of approbation.

All this got through, at the moment I expected to be, at last, placed according to my wishes, they turned me out of doors with something more than twenty livres in small money, which the gathering produced. They recommended to me to live a good

J.-J. AT SIXTEEN

Christian, be faithful to grace; they wished me good luck, shut the door on me, and everyone disappeared.

Thus, in an instant, were all my grand expectations at an end, and nothing remained of the selfish steps I had taken, but the remembrance of having been, at once, an apostate and a dupe. It is easy to guess what a sudden revolution must have been caused in my ideas, when, from my shining projects of fortune, I saw myself descend to the completest misery, and that, after deliberating, in the morning, on the choice of the palace I should inhabit, I saw myself, at night, reduced to lie in the street. You would think I began to give myself up to a despair, so much the more cruel, as the sorrow for my faults must have been heightened by a conviction that my misfortunes were of my own seeking. Not a bit of all that. I had been, for the first time in my days, shut up more than two months. The first sentiment that struck me was that of the liberty I recovered. After a long slavery, again become master of myself and my actions, I saw myself in a great city abounding in resources, full of people of quality, whereof my talents and merit could not fail to make me welcome as soon as they heard of me. I had, besides, time to wait, and twenty livres I had in my pocket seemed a treasure which would never be exhausted. I could dispose of it at my fancy, without rendering account to anyone. It was the first time I found myself so rich. Far from falling into despondency and tears, I only changed my hopes; and self-love lost nothing by it. Never did I feel so much confidence and security: I thought my fortune already made; and was pleased that the obligation was to myself alone.

The first thing I did was to satisfy my curiosity in running all over the city, though it should be but as an act of my liberty. I went to see them mount guard; the military instruments pleased me much. I followed processions; I liked the faux-bourdon of the priests. I went to see the king's palace: I approached it with dread; but seeing other people go in, I did like them; they let me go in: perhaps I was indebted for this favour to the little bundle under my arm. Be that as it may, I conceived a great opinion of myself in being in the palace; I already looked on myself as almost an inhabitant there.

At length, by running backwards and forwards, I grew tired; I was hungry: it was hot; I go to a milk-shop: they brought me some curds and milk, and with two slices of the charming Piedmont bread, which I prefer to any other, I made, for five or six sous, one of the best dinners I ever made in my life.

It was time to seek a lodging. As I already knew enough of the Piedmont tongue to make myself understood, there was no great difficulty in finding one; and I had the prudence to choose it more adapted to my purse than my taste. I was told of a soldier's wife, in the Po-street, who received servants out of place, at one sou per night. I found there, empty, a bed, and took possession of it. She was young, and just married, though she already had five or six children. We all slept in the same room, mother, children, and lodgers; and it continued in this manner whilst I remained with her. As for the rest, she was a good-natured woman, swearing like a carter, breasts always open, and cap off, but a feeling heart, obliging, and inclined to serve me, and was even useful to me.

I spent several days in giving myself up wholly to the pleasure of independence and curiosity. I went wandering within and without the city, ferreting out and visiting everything which seemed curious or new, and everything was so for a young lad coming from his nest, who had never seen a capital. I was very exact in paying my court, and regularly assisting every morning at the King's mass. I thought it fine to be in the same chapel with this prince and his retinue; but my passion for music, which began to show itself, had more share in my assiduity than the splendour of the court, which, soon seen and always the same, did not strike me long. The King of Sardinia had, at that time, the best orchestra in Europe. Somis, Desjardins, and the Besouzzi, shone there alternately. Less would have been sufficient to draw a young fellow, that the sound of the least instrument, provided it was just, transported with gladness. Besides, I had only a stupid admiration for the magnificence which struck my sight, without desire. The only thing I thought of in all the pomp of the court, was to find a young princess there who deserved my respect, and with whom I could act a romance.

I was not far from beginning one in a situation less brilliant; but where, had I brought it to a conclusion, I had found pleasures a thousand times more delicious.

Though I lived with great economy, my purse insensibly grew lighter. This economy, however, was less the effect of prudence than of a simplicity of taste, which even at this day the use of plentiful tables has not altered. I did not know, or do not yet know, a better feast than a country meal. With milk-diet, eggs, herbs, cheese, brown bread, and tolerable wine, you are sure to regale me well; a good appetite will do the rest, if a steward and the servants around me do not satiate me with their impertinent aspect. I then made much better meals at the expense of six or seven sous, than I have since made for six or seven livres. I was therefore sober, for want of a temptation to be otherwise. I am still to blame to call it sobriety, for I employed all possible sensuality. My pears, my curds, my cheese, my bread, and a few glasses of Montferrat wine, that you might cut with a knife, rendered me the happiest of gluttons. But still, with all that, it was possible to see the end of twenty livres; this I from day to day more sensibly

perceived, and, in spite of the giddiness of my age, my uneasiness
for the hereafter was inclining to terror. Of all my castles in the
air, there only remained that of seeking an occupation I could live
by, and that was not very easily realised. I thought of my old
trade, but knew not enough of it to work with a master; besides,
masters do not abound at Turin. I therefore, while waiting something better, took a resolution of offering, from shop to shop, to
engrave a cypher, or coats of arms, on plates or dishes, hoping to
tempt people by cheapness, in submitting to their discretion. This
expedient was not very happy. I was almost everywhere denied,
and what I got to do was so trifling, I could hardly earn a meal.
One day, however, passing pretty early in the Contra nova, I saw,
through the windows of a counter, a young tradeswoman, so
graceful and of so attractive a countenance, that, in spite of my
timidity towards ladies, I did not hesitate to go in and offer my
talent. She did not discourage me, made me sit down, tell her my
little story, pitied me, told me to be of good cheer, and that good
Christians would never abandon me: then, while she sent for the
tools I wanted to a jeweller's of the neighbourhood, she went into
the kitchen, and herself brought me some breakfast. This beginning seemed to promise well enough; the end did not contradict it.
She seemed satisfied with my little labours; much more with my
prattle, when I had a little collected myself: for she was brilliant
and dressy, and, in spite of her graceful countenance, this lustre
had imposed on me. But her reception full of good nature, her
compassionate tone, her gentle and caressing manner, soon
brought me to myself. I saw I succeeded, and that made me succeed the more; but though an Italian, and too pretty not to be a
little of the coquette, she was nevertheless so modest, and I so
timid, that it was difficult to bring our acquaintance to any good.
They did not give us time to finish the adventure. I recollect with
a greater pleasure only the short moments I passed with her, and
I can say I there tasted in their prime the softest and the purest
pleasures of love.

She was a brown girl, extremely smart, but whose natural
goodness, painted in her pretty face, rendered her vivacity touching. Her name was Madame Basile. Her husband, older than she
was, and tolerably jealous, left her during his absence under the
care of a clerk, too disagreeable to be dangerous, but who nevertheless had pretensions of his own, which he rarely showed but
by ill-humour. He showed me a great deal, though I was fond of
hearing him play the flute, which he did pretty well. This second

Ægisthus always grumbled whenever he saw me go into his lady's room: he treated me with a disdain which she heartily returned him. She seemed as if she took a pleasure in tormenting him, by caressing me in his presence; and this sort of vengeance, though much to my wish, would have been much more so in a tête-à-tête. But she did not carry it quite so far; or rather, it was not in the same manner. Whether she thought me too young, whether she could not make the advances, or whether she would seriously be prudent, she had, at those times, a sort of reserve which was not unkind, but which intimidated me without my knowing the cause. Though I did not feel for her the same real and tender respect which I felt for Madame de Warens, I felt more fear and less familiarity. I was perplexed and trembling; I dared not look at her; I dared not breathe before her; I nevertheless dreaded leaving her more than death. I devoured, with greedy looks, all I could see without being perceived; the flowers of her gown, the end of her pretty foot, the interval of a white and compact arm which appeared between her glove and her ruffle, and that which happened, sometimes, between the contour of her neck and her handkerchief. Each object added to the impression of others. By dint of looking at what was to be seen, and even more than was to be seen, my eyes were confused, my heart was oppressed, my respiration, every instant more and more impeded, was with trouble kept down, and all I was able to do was to stifle, without noise, the sighs which were very troublesome to me during the silence we often were in. Happily, Madame Basile, employed at her work, did not seem to perceive it. I, however, sometimes saw, by a sort of sympathy, her handkerchief swell frequently enough. This dangerous sight finished my patience; and when I was ready to give way to my transport, she directed a few words to me in an easy voice, which in an instant made me come to myself.

I saw her in this manner several times alone, without there being a word, a motion, or even a look too expressive, which could denote between us the least intelligence. This state, too torturing for me, caused, however, my delight; and I could hardly, in the simplicity of my heart, imagine why I was thus tortured. It seemed these little tête-à-têtes did not displease her neither; at least, she rendered the occasion frequent enough; an attention gratuitous certainly in her, for the use she made of it, or let me make of it.

One day, being tired of the clerk's foolish chatter, and retiring to her chamber, I hastened to finish my task in the back shop where I was, and followed her. Her chamber-door was half open;

I went in without being perceived. She was embroidering near the window, facing that side of the room opposite the door. She could not see me go in, or hear me for the noise of the carts in the street. She was always neatly dressed; that day her attire bordered on coquetry. Her attitude was graceful; her head, inclining a little forward, exposed to view the whiteness of her neck; her hair, set off with elegance, was decorated with flowers: there reigned all over her person a charm I had time to examine, and which carried me beyond myself. I threw myself on my knees at the entrance of the room, stretching my hands towards her with amorous ecstasy, quite certain she could not hear me, and not imagining she could see me; but there was a glass at the chimney which betrayed me. I do not know what effect this transport had on her; she did not look at me, or speak to me; but, turning her side-face, by a simple motion of the finger, she showed me the mat at her feet. To leap up, cry out, and fly to the place she pointed to, was all done in the same instant; but it will be hardly believed, I dared undertake nothing farther, or say a single word, or raise my eyes towards her, or even touch her, in an attitude so constrained, to lean one moment on her knee. I was dumb and immovable, but not composed assuredly: everything painted in me agitation, joy, gratitude, and ardent desires uncertain of their object, and restrained by the dread of displeasing, on which my young heart could not reassure itself.

She did not appear calmer or less timid than I. Uneasy at seeing me there, confounded at having drawn me there, and beginning to feel all the consequence of a sign which escaped her doubtless without reflection, she neither encouraged nor discouraged me; she did not take her eyes from her work; she endeavoured to act as if she did not see me at her feet, but all my stupidity did not prevent me from judging that she partook of my trouble, perhaps of my desires, and that she was withheld by a shame like mine, without its giving me the power of surmounting it. Five or six years old than I, she ought, in my opinion, to take all the freedom herself; and I said to myself, Since she does nothing to excite mine, she does not choose I should take any. And at this day I believe I thought right; and surely she had too much sense not to see that a novice like me had occasion not only for encouragement, but instruction.

I do not know how this lively and dumb scene would have ended, or how long I might have remained immovable in this ridiculous and delightful situation, had we not been interrupted.

In the strongest of my agitations I heard the kitchen door open, which joined the chamber we were in, and Madame Basile, alarmed, says to me with hasty voice and gesture, Get up, there is Rosina. In rising in a hurry, I seized her hand, which she held out; I gave it two eager kisses, at the second of which I felt this charming hand press a little against my lips. In my days I never knew so sweet a moment; but the occasion I had lost offered no more, and our young amours stopped there.

This is, perhaps, the reason the image of this amiable woman remains imprinted on the bottom of my heart in so lively colours. It is heightened even since I know the world and women better. If she had had the least experience, she would have taken another method to animate a young fellow: but although her heart was weak, it was honest; she involuntarily yielded to an inclination which hurried her away; it was, to all appearance, her first infidelity, and I should have found, perhaps, more to do in vanquishing her modesty than my own. Without going so far, I tasted in her company inexpressible delights. Nothing I ever felt from the possession of women is worth the two minutes I spent at her feet, without even daring to touch her gown. No, there is no enjoyment like that we find in an honest woman we esteem; all is favour with her. A trifling sign of the finger, a hand lightly pressed against my mouth, are the only favours I ever received of Madame Basile; and the remembrance of these favours, so trifling, still transports me when I think of them.

In vain I sought a second tête-à-tête the two following days; it was impossible for me to find an opportunity, and I perceived no inclination in her to favour it. She had even a countenance, not more indifferent, but more reserved than ordinary; and I believe she avoided my looks, for fear of not being able sufficiently to govern hers. Her cursed clerk was more mortifying than ever. He became even a banterer and jocose; he told me I should make my way amongst the ladies. I trembled lest I should have been guilty of an indiscretion; and looking upon myself as already familiar with her, I would have made a mystery of an inclination which till then did not much want it. This made me more circumspect in laying hold of the occasions of satisfying it, and in endeavouring to be certain of some, I found none at all.

This is likewise another romantic folly I could never get the better of, and which, added to my natural timidity, has greatly contradicted the clerk's predictions. I loved too sincerely, too perfectly, I dare say it, to be easily happy. Never were passions more lively, and at the same time more pure than mine; never was love more tender, more real, and more disinterested. I would have sacrificed a thousand times my happiness to that of the person I loved: her reputation was dearer to me than life, and never, for all the pleasure of enjoyment, would I have compromised for a moment her peace. This has made me so cautious, so secret, and so careful in my undertakings, that none have ever succeeded. My little success with women was always caused by loving them too much.

To return to the Ægisthus the fluter: it was most singular, that, in becoming more insupportable, the traitor became more complaisant. From the first minute his lady showed me kindness, she thought of making me useful in the warehouse. I knew arithmetic pretty well; she proposed his teaching me book-keeping: but the cross fellow received the proposal extremely ill, fearing, perhaps, he might be supplanted. Thus all my work, after engraving, was to copy some accounts and bills, to write over fairly a few books, and translate commercial letters from Italian into French. All at once our man took it in his head to return to the proposal which was made and rejected, and said he would teach me accounts by double entry, and make me capable of offering my services to M. Basile on his return. There was something in his tone and looks, though I cannot tell what, false, artful, and ironical, which did not inspire confidence. Madame Basile, without waiting my answer, told him coldly, I was much obliged to him for his offers, that she hoped fortune would favour my deserts, and that it would be a great pity that one of so much sense should be nothing but a clerk.

She several times told me she would make me acquainted with those who could serve me. She prudently thought it time to send me from her. Our dumb declarations happened on Thursday. On Sunday she gave a dinner, at which I was present; and likewise a Dominican friar of a good appearance, to whom she presented me. The monk treated me very affectionately, complimented me on my conversion, and told me several parts of my history which showed that she had given him the particulars of it: then giving me two little strokes on the cheek with the back of his hand, he told me to be good, to cheer up, and to go and see him, in order to talk with more leisure together. I judged, by the respect everyone paid him, that he was a person of importance, and, by his paternal tone of voice to Madame Basile, that he was her confessor. I recollect also his decent familiarity was mixed with marks of esteem and even respect for his penitent, which at that time made less impression on me than now. Had I had more understanding, how much should I have been touched to have rendered sensible a young woman respected by her confessor!

The table was not large enough for all of us. A side-table was necessary, at which I had the agreeable conversation of the clerk. I lost nothing on the side of attention and good eating; several plates were sent to the side-table which certainly were not intended for him. Everything went well so far; the ladies were very merry, the gentlemen very polite: Madame Basile did the honours of the repast with a charming grace. In the midst of the dinner a chaise was heard to stop at the door; someone comes up; it is M. Basile. I see him as if entering this moment, in a scarlet coat with gold buttons; a colour I have since that day detested. M. Basile was a tall, fine man, with an extremely good presence. He comes in hastily, and with the air of one who surprises his company, though none were there but his friends. His wife clings around his neck, takes hold of his hands, gives him a thousand caresses, which he receives without returning them. He salutes the company, a plate is brought, he eats. They had scarcely begun talking of his journey, but throwing his eyes on the side-table, he asks, in a severe tone, who that little boy is he sees there? Madame Basile tells him ingenuously. He asks if I lodge in the house. He is told no. Why not? replies he in a rough manner: since he is here in the day-time, he may as well be here at night. The monk took up the conversation, and after a grave and sincere panegyric on Madame Basile, he made mine in a few words; adding that, far from blaming the pious charity of his wife, he should be forward in assisting it, since nothing had passed the bounds of discretion. The husband replied in a tone of humour, half of which was stifled, restrained by the presence of the monk, but which was sufficient to let me know he had been informed of me, and that the clerk had served me a trick in his way.

They were scarcely risen from table, but this last, despatched by his master, came in triumph to signify to me from him, that I must leave the house that instant, and never more set my foot there. He seasoned his commission with everything which could render it insulting and cruel. I went off without a word, but with a sorrowful heart, not so much at leaving this amiable woman, as at leaving her a prey to the brutality of her husband. He certainly had a right to take care she was not unfaithful; for although she was prudent, and of good birth, she was an Italian, that is, tender and vindictive; and it was a fault in him, in my opinion, to make use of those means the most likely to bring on the misfortune he dreaded.

Such was the success of my first adventure. I endeavoured, by passing and repassing two or three times in the street, to see, at least, her whom my heart grieved for without ceasing: but, instead of her, I saw none but the husband and the vigilant clerk, who, on perceiving me, made a motion with the ell in the shop, more expressive than inviting. Finding I was so well watched, I lost courage and went no more. I wished to see, however, the patron she had procured me. Unfortunately I knew not his name. I rambled several times, in vain, round the convent to endeavour to meet him. At last, other adventures banished the charming remembrance of Madame Basile; and in a short time I so far forgot her, that, as simple and as much a novice as I was before, I did not remain in danger of pretty women.

Her liberalities had, however, again stocked me a little; very modestly nevertheless, and with the precaution of a prudent woman, who looked on decency rather than dress, and who would prevent me from suffering rather than deck me out. The coat I brought from Geneva was still good and wearable; she added only a hat and a little linen. I had no ruffles; she would give me none, though I greatly desired them. She thought it sufficient for me to be clean; but this was an attention she need not have recommended while I appeared before her.

A few days after my catastrophe, my hostess, who, as I have said, had shown me friendship, told me she had perhaps got me a place, and that a lady of quality wanted to see me. At this word, I thought myself entirely in the road to great adventures, for that was always uppermost in my thoughts. This was not so brilliant as I had figured it. I went to the lady's with the servant who had spoken to her of me. She questioned me, examined me; I did not displease her; and immediately entered into her service, not absolutely in quality of a favourite, but in quality of a footman. I was clothed in the colour of her people; the only distinction was their wearing a shoulder-knot, and I had none: as there was no lace to the livery, it was nearly a tradesman's coat. Here was the unexpected term to which, at last, were pointed all my brilliant hopes.

Madame la Comtesse de Vercellis, whom I served, was a widow without children; her husband was a Piedmontese. I always thought her a Savoyard, not being able to persuade myself a Piedmontese could speak so good French with so pure an accent. She was of a middle age, of a noble presence, a mind well adorned, fond of French literature, and well versed in it. She wrote much, and always in French. Her letters had the expression, and almost the grace, of Madame de Sévigné's. You might have mistaken some of them for hers. My principal employment, which did not displease me, was to write them from her dictating; a cancer in the breast, of which she greatly suffered, not permitting her any longer to write herself.

Madame de Vercellis had not only much wit, but an elevated and strong mind. I attended her last illness. I saw her suffer and die without once showing the least weakness, without making the least effort of constraint, without quitting her female character, and without imagining any philosophy in all this; a word not then in vogue, and which she was not even acquainted with in the sense it now bears. This strength of character was sometimes carried to rudeness. She always appeared to me to feel as little for others as for herself; and when she did a kindness to the unfortunate, it was to do what was good in itself, rather than from true compassion. I experienced a little of this insensibility during the three months I passed with her. It was natural she should show some kindness to a young person of some views who was incessantly under her eye, and think, finding herself dying, that after her death he would want some assistance and support: however, whether she did not judge me worthy any particular attention, or whether those who surrounded her did not permit her to think of any but themselves, she did nothing for me.

I remember, however, very well, her showing some curiosity to know me. She questioned me sometimes; was glad to see the letters I wrote to Madame de Warens, to receive an account of my sentiments. But she surely did not take the right method, by never showing me hers. My heart loved to open itself, provided it met with another equally open. Interrogations dry and cold, without any sign of approbation or blame on my answers, gave me no confidence. When nothing told me whether my chatter pleased or displeased, I was always in fear, and I sought not so much to show my thoughts as to say nothing which could hurt me. I have since observed, that this dry manner of interrogating people to know them, is a common trick amongst women who pique themselves on sense. They imagine that, in not letting their own sentiments appear, they will arrive at penetrating yours the better; but they do not see that they thus take away the resolution of exposing them. A man who is questioned, begins, for that reason only, to put himself on his guard; and if he imagines, that, without taking a real interest in him, they only want to make him prate, he lies, or conceals, or deliberately goes back on himself, and had rather pass for a fool than be duped in satisfying your curiosity. In fine, it is always a bad method of reading the hearts of others to affect to hide your own.

Madame de Vercellis never said one word to me that felt of affection, pity, or benevolence. She questioned me coldly. I answered with reserve. My answers were so timid she must have found them mean, and grew tired of them. Towards the last she questioned me no more, and talked of nothing but her service. She judged me less on what I was, than what she had made me; and by dint of seeing me in no other light than that of a footman, she prevented me from appearing anything else.

I believe I experienced at that time the arch game of underhand interests, which has thwarted me all my lifetime, and given me a very natural aversion for the apparent order which produces it. Madame de Vercellis having no children, her heir was her nephew, the Count de la Roque, who assiduously paid her his court. Besides that, her principal servants, who saw her draw near her end, did not forget themselves; and there were so many assiduous people about her, it was difficult for her to think of me. At the head of her affairs was one M. Lorenzi, an artful fellow, and whose wife, who was still more artful, had so much insinuated herself into the good graces of her mistress, she was with her rather as a companion, than a woman who received wages. She had placed her niece with her as her chamber-maid; her name was Mademoiselle Pontal; a cunning jade, who gave herself the airs of a waiting gentlewoman, and assisted her aunt in so well besetting their mistress, that she saw but through their eyes, and acted but through their hands. I had not the happiness to please these three personages: I obeyed them, but did not serve them; I did not think that, besides the service of our common mistress, I must be the valet of her valets. I was, besides, a troublesome person to them. They plainly saw I was not in my proper place: they dreaded their lady might see it likewise, and that, if she put me there, it might decrease their portions; for these sort of people, too covetous to be just, regard every legacy left to others as taken from their right. They therefore united to keep me from her sight. She was fond of writing letters; it was an amusement for her in her state; they disgusted her of it, and got the physician to dissuade her, pretending it fatigued her. By pretending I did not know service, they employed in my stead two great clowns of chairmen to be with her: in fine, they managed it so well, that they kept me a week from her chamber before she made her will. It is true, I went in afterwards as usual, and was even more assiduous there than anyone: for the pains of this poor lady grieved me; the constancy with which she suffered rendered her extremely respectable and dear to me; and I have, in her chamber, shed many sincere tears, without her or anyone else having perceived it.

We lost her at last. I saw her expire. Her life had been that of a woman of wit and sense; her death was that of a sage. I can say she rendered the Catholic religion amiable to me, by the serenity of soul with which she fulfilled the duties of it, without neglect or affectation. She was naturally serious. Towards her latter end, she took up a sort of cheerfulness too equal to be affected, and which was nothing but a counterbalance given by reason itself against the sadness of her situation. She kept her bed the two last days only, and did not cease conversing peaceably with everyone. At last, her speech being gone, and already combating the agonies of death, she broke wind loudly. Good, says she, and turned in her bed; she who breaks wind is not dead. These were the last words she pronounced.

She left a year's wages to her under-servants; but, not being set down as one of her family, I had nothing. But the Count de la Roque ordered me thirty livres, and gave me the new coat I had on, and which M. Lorenzi would have taken off. He likewise promised to seek me a place, and permitted me to see him. I went two or three times to his house, without being able to speak to him. I was easily discouraged, I went no more. You will presently see I was to blame.

Had I but finished all I had to say concerning my abode with Madame de Vercellis! But, though my apparent situation remained the same, I did not come out of her house as I went into it. I carried away from thence the long remembrance of crimes, and the insupportable weight of remorse, with which, though forty years since, my conscience is still loaded, and whose bitter sense, far from growing weaker, grows stronger as I grow older. Who could believe that the fault of a child could have such cruel effects? It is these effects, more than probable, that have caused my heart to get no ease. I have, perhaps, murdered with ignominy and misery an amiable, honest, and estimable girl, who was assuredly much better than I.

The dissolution of a family seldom happens without causing some confusion in the house, and many things to be missed. Such, however, was the fidelity of the servants, and the vigilance of M. and Madame Lorenzi, that nothing was found short at the inventory. Mademoiselle Pontal, only, lost a riband of a white and rose colour, already much worn. Many better things were within my reach: this riband only tempted me. I stole it, and, as I did not much hide it, they soon found it on me. They wanted to know whence I got it. I am confused, I hesitate, I stutter, and at last I said, with redness in my face, It was Marion gave it me. Marion was a young girl from Maurienne, whom Madame de Vercellis had made her cook, when, ceasing to give entertainments, she had discharged her own, having more occasion for good broths than fine ragouts. Marion was not only pretty, but had a freshness of colour to be found only in the mountains, and particularly an air of modesty and mildness that one could not see without loving; besides, a good girl, prudent, and of an approved fidelity. This surprised them when I named her. They had almost as much confidence in me as in her, and it was judged of importance to know which of the two was the thief. She was sent for; the company was numerous, the Count de la Roque was present. She comes, they show her the riband, I accuse her boldly; she remains speechless and astonished, casts a look at me which would have appeased a devil, but which my barbarous heart resists. She denies, in fine, with assurance, but without anger, turns toward me, begs me to consider, not disgrace an innocent girl who never wished me ill; and I, with an infernal impudence, confirm my declaration, and maintain to her face that she gave me the riband. The poor creature began crying, and said but these words, Ah! Rousseau! I thought you of a good disposition; you reduce me to misery, but I would not be in your place. That was all. She continued defending herself with as much simplicity as steadiness, but without using against me the least invective. This moderation, compared to my decisive tone, hurt her. It did not seem natural to suppose on one side an audaciousness so diabolical, and on the other a mildness so angelical. They did not seem to determine entirely, but prejudice was for me. In the bustle they were engaged in, they did not give themselves time to sound the affair; and the Count de la Roque, in sending us both away, contented himself with saying, the conscience of the culpable would revenge the innocent. His prediction was not vain; it does not cease one single day to be fulfilled.

I do not know what became of this victim of my calumny; but there is little appearance of her having been able, after that, easily to get a good place. She carried with her an imputation cruel to her honour in every manner. The theft was but a trifle, but however it was theft, and, what is worse, made use of to decoy a young fellow: in fine, lies and obstinacy left no hope for her in whom so many vices were united. I do not look even on her misery and being an outcast as the greatest dangers I exposed her to. Who knows, at her age, what despondency and innocence contemned may have led her to. Ah! if the remorse of having made her unhappy is insupportable, judge how much more cutting it must be to me for having made her still worse than myself.

This cruel remembrance troubles me sometimes, and disorders me to such a degree, that I perceive, in my endeavours to sleep, this poor girl coming to upbraid me of my crime, as if it was committed yesterday. Whilst I lived happy, it tormented me less; but, in the midst of a life of troubles, it robs me of the sweet consolation of persecuted innocence: it makes me feel to the quick what I believe I have mentioned in one of my works, that remorse sleeps during a prosperous life, but awakens in adversity. I never could determine, however, to disburden my heart of this load in the breast of a friend. The strictest intimacy never induced me to tell it anyone, not even to Madame de Warens: the most I could do was to own I upbraided myself of an atrocious action, but never said in what it consisted. This weight has therefore remained to this day on my conscience without alleviation; and I may say that the desire of delivering myself from it in some degree, has greatly contributed to the resolution I have taken of writing my Confessions.

I have proceeded openly in that I have just made, and it cannot be thought, certainly, that I have here palliated the heinousness of my crime. But I should not fulfil the object of this book, did I not expose, at the same time, my interior dispositions, and dread to excuse myself in what is conformable to truth. Never was villainy farther from me than in that cruel hour; and when I accused this unfortunate girl, it is strange, but it is true, my friendship for her was the cause of it. She was present in my thoughts; I excused myself on the first object which offered. I accused her of having done what I intended to do, of giving me the riband, because my intention was to give it her. When I saw her afterwards appear, my heart was racked, but the presence of so many people was stronger than my repentance. I little feared punishment, I dreaded the shame only; but I dreaded it more than death, more than the crime, more than the whole world. I had been glad to have sunk, stifled in the bosom of the earth: invincible shame overcame all; shame only caused my impudence; and the more I became criminal, the more the terror of acknowledging it rendered me intrepid. I saw nothing but the horror of being discovered, publicly denounced, myself present, a robber, liar, and calumniator. A universal perturbation banished every other feeling. Had they let me recover myself, I had certainly declared the whole. Had M. de la Roque taken me aside, and said to me: Do not destroy the poor girl; if you are guilty, acknowledge it to me; I had instantly thrown myself at his feet; I am perfectly sure of it. But they only intimidated, instead of encouraging me. My age is likewise an allowance it is but just to make. I had scarcely quitted childhood, or rather was still a child. In youth enormous crimes are still more criminal than in an age of maturity; but mere weakness is much less so, and my fault at bottom was very little more. For this reason, its remembrance afflicts me much less on account of the mischief itself, than for that which it must have caused. It has even done me this good, of keeping me, for the rest of my life, from every act which tends towards crime, by the terrible impression I still retain of the only one I ever was guilty of; and I think I feel my aversion to falsehood grow in a great measure from the regret of having been able to commit so black a one. If it is a crime that can be expiated, as I hope it is, all the misfortunes which overwhelm me in the decline of life must have done it, added to forty years of uprightness and honour on difficult occasions; and poor Marion having so many avengers in this world, however great my offence was towards her, I have little dread of carrying its guilt with me. This is all I had to say on this article. Let me be permitted never to speak of it more.

BOOK THREE

Leaving Madame de Vercellis's nearly as I went there, I returned to my old landlady, and remained there five or six weeks, in which time health, youth, and laziness often rendered my constitution importunate. I was uneasy, absent, and pensive; cried, sighed, desired a happiness I had no idea of, but whose privation, however, I felt. This situation cannot be described, and few men can even imagine it; because the greatest part have prevented this plentitude of life, at the same time tormenting and delightful, which, in the drunkenness of desire, gives a foretaste of enjoyment. My fired blood incessantly filled my head with girls and women; but not knowing their real use, I possessed them whimsically in idea to my fancy without knowing what more to do with them; and these ideas kept my senses in a disagreeable activity, from which, fortunately, they did not teach me to deliver myself. I had given my life to have met, for a quarter of an hour, a Mlle. Goton. But the time was past when children's games went that way as if of themselves. Shame, the companion of a bad conscience, accompanied my years; it had strengthened my natural timidity to the degree of rendering it invincible, and never, at that time or since, could I arrive at making a lascivious proposal; unless she I made it to constrained me to it, in a manner, by her advances; though certain she was not scrupulous, and almost sure of being taken at my word.

My agitation increased to such a degree that, since I could not satisfy my desires, I enflamed them by the most far-fetched expedients. I sought out dark passages and hidden nooks where I could expose myself at a distance to those of the fair sex in that state in which I should have wished to be in their presence. What they saw was no obscene object, I never even dreamed of such a thing; it was a ridiculous one. The stupid pleasure I had in displaying it to their sight cannot be described. From this it was but a step to experiencing the desired treatment, and no doubt some bold hussy, passing, would have given me that amusement, had I had the boldness but to wait for one. This madness had a catastrophe rather comic, but not too pleasant for me.

One day I went to take my position at the end of a yard, in which was a well where the young women of the house often came for water. At this end was a little slope which led down by several

passages to some cellars. I explored these subterranean passages
in the darkness, and, finding them long and obscure, supposed
that they were endless, and that, if seen and surprised, I should
find in them a safe refuge. In this confidence, I offered to the girls
who came to the well a spectacle laughable rather than seductive.
The wiser ones pretended to see nothing; others began to laugh;
others ran off, insulted, and raised a disturbance. I took refuge in
my retreat; I was followed. I heard a man's voice, a thing I had
not counted on, and one that alarmed me. I huddled underground
at the risk of being lost; the noise, voices, the man's voice, still
followed me. I had expected darkness; I saw light. I trembled,
and hid further in. A wall stopped me, and, unable to go further,
I must there await my fate. In a moment I was found and seized by
a large man with a big moustache, a large hat, and a large sword,
escorted by four or five old women each armed with a broom-
handle; among them I perceived the little rogue who had un-
masked me, and who desired doubtless to see my face.

The man with the sword, taking me by the arm, asked roughly
what was I doing there. My reply, you may be sure, was not
ready. I collected myself, however; and, putting forth all my wit
at this critical moment, I drew out of my head a romantic expedient which succeeded. I asked him, in the tone of a suppliant, to
pity my age and condition; I was a young foreigner of high birth,
whose brain was turned; I had escaped from my father's house
because they sought to shut me up; if he made me known, I was
lost; but, if he would let me go, I might one day be able to show
my gratitude for the favour. Against all likelihood, my words and
mien had effect; the dreadful man was moved; and after a short
reprimand, he let me go gently without further question. By the
way in which the women looked at me as I went, I judged that the
man I had so feared had been very useful to me, and that had it
been left to them I should not have got off so cheap. I heard them
mutter I don't know what, but cared little for it; for, provided
the sword and the man did not meddle with me, I was sure enough,
lusty and vigorous as I was, of getting free soon enough from them
and their cudgels.

Some days after, passing through a street with a young clergyman my neighbour, I came face to face with the man of the sword.
He knew me, and mocking me in a railing voice, *I am a prince,
I am a prince,* said he; *and I, I am a poltroon; but let His Highness
not come back.* He added nothing more, and I slipped away, low-
ering my head and thanking him, in my heart, for his discretion.

I supposed those cursed old women had made him ashamed of his credulity. Be that as it may, Piedmontese as he was, he was a good fellow, and I never think of him without a motion of gratitude; for the story was so amusing that, if only from desire to raise a laugh, another man in his place would have shamed me. This adventure, though it had not the end I might have feared, did not fail to make me prudent for a long time.

My stay with Madame de Vercellis procured me a few acquaintances I kept in with in hopes of making them useful. I went to see, sometimes, among others, a Savoyard parson, named M. Gaime, preceptor to the Count of Mellarède's children. He was a young man little known, but of good sense, probity, and understanding, and one of the honestest men I ever knew. He was of no use as to the object which sent me to him; he had not credit enough to place me: but I received more precious advantages from him, by which my whole life has profited; the lessons of a sound morality, and the maxims of a right reason. In the successive order of my inclinations I had always been too high or too low; Achilles or Thersites; sometimes a hero, sometimes a villain. M. Gaime took the pains to put me in my proper place, and to show me to myself without sparing or discouraging me. He spoke to me very honourably of my talents and my genius; but he added, that he saw obstacles arise from them which would prevent me from making the best of them, so that they would, according to him, serve me much less in the attainment of fortune, than in resources to do without it. He painted me the true picture of human life, of which I had but wrong ideas: he explained to me, how in adversity a wise man may always attain happiness, and gain that wind which blows him there; how there is no happiness without prudence, and how it is that prudence belongs to every condition. He greatly deadened my admiration for grandeur, in proving to me, that those who lorded it over others were neither wiser nor happier than they were. He told me one thing, which often occurs to my memory; and that is, if each man could read the hearts of others, there would be more people wish to descend than ascend. This reflection, whose reality strikes, and has nothing forced, has been very useful to me in the course of my life, in making me keep to my lot peaceably. He gave me the first true ideas of honesty, which my bombastic genius had only known to excess. He made me understand, that the enthusiasm for sublime virtue was of little use in society; that in aiming too high you are subject to fall; that the continuity of little duties well fulfilled demanded no less strength than heroic actions; that you find your account in it much better, both in respect to reputation and happiness; and that the continual esteem of mankind was infinitely better than sometimes their admiration.

To establish the duties of man, you must remount to their first principles. Besides, the step I had taken, whereof my present situation was the consequence, led us on to talk of religion. It is readily conceived that the honest M. Gaime is, at least in a great measure, the original of the *Vicaire Savoyard*. Prudence, only, obliged him to speak with more reserve; he explained himself less openly on certain points; but as to the rest, his maxims, his sentiments, and his advice, were the same, and even the counselling me to return home, everything happened just as I have given it since to the public. Thus, without dwelling on conversations of which everyone may see the substance, I shall say that his lessons, prudent, though without an immediate effect, were as so many seeds of virtue and religion in my heart, which were never extinguished, and which waited, to fructify, only a more lovely hand.

Though till then my conversion was not very solid, I was nevertheless moved. So far from being tired of his discourses, I relished them on account of their clearness, their simplicity, and particularly for a certain interest of the heart of which I saw them full. I have an affectionate turn, and was always endeared to people less in proportion to the good they do me, than that they wish to do me, and I am seldom mistaken in them. I, therefore, was very fond of M. Gaime; I was in a manner his second disciple, and it produced for the moment the inestimable good of turning me from the inclination to vice my idle life was drawing me into.

One day, thinking of nothing less, I was sent for by the Count de la Roque. By continually going, and not seeing him, I grew tired, and went no more: I thought he had forgot me, or that he had an ill opinion of me. I was mistaken. He was witness, more than once, of the pleasure I took in fulfilling my duty to his aunt; he even told her of it, and he repeated it to me when I thought little of it. He received me well: told me that, without amusing me with empty promises, he had sought to get me a place; that he had succeeded; that he would put me in the road of becoming something, and that I must do the rest; that the family he recommended me to was powerful and respectable; that I should want no other help to preferment; and that, though treated at first as a simple servant, as before, I might be assured, that, should I be judged by my sentiments and conduct above this state, they were

disposed not to leave me in it. The end of this discourse cruelly
contradicted the brilliant hopes I had conceived at the beginning
of it. What! always a footman? said I to myself with a bitter indignation, which confidence soon wiped away. I thought myself
too little made for this place to dread their leaving me there.

TURIN: CATHEDRAL OF ST. JOHN

He took me to the Count of Gouvon, master of the horse to the
Queen, and chief of the illustrious house of Solar. The dignified
air of this respectable old gentleman rendered the affability of the
reception more affecting. He questioned me with concern, and I
answered him with sincerity. He said to the Count de la Roque,
I had an agreeable physiognomy which promised wit; that it
seemed to him I had enough, but that was not all, and that he
must see the rest. Then, turning towards me, Child, said he, the
beginnings of almost all things are difficult; yours, however, shall
not be much so. Be prudent, and try to please all here; this is for
the present your whole business. As to the rest, take courage; we
will take care of you. He immediately went to the Marchioness
of Breil, his daughter-in-law, and presented me to her, and afterwards to the Abbé de Gouvon, his son. This beginning I liked.

I had already knowledge enough to know so much ceremony was not used at the reception of a footman. In fact, I was not treated as one. I dined at the steward's table; had no livery; and the Count of Favria, a giddy young man, ordering me behind his coach, his grandfather forbade my going behind any coach, or following anybody out of the house. I waited at table, however, and did in the house nearly the service of a footman; but I did it in some respect with liberty, without being bound particularly to anyone. Except a few letters dictated to me, and some images I cut for the Count of Favria, I was master of almost my whole time. This method of acting, which I did not perceive, was surely very dangerous; it was not even very kind; for this extremely idle life might have made me contract vices I should not have had without it.

But, luckily, this did not happen. M. Gaime's lessons had made an impression on my heart, and I so much liked them, I stole away sometimes to hear more of them. I fancy those who saw me steal out, little imagined where I ran to. Nothing could be more sensible than the advice he gave me on my conduct. My beginnings were admirable; I was of an assiduity, an attention, a zeal, which charmed everyone. The Abbé Gaime prudently advised me to moderate this first fervour, for fear it should relax, and they should take notice of it. Your beginning, said he, is a rule of what they will expect of you: endeavour to spare yourself something to be done hereafter, but take care never to do less than you do now.

As they had examined me but little on my trifling talents, and supposed I had no more than nature had given me, it did not appear, although the Count of Gouvon had promised, that they intended anything for me. Things happened cross, and I was nearly forgot. The Marquis of Breil, son to the Count of Gouvon, was at that time ambassador at Vienna. Some unexpected business happened at court, which was felt in the family; and they were some weeks in an agitation which left little time to think of me. However, till then I had relaxed but little. One thing did me good and harm; by keeping me from all external dissipation, and by rendering me a little more inattentive to my duty.

Mlle. de Breil was a young lady about my age, well made, handsome enough, extremely fair, with very black hair, and, though black-eyed, had in her countenance the mild look of a fair woman, which my heart could never resist. The court dress, so favourable to young people, showed her pretty stature, exposed

her breasts and shoulders, and rendered her complexion still more
dazzling from the mourning then worn. You will say, it is not a
servant's place to perceive those things. I was, without doubt, to
blame, but I did perceive them, and I was not the only one. The
steward and valets de chambre talked of them sometimes at table,
with a rudeness which hurt me greatly. My head was not, however, so far lost as to be quite in love. I did not forget myself, I kept
my distance, and even my desires did not turn to liberties. I was
happy to see Mlle. de Breil; to hear her say anything which
showed wit, sense, or modesty: my ambition, confined to the
pleasure of serving her, did not go beyond its bounds. At table
I was attentive in making use of them. If her footman quitted, a
moment, her chair, you saw me placed there that instant; when
not there, I was always opposite her; I sought in her looks what
she wanted; I watched the moment of changing her plate. What
would not I have given that she would deign to command me, look
at me, speak to me but a word! But no; I had the mortification of
being a cypher in her eyes; she did not even know I was there.
However, her brother, who sometimes spoke to me at table, having said some words not very obliging, I made him so smart and
well-turned an answer, she remarked it, and threw her eyes on
me. This look, which was but short, did not fail to transport me.
The next day a second occasion offered, and I made use of it.
There was much company to dinner, when, for the first time, to
my great surprise, I saw the steward wait, his sword by his side,
and his hat on his head. The conversation by chance turned on
the motto of the house of Solar, which was on the tapestry in the
room with the arms, *Tel fiert qui ne tue pas*. As the Piedmontese
are not in general versed in the French language, some of them
found in this motto an orthographical error, and said that in the
word *fiert* there should be no *t*.

The old Count of Gouvon was going to answer, when, looking
towards me, he saw I smiled without daring to say anything: he
ordered me to speak. I then said, I did not think the *t* too much —
that *fiert* was an old French word, which did not derive from the
noun *ferus*, fierce, threatening, but from the verb *ferit*, he strikes,
he wounds — that the motto, therefore, did not appear to me to
say, Many a one threatens, but Many a one strikes, who does
not kill.

The whole company stared at me, and stared at each other,
without saying a word. Never was so great a surprise. But what
flattered me most was to see plainly an air of satisfaction in the

countenance of Mlle. de Breil. This disdainful person conde-
scended to cast at me a second look, which was at least worth the
first; then, turning her eyes towards her grandpapa, she seemed
to expect with a sort of impatience the commendation he owed
me, and which he gave me in fact so full and so entire, and with
an air so full of satisfaction, that the whole table was eager to
join in chorus. This instant was short, but delicious in every respect. This was one of those uncommon moments which bring
back things to their natural order, and revenge merit abased by
the injury of fortune. A few minutes afterwards, Mlle. de Breil,
raising her eyes once more on me, begged me, in a voice as timid
as it was affable, to bring her something to drink. You may judge
I did not make her wait. But in approaching I was seized with so
great a trembling, that, having filled her glass too full, I spilt
some of the water on her plate and even on herself. Her brother
giddily asked me why I shook so? This question did not serve to
recover me, and Mlle. de Breil reddened like a turkey.

Here finished the romance; where you will remark, as with
Madame Basile, and in the whole course of my history, that I am
not happy in the conclusion of my amours. I in vain attended the
antechamber of Madame de Breil; I never more obtained one
mark of attention from her daughter. She went out and in without looking at me, and, for my part, I hardly dared look towards
her. I was even so stupid and so unskilled, that when one day in
passing she let fall her glove, instead of flying to the glove which
I could have covered with kisses, I dared not stir from my place,
and suffered it to be taken up by a great lubber of a valet, whom
I could have knocked down with pleasure. That I might be entirely intimidated, I saw that I had not the good fortune to please
Madame de Breil. She not only never ordered my service, but
never accepted it; and finding me twice in her antechamber, she
asked me very coldly if I had nothing to do? I was obliged to leave
this dear antechamber: at first I was sorry; but other things
happening, I soon thought no more of it.

I had ample amends for the disdain of Madame de Breil in the
bounty of her father-in-law, who at last perceived I was there.
On the evening of the dinner I spoke of, he held a conversation
with me half an hour, with which he seemed satisfied, and which
highly delighted me. This good old gentleman, though a man of
sense, had less than Madame de Vercellis, but he was more compassionate; I therefore succeeded better with him. He told me to
attend the Abbé de Gouvon, his son, who was inclined to serve

me; that this inclination, if I would improve it, might be useful
to me, in helping me to acquire what I wanted for the destination
they intended me. The next morning I ran to the Abbé. He did not
receive me as a servant; made me sit down at the corner of his
fire; and, questioning me with the greatest mildness, he found
my education, which had attempted too many things, had completed none. Seeing particularly I knew a little Latin, he undertook to teach me more. It was agreed I should go to him every
morning, and I began the next day. Thus, by one of those caprices
you will often meet in the course of my life, at the same time
above and below my condition, I was disciple and valet to the
same family, and in my servitude I had nevertheless a preceptor
whose birth entitled him to be a preceptor to the sons of kings only.

The Abbé de Gouvon was a younger son, and designed by his
family to a bishopric; his studies, for this reason, had been carried
farther than is usual to children of quality. He had been sent to the
university of Siena, where he remained several years, and from
whence he brought a pretty strong dose of Cruscantism,[1] in order
to be at Turin what formerly the Abbé de Dangeau[2] was at Paris.
A disgust of theology threw him into the belles-lettres; this is
common enough in Italy to those who enter the career of prelacy.
He had, particularly, read the poets; he wrote Latin and Italian
verse pretty well. He had, in a word, the necessary taste for forming mine, and giving some choice to the medley with which I had
stuffed my head. But, whether my chatter had deceived him on
my knowledge, whether he could not support the tediousness of
elementary Latin, he put me too forward; I had scarcely translated a few fables of Phædrus, but he threw me into Virgil, where
I hardly understood anything. It was my fate, as will be seen in
the sequel, often to be taught Latin, and never to know it. I, nevertheless, laboured zealously enough; and the Abbé lavished his
attention with a kindness whose remembrance yet moves me.
I spent a good part of the morning with him, as well for my instruction as for his service; not for that of his person, for he never
suffered me to do any; but to write under his direction, and to
copy. My function of secretary was much more useful to me than
that of pupil. I learnt not only Italian in its purity, but it gave me
a taste for literature, and some discernment of good authors which

---

[1] Purism. The *Accademia della Crusca* was established at Florence in 1581
for the improvement of the Italian language.

[2] A seventeenth-century French grammarian.

was not acquired at la Tribu's, and which was afterwards useful
to me, when I worked alone.

These days were those of my life when I could, without romantic projects, most reasonably give into the hope of preferment.
The Abbé, well satisfied with me, told everyone so; and I was so
singularly in his father's favour, the Count of Favria told me he
had talked of me to the King. Madame de Breil had likewise left
off treating me with that air of contempt. In fine, I became a sort
of favourite in the family, to the great jealousy of the rest of the
servants, who, seeing me honoured by the instructions of their
master's son, felt plainly I was not long to remain their equal.

As much as I could judge of the views they had for me by a few
words dropped at random, but on which I did not reflect till afterwards, it appeared to me, the house of Solar, wishing to run the
career of embassies, and perhaps open, in time, the road to the
ministry, might have been glad to form, before-hand, a person of
merit and talents, who, depending entirely on them, had been
able, in time, to have obtained its confidence, and serve it essentially. This project of the Count de Gouvon was noble, judicious,
magnanimous, and truly worthy a great, good, and prudent man;
but, besides that I did not then see its whole extent, it was too
judicious for my brain, and required too much constraint. My
stupid ambition sought fortune through adventures only; and
seeing no woman in all this, this method of preferment seemed
slow, painful, and dull; though I ought to have seen it much more
honourable and certain, as women had no hand in it: the species
of merit they protect, being not, certainly, equal to what was
supposed in me.

Everything went on miraculously. I had obtained, almost forced
the esteem of everyone: the proofs were got through, and I was
generally regarded in the family as a young man who had the
greatest hopes, who was not in his place, but expected to be there.
But my place was not that assigned me by mankind; I was to
reach it by a quite different road. I come to one of the characteris-
tical touches peculiar to me, which it is sufficient to show the
reader, without adding a reflection.

Although there were many new converts of my species at Turin,
I was not fond of, nor ever would see one of them. But I saw some
Genevese who were not of them; among others a M. Mussard,
nicknamed Wrychops, a miniature painter, and a distant relation.
This M. Mussard found out my abode with the Count de Gouvon,
and came to see me with another Genevese named Bâcle, whose

companion I had been during my apprenticeship. Bâcle was a very amusing, sprightly young fellow, full of jocose sallies his youth rendered extremely agreeable. I am at once infatuated by M. Bâcle, but so much infatuated as not to be able to quit him. He was soon to depart on his return to Geneva. What a loss I was going to suffer! I felt its whole weight. The better, however, to engross the whole time he stayed, I never left him, or rather he never left me; for I was not at first so far lost as to go out without leave and spend the day with him: but very soon, observing he continually beset me, he was forbid the house. I was so much heated, that, forgetting everything except my friend Bâcle, I never went to the Abbé nor the Count, nor was to be found any longer in the house. I was reprimanded, but did not listen to it. They threatened to dismiss me. This threat was my ruin; it let me perceive it possible Bâcle might not go alone. From that time I saw no other pleasure, no other fate, no other happiness, than that of making a like journey; and I saw in it but the ineffable felicity of the journey, at the end of which, to complete it, I discovered Madame de Warens, but at an immense distance; for returning to Geneva I never thought of. The mountains, the fields, the woods, the rivulets, the villages, succeeded each other without end and without ceasing, with fresh delights: this heavenly jaunt seemed to say it would absorb my whole life. I recollected with raptures how much this journey delighted me before. What must it be, when, to all the charms of independence, would be joined that of going with a companion of my age, of my inclinations, and of good humour, without restraint, without obligation of going on or resting but as we pleased? A man must be a fool, to sacrifice a like occasion to projects of ambition of a tardy, difficult, and uncertain execution, and which, suppose them one day realised, were not worth, in all their splendour, a quarter of an hour's real pleasure and freedom in youth.

Full of this wise fancy, I conducted myself so well, I brought about to get myself turned out, and, to say truth, it was not without trouble. One evening, on coming home, the steward signified to me my dismission by the Count's order. It was precisely what I wanted; for seeing, in spite of myself, the extravagance of my conduct, I added, to excuse it, injustice and ingratitude, thus imagining to throw the blame on others, and be justified in my own eyes in an act of necessity. I was told from the Count of Favria to speak to him the next morning before my departure; but as they perceived my brain was turned, and that I was

capable of not observing it, the steward put off till after this
visit a present intended me, and which assuredly I had badly
earned; for, not having left me in the state of a valet, I had no
fixed wages.

The Count of Favria, young and giddy as he was, showed on
this occasion the most reasonable language, and, I almost dare
advance, the tenderest; so much did he recall, in the most flattering and touching manner, the attention of his uncle and the
intention of his grandfather. In fine, having brought, in lively
colours, to my view, what I sacrificed to my ruin, he offered to
make my peace, exacting, as the only condition, that I no more
saw the sorry wretch who had seduced me.

It was so plain he did not say this of himself, that, in spite of
my stupid inconsiderateness, I felt all the bounty of my old
master, and it touched me: but this dear journey was so imprinted
on my imagination, that nothing could balance its charms. I was
absolutely beyond my wits; I grew stouter, more hardened, affected haughtiness, and arrogantly answered that, as they had
given me my dismission, I had taken it; that it was too late to
retract; and that, whatever might happen to me, I was resolved
never to be turned twice out of the same house. At this, the young
man was justly irritated, gave me the epithets I deserved, turned
me out of his room by the shoulders, and shut the door on my
heels. For my part, I went off triumphantly, as one who had
gained the greatest victory; and, for fear of having a second combat to sustain, I had the baseness to depart without going to thank
the Abbé for his kindness.

To conceive how far I carried my delirium at this time, you
should be acquainted to what a point my mind is subject to be
heated by the least trifle, and with what force it plunges into the
idea of an object which attracts it, however vain this object might
sometimes be. The most foolish, the most childish, the most unac-
countable plans, soothe my favourite idea, and show me such a
probability as to give into them. Would one believe, that, at near
nineteen,[1] I should build my hopes on an empty phial for the subsistence of the rest of my days? Well, hearken.

The Abbé de Gouvon made me a present, a few weeks before,
of an Hero-fountain,[2] very pretty, which delighted me. By con-

---

[1] He was then seventeen.

[2] A compression-fountain supposed to have been invented by Hero of Alex-
andria (2nd cent. B.C.).

tinually playing this fountain, and talking of our journey, we
imagined, the wise Bâcle and I, that one might assist the other,
and prolong it. What in the world could be so curious as an Hero-
fountain? This principle was the foundation on which we built
our fortune. We were to assemble the country-people of each
village around our fountain, and there meals and good living were
to fall on us in greater abundance, as we were both persuaded
provisions cost those who gather them nothing, and that when
they did not stuff strangers with them, it was mere ill-nature. We
imagined everywhere feasting and rejoicings, supposing that,
without any other expense than the wind of our lungs, and the
water of our fountain, we should be defrayed in Piedmont, in
Savoy, in France, and all over the world. We laid out endless
projects for our journey, and directed our course northward,
rather for the pleasure of crossing the Alps, than for the supposed
necessity of stopping at last anywhere.

This was the plan on which I began the campaign, abandoning, without regret, my protector, my preceptor, my studies, my
hopes, and the expectation of an almost certain fortune, to begin
the life of an absolute vagabond. Farewell the capital, farewell
the court, ambition, vanity, love, the fair, and all the brilliant
fortune whose hopes had guided me the preceding year! I set off
with my fountain and my friend Bâcle, a purse scantily garnished,
but a heart leaping with joy, and thinking of nothing farther than
this strolling felicity to which I had all at once confined my
shining projects.

I made this extravagant journey almost as agreeably, however,
as I expected, but not exactly in the same manner; for, although
our fountain amused, a few minutes, in the public-houses, the
landlord and his waiters, we must, nevertheless, pay at parting.
But that troubled us little: we thought to make use heartily of this
resource when our money failed only. An accident saved us the
trouble; the fountain broke near Bramant, and it was quite time;
for we felt, without daring to say so, that it began to tire us. This
misfortune rendered us gayer than before, and we laughed heartily at our inconsiderateness in having forgot that our clothes and
shoes were wearing, or imagining we could replace them by the
diversion of our fountain. We continued our journey as merrily
as we began it, but drawing a little nearer the time when our
exhausted purses made it necessary to arrive.

At Chambéry I became pensive, not on the folly I had committed; never did man so soon or so well make up his mind on the

past; but on the reception which awaited me at Madame de Warens's; for I looked on her house exactly as my paternal one. I wrote to her on my entrance at the Count de Gouvon's; she knew the footing I was on, and in complimenting me she gave me some wise lessons on the manner in which I ought to answer the kindness they showed me. She looked on my fortune as certain, did I not destroy it by my own fault. What would she say on seeing me? It never once came into my head that she might shut her door against me; but I dreaded the vexation I should cause her; I dreaded her reproaches, sharper to me than want. I resolved to endure all in silence, and do everything to appease her. I saw in the universe but her alone; to live out of her favour could not be.

I was most uneasy about the companion of my journey, whom I did not wish to tell that I had had enough of him, and whom I dreaded I should not be able easily to get rid of. I prepared this separation by living coolly with him the last day: the droll fellow comprehended me; he was more crazy than sottish. I imagined this change would affect him; I was wrong; my friend Bâcle was not to be affected. We had hardly set our foot in Annecy, but he says to me, Thou art at home, shook me by the hand, bid me farewell, turned on his heel, and went off. I never heard of him since. Our acquaintance and our friendship lasted together about six weeks; but the effects have lasted as long as myself.

How did my heart beat in approaching the house of Madame de Warens! My legs trembled under me, my sight was overcast; I saw nothing, heard nothing, nor should have known anyone; I was forced to stop several times to breathe and recover my senses. Was it the fear of not obtaining the aid I wanted that troubled me to this degree? At the age I was of, does the dread of starving produce those alarms? No, no; I speak it with as much truth as pride; never at any time of my life could interest or indigence boast of having rejoiced or oppressed my heart. In the course of a life unequal and memorable by its vicissitudes, often without an asylum or bread, I always saw with the same eye both opulence and misery. At a pinch I had begged or stole like another, but feel no uneasiness at being reduced to it. Few men have suffered like me, few have shed so many tears in their lifetime; but never did poverty, or the dread of falling into it, cause me to heave a sigh or drop a tear. My soul, proof against fortune, acknowledged no true happiness or real misery but those which did not depend on her, and it was when nothing was wanting on the side of necessaries I felt myself the unhappiest of mortals.

I had scarcely appeared before Madame de Warens but her countenance cheered me. I leaped at the first sound of her voice, I ran to her feet, and in the transports of melting joy I pressed my lips to her hand. For her part, I do not know whether she had heard of my affair, but I saw little surprise in her countenance, and not the least uneasiness. Poor little fellow! says she, in a soothing tone, you are here again then! I knew very well you were too young for this journey; I am very glad, however, it did not turn out so bad as I dreaded. She afterwards made me tell my whole story, which was not long, and I told it very faithfully, concealing, however, a few articles, but without sparing or excusing myself.

The question was my lodging. She consulted her maid. I dared not breathe during this deliberation; but when I heard I was to sleep in the house, it was with trouble I contained myself; and I saw my little bundle carried to the room intended for me, nearly as Saint-Preux saw his chair carried back to Madame de Wolmar's.[1] I had, to complete it, the pleasure of learning that this favour was not to be transient, and, at a time they thought me attentive to other things, I heard her say, They may talk as they will, but since Providence has brought me him again, I am determined not to abandon him.

Here I am then, at last, fixed at her house. It is not, however, from hence I date the happy part of my life, but it served to prepare it. Although this sensibility of heart, which makes us really enjoy each other, is the work of nature, and perhaps a production of organization, it calls for a situation to unfold itself. Without these occasional causes, a man born with fine feelings would feel nothing, and go out of the world without having known his existence. Such, nearly, had I been till then, and such had I perhaps always been, had I never known Madame de Warens, or if, having known her, I had not lived long enough with her to contract the gentle use of the affectionate sentiments she inspired me with. I dare advance, he who feels only love, does not feel the greatest charms of this life. I am acquainted with another feeling, less impetuous perhaps, but more delightful a thousand times, which sometimes goes with love, and is sometimes separated from it. This sentiment is not friendship alone neither; it is more luxurious, and tenderer: I do not imagine it can act for one of the same sex; at least, I know friendship if ever man knew it, and never

---

[1] Saint-Preux and Mme. de Wolmar are two of the characters of *Julie*.

felt it for any one of my friends. This is not clear, but it will be in what follows: feelings are not to be thoroughly described but by their effects.

She lived in an old house, but large enough to have a room of reserve, in which she received company, and in which she lodged me. This room was in the passage where I have said we had our first conference, and beyond the little brook and gardens you perceived the country. This sight was to the young inhabitant not an indifferent thing. It was, since Bossey, the first verdure I had seen before my window. Always enclosed by walls, I had never before my eyes but the tiles or the street. How charming and sweet was

J.-J. AND "MAMMA"

this novelty! It very much increased my disposition to tenderness. I looked on this pleasing landscape as one of the favours of my dear protectress: it seemed she placed it there on purpose for me; I placed myself peaceably there by her side; I saw her everywhere between the flowers and the verdure; her charms and those of the spring were blended in my eyes. My heart, till then compressed, found itself more expanded in this space, and my sighs were breathed with more freedom among these orchards.

The magnificence I had seen at Turin was not found at Madame

de Warens's, but I found cleanliness, decency, and a patriarchal
abundance that ostentation never reaches. She had very little
plate, no china, no game in her kitchen, or foreign wine in her
cellar; but both were well furnished, at everyone's service, and in
her earthen cups she offered excellent coffee. Whoever came there
was invited to dine with her or at her house, and never workman,
messenger, or traveller went away without eating or drinking.
Her household was composed of her own maid from Fribourg,
pretty enough, named Merceret, a valet from her own country,
named Claude Anet, whom we shall speak of afterwards, a cook,
and two hackney porters for her visits, which happened rarely.
This is a great deal for two thousand livres a year; her little income, if well managed, would have nevertheless sufficed to all
this, in a country where the land is extremely good, and money
very scarce. Unhappily, economy was never her favourite virtue;
she ran in debt, she paid; money passed backwards and forwards,
and so it went on.

The manner her house was conducted was precisely what I
would have chosen; you may think I took the advantage of it with
pleasure. I was least pleased with sitting so long at table. She with
trouble supported the first smell of soup or meat. This smell
almost made her faint, and her disgust lasted some time. She came
to by degrees, chattered, but did not eat. It was half an hour before she tried the first bit. I had dined three times in this time; my
meal was finished long before she began hers. I began again to
keep her company, and thus ate for two without finding myself
worse for it. In fine, I gave it to the agreeable sentiment of the
well-being I found with her, so much the readier, as this well-
being I enjoyed was mixed with no uneasiness on the means of
supporting it. Not being yet in the strict confidence of her affairs,
I supposed her in a state of always continuing the same. I found
the same pleasure in her house afterwards; but, better informed
of her real situation, and seeing she anticipated on her income,
I did not enjoy it with the same tranquillity. Foresight has always,
with me, spoiled enjoyment. I saw futurity in vain; I never could
avoid it.

From the first day the easiest familiarity was entertained between us to the same degree it continued during the rest of her
life. *Little Dear* was my name, *Mamma* hers; and we always remained *Little Dear* and *Mamma*, even when years had almost
effaced the difference between us. I find that these two names
marvellously render the idea of our tones, the simplicity of our

manners, and particularly the relation of our hearts. She was to me the tenderest of mothers, who never sought her pleasure, but always my good; and if sense formed a part in my passion for her, it was not to change its nature, but only to render it more exquisite, to infatuate me with the charm of having a mamma young and pretty, whom it delighted me to caress; I say to caress, in a literal sense; for she never thought of sparing her kisses or the tenderest maternal caresses, and it never entered my heart to abuse it. You will say we had, however, at last, relations of another sort: agreed; but stay a little; I cannot say all at once.

The sight of her, at our first interview, was the only instant truly passionate she ever caused me; and even that instant was the work of surprise. My indiscreet looks were never busied under her handkerchief, though a plumpness little covered in this part might very well have drawn them there. I had neither transports nor desires with her; I was in a ravishing calm, enjoying without knowing what. I could thus have spent my life and eternity without being tired an instant. She was the only person with whom I never found a dryness of conversation, which is the greatest of punishments, from the obligation of supporting it. Our tête-à-têtes were not so much discourse as an inexhaustible prattle, which to put an end to must be interrupted. So far from the obligation of talking, I was rather obliged to impose on myself that of forbearing. By long contemplating her projects, she often lost herself in thought. Well, I let her remain so; I said nothing, I gazed on her, and was the happiest of men. I had, besides, another singular trick. Without pretending to the favours of privacy, I continually sought it, and enjoyed it with a passion which degenerated to fury, if it was interrupted. As soon as anyone came in, man or woman, it was equal to me, I went out murmuring, not being able to remain a third in her company. I went and counted the minutes in her antechamber, cursing, a thousand times, these eternal visitors; nor could I conceive how they had so much to say, because I had still more.

I never felt my whole passion for her, but when I did not see her. When I saw her I was contented only; but my uneasiness at her absence carried me to a degree of grief. The necessity of living with her gave me transports so melting as often to draw tears. I shall never forget one great holiday, whilst she was at vespers, I took a walk out of town, my mind filled with her image and an ardent desire to spend my days with her. I had sense enough to see that, at present, it was not possible, and that a happiness I so well relished would be short. This gave my contemplation a sorrowfulness which had, however, nothing gloomy in it, and which was allayed by flattering hope. The sound of the bells, which always singularly affected me, the singing of birds, the clearness of the weather, the sweetness of the landscape, the houses scattered and rural, in which I placed in idea our common abode; all this struck me with an impression so lively, so tender, so pensive, and so touching, that I saw myself, as in ecstasy, transported to those happy times, and in those happy abodes, where my heart, possessing every felicity that could delight it, tasted them in raptures inexpressible, without ever thinking of sensual voluptuousness. I never remember to have launched into futurity so forcibly, and with such illusions, as at that time; and what struck me most in the recollection of this conceit, when it was realized, was to find the objects exactly such as I had imagined them. If ever the dream of a man awake had the air of a prophetic vision, it was certainly this. I was deceived in its imaginary duration only; for the days, and the years, and the whole life, passed in an unalterable tranquillity, but in effect it all lasted but an instant. Alas! my most certain happiness was but a dream. Its accomplishment was almost instantly followed by sleeping no more.

I should never end, were I to enter into the particulars of all the follies the remembrance of this dear Mamma caused me to act, when I was not in her sight. How many times I have kissed my bed, in thinking she had lain there; my curtains, all the furniture of the room, in thinking they were hers, that her dear hand had touched them; even the floor on which I laid myself, thinking she had walked there. Sometimes, even in her presence, the greatest extravagances have fallen from me, that only the most violent passion seemed able to inspire. One day at table, at the time of her putting a bit in her mouth, I cry out I see a hair in it; she spits it out on her plate; I greedily lay hold of and swallow it. In a word, between me and the most passionate lover there was but only one essential difference, and that renders my state almost inconceivable to reason.

I was returned from Italy, not altogether as I went, but as, perhaps, never at my age anyone came back. I brought back from thence, not my virginity, but my maidenhead. I had felt the progress of years; my troublesome constitution at last declared itself; and its first eruption, extremely involuntarily, gave me apprehensions for my health, which paint, better than anything else, the innocence in which I had lived till that time. But my

fears being soon removed, I learnt that dangerous supplement
which diverts the course of nature, and saves young people of my
humour many disorders at the expense of their health, their
vigour, and sometimes their life. This vice, which shame and
timidity find so convenient, has, besides, a great enticement for
lively imaginations; that is, to dispose, in a manner, at will, of
the whole sex, and to make the beauties which tempt them serve
their pleasures without the necessity of obtaining their consent.
Seduced by this fatal advantage, I laboured to destroy the sound
constitution nature had given me, and which I had given time to
form strongly. Add to this disposition the locality of my present
situation; lodged at a pretty woman's, caressing her image in my
heart, seeing her incessantly in the day-time, at night surrounded
by objects which recall her to my mind, sleeping in the bed I
know she has slept in. What stimulants! Whatever reader repre-
sents them to himself, looks on me as already half dead. Quite the
contrary: that which should have destroyed me, precisely saved
me, at least for some time. Drowned in the pleasure of her company, the ardent desire of passing my days in it, absent or present,
I always saw in her a tender mother, a beloved sister, a delightful
friend, and nothing farther. I always saw her so, continually the
same, and saw nothing but her. Her image, always present, left
room for no other; she was, to me, the only woman existing; and
the extreme gentleness of sentiment with which she inspired me,
not allowing my senses time to awaken for others, defended me
from her and the whole sex. In a word, I was moderate because
I loved her. From these effects, which I badly relate, tell me who
can, of what species was my passion for her? For my part, all I
can say of it is, that, if this seems very extraordinary, what follows
will appear much more so.

I spent my time the most agreeably, employed on things which
pleased me least. There were either plans to adjust, bills to write
out, receipts to transcribe: there were herbs to pick, drugs to
pound, stills to watch: and in the midst of all this came crowds
of travellers, beggars, visits of all sorts. We must entertain, all at
once, a soldier, an apothecary, a prebendary, a lady of fashion,
and a lay brother. I inveighed, I grumbled, I swore, I wished all
this cursed medley at the devil. For her, who took everything
gaily, my fury made her laugh till tears came down her cheeks;
and that which made her laugh still more was, to see me grow the
more furious, as I could not help laughing myself. These little
intervals, which gave me the pleasure of growling, were delight-

ful; and if a chance guest came in during the dispute, she knew
how to make the most of it for amusement, in maliciously prolonging the visit, and casting now and then a glance at me, when
I could willingly have beat her. She could hardly abstain from
bursting, on seeing me, constrained and moderate from decency,
give her the looks of a demon, whilst, from my heart, even in
spite of me, I thought it all exceeding comic.

ANNECY: THE CHATEAU

All these things, without pleasing me in themselves, nevertheless amused me, because they made a part of a manner of being
which charmed me. Nothing that was done around me, nothing
they made me do, was after my taste, but everything was after
my heart. I believe I should have arrived at a fondness for medicine, had not my disgust to it produced toying scenes which
incessantly diverted us: it was, perhaps, the first time this art
produced a like effect. I pretended to know by the smell a book
of medicine, and it is pleasant to think I was seldom mistaken. She
forced me to take the most detestable drugs. It was in vain I ran
off, or would have contended; in spite of my resistance and my
horrible grimaces, in spite of myself and my teeth, when I saw
those lovely besmeared fingers approach my mouth, I must open
it and suck. When all her little apparatus was assembled in one
room, to hear us run and halloo amidst the burstings of laughter,
you would have thought we were acting a farce, instead of making
opiate or elixir.

My time was not, however, spent entirely in this foolery. I had
found a few books in the room I slept in: the *Spectator*, Puffen-

dorf, Saint-Evremond, the *Henriade*. Though I did not preserve
my old passion for reading, yet, to fill my leisure, I read a little
of all these. The *Spectator*, particularly, pleased me much, and
was useful to me. The Abbé de Gouvon had taught me to read less
eagerly, and with more reflection; I was edified more by study.
I accustomed myself to reflect on the elocution, and on the elegant
construction; I exercised myself in discerning pure French from
my country dialect. For instance, I was corrected in an orthographical fault I made with all our Genevese, by these two verses
of the *Henriade:*

Soit qu'un ancien respect pour le sang de leurs maîtres
Parlât encor pour lui dans le cœur de ces traîtres.

The word *parlât*, which struck me, taught me that there must be
a *t* in the third person of the subjunctive; instead of which I had
written and pronounced *parla*, as in the perfect and the indicative.

Sometimes I chattered with Mamma on my study; sometimes
read to her; I took great pleasure in it; I exercised myself in reading well, and it was useful to me. I have said she had a well-
cultivated understanding. It was then in all its prime. Several
men of letters had endeavoured to render themselves agreeable to
her, and had taught her to judge of works of merit. She had, if
I am allowed to say it, a taste a little Protestant; she talked of
none but Bayle, and extolled Saint-Evremond, who had been long
dead in France. But that did not prevent her from knowing good
literature, and conversing very well on it. She had been brought
up in choice society, and coming to Savoy still young, she had lost,
in the pleasing company of the nobility of the country, the affected
tone of the country of Vaud, where the ladies take wit for sense,
and cannot speak but in epigrams.

Though she had seen the court but little, she had thrown a
rapid glance around it, which was, to her, sufficient to know it.
She always kept friends there, and, in spite of secret jealousy, in
spite of the murmurs her conduct and debts excited, she never lost
her pension. She had a knowledge of the world, and the spirit of
reflection which knows to draw advantages from that knowledge.
It was the favourite subject of her conversations, and precisely,
considering my chimerical notions, the sort of instruction I most
wanted. We read together La Bruyère: he pleased her more than
La Rochefoucauld, a dull and mortifying book, principally for
youth, who do not love to see man as he is. When she moralised,
she sometimes lost herself a little by wandering; but, with a kiss

now and then of the lips or hands, I kept my patience, and her tediousness was not tiresome.

This life was too pleasing to last. I saw it, and the uneasiness of seeing it terminate was the only thing which disturbed its enjoyment. With all our foolery, Mamma studied me, observed me, questioned me, and built up for my fortune many projects which I could very well have done without. Happily, it was not sufficient to be acquainted with my inclinations, my tastes, and my trifling talents; occasions were to be sought to make them useful, and these were not the business of a day. Even the prejudices the poor thing had conceived in favour of my merit, retarded the time of employing it, by making her more difficult on the choice of the means. In fine, all went as I could wish, thanks to the good opinion she had of me; but it was to be lowered, and then farewell ease! One of her relations, named M. d'Aubonne, came to see her. He was a man of great understanding, cunning, and a genius for projects like herself, but did not ruin himself by them, a sort of adventurer. He came from offering the Cardinal of Fleury the plan of a lottery, extremely well composed, but which was not relished. He was going to offer it the court of Turin, where it was adopted and put in execution. He stayed some time at Annecy, and became enamoured with the Intendant's wife, who was a very amiable person, very much to my taste, and the only one I saw with pleasure at Mamma's. M. d'Aubonne saw me, his kinswoman talked to him about me; he undertook to examine me, to see what I was proper for, and, if he found any genius in me, endeavour to place me.

Madame de Warens sent me to him two or three mornings following, on pretext of an errand, and without acquainting me with anything of it beforehand. He took an excellent method of making me chatter, spoke freely with me, put me under as little restraint as possible, talked to me of trifles and on all sorts of subjects; all without seeming to observe me, without the least affectation, and as if, pleased with me, he would converse without restraint. I was delighted with him. The result of his observations was, that, whatever my exterior and my animated physiognomy might promise, I was, if not absolutely a fool, at least a boy of very little sense, without ideas, almost without acquirements; in a word, a very shallow fellow in all respects; and that the honour of becoming some day the parson of a village was the greatest fortune I ought to aspire to. Such was the account he gave me to Madame de Warens. This was the second or third time I was thus judged; it was not the last, and the decree of M. Masseron has been often confirmed.

The cause of these judgements is too much connected with my character not to want an explanation: for, in conscience, it is plainly seen I cannot sincerely subscribe to them; and that, with all possible impartiality, whatever Messieurs Masseron, d'Aubonne, and many others have said, I cannot take their word for them.

Two things, almost inalliable, unite in me, without my being able to conceive the manner. A constitution extremely violent, impetuous and lively passions, and ideas slowly produced, confused, and which never offer till after the proper time. You would think my heart and mind do not belong to the same individual. Sentiment quicker than light fills my soul, but, instead of enlightening, it fires and dazzles me. I feel everything and see nothing. I am transported, but stupid; I must be cool to think. What astonishes is, that I have my feeling pretty sure, penetration, and even delicate wit, provided you will wait for me: I can make an excellent impromptu at leisure, but in an instant I never wrote or said anything clever. I could hold a pretty conversation by the post, as the Spaniards, it is said, play at chess. When I read that stroke of the Duke of Savoy's, who turned round, keeping on his journey, to cry out, *At your throat, Paris merchant!* I said, That is I.

This slowness of thought, joined to the vivacity of feeling, is not in my conversation only; I have it when alone also, and when I write. My ideas are disposed in my head with the greatest difficulty: they circulate dully; they ferment till they move me, heat me, give me palpitations; and, amidst all this emotion, I see nothing clearly; I cannot write a single word; I must wait. Insensibly this vast emotion is suppressed, the chaos is dispersed; each thing takes its place, but slowly, and after a long and confused agitation. Have you not sometimes seen an opera in Italy? In changing the scenes there reigns a disagreeable disorder on these grand theatres, which lasts a considerable time: the decorations are all intermixed; you see in every part a pulling and hauling about which gives pain; you think the whole is turning topsy-turvy. By degrees, everything is, however, brought to its place, nothing is wanting, and you are greatly surprised to find a ravishing sight succeed this long tumult. This piece of work nearly resembles that which operates in my brain, when I would write. Had I known how first to wait, and then render, with all their beauties, the things thus painted there, few authors would have surpassed me.

Thence comes the extreme difficulty I find in writing. My manuscripts, scratched out, blotted, mixed, not legible, attest the trouble they cost me. Not one but I was obliged to transcribe four or five times before it went to the press. I never could do anything, the pen in hand, opposite a table and paper: it was in my walks, amidst rocks and woods; it was in the night, abed, when I could not sleep, I wrote in my brain; you may judge how slowly, particularly to a man deprived of verbal memory, and who, in his life, never could retain six verses by heart. Some of my periods have been turned and winded five or six nights in my head before they were in a state for going on paper. From thence, likewise, I succeed better in works which demand labour, than in those which must have a certain airiness; as letters, a style I could never get the tone of, and whose occupation is to me the greatest of punishments. I write no letters on the most trifling subject, which do not cost me hours of fatigue; or, if I would write immediately what strikes me, I can neither begin nor end; my letter is a long and confused verbosity; with trouble I am understood when it is read.

I am not only troubled to render my ideas, but even in receiving them. I have studied mankind, and think myself a tolerable good observator: nevertheless, I cannot see anything in that I perceive; I see clearly only that I recollect, and I have no knowledge but in my recollections. Of all that is said, of all that is done, of all that passes in my presence, I know nothing, I penetrate nothing. The external sign is all that strikes me. But afterwards the whole returns again; I call to mind the time, place, tone, look, gesture, circumstance; nothing escapes me. Then, from what they said or did, I find out what they thought, and it is very seldom I mistake.

So little master of my judgement alone by myself, judge what I must be in conversation, when, to speak apropos, you must think at one and the same time of a thousand things. The sole idea of so many conformities, of which I am sure to forget at least some one, suffices to intimidate me. I do not even comprehend how they dare talk in company: for at each word you must pass in review every person there; you must be acquainted with every man's character, know their history, to be assured of saying nothing which might offend some of them; in which those who frequent the world have a great advantage: knowing better on what to be silent, they are surer of what they say; and with all that, they often let fall absurdities. Judge, therefore, of him who falls there from the clouds! It is almost impossible he should talk a minute with impunity. In private conversations there is another inconvenience I think worse; the necessity of always talking. When you are spoke to, you must answer; and if nothing is said, you must revive the conversation. This insupportable constraint only would have disgusted me of society. I find no torture like that of the obligation of speaking instantly and continually. I do not know whether this proceeds from my mortal aversion to all subjection; but it is sufficient that if I must absolutely talk, I infallibly talk nonsense.

What still is more fatal, instead of knowing when to be silent, if I have nothing to say, it is then, the sooner to pay my debt, I have the frenzy of wanting to talk. I hasten to stammer quickly words without ideas, very happy when they mean nothing at all. Striving to conquer or hide my folly, I seldom fail to show it.

Of a thousand examples I might give, here is one; not from my youth, but from a time when, having lived several years in society, I should have taken its easy tone, were that at all possible. I was one evening with two fine ladies and a man — I can give his name: the Duke of Gontaut. No one else was in the room; I was compelled to speak a few words, what they were God only knows, in a conversation among four persons, of whom three certainly needed no help from me. The lady of the house had an opiate brought which she took, twice every day, for her stomach. The other lady, seeing her make a grimace, said laughing: Is that M. Tronchin's opiate? I think not, replied the former in the same tone. I think it can hardly be better, gallantly added the witty Rousseau. Everyone stopped astonished; not the smallest word or smile escaped, and the next instant the conversation took another turn. Addressed to any other, the stupid remark might have been but a pleasantry; but to a woman too amiable not to have made herself a little talked of, it was terrible; and I think the two witnesses, man and woman, with difficulty refrained from a burst of laughter. Such is one of those efforts of wit which escape me through desiring to speak when I have nothing to say. I shall not easily forget it; for, besides being very memorable in itself, I fancy that it had consequences which recall it to me but too often.

I believe here is enough to make it understood, how, without being a fool, I have nevertheless often passed for one, even with people who were thought good judges; so much the more un-

happily, as my physiognomy and eyes promised more, and that
this expectation frustrated, renders to others my stupidity more
shocking. This detail, which a peculiar occasion gave birth to, is
not unnecessary to what follows. It contains the key to many
extraordinary things I have been observed to do, which is attributed to a savage humour I have not. I should love society like
another, was I not certain of appearing there, not only to disadvantage, but quite different to what I am. My determination to
write and hide myself from the world is precisely that which suits
me. Myself present, my parts had never been known, or even
suspected; and this happened to Madame Dupin, though a woman
of sense, and though I lived in her house several years. She has
often told me so herself since that time. However, all this suffers
certain exceptions, and I shall come over it again in the course
of the work.

The measure of my talents thus fixed, the state I was fit for thus
designed, there was no farther question, for the second time, but
the fulfilling my vocation. The difficulty was my not having gone
through my studies, or knowing Latin enough even to become a
priest. Madame de Warens proposed sending me to be instructed
some time at the Seminary. She mentioned it to the Superior; he
was a Lazarist, named M. Gros, a good-natured, half-blind,
meagre, grey-haired little man, the most spiritual and the least
pedantic Lazarist I have known; which, in fact, is not saying
much.

He sometimes came to Mamma's, who welcomed him, caressed
him, even allured him, and sometimes let him lace her stays; an
employment he willingly undertook. Whilst he was thus in office,
she ran from one side of the room to the other, doing sometimes
one thing, sometimes another. Drawn by the lace, the Superior
followed grumbling, and saying every minute, Well, Madame,
hold still then. It produced a scene funny enough.

M. Gros heartily gave into Mamma's project. He was contented with a moderate salary, and undertook my instruction.
Nothing was wanting but the Bishop's consent, who not only
granted it, but would pay it himself. He likewise permitted me
to remain in the secular habit, till they could judge by a trial of
the success they might hope.

What a change! I must submit. I went to the Seminary as to the
place of execution. What a doleful place is a seminary; especially
to him that comes from the house of a pretty woman! I carried
one book only, which I begged Mamma to lend me, and which

was a great resource to me. You would not guess what sort of a book this was; a music book. Among the talents she cultivated, music was not forgot. She had voice, sung passably, and played the harpsichord a little. She had had the complaisance to give me a few lessons of music, and she was obliged to bring me from far, for I hardly knew the music of our psalms. Eight or ten lessons from a woman, and those much interrupted, far from enabling me to sol-fa, taught me not a quarter of the musical signs. I had, nevertheless, so great a passion for this art, I wanted to make a trial of exercising myself alone. The book I carried with me was not of the easiest neither; it was Clérambault's cantatas. My application and obstinacy may be conceived, when I tell you, that, without knowing either transposition or quantity, I arrived at deciphering and singing the first recitative and the first air of the cantata of *Alpheus and Arethusa:* it is true, this air is scanned so just, you need only recite the verses with their measure to catch the air.

There was a cursed Lazarist at the Seminary who undertook me, and made me detest the Latin he would have taught me. He had flat, thick, black hair, a gingerbread face, a bull's voice, the looks of a polecat, a wild boar's bristles instead of a beard; his smile was sardonic; his limbs played like pullies in a puppet-

show: I have forgot his odious name; but his frightful, precise
figure I have retained; it is with trouble I recollect him without
horror. I think I see him yet in the passage, pulling forward with
grace his old square bonnet as a sign to come into his room, more
dreadful to me than a cell. Judge of the contrast with such a
master for the disciple of a Court Abbé!

Had I remained two months at the mercy of this monster, I am
persuaded my head would not have resisted. But the good-natured
M. Gros, who perceived I was dull, ate nothing, and grew thin,
guessed the cause of my uneasiness; it was not difficult. He took
me from the clutches of the animal, and by a still more striking
contrast put me to the mildest of men. He was a young Abbé from
Faucigny, named M. Gâtier, who studied at the Seminary, and,
from complaisance for M. Gros, and I believe from humanity,
was so kind as to take from his own studies that time he gave to the
direction of mine. I never saw a physiognomy more touching than
M. Gâtier's. He was fair, with a beard inclining to carroty. He
had the common appearance of people of his province, who under
a heavy outside hide a deal of good sense; but that which truly
characterised him was a sensible, kind, and affable heart. He had
in his large blue eyes a mixture of good temper, tenderness, and
sadness, which engaged one to wish him well. In the looks, in the
tone of this poor young man, you would have said he foresaw his
destiny, and that he felt himself born to misfortune.

His character did not contradict his physiognomy. Made up of
patience and complaisance, he seemed to study with me rather
than instruct me. Less would have done to have gained my esteem;
his predecessor had rendered that extremely easy. Nevertheless,
though he bestowed so much time on me, and though each of us
did all in his power, and although he took an exceeding good
method, I advanced little with much labour. It is singular, that,
with conception enough, I could never learn anything by masters,
except my father and M. Lambercier. The little I have got since,
I learnt alone, as you will see. My reason, disclaiming every kind
of yoke, cannot submit to the law of the moment. Even the dread
of not learning prevents my attention. For fear of tiring him who
speaks, I feign to understand him; he goes on, and I understand
nothing of it. My reason will march at its own hour; it cannot
submit to another's.

The time of ordination being arrived, M. Gâtier returned to
his province a deacon. He carried with him my grief, my attachment, and my gratitude. I sent up prayers for him, which were no

more heard than those I made for myself. A few years afterwards I heard, that, being curate of a parish, he had a child by a girl, the only one, though he had an extremely tender heart, he had ever known. This was a dreadful scandal in a diocese so severely governed. Priests, according to what is right, must get none but married women with child. Because he failed in this law of conveniency, he was sent to prison, defamed, and turned out. I do not know whether afterwards he was able to settle his affairs; but the sense of his misfortunes, deeply graven on my mind, returned when I wrote *Emile*, and, uniting M. Gâtier with M. Gaime, I made of these two worthy priests the original of the Vicaire Savoyard. I flatter myself the imitation did not disgrace its models.

Whilst I was at the Seminary, M. d'Aubonne was obliged to leave Annecy. The Intendant took it in his head to be angry that he made love to his wife. It was imitating the gardener's dog; for though Madame Corvezi was amiable, he lived on poor terms with her; his ultramontane tastes[1] made her useless to him, and he treated her so brutally, a separation was talked of. M. Corvezi was an ugly fellow, black as a mole, knavish as an owl, and who by dint of oppressions ended by being himself driven out. It is said the Provençals revenge themselves on their enemies by songs; M. d'Aubonne revenged himself on his by a comedy: he sent this piece to Madame de Warens, who showed it me. It pleased me, and inspired me with a fancy to write one, to try whether I was in effect that blockhead the author had pronounced me; but it was not till I came to Chambéry I executed this project, in writing *The Lover of Himself*.[2] Thus when I said, in the preface to that work, I wrote it at eighteen, I curtailed a few years.

It was about this time an adventure refers to, of little importance in itself, but which in respect to me has had effects, and has made a noise in the world when I had forgot it. I had, every week, permission to go out. I have no occasion to mention the use I made of it. One Sunday, being at Mamma's, a fire broke out in a building of the Cordeliers, joining the house she occupied. This building, in which was their oven, was stuffed full of dry faggots. The whole was in a short time on fire. The house was in great danger, covered by the flames the wind brought there. They began to remove in haste, and carry the goods into the garden, which was opposite my former windows, and beyond the brook I have already

---

[1] Pederasty.

[2] *Narcisse, ou l'Amant de lui-même*, played Dec. 18th, 1752, and published 1753.

spoken of. I was so affrighted, I threw indifferently out at the
window everything I laid hold of, even a large stone mortar,
which at any other time I could hardly have lifted: I was going
to throw, equally, a large looking-glass, if someone had not held
me. The good Bishop, who that day came to see Mamma, did not
remain idle neither. He took her to the garden, where he began
prayers with her and all those who were there; so that, coming
up some time afterwards, I saw everyone on their knees, and
I fell on mine. During the holy man's prayer, the wind changed,
but so suddenly and so àpropos, that the flames, which covered
the house, and had already entered the windows, were driven to
the other side of the court, and the house received no damage.
Two[1] years afterwards, M. de Bernex being dead, the Antonines,
his old brethren, began to collect the pieces which might serve towards his beatification. At the instance of Father Boudet, I joined
to these pieces an attestation of the fact I have just stated, in which
I did well; but that in which I did ill was giving this fact as a
miracle. I had seen the bishop at prayers, and during his prayers
I saw the wind change, and even extremely àpropos: this I might
have said and certified; but that one of these two things was the
cause of the other, I ought not to have attested, because I could
not know it. However, as far as I can recollect my ideas at that
time, a sincere Catholic I was in earnest. The fondness for miracles
so natural to the human heart, my veneration for this virtuous
prelate, the secret pride of having myself contributed to the miracle, aided in seducing me; and if this miracle had been the effect
of the most ardent prayers, it is certain I might have attributed
to myself a part of it.

More than thirty years afterwards, when I published the *Letters
from the Mountain*, M. Fréron discovered this certificate, I do
not know by what means, and made use of it in his paper. I must
own the discovery was fortunate, and the patness appeared even
to me extremely pleasant.

I was fated to be the outcast of all conditions. Although M.
Gâtier gave the least unfavourable account possible of my progress, they saw it was not proportioned to my labour, which had
nothing encouraging to carry my studies farther. The Bishop and
the Superior, therefore, gave me over, and I was returned to
Madame de Warens as a person not worth the making even a
priest of; in other respects a good lad, say they, and not vicious:

---

[1] Actually twelve — M. de Bernex died in April 1734.

this caused her, in spite of every dispiriting prejudice against me, not to abandon me.

I brought back to her, in triumph, the music-book I had made so good use of. My air of *Alpheus and Arethusa* was nearly all I had learnt at the Seminary. My remarkable taste to this art gave rise to a thought of making me a musician. The occasion was convenient. She had music at least once a week at her house, and the music-master of the cathedral, who directed this little concert, came very often to see her. He was a Parisian, named M. Le Maître, a good composer, very lively, very gay, still young, pretty well made, little sense, but on the whole a very good kind of man. Mamma made me acquainted with him; I was all to him, and did not displease him: the salary was mentioned; it was agreed on. In short, I went to him, passed the winter there the more agreeably as the school was not more than twenty paces from Mamma's; we were with her in a moment, and supped there very often together.

You may judge, the life of the music-school, always singing and gay, with the musicians and the singing-boys of the choir, pleased me more than the Seminary and the fathers of St. Lazarus. However, this life, though more free, was not less even and regular. I was made to love independence, and never abuse it. During an entire six months, I never went out once, but to Mamma's or church; nor did I even wish it. This interval is one of those in which I lived in the greatest calm, and that I recollect with the greatest pleasure. In the divers situations I have found myself, some of them have been marked with such a sentiment of well-being, that, in bringing them again to my memory, I am as affected by them as if I was still there. I not only recall time, place, and persons, but every encompassing object, the temperature of the air, its smell, its colour, a certain local impression which is not felt but there, and whose lively remembrance carries me there again. For instance, all they repeated at the school, all they sung at the choir, all they did there, the charming and noble dress of the canons, the priests' chasubles, the chanters' mitres, the musicians' persons, an old lame carpenter who played the counter-bass, a little spark of an abbé who played the violin, the tattered cassock which, after laying down his sword, M. Le Maître put over his secular coat, and the beautiful fine surplice with which he covered the tatters to go to the choir; the loftiness with which I went, holding my little flute, placing myself in the orchestra at the stand, for a little scrap of a recitative M. Le Maître had composed on purpose for me; the good eating that awaited us afterwards, the good appetite we carried there; this concourse of objects, brought back in a lively manner, has a hundred times charmed me in my memory, as much or more than in reality. I have always retained a feeling inclination for a certain air of *Conditor alme siderum,* which goes by iambics; because, one Sunday in Advent, I heard from my bed this hymn sung before day, on the steps of the cathedral, according to a custom of this church. Mlle. Merceret, Mamma's woman, knew a little of music: I shall never forget the little anthem *Afferte* which M. Le Maître obliged me to sing with her, and which his mistress heard with so much pleasure. In fine, all down to the good-natured girl Perrine, who was so good a girl, and whom the singing-boys teased to madness, everything of the remembrance of those times of happiness and innocence often returns to enrapture and afflict me.

I lived at Annecy almost a twelvemonth without the least reproach; everyone was satisfied with me. Since my return from Turin I had committed no follies, nor did I commit any whilst I was with Mamma. She always conducted me properly; my attachment to her was become my sole passion, and a proof it was not a foolish passion, my heart formed my reason. It is true, this only sentiment, absorbing, in a manner, all my faculties, put it out of my power to learn anything, even music, though I made every effort. But it was not my fault; none could be more willing;

assiduity was not wanting. I was inattentive and pensive; I sighed; what could I do? Nothing was wanting to my progress which depended on me; but that I might commit fresh follies, a subject only was necessary. This subject presented itself; chance settled all, and, as you will afterwards see, my foolish head made use of it.

One evening, in the month of February, in very cold weather, as we were all around the fire, we heard a knocking at the street door. Perrine takes the lantern, goes down, and opens: a young man comes in with her, comes upstairs, introduces himself with an easy air, and pays M. Le Maître a short and well-turned compliment; says he is a French musician, that the bad state of his purse obliged him to act the vicar,[1] to get on his road. At this word of French musician, M. Le Maître's good-natured heart leaped for joy; he was passionately fond of his country and his art. He receives the young traveller, offers a lodging he seemed much to want, and accepted without much ceremony. I observed him, whilst he warmed himself and chattered till supper time. Short of stature, but very square; he had I know not what ill in his make, without any particular deformity; he was, one may say, hump-backed with flat shoulders, but I believe he limped a little. He had on a black coat rather worn than old, which was falling to pieces, a very fine but very dirty shirt, beautiful fringed ruffles, spatterdashes into each of which he might have put both his legs, and, to keep the snow from him, a little hat to carry under his arm. In this odd equipage he had, nevertheless, something noble which his conversation did not contradict; his look was delicate and agreeable; he talked with ease and well, but not very modestly. Everything showed him a young libertine, who had education, and did not go begging as a beggar, but as a fool. He told us his name was Venture de Villeneuve, that he came from Paris, that he had lost his way, and, forgetting a little his story of musician, he added he was going to Grenoble, to see a relation who was of the parliament.

During supper music was talked of, and he talked well. He knew all the greatest virtuosi, all the famous works, every actor, every actress, every pretty woman, every nobleman. He seemed perfectly acquainted with all that was said; but a subject was scarcely begun, but he threw into the conversation some joke which made them laugh and forget all they had said. This was on Saturday; the next day we had music at the cathedral. M. Le

---

[1] *vicarier;* a word used of the perambulations from town to town of unemployed musicians in search of work.

Maître asked him to sing there: *With all my heart;* asks him his part: *The counter-tenor*, and talks of something else. Before going to church they offer him his part to peruse; he did not look at it. This gasconnade surprised Le Maître: he whispers to me and says, You'll see he does not know a single note in music. I am much afraid of it, say I. I follow them, extremely uneasy. When they began, my heart beat with terrible force; for I was very much inclined to wish him success.

I had soon reason to recover myself. He chanted his two recitatives with all the justice and taste imaginable, and what is more, with an extremely pretty voice. I was hardly ever more agreeably surprised. After mass, M. Venture was complimented to the skies, by the canons and musicians, to which he replied joking, but always with a deal of grace. M. Le Maître embraced him heartily; I did the same: he saw I was very glad, and it seemed to give him pleasure.

You will agree, I am sure, that, after being infatuated by M. Bâcle, who, take him together, was but a booby, I might be infatuated with M. Venture, who had education, talents, wit, and the knowledge of the world, and who might pass as a pleasing libertine. It was what happened to me, and what might have happened, I believe, to any other young man in my place; so much the more readily too, if he had a better knack of perceiving merit, and a better relish to be engaged by it: for Venture had merit beyond contradiction, and he had a very rare one at his age, that of not being forward in showing his acquirements. It is true, he boasted of many things he knew nothing of; but of those he knew, which were pretty numerous, he said nothing: he waited the occasion of showing them; he made use of them without forwardness, and this had the greatest effect. As he stopped at each thing without speaking of the rest, you could not tell when he would finish. Sportful, waggish, inexhaustible, ensnaring in his conversation, always smiling, never laughing, he said in a most elegant tone of voice the rudest things, and made them pass. Even the modestest women were astonished at what they suffered from him. It was in vain they knew they should be angry, they had not the power. He desired none but prostitutes; I do not believe he was made for fortune, but he was made for rendering infinitely agreeable the society of those who had it. It was unlikely, that, with so many agreeable talents, in a country where they are well understood and cherished, he would long remain within the sphere of a musician.

My inclination to M. Venture, more reasonable in its cause, was likewise less extravagant in its effects, though more active and more durable, than that I had towards M. Bâcle. I loved to see him, hear him; all he did seemed charming, all he said seemed oracles: but my infatuation did not extend so far as not to be able to be separated from him. I had in the neighbourhood a good preservative against this excess. Besides, finding his maxims very good for him, I saw they were not for me to make use of: I wanted another kind of pleasure, of which he had no idea, and of which I dared not speak to him, certain he would have ridiculed me. However, I wanted to ally this attachment to that which governed me. I spoke of him with transport to Mamma; Le Maître spoke to her of him with commendation. She consented to his introduction; but the interview did not succeed at all: he thought her formal: she saw him a libertine; and being alarmed at my making so bad an acquaintance, she not only forbade my bringing him there again, but so strongly pointed out to me the danger of this young man, I became a little more circumspect towards him, and, very happily for my morals and my brains, we were soon separated.

M. Le Maître had the tastes of his art: he loved wine. At table, however, he was sober; but at work in his closet he must drink. His maid knew it so well, that, as soon as he prepared his paper for composing, and had taken his violoncello, his pot and glass arrived an instant afterwards, and the pot was replenished from time to time. Without ever being absolutely drunk, he was almost always fuddled; and faith it was pity, for he was a person essentially good, and so merry, Mamma called him no other than *Little Cat*. Unfortunately, he was fond of his talent, worked much, and drank the same. This reached his health, and at last his humour; he was sometimes suspicious, and easily offended. Incapable of rudeness, incapable of disrespect to anyone, he never spoke an ill word, even to his singing-boys. But neither would he be treated disrespectfully; that was but just. The evil lay in his having little knowledge; he did not distinguish tone or character, and often took the huff at nothing.

The ancient chapter of Geneva, where formerly so many princes and bishops thought it an honour to sit, has lost, in its exile,[1] its ancient splendour, but has preserved its loftiness. To be admitted, you must be either a gentleman or a doctor of Sorbonne. If there is a pardonable pride after that derived from personal merit, it

---

[1] At Annecy, where they resided after the conversation of Geneva to Protestantism.

is that merit birth gives. Besides, all priests, who have laity in their pay, treat them, in general, haughtily enough. It was thus the canons often treated poor Le Maître. The chanter particularly, named M. l'Abbé de Vidonne, who in other respects was a very accomplished man, but too full of his noblesse, had not always that respect for him his talents merited; the other could not well put up with his disdain. In the Holy week of this year they had a sharper dispute than usual at a dinner of institution the Bishop invited the canons to, and where Le Maître was always asked. The chanter did him some injustice, and said something harsh, which the other could not digest. He that moment took a resolution of leaving them the following night, and nothing could make him desist from it, though Madame de Warens, whom he went to take leave of, did all in her power to appease him. He could not renounce the pleasure of being revenged on his tyrants, in leaving them distressed in the Easter holidays, a time when they were in the greatest want of him. But that which distressed him likewise, was his music he would take with him; this was not easy. It formed a chest pretty large and very heavy, not to be taken under one's arm.

Mamma did as I had done, and would yet do in her place. After many useless efforts to retain him, seeing him resolved to go at all events, she determined to help him as much as depended on her. I dare advance she owed it him. Le Maître had devoted himself, in a manner, to her service. Whether in what belonged to his art, or what depended on attention, he was entirely at her commands; and the heart, which went with it, gave his complaisance an additional value. She therefore did no more than return a friend, on an essential occasion, what he had done for her, in detail, during three or four years; but she had a soul, which, to fulfil such duties, had no occasion to be told it was for her. She sent for me, ordered me to follow M. Le Maître at least as far as Lyons, and to remain with him as long as he wanted me. She has told me since, that the desire of removing me from Venture had a great share in this business. She consulted Claude Anet, her faithful servant, as to the conveyance of the chest. His advice was, that instead of taking a pack-horse at Annecy, which would infallibly discover us, we must, at dark, carry the chest on our shoulders to a certain distance, and then hire an ass in some village, to carry it to Seyssel, when, being in the French territories, we had nothing more to fear. This counsel was followed: we departed at seven the same evening, and Mamma, on pretext of paying my expenses, swelled the petty purse of the poor *Little Cat* by an addition which was not useless. Claude Anet, the gardener, and I, carried the chest as we could to the nearest village, where an ass relieved us, and the same night we reached Seyssel.

I think I have observed somewhere, that there are instants in which I so little resemble myself, I might be taken for another man of a quite opposite character. You are going to see an example of this. M. Reydelet, vicar of Seyssel, was a canon of St. Peter's, of course M. Le Maître's acquaintance, and one of those he should hide himself most from. My advice was, on the contrary, to go and introduce ourselves there, ask him to lodge us on some pretext, as coming by consent of the chapter. Le Maître relished this notion, which rendered his vengeance mocking and pleasant. We therefore went boldly to M. Reydelet's, who received us well. Le Maître told him he was going to Belley, by desire of the Bishop, to direct his music in the Easter holidays; that he should return in a few days: and, in support of this lie, I stuffed in a hundred more, so natural, that M. Reydelet thought me a smart lad, and showed me kindness with a thousand caresses. We were well treated, well lodged; M. Reydelet did not know how to make enough of us; and we separated the best friends in the world, promising to stay longer on our return. We could hardly stay till we were alone to burst with laughing, and I declare it takes me again now on thinking of it; for you could not imagine a trick better supported or more happy. It had made us merry the whole journey, had not M. Le Maître, who incessantly drank, and reeled about, been attacked two or three times by a fit, to which he became very subject, very much resembling an epilepsy. This threw me into a disorder that affrighted me, and which I thought to extricate myself from as I could.

We went to Belley to pass the Easter holidays, as we had told M. Reydelet; and though we were not expected, we were received by the music-master, and welcomed by everyone, with the greatest pleasure. M. Le Maître was esteemed for his skill, and merited it. The music-master at Belley honoured him with his best compositions, and endeavoured to obtain the approbation of so good a judge; for, besides being a connoisseur, Le Maître was equitable, not at all jealous, no flattering parasite. He was so superior to all those provincial music-masters, and they so well knew it, they regarded him less as a brother artist than as their head.

Having passed, very agreeably, four or five days at Belley, we left it, and continued our journey, without any other accident than those just mentioned. Arrived at Lyons we were lodged at Notre Dame de Pitié; and while waiting for the chest, that, favoured by another falsity, we had embarked on the Rhone, by the care of our good protector, M. Reydelet, M. Le Maître went to see his acquaintances, among others Father Caton, a Cordelier, of whom we shall speak afterwards, and the Abbé Dortan, Count of Lyons. Both received him well, but betrayed him, as you will presently see; his good fortune ended at M. Reydelet's.

Two days after our arrival at Lyons, as we were passing up a little street, not far from our inn, Le Maître was taken with one of his fits; this was so violent, I was seized with terror. I cried out, called help, named his inn, and begged he might be carried there; then, whilst they assembled and crowded around a man fallen without sense and foaming in the middle of the street, the only friend on which he depended left him. I took the instant when no one thought of me, turned the corner of the street, and disappeared. Thanks to Heaven, I have finished this third painful declaration! Did many more remain, I should abandon the work I have begun.

Of all I have hitherto said, a few vestiges are to be found in the places I have lived; but that I mean to speak of in the following book is almost entirely unknown. They are the greatest extravagances of my life, and it was lucky they did not finish worse. But my head, raised to the tone of a foreign instrument, got out of its diapason; it came back of itself; I then quitted my follies, or at least I committed those which better agreed with my natural disposition. This period of my youth is that I have the most confused idea of. Nothing almost passed at this time which sufficiently engaged my heart to trace in a lively manner its remembrance; and it will be strange, if, in so many turnings and windings, in so many successive changes, I do not transpose sometimes time or place. I write absolutely from memory, without notes, without matter which might remind me of it. There are events of my life as present as when they happened; but there are gaps and voids I cannot fill up but by the assistance of recitals as confused as their remaining remembrance. I may, therefore, have erred, and may err again on trifles, until the time I have more certain marks to conduct me; but in that which is of real import to the subject, I am sure of being exact and faithful, as I shall always endeavour to be on everything: this may be depended on.

As soon as I had quitted M. Le Maître, my resolution was taken, and I set out on my return to Annecy. The cause and the mystery of our departure had given me great concern for the safety of our retreat; and this concern, wholly employing me, had caused a diversion for some days from that which called me back again: but the moment security had produced tranquillity, the governing sentiment took its place again. Nothing flattered me, nothing tempted me; I had no other desire than that of returning to Mamma. The tenderness and reality of my affection for her had rooted from my heart all imaginary projects, all the follies of

ambition. I saw no other happiness than that of living with her, nor did I take one step without feeling I was removing from this happiness. I therefore returned there as fast as possible. My return was so quick, and my mind so distracted, that, although I recollect with so much pleasure all my other journeys, I have not the least remembrance of this. I recollect nothing at all of it, except my departure from Lyons, and my arrival at Annecy. Judge if this last period could ever quit my memory: at my arrival, I found Madame de Warens was no more there; she was gone to Paris.

I never rightly knew the secret of this journey. She would have told me, I am very certain, had I pressed her; but never was man less curious of knowing the secrets of friends. My mind solely employed on the present, it fills up its whole extent, its whole space, and, except past pleasures, which are henceforth my sole enjoyments, there is not the least spare corner for that which exists no more. All I thought I perceived in the little she said to me of it was that, by the revolution caused at Turin in the abdication of the King of Sardinia, she dreaded being forgot, and wanted, favoured by the intrigues of M. d'Aubonne, to get the same support of the Court of France, which, she has often told me, she would have preferred; because the multiplicity of great interests prevents one's being so disagreeably watched. If it was so, it is surprising that, on her return, they did not receive her with more indifference, and that she always enjoyed her pension without interruption. Many people thought her charged with some secret commission, either from the Bishop, who at that time had some affairs at the Court of France, where he himself was obliged to go, or from some one still more powerful, who knew to prepare for her a happy return. It is certain, if that was so, the Ambassadress was not badly chosen, and that, still young and beautiful, she had every necessary talent for succeeding in a negotiation.

BOOK FOUR

I ARRIVE and do not find her there. Judge of my surprise and my affliction! It was then the regret of having shamefully abandoned M. Le Maître began to pinch. It was still sharper when I learnt the accident that had happened to him. His chest of music, which contained his whole fortune, this choice chest, saved with so much trouble, had been seized on coming into Lyons by the vigilance of the Count Dortan, to whom the Chapter had written to apprise him of this private theft. Le Maître claimed, in vain, his property, his livelihood, the labour of his whole life. The property of this chest was at least subject to dispute; there was none. The affair was decided in the very instant by the law of the strongest, and poor Le Maître thus lost the fruit of his talents, the labours of his youth, and the dependence of his old age.

Nothing was wanting to the shock I received to render it overwhelming. But I was of an age when great grief has little power, and soon forged myself consolation. I expected to hear very soon from Madame de Warens, though I did not know her direction,

and she was ignorant of my return; and as to my desertion, everything reckoned, I did not think it so culpable. I had been useful to
M. Le Maître in his retreat; it was the only service I could do.
Had I remained with him in France, I could not have cured his
disorder, I could not have saved his chest; I should only have
doubled his expenses, without being able to serve him in the least.
Thus it was I then saw the affair; I now see it otherwise. It is not
when a dirty action is just committed, it torments us; it is on the
recollection of it long afterwards; for its remembrance does not die.

The only means of hearing from Mamma was to wait; for how
was I to seek for her at Paris, and with what make the journey?
There was no place so certain as Annecy to know sooner or later
where she was. I therefore remained there. But I conducted myself badly enough. I did not go to see the Bishop, who had patronised me, and might still have patronised me. My protector was no
more with me, and I dreaded a reprimand on our evasion. I went
still less to the Seminary. M. Gros was gone. I saw none of my
friends: I should have gone with pleasure to see the Intendant's
lady, but dared not. I did worse than all that. I found out M. Venture again, of whom, though so much delighted with him, I had
not thought since my departure. I found him again shining and
welcomed in every part of Annecy, the ladies tearing him from
each other. This success quite turned my head. I saw nothing but
M. Venture, and he almost made me forget Madame de Warens.
The better to benefit by his lessons, I proposed lodging with him;
he consented. He lodged at a shoemaker's; a droll, pleasant fellow,
who in his gibberish called his wife nothing but slut; a name she
much deserved. He had wranglings with her, which Venture took
care to promote, in seeming to wish the contrary. He had the
strangest dry sayings, which in his country accent had the finest
effect; it was scenes which would make one burst with laughing.
Thus passed the mornings without thought. At two or three we
ate a bit of something. Venture went out into companies, where he
supped; and I went a-walking alone, meditating on his great merit,
admiring and coveting his rare talents, and cursing my ugly stars,
that had not called me to this happy life. Ah! how little I knew of
it! Mine had been a hundred times more charming, had I been
less a fool, and known better how to enjoy it.

Madame de Warens had taken with her Anet only; she had
left Merceret, her chamber-maid, of whom I have already spoken.
I found her still occupying her mistress's apartment. Mlle. Merceret was a little older than myself, not pretty, but agreeable

enough; a good-natured girl from Fribourg, without malice, and in whom I knew no other fault than muttering a little at her mistress. I went to see her pretty often; she was an old acquaintance, whose sight called to my mind one more dear, and made me love her. She had several acquaintances; among others, a Mlle. Giraud, of Geneva, who, for my sins, took it in her head to have an inclination for me. She continually begged Merceret to bring me to her house; I consented to go, because I loved Merceret well enough, and that we found other young people there I saw with pleasure. As for Mlle. Giraud, who did nothing but ogle me, nothing can be added to the aversion I had for her. When she came near my face with her hard black snout besmeared with Spanish snuff, I could hardly abstain from spitting at it. But I took patience, and, except that, I was well enough pleased with these girls; whether to court Mlle. Giraud, or myself, each strove to surpass the other in feasting me. I saw nothing but friendship in all this. I have since thought it my own fault I did not see more; but then I did not think so.

Besides, mantua-makers, chamber-maids, little tradeswomen, did not tempt me much. I wanted young ladies. Everyone to his fancy, that was always mine, nor do I think with Horace on that point. It is not, however, at all, the vanity of estate and rank which attracts me; it is a complexion better preserved, prettier hands, a more graceful attire, an air of delicacy and neatness over all their person, more taste in the manner of their dress and their expression, a gown finer and better made, a leg and foot more delicately formed, ribbands, lace, hair better disposed. I should always prefer less beauty, having more of all this. I myself find this preference very ridiculous; but my heart gives in to it in spite of me.

Well, this advantage offered too, and it depended on me only to lay hold of it. How I love to fall from time to time on the agreeable minutes of my youth! They were so sweet, so short, so rare, and I tasted them at so cheap a rate! Ah! their remembrance only brings back to my heart pure delights I greatly stand in need of to revive my spirits, and support the sorrows of my remaining years.

Aurora one morning appeared so beautiful, that, dressing myself precipitately, I hasted into the country to see the rising sun. I relished this pleasure with all its charms; it was the week after Midsummer-day. The earth in its gayest clothing was covered with herbs and flowers; the nightingales, whose warbling grew near its end, seemed to outvie each other in raising their lovely notes; the whole of the feathered race, bidding in chorus farewell to spring, welcomed the birth of a fine summer's day, of one of those heavenly days which are not seen at my age, and which the pensive soil I now inhabit[1] never saw.

I insensibly left the city, the heat increased, and I walked under the shade in a valley by the side of a brook. I hear behind me the steps of horses, and the voice of some girls, who seemed in trouble, but who did not laugh less heartily. I turn round, they call me by my name; I approach, and see two young people of my acquaintance, Mlle. de Graffenried and Mlle. Galley, who, not being the best of horsewomen, knew not how to get their horses across the brook. Mlle. de Graffenried was a young lady from Berne, very amiable, who, for some folly of her age, having been sent out of her country, had imitated Madame de Warens, where I had sometimes seen her; but not, like her, getting a pension, she was very happy in her acquaintance with Mlle. Galley, who, having contracted a friendship for her, engaged her mother to let her have her as a companion, until something could be done with her. Mlle. Galley, one year younger than she, was even prettier; she had something of I know not what more delicate and smart about her; she was likewise at the same time slender and well shaped, which is for a girl a happy thing. They were tenderly fond of each other, and the kind character of the one and the other must long entertain this harmony, if no lover came to disturb it. They told me they were going to Toune, an old castle belonging to Madame Galley; they begged my assistance in making their horses go on, not being able to do it themselves. I would have whipped their horses, but they feared my being kicked, and their being thrown. I had recourse to another expedient: I took the bridle of Mlle. Galley's horse, and pulling him after me, I crossed the brook with the water half up my legs; the other horse followed without difficulty. This done, I would have saluted the ladies, and gone off like a booby; they spoke softly to each other, and Mlle. de Graffenried, addressing herself to me, No, no, said she, you must not leave us in that manner. You have wetted yourself to serve us, and we ought, in conscience, to take care and dry you: please to come with us, we take you prisoner. My heart beat; I looked at Mlle. Galley. Yes, yes, said she, laughing at my bewildered look, prisoner of war: get up behind her; we will give

[1] Note in Paris MS.: "At Wootton, in Staffordshire."

an account of you. But, Miss, I have not the honour of being known to your mother; what will she say on seeing me there? Her mother, replied Mlle. de Graffenried, is not at Toune; we are alone: we return to-night, and you shall come back with us.

The effect of electricity is not quicker than that these words had on me. In leaping on Mlle. de Graffenried's horse, I trembled with joy, and when I had to embrace her to hold myself on, my heart beat so strong she perceived it: she told me hers beat likewise through fear of falling; this was, in my posture, an invitation to verify the affair: I never dared; during the whole ride my two arms served her as a girdle, extremely tight, but without changing, one moment, their position. Some women who read this would box my ears with pleasure, and would not be to blame.

The pleasure of the journey, and these girls' chatter, so much sharpened mine, that till the evening, and the whole time we were together, we were never silent a moment. They made everything so agreeable, my tongue said as much as my eyes, though not the same things. A few instants only, whilst I was alone with one or the other, the conversation was a little embarrassed; but the absent one soon returned, and did not give us time to explain this confusion.

Arrived at Toune, and I well dried, we breakfasted; after which they must proceed to the important business of getting the dinner ready. The two young ladies, while cooking, kissed, now and then, the farmer's children, and the poor scullion saw it, biting his lips. They had sent provisions from the town, which sufficed to make an exceeding good dinner, particularly in dainties; but, unfortunately, they had forgot the wine. This forgetfulness was not surprising in girls who drank little; but I was sorry, for I depended a little on its assistance to embolden me. They, likewise, were sorry for it, and perhaps for the same reason; but I do not think so. Their lively and charming mirth was innocence itself; besides, what could they have done with me between them? They sent for wine everywhere: none was to be had, so sober and poor are these peasants. As they remarked to me their uneasiness at it, I told them not to give themselves the least trouble about it; that they had no occasion for wine to make me drunk. This was the only gallantry I dared pronounce the whole day; however, I believe the rogues saw plainly this gallantry was a truth.

We dined in the farmer's kitchen; the two friends sat on benches which were on each side the table, and their visitor between them on a three-legged stool. What a dinner! What a remembrance full of charms! How, when we can, at so trifling an expense, taste pleasures so pure and so real, want to seek others! Never was dinner at the Mad-house of Paris to be compared to this meal; I do not mean for mirth only, for pleasing joy, but I mean for sensuality.

After dinner we thought of economy. Instead of taking the coffee that remained from breakfast, we kept it for the afternoon, with cream and cakes they had brought from town; and to keep our appetite sharp, we went to finish our dessert on cherries in the orchard. I got up the trees, from whence I threw them clusters, whose stones they returned through the branches. Once Mlle. Galley, holding her apron forward, and her head backward, stood so fair, and I aimed so well, I caused a bunch to drop in her bosom; at which she laughed. Said I to myself, Why are not my lips cherries? How readily would I throw them there likewise!

The day passed thus in romping with the greatest liberty, and always with the greatest decency. Not one equivocal word, not one free expression; we did not impose this decency on ourselves; it came of itself; we followed the manner our hearts taught us. In fine, my modesty, others will say my stupidity, was such, that the greatest liberty that escaped me was kissing, once, Mlle. Galley's hand. It is true, the circumstance made this trifling favour valuable. We were alone; I breathed with difficulty; her eyes were turned to the ground. My lips, instead of seeking words, resolved to fix on her hand, which she gently drew away, after it was kissed, with a look which was not an angry one. I know not what I should have said to her: her friend came in, and I thought her ugly at that instant.

In fine, they remembered that, if they stayed too late, the city gates would be shut. We had only time sufficient to get in by daylight, and hasted to set off, distributing ourselves as we came. Had I dared, I had transposed this order; for the look from Mlle. Galley had greatly inflamed me; but I could say nothing, and she could not propose it. On our march we said the day was to blame to end; but, far from complaining of its shortness, we saw we had found the secret of prolonging it by every amusement we were able to invent.

I left them near the place they had taken me up. With what regret did we separate! With what pleasure did we plan another interview! Twelve hours spent together were worth ages of familiarity. The sweet recollection of this day could never torture the hearts of these amiable girls; the tender harmony which reigned amongst us three, was equal to livelier pleasures, and could not have subsisted with them: our fondness for each other was without mystery or disgrace, and we wanted to retain this fondness for ever. Innocence of manners has its sensuality, which is at least of a price with the other, because it has no void, and acts continually. For my part, I know that the remembrance of so delightful a day touches and charms me more, comes back again more to my heart, than that of any pleasures I ever tasted. I did not well know what I wanted of these two charming girls, but each very much engaged me. I do not say that, had I been master in this business, my heart would have been divided; I was sensible of a preference. I had been happy in having Mlle. de Graffenried for a mistress; but if I had had my choice, I should have liked her better as a confidante. Be that as it may, it seemed, on quitting them, I could not live without the one and the other. Who would think I should never see them more, and that here ended our ephemeral amours?

Those who read this will not fail to laugh at my gallant adventures, on remarking that, after many preliminaries, the most advanced ended in a kiss of the hand. O readers, you may mistake! I have, perhaps, had more pleasure in my amours in ending at this kissed hand, than you will ever have in beginning at least there.

Venture, who went very late to bed the night before, came in a little after me. This once I did not see him with the same pleasure as usual; I took care not to tell him how I had passed the day. The young ladies spoke of him with little esteem, and seemed discontented at my being in so bad hands; this hurt him with me: besides, everything which diverted me from them must be disagreeable to me. However, he soon recalled me to him and myself by talking of my situation. It was too critical to last. Though I spent very little, my little savings were exhausted; I was without resources. No news of Mamma; I knew not what to do, and I felt a cruel heart-breaking at seeing Mlle. Galley's friend reduced to beggary.

Venture told me he had spoken of me to the Chief Justice;[1] that he would take me there to dinner on the morrow; that he was a man who could do me service through his friends; besides, a good acquaintance to make, a man of sense and letters, a very agreeable man in conversation, who had talents and favoured them; then mixing, as usual, the most trifling frivolousness with the most serious affairs, he showed me a pretty couplet from Paris,

---

[1] The *Juge-Mage*, a civil magistrate of first instance.

to the air of an opera of Mouret, acted at that time. This couplet had so much pleased M. Simon (the Chief Justice's name), he wanted to compose another in answer, to the same air: he told Venture to compose one likewise; he was so taken with his folly, as to make me compose a third, in order, says he, that they may see couplets arrive the next day, like the chairs of the *Roman comique.*

At night, not being able to sleep, I composed, as well as I could, my couplet. For the first verses I had made, they were passable, better even, or at least with more taste, than I should have made them in the evening; the subject running on a very feeling situation, to which my heart was already much disposed. In the morning I showed my couplet to Venture, who, thinking it pretty, put it into his pocket, without telling me whether he had composed his or not. We went to dinner at M. Simon's, who received us well. The conversation was agreeable; it could not fail where two men of sense were met, edified by reading. As for me, I acted my part; I listened and said nothing. Neither of them talked of couplets, I said nothing of them neither; and never, that I heard, was any mention made of mine.

M. Simon seemed satisfied with my appearance: it was nearly the whole he saw of me during this interview. He had seen me, several times, at Madame de Warens's, without taking much notice of me: so that from this dinner I must date his acquaintance, which was of no service to me as to the object that caused it, but from which I, afterwards, drew other advantages, which recall his memory with pleasure.

I should be wrong in not speaking of his person which from his quality of magistrate, and the learning on which he piqued himself, could not be guessed if I said nothing of it. The Chief Justice Simon was not, assuredly, two[1] feet high: his legs straight, small, and even pretty long, would have made him taller, had they been perpendicular; but they stood stretched like a pair of compasses widely opened. His body was not only short, but thin, and in every sense of a most inconceivable smallness. He must appear like a grasshopper when naked. His head, of a natural size, with a face well formed, a noble air, pretty good eyes, seemed a false one planted on a stump. He might have spared the expense of dress; for his large periwig alone covered him from top to toe.

He had two voices quite different, which incessantly mixed in

---

[1] Paris MS.: "three feet."

his conversation, with a contrast at first extremely pleasing, but soon became as disagreeable. One grave and sonorous; this was, if I may say so, the voice of his head; the other, clear, sharp and piercing, was the voice of his body. Whenever he minced his words, took care to speak with composure, and governed his breath, he could always speak with his coarse voice; but, the least heated, and if a higher accent caught him, this accent became like the whistling of a key, and he had the greatest trouble in the world to come to his bass again.

J.-J. WITH M. SIMON

With the figure I have just drawn, and which I have not exaggerated, M. Simon was a courtier, always ready with his amorous discourses, and carried even to coquetry his attention to his person.

As he sought his advantages, he the more readily gave morning audiences in bed; for when a good head was perceived on the pillow, no one imagined there was nothing more. This sometimes gave rise to scenes which I am certain all Annecy still remembers.

One morning waiting in his bed, or rather on his bed, the arrival of some people who had suits at law, in a beautiful night-cap, very fine and white, garnished with two large knots of rose-coloured ribband, a countryman comes in, taps at the door. The maid was gone out. The Chief Justice, hearing it increase, cries, Come in: and this, spoken a little too quick, shot from his shrill voice. The man goes in, and examines from whence came the woman's voice, and perceiving in the bed a woman's cap and a top-knot, he was going out again, asking the lady a thousand pardons. M. Simon grows angry, and cries so much the shriller. The countryman, confirmed in his idea, and thinking himself insulted, returns it, telling him, she is nothing but a prostitute, and that the Chief Justice does not set good examples in his house. The Justice, in fury, and having no other arms than his chamber-pot, was going to throw it at the poor man's head, when his housekeeper came in.

This little dwarf, so disgraced by nature in his body, was amply rewarded by a well-endowed mind: it was naturally agreeable, and he had taken care to adorn it. Though he was, as was said, a very great lawyer, he was not fond of his business. He had taken a turn to polite literature, and had succeeded. He had particularly laid hold of that superficial brilliancy, that airiness, which spreads delights in society, even with women. He had got by heart all the little strokes of the *Ana*, and such like: he had the art of making the most of them, in telling to advantage, with mystery, and as the anecdote of the evening, that which happened sixty years ago. He knew music, and sung agreeably with his man's voice: in fine, he had many pretty talents for a magistrate. By dint of cajoling the ladies of Annecy, he was in favour with them; they had him at their tail like a little monkey. He pretended even to fortune, and that amused them. A Madame d'Epagny said, that the greatest favour for him, was to kiss a woman on her knees.

As he knew good authors, and talked much of them, his conversation was not only amusing but instructive. In length of time, when I had taken a turn to study, I cultivated his acquaintance, and found it very useful. I sometimes went from Chambéry to see him, where I was at that time. He commended, animated my emulation, and gave me on my studies good advice, which I have often benefited by. Unfortunately, this weakly body contained

a tender soul. A few years afterwards he had I do not know what
trouble, which grieved him, and of which he died. It was a loss; he
was certainly a good-natured little man, whom you began with
by laughing at and ended by esteeming. Though his life had little
to do with mine, as he had given me useful lessons, I thought
I might from gratitude bestow a little corner in remembrance
of him.

The moment I was at liberty I ran to the street where lived
Mlle. Galley, hoping to see someone go in or out, or opening a
window. Nothing, not even a cat, stirred; and all the time I was
there the house remained as close as if uninhabited. The street
was little, and no one stirring in it. A man was remarked there:
now and then someone passed, or came in or out of the neighbourhood. I was much troubled with my person; it seemed to me they
guessed my business there, and this idea tortured me: for I always
preferred to my pleasures the honour and repose of those who
were dear to me.

In fine, tired of acting the Spanish lover, and having no guitar,
I resolved to go home, and write to Mlle. de Graffenried. I had
preferred writing to her acquaintance; but I dared not, and it
was more becoming to write to her to whom I was indebted for the
other's acquaintance, and with whom I was more familiar. My
letter finished, I carried to to Mlle. Giraud's, as was agreed between the young ladies and me at parting. They themselves gave
me this expedient. Mlle. Giraud was a quilter, who working sometimes at Madame Galley's, could easily get in there. The messenger did not, however, appear to me well chosen; but I was fearful,
if I started the least difficulty on this, they would propose no other.
Besides, I dared not hint that she would labour in her own behalf.
I felt myself mortified at her imagining herself, for me, of the
same sex as those ladies. In fine, I chose that repository rather
than none, and stuck to it at all hazards.

At the first word the Giraud guessed me: it was not very difficult. If a letter to be carried to a young lady did not speak for itself,
my sottish and confused looks had alone discovered me. You may
think this errand was not very pleasing to her; she, nevertheless,
undertook it, and executed it faithfully. The next morning I ran
to her house and found my answer. How did I hasten to get out to
read and kiss it at pleasure! That has no occasion to be told; but
the part Mlle. Giraud acted has, in whom I found more delicacy
and moderation than I expected. Having sense enough to perceive,
that, with her thirty-seven, the eyes of a leveret, a besmeared nose,

shrill voice, and black skin, she had little chance against two young graceful girls in all the splendour of beauty, she would neither betray nor serve them, and chose, rather, to lose me than procure me for them.

Merceret, receiving no news of her mistress, had some time intended returning to Fribourg; she entirely determined on it. She did more; she hinted to her it would not be amiss that someone conducted her to her father's, and proposed me. Little Merceret, who did not dislike me, thought this idea might be easily executed. They spoke to me of it the same day as an affair settled; and as I found nothing displeasing in this manner of disposing of myself, I consented, regarding this journey as an affair of eight days at most. Giraud, who did not think with me, settled all. I was obliged to own the state of my purse. They provided for it, Merceret undertook to defray my expenses; and to gain on one side what they lost on the other, at my instance it was determined to send her little luggage forward, and that we should go slowly on foot. This was done.

I am sorry to make so many girls in love with me; but as there is no great subject of vanity in the advantage I took of these amours, I think I may tell the truth without scruple. Merceret, younger and less artful than Giraud, never used so strong enticement: but she imitated my voice, my accent, repeated my words, had for me the attention I should have had for her, and always took great care, as she was very fearful, that we lay in the same chamber; a matter which seldom rests there, between a young fellow of twenty and a girl of twenty-five.

It rested there, however, this time. My simplicity was such, that, though Merceret was not disagreeable, there never came in my head during the whole journey, I do not say the least temptation of gallantry, but even the least idea that had any relation to it; and if this idea had struck me, I was too stupid to turn it to advantage. I did not imagine how a girl and a young fellow arrived at lying together; I thought it required ages to prepare this wondrous affair. If poor Merceret in defraying my expenses expected some equivalent, she was bit; for we arrived at Fribourg exactly as we set out from Annecy.

In passing through Geneva, I went to see no one; but I almost fainted on the bridges. I never saw the walls of this happy town, never went into it, without feeling a kind of sinking of the heart, which proceeded from tenderness to excess. At the same time the noble image of liberty elevated the mind, those of equality, of union, of mildness of manners, touched me even to tears, and inspired a lively sorrow at having lost all these blessings. What an error, but still how natural! I thought I saw all this in my native country, because I felt it in my heart.

We must pass through Nyon. What, without seeing my good father! If I had had the courage to do this, I should have died with grief. I left Merceret at the inn, and went to see him at every hazard. Ah! was I not to blame to dread him? His heart, on seeing me, opened to those paternal sentiments with which it was filled. What tears were shed in our embraces! He thought, at first, I was returned to him. I told him my story and my resolution. He feebly opposed it. He showed me the dangers to which I exposed myself, and told me the least follies were best. As to the rest, he was not the least tempted to retain me by force, and in that I think he was right; but it is certain he did not, to recall me, do all he might have done, whether he judged from the steps I had taken I should not have returned, whether he was puzzled to know, at my age, what to do with me. I have since learnt he had an opinion of my travelling companion, very unjust and very far from truth, but, however, natural enough. My mother-in-law, a good woman, a little sweetening, pretended to oblige me to sup there. I did not stay; but I told them I intended to stay longer with them on my return, and left them, as a deposit, my little bundle I had sent by the boat, and which encumbered me. The next morning I set off early, very happy to have seen my father, and to have dared to do my duty.

We happily arrived at Fribourg. Towards the end of the journey, the officiousness of Mlle. Merceret decreased a little. After our arrival, she showed me nothing but coolness, and her father, who did not swim in opulence, did not give me a very good reception; I went to lodge at a public-house. I returned to see them the next day; they offered me a dinner, I accepted it. We separated with dry eyes; I returned at night to my lodging-house, and left the place two days after my arrival, without well knowing which way I intended to go.

Here is another circumstance of my life, where Providence offered me precisely what I wanted to see happy days. Merceret was a very good girl, not brilliant or handsome, but she was not ugly; not passionate; a reasonable girl, except a few trifling humours, which went off with a cry, and never had any stormy effects. She had a real inclination to me; I might have married her without trouble, and followed the trade of her father. My taste

for music would have made me love it. I should have settled at
Fribourg, a small city, not pretty, but inhabited by very good
people. I should have, without doubt, missed a deal of pleasure,
but I should have lived in peace to my last hour; and I ought to
know, better than anyone, I should not have hesitated at this
bargain.

I returned, not to Nyon, but to Lausanne. I wanted to have a
thorough view of the beautiful lake, which is seen there in its
utmost extent. The greatest part of my secret determining motives
have not been solider. Distant views are seldom powerful enough
to make me act. The uncertainty of future times has always made
me regard projects of long execution as the lures of deceit. I give
in to hope like another, provided it costs me nothing to entertain
it; but if it requires a long and painful attendance, I have done
with it. The least trifling pleasure within my reach tempts me
more than the joys of Paradise. I except, however, the pleasures
which are followed by pain: those do not tempt me, because I love
only pure enjoyments, and we never have them so when we know
we prepare for repentance.

It was necessary I should arrive somewhere, and the nearest
place was the best; for, having lost my road, I found I was in the
evening at Moudon, where I spent the little I had left, except ten
kreutzers,[1] which went the next day at dinner: and coming in the
evening to a little village near Lausanne, I went into a public-
house without a sou to pay my lodging, and without knowing
what would become of me. I was very hungry; I put on a good
face, and asked for supper as if I had wherewithal to pay for it.
I went to bed without thinking of anything; I slept soundly; and
having breakfasted in the morning, and reckoned with the landlord, I wanted, for seven batz,[2] which my expenses amounted to,
to leave my waistcoat in pledge. This honest man refused it: he
told me that, thanks to God, he had never stripped anyone; that
he would not begin for seven batz; that I might keep my waistcoat, and pay him when I could. I was touched with his goodness;
but less than I ought to have been, and have been since on its
remembrance. It was not long before I sent him his money, with
thanks, by a safe hand; but fifteen years afterwards, returning
from Italy by way of Lausanne, I was extremely sorry to have forgot the name of the house and the landlord. I should have gone to
see him: it would have given me great pleasure to have reminded

[1] The kreutzer was a German copper coin, current in Switzerland, worth
four centimes.
[2] The batz, a local coin of which thirty made an écu or crown.

him of his charity, and to prove to him it was not badly placed. Services, more important, without doubt, but rendered with more ostentation, did not appear to me so worthy acknowledgement, as the humanity, simple and without parade, of this honest man.

In drawing near Lausanne, I mused on the distress I was in, and the means of extricating myself without acquainting my mother-in-law of my misery; and I compared myself in this walking pilgrimage to my friend Venture on his arrival at Annecy. I was so heated with this idea, that, without thinking I had neither his gentility, nor his talents, I took it in my head to act at Lausanne the little Venture, to teach music I knew nothing of, and to call myself of Paris, where I had never been. In consequence of this noble project, as there was no music-school where I could act the vicar, and that besides I took care not to run myself amongst those of the art, I began to inform myself of some public-house where one could be well served at a cheap rate. I was directed to one Perrotet, who took boarders. This Perrotet happened to be one of the best men in the world, and received me well. I told him over all my pretty lies as I had prepared them. He promised to speak of me, and endeavour to procure me some pupils: he told me he should not ask me for money until I had earned it. His board was five white crowns; this was little for the things, but a great deal for me. He advised me to begin by the half-board, which consisted at dinner of good soup and no more, but a plentiful supper. I agreed. This poor Perrotet advanced me all these things with all the good-nature possible, and spared no pains to serve me.

How is it that, having met with so many good people in my youth, I find so few in an advanced age? Is their race extinct? No; but the rank in which I am obliged to seek them now, is not that I found them in then. Amongst the people, where the great passions declare themselves but by intervals, the feelings of nature make themselves oftener heard: in more elevated situations they are absolutely stifled, and, under the masks of sentiment, it is only interest or vanity which speaks.

I wrote from Lausanne to my father, who sent my bundle, and wrote me excellent instruction I ought to have made better use of. I have already noted instants of inconceivable delirium when I was no longer myself. Here is another the most remarkable. To comprehend to what a point my brain was turned at that time, and to what degree I was, as one may say, *venturized*, it will be only necessary to show how many extravagances I gave in to at one and the same time. I am a singing-master, without knowing how to read a tune; for, had I benefited of the six months I passed

with Le Maître, they could not have sufficed: besides this, I was
taught by a master, which was enough to learn indifferently. A
Parisian of Geneva, and a Catholic in a Protestant country, I
thought I might change my name as well as my religion and my

LAUSANNE

country. I always followed my grand model as near as I could.
He called himself Venture de Villeneuve, and I turned by ana-
gram the name of Rousseau into that of Vaussore, and called myself Vaussore de Villeneuve. Venture could compose, though he
had said nothing of it; and I, who knew nothing of it, boasted to
all the world I understood it very well; and, without being able
to prick the commonest song, gave out I was a composer. This is
not all: having been presented to M. de Treytorens, professor in
law, who was fond of music, and had concerts at his house, I must
give him a sample of my talents, and set about composing a piece
for his concert, with as much effrontery as if I had understood it.
I had the constancy to labour, a fortnight, at this charming work,
to write it fair, to draw out the parts, and distribute them with
as much assurance as if it had been a masterpiece of harmony.
In fine, that which will be scarcely believed, but which is certain,
worthily to crown this sublime production, I added at the end a
pretty minuet, sung in the street, and which perhaps everyone
still recollects, to these words, formerly so well known:

> *Quel caprice!*
> *Quelle injustice!*
> *Quoi, ta Clarisse*
> *Trahiroit tes feux! &c.*

Venture had taught me this air, with the bass, to other infamous words, by which aid I had retained it. I therefore added, at the end of my composition, this minuet and the bass, suppressing the words, and gave it out as my own, as resolutely as if I had talked to the inhabitants of the moon.

They assemble to execute my piece; I explain to each one the motion, manner of execution, and references to parts: I had enough to do. They accord for five or six minutes, which to me were five or six ages. In fine, everything ready, I strike, with a fine roll of paper, my magisterial desk five or six strokes of *Get ready*. There is a silence. I gravely begin to beat time, they begin . . . no, never since French opera existed, in your life did you hear such a horrid jumble. Whatever they had thought of my pretended talents, the effect was worse than they seemed to expect. The musicians were stifled with laughter; the auditors stared, and would have been glad to have stopped their ears; but there was no possibility. My butchers of performers, who were determined to have fun enough, continued scraping so as to pierce the tympanum of him who was born deaf. I had constancy enough to continue at the same rate, sweating, it is true, large drops; but, kept to it by shame, not daring to run off, I remained nailed there. For my comfort, I heard around me the company whispering in each other's ear, or rather in mine, This is insupportable! another says, What outrageous music! another, What a devilish caterwauling! Poor Jean-Jacques, in this cruel moment you had no great hopes that there might come a day, when, before the King of France and his whole Court, your sounds would excite whispers of surprise and applause, and that, in every box around you, the most amiable women would say to themselves in a low voice, What delightful sounds! What enchanting music! Every note reaches the heart.

But it was the minuet brought them back to good humour. They had scarcely played a measure or two, when I heard burstings of laughter from every part of the room. Everyone complimented me on my taste for music: they assured me this minuet would make me talked of, and that I merited praise from every quarter of the globe. It is unnecessary to paint my feelings, or to own I well deserved them.

The next day one of my orchestra, named Lutold, came to see me; he had good nature enough not to compliment me on my success. The deep sense of my impertinence, the shame, grief, despair of the situation to which I was reduced, the impossibility of keeping my troubled heart shut, caused me to open it to him; I gave a loose to tears, and, instead of contenting myself with owning my ignorance, I told him everything, begging him to keep the secret, which he promised, and which he kept as everyone may guess. The same evening all Lausanne knew who I was, but, what was most remarkable, nobody pretended to know it, not even the good-natured Perrotet, who did not on that account discontinue lodging and boarding me.

I lived, but very sorrowfully. The effects of such a beginning did not render Lausanne a very agreeable residence to me. Pupils did not come in crowds; not a single female one, and no one of the city. I had only two or three big Germans, as stupid as I was ignorant, who tired me to death, and who, under my hands, did not become great note-wielders. I was sent for to one house only, where a little serpent of a girl took pleasure in showing me a deal of music of which I could not read a single note, and which she was malicious enough to sing afterwards to her master, to show him how it should be executed. I was so little capable of reading an air on first sight, that, in the brilliant concert I have spoken of, it was not in my power to follow the execution a moment, to know whether what I had under my eye, and which I myself had composed, was well played.

Amidst so many mortifications, I had the sweet consolation of receiving, from time to time, letters from my two charming acquaintances. I have always found a consoling virtue in the fair, and nothing so much softens my afflictions in disgrace, as to see they affect an amiable person. This correspondence ceased, however, soon afterwards, and was never renewed; but that was my fault. In changing my abode, I neglected sending my direction; and forced by necessity to think continually of myself, I very soon forgot them.

It is long since I mentioned my poor Mamma; but if it is thought I had forgot her, it is a mistake. I never ceased thinking of her, and wishing to find her again, not to supply the wants of a subsistence, but those of my heart. My affection for her, however lively, however tender, did not prevent me from loving others; but not in the same manner. All equally owed my passion to their charms, but it solely depended on those of others, and had not survived them; but Mamma might grow old and ugly without my loving her less tenderly. My heart had entirely transmitted to her person the homage it immediately paid her beauty, and whatever change she suffered, provided it was still herself, my feelings could never change. I know I owed her gratitude; but I really did not think of it. Whatever she had done, or had not done for me, it would have been the same. I did not love her from duty, interest, or convenience; I loved her because I was born to love her. When I became amorous of another, it caused a diversion I own, and I thought less of her: but I thought of her with the same pleasure; and never, amorous or not, did I think of her without feeling that there was no true happiness for me in this life, so long as I should be separated from her.

Though I had so long been without news of her, I never imagined I had quite lost her, or that she could have forgot me. I said to myself, she will know, sooner or later, that I am wandering about, and will let me know she is alive; I shall find her again, I am sure of it. In the meanwhile it was a comfort to me to be in her country, to pass down those streets she had passed, before those houses she had lived in, and the whole through mere conjecture; for one of my stupid humours was that of not daring to inform myself of her, or to pronounce her name without the most absolute necessity. It seemed to me that, in naming her, I said all she inspired me with, that my lips revealed the secret of my heart, and that I in some sort exposed her. I believe there was in all this a mixture of fear lest someone should speak ill of her. Much had been said of her proceedings, and something of her conduct. Fearing they might not say of her what I could wish to hear, I rather chose they should not talk about her.

As my pupils did not greatly employ me, and her city was but four leagues from Lausanne, I took a turn there of three or four days; during this time, the most agreeable perturbation never left me. The aspect of the lake of Geneva, and its admirable borders, had always, in my eyes, a peculiar attraction I cannot explain, which proceeds, not only from the beauty of the prospect, but from I know not what more interesting which affects and melts me. Every time I approach the country of Vaud, I feel an impression composed of the remembrance of Madame de Warens who was born there, my father who lived there, Mlle. de Vulson who had there the first fruits of my heart, of several pleasure journeys I made there in my childhood, and, it would seem, of some other more secret and more powerful cause than all these. When the ardent desire of the mild and happy life which eludes me, and for which I was born, returns to fire my imagination, it is always in the country of Vaud, near the lake, in delightful fields, it fixes. I must absolutely have an orchard on the borders of this lake and no other; I must have a friend to be depended on, an amiable woman, a cow, and a little boat. I shall never enjoy perfect happiness on earth till I have these. I laugh at the simplicity with which I have several times gone into this country solely to find this imaginary blessing. I was always surprised to find the inhabitants, particularly the women, of a quite different character to those I sought. How ill-matched that appeared to me! The country and the people who cover it never seemed to me made for each other.

CASTLE OF CHILLON

In this journey to Vevey, in walking along these beautiful banks, I abandoned myself to the gentlest melancholy. My heart launched with eagerness into a thousand innocent pleasures; I was moved, I sighed, and shed tears like a child. How many times, stopping to cry with more ease, seated on a large stone, have I not been amused, by seeing my tears drop into the stream?

At Vevey I lodged at the *Key*, and, in the two days I stayed there without visiting anyone, I contracted a fondness for this city that has followed me in all my travels, and which in fine caused me to fix there the hero of my romance.[1] I should readily say to those who have taste and feelings, Go to Vevey, visit the country, examine its position, take a turn on the lake, and say whether Nature did not make this beautiful country for a Julie, for a Claire,

---

[1] *Julie.*

and for a Saint-Preux; but do not seek them there. I return to my history.

As I was a Catholic, and owned it, I followed without mystery or scruple the doctrine I had embraced. On Sundays, in fine weather, I went to mass at Assens, two leagues from Lausanne. I generally took this trip with other Catholics, particularly a Parisian embroiderer, whose name I have forgot. He was not such a Parisian as myself, but a real Parisian of Paris, one of God Almighty's arch-Parisians, as good-natured as a Champenois. He was so fond of his country he would not doubt I was of it, for fear of losing an opportunity of talking of it. M. de Crouzas, lieutenant of the bailiwick, had a gardener, likewise from Paris; but less complaisant, and who thought the glory of his country questioned in daring to say you were of it, when you had not that honour. He questioned me as a man sure of catching me, and then smiled maliciously. He asked me, once, what there was remarkable at the New Market. I was lost, as you may imagine. Having lived twenty years at Paris, I ought at present to know that city. If, however, I was now asked a like question, I should be no less troubled to answer, and by this difficulty it might be equally concluded I had never been at Paris. So much, even though you meet truth, is one subject to build on false principles!

I cannot exactly say how long I stayed at Lausanne. I did not take from this city anything worthy recollection. I only know that, not finding a livelihood, I went from thence to Neufchâtel, and passed the winter. I succeeded better in this last city; I had some pupils, and gained enough to pay off my good friend Perrotet, who had faithfully sent my bundle, though I was considerably in his debt.

I insensibly learnt music in teaching it. I lived happy enough; a reasonable man had been satisfied: but my uneasy mind wanted something more. On Sundays and holidays, when at liberty, I ran over the fields and woods of the environs, continually wandering, musing, sighing, and, once out of the city, never came in till evening. One day, being at Boudry, I went to a public-house to dine: I saw there a man with a long beard, a violet-coloured coat in the Greek taste, a furred cap, a noble air and garb, and who had often much difficulty to make himself understood, speaking but a gibberish almost unintelligible, that resembled, however, Italian more than any other language. I understood nearly all he said, and I was the only one; he could express himself only by signs to the landlord and the country-people. I spoke a few words of Italian to him which he perfectly understood; he got up and embraced me with transport. The connexion was soon made, and from that instant I served him as interpreter. He had a good dinner; mine was worse than indifferent: he invited me to his table; I made little ceremony. By drinking and talking we began to be familiar, and at the end of the repast we were inseparable. He told me he was a Greek prelate, and archimandrite of Jerusalem; that he was commanded to make a gathering in Europe for repairing the Holy Sepulchre. He showed me beautiful patents from the Czarina and the Emperor; he had some from many other Sovereigns. He was well enough satisfied with what he had already got together, but he had met incredible difficulties in Germany, not understanding a word of German, Latin, or French, and reduced to his Greek, Turkish, and lingua franca, as his whole resource, which procured him little in the country he was just beginning on. He proposed my accompanying him as secretary and interpreter. Though I had a smart violet coat, lately purchased, which squared pretty well with my new employment, I had so shabby a look he thought me easily gained; he was not mistaken. Our agreement was soon made; I asked nothing, he promised much. Without security, without bond, without acquaintance, I submit to be conducted by him, and the very next morning here I go for Jerusalem.

We began our tour by the canton of Fribourg, where he did little. The episcopal dignity could not admit of acting the beggar, and gather of individuals; but we presented his commission to the Senate, who gave him a trifling sum. From thence we went to Berne. Here more ceremony was needed, and the examination of his titles was not the business of a single day. We lodged at the *Falcon*, at that time a good inn, where good company were found. There were many people at table, and it was well served. I had long fared very poorly; I had occasion enough to renew myself: I had the opportunity, and made good use of it. My Lord archimandrite himself was very good company, fond enough of a good table, gay, conversed well with those who understood him, not wanting in certain sciences, and adapting his Greek erudition agreeably enough. One day, cracking nuts at the dessert, he cut his finger very deep; and as the blood gushed out in abundance, he held up his finger to the company, and says with a laugh: *Mirate, Signori; questo è sangue Pelasgo.*

At Berne my functions were not useless to him, and I did much better than I expected. I was much more courageous, and spoke

better than I should have done for myself. Things did not pass so
simply as at Fribourg. Long and frequent conferences with the
first men of the State, and the examination of his titles, were not
the work of a day. At last, everything being settled, he was admitted to an audience of the Senate. I went with him as his interpreter, and was commanded to speak. I did not expect anything
less; it did not come into my head that, after having long conferred with the members separately, the assembly must be addressed as if nothing had been said. Judge of my embarrassment!
For so bashful a man to speak, not only in public, but before the
Senate of Berne, and speak extempore, without having had a
single minute to prepare myself; this was enough to annihilate
me. I was not even intimidated. I represented succinctly and
clearly the archimandrite's commission. I praised the piety of
those princes who had contributed to the gathering he was come
to make. Sharpening with emulation that of their Excellencies,
I said, no less could be expected from their accustomed munificence; and then endeavouring to prove this charitable work to be
equally so for all Christians without distinction of sect, I ended
by promising the blessings of Heaven to those who should contribute to it. I shall not say my speech had any effect; but it is
certain it was relished, and that after the audience the archimandrite received an honourable present, and more, on the parts of
his secretary, compliments which I had the agreeable office of
interpreting, but which I dared not literally render. This is the
only time of my life I spoke in public, and before a sovereign; and,
perhaps, the only time likewise I spoke boldly and well. What
difference in the dispositions of the same man! It is three years
since I went to see at Yverdun my old friend M. Roguin, and received a deputation of thanks for some books I had made a present
of to the library of this city. The Swiss are much for harangues;
these gentlemen harangued me. I thought myself obliged to
answer, but I was so embarrassed in my answer, and my head
was so confused, I stopped short, and got myself laughed at.
Though naturally timid, I have been sometimes confident in my
youth; never in my advanced age. The more I see of the world,
the less I can form myself to its manner.

On leaving Berne, we went to Soleure; for the design of the
archimandrite was to take the road of Germany, and return by
Hungary or Poland: this was an immense tour; but as in journey-
ing his purse filled rather than emptied, he little dreaded a winding course. For my part, who was almost as much pleased on

horseback as on foot, I desired no better than thus to travel my whole lifetime; but it was written I should not go so far.

The first thing we did on our arrival at Soleure, was to pay our respects to the Ambassador of France. Unfortunately for our Bishop, the Ambassador was the Marquis of Bonac, who had been Ambassador at the Porte, and who must be well acquainted with everything regarding the Holy Sepulchre. The archimandrite had an audience of a quarter of an hour where I was not admitted, as the Ambassador understood the lingua franca, and spoke Italian as least as well as I. On my Greek's departure I was following him; I was stopped: it was my turn. Having passed as a Parisian, I was, as such, under the jurisdiction of his Excellency. He asked me who I was, exhorting me to tell the truth; I promised it, on asking a private audience, which was granted. The Ambassador took me to his closet, and shut the door, and there, throwing myself at his feet, I kept my word. I had not said less, though I had promised nothing; for a continual inclination to disclose my heart brings every instant my thoughts on my lips, and having opened myself without reserve to the musician Lutold, I had no occasion for any mystery to the Marquis of Bonac. He was so satisfied with my story, and the effusion of heart which he saw accompanied it, he took me by the hand, led me to the Ambassadress, and introduced me to her, in giving an abridgement of my recital. Madame

de Bonac received me with kindness, and said they must not let me go with this Greek monk. It was determined I should remain at the hotel until they saw what might be done with me. I wanted to go take my leave of my poor archimandrite, for whom I had conceived a friendship: it was not permitted. They sent him notice of my arrest, and in a quarter of an hour I saw my little bundle brought in. M. de la Martinière, secretary to the embassy, had in some sort the care of me. In conducting me to the room intended for me, he said to me, This room was occupied under the Count du Luc, by a celebrated man of the same name as yourself.[1] It depends on you to replace him in every manner, that it may be one day said, Rousseau the First, Rousseau the Second. This conformity, which at that time I had little hopes of, had less flattered my wishes, had I been able to foresee how dear I should one day pay for it.

M. de la Martinière's words excited my curiosity. I read the works of him whose room I occupied, and, on the compliment paid me, imagining I had a taste for poesy, I made for my trial a cantata in praise of Madame de Bonac. This turn flagged. I have now and then made indifferent verse; it is a good exercise enough to break one's self into elegant inversions, and teach one to write better prose; but I never found charms sufficient in French poetry to give myself entirely to it.

M. de la Martinière wanted to see my style, and asked me the same particulars in writing I had told the Ambassador. I wrote him a long letter, which I learn was preserved by M. de Marianne, who was a long while with the Marquis de Bonac, and who has since succeeded M. de la Martinière in M. de Courteilles' embassy. I have begged M. de Malesherbes to endeavour to procure me a copy of this letter. If I get it by him or others, it will be found in the collection which I intend shall accompany my Confessions.

The experience I began to have, moderated by degrees my romantic projects; and as a proof, not only I did not fall in love with Madame de Bonac, but immediately saw I should do but little in her husband's family. M. de la Martinière in place, and M. de Marianne in survivance, as one may say, left me no farther hopes for my fortune than the place of under-secretary, which little tempted me. This was the cause, that, when I was consulted on what I should like, I showed a great inclination to go to Paris. The Ambassador relished this idea, which tended, at least, to his

---

[1] Jean-Baptiste Rousseau (1670-1741), French lyric and dramatic poet.

getting rid of me. M. de Merveilleux, secretary and interpreter to the embassy, said his friend M. Godard, a Swiss colonel in the service of France, wanted someone to be with his nephew, who entered very young into the service, and thought I might suit him. On this notion, slightly enough taken, my departure was resolved; and I, who saw a journey in the case, and Paris at the end, was as joyful as joy could make me. They gave me some letters, a hundred livres for my journey, accompanied by very good advice, and I set off.

I was on this journey fifteen days, which I may reckon among the happy ones of my life. I had youth, health, money enough, great hopes, travelled alone. You will be surprised to see me reckon this an advantage, if you were not already familiar with my humour. My pleasing chimeras kept me company, and never did the heat of my imagination give birth to any so magnificent. If I was offered an empty place in a carriage, or anyone accosted me on the road, my temper grew sour at seeing my fortune crossed, whose edifice I built up as I walked. This time my notions were martial: I was going to engage to a military man, and become a military man myself; for it was settled I should begin by entering a cadet. I thought I already saw myself in an officer's dress, with a fine white feather in my hat. My heart swelled at this noble idea. I had a little smattering of geometry and fortification; I had an uncle an engineer; I was, in some sort, of the bullet family. My near sight offered a few obstacles, which never troubled me; and I supposed that presence of mind and intrepidity would supply this failing. I had read that Marshal Schomberg was near-sighted; why might not Marshal Rousseau be so? I so heated myself by these follies, I saw nothing but armies, ramparts, gabions, batteries, and myself amidst fire and smoke, coolly giving orders, my spying-glass in my hand. However, when I passed through agreeable fields, and saw groves and rivulets, the striking scene drew sighs of sorrow; I felt, amidst all this glory, my heart was not inclined to so much havoc; and soon, not knowing how, I returned to my beloved sheep-folds, for ever renouncing the labours of Mars.

How much did the first sight of Paris belie the idea I had of it! The external decoration I had seen at Turin, the beauty of the streets, the symmetry and squareness of the houses, induced me to seek at Paris still more. I had figured to myself a city as beautiful as large, of the most imposing aspect, where nothing was seen but superb streets and marble or golden palaces. Coming in at the

suburb St. Marceau, I saw none but little, dirty, stinking streets,
ugly black houses, the appearance of nastiness, poverty, beggars,
carters, old clothes botchers, cries of ptisan and old hats. All these
things struck me, at first, to such a degree, that all I have since
seen at Paris, really magnificent, has not been able to destroy this
first impression, and that there still remains a secret disgust to the
residence of this capital. I can say the whole time I afterwards
remained there, was employed in seeking resources which might
enable me to live far from it. Such is the fruit of a too active imagination, which exaggerates beyond the exaggerations of mankind,
and always sees more in a thing than has been heard. I had heard
Paris so much boasted of, I looked on it like ancient Babylon, from
which I should, perhaps, have found full as much to deduct, had
I seen it, from the picture I had drawn of it. The same thing happened to me at the opera, where I hastened to go the morrow of
my arrival: the same afterwards happened at Versailles; after
that, likewise, on seeing the sea; and the same thing will always
happen to me, on seeing anything too much extolled; for it is
impossible to mankind, and difficult to Nature itself, to surpass
the richness of my imagination.

From the manner I was received by all those for whom I had
letters, I thought my fortune made. Him I was most recommended
to, and least caressed by, was M. de Surbeck, retired from the
service, and living philosophically at Bagneux, where I went
several times to see him, without his once offering me even a
glass of water. I was better received by Madame de Merveilleux,
sister-in-law to the interpreter, and by his nephew, an officer in
the guards. The mother and son not only received me well, but
offered me their table, of which I often benefited during my stay
at Paris. Madame de Merveilleux appeared to me to have been
handsome; her hair was a beautiful black, and formed, in the old
fashion, ringlets on her forehead. That which does not perish with
beauty still remained, an agreeable mind. She seemed pleased
with mine, and did all in her power to serve me; but no one
seconded her, and I was soon undeceived on all this great interest
they appeared to take in my behalf. I must, however, do the
French justice; they do not smother you with protestations, as is
said of them; and those they make are almost always sincere; but
they have a manner of interesting themselves in your favour,
which deceives you more than words. The coarse compliments of
the Swiss can impose on fools only. The French manners are
more seducing, if only because they are more simple; you think

they do not tell you all they intend to do for you, to surprise you more agreeably. I will go farther: they are not false in their demonstrations; they are naturally officious, humane, benevolent, and even, whatever may be said of it, more downright than any other nation; but they are light and airy. They have, in effect, the sentiment they express; but this sentiment goes off as it came. While speaking to you, they are full of you; go out of their sight, they have forgot you. Nothing is permanent in them; everything with them lasts but a moment.

I was therefore flattered much, served little. That Colonel Godard, whose nephew I was to be with, turned out a miserly old rogue, and, seeing my distress, although rolling in riches, wanted me for nothing. He pretended that I should be with his nephew a kind of valet without wages rather than a real tutor. Continually engaged with him, and by that dispensed from duty, I must live on my cadet's pay, that is, a soldier's; it was with trouble he consented to give me a uniform; he had been glad to put me off with that of the regiment. Madame de Merveilleux, enraged at his proposals, advised me herself not to accept them; her son was of the same opinion. Other things were sought, but nothing found. I began, however, to be in want; a hundred livres, on which I had made my journey, could not carry me far. Happily, I received from the Ambassador a trifling remittance, which was very useful; and I believe he had not discarded me, had I had more patience: but to languish, wait, solicit, are to me impossibilities. I was discouraged, appeared no more, and all was at an end. I had not forgot my poor Mamma; but how to find her? where seek her? Madame de Merveilleux, who knew my story, assisted me in the research, but long to no purpose. At last she told me that Madame de Warens had been gone more than two months,[1] but it was not known whether to Savoy or Turin, and that some said she was returned to Switzerland. Nothing more was necessary to determine me to follow her, certain that, wherever she might be, I should find her in the country much easier than I could have done at Paris.

Before my departure, I exercised my new poetical talent, in an epistle to Colonel Godard, in which I bantered him as well as I could. I showed this scrawl to Madame de Merveilleux, who, instead of censuring me, as she ought, laughed heartily at my sarcasms, and her son alike, who, I believe, did not love M. Godard;

---

[1] It was now the end of 1731; Mme. de Warens had left Paris in July 1730.

it must be owned he was not amiable. I was tempted to send him my verses, they encouraged me: I made a parcel of them directed to him; and, as there was no penny-post then at Paris, I put it in my pocket, and sent it from Auxerre in passing through that place. I laugh yet, sometimes, on thinking of the grimaces he must have made on reading his panegyric, where he was painted stroke by stroke. It began thus:

> *Tu croyois, vieux Pénard, qu'une folle manie*
> *D'élever ton neveu m'inspireroit l'envie.*

This little piece, badly composed in fact, but which did not want salt, and which showed a talent for satire, is nevertheless the only satirical work that ever came from my pen. My mind is too little inclined to hatred to glory in this kind of talent; but I fancy you may judge by some pieces of controversy, written from time to time in my defence, that, had I been of a warring humour, my aggressors had seldom had the laughers on their side.

What I most regret in the particulars of my life, which I do not remember, is not having kept a journal of my travels. Never did I think, exist, live, or was myself, if I may say so, so much as in those I made alone and on foot. Walking has something which animates and enlivens my ideas: I can scarcely think when I stand still; my body must stir in order to stir my mind. The view of the country, the succession of agreeable sights, a good air, a good appetite, and the good health I get by walking; the freedom of inns, the distance of those objects which force me to feel my subjection, of everything which reminds me of my condition, the whole gives a loose to my soul, gives me more boldness of thought, carries me, in a manner, into the immensity of beings, so that I combine them, choose them, appropriate them to my will, without fear or restraint. I imperiously dispose of all Nature: my heart, wandering from object to object, unites, becomes the same with those which engage it, is compassed about by delightful images, grows drunk with delicious sensations. If to determine them, I divert myself by painting them in my mind, what vigorous touches, what resplendent colouring, what energy of expression do I not give them! We have, you will say, seen all this in your works, though written in the decline of life. Oh! had you known those of the flower of my youth, those I made during my travels, those I composed but never wrote... Why, say you, did you not write them? And why write them, I answer you; why withdraw myself from the actual charms of enjoyment, to tell others I did enjoy? What cared I for readers, the public, and the whole earth, while I was swimming in the heavens? Besides, did I carry ink and paper? Had I thought of all these things, nothing had struck me. I did not foresee I should have ideas; they come when they please, not when I please; they come either not at all, or else in a crowd, to overwhelm me with number and force. Ten volumes a day had not sufficed. Where borrow time to write them? On arriving I thought of nothing but a hearty dinner. On departing I thought of nothing but trudging on. I saw a new Paradise awaited me at the door, I ran off to catch it.

I never felt all this so much as in the journey I am speaking of. In coming to Paris I was confined to ideas relative to the business I was going on. I launched into the career I was going to run, and should have run through it with glory enough, but this career was not that my heart called me to, and real beings prejudiced imaginary ones. Colonel Godard and his nephew made poor figures when opposed to a hero like me. Thanks to Heaven! I was now delivered from all these obstacles; I could plunge at will into the land of chimeras, for nothing more was seen before me. And I was so far bewildered in it, I really lost, several times, my road. I had been very sorry to have gone straighter; for finding, at Lyons, I was almost on earth again, I had been glad never to have reached it.

One day among others, going on purpose out of my road, the better to see a spot which appeared admirable, I was so delighted with it, and went around it so often, I entirely lost myself. After running backwards and forwards several hours in vain, tired and dying of hunger and thirst, I went to a country person's, whose house had not a very good appearance, but it was the only one I saw near me. I thought it was as it is at Geneva or Switzerland, where every inhabitant, who could afford it, might exercise hospitality. I begged this man to let me dine with him for my money. He offered me some skimmed milk and coarse barley bread, and told me it was all he had. I drank the milk with pleasure, and ate the bread, straw and all; but this was not very strengthening to a man exhausted with fatigue. The countryman, who examined me, judged of the truth of my story by that of my appetite. Suddenly, having told me that he very well saw[1] I was a good-natured, honest young man, who was not come there to betray him, he opened a little trap-door near the kitchen, went down, and in an

---

[1] It seems I had not, at that time, the physiognomy they have since given me in my portraits. (*Note by Rousseau.*)

instant came back with a good household loaf of pure wheat, a gammon of bacon very enticing, though already cut, and a bottle of wine, whose appearance raised my spirits more than all the rest. An omelet pretty thick was added to these, and I made a dinner such as those only who travel on foot were ever acquainted with. When I offered to pay, his uneasiness and fears came on him again, he would not take my money; he returned it with extraordinary agitation; and the pleasantest of all was, I would not imagine what he had to dread. At last he pronounced with trembling words, Officers and Cellar-rats. He made me understand that he hid his wine for fear of the excise, his bread for fear of the poll-tax, and that he was a ruined man, had they the least doubt but that he was starving with hunger. Everything he told me on this subject, of which I had not the least idea, made an impression on me that will never wear away. This was the spring and source of that inextinguishable hatred which hath since unfolded itself in my heart against the vexations the poor people experience, and against their oppressors. This man, though in easy circumstances, dared not eat the bread he had earned by the sweat of his brow, and could escape ruin solely by an appearance of that want which was seen all around him. I went from his house with as much indignation as pity, deploring the fate of these beautiful countries to which Nature has been lavish in her gifts, only to make them a prey to barbarous publicans.

This is the only thing I distinctly remember of all that happened in this journey. I recollect only one thing more, that, in approaching Lyons, I was tempted to prolong my travels by going to see the borders of the Lignon: for among the romances I had read at my father's, *Astrée* had not been forgotten; it came more frequently to my mind than any other thing. I asked the road to Forez, and, in chatting with a landlady, she told me it was a rare country for workmen, that it contained many forges, and that good iron work was done there. This encomium at once calmed my romantic curiosity; I did not think proper to go to seek Dianas and Sylvanders amidst a generation of blacksmiths. The good old woman who encouraged me in this manner, certainly took me for a journeyman locksmith.

I did not quite go to Lyons without some view. On my arrival, I went to see, at the Chasottes, Mlle. du Châtelet, an acquaintance of Madame de Warens, and for whom she had given me a letter when I came with M. Le Maître; it was, therefore, an acquaintance already made. Mlle. du Châtelet told me, that, in fact, her friend had passed through Lyons, but she could not tell whether she had continued her road as far as Piedmont, and that she was uncertain herself, at her departure, whether or no she should not stop in Savoy; that, if I chose, she would write in order to learn something of her, and that the best way was for me to wait the answer at Lyons. I accepted the offer; but dared not tell Mlle. du Châtelet a speedy answer was necessary; and that my little exhausted purse did not leave me in a condition to wait long. It was not her bad reception that withheld me. On the contrary, she showed me much kindness, and treated me in a style of equality that disheartened me from letting her see my situation, and descending from the state of good company to that of a beggar.

I think I clearly see the agreement of all I have mentioned in this book. I, nevertheless, seem to recollect, in the same interval, another journey to Lyons, whose place I cannot fix, and in which I was much straitened.

A little story, not easy of telling, will never allow me to forget it. One evening I was sitting at Bellecour, after a very scanty supper, thinking over ways of getting out of a difficulty, when a man in a cap sat down by my side; he seemed to be one of those silk workers who are called at Lyons *taffetatiers*. He spoke to me; I replied; a conversation began. We had hardly talked for a quarter of an hour, when, with the same coolness and without his changing his tone, he proposed that we should amuse ourselves together. I waited for him to explain what this amusement should be; but, without adding a word, he got himself ready to give me the example. We were almost touching, and the night was not dark enough to prevent my seeing for what he was preparing. He did not want my body; at least, nothing suggested that attention, and the place was not a favourable one. He wanted only, as he had said, to amuse himself, and that I should amuse myself, each on his own account; and it seemed to him quite simple, for he had not even imagined that it would not seem the same to me as to him. I was so aghast at this impudence that without replying I got up and hastened to flee with all speed, thinking I had the wretch at my heels. I was so disturbed that instead of reaching my lodgings in St. Dominic's street, I ran beside the quay, and stopped only beyond the wooden bridge, trembling as if I had but just committed a crime. I was subject to the same vice; this remembrance cured me of it for a long time.

On this journey I had another adventure much of the same sort, but which put me in greater danger. Perceiving my money

drew to its end, I husbanded what little remained. I took meals
less often at my inn, and often took nothing at all, since for five or
six sous I could regale myself at a public-house as well as I could
there for twenty-five. No longer eating there, I knew not how to
sleep there, not that I was much in debt, but that I was ashamed
to occupy a room without bringing my host any profit. The
weather was fine. One evening, when it was very hot, I determined to pass the night in the square, and was already established on a bench, when an abbé who was passing, seeing me
lying thus, approached and asked if I had no place to sleep. I
opened my case to him, he seemed touched by it; he sat down at
my side, and we talked together. He spoke pleasantly; all that
he said gave me the best opinion of him in the world. Seeing me
well disposed, he told me that his lodging was not a large one,
that he had but one room, but that he would certainly not let me
lie thus in the square; that it was late to find me a lodging, and
that he offered me for that night half of his own bed. I accept the
offer, hoping to make a friend who may be of use to me. His room
seems clean, small though it is; he does me the honours of it very
politely. He takes from a cupboard a glass pot in which are cherries
in spirit; we each eat a couple of them, and go to bed.

This man's tastes were those of my Jew at the hospital, though
he did not declare them in so brutal a fashion. Whether, knowing
I might be heard, he feared to force me to defend myself, or
whether, in fine, he was less determined in his projects, he dared
not propose to me openly their execution, and sought to move me
without disturbing me. More instructed than on the previous
occasion, I soon understood his plan, and shuddered at it; knowing not in what house nor in whose hands I was, I feared, if
I made a noise, to pay for it with my life. I feigned not to know
what he wanted of me; but seeming much troubled by his caresses
and entirely determined not to endure their progress, I dealt so
that he was compelled to contain himself. Then I spoke to him
with all the gentleness and firmness of which I was capable; and,
without seeming to suspect anything, excused myself for the inquietude I had shown by my former adventure, which I affected
to relate to him in terms so full of disgust and horror that I made
him, I believe, himself sick, and he renounced altogether his dirty
design. The rest of the night was passed in quiet. He likewise said
a number of good and sensible things to me, and was certainly not
a man without merit, great blackguard as he was.

In the morning, M. l'Abbé, not willing to seem disappointed, spoke of breakfast, and asked one of the daughters of his landlady, a pretty girl, to bring it. She told him she had no time; he addressed himself to her sister, who did not even condescend to answer him. We both waited; but no breakfast. At last we went into the room of the young ladies. They received M. l'Abbé with a poor welcome; I had even less reason to be pleased with mine. The elder, turning round, planted her pointed heel on the toe of my foot, where a very painful corn had made me cut my shoe; the other came behind me and roughly moved away a chair on which I was about to sit down; their mother, in throwing water out of the window, sprinkled my face with it; wherever I placed myself, they made me move in order to look for something; never in my days had I spent such a time. In their insulting and mocking looks I saw a hidden anger which I was stupid enough not to comprehend. Astounded, stupefied, ready to suppose them all possessed, I began once more to be affrighted, when the Abbé, who did not appear to see or hear anything, concluding that there was no breakfast to be hoped for, made a move to go out, and I hastened to follow him, very content to escape from these three furies. As we went he suggested that we should breakfast at a coffee-house. Though I was extremely hungry, I did not accept this offer; he did not insist on it neither, and we separated at the third or fourth street-corner; I charmed at being out of sight of everything that attached to that accursed house; and he very pleased, as I suppose, at having got me far enough away from it for it not to be easy to recognise it. As neither at Paris nor in any other town has anything like these two adventures ever happened to me, there has remained with me a not very favourable impression of the people of Lyons, and I have always thought this town of all those in Europe the one where the most terrible corruption reigns.

The remembrance of the extremities to which I was reduced, does not contribute any more to recall it agreeably to my memory. Had I done like some others, had I possessed the talent of borrowing and running in debt at my lodging, I had easily got through; but in this my unaptness equalled my repugnance; and to imagine the point to which I carried both one and the other, it is sufficient to know that, having spent almost my whole life in hardships, and often at the point of wanting bread, it never happened to me, once in my life, to be asked, by a creditor, for money, without giving it him that instant.[1] I never could contract bawling debts, and was always fonder of suffering than owing.

---

[1] The Paris MS. adds: "or to make a workman come twice for his money."

To be reduced to lie in the street was certainly suffering, and this happened to me several times at Lyons. I chose to employ the few halfpence that remained, in paying for bread rather than a lodging; because, after all, I run less hazard of dying for want of sleep than bread. It is surprising that, in this cruel situation, I was neither uneasy nor dull. I had not the least care for future days. I waited the answers Mlle. du Châtelet was to receive, lodging in the open air, and sleeping stretched on the earth, or on a bench, with the same ease as on a bed of down. I remember to have passed even a delightful night out of the city, on a road which borders the Rhône or the Saône, I do not recollect which of the two. Gardens forming terraces bordered the road on the opposite side. It had been extremely hot that day; the evening was charming; the dew moistened the drooping grass; no wind, a still night; the air was fresh, but not cold; the sun being set had left red vapours in the heavens whose reflection gave to the water the colour of a rose; the trees on the terrace were covered with nightingales, who answered each other's notes. I walked about in a sort of ecstasy, giving up my feelings and heart to the enjoyment of the whole, and sighing a little with grief at enjoying it alone. Absorbed in delightful meditation, the night was far advanced before I perceived my lengthened walk had tired my weary limbs. I perceived it at last. I laid myself luxuriously on the step of a sort of niche or false door in the terrace walk: the canopy of my bed was formed by the tops of trees; a nightingale was precisely over my head; his music lulled me asleep: my slumbers were soft, my awaking was more so. It was broad day; my eyes, on opening, saw water, verdure, and an admirable landscape. I got up, shook myself, hunger seized me. I made, gaily, the best of my way towards town, resolved to spend on a good breakfast the last two pieces I had left. I was in so excellent a humour as to go singing along all the way, and I even remember, I sung a cantata of Batistin[1] I had by heart, entitled the *Baths of Thomery*. God bless the good Batistin and his good cantata, which brought me a better breakfast than what I expected, and still a better dinner, which I did not expect at all. In the height of my walking and singing, I heard someone behind me. I look round, I see an Antonine following me, and seeming to listen to me with pleasure. He accosts me, bids me good-morning, and asks if I know music. I answered, *a little*, to make it believed a great deal. He continues to question me: I

---

[1] Stück, a Florentine musician, who died in Paris 1755, was so called in France.

tell a part of my story. He asks me whether I ever copied music. Often, say I, which was true; my best method of learning was by copying. Well, says he, come with me; I can employ you a few days, during which time you shall want nothing, provided you consent to not going out of the room. I willingly acquiesced, and followed him.

This Antonine was named Rolichon, was fond of music, understood it, and sung in little concerts he gave his friends. There was nothing in this but innocence and decency; but this taste seemed to degenerate into passion, of which he was obliged to conceal a part. He conducted me to a little room I occupied, where I found a deal of music he had copied. He gave me more to copy, particularly the cantata I sung, and which he intended to sing in a little time. I stayed there three or four days, copying the whole time I did not eat; for in my life I never was so hungry or better fed. He brought my meals himself from the kitchen; they must have had a good one, if their living was equal to mine. In my days I have not eaten with so much pleasure; and I must own these bits came in the nick of time, for I was as dry as wood. I worked with nearly as good a heart as I ate, which is not saying a little. It is true I was not so correct as diligent. Some days after, M. Rolichon, whom I met in the street, told me my parts could not be performed on account of omissions, duplications, and transpositions. I must own I have, in choosing that, chose the one science in the world for which I was least calculated. Not but that my notes were good, and that I copied very clean; but the tediousness of a long job distracts me so much, that I spend more time in scratching out than in noting; and if I do not use the greatest attention in comparing my parts, they always cause the performance to fail. I, therefore, in endeavouring to do well, did very ill, and to get on quickly, I went cross. This did not prevent M. Rolichon from treating me well the whole time, and giving me, on leaving him, half-a-crown I little deserved, but which set me quite on foot again; for in a few days after I received news from Mamma, who was at Chambéry, and money to carry me to her: this journey I made with transport. Since those times my finances have often been very low; but never so as to go without bread. I mention this period with a heart sensible of the attention of Providence. It was the last time of my life I felt hunger and misery.

I stayed at Lyons seven or eight days more, waiting the things which Mamma had desired Mlle. du Châtelet to get for her. I attended this lady more assiduously, during this time, than before,

LYONS: OLD BRIDGE OVER THE SAÔNE

having the pleasure of talking with her of her friend, without being any longer taken off by those cruel reflections on my situation which forced me to conceal it. Mlle. du Châtelet was neither young nor pretty, but she did not want agreeableness; she was easy and familiar, and her wit gave a price to this familiarity. She had the faculty of observing morals, which teaches to study mankind; and it is from her in its first origin I derive this taste. She was fond of Le Sage's romances, and particularly *Gil Blas;* she spoke to me of it, lent it me, and I read it with pleasure; but I was not then ripe for this kind of reading: I wanted romances of flighty sentiments. I thus passed my time at the grate of Mlle. du Châtelet with as much pleasure as profit; it is certain the interesting and sensible conversations of a woman of merit are more proper to form a young man, than all the pedantic philosophy of books. I got acquainted at the Chasottes with other boarders and their friends; among others, with a young person of fourteen, named Mlle. Serre, to whom I did not, at first, pay much attention; but whom I grew fond of eight or nine years afterwards, and with reason; she was a charming girl.

Occupied with the expectation of soon seeing again my dear Mamma, I made a little truce with my chimeras; and the true happiness that awaited me dispensed me with seeking them in visions. I not only found her again, but I found with her, and by her means, an agreeable situation; for she wrote me word she had got me an occupation she hoped could suit me, without separating from her. I spent myself in conjectures in guessing what this occupation could be, and it was necessary to guess, in fact, in order to meet it exactly. I had money sufficient to travel conveniently. Mlle. du Châtelet would have had me take a horse; I could not consent, and had reason on my side: I had missed the pleasure of the last journey on foot I ever made; for I cannot call by this name the excursions I often made round my neighbourhood, when I lived at Motiers.

It is a singular thing, that my imagination never rises more agreeably than when my condition is the least so; and that, on the contrary, it is less smiling when everything smiles around me. My stubborn head cannot submit to things; it cannot embellish, it will create. Real objects are shown there at most but as they are; it can dress out none but imaginary objects. Would I paint spring, it must be in winter; would I describe a beautiful landscape, I must be shut up; and I have an hundred times said that, if ever they put me into the Bastille, I should compose the picture of Liberty. On leaving Lyons I saw nothing but future delights; I was as happy, and had every reason to be so, as I was the reverse on leaving Paris. I nevertheless had none of those delightful meditations in this journey I had in the other. My heart was at ease, and that was all. I drew near that excellent friend I was going to see again with melting fondness. I tasted beforehand, but without ebriety, the pleasure of living with her: I always expected it: it was as if nothing new had happened. I was disquieted at what I was going to do as if it had been very disquieting. My ideas were peaceable and mild, not celestial and ravishing. All passing objects struck my sight; I gave attention to the landscapes; I observed the trees, the houses, the brooks; I considered at the crossing of roads; I feared losing myself, but did not. In a word I was no longer in the empyrean; I was sometimes where I was, sometimes where I was going to, never farther.

I am in recounting my travels as I was in making them: I cannot arrive. My heart beat with joy when I drew near my dear Mamma, but I went no faster for that. I love to walk at my ease, and stop when I please. I love a strolling life. Make a journey on foot in fine weather, in a fine country, without hurry, and an agreeable object at the end of it; this is of all the manners of living the most to my taste. As to the rest, it is understood what I mean by a fine country. Never a champaign country, however fine it may be, appeared so in my eyes. I must have torrents, rocks, fir-trees, gloomy woods, mountains, roads which are rugged to go up or down, precipices on each side which affright me. I had this pleasure, and tasted all its delights, in approaching Chambéry.

Not far from a cut mountain, called the Pas-de-l'Echelle, at the bottom of a great road cut through the rock, at a place called Chailles, is a little river, which runs and spouts into dreadful abysses which it seems to have taken thousands of ages to hollow out. They have bordered the road by a parapet to prevent accidents: by this means I could contemplate the bottom, and make myself giddy at my ease; for what is most pleasant in my taste for steep places, is that they make my head run round, and that I am very fond of this turning round, provided I am safe. Leaning firmly on the parapet, I advanced my head, and remained there whole hours, perceiving from time to time the froth and the blue water, whose roaring I heard amidst the cries of ravens and birds of prey, which flew from rock to rock, and from thicket to thicket, between six and seven hundred feet below me. In those places where the descent was pretty regular, and the bushes thin enough to let stones pass, I fetched some from a pretty good distance, as large as I could carry, piled them on a heap on the parapet, then throwing them one after the other, I was delighted to see them roll, bound, and fly into a thousand pieces before they reached the bottom.

Nearer Chambéry I had a like sight in a contrary sense. The road passes at the foot of the finest cascade I have ever seen. The mountain is so steep, that the water flies off neat, and falls in the form of an arcade so wide that you can pass between the cascade and the rock, sometimes without being wetted. But, if you do not take your measures well, you may be taken in, as I was; for, from the extreme height, the water divides and falls into a mist, and when you approach this cloud a little, without immediately perceiving you are wet, in an instant you are well soaked.

I arrive at last; I see her again. She was not alone. The Intendant-general was in her room at the time I came in. Without speaking to me, she takes me by the hand, and presents me to him with that grace which opens to her every heart. Here he is, Sir, poor young fellow; condescend to patronize him as long as he deserves it; I am under no apprehension for him the rest of his life. Then turning to me, Child, says she, you belong to the King: thank the Intendant, who has provided you bread. I stared without speaking a word, or without very well knowing what to think: growing ambition, with a trifling addition, would have turned my head, and made me immediately act the little Intendant. My fortune I found less brilliant than I imagined from this beginning; but for the present it was a living, which, for me, was a great deal. This was the affair.

King Victor-Amédée, judging by the fate of the preceding wars, and by the position of the ancient inheritance of his forefathers, it might some time or other slip from him, thought only how he might exhaust it. He had resolved a few years before to tax the nobility, he ordered a general survey of the lands of the whole country, in order, that by laying the tax on land, he might divide it with more equity. This work, begun under the father, was finished under the son. Two or three hundred people, as well surveyors, who were called Geometers, as writers, who were called Secretaries, were employed on this work: it was among these last Mamma had got my name entered. The post, though not lucrative, was sufficient to live well upon in that country. The worst was, the employment was only for a term; but it put one forward in seeking and waiting, and it was by way of forecast she endeavoured to obtain his private patronage for me, in order to get a more permanent employment when the term of this should be expired.

I entered into office a few days after my arrival. There was nothing difficult in this work; I was soon master of it. It was thus, after four or five years running about in follies and sufferings, since I left Geneva, I began, for the first time, to get my bread with credit.

These long particulars of my youth may have appeared very puerile; I am sorry for it: though born a man in many respects, I was long a child, and am so yet in many others. I did not promise to hold up to the public a great personage; I promised to paint myself such as I am; for to know me well in my advanced age, it is necessary to have known me in my youth. As, in general, objects make less impression on me than their remembrance, and all my ideas are in images, the first strokes which were engraven on my mind have remained there, and those which were imprinted afterwards have rather joined than effaced them. There was a certain succession of affections and ideas which modify those which follow, and which it is necessary to be acquainted with, in order properly to judge of them. I strive, everywhere, to lay the first causes quite open, to make you feel connexion of effects. I want to be able, if I could, by some means to render my heart transparent to the sight of the reader; and this is the reason I endeavour to show it him in every point of view, to lead him by every path, to speak in such a manner that a single movement shall not pass but he shall perceive it, in order that he may judge himself of the principle which produces it.

Did I take the result on myself, and say, Such is my character, he might think, if I would not deceive him, that I might deceive myself. But in particularising with simplicity everything that has happened to me, all my actions, all my thoughts, all my feelings, I cannot lead him to error, unless I will; and even if I would, I should not easily attain it in this manner. It is he must assemble the elements and determine the being they compose; the result must be his work; and if he then mistakes, all the error will be his own. Now, it is not sufficient to this end that my recitals are faithful; they must be exact. It is not for me to judge of the importance of the facts; I must tell them all, and leave the care of the choice to him. I have endeavoured to do it hitherto with all my courage, and I shall not relax in what follows. But the memory of the middle age is always weaker than that of our younger years. I began by making the best I possibly could of these last. If the other come back with the same force, some impatient readers may perhaps grow tired; but for my part, I shall not be sorry for my labour. I have only one thing to fear in this undertaking; it is not saying too much, or telling falsities; but it is, not saying all, or being silent on truths.

BOOK FIVE

IT was, I think, in 1732, I arrived at Chambéry, as I have just said; and that I commenced my employment of registering land for the King. I had passed my twentieth year, and was almost one-and-twenty. I was, for my age, well enough formed as to the mind; but my judgement was far from being so, and I had great occasion for those into whose hands I fell to learn a proper conduct: for a few years of experience had not yet cured me radically of my romantic visions; and though I had suffered so many evils, I knew as little of the world and mankind as if I had not paid for such instruction.

I lay at my own house, that is at Mamma's; but I did not find a second Annecy: no more gardens, no more brooks, no more landscapes. The house she lived in was dark and dismal, and my room was the darkest and most dismal of the whole house. A wall the only prospect, an alley instead of a street, little air, little light, little room, iron bars, rats and a rotten floor; these things could not form a pleasant habitation. But I was at her house, with her; incessantly at my desk or in her chamber, I little perceived the hideousness of my own. I had not time to think of it. It will seem singular that she should have fixed on Chambéry on purpose to live in this disagreeable house: this was a mark of her cleverness I ought not to pass over. She went to Turin with repugnance, well knowing that, on so recent revolutions, and the agitation in which the court then was, she could not be favourably received. Her affairs, nevertheless, demanded her presence there; she feared being forgotten or ill-used. She particularly knew that the Count of Saint-Laurent, intendant-general of the finances, did not favour her. He had at Chambéry an old house, badly constructed, and in so nasty a position it always remained empty; she took it and lived there. This succeeded better than a journey; her pension was not struck off, and since that time the Count of Saint-Laurent was always of her friends.

I found her household nearly on the old footing; and the faithful Claude Anet still with her. He was, as I think I have already said, a peasant of Moutru,[1] who in his childhood gathered simples in Jura for making Swiss tea, and whom she had taken into her service for his knowledge in drugs, finding it convenient to have a herbalist among her domestics. He was so passionately fond of the study of plants, and she so much favoured his turn, that he became a real botanist; and, had he not died young, he had been famed in this science as much as he deserved to be as an honest man. He being serious, even grave, and I younger than he, he was to me a kind of tutor, and saved me from many follies; for he imposed respect; I dared not forget myself before him. He imposed it equally on his mistress, who was acquainted with his profound sense, his uprightness, his inviolable attachment to her, who so justly returned it. Claude Anet was beyond contradiction an uncommon man, and the only one I have ever seen of the sort. Slow, staid, deliberate, circumspect in his conduct, reserved in his manner, concise and pithy in his discourse, he was in his passion of an impetuosity he never allowed to appear, but which preyed upon him inwardly, and which never but once in his life hurried him into extravagance; but this once was terrible; it was poisoning himself. This tragic scene passed soon after my arrival, and neces-

[1] He was born at Montreux in 1706.

sary enough it was to teach me the intimacy of this young fellow with his mistress; for had she not herself told me of it, I should never have suspected it. Assuredly, if attachment, zeal, and fidelity, could merit such a reward, it was due to him, and what proves he was worthy of it, he never abused it. They very seldom disputed, and their disputes always ended well. They had, however, one which ended ill: his mistress, in her anger, said something affronting to him, which he never could digest. He consulted despair only, and finding, ready to his hand, a vial of laudanum, he drank it, then went quietly to bed, thinking to awake no more. Happily Madame de Warens, uneasy, herself agitated, wandering about the house, found the vial empty, and guessed the rest. In flying to his assistance her screams drew me after her; she confessed everything to me, implored my help, and was, with a deal of trouble, so fortunate as to make him throw up the opium. Witness to this scene, I admired my stupidity at never in the least suspecting the connexions she acquainted me of. But Claude Anet was so discreet that the most penetrating might have been deceived. Their reconciliation was such that myself was extremely affected at it; and since this time, adding respect to the esteem I had for him, I became, in some measure, his pupil, and did not find myself worse for it.

I learnt, however, not without pain, that another could live with her in closer intimacy than myself. I never even thought of desiring this place, but it hurt me to see it filled by another; that was very natural. However, instead of hating him who had jostled me, I really felt the attachment I had for her extend to him. All I desired was that she might be happy, and since she had occasion for him to make her so, I was satisfied at his being happy likewise. For his part, he entered perfectly into the views of his mistress, and contracted a sincere friendship for the friend she had chosen.

Without affecting the authority his post gave him over me, he naturally took that his judgement had over mine. I dared do nothing he seemed to disapprove, and he disapproved only what was wrong. We thus lived in a union which made us all happy, and which nothing but death was able to destroy. One proof of the excellence of this amiable woman was, that all those who loved her, loved each other. Jealousy, rivalship even, gave way to the ruling sentiment she inspired, and I never saw any of those who surrounded her with each other ill. Let those who read me stop this reading a moment at this encomium, and if they find, on recollection, any other woman of whom the same things can be said, let them adhere to her for the repose of their days, were she even the lowest of whores.

Here begins an interval of eight or nine years, from my arrival at Chambéry until my departure for Paris in 1741, during which time I shall have few adventures to write, because my life was as simple as pleasant, and this uniformity was precisely what I most wanted to finish the forming my character, which continual troubles prevented from fixing. It was during this precious interval my education, mixed and without connexion, having taken a consistency, was the cause that I have never ceased to be amidst the storms which awaited me. The progress was insensible and slow, attended by few memorable events; but it deserves, nevertheless, to be followed and unfolded.

At first I was employed in little more than my office; the constraint of a desk left no room for other thoughts. The little time I was at liberty was spent with the dear Mamma, and not having even any for reading, the thought did not reach me. But when my business, becoming a kind of daily round, occupied my mind less, uneasiness found its way again, study was once more necessary, and, as if this desire was always irritated by the difficulty of satisfying it, it would have become a passion, as it did when with my master, had not other inclinations, interposing, diverted that one.

Although our operations did not demand an arithmetic very transcendent, they demanded enough to embarrass me sometimes. To vanquish this difficulty, I bought arithmetical books, and I learnt well; for I learnt alone. Practical arithmetic extends farther than is thought, if you would have an exact precision. There are operations of an extreme length, in which I have sometimes seen good geometricians lose themselves. Reflection joined to practice gives clear ideas; then you find out abridged methods whose invention flatters self-sufficiency, whose exactness satisfies the mind, and which render pleasant a work of itself unprofitable. I went so deeply into it, there was not a question solvable by arithmetical calculation alone that embarrassed me; and now that everything I knew wears daily from my memory, this acquirement still remains in part, after an interruption of thirty years. A few days ago, in a journey I made to Davenport, being present with my landlord at an arithmetical lesson of his children, I did without errors, with an incredible pleasure, a work the most complicated. It seemed to me, on setting down my figures, I was still at Chambéry, in my happy days. This was coming back on my steps from afar.

Applying colour-wash to the maps of our geometricians had also given me a taste for drawing. I bought colours, and set myself to drawing flowers and landscapes. It was a pity I found in myself few talents for this art; my inclination was entirely disposed to it. Amidst my crayons and pencils I had passed whole months without going out of doors. This employment engaging me too much, they were obliged to force me from it. It is thus with every fancy I give in to; it augments, becomes a passion, and I soon see nothing but the amusement in which I am occupied. Years have not cured me of this fault; they have not even abated it; and now that I am writing this you have an old dotard, infatuated by another useless study, of which I understand nothing, and which those who have given their youthful days to it, have been obliged to abandon at the age I am beginning it.

At that time it might have been in its place; the opportunity was fine, and I had some temptation to benefit by it. The satisfaction I saw in the countenance of Anet, coming home loaded with new plants, set me two or three times on the point of going to herbalize with him. I am almost assured, had I gone once only, I had been caught, and should, perhaps, this day be an excellent botanist; for I know no study so well associated to my natural tastes as that of plants: the life I lead these ten years in the country, is scarcely any other than that of a continual herbalist, in reality without object or progress; but having at that time no idea of botany, I almost despised, and was even disgusted at it; I considered it only as the study of an apothecary. Mamma, who was fond of it, made herself no other use of it; she sought none but common plants to employ them in her drugs. Thus botany, chemistry, and anatomy, confounded in my brain under the denomination of medicine, served only to furnish matter for pleasant sarcasms the whole day; and draw on me, from time to time, a box on the ear. Besides, a different and too opposed taste grew up in me by degrees, and absorbed every other — I mean music. I was certainly born for this art; for my fondness for it was from my childhood, and it is the only one I constantly loved at every age. What is most astonishing, is, that the art for which I was born should have nevertheless cost me so much pains to learn it, and with a success so slow, that, after practising my whole life, I never could attain to sing with certainty on opening a book. What rendered this study more agreeable to me in especial at that time was, my being able to follow it with Mamma. Though in other respects our tastes differed, music was a point of union I loved to

make use of. She was not averse to it; I was then almost as far
advanced as she; in two or three trials we deciphered an air. Sometimes seeing her busied round her furnace, I said to her, Mamma,
here is a charming duet, that seems inclined to spoil your drugs.
Why faith, says she, if thou dost make me burn them, I'll make
thee eat them. Thus in disputing I drew her to her harpsichord;
the furnace was forgot; the extract of juniper or wormwood was
calcined; she smeared it over my face; and all this was delightful.

You see, with little leisure I had things enough to fill it up. One
amusement more, however, found room, which gave a price to all
the others.

We lived in so close a dungeon, it was necessary sometimes to
get a little air on earth. Anet engaged Mamma to hire a garden in
the suburbs for plants. To this garden was added a snug box,
pretty enough, which was furnished according to order. A bed was
sent; we often dined, and I sometimes lay there. Insensibly I was
infatuated with this little retirement; I put a few books and many
prints in it; I spent a part of my time in ornamenting it, and preparing those things that might agreeably surprise Mamma when
she came there. I left her, that I might employ my thoughts on
her, that I might think of her with more pleasure; another caprice
I neither excuse nor explain, but which I acknowledge, because
it was so. I remember Madame de Luxembourg speaking to me in
raillery of a man who left his mistress to write to her. I told her
I could have been that man, and might have added, I had been
such a one sometimes. I never, however, found in Mamma's company the necessity of leaving it to love her more; for in a tête-à-
tête with her I was as perfectly free as alone, which I never found
in any other's company, man or woman, how strong soever my
affection might be. But she was so often surrounded, and by people
so little agreeable to me, that indignation and their tiresome company drove me to my asylum, where I had her as I pleased, without fear of being followed by the importunate.

Whilst thus divided between business, pleasure, and instruction, I lived in the sweetest repose; Europe was not so quiet. France
and the Emperor had mutually declared war with each other: the
King of Sardinia entered into the quarrel, and the French army
filed into Piedmont, to enter the Milanese territories. One of their
columns came through Chambéry, and, among the rest, the regiment of Champagne, whose colonel was the Duke of la Trimouille,
to whom I was introduced, who promised me many things, and
who certainly never more thought of me. Our little garden was

exactly at that end of the suburbs by which the troops entered, in such a manner that I was fully satisfied with the pleasure of seeing them pass; and I was as desirous for the success of this war as if it had nearly concerned me. Till then I never took in my head to think of public affairs, and I began to read newspapers for the first time, but with so much partiality to France, that my heart beat for joy at their most trifling advantages, and that their reverses afflicted me as if they had fallen on me. Had this folly been passing, I had not thought it worth notice; but it is so rooted in me without any reason, that, when I afterwards acted at Paris the anti-despot and the proud republican, I felt, in spite of myself, a secret predilection for the very nation I saw servile, and for the government I affected to oppose. The pleasantest of all was, that, being ashamed to own an inclination so contrary to my maxims, I dared not own it to anyone; and I rallied the French on their defeats, whilst my heart was more grieved at them than theirs. I am certainly the first, who, living with people that treated him well, and whom he adored, took on him, in their own country, a borrowed air of despising them. In fine, this inclination has proved itself so disinterested, so strong, so constant, so invincible in me, that, even since my leaving the kingdom, since government, magistrates, authors, have outvied each other against me, since it is become genteel to load me with injustice and abuse, I have not been able to cure myself of my folly. I love them in spite of myself, though they use me ill. Now that I see that decadence of England, which I have predicted, already beginning in the midst of her triumphs, I lull myself with the foolish hope that the French nation, victorious in her turn, will one day come to deliver me from the sad captivity I live in.

I long sought the cause of this partiality; I have been able to find it only in the occasion which gave it birth. A rising taste for literature attached me to French books, to the authors of those books, and to the country of those authors. At the instant the French army was filing off under my eyes, I was reading Brantôme's *Great Captains:* my head was full of the Clissons, Bayards, Lautrecs, Colignys, Montmorencys, and La Trimouilles; and I loved their descendants as the heirs of their merit and great courage. In each regiment that passed I thought I saw those famous black bands who formerly had done so many exploits in Piedmont. In fine, I applied to that I saw the ideas I gathered from books; my studies continued, and, still taken from the same nation, nourished my friendship for her, and at last grew to a blind passion which nothing has been able to overcome. I have had occasion, several times, in the sequel, to remark in my travels, that this impression was not peculiar to me, and that, more or less active, in every country, on that part of the nation who were fond of literature and cultivated learning, it balanced the general hatred the conceited air of the French inspires. Their romances, more than their men, attract the women of every country; their dramatic *chefs-d'œuvre* create a fondness in youth for their theatres. The reputation of that of Paris draws to it crowds of strangers, who come back enthusiasts. In fine, the excellent taste of their literature captivates the senses of every man who has any; and in the so unfortunate war they have just ended, I saw their authors and philosophers maintain the glory of France so tarnished by their warriors.

I was, therefore, an ardent Frenchman, and that rendered me a news-monger. I went with the throng of bubble-gulpers to wait in the square the arrival of the post; and, more sot than the ass of the fable, I was very uneasy to know whose pack-saddle I should have the honour to carry: for it was at that time pretended we should belong to France, and Savoy was to be given in exchange for Milan. I must, however, own I had some cause of uneasiness; for, had this war ended badly for the allies, Mamma's pension was in great danger. But I had full confidence in my good friends; and for once, in spite of the surprise of M. de Broglie, this confidence was not vain, thanks to the King of Sardinia, whom I never thought of.

While they were fighting in Italy, they were singing in France. The operas of Rameau began to make a noise, and again raised up his theoretic works, which were within the reach of but few on account of their obscurity. By chance I heard of his *Treatise on Harmony;* I had no rest till I had purchased this book. By another hazard I fell ill. The illness was inflammatory; it was sharp and short; but my convalescence was long, it was a month before I was able to go out. During this time I sketched, I devoured my *Treatise on Harmony;* but it was so long, so diffuse, so badly disposed, I found it would take me a considerable time to study and unravel it. I suspended my application, and recreated my sight with music. The cantatas of Bernier, in which I exercised myself, were never from my mind. I learnt four or five by heart; among the rest, that of the *Amours dormants,* which I have never seen since that time, and which I still retain almost entirely, as well as *L'Amour piqué par une Abeille,* a very pretty cantata by Clérambault, which I learnt in nearly the same time.

To complete me, there came from Val d'Aosta a young organist, named Abbé Palais, a good musician, a good-natured man, who accompanied extremely well with the harpsichord. I get acquainted with him; we become inseparable. He was pupil to an Italian monk, a great organist. He talked of his elements: I compared them with those of my Rameau: I stuffed my head with accompanying, concord, and harmony. It was necessary to form the ear to all these: I proposed to Mamma a little concert every month; she consented. I am so full of this concert, that night or day I was employed on nothing else; but that really employed me, and very much, to get the music, the musicians, the instruments together, make out the parts, etc. Mamma sang; Father Caton, whom I have already spoken of, and whom I shall again have occasion to speak of, sang likewise; a dancing master, named Roche, and his son, played the violin; Canavas, a musician from Piedmont, employed at the Registry, who is since married at Paris, played the violoncello; the Abbé Palais accompanied on the harpsichord: I had the honour of conducting the music, without forgetting the woodcleaver's beetle. The charms of all this may be guessed! Not altogether as at M. de Treytorens', but pretty near it.

The little concert at Madame de Warens's, newly converted, and living, said they, on the King's charity, made the crew of devotees murmur; but for many genteel people it was an agreeable amusement. I put at their head, on this occasion, one who would not be readily guessed; a monk, but a monk of merit, and even amiable, whose misfortunes did in the end extremely affect me, and whose memory, connected with that of my happy days, is yet dear. I am speaking of Father Caton, a Franciscan friar, who, together with the Count Dortan, got the music of the poor *little cat* seized at Lyons, which is not the best action of his life. He was a bachelor of Sorbonne: he lived a long while at Paris amidst the best families, and was particularly very friendly received at the Marquis of Antremont's, then Ambassador from Sardinia. He was tall and well made, a full face, full eyes, black hair, which without affectation formed a ringlet on the side of his forehead, a countenance at the same time noble, open, modest, a simple but good presence, having neither the hypocritical nor the impudent carriage of a monk, nor the imperious appearance of a man of fashion, though he was very much so, but the assurance of a gentleman, who, without blushing at his gown, does honour to himself, and knows his place is in genteel company. Though Father Caton had not much learning for a doctor, he had a great deal for a man of society; and, not being very forward to show his parts, he used them so advantageously as to appear more than they were. As he had been accustomed to company, his application was rather to agreeable talents than solid knowledge. He had sense, made verses, conversed well, sung better, had a good voice, played the organ and harpsichord. Less would have made him courted; he was so; but it caused him so little to neglect the duties of his order, that he obtained, though he had extremely jealous competitors, the election as a Definitor of his province.

This Father Caton became acquainted with Mamma at the Marquis of Antremont's. He heard of our concerts, he wished to be of them; he was so, and rendered them brilliant. We were soon connected by our common taste for music, which in each of us was a lively passion, with this difference, that he was really a musician, and I only a scribbler. We went with Canavas, and the Abbé Palais, to play at his room, and sometimes at his organ on holidays. We often dined at his little table; for, which is more surprising in a monk, he was generous, sumptuous, and sensual without grossness. On our concert days he supped at Mamma's. These suppers were extremely gay, very agreeable; there was good and witty talk, duets were sung: I was quite at ease, I had wit and flights; Father Caton was charming company; Mamma was adorable; the Abbé Palais, with his bull's voice, was our butt. Delightful moments of gay youth, what a while have you and I been parted!

As I shall have no occasion to speak again of our old Father Caton, let me here, in a few words, finish his doleful history. The rest of the monks, jealous, or rather furious, at seeing his merit, and an elegance of manners which had nothing of the monastic crapulence, detested him, because he was not, like them, detestable. The heads entered into a combination against him, and stirred up the little underling monks that wanted his place, who before dared not look towards him. They gave him a thousand affronts; got his place; turned him out of his chamber, which he had furnished with taste, though with simplicity; confined him I know not where: in fine, these miscreants heaped on him so many wrongs, that his honest heart, with justice lofty, could resist no longer; and, after having been the delight of the most amiable societies, he died with grief on an old couch, thrust into some cell or dungeon, lamented and bewailed by every good man who knew him, and who saw no other fault in him than being a monk.

With this sort of life, I got so forward in a very short time, that, entirely drowned in music, I found myself in no situation to think of other things. I no longer went to our office but with an ill will; constraint and assiduity to business made it to me a punishment not to be supported, and it brought me at last to wish to quit my employment, to give myself up entirely to music. It may easily be guessed this folly did not pass without opposition. To leave an honourable post, and a certain revenue, to run after uncertain pupils, was a little too senseless to please Mamma. Even supposing my future progress as great as I figured to myself, it was very modestly confining my ambition, to reduce me for life to the state of a musician. She who formed none but magnificent projects, and who did not take me altogether at M. d'Aubonne's word, with pain saw me seriously occupied in a talent she thought so frivolous, and often reminded me of this provincial proverb, not so well adapted to Paris: *He who sings well, and well dances, does that which not much advances.* She saw me, on the other hand, carried away by an irresistible inclination; my passion for music became enthusiasm; it was therefore to be feared that my employment, suffering by my inattention, might draw on me a dismission, which it was better I myself should forestall. I likewise represented to her, that this employment would not last long; that I wanted a mode of subsistence; that I was more likely to succeed by practice in that my inclination led me to, and which she had chosen for me, than to be at the mercy of patronage, or to make new experiments which might succeed indifferently, and leave me, after having passed the age of being taught, without a way to earn my bread. In fact, I extorted her consent, rather by the power of importunity and caresses, than by reasoning which satisfied her. I instantly ran to thank, haughtily, M. Coccelli, Director General of the Registry, as if I had done the most heroic action, and voluntarily left my employment without cause, without reason, without pretext, with as much and more joy than I entered on it not quite two years before.

This step, as foolish as it was, drew on me in the country a sort of respect which was useful to me. Some thought I had a fortune I had not; others, seeing me devoted entirely to music, judged of my talents by the sacrifice I made, and supposed that with so great a passion for the art, I must possess it in a superior degree. In blindman's kingdom squinters wear crowns; I there passed for an experienced master, because they had none but poor ones. Having, nevertheless, a taste in singing, favoured besides by youth and person, I had soon more female scholars than needed to replace my salary of secretary.

It is certain that, for an agreeable life, you could not pass more rapidly from one extremity to the other. At the office, employed eight hours a day in the most disagreeable business, with people still more disagreeable; shut up in a pitiful office, stinking with the breath and sweat of so many clowns, most of them not combed and very dirty, I sometimes felt myself oppressed even to dizziness by attention, stench, constraint, and weariness. Instead of this, I am immediately thrown amongst the beau monde, admitted, sent for to the first families; everywhere a kind and gracious reception, an air of welcome: amiable young girls, neatly dressed, wait my arrival, receive me officiously; I see none but charming objects, smell nothing but rose and orange flower waters; we sing, we converse, we laugh, we divert ourselves; I go from there only to do the same elsewhere. It must be agreed that, as to advantage, one could not hesitate a moment in the choice. I so much approved of mine, I never once repented; neither do I repent at this instant, when I weigh in the balance of reason the actions of my life, and when I am freed of those motives, senseless enough, which governed me.

This is almost the only time that, listening to my inclinations only, I was not deceived in my expectations. The unaffected reception, the easy temper, the complying humours of the inhabitants of the country, rendered an intercourse with the world amiable to me; and the satisfaction I then had in it, proves to me beyond a doubt that, if I cannot live amongst mankind, it is less my fault than theirs.

It is a pity the Savoyards are not rich, or, perhaps, it would be a pity they were; for as they are, they are the best and the most sociable people I am acquainted with. If there is a little city in the world where the comforts of life are tasted through an agreeable intercourse, it is Chambéry. The nobility of the province gathered there have no more fortune than will support them; they have not enough to aspire after ambition, and not being able to give themselves up to it, they follow, from necessity, the counsel of Cyneas.[1] Their youth they devote to a military life; then return, and peaceably grow old at home. Honour and reason preside at this division. The women have beauty, but could do without it; they possess all that makes beauty valuable, or that takes its place. It is singular that, my situation introducing me into the company of young women, I do not remember to have seen one at Chambéry who had not charms. You will say I was disposed to think so: that may be; but it required no effort of mine. I cannot really recall, without pleasure, the remembrance of my young scholars. Why cannot I, whilst I am naming the most amiable, call them back with myself to that happy youth, when we spent days together as sweet as they were innocent! The first was Mademoiselle de Mellarède, my neighbour, sister to the pupil of M. Gaime. She was a black-eyed girl, and very lively; but her vivacity was very caressing, full of grace, and without giddiness. She was rather thin, as most girls of her age are; but her sparkling eyes, fine shape, and attractive air, wanted no *embonpoint* to make her pleasing. I went there in the morning; she was generally in a deshabille, without any other headdress than her hair carelessly turned up, adorned with some flowers, which were put on at my arrival, and taken off at my departure. I fear nothing so much as a pretty woman in an undress; I should have dreaded her a hundred times less in her dress. Mademoiselle de Menthon, whom I attended in the afternoon, was always dressed; she made as soft an impression on me, but in a very different manner. Her hair was of an ash-coloured white: she was extremely delicate, extremely timid, and extremely fair; a clear, just, and soft voice, but which dared not display itself. She had a mark on her bosom from a scald of boiling water, which a blue corded handkerchief did not well hide. This mark

---

[1] The minister of Pyrrhus, King of Epirus.

sometimes drew my attention that way, which was soon drawn to
something else besides the scar. Mademoiselle de Challes, another
of my neighbours, was a girl grown up, tall, a fine chest, fleshy;
very clever. She was not a beauty; but might be cited as graceful,
even-tempered, and good-natured. Her sister, Madame de Charly,
the finest woman in Chambéry, no longer learnt music, but had
her daughter taught, who was yet very young, but whose rising
beauty promised to equal her mother's, had she not unfortunately
been a little carroty. I had, at the Visitation, a little French lady,
whose name I have forgot, but who merits a place in the list of my
preferences. She had taken the slow drawling tone of the nuns,
and with this drawling tone she said very smart things, which did
not seem to belong to her character. As to the rest, she was lazy,
did not love to be at the trouble of showing her wit, and it was a
favour she did not grant everyone. It was not till after a month or
two's lessons and negligence she chose this expedient to make me
more assiduous; for I never could determine to be so. I was pleased
with my lessons when at them, but did not like to be obliged to go
or be governed by the clock: at all times constraint and subjection
are, to me, insupportable; they would make me hate pleasure itself. They say, that, with the Mahometans, a man passes, at day-
break, through the streets, to order husbands to do their duty to
their wives; I should make a bad Turk at those hours.

I had also a few scholars of the middle rank, and one amongst
the rest who was the indirect cause of a change of correspondence
I shall speak of, as I have promised to tell all. She was a grocer's
daughter, whose name was Mlle. Lard, the true model of a Greek
statue, whom I should cite as the finest girl I ever saw, was there
a real beauty without life or soul. Her indolence, her coldness, her
insensibility, were carried to a degree almost incredible. It was as
impossible to please as to anger her; and I am persuaded that, had
an attempt been made on her, she had let it be done, not by inclination, but through stupidity. Her mother, who would not run
the risk of it, never left her a moment. By having her taught to
sing, sending her a young master, she did all in her power to stir
her up; but it did not succeed. Whilst the master ogled the daughter, the mother ogled the master, and that did not succeed much
better. Madame Lard added to her natural vivacity all her daughter should have had. She had a little sharp rough face, pitted with
the smallpox; small eyes extremely piercing, and a little red,
because they were almost always sore. Every morning, on my
arrival, I found my coffee and cream always ready; and the

mother never failed welcoming me with a kiss well applied to the lips, and which, from curiosity, I would have wished to have returned to the daughter, to see how she would have taken it. However, the whole was done so simply, and with so little consequence, that when M. Lard were there the ogles and kisses went on in the same manner. He was a good honest fellow; the real father of his daughter, whom his wife did not deceive, because there was no occasion for it.

I gave into all these caresses with my usual blockishness, taking them good-naturedly as marks of sincere friendship. They were, however, sometimes troublesome, for the lively Mme. Lard was nothing less than very urgent; and if, in the course of the day, I had passed by the shop without stopping, there would have been a stir about it. I was obliged, if in a hurry, to go round by another street, well assured it was not so easy to get out of her house as to go into it.

Madame Lard took too much notice of me not to have some taken of her. Her attention touched me greatly: I spoke of it to Mamma, as of a thing without mystery, and had there been any, I had equally told her of it; for to keep any kind of secret from her was, to me, an impossibility; my heart was open to her as to God. She did not see the affair with quite the same simplicity as I did. She saw advances where I saw nothing but friendship; she judged that Madame Lard, making a point of honour of leaving me less stupid than she found me, would arrive, by some means or other, at making herself understood; and, besides that it was not just any other woman should take charge of her pupil, she had motives more worthy of her to secure me from the traps my age and profession exposed me to. At the same time another was laid of a different kind, which I escaped; but which let her see, that the dangers which incessantly threatened me rendered every preservative in her power necessary.

The Countess of Menthon, mother of one of my scholars, was a woman of much wit, and was said to have as much ill nature. She was the cause, it was said, of many disputes, and, amongst others, one whose consequences had been fatal to the House of d'Antremont. Mamma had been sufficiently connected with her to know her character: having very innocently inspired an inclination in one on whom Madame de Menthon had pretensions, she was charged by her with the crime of this preference, though she was neither sought nor accepted; and Madame de Menthon endeavoured, from that time, to play her rival many tricks, of which not one succeeded. I shall relate one of the oddest by way of sample. They were together in the country with several gentlemen of the neighbourhood, and amongst them the candidate in question. Madame de Menthon one day said to one of the gentlemen, that Madame de Warens was but a formal creature, without taste, dressed badly, and covered her neck like a tradeswoman. As to the last article, says the gentleman, who was a witty fellow, she has her reasons; for I know she has a great ugly rat marked on her breast, but so natural, that you would think it was running along. Hatred, like love, renders us credulous. Madame de Menthon resolved to make something of this discovery; and one day, when Mamma was at cards with the ungrateful favourite of the lady, this last took the opportunity of going behind her rival, and turning her chair half over, she artfully drew off her handkerchief. But, instead of a great rat, the gentleman saw a very different object, which it was not easier to forget than perceive. This did not at all answer the lady's intention.

I was not a person fit to occupy the thoughts of Madame de Menthon, who would have none but bright sparks about her. However, she showed me some attention; not for my person, for which, certainly, she cared not a fig, but for the wit it was supposed I had, which might have rendered me useful to her inclinations. Hers was satirical enough. She was fond of composing songs and verses on those who displeased her. If she had thought my talents sufficient to assist her in her verses, and that I had complaisance to write them, between her and me Chambéry had soon been turned upside down. The source of these libels would soon have been traced; Madame de Menthon would have got out of the hobble by sacrificing me, and I had been shut up, perhaps, the remainder of my days, to teach me to act the Phoebus with the ladies.

Luckily nothing of all this happened. Madame de Menthon kept me to dinner two or three times, to make me chatter, and found I was a stupid fellow. I felt it myself, and trembled, envying the talents of my friend Venture, when I ought to have thanked my blockishness for saving me from such perils. I remained the singing-master of Madame de Menthon's daughter, nothing farther; but I lived in tranquillity, and always welcomed in Chambéry. That was better than being a wit to her, and a serpent to the rest of the country.

Be that as it may, Mamma saw that, to keep me from the dangers of youth, it was time to treat me as a man; and so she did, but in the most singular manner any woman thought of on a like occasion. I found her looks more grave, and her conversation more moral than usual. To the frolicsome gaiety with which she generally mixed her instruction, all at once succeeded a regular voice, which was neither familiar nor severe, but which seemed to prepare an explanation. Having vainly sought in myself the reason of this change, I asked it her; this was what she expected. She proposed a walk in the little garden for the morrow; we were there early. She had taken her measures that we might be alone the whole day: she made use of it to prepare me for the kindness she intended showing me, not, like other women, by managing and ogling me, but by a conversation full of sentiment and reason, more adapted to instruct than seduce me, and which spoke more to my heart than my senses. However excellent and useful her discourse to me might be, and though it was neither cold nor tiresome, I did not pay it the attention it deserved; nor did I imprint it in my memory, as I should have done at other times. Her introduction, her method of preparing, made me uneasy: whilst she was talking, thoughtful and inattentive, in spite of myself, I thought on what she said less than on what she intended to say, and as soon as I understood her, which was not very easy, the novelty of the idea, which since I lived with her never once struck me, immediately employed my thoughts so much, it did not leave me master of giving the least attention to what she spoke of. I thought of her only, and did not listen to her.

Wanting to make young people attentive to what you would tell them, by showing them at the end an object which much concerns them, is an error teachers are very apt to fall into, and which I myself have not avoided in my *Emile*. A young man, struck with the object before him, is entirely employed on it, and takes large strides over your preliminary discourse, to grasp at once the end to which, in his opinion, you lead him too slowly. If you would render him attentive, do not let him penetrate you beforehand, and in this Mamma was very awkward. By a singularity which was part of her systematical temper, she stook the very vain precaution of proposing conditions; but, as soon as I saw the prize, I thought no more of them, and hastened to consent to everything. I even much doubt whether, in such a case, there is on the earth a man frank enough, or who has fortitude, to dare hesitate; or a single woman who, if he did, could forgive him. From a consequence of this humour, she added to this agreement the gravest formalities, and gave me eight days to think of it, of which I falsely

assured her I had no occasion; for, to fill up the measure of singularity, I was glad of them, so much did the novelty of these
ideas strike me, and so total a confusion did I feel in mine, that it
required time to arrange them!

You would think these eight days were to me eight ages. No
such thing; I should have been glad if they had lasted so long. I am
at a loss to describe the situation I was in, filled with a kind of
dread mixed with impatience, fearing what I desired, so much as
at times heartily to seek for some honourable means of avoiding
happiness. Let anyone represent to himself my warm and lascivious constitution, my blood inflamed, my heart intoxicated with
love, my vigour, my health, my age; think that in this state,
greedy with desire for women, I had not yet come near one; that
imagination, necessity, vanity, and curiosity, united to devour
me with the ardent wish of being a man, and appearing one; add,
above all, for it should not be forgot, that my lively and tender
attachment for her, far from cooling, had daily increased; that I
was never easy but with her; that I never left her but to think of
her; that my heart was full, not only of her kindness and her
amiable character, but of her sex, her face, her person, in a word,
of herself, under every view in which she could be dear to me:
and let it not be imagined that, for the ten or twelve years I was
younger than her, she was grown old, or appeared so to me. Since
the five or six years I felt the soft transports on her first sight, she
was really very little altered, and did not seem to me to be so at all.
She has always appeared charming to me, and was still so to
everyone. Her waist only was grown a little thicker. There remained the same eye, the same skin, the same neck, the same
features, the same fine flaxen hair, the same gaiety, everything
the same even to her voice, the clear voice of youth, which always
made on me so great an impression, that to this day I cannot hear
without emotion the sound of a girl's fine voice.

In fact, the most I had to fear in waiting for the possession of
so lovely a person, was anticipation, and not being able sufficiently
to govern my desires and my imagination to be master of myself.
You will see that, in an advanced age, the thought only of a
trifling favour which awaited me from the beloved person, fired
my blood to a degree of rendering impossible the going over with
impunity the short space that separated me from her. How, and
by what prodigy, in the flower of my youth, had I so little desire
to the first possession? How could I see the hour approach with
more pain than pleasure? How, instead of delights which should

have intoxicated me, did I feel almost repugnance and fear? There
is not the least doubt of my having flown from this happiness with
all my heart, could I have done it with decency. I promised extravagances in the history of my affection for her; this is certainly
one little to be expected.

The reader, already shocked, judges that, having been possessed
by another, she had debased herself in my eyes, by dividing her
affection, and that a sentiment of disesteem had cooled those she
had before inspired: he is mistaken. This division, it is true, gave
me great pain, as well from natural delicacy, as because, in fact,
I thought it unworthy herself or me; but as to my feelings for her,
it did not change them; and I can swear that never did I love her
more tenderly than when I so little desired to possess her. I was too
well acquainted with the chastity of her heart, and her frozen
constitution, to think for a moment the pleasures of sense had any
part in this abandoning herself: I was perfectly sure, that her
attention to tearing me from dangers otherwise inevitable, and to
keeping me entirely to myself and my devoirs, made her break
through one which she did not regard from the same point of view
as other women, as we shall hereafter see. I pitied her, and pitied
myself. I had an inclination to tell her, No, Mamma, it is not
necessary; I can answer for myself without it. But I dared not;
first, because it was a thing to be said, and that at the bottom I
knew it was not true; and that, in fact, a woman was necessary to
keep me from other women, and secure me from temptation.
Without wishing to possess her, I was glad she prevented me from
wishing to possess others; so much did I look on everything which
could divert me from her as a misfortune.

The long habit of living together, and living innocently, far
from weakening my feelings for her, strengthened them, but at
the same time had given them another turn, which rendered them
more affectionate, tenderer perhaps, but less sensual. By continually calling her Mamma, continually using with her the
familiarity of a son, I had grown accustomed to think myself so.
I believe this is the true cause of the little desire I had to possess
her, though she was so dear to me. I very well remember that my
first feelings, without being more lively, were more voluptuous.
At Annecy I was infatuated; at Chambéry I was no longer so.
I loved her as passionately as it was possible; but I loved her more
for herself and less for me, or rather I sought my happiness more
than my pleasure in her company: she was more to me than a
sister, more than a mother, more than a friend, even more than a

mistress, and that was the cause she was not a mistress. In fine, I loved her too much to covet her: this is the clearest of anything I have in my ideas.

The day, rather dreaded than awaited, at last came. I promised everything, and kept my promise. My heart confirmed my engagements, without wishing the reward. I obtained it nevertheless; I found myself, for the first time, in a woman's arms, and that the woman I adored. Was I happy? No, I tasted pleasure. I do not know what invincible sadness poisoned its charms. I was as if I had committed incest. Two or three times, pressing her with transport to my arms, I poured on her breast a torrent of tears. As for her, she was neither happy nor unhappy; she was caressing and calm. As she was little sensual, and did not wish for sensual pleasures, she had not its delights, nor has ever felt its remorse.

I repeat it; all her faults proceeded from error, never from her passions. She was of a good family; her heart was uncorrupt; she loved good manners; her inclinations were upright and virtuous, her taste delicate: she was born to an elegance of morals she always loved and never followed; for, instead of listening to her heart, which led her right, she obeyed her reason, which led her wrong. When false principles had led her astray, her true feelings always contradicted them; but unhappily, she piqued herself on philosophy, and the morals she had built for herself infected those her heart dictated.

M. de Tavel, her first lover, was her teacher in philosophy, and the principles he instilled in her were those which were necessary to seduce her. Finding her true to her husband and her duty, reserved, reasoning and unattackable through the senses, he attacked her by his sophisms, and arrived at exposing her duties, to which she was so attached, as the prating of a catechism invented only to amuse children; the union of the sexes as an act most indifferent in itself; conjugal faith as binding in appearance, whose only morality regarded opinion; the repose of a husband as the only rule of a wife's duty; so that secret infidelity, without existence for the offended person, was so likewise for the conscience: in fine, he persuaded her that the thing in itself was nothing, that it took its existence from scandal only, and that every woman who appeared prudent was effectually so. It was thus the scoundrel arrived at corrupting the reason of a child, whose heart he could not corrupt. His punishment was a consuming jealousy, persuaded she treated him as he had taught her to treat her husband. I do not know that he was mistaken. The minister Perret passed as his successor. Thus much I know, the cold constitution of this young woman, which should have guarded her from such a system, was the very thing that prevented her from quitting it afterwards. She could not conceive how a thing could be treated with such importance, which was of none to her. She never honoured with the name of virtue an abstinence which cost her so little.

She had, therefore, hardly made an ill use of these false principles for herself; but she made an ill use of them for others, and that from almost as false a maxim, but more agreeable to the goodness of her heart. She always believed nothing so much attached a man to a woman as possession; and although she loved her friends but with friendship, it was a friendship so tender, she made use of every means in her power to attach them to her more strongly. The most extraordinary is her almost always having succeeded. She was so really amiable, that the greater the intimacy with her, the more you found new subjects for loving her. Another thing worthy remark; after her first weakness, she seldom favoured any but the unfortunate: shining sparks had all their trouble for nothing, but the man she began by pitying, must have had very few amiable qualities, if she did not end by loving him. When her choice was not worthy her, far from its proceeding from low inclinations, which never reached her noble heart, it was solely from her character, too generous, too humane, too compassionate, too tender, which she did not always govern with discernment.

If a few false principles led her astray, how many amiable ones had she not which she never departed from? By how many virtues did she not redeem her weaknesses, if errors can be called by this name, where sense had so little share! The same man who deceived her in one point, had excellently instructed her in a thousand others; and her passions not being warm, and always permitting her to follow her understanding, she did right when his sophisms did not lead her away. Her motives were praiseworthy even in her faults; through mistake she might do ill, but it was out of her power to wish to do ill. She abhorred duplicity and lies: she was just, equitable, humane, disinterested, faithful to her word, to her friends, to duties she acknowledged to be such, incapable of vengeance or hatred, and could not even conceive there was the least merit in pardoning. In fine, to return to that which was least excuseable in her, without esteeming her favours of any price, she never made a base traffic of them; she bestowed them plentifully, but never sold them, though she was very often at the last penny; and I dare advance, that if Socrates could esteem Aspasia, he would have respected Madame de Warens.

I know beforehand that, in giving her a character of tenderness and a cold constitution, I shall be accused of contradiction, as usual, and with as much reason. Nature might have been to blame, and they ought not, perhaps, to have met; I only know that so it was. All those who were acquainted with Madame de Warens, whereof a great number still exist, know that thus she was. I dare add she knew but one sole pleasure; it was giving it those she loved. Everyone, however, has a right to argue on it at pleasure, and learnedly to prove it false. My function is to tell truth, but not to make it believed.

I learnt, from time to time, what I have just said, in conversations which followed our union, and which only rendered it delightful. She was right when she thought her complaisance might be useful to me for my instruction; I drew great benefit from it. She had till then talked of myself alone as to a child. She began to treat me as a man, and to talk of herself. Everything she said concerned me so much, I found myself so touched by it, that, turning it in my mind, I applied her confidence to my advantage more than I had done her lessons. When we really feel the heart speak, ours opens to receive its overflowings, and never will all the morality of a pedagogue equal the tender and affectionate prattle of a sensible woman for whom you have an attachment.

The intimacy in which I lived with her, having enabled her to judge more advantageously of me than before, she judged that, in spite of my awkward look, I was worth the trouble of putting forward in the world, and that could I once reach it I should make my road. On this idea she undertook, not only to form my judgement, but my exterior, my manners, to render me amiable as well as estimable; and if it is true that success in the world can be allied to virtue, which is what I do not believe, I am certain, at least, there is no other road than that she had taken, and would have led me: for Madame de Warens knew mankind, and understood, in a superior degree, the art of treating with them without falsehood or imprudence, without deceiving or angering them. But this art was in her character more than her lessons; she better knew to practise than teach it, and I was of all men the least apt to learn it. Thus all she did in this respect was almost thrown away, as well as her attention in procuring me dancing and fencing masters. Though light and well enough made, I could not learn to dance a minuet. I had so far got a habit, on account of my corns, of

walking on my heels, Roche could not break me of it, and never,
with my nimble appearance, could I leap over a middling ditch.
It was worse at the fencing-school. After three months' lessons,
I was still at the mark, unable to fence; nor ever had a hand supple
enough, or an arm strong enough, to hold a foil, whenever my
master chose to make it fly. Add to this, I had a mortal hatred to
the exercise, and for the master who endeavoured to teach me.
I could not have believed a man could be so proud of the art of
killing a man. To bring his vast genius within my reach, he expressed himself only by comparisons from music, which he did
not understand. He found a striking analogy between tierce and
quart, and the musical intervals of the same name. When he intended a feint, he told me to look out for the sharp, because formerly the sharp was called a *feint:* when he had made my foil
fly, he said, with a sneer, that was a *stop*. In fine, I never in my
life saw a pedant so insupportable as this poor creature with his
plume and his fencing-jacket.

I therefore made little progress in my exercises, which I soon
quitted from pure disgust; but I did better in a more useful art,
that of being contented with my lot, without desiring one more
brilliant, for which I began to see I was not made. Entirely given
up to the desire of making Mamma's days happy, I always took
pleasure in her company; and when I was obliged to leave her to
run to town, in spite of my passion for music, I began to feel the
constraint of my lessons.

I do not know whether Claude Anet perceived the intimacy
between us. I have reason to believe it was not hid from him. He

was a young fellow who could see clearly, but discreetly; who never spoke contrary to his thoughts, but did not always speak them. Without taking the least notice to me that he knew it, by his conduct he seemed to me to be acquainted with it; and this conduct did not certainly proceed from meanness of spirit, but, having given in to the principles of his mistress, he could not disapprove of her acting in consequence of them. Although he was as young as she, he was so staid and so grave, he regarded us almost as two children worthy indulgence, and we regarded him, each of us, as a respectable man, whose esteem we would merit. It was not till after her unfaithfulness to him I was acquainted with the whole attachment she had for him. As she knew I thought, felt, or breathed by her only, she let me perceive how much she loved him, that I might love him likewise; she dwelt less on her friendship than her esteem for him, as it was the sentiment I could more fully partake of. How many times did she not melt our hearts and make us embrace each other with tears, telling us we were both necessary to the happiness of her life! But let not those women who read this, ill-naturedly smile; with the constitution she had, this necessity was not equivocal; it was solely that of her heart.

Thus was established amongst us three a society without perhaps other example on earth. All our wishes, our cares, our hearts, were one. None of them passed beyond this little circle. The habit of living together, and living exclusively, became so great, that if at our meals, one of the three was wanting, or a fourth came in, all was confusion, and, in spite of our particular connexion, tête-à-têtes were less charming than our reunion. That which prevented constraint amongst us was our extreme reciprocal confidence, and that which prevented dulness was our being always employed. Mamma, always projecting and continually active, left neither of us very idle; we had each of us separately enough to fill up all our time. In my opinion, idleness is no less the pest of society than of solitude. Nothing contracts the mind, nothing engenders trifles, tales, backbitings, slander, and falsities, so much as being for ever shut up in a room opposite each other, reduced to no other occupation than the necessity of continually chattering. When everyone is employed, one speaks only when one has something to say; but if you are doing nothing, you must absolutely talk incessantly, and this of all constraints is the most troublesome and the most dangerous. I dare go even farther, and maintain that, to render a circle truly agreeable, everyone must be not only doing something, but something which requires a little attention.

To make knots is to make nothing; and it is as necessary to amuse a woman who is making knots, as when she holds her arms across. But when she is embroidering, that is another thing; she is sufficiently employed to fill up the intervals of silence. The most shocking and ridiculous is, to see, during that time, a dozen awkward fellows get up, sit down, go, come, turn on their heels, take up a hundred times the apes on the chimney-piece, and tire their Minerva to support an inexhaustible flow of words; a fine occupation! These people, do what they can, will always be a burden to others and to themselves. When I was at Motiers, I sat down with my neighbours to make laces: should I once more mix with the world, I will carry in my pocket a cup and ball, to play with it the whole day, to dispense me from talking when I have nothing to say. If everyone did so, mankind would be less wicked, their friendship more certain, and I believe more agreeable. In fine, let wags laugh if they will; I maintain that the only morals within the reach of the present age are cup and ball morals.

However, avoiding dulness was not left entirely to ourselves; troublesome visitors caused us too much by their numbers to leave us any when alone. The uneasiness they gave me of old was not decreased; the whole difference consisted in my having less time to think of it. Poor Mamma had not got rid of her old fancy for projects and systems. On the contrary, the more her domestic wants became pressing, the more, to provide for them, she gave in to her visions. The less present resources she had, the more she expected in future. The progress of years only increased this passion in her; and still, as she lost her taste for the pleasures of youth and the world, she replaced them by secrets and projects. The house was not cleared of quacks, manufacturers, seekers of the philosophers' stone, jacks of all trades, who, distributing fortune by millions, ended in wanting half a crown. None went from her empty, and that which astonished me was, that she could suffice so long to so much profusion, without draining the source, and tiring her creditors.

The plan which most employed her at the time I speak of, and which was not one of her most unreasonable ones, was to form at Chambéry a royal garden of botany, with a paid Demonstrator: the person intended for this place may be easily guessed. The position of this city, in the centre of the Alps, was extremely favourable to botany; and Mamma, who made one project easy by another, added to it that of a college of pharmacy, which really seemed extremely useful in so poor a country, where apothecaries are almost the sole physicians. The Proto-physician Grossi's retiring to Chambéry, after the death of King Victor, seemed greatly to favour this idea, and perhaps suggested it to her. Be that as it may, she set about cajoling Grossi, who was not, however, very cajolable; for he was the most caustic and the most brutal gentleman I have ever been acquainted with. You may judge of him by two or three stories I shall give you by way of sample.

He was once in consultation with some other physicians, and, amongst them, one who had been sent for from Annecy, and who was the sick person's usual physician. This young man, but yet little learned for a physician, dared to be of a different opinion from M. Proto. This last, in answer, asked him, when he returned home, which road he took, and what carriage he should go in. The other, having satisfied him, asked him, in his turn, whether there was anything he could do for him. Nothing, nothing, said Grossi, only I will go to some window to see an ass go by on horseback. He was as avaricious as rich and hard-hearted. One day a friend of his wanted to borrow some money of him on good security. My friend, says he to him, squeezing his arms, and at the same time grinning, should St. Peter come down from Heaven to borrow of me ten pistoles, and the Trinity would be bound for the payment, I would not lend him the money. Being invited to dine one day with the Count Picon, Governor of Savoy, and extremely devout, he came before the hour; his Excellency, being occupied at his prayers, proposed the same amusement to him. Not knowing what to say, he makes a wry face, and falls on his knees. But he had scarcely said two *Ave Marias*, when, not being able to hold any longer, he gets up in a hurry, takes his cane, and goes off without a word. Count Picon runs after him, and cries out, Stay, M. Grossi, stay; they have got below an excellent red partridge on the spit. Count! says he, and turns round, if you had a roasted angel I would not stay. This was the character of the Proto-physician Grossi, whom Mamma undertook and succeeded in taming. Though extremely occupied, he often used to call on her, had a friendship for Anet, seemed to think him intelligent, spoke of him with esteem, and, what would not be expected from such a bear, affected to treat him with consideration, to wipe off the impression of the past. For though Anet was not now on the footing of a servant, it was known he had been one, and nothing less than the example and authority of the Proto-physician was necessary to authorize a tone which otherwise would not have been relished. Claude Anet, with a black coat, a well-dressed wig, a grave and decent carriage, a prudent and circumspect bearing, a knowledge pretty extensive in medicinal and botanical matters, and favoured by the head of the faculty, might reasonably hope to fill with applause the place of Demonstrator royal of plants, if the proposed institution took place; and Grossi really relished the plan, had adopted it, and to propose it to government waited only until peace should permit it to think of useful things, and give opportunity to assist it with the necessary supplies.

But this project, whose execution had probably thrown me into botany, for which it seems to me I was born, failed by one of those unexpected strokes which overturn the best-concerted plans. I was fated to become, by degrees, an example of human miseries. One would think Providence, which invited me to these great trials, dispelled with its hand everything that could prevent me from falling into them. In a trip Anet made to the top of the mountains to look for genipi, a scarce plant which grows only on the Alps, and which M. Grossi wanted, the poor fellow so far heated himself as to bring on a pleurisy, of which the genipi could not cure him, though it is, they say, specifical for it; and with all the art of Grossi, who was certainly an able man, the infinite care taken of him by his kind mistress and me, he died the fifth day, under our hands, after the most cruel sufferings, during which he had no other exhortations than mine, but which were given with affectionate zeal and anguish, such as, had he been in a situation of understanding them, must have been of some consolation to him. Thus I lost the most solid friend I ever had; a man valuable and scarce, in whom Nature supplied the place of education, who cherished in servitude all the virtues of illustrious men, and to whom nothing more perhaps was wanting to show himself such to the world, than life and a place.

The next day I talked of him to Mamma with a lively and sincere affliction; and, all at once, in the midst of the conversation, I had the base and unworthy thought of my succeeding to his clothes, and particularly a neat black coat which I fancied. I thought so, and consequently said so; for with her it was to me the same thing. Nothing so plainly showed her the loss she had sustained, as this sordid, odious word; disinterestedness and a noble soul being qualities the deceased had eminently possessed. The poor creature, without answering, turned her head away and cried bitterly. Dear and precious tears! They were felt and ran all to my inward soul; they washed from it every trace of base and dishonest sentiment; none ever entered there since that time.

This loss was as prejudicial as painful to Mamma. From this instant her affairs incessantly declined. Anet was an exact, orderly young man, who took care there was regularity in his mistress's house. They dreaded his vigilance, and there was less waste. She herself dreaded his censure, and contracted her dissipations. His attachment was not sufficient for her; she would have his esteem; and she feared the just reproach he sometimes dared to cast at her, telling her she wasted the good of others as well as her own. I thought the same as he, and even said so; but I had not the same influence over her, and my words were not as weighty as his. When he was no more, I was forced to take his place, for which I had as little aptitude as inclination; I filled it ill. I was not careful, very timid, and grumbling to myself only, I let all go on as it would. Besides, though I had gained the same confidence, I had not the same authority. I saw the disorder; I trembled at it, complained, but was not listened to. I was too young and too hasty to claim a right to reason; and when I took on me to act the reformer, Mamma gave me caressing boxes on the ear, called me her little Mentor, and obliged me to return to the part for which I was better suited.

The deep sense of the distress her unmeasured expenses must sooner or later bring her to, made the stronger impression on me as, being now the inspector of her house, I judged myself of the disproportion of the debtor and creditor side of the question. I date from this period the inclination I have always found to avarice since that time. I never was foolishly prodigal but by fits; but till then I gave myself little trouble about how little or how much money I had. I began to give this attention, and be careful of my purse. I became mean from a noble motive; for I really thought only to keep a little resource for Mamma in the catastrophe I foresaw. I feared her creditors might seize her pension, or that it might be entirely taken off; and I imagined, according to my narrow views, that my little hoard might then greatly assist her. But to form it, and particularly to preserve it, I must hide it from her; for it would not have been safe, when she was at the last expedient, that she should be acquainted with my little treasure. I therefore sought sly places here and there to thrust a few guineas into as a deposit, intending to increase the deposit incessantly, until the instant I threw it into her lap. But I was so awkward in the choice of my hiding-holes, that she always discovered them; and to let me know she had found them, she took out the gold, and put in a larger sum in different coin. I posted, quite ashamed, to bring back my little treasure to the common purse; but she never failed laying it out to my advantage in clothes, or other things, as a silver-hilted sword, watch, or some such thing.

Well convinced that I should never succeed in accumulating, and that it would be but a slender resource for her, I saw, in fine, I had no other against the misfortune I dreaded than to put myself in a situation of providing for her subsistence, when, ceasing to support me, she might see herself in want of bread. Unhappily, making my projects subservient to my inclinations, I persisted in foolishly seeking my fortune in music, and finding ideas and tunes rise in my brain, I thought that as soon as I should begin to get money by it, I should become a man of note, a modern Orpheus, whose notes would attract all the money of Peru. The question was, as I began to read music passably, how to learn composition. The difficulty lay in getting someone to teach me; for with my Rameau only I could not expect to attain it alone, and after the departure of M. Le Maître, there was no one in Savoy who understood the least of harmony.

Here you will see another of those inconsequences with which my whole life is filled, and which have so often led me from my object, even when I thought I was going directly to it. Venture had said a great deal to me of the Abbé Blanchard, who taught him to compose; a man of merit and great talents, then music-master to the cathedral of Besançon, and now to the cappella of Versailles. I took it in my head to go to Besançon to take a lesson of the Abbé Blanchard: the idea appeared so reasonable to me, I persuaded Mamma to think so likewise. She sets to work to equip me, and with the profusion she showed in everything. Thus continually planning how to prevent a bankruptcy, and to repair in future the work of her dissipation, I was at that instant putting her to an expense of eight hundred livres: I accelerated her ruin to put me in a situation to prevent it. However silly this conduct might be, the illusion got entirely hold of me, and even of her. We were both equally persuaded, I that I was usefully labouring for her good, and she that I was usefully labouring for my own.

I expected to find Venture still at Annecy, and to ask him for a letter to the Abbé Blanchard, He was gone. I was obliged to content myself as my only instructor, with a four-part mass of his composing, and which he had left with me. With this recommendation I go to Besançon, by way of Geneva, where I saw my relations, and through Nyon, where I saw my father, who received me as usual, and undertook to send my portmanteau, which was coming after me, as I was on horseback. I arrive at Besançon. The Abbé Blanchard receives me well, promises to instruct me, and offers me his services. We were just beginning, when I learn from my father that my portmanteau had been stopped, and confiscated at Rousses, a post of France on the frontiers of Switzerland. Affrighted at this news, I make use of the acquaintance I had made at Besançon to know the motive of this confiscation; for being certain of its having nothing prohibited, I could not conceive on what pretext they could seize it. I learnt it at last: it must be told, for it is a curious affair.

I went to see at Chambéry an old man from Lyons, a very good sort of man; his name was Duvivier; he had been employed in the Chancery under the Regency, and, for want of employment, came to assist at the Registry of the lands. He had lived well; had talents, some knowledge, was mild, polite, knew music, and, as we were of the same room, we preferred each other's company to that of the unlicked bears who surrounded us. He had correspondents at Paris, who supplied him with those trifles, those ephemeral novelties, which have a day's run one cannot tell why, which die one cannot tell how, without anyone's ever thinking of them after they have ceased talking of them. As I sometimes took him to dinner to Mamma's, he in some sort made his court to me, and, to make himself agreeable, he endeavoured to give me a taste for this rubbish, for which I had so great a disgust. I have never in my life read one when alone. To make myself agreeable to him, I took these precious scraps of paper, thrust them into my pocket, and thought no more of them except for the only purpose for which they were fitted. Unfortunately, one of these cursed papers was left in the waistcoat-pocket of a new suit I had worn but two or three times, in order to make all regular with the officials. The paper was a Jansenist parody, flat enough, of the beautiful scene of Racine's *Mithridate*. I had not read ten verses, and left it through forgetfulness in my pocket. This caused the seizure of my whole equipment. The officials placed at the top of the inventory of my portmanteau a magnificent *procès-verbal*, wherein, imagining the writing came from Geneva to be printed and distributed in France, they gave scope to holy invectives against the enemies of God and the Church, and to praises of their pious vigilance who had stopped the execution of this infernal project. They doubtless found likewise my shirts smell of heresy; for, by virtue of this terrible paper, all was confiscated without

my ever, for all I could do, having had account or news of my
poor little bundle. The Farmers-general, who were applied to,
demanded so many documents, informations, certificates, memorials, that, losing myself a thousand times in this labyrinth, I
was constrained to abandon all together. I have often regretted
I did not keep the *procès-verbal* of the post of Rousses. It was a
piece which might figure with distinction amidst those of which a
collection accompanies this work.

This loss obliged me to return to Chambéry immediately, without having done anything with the Abbé Blanchard; and, all
things weighed, seeing misfortune attend all my undertakings,
I resolved to keep entirely to Mamma, to share her fortune, and
not make myself in vain uneasy for an hereafter about which I
saw I could no nothing. She received me as if I had brought her
treasures, replaced by degrees my little wardrobe, and my misfortune, bad enough for both of us, was almost as soon forgot as
it happened.

Although this accident cooled me as to my schemes of music,
I did not, nevertheless, neglect to study continually my Rameau,
and by repeated efforts I arrived at last at understanding him,
and making a few trials at composing, whose success encouraged
me. The Count of Bellegarde, son to the Marquis of Antremont,
was returned from Dresden, after the death of King Augustus.
He had lived a great while at Paris, was very fond of music, and
passionately so of Rameau's. His brother, the Count of Nangis,
played the violin, Madame the Countess of la Tour, their sister,

sang a little. These things brought music in fashion at Chambéry, and a sort of public concert was begun, of which they intended to have given me the direction, but soon perceived it surpassed my strength, and settled it otherwise. I nevertheless gave some trifling pieces in my manner, particularly a cantata, which greatly pleased. It was not a good piece, but it was filled with new tunes, and things of effect, which were not expected from me. These gentlemen could not believe that, reading music so ill, I was capable of composing it passably, and did not doubt but I had honoured myself with the goods of my neighbours. To verify it, M. de Nangis came to me one morning with a cantata of Clérambault he had transposed, as he said, for the convenience of the voice, and to which another bass was necessary, the transposition rendering that of Clérambault impracticable on the instrument. I answered it was a considerable labour, and could not be done immediately. He thought I sought to put him off, and pressed me to do at least the bass of a recitative. I therefore did it, ill undoubtedly, because in all things, in order to succeed well, I must have ease and liberty; but I did it at least according to rule, and, as he was present, he could not doubt my knowledge of the elements of composing. Thus I did not lose my scholars, but I cooled a little on music, seeing they had a concert, and did not choose me.

It was about this time, peace being concluded, the French army repassed the mountains. Several officers came to visit Mamma; among the rest the Count de Lautrec, Colonel of the regiment of Orleans, since Plenipotentiary at Geneva, and afterwards Marshal of France, to whom she presented me. On what she said to him, he seemed to take much notice of me, and promised me many things, which he never thought of till the last year of his life, when I had no occasion for him. The young Marquis of Sennecterre, whose father was then Ambassador at Turin, passed at the same time through Chambéry. He dined at Madame de Menthon's; I dined there likewise that day. After dinner they talked of music; he knew it well. The opera of *Jephté*[1] was then new; he talked of it, it was brought him. He made me tremble on proposing that we should execute this opera; and, on opening the book, he fell on this celebrated piece with a double chorus:

> *La Terre, l'Enfer, le Ciel même,*
> *Tout tremble devant le Seigneur.*

---

[1] By the Abbé Pellegrin, with music by Monteclaire.

He says to me, how many parts do you take? I shall take, for my share, these six. I was not then acquainted with French petulancy; and although I had sometimes given out partitions, I did not comprehend how the same person could, at the same time, do six parts, or even two. Nothing has perplexed me so much in the exercise of music, as skipping thus lightly from one part to another, and keeping at the same time the eye on a whole partition. From my manner of acting in this affair, M. de Sennecterre must have been tempted to think I did not know music. It was, perhaps, to verify this doubt, that he proposed my noting a song he wanted to give Mademoiselle de Menthon. I could not deny him. He sung the tune; I pricked it, without even making him repeat it often. He afterwards read, and found it, as it really was, very correctly noted. He saw the trouble I was in; he took pleasure in making the most of this trifling success. It was a thing, however, extremely simple. At the bottom I knew music well; I wanted nothing but that quickness at a first glance, which I never possessed in anything, and which is acquired in music but by consummate practice. Be it as it may, I was sensible of his obliging attention in wiping from the mind of others, and from mine, the little shame it had caused me. Twelve or fifteen years afterwards, meeting in different companies at Paris, I was several times tempted to remind him of this trifling anecdote, to show him I still remembered it. But he had lost his sight since that. I was afraid of renewing his sorrow, by recalling to him the use he had known how to make of it; so I was silent.

I draw near the moment which begins to connect my past existence with the present. A few acquaintances of those times, prolonged to these, are become precious to me. They have often made me regret the happy obscurity in which those who called themselves my friends, were so, and loved me for myself, from pure kindness, not for the vanity of being connected with a man of some reputation, or from the secret desire of seeking more occasion to do him mischief. It is here I date my first acquaintance with my old friend Gauffecourt, who is still mine, in spite of the efforts people have made to take him from me. Still mine! No. Alas! I have just lost him. But he ceased to love me only when he ceased to live, and our friendship ended only when he died. M. de Gauffecourt was one of the most amiable men that ever existed. It was impossible to see him without esteeming him, or to live with him without an absolute attachment. I never in my life saw a countenance more open, more caressing, that had more serenity,

which marked so much sentiment and understanding, or inspired
more confidence. However reserved a man might be, he could not,
from first sight, help being as familiar with him as if he had
known him twenty years; and I, who had so much trouble to be
without restraint among new faces, was so with him from the
first moment. His tone of voice, his accent, his conversation, perfectly accompanied his physiognomy. The sound of his voice was
clear, full, and powerful; a fine bass voice, sharp and strong,
which filled the ear, and sounded to the heart. It is impossible to
be possessed of milder and more equal mirth, a truer and more
simple grace, talents more natural or cultivated with more taste.
Join to these an affectionate heart, but a little too affectionate to
all; an officious character, with little choice, serving his friends
with zeal, or rather making himself the friend of those he could
serve, and cunningly managing his own affairs, in ardently managing those of another. Gauffecourt was the son of a watchmaker
only, and had been a watchmaker himself; but his person and
merit called him to another sphere, into which he soon entered.
He became acquainted with M. de la Closure, the French Resident at Geneva, who took him to his friendship. He procured him,
at Paris, other useful acquaintances, by whom he obtained the
supplying Valais with salt, worth twenty thousand livres a year.
His fortune, brilliant enough, was bounded here as to mankind;
but on the side of women it was very different, he had his choice,
and did as he thought proper. The most extraordinary and the
most honourable for him of all was, that, having connexions with
all conditions, he was beloved by all, his friendship coveted by
everyone, without ever being envied or hated, and I believe he
died without ever having had in his life one enemy. Happy man!
He came every year to the baths of Aix, where good company
from the neighbouring country resorted. Connected with all the
nobility of Savoy, he came from Aix to Chambéry to visit the
Count of Bellegarde, and his father, the Marquis of Antremont,
at whose house Mamma made and procured me his acquaintance.
This acquaintance, which seemed to have no view, and was many
years interrupted, was renewed on an occasion I shall mention,
and became a true attachment. This is enough to authorize me to
speak of a friend with whom I was so closely connected; but, had
I no personal interest in his memory, he was so amiable a man,
and of so happy a turn, that, for the honour of the human species,
I should think it right to preserve it. This so bewitching a man
had, however, like others, his faults, as will be seen hereafter;

but, if he had not had them, he had perhaps been less amiable. To make him as interesting as possible, it was necessary he should have something to be pardoned in him.

Another friendship of the same time is not extinct, and still lulls me with that hope of temporal happiness which with difficulty dies from the heart of man. M. de Conzié, a gentleman of Savoy, then young and amiable, had a fancy to learn music, or rather to be acquainted with one who taught it. With judgement and taste for polite learning, M. Conzié joined a mildness of character which rendered him extremely complying, and I myself was much so with those in whom I found it. This connexion was soon formed.[1] The seeds of literature and philosophy, which began to ferment in my brain, and waited only a little cultivation and emulation entirely to unfold themselves, found them in him. M. de Conzié had little disposition for music; this was lucky for me: the hours of lesson were spent in quite other things than sol-faing. We breakfasted, we chatted, we read new things, and not a word of music. Voltaire's correspondence with the Prince Royal[2] of Prussia then made a noise; we often entertained ourselves on these celebrated men, whereof one, soon after on the throne,[3] already announced himself such as he would soon show himself; and the other, as much in discredit as he is now admired, made us sincerely lament the misfortunes which seemed to pursue him, and which we so often see are the portion of great talents. The Prince of Prussia had been rather unsuccessful in his youth, and Voltaire seemed born to be never so. Our concern for them extended to everything which related to them. Nothing Voltaire wrote escaped us. The relish I had for these writings inspired me with a desire of writing with elegance, and of endeavouring to imitate the beautiful colouring of this author, with whom I was enraptured. Some time afterwards his *Philosophical Letters*[4] appeared: though they certainly are not his best works, it was those which mostly drew me towards study; and this rising taste has not been extinguished since that time.

But the time to give myself entirely up to it was not yet come. There still remained a humour a little inconstant, a desire of

---

[1] The Paris MS. adds a note here: "I have seen him again since, and found him completely transformed. What a great magician was M. de Choiseul! None of my old acquaintance has escaped the changes he has brought about!"

[2] Paris MS.: "King."

[3] Frederick II became King of Prussia in 1740.

[4] They appeared in 1734.

coming and going, which was more restrained than extinguished, which was fed by the course of Madame de Warens's house, too noisy for my solitary humour. The jumble of strange faces which daily flowed in from all parts, and the persuasion I was in of these fellows seeking no more than to dupe her, each one in his way, made my habitation a place of torments. Since I had succeeded Claude Anet in the confidence of his mistress, I followed up more closely the state of her affairs; I perceived a progress towards evil which affrighted me. I an hundred times remonstrated, begged, pressed, conjured, and always in vain. I threw myself on my knees, strongly representing the catastrophe which threatened her, sharply exhorting her to reform her expenses, to begin by me, rather to suffer a little whilst she was yet young, than, by continually increasing her debts and her creditors, to expose herself in her old age to oppression and misery. Sensible of the sincerity of my zeal, she relented with me, promising me the finest things in the world. Did a sponger come in? that instant all was forgotten. After a thousand proofs of the inutility of my remonstrances, what remained to be done, but turn my eyes from the evil I could not prevent? I withdrew from the house whose door I could not keep. I took little journeys to Nyon, Geneva, Lyons, which, drowning the secret pains, increased at the same time the cause by my expenses. I can swear I could have suffered all retrenchments with joy, had Mamma really benefited by the saving; but certain that what I refused myself went to knaves, I abused her indulgence to partake with them, and, like the dog which comes from the shambles, I took off a morsel from the piece I could not save.

Pretexts were never wanting for any of these excursions, and Mamma alone had supplied me with more than necessary, as she had, everywhere, so many connexions, negotiations, affairs, commissions to send by some sure hand. She was glad to send me, I was glad to go; this could not fail to form a pretty errant life. These journeys brought within my reach a few acquaintances who were afterwards agreeable or useful: among others, at Lyons, that of M. Perrichon, which I reproach myself for not having sufficiently cultivated, considering the kindness he showed me; that of the good-natured Parisot, which I shall speak of in its place: at Grenoble, that of Madame Deybens, and of Madame la Présidente de Bardonanche, a woman of great sense, and who had taken me to her friendship, could I have made it convenient to see her oftener: at Geneva, that of M. de la Closure, the French

Resident, who often talked to me of my mother, from whom, in spite of death and time, his heart was not detached; that of the two Barillots, whose father, that called me his grandson, was most amiable company, and one of the worthiest men I ever knew. During the troubles in the Republic, these two citizens took a contrary part: the son that of the citizens; the father that of the magistrates: and when they took up arms in 1737, I saw, being then at Geneva, the father and son go out armed from the same house, one for the Town-house, the other for his quarter, sure to meet within two hours afterwards, facing each other, exposed to blowing each other's brains out. This dreadful sight made so lively an impression on me, I swore never to imbrue my hands in civil war, and never to support internal liberty by force of arms, neither personally nor by consent, if ever I returned to my rights of citizen. I render myself the testimony of having kept my oath on a trying occasion; and it will be found, at least I think so, that this moderation was of some value.

But I had not yet reached the first fermentation of patriotism which Geneva in arms excited in my heart. It may be judged how far I was from it, by a most serious fact I was charged with, which I forgot to put in its place, and which ought not to be omitted.

My uncle Bernard had been several years gone to Carolina, to build the city of Charlestown, of which he had given the plan. He died there soon afterwards; my poor cousin was likewise dead in the King of Prussia's service: thus my aunt lost her son and husband almost at the same time. These losses warmed her friendship a little for the nearest relation left her, which was myself. When I went to Geneva, I slept at her house, and amused myself in ferreting out and turning over the books and papers my uncle had left. I found many curious pieces and letters of which surely they little thought. My aunt, who made nothing of these waste papers, would have let me carry all off, if I had chosen it. I contented myself with two or three books commented by the hand of my grandfather Bernard the minister, and, among others, the posthumous works of Rohault, in quarto, whose margin was filled with excellent scholia, which gave me a fondness for mathematics. This book remained with those of Madame de Warens; I have ever since been sorry I did not keep it. To these books I joined five or six manuscripts, and one only printed, which was of the famous Micheli Ducret; a man of great talents, learned, enlightened, but too restless, cruelly treated by the magistrates of Geneva, and who died lately in the fortress of Arberg, where he had been shut up many years, for having, they said, been concerned in the conspiracy of Berne.

This memoir was a criticism, judicious enough, on the grand and ridiculous plan of fortification which has been partly executed at Geneva, to the mockery of every man of the art, who was not acquainted with the private end the Council proposed in the execution of this magnificent undertaking. M. Micheli, having been excluded from the Chamber of Fortification, for blaming this plan, thought, as member of the Two Hundred, and even as a citizen, he could give his advice more at length: this he did by this memoir, which he had the imprudence to put in print, but not publish; for he only had the number of sets printed he sent to the Two Hundred, which were all intercepted in the post by order of the under council. I found this memoir among the papers of my uncle, with the answer he had been charged to give; I took both away. I made this journey soon after I left the office for registering the lands, and remained connected with the advocate Coccelli who conducted it. Some time after, the director of the customhouse took it in his head to beg I would be godfather to a child, and Madame Coccelli was godmother. The honour turned my brain; and, proud so nearly to belong to the advocate, I endeavoured to act the man of importance, to show myself worthy the glory.

With this notion I thought I could not do better than to show him my memoir in print by M. Micheli, which was really a scarce thing, to prove to him I belonged to the eminent people of Geneva who knew the secrets of the state. However, from a half reserve, of which I should be troubled to give a reason, I did not show him my uncle's answer to this memoir; perhaps because it was a manuscript, and that the advocate must have nothing but print. He, however, so well saw the value of the writing I had the stupidity to entrust him with, I could never get it or see it any more; and, being well convinced of the inutility of my efforts, I made a merit of the business, by transforming the robbery into a present. I have not the least doubt of his having made, at the court of Turin, the best of this piece, more curious however than useful; and that he has taken great care to get himself repaid, by some means or other, the money it must have cost him to obtain it. Happily, of all future contingents, one of the least probable is, that some day or other the King of Sardinia will besiege Geneva: but as there is no impossibility in the thing, I shall always reproach my foolish vanity for having shown the greatest defects of this place to its most ancient enemy.

I spent two or three years in this manner between music, prescriptions, projects, journeys, incessantly floating between one thing and the other, seeking to fix without knowing at what, but inclining however by degrees towards study, visiting men of learning, hearing conversations on literature, sometimes taking on me to talk of it likewise, and taking rather the jargon of books than the knowledge they contained. In my trips to Geneva, I called from time to time on my old good friend M. Simon as I went by, who greatly stirred up my rising emulation by quite fresh news of the republic of letters, from Baillet or Colomiès. I likewise very often saw at Chambéry a Dominican professor of physic; a good kind of a monk, whose name I have forgot, and who often made little experiments which greatly amused me. I wanted by his example[1] to make some sympathetic ink. For this purpose, having filled a bottle more than half with quick-lime, orpiment, and water, I corked it well. The ebullition began almost instantly with extreme violence. I ran to uncork the bottle, but was not in time enough; it flew in my face like a bomb. I swallowed orpiment and lime; it had nearly killed me.[2] I was blind more than six weeks, and thus learnt never to meddle with experimental physic without knowing its elements.

This adventure happened very unluckily for my health, which for some time was sensibly changed. I cannot tell how it was, that, being well formed as to the chest, and running to no excess of any kind, I decayed visibly. I am pretty square, have a large breast, my lungs should move at ease: I had, nevertheless, short breath; felt myself oppressed; sighed involuntarily, had palpitations, spat blood; a lingering fever came on of which I never got quite rid. How can a man in the prime of life fall into such a state, without having any intestine vitiated, without having done the least thing to destroy his health?

The sword wears out the sheath, they say sometimes. This is my history. My passions kept me alive, and my passions killed me. What passions, you will ask me? Why, trifles, the most childish things in the world, but which engaged me as much as the possession of Helen, or the throne of the universe, would have done. First, women. When I had one, my senses were easy, but my heart never was. The necessities of love devoured me in the bosom of enjoyment. I had a tender mother, a beloved friend, but

---

[1] Paris MS. adds: "and assisted by Ozanam's *Mathematical Recreations.*"
[2] Rousseau actually made a will on this day (June 27, 1737).

I wanted a mistress. I figured her to myself as such; I represented her a thousand ways, to delude myself. Had I thought I held Mamma in my arms when I held her there, my embraces had not been less close, but every desire had been extinguished; I had sobbed with tenderness, but had not enjoyed. Enjoyed! Is this the lot of man? Ah! had I once only in my life tasted in their fulness all the delights of love, I do not imagine my frail existence could have borne it; I had died in the act.

I therefore was burning with love without an object, and perhaps it is thus it exhausts the most. I was uneasy, tortured with the bad situation of my poor Mamma's affairs and her imprudent conduct, which could not fail to work her total ruin in a little time. My cruel imagination, which always outruns misfortune, incessantly showed it me, in all its excess, and all its consequences. I saw myself, beforehand, forcibly separated by want from her to whom I had consecrated my days, and without whom I could have no enjoyment Thus my mind was continually agitated. Desires and fears alternately consumed me.

Music was to me a passion less transporting, but not less consuming, from the ardour with which I gave myself up to it, from the obstinate study of the obscure books of Rameau, from my invincible determination of loading my memory, which still refused, with them, from my continual runnings about, from the immense compilations I heaped up, often passing whole nights in copying. And why stop at permanent things; while every folly which passed through my unconstant brain, the fugitive inclinations of a single day, a journey, a concert, a supper, a proposed walk, a romance to read, a comedy to see, anything the least premeditated in pleasure or business, became so many violent passions, which by their ridiculous impetuosity gave me real torment? Reading the imaginary misfortunes of Cleveland, sometimes in fury and often interrupted, caused me, I believe, as much bad blood as my own.

There was a Genevese, named M. Bagueret, who had been employed under Peter the Great at the Court of Russia; one of the meanest fellows and the greatest fools I ever saw, always full of projects as foolish as himself, which brought millions down like rain, and to whom ciphers cost but little. This man, being come to Chambéry for some suit at the senate, took possession of Mamma of course, and for the treasures in ciphers he so generously threw about, drew her poor shillings from her piece by piece. I did not like him, he saw it; with me that it is not difficult: there was no kind

of baseness he did not make use of to cajole me. He took it in his
head to propose teaching me chess, which he played a little. I tried
almost against my will; and having well or ill learnt the moves,
my progress was so rapid, that at the first sitting I gave him the
rook he had given me at the beginning. I wanted no more; I become a madman after chess. I buy a chessboard; I buy Calabrais;[1]
I shut myself up in my room; I pass nights and days in seeking
to learn by heart every game, to force them into my head right or
wrong, in playing alone, without ceasing or end. After two or
three months of this charming exercise and every imaginable
effort, I go to the coffee-house, haggard, yellow, and almost stupid.
I try, I again play with M. Bagueret; he beats me once, twice,
twenty times: so many combinations were jumbled in my brain,
and my imagination was so deadened, I saw nothing but clouds
before me. Every time I exercised myself in studying the game
by Philidor's or Stamma's books, the same thing happened, and,
after having spent myself with fatigue, I found I played worse
than at first. But whether I left off playing, or whether in playing
I would recover a little breath, I never advanced one hair from
the first sitting, and always found myself at the same point as
when I left off. I might exercise myself a thousand ages, I could
give Bagueret the rook, but nothing more. This was employing
time well, you will say! and I employed a good deal so. I ended
this first trial only when I had not strength to support it longer.
When I left my chamber to show myself, I looked like one from
the grave, and, had I continued this life, I should not have remained from it long. It must be agreed to be difficult, particularly
in the heat of youth, that such a brain should keep the body
always in health.

The change in mine affected my humour, and moderated the
heat of my fancies. Finding myself weakened, I became more
tranquil, and cooled in my passion for travelling. More sedentary,
I was laid hold of, not by care, but melancholy; the vapours succeeded passion, my languor became dulness; I wept and sighed
with little cause; I found life leaving me before I had tasted it;
I bewailed the state in which I was leaving poor Mamma, and
that I saw her falling into; I can truly say, that to leave her, and
in an uncomfortable situation, was all I regretted. In fine, I fell
quite ill. She nursed me as never mother nursed a child; this was
of service to her too, by diverting her from her projects, and keep-

---

[1] A treatise on chess by the Italian chess-player Gioacchino Greco, nicknamed "le Calabrais."

ing off projectors. How sweet a death, had death come then!
Though I had tasted little of the blessings of life, I had felt few
of its curses. My peaceful soul might depart without the cruel
knowledge of man's injustice, which mars both life and death. I
had the consolation of surviving in my best moiety; it was scarcely

dying. Without the uneasiness her fate caused me, I should have
died with the same ease I should have slept; and even these un-
easinesses had an object so affectionate and tender, it allayed in
some measure their bitterness. I told her, You are trustee of all
my being; act so as to make me happy. Two or three times, when
I was at the worst, I got up in the night, and crawled to her room,
to give her advice on her conduct, I may say exact and sensible,
but in which the interest I took in her fate was more apparent
than anything else. As if tears were my food and medicine, I
gained strength by those I shed near her and with her, seated on
her bed, and holding her hands in mine. Hours glided away in
these nocturnal conversations, and I returned better than I came:
contented and calm from the promises she made me, in the hopes
she had given me, I slept with tranquillity of mind and resignation to Providence. Would to God, after so many reasons for hating life, so many storms which have agitated mine, and which
make it but a troublesome burden, death, which must terminate
it, may be as little unwelcome as it would have been at that time!

By dint of care, vigilance, and incredible trouble, she saved me, and certain it is that she alone could save me. I have little faith in the medicine of physicians, but a great deal in that of true friends: things on which our happiness depends are always better performed than any other. If there is in life a delightful sentiment, it is that we experience in being each other's again. Our mutual attachment did not increase, it was not possible; but it took on something of I do not know what more cordial, more touching, from its great simplicity. I became entirely her work, entirely her child, and more than if she had been my real mother. We began, without thinking of it, never to separate more from each other; to render, in some sort, our existence common: and, reciprocally feeling we were not only necessary, but sufficient to each other, we accustomed ourselves to think of nothing foreign to us, and absolutely to limit our happiness and desires to this mutual possession, perhaps unique amongst the human species, which was not, as I have said, that of love, but a more essential possession, which, without depending on sex, age, face, or senses, depends on all that makes us to be ourselves, and which we cannot lose but in ceasing to be.

What prevented this precious crisis from producing the happiness of the rest of her days and mine? Not I, I render myself the consoling justice. Neither did she; at least, her will did not. It was written that invincible Nature should soon recover its empire. But this fatal return did not operate all at once. There was, thanks to Heaven, an interval; short, but precious interval! which did not end by my fault, and which I shall not reproach myself with having badly employed.

Though recovered from my great illness, I had not regained my strength. My lungs were not healed; a remnant of the fever hung about me, and kept me weak. I had no inclination to anything but ending my days with her who was so dear to me, containing her in her prudent resolutions, making her feel in what consisted the true charms of a happy life, rendering hers such as much as depended on me. But I saw, I felt even, that in a dull and dismal house, the continual solitude of a tête-à-tête would become dull likewise. A remedy to this was presented as of itself. Mamma had ordered me milk, and would have me take it in the country. I consented, provided she went with me. Nothing more was necessary to determine her; the only question was to choose the place. The suburb garden was not properly in the country; encompassed by houses and other gardens, it had not the charms of a country retreat. Besides, after the death of Anet, we had left this garden from economy, having plants no longer at heart, and other views making us little regret this corner.

Taking immediate advantage of the disgust I found in her for the town, I proposed leaving it entirely, and fixing ourselves in an agreeable solitude, in some little house far enough away to defeat the designs of troublesome visitors. She would have done it, and this expedient, which her good angel and mine suggested, had probably assured us a life of happiness and tranquillity, until the moment death should separate us. But this was not the state we were called to. Mamma must experience every anguish of indigence, and every inconvenience in life, after having passed her days in abundance, to make her quit it with less regret; and I, by the union of all kinds of misfortunes, was to become one day an example to whoever, inspired by the sole love of justice and public good, dare, supported only by innocence, openly tell mankind the truth, without the prop of faction, without having formed a party for his protection.

An unhappy fear detained her. She dared not quit this old house, for fear of angering the proprietor. Thy plan of retreat is charming, said she, and much to my taste; but in this retreat one must live. In quitting my prison I am in danger of losing my bread; and when there is no more to be had in the wood, we must return to seek it in the town. That we may not be necessitated to come back, do not let us entirely quit it. Let us pay the Count of Saint-Laurent this little pension, that he may leave me mine. Let us seek some corner far enough from town to live in peace, and near enough to return to it whenever it may be necessary. This was done. Having looked round a little, we fixed on les Charmettes, on the estate of M. de Conzié, close to Chambéry, but as retired and solitary as if it had been at an hundred leagues from it. Between two pretty high hills is a little valley, north and south, at the end of which runs a water amongst stones and trees. Along this valley, on the side of the hill, are a few straggling houses, very agreeable to those who are fond of a retreat a little wild and retired. Having looked at two or three of these houses, we at last chose the prettiest, belonging to a gentleman of the army, M. Noiret. The house was very convenient: in the front, a garden forming a terrace, a vineyard above, and an orchard below it, opposite a little wood of chestnut-trees, a fountain handy; higher up the hill, meadows for feeding cattle; in fine, every necessary for the little country establishment we proposed. As near as I can recollect the time and

date, we took possession about the end of the summer of 1736.[1]
I was in transports the first night we lay there. O Mamma! said
I to this dear friend, embracing and drowning her in tears of joy
and melting tenderness, this is the abode of happiness and innocence. If we do not find both here, we must seek them nowhere.

BOOK SIX

Hoc erat in votis: modus agri non ita magnus,
Hortus ubi et tecto vicinus jugis aquae fons,
Et paulum sylvae super his foret....

Horace, Satires, II, 6.

I CANNOT add, *auctius atque Dî melius fecere:* no matter, I
wanted no more; I did not even wish to be the proprietor, the
enjoyment of it was sufficient to me; I have long said and thought
the proprietor and possessor are often two different people, putting
husbands and gallants out of the question.

Here begins the short happiness of my life; now come the peaceable, but rapid moments which give me a right to say I have
lived. Precious and regretted moments! Ah, begin again your
lovely course; glide more gently through my memory, if possible,
than you really did in your fugitive succession. What shall I do
to prolong to my wish this recital so touching and so simple; to tell
over and over the same things, and not tire my readers by repeating them more than I myself was tired by incessantly recommencing them! Besides, did this consist in deeds, in actions, in words,
I might describe and render them somehow; but how say that
which was neither said, nor done, nor thought, but tasted, but
felt, without my being able to express any other object of my
happiness but this feeling only? I rose with the sun, and was
happy; I walked, and was happy; I saw Mamma, and was happy;
I quitted her, and was happy; I ran over the woods, the hills,
strayed through the valleys, I read, rested, worked in the garden,
gathered fruit, assisted in the house, and happiness followed me

---

[1] The lease was dated 6 July, 1738: the occupation began on 24 June, 1738.

to every place; it was not in anything assignable, it was all within me, it could not leave me a single instant.

Not the least thing which happened to me during this lovely period, nothing I did, said, or thought all the while it lasted, has escaped my memory. The years which precede or follow it present themselves at intervals; I recollect them unequally and confusedly; but this I entirely remember, as if it still existed. My imagination, which in my youth was always beforehand, and now retrogrades, compensates by this sweet recollection the hope I have for ever lost. I see nothing in futurity that can tempt me; reflecting only on the past can soothe me; and this reflection so lively and so real in the period I speak of, often makes my life comfortable in spite of my misfortunes.

I shall give one example only of these recollections, which will enable one to judge of their force and reality. The first day we went to sleep at les Charmettes, Mamma was in a sedan chair; I followed her on foot. It was a rising road, she was pretty heavy, and, fearing to fatigue the chairmen, she got out about half-way thither, to walk the other half. Going along, she saw something blue in the hedge, and says, Here is some periwinkle yet in bloom! I had never seen any periwinkle; I did not stoop to examine it; I am too short-sighted to distinguish herbs on the ground when I stand upright. I just glanced at this as I passed along. Near thirty years had passed before I saw any periwinkle again, or that I took notice of it. In 1764, being at Cressier with my friend M. du Peyrou, we went up a little mountain, at whose summit there is a pretty hall, justly called Belle-Vue. I was then beginning to herbalize a little. Looking, as I ascended, amidst the bushes, I joyfully cry out, *Ah, there is some periwinkle!* and in effect it was so. Du Peyrou perceived the transport, but was ignorant of the cause: I hope he will learn it, when one day or other he reads this book. The reader may judge, from the impression of so trifling an object, what all those produced which have relation to this period.

The country air did not, however, restore my former health. I languished, and became worse. I could not support milk, I was obliged to leave it. Water was then in fashion as the only remedy; I followed it, and with so little discretion, that I had nearly been cured, not of my complaints, but of life. Every morning at rising I went to the fountain with a large tumbler, and successively drank, in walking about, the value of two bottles. I left off wine at my meals. The water I drank was a little raw and difficult to pass, as are generally waters from the hills. To be brief, I managed so well, that in less than two months I totally destroyed my stomach, so strong till then. No longer digesting, I understood there were no farther hopes of a cure. At the same time, an accident happened to me, as singular in itself as in its effects, which will end but with me.

One morning that I was not worse than usual, fixing a small table on its foot, I felt all over my body a sudden and almost inconceivable revolution. I cannot better compare it than to a kind of tempest, which took rise in my blood, and in an instant reached every member. My arteries began beating with so great a force, that I not only felt them beat, but heard them too, and particularly that of the carotids. A vast noise in the ears attended it; and this noise was treble, or rather quadruple, that is, a dull hollow buzzing, a clearer murmur like running water, a whistling extremely sharp, and the beating I have just mentioned, whose strokes I could easily count, without feeling my pulse, or touching my body with my hands. This internal noise was so great, it deprived me of the quickness of hearing I had before, and rendered me not quite deaf, but hard of hearing, as I am since that time.

You may judge of my surprise and terror. I thought myself dead; I went to bed; the physician was called; I told him my case with horror, judging it without remedy. I believe he thought so too, but he acted the doctor: he gave me a long string of reasonings, of which I comprehended nothing; and then, in consequence of his sublime theory, he began, *in anima vili*, the experimental cure he thought proper to try. It was so painful, so disgustful, and operated so little, I soon grew tired of it; and in a few weeks, seeing I grew neither better nor worse, I got up, and returned to my ordinary manner of living, with my beating arteries and my buzzings, which from that time, that is, during thirty years, have never left me a minute.

Till then I was a great sleeper. The total privation of sleep, added to these symptoms, and which has constantly accompanied them till now, completed the persuasion I was in of having but a few days to live. This persuasion took off for a time my care for a recovery. Not being able to prolong my life, I resolved to make as much as I could of the little that remained of it; this I was enabled to do by a singular favour of nature, which in so melancholy a state exempted me from the pains that I expected it would have brought on. I was troubled with the noise, but did not suffer: it was accompanied by no other habitual inconvenience than want of sleep in the night, and at all times a short breath, which did not reach an asthma, nor was ever felt but when I ran or exerted myself a little.

This accident, which might have killed the body, killed only the passions; and I every day thanked heaven for the happy effects it produced on my mind. I may safely say I began to live only when I thought myself dead. Esteeming the things, to which I was going to bid farewell, at their true value, I began to employ my mind in more noble cares, as anticipating those I should soon have to attend, and which I had till then much neglected. I had often burlesqued religion in my manner, but I had never been entirely without religion. It was less painful to me to return to this subject, so melancholy to many people, but so sweet to those who make it an object of consolation and hope. Mamma was more useful to me on this occasion than all the theologians in the world would have been.

She who brought everything to system, did not fail to bring religion within a system likewise; it was composed of very mixed ideas, some sound, some foolish, of sentiments relative to her character, and prejudices proceeding from education. Believers generally make God as they are themselves: good people make him good, the wicked make him mischievous; choleric and spiteful bigots see nothing but hell, because they would be glad to damn everybody; mild and friendly souls believe little in it, and one of the astonishments I cannot get the better of is, to perceive the good Fénelon speak of it, in his *Telemachus*, as if he really believed in it: but I hope he told a lie; for, in fact, however veridical a man may be, he must lie a little sometimes if he is a bishop. Mamma did not do so with me; and her soul, without spleen, which could not imagine a vindictive and continually angry God, saw nothing but clemency and mercy where bigots see nothing but justice and punishment. She often said, that there would be no justice in God in being equitable towards us; for not having given us that which must make us so, it would be demanding more of us than he has given. The most whimsical of all was her believing in purgatory, but not in hell. This proceeded from her not knowing how to dispose of the wicked, as she could neither damn them nor place them with the good until they were become so; and it must be owned the wicked are, both in this world and the next, extremely embarrassing.

Another extravagance. This system destroys the whole doctrine of original sin and redemption, shakes the foundation of vulgar Christianity, and Catholicism at any rate cannot subsist. Mamma, however, was a good Catholic, or pretended to be one; and certain it is, her pretensions were made in good faith. The scriptures seemed to her to be too literally and too harshly explained. All we read there of eternal torments appeared to her comminatory or figurative. The death of Jesus Christ seemed to her an example of charity, truly divine, to teach men to love God and each other. In a word, faithful to the religion she had embraced, she sincerely admitted the whole profession of faith; but when she came to the discussion of each article, it appeared she believed quite differently from the Church, though still submitting to it.

She had on that head a simplicity of heart, a frankness more eloquent than cavillings, and which often embarrassed even her confessor; for she hid nothing from him. I am a good Catholic, said she to him, and will always be so; I adopt, with all the powers of my soul, the decisions of our Holy Mother the Church. I am not mistress of my faith, but am of my will. I give it up without reserve, and will to believe everything. What more do you ask?

Had there been no Christian morality, I believe she had followed it; so much was it adapted to her character. She did all that was commanded; but she had equally done so, had it not been commanded. In things indifferent she was fond of obeying, and, had she not been permitted, prescribed even, to eat meat, she had fasted between God and herself, without prudence having anything to do with the matter. But all this morality was subordinate to the principles of M. de Tavel, or rather she pretended to see nothing contrary to them. She could have lain every day with twenty men, and have had a conscience at ease, without even having more scruples than desires. I know that many devotees are not more scrupulous on this point; the difference is in their being seduced by their passions, and she by her sophisms only. In the most pathetic conversations, and, I may add, the most edifying, she has fallen on this point without changing either air or tone, and without believing she contradicted herself. She would have, if necessary, interrupted them for a time, and taken them up again with the same serenity as before; so much was she heartily persuaded that all this was only a maxim of social order, which every sensible person might interpret, apply, except, according to the spirit of the thing, without the least danger of offending God. Though I assuredly did not, on this point, think with her, I own I dared not oppose it, ashamed of the very unpolite part I must have acted in support of my argument. I should have been glad to have established these rules for others, and excepted myself;

but, besides that her constitution sufficiently prevented the abuse of her notions, I know she was not a woman to be deceived, and that claiming an exception for myself was claiming it for all those who pleased her. However, I add here, by occasion, this inconsequence to the rest, though it never had much effect on her conduct, and at that time none; but I promised to expose exactly her principles, and will keep my word. I now return to myself.

Finding in her every maxim necessary to ease me of the terrors of death and futurity, I dived with security into this source of confidence. I attached myself more than ever to her. I wished to convey into her the life I felt was just leaving me. From this additional attachment to her, the persuasion I was in of having a short time to live, my profound security on my future state, resulted an habitual state extremely calm, and even sensual; for that, deadening every passion which bears too far our hopes and fears, it enabled me to enjoy without uneasiness or trouble my few remaining days. One thing contributed to render them more agreeable; it was the attention I gave to fostering her taste for the country by every amusement I could collect. By giving her a fondness for her garden, poultry, pigeons, cows, I grew fond of them likewise; and these trifling occupations, which filled up the day without troubling my tranquillity, were of more service than milk, or any other remedy, for the preservation of my poor carcase, and its recovery too, as far as that could be done.

The vintage and gathering in the fruits diverted us the rest of the year, and we grew more and more inclined to this rustic life amidst the good people who surrounded us. We saw winter approach with regret, and returned to town as if we had been going into exile; I particularly, who, doubting of seeing another spring, thought I bade for ever adieu to les Charmettes. I did not leave it without kissing the ground and the trees, and looking several times back as we drew from it. Having long left my scholars, having lost a taste for the amusement and society of the town, I no longer went out, or saw anybody, except Mamma, and M. Salomon, lately become her physician and mine, an honest man, a man of sense, and a great Cartesian, who talked well on the system of the world, and whose agreeable and instructive conversation did me more good than all his prescriptions. I could never support the silly, sottish fillings-up of ordinary conversation; but useful and solid conversations always gave me great pleasure, and I have never refused them. I very much relished M. Salomon's; methought I anticipated with him the great knowledge my soul

LES CHARMETTES

would acquire when divested of its fetters. The inclination I had for him extended to the subjects he treated, and I began to seek those books which might help me the better to understand him. Those which mixed devotion with knowledge were the most agreeable to me; such were, peculiarly, those of the Oratory and of Port-Royal. I began to read, or rather devour them. One of them fell into my hands, by Father Lamy, entitled, *Entretiens sur les Sciences.* It was a sort of introduction to the knowledge of the books which treat of them. I read it over and over a hundred times: I resolved to make it my guide. In fine, I felt myself carried away by degrees, in spite of the state I was in, or rather by this state, towards study, with an irresistible force; still looking on each day as my last, I studied with as much ardour as one who thought to live for ever. It was said it did me great hurt; I think it did me great good, not only to my mind but to my body; for this application, of which I was so fond, became so delightful, that, no longer thinking of my illness, I was much less affected by it. It is, however, certain, that nothing procured me real ease; but sharp pain having left me, I accustomed myself to weakness, no sleep, to think instead of act, and, in fine, to look on the successive and lingering decay of my carcase as an inevitable progress which nothing but death would stop.

This opinion not only withdrew me from every vain care for life, but delivered me from the trouble of medicine, to which I was, till then, obliged to submit against my will. Salomon, convinced his drugs could not save me, spared me their draught, and contented himself with amusing the uneasiness of my poor Mamma, by a few of those indifferent prescriptions which keep up the patient's hopes and the doctor's credit. I quitted the strict regimen, and returned to the use of wine, and the whole course of life of a man in health, according to the measure of my strength, sober in all things, but abstaining from nothing. I went out too, and began to see my friends again, particularly M. de Conzié, whose acquaintance pleased me much. In fine, whether it seemed noble to learn to my last breath, or whether some hidden hope of life was at the bottom, the expectation of death, far from relaxing my relish for study, seemed to animate it, and I hurried to collect a little knowledge for the other world as one who thought to find no more there than he carried with him. I took a liking to the shop of a bookseller whose name was Bauchard, where a few people of learning resorted; and the spring, which I thought I never should see again, approaching, I looked out a few books for les Charmettes, in case I should have the good fortune to return there.

I had this good fortune, and made the best of it. My joy on seeing the first buds is inexpressible. To see another spring was to me a resurrection into paradise. The snow had scarce begun to melt, but we crept from our dungeon and went immediately to les Charmettes, to hear the first note of the nightingale. Then I thought of death no more; and really it is singular I never was very ill in the country. I have felt great pain, but never so as to keep my bed. I often said, finding myself worse than ordinary, When you see me at death's door, carry me under a shady oak; I give you my word, I shall be better.

Though feeble, I returned to my rustic functions, but in a manner proportioned to my strength. I was greatly vexed at not being able to do the garden alone; but on digging five or six spades, I was out of breath, the sweat ran down me, and I could do no more. When I stooped, my beatings redoubled, and the blood came into my face with such force, I was obliged hastily to stand up. Restrained to less fatiguing cares, I undertook, among others, that of the pigeon-house, and took so great delight in it I often spent several hours together there, without being tired a moment. Pigeons are very timid, and very difficult to tame. I, however, found means to inspire mine with so much confidence, they followed me everywhere, and let me take them whenever I chose it.

I could not stir in the garden or court, without having two or three of them instantly on my arms and head; and at last, though I took so much pleasure in them, this retinue became so troublesome, I was obliged to deprive them of this familiarity. I always took singular pleasure in taming animals, particularly those which are fearful and wild. It seemed delightful to me to inspire them with a confidence I never abused. I wanted them to love me in liberty.

I said I carried books with me. I made use of them; but in a manner much less to instruct than weary me. The false notion I had of things persuaded me that, to read a book profitably, a man should have all the knowledge it supposes; far from thinking that often the author has it not himself, but fished it from other books as he wanted it. With this foolish notion I was stopped every instant, forced incessantly to run from book to book, and sometimes, before I reached the tenth page of that I was studying, I was obliged to run over libraries. Nevertheless, I was so determined on this extravagant method, I lost an infinite deal of time, and had almost puzzled my brains to a degree of not being able to perceive or understand anything. I happily saw I was taking a wrong road, which led me into an immense labyrinth; I got out of it before I was quite lost.

When a man has a little true relish for the sciences, the first thing he finds in his pursuit is their connexion, which causes them mutually to attract, assist, and enlighten each other, and that one cannot do without the other. Though the human mind is not sufficient to all, and must always prefer one as the principal, yet if it has not some notion of the others, it often finds itself in obscurity even with that it has chosen. I knew that what I had undertaken was good and useful in itself, and that nothing but a change of method was necessary. Beginning with the *Encyclopedia*, I went on, dividing it into branches; I saw the contrary was necessary, to take them each one separately, and follow them each one by itself to the point at which they unite. Thus I came back to the ordinary synthesis; but I came back as a man who knows what he is doing. In this, meditation served me in lieu of understanding, and a very natural reflection assisted me in conducting me aright. Whether I lived or died, there was no time to lose. To know nothing, and want to know everything, at five-and-twenty, was engaging to make good use of one's time. Not knowing at what point fate or death might put an end to my zeal, I wanted at all events to acquire notions of everything, as well to sound my natural disposition, as to judge by myself of that which most deserved cultivation.

I found, in the execution of this plan, another advantage I had not thought of; that of making good use of a great deal of time. I could not be born for study; for a long application fatigues me to a degree of making it impossible to employ myself half an hour together with force on the same subject, especially by following the ideas of another; for it has sometimes happened to me to follow my own longer, and that with pretty good success. When I have followed a few pages of an author who must be read with attention, my imagination deserts him, and is lost in the clouds. If I am obstinate, I weary myself in vain; a dimness comes over me, and I can see nothing. But let different subjects succeed each other, even without interruption, one is a relaxation to the other, and, without the necessity of discontinuing, I pursue them with more ease. I benefited by this observation in the plan of my studies, and so intermixed them, I employed myself the whole day without the least fatigue. It is true, rural and domestic occupations usefully diverted me; but in my increasing fervour I soon found means to take from them time for study, and employed myself in two businesses at once, without dreaming that each was the worse for it.

In so many trifling details which delight me, and with which I often tire my reader's patience, I use however a discretion he would not think of, did not I take care to acquaint him. Here, for instance, I remember with delight all the different trials I made to distribute my time in such a manner as to find at the same time as much pleasure and utility as possible; and I can say, the time I spent in retirement, and always ill, was that of my days in which I was least idle and least sorrowful. Two or three months thus passed in trying the bent of my genius, and enjoying, in the finest season of the year, and in a place it rendered enchanting, the charms of a life whose price I so well knew, those of a society as free as it was gentle, if the name of society can be given to so perfect a union, and those of knowledge and learning I proposed to acquire; for they were to me as if I already possessed them; or, rather, it was still better, since the pleasure of learning them formed a great part of my happiness.

I must pass over these trials which were to me so many enjoyments, but too simple to be explained. Once more, true happiness is not to be described, it is felt, and so much the more felt as it cannot be described, because it is not the result of a collection of

acts, but a permanent state. I often repeat things, but should repeat them oftener, did I say the same things whenever they struck
me. When at last my manner of life, often varied, had taken a
uniform course, this was nearly the mode of dividing it.

I rose every morning before the sun. I passed through a neighbouring orchard into a very pretty road above the vineyard, which
I followed to Chambéry. There, still walking on, I said my prayer,
which did not consist in a vain mumbling of the lips, but in a
sincere raising the thoughts to the Author of this lovely nature
whose beauties were under my eye. I never loved praying in my
room; the walls and other trifling works of man seemed to thrust
themselves between God and me. I love to contemplate him in his
works, whilst my soul is lifted up to him. My prayers were pure,
I dare advance it, and therefore worthy to be heard. I begged for
myself, and her from whom my wishes were never separated, but
an innocent and quiet life, exempt from vice, pain, and want, the
death of the just, and their lot in futurity. However, this act passed
more in admiration and contemplation than in petitions; for I
knew that, with the Dispenser of real blessings, the best means
of obtaining those which are necessary for us is not so much to
ask for them, as to deserve them. I returned from my walk by a
roundabout road, employed in considering with affection and
voluptuousness the rural objects by which I was surrounded, the
only ones with which the eye and heart are never tired. I examined at a distance if Mamma was up; if I saw her windows open, I
leaped with joy, and ran towards them. When they were shut,
I went into the garden to wait her stirring, reflecting on what I
had learnt the eve, or gardening. The window open, I run to
embrace her in her bed, often half awake; and this embracing, as
pure as it was tender, drew, from its innocence only, a charm
which the voluptuousness of the senses never felt.

We generally breakfasted on milk and coffee. It was the part of
the day we were most ourselves, and where we could chatter at
our ease. These sittings, in general pretty long, have given me a
great relish to breakfasts; and I infinitely prefer the custom of
England and Switzerland, where the breakfast is a real repast
which assembles everyone, to that of France, where each one
breakfasts alone in his room, or oftener does not breakfast at all.
After an hour or two's chat, I went to my books till dinner. I began with some author on philosophy, as the *Logic* of Port-Royal,
Locke's *Essay*, Malebranche, Leibnitz, Descartes, etc. I soon perceived these authors were in an almost perpetual contradiction

with each other, and I formed the chimerical project of reconciling them, which greatly fatigued me, and caused the loss of a deal of time. I confused my brain, and did not get forward. In fine, renouncing this method likewise, I took a much better, to which I attribute all the progress I may have made in spite of my trifling capacity; for it is certain I never had much for study. In reading each author, I made it a rule to adopt and follow all his notions, without mixing my own or those of another with them, and without ever quarrelling with him. I said to myself, Let us begin by forming a magazine of notions, true or false, but clear, until my head shall be sufficiently furnished to be able to compare and choose. This method is not without inconveniences; I know it; but it answered my purpose as to my object of instruction. At the end of several years spent in thinking exactly with others, without reflection, in a manner, and almost without reasoning, I found I had a good stock of knowledge to suffice to myself, and think without another's help. Then, when travelling and business deprived me of the means of consulting books, I amused myself by calling over and comparing what I had read, weighing each thing in the balance of reason, and sometimes judging my masters. I did not find that beginning to exercise my judicial faculties late had caused them in the least to lose their vigour; and when I had published my own ideas, I was not accused of being a servile disciple, and swearing *in verba magistri*.

I passed from thence to elementary geometry; for I never went farther, determining to overcome my short memory by means of going a hundred and a hundred times over the same thing, and incessantly recommencing the same route. I did not relish Euclid, who rather seeks the string of demonstrations than the connection of ideas; I preferred the geometry of Father Lamy, who from that time became one of my favourite authors, whose works I still read over again with pleasure. Algebra followed, and it was still Father Lamy I took for a guide: when I was a little forwarder I took Father Reynaud's *Science of Calculation*, and afterwards his *Analysis Demonstrated*, which I only ran over. I never went far enough sufficiently to understand the application of algebra to geometry. I was not fond of this method of operation without seeing what one is about; it seemed to me that to resolve a problem in geometry by equation, was playing a tune by turning round a handle. The first time I found, by calculation, that the square of a binomial figure was composed of the square of each of its parts, and of the double product of one by the other, although my multiplication was right, I would not believe it till I had made the figure. Not but I had a great taste to algebra, considered as to abstract quantity; but, applied to dimension, I must see the operation on the lines, otherwise I comprehended nothing of it.

After this came Latin. It was my most painful study, in which I never made great progress. I first applied myself to the Latin method of Port-Royal, but fruitlessly. Their barbarous verses sickened me, and could not reach my ear. I lost myself in so great a jumble of rules; for in learning the last, I forgot all which preceded it. The study of words is not for a man without memory, and it was precisely to force my memory to capacity I was obstinate in continuing this study. I was obliged to abandon it at last. I could construe well enough to read an easy author by the help of a dictionary. I followed this route, and found it did very well. I applied to translation, not in writing, but mental, and kept to it. By time and exercise I attained reading off-hand pretty well the Latin authors, but never was able to speak or write that language; which has often confused me, when I was, I know not how, enrolled among men of letters. Another inconvenience in consequence of this method of learning is, I never knew prosody, much less the rules of versification. Desiring, however, to feel the harmony of the language in verse and prose, I have made many attempts to attain it; but am convinced that without a master it is almost impossible. Having learnt the composition of the easiest of all verse, which is the hexameter, I had the patience to scan almost all Virgil, and measure feet and quantity: then, when I was in doubt of a syllable's being long or short, it was my Virgil I consulted. This, as may be imagined, led me into many errors, because of the alterations permitted by the rules of versification. But if there is any advantage in studying alone, there are likewise great inconveniences, especially a difficulty past belief. I know it better than anyone.

Before noon I quitted my books, and if dinner was not ready, I paid a visit to my friends the pigeons, or worked in the garden till that hour. When I heard myself called, I ran up very happy, and provided with a good appetite; for it is worthy notice that, however ill I may be, my appetite never fails. We dined very agreeably, chattering on our affairs, till Mamma could eat. Two or three times a week, when it was fine, we went behind the house to take coffee in a little cabin, cool and bushy, which I had garnished with hops, that gave us great pleasure during the heat; we spent a short hour there, examining our vegetables and flowers, and in conversations relative to our manner of life, which caused us the more to feel its sweetness. I had another little family at the end of the garden; this was bees. I seldom failed, and often Mamma with me, to pay them a visit; I was much delighted with their labour; I was infinitely amused in seeing them return from plundering, their little thighs sometimes so loaded they could hardly move. At first, my curiosity made me indiscreet, and I was stung two or three times; but we afterwards got so well acquainted that, however near I went, they did not trouble me, and however full the hives might be, ready to swarm, I was sometimes encompassed by them, they came on my hands and face, without one of them ever stinging me. All animals mistrust man, and cannot be blamed; but are they once sure he will not injure them, their confidence becomes so great, he must be more than a barbarian that abuses it.

I returned to my books; but my occupations of the afternoon deserved much less the name of labour and study than of recreation and amusement. I never could bear the application of the closet after dinner, and in general all trouble hangs heavy during the heat of the day. I employed myself, however, but without constraint, and almost without rule, in reading without studying. The things I followed most punctually were history and geography, and, as they did not demand mental disputing, I made as much progress in them as my bad memory permitted. I wanted to study Father Pétau, and descended into the obscure mansions of chronology: but I grew disgusted at the critical parts which have neither bottom nor banks; and I was inclined to prefer the exact measure of time, and the motion of the celestial bodies. I should have even taken a taste to astronomy, had I had any instruments; but I must be contented with a few elements taken from books, and a few rough observations made with a telescope, only to know the general situation of the heavens: for my short sight does not permit me to distinguish the stars clearly with the naked eye. I recollect an adventure on this subject whose remembrance has often made me laugh. I bought a celestial planisphere to study the constellations. I placed this planisphere on a frame; on nights when the heavens were serene, I went into the garden to fix my frame on four stakes of my own height, the planisphere turned downwards, and to light it that the wind did not blow out my candle, I put it into a bucket on the ground between the four stakes; then looking alternately at the planisphere with my eye, and the stars with my telescope, I exercised myself in recognising

the stars and discerning the constellations. I think I have mentioned the garden of M. Noiret forming a terrace; you could see
from the road everything which passed. One evening some peasants going by pretty late, saw me, in a grotesque attire, employed
at this operation. The glimmering light which gave down on my
planisphere, of which they did not see the cause, because the
candle was hid from them by the sides of the bucket, the four
stakes, the large paper besmeared with figures, the frame, and
the motion of my telescope they saw go backwards and forwards,
gave to the whole affair an air of conjuration which terrified them.
My dress was not adapted to remove their fears: a flapped hat
over my cap, and a padded hood of Mamma's she had obliged
me to put on, offered to their view the image of a true sorcerer,
and, as it was near midnight, they did not in the least doubt but
the assembly of devils was commencing. Not very curious to see
more of it, they ran off extremely alarmed, awakened their neighbours to inform them of their vision; and the story ran about so
fast, that the next day everyone in the neighbourhood knew that
the nocturnal assembly of witches was held at M. Noiret's. I do
not know what this rumour might have produced, had not one
of the peasants, witness to my conjurations, carried his complaints
the next day to two Jesuits who visited us, and, without knowing
the real affair, provisionally undeceived them. They told us the
story, I told them the cause, and we laughed heartily. It was however resolved, for fear of a relapse, that I should, in future, make
my observations without light, and consult the planisphere in the
house. Those who have read, in the *Lettres de la Montagne*, my
magic of Venice, will find, I am sure, I had of long standing a
mighty calling to sorcery.

This was my course of life at les Charmettes, when I was not
employed in any rural occupation; for that had always the preference, and in anything which did not exceed my strength, I worked
like a labourer: it is true, indeed, my extreme weakness left me on
this article little more than the will. Besides, I would do two
things at once, for which reason neither of them was done well.
I had put it into my head to gain memory by force; I still persisted
in wanting to learn a deal by heart. In order to do this, I always
carried a book with me, which with incredible trouble I studied
and called over as I worked. I do not know why the obstinacy of
these vain and continual efforts did not render me stupid. I certainly have learned Virgil's eclogues over and over twenty times,
of which I do not know a single word. I lost or mis-sorted a mul-

titude of books, from the habit I had of carrying them everywhere with me, to the dove-house, the garden, the orchard or the vineyard. Employed on other things, I put my book at the foot of a tree or hedge; forgot to bring it from any place I had laid it; and often, in a fortnight after, I have found it rotten or eaten by pismires or snails. This ardour for learning became a passion which made a blockhead of me, incessantly occupied as I was mumbling something between my lips.

The writings of Port-Royal and the Oratory, being those I mostly read, had almost made me half a Jansenist, and, in spite of all my confidence, their tough theology sometimes terrified me. The terrors of hell, that till then I very little dreaded, troubled my security by degrees, and, had not Mamma given ease to my mind, this frightful doctrine had at last quite disordered me. My confessor, who was likewise hers, contributed his share in keeping me steady. It was Father Hemet, a Jesuit, a good and sage old man, whose memory I shall always revere. Though a Jesuit, he had the simplicity of a child, and his morality, less relaxed than mild, was precisely necessary to balance the melancholy impressions of Jansenism. This good man, and his companion, Father Coppier, came often to see us at les Charmettes, though the road was very rough and pretty long for people of their age. Their visits were of great service to me: I hope God will return it their souls; for they were then too old to presume them still alive. I went also to see them at Chambéry; I grew by degrees familiar in their house; their library was at my service. The remembrance of these happy times is connected with the Jesuits so as to make me love one for the other; and though their doctrine always appeared to me dangerous, I never could find in me sincerely to hate them.

I should like to know whether there pass in the minds of other men the like puerile notions which sometimes passed in mine. Amidst my studies, and a life as innocent as man could read, and in spite of all they said to me, the fear of hell nevertheless often agitated me. I questioned myself thus: In what situation am I? Were I to die now, should I be damned? According to my Jansenists, the thing was indubitable; but according to my conscience, it appeared otherwise. Always in fear, and floating in this cruel uncertainty, I had recourse, to get out of it, to the most laughable expedients, for which I would willingly shut a man up, were I to see him do the same. One day, musing on this melancholy subject, I exercised myself mechanically in throwing stones at the trunks of trees, and that with my usual address, that is, without hitting one of them. All at once, in the middle of this pretty exercise, I took it in my head to invent a kind of prognostic to calm my uneasiness. I say to myself, I will go now and throw this stone at the tree which faces me: if I hit it, sign of salvation; if I miss it, sign of hell. In saying thus I throw my stone with a trembling hand, and with a horrible beating of the heart, but so fortunately, it went straight to the body of the tree; which in fact was not very difficult; for I had taken care to choose it very large and very near. Since this I have never doubted of salvation. I do not know in recalling this action whether I should laugh or lament over myself. You great and eminent men, you laugh of course; congratulate yourselves, but do not insult my wretchedness, for I swear to you I feel it sufficiently.

As to the rest, these alarms, inseparable perhaps from devotion, were not permanent. I was commonly pretty easy, and the impression the idea of an approaching death made on my mind was not so much melancholy as a peaceable languor, which had its delights too. I have lately found, among some old papers, a sort of exhortation I made to myself, where I congratulated myself on dying at an age in which we have courage to face death, before I had experienced in life great ills of body or mind. How well I reasoned! A misgiving made me fear life for its sufferings. It seemed I foresaw the fate which awaited my old age. I was never so near wisdom as at this happy period. Without great remorse for the past, delivered from the care of futurity, the ruling sentiment of my mind was to enjoy the present. Devotees have in general a little sensuality, extremely keen, which makes them savour with delight the innocent pleasures permitted them. Worldlings impute it to them as a crime, I know not why, or rather I do know. It is because they envy others the enjoyment of the simple pleasures for which they have lost all taste. I had this taste, and found it pleasing to satisfy it in surety of conscience. My heart, as yet new, gave in to all with the pleasure of a child, or rather, if I dare say so, with the voluptuousness of an angel; for really these tranquil enjoyments have the serenity of those of Paradise. Dinners dressed on the grass at Montagnole, suppers in the arbour, gathering in the fruits, vintage, peeling flax in the evening with our people, these things were to us so many holidays, in which Mamma took as much pleasure as myself. More solitary walks had still greater charms, because the mind could expand itself more freely. We took one amongst others, which forms an epoch in my memory, one St. Louis's Day, whose name Mamma bore. We set out

together, by ourselves, early in the morning after mass a Car-
melite came to say for us at break of day in a chapel adjoining
the house. I proposed going on the opposite side to that we were
on, which we had not yet seen. We sent our provisions before us,
for the outing was to last the whole day. Mamma, though a little
round and fat, did not walk ill; we went from hill to hill, and
from copse to copse, sometimes in the sun, and often in the shade;
reposing from time to time, and forgetting ourselves for hours
together; chatting of ourselves, our union, the mildness of our
fate, and making prayers for its duration which were not heard.
Everything seemed to conspire to the happiness of this day. It had
lately rained, no dust, and brooks which finely purled. A gentle
wind disturbed the leaves, the air was pure, the horizon without a

J.-J.'S ROOM AT LES CHARMETTES

cloud; serenity reigned in the heavens as in our minds. Our dinner
was dressed at a peasant's, and divided with his family, who
heartily blessed us. What good kind of people these poor Savoyards are! After dinner we got under the shade of some large trees,
where, whilst I gathered some bits of dry wood to make the coffee,
Mamma amused herself herbalizing amongst the bushes, and
with the flowers of a nosegay that in going along I had picked her
up: she remarked to me, in their structure, a thousand curious
things which greatly delighted me, and ought to have given me a
relish for botany; but the time was not yet come; I was taken off
by too many other studies. An idea which struck me diverted me
from flowers and plants. The situation of mind I was in, all we
said and did that day, every object which struck me, brought to

my remembrance the sort of dream which, quite awake, I had
at Annecy seven or eight years before, of which I gave an account
in its place. The affinity was so striking, that in reflecting on it
I was moved to tears. In transports of tenderness I embraced my
lovely friend. Mamma, Mamma, said I to her with fondness, this
day has been long promised me, and I see nothing which can
surpass it. My happiness, thanks to you, is now at its meridian;
may it never more decline! May it last as long as I conserve the
wish for it! it will finish but with me.

Thus my happy hours glided away, and so much the happier,
as I perceived nothing that could trouble them; I expected their
end, in fact, only with mine. Not that the source of my cares was
absolutely stopped; but I saw it take another course, which I
directed, as well as I could, towards useful objects, in order that
it might carry its remedy with it. Mamma was naturally fond of
the country, and this inclination did not cool in me. By little and
little she inclined to rural cares; she loved the cultivation of land,
and had some knowledge of it, which she made use of with delight. Not contented with that which belonged to the house she
had taken, she sometimes hired a field, sometimes a meadow. In
fine, carrying her enterprising humour to objects of agriculture,
instead of remaining unemployed in her house, she took the road
to becoming a great farmer. I was not fond of seeing her thus
extend her views, and opposed it with all my might; certain she
would be continually cheated, and that her liberal and prodigal
humour would always carry the expense beyond the produce.
However, I consoled myself by thinking that this produce would
at least not be useless, and would help her to live. Of all the undertakings she could form, this appeared to be the least ruinous; and
without looking on it, as she did, as an object of profit, I saw it as
a continual occupation which would shield her against worse
business and sharpers. In this notion I ardently desired to recover
as much health and strength as would be necessary to mind her
business, to be overseer of her labourers, or her head-labourer;
and, naturally, the exercise it caused me, taking me often from
my books and diverting me from my condition, must have made
it easier.

The following winter, Barillot, returning from Italy, brought
me a few books, amongst them the *Bontempi* and the *Cartella per
Musica* of Father Banchieri, which gave me a relish for the history
of music and the theoretical researches on this charming art.
Barillot remained some time with us, and as I was of age some

months since,[1] it was agreed I should go the following spring to Geneva, to receive my mother's heritage, or at least that part which belonged to me, till it could be known what was become of my brother. It was put in execution, as had been resolved. I went to Geneva; my father came there also. For a long while he had come there again as he pleased, without their opposing it, though he had not justified himself of the accusation; but as they esteemed his courage, and respected his probity, they feigned to have forgotten the affair, and the magistrates, employed on the grand project which appeared soon after, would not rouse the citizens before the time, in renewing mal-à-propos their ancient partiality.

I feared meeting difficulties as to the change of my religion; they did not make one. The laws of Geneva are in this respect less rigid than those of Berne, where whoever changes his religion loses not only his freedom, but his estate. Mine was not therefore disputed, but was reduced, I know not how, to a very trifle.[2] Though they were almost sure of the death of my brother, there was no legal proof: I was not sufficiently entitled to claim his share, and left it without regret to assist my father, who enjoyed it till his death. As soon as the formality of justice was got through, and I had received my money, I laid some of it out on books, and ran to carry the rest to Mamma. My heart beat with joy on the road, and the moment I put this money into her hands was a thousand times more charming than that which brought it into mine. She received it with the simplicity of noble minds, which, doing things of that sort without effort, see them without admiration. Almost all this money was laid out on me, and that with the same simplicity. Its use had been the same, had it come from any other quarter.

I did not, however, recover my health. I, on the contrary, decayed visibly. I was as pale as death, and as thin as a skeleton. My beating of the arteries was terrible, my palpitations more frequent; I was continually oppressed, and my weakness became at last so great, I moved with trouble; I could not hasten my steps without stifling, I could not stoop without giddiness, I could not lift the lightest thing; I was reduced to the most torturing inaction, for a stirring man like me. It is certain the vapours made a

---

[1] There is confusion here. So far this book has dealt with Rousseau's two periods of residence at les Charmettes in 1738-9; from this point the story goes back to 1737, on the 28th of June in which year Rousseau, at the age of twenty-five, attained his majority by Genevese custom.

[2] Rousseau received 6500 florins by his mother's death.

part of all this. Vapours is the disease of happy minds; it was mine: the tears I often shed without subject, the violent dread at the noise of a leaf or bird, the unequal humour in the calm of a happy life, all these things proved the heaviness of an easy being, which makes, in a manner, sensibility grow dotish. We are so little made for happiness here below, it is necessary the mind or body should suffer, if not both; and the good condition of one generally hurts the other. Had I been able deliciously to enjoy life, my decaying frame prevented it, without the possibility of knowing the true seat of the cause of the disorder. In process of time, in spite of declining age and real and very serious illness, my body seems to recover its strength, the better to feel its misery; and now that I am writing this, infirm and near sixty, over-whelmed with affliction of every sort, I find in myself, for suffer-ing, more vigour and life than I had for enjoyment in the flower of youth, and in the bosom of real happiness.

To finish my own history, having brought a little physiology into my studies, I began to study anatomy; and reviewing the multitude and action of the pieces which composed my own frame, I expected to feel it disjointed twenty times a day; far from being surprised that I was dying, I was surprised I was alive, and never read the description of a disorder which I did not think my own. I am certain that, had I not been ill, this fatal study would have made me so. Finding in each disorder symptoms of mine, I thought I had them all, and got one still more cruel, of which I thought I was delivered; the notion of being curable: it is a difficult one to avoid, when you read treatises on medicine. By dint of searching, reflecting, comparing, I was on the point of imagining the basis of my disorder was a polypus on the heart, and Salomon himself seemed struck with this idea. I ought reasonably to have departed from this opinion, to confirm myself in my preceding resolution. I did not do so. I set all the springs of my mind to work to find a cure for a polypus on the heart, resolved to undertake this mar-vellous cure. In a journey Anet made to Montpellier to see the Garden of Plants and the Demonstrator M. Sauvage, he heard there that M. Fizes cured a like polypus. Mamma remembered and spoke to me of it. I wanted nothing more to fill me with a desire of going to consult M. Fizes. The hopes of recovering made courage and strength return to undertake the journey. The money from Geneva furnished the means. Mamma, far from dissuading, exhorts me into it; so I am off for Montpellier.

I had no occasion to go so far to find the doctor I wanted. The horse tiring me too much, I took a chaise at Grenoble. At Moirans five or six other chaises came up behind mine. Now it was really the chair adventure.[1] The greater part of these chaises were the retinue of a new-married woman, whose name was Madame du Colombier. With her was another lady, Madame de Larnage, not so young or pretty as Madame du Colombier, but as amiable, and who was to continue her journey from Romans, where the first lady was to stop, as far as Bourg-Saint-Andéol, near Pont-Saint-Esprit. With the timidity I am known to have, it is expected an acquaintance was not soon made with brilliant ladies and the suite which accompanied them; but at last, going the same road, lodging at the same inns, and, on pain of passing for an unsociable fellow, obliged to come to the same table, this acquaintance was forcibly made. It was made then, and even sooner than I desired; for all this noise and figure did not much suit a sick man, and particularly a sick man of my humour. But curiosity makes the jades so insinuating that, in order to know a man, they begin by turning his brain. Thus it happened to me. Madame du Colombier, too much surrounded by her young curs, had not much time to eye me, and besides, it was not worth while, as we were separating; but Madame de Larnage, not so beset, had a provision to make for her journey. Madame de Larnage undertakes me, so farewell poor Jean-Jacques, or rather farewell fever, vapours, polypus; all depart at her presence, except certain palpitations which remained, of which she would not cure me. The bad state of my health was the first text of our acquaintance. They saw I was ill, knew I was going to Montpellier, and my look and manner could not have announced a debauchee, for it was clear by the sequel they did not suspect I was going to the gruel warehouse.[2] Though an ill state of health in a man is no great recommendation to the ladies, it rendered me interesting to them. In the morning they sent to ask after my health, and to invite me to take chocolate with them; they must know how I had passed the night. Once, according to my laudable custom of speaking before I thought, I told them I did not know. This answer inclined them to think me silly; they examined me farther, and this examination was not unfavourable to me. I once heard Madame du Colombier say to her friend, He is unacquainted with the world, but he is amiable. This encouraged me much, and caused me to become so in effect.

[1] In Scarron's *Roman comique; cf.* above, p. 126.
[2] *Faire un tour de casserole:* a familiar phrase signifying to undergo treatment for venereal disease.

Growing familiar, I must speak of myself, say where I came from, who I was. This embarrassed me; for I knew very well that, in good company, and with coquettes, this word of a new convert would destroy me. I know not from what whimsy I took it in my head to pass for an Englishman. I called myself a Jacobite, they took me as such; I said my name was Dudding, and was called M. Dudding. A cursed Marquis of Torignan, who was there, ill like me, older too, and ill-natured enough, must begin a conversation with M. Dudding. He talked to me of King James, of the Pretender, of the ancient Court of St. Germain; I was on thorns. I knew no more of it than I had read in Count Hamilton,[1] and in the newspapers; I however made so good use of this little, I got out of the hobble: happy on not being questioned on the English language, of which I did not know a single word.

Every one of the company was very agreeable, and saw with regret the hour of separation. We went a snail's journey. We came to Saint-Marcellin on a Sunday; Madame de Larnage would go to Mass; I went with her; that had nearly spoiled all. I behaved as I have always done. By my modest and reserved countenance she thought me devout, and began to have a poor opinion of me, as she owned two days afterwards. I was under the necessity of a deal of gallantry to wipe off this bad impression; or rather Madame de Larnage, like an experienced woman, who was not easily repulsed, thought proper to run the hazard of her advances to see how I might behave. She made me many, and such that, far from presuming on my person, I thought she jeered me. From this folly there was not a blunder but I was guilty of; it was worse than the Marquis du Legs.[2] Madame de Larnage held it out, gave me so many glances, said such tender things, a man much less stupid had been puzzled to take it seriously. The more she did, the more she confirmed my idea; and that which tortured me most was, that I took fire in earnest. I said to myself, and to her with a sigh, Ah! why is not this true? I should be the happiest of men. I believe my simplicity as a novice did but irritate her fancy; she would not be disappointed.

We left Madame du Colombier and her attendants at Romans. We continued our road as slowly and agreeably as possible, Madame de Larnage, the Marquis of Torignan, and myself. The Marquis, though ill and grumbling, was a good sort of a man, but who did not love to eat bread with roast meat in sight. Madame

---

[1] 1646-1720; author of the *Mémoires de Gramont*.
[2] A timid lover in a comedy by Marivaux.

de Larnage took so little pains to hide her inclination to me, that he perceived it before me, and his arch sarcasms ought at least to have created more confidence than I had in the lady's kindness, if by an untoward thought, whereof I alone was capable, I had not imagined they had agreed to ridicule me. This stupid idea quite turned my head, and made me act the flattest personage, in a situation where my heart, being really caught, might have dictated a brilliant one. I cannot conceive how Madame de Larnage was not disgusted at my awkward figure, or did not dismiss me in the greatest disdain. But she was a woman of sense, who could discern her man, and who plainly saw there was more stupidity than coolness in my proceedings.

She at last made herself understood; but it was not without trouble. We arrived at Valence to dinner, and, according to our laudable custom, we spent the rest of the day there. We lodged without the city, at St. Jacques. I shall for ever remember that inn, as well as the room Madame de Larnage had taken. After dinner she would take a turn; she knew the Marquis would not go out: it was the method of procuring a tête-à-tête, of which she was resolved to make the best; for no more time could be lost were some to remain for use. We walked round the outside of the city, along the ditch. There I returned to my long story of complaints, to which she replied in so tender a tone, squeezing my hand, which she held, sometimes to her heart, that nothing but a stupidity like mine could suspect her being serious. The most extraordinary of all was myself being excessively moved. I have already said she was amiable; love made her charming, and rendered her all the splendour of her prime of youth, and she ordered her glancings with so much art, she had seduced a statue. I was therefore very little at my ease, and always on the point of licentiousness. But the fear of offending or displeasing, the still greater dread of being hooted, hissed, laughed at, being the talk at table, being complimented on my success by the unmerciful Marquis, made me full of indignation against myself for my stupid bashfulness, which I was not able to overcome by reproaching myself. I was on the rack; I had already left off my talk in Céladon's fashion,[1] feeling how ridiculous it was in so fine a train; not knowing what countenance to keep or say, I said nothing, I had the air of a discontented person; in fine, I did everything necessary to draw on myself the

[1] Céladon is a devoted but bashful lover who appears in Honoré d'Urfé's play *Astrée*.

treatment I dreaded. Luckily, Madame de Larnage took a more humane method. She hastily broke this silence by throwing her arm round my neck, and in an instant her lips spoke too plainly on mine to leave me any longer in error. The crisis could not happen more àpropos. I became loving. It was time. She gave me that confidence, the want of which has always hindered me from being myself. I was so this time. Never had my eyes, senses, heart, or mouth, spoken so well before; never did I so amply repair my faults; and, if this trifling conquest cost Madame de Larnage some trouble, I had reason to think she did not regret it.

Were I to live a hundred years, I should always recall with pleasure the remembrance of this charming woman. I say charming, though she was neither pretty nor young; but not being ugly or old, she had nothing in her person which prevented her wit and grace from having all their effect. Quite contrary to other women, her freshness appeared least in her face; I believe rouge had spoiled it. She had reasons for her facility; it was the method of showing herself to advantage. You might see her and not love her, but not possess her without adoring her; which proves, I think, she was not always so prodigal of her kindness as with me. She had a taste too prompt and violent to be excusable, but where the heart went at least as much as the senses; and during the short and delightful instants I passed with her, I had reason to believe, by the forced restraints she imposed on me, that, though sensual and voluptuous, she loved my health more than her pleasure.

Our understanding did not escape the Marquis. He did not banter me the less: on the contrary, he treated me more than ever as a poor chilled lover, a martyr to the rigours of his mistress. He never let fall a word, a smile, a look, which could make me suspect he guessed us; and I had believed him our dupe, had not Madame de Larnage, who saw farther than I, told me he was not, but that he was a gentleman; in fact, it was impossible for a man to carry himself genteeler or behave with more politeness than he always did, even towards me, except his pleasantry, particularly since my success: he attributed the honour, perhaps, to me, and supposed me less a blockhead than I appeared; he was mistaken, as you have seen, but no matter; I benefited by his error, and it is certain that I, being then on the right side, laughed heartily and with a good grace at his epigrams, and sometimes returned them happily enough, quite proud of claiming the honour, in Madame de Larnage's company, of the wit she gave me. I was no longer the same man.

We were in a country and a season of plenty. We enjoyed it excellently everywhere, thanks to the kind offices of the Marquis. I had wished, however, he had not extended them quite to our chambers; but he always sent his lackey forward to take them, and the rogue, whether of himself, or whether by order of his master, always put him next to Madame de Larnage, and thrust me into the farther end of the house; but that gave me little trouble, for our meetings were the more poignant. This delightful life lasted four or five days, during which I was intoxicated with the most charming pleasure. I tasted it pure, lively, without the least mixture of pain. This was the first and the sole I have thus tasted; and I may say, I am indebted to Madame de Larnage for not having died without knowing pleasure.

If what I felt for her was not precisely love, it was at least so tender a return for that she showed me, it was a sensuality so heated by pleasure, and an intimacy so sweet in conversation, it had all the charms of passion without its delirium, which turns the brain and prevents enjoyment. I never felt true love but once in my life, and that was not with her. I did not love her, neither, as I had loved and as I did love Madame de Warens; but that was the only reason I possessed her a thousand times more. With Mamma, my pleasure was always troubled by sadness, by a secret oppression of the heart I could not surmount without pain: instead of congratulating myself on possessing her, I reproached myself with having debased her. With Madame de Larnage, on the contrary, proud of being a man and happy, I gave in to sense with joy, with confidence; I partook of the impression I made on hers; I was enough myself to contemplate my triumph with as much vanity as voluptuousness, and to draw from that sufficient to redouble it.

I do not recollect where we quitted the Marquis, who was of that country; but we were alone before we arrived at Montélimart, and then Madame de Larnage fixed her maid in my chaise, and I went with her in hers. I assure you we were not tired of the length of our journey in this manner, and I should be troubled to give the least account of the country we passed through. At Montélimart she had business, which detained her three days, during which she quitted me, however, but a quarter of an hour for a visit, which brought on her some mortifying importunities and invitations she took care not to accept. Her pretext was indisposition, which nevertheless did not prevent us taking a turn every day by ourselves in the finest country and in the finest

climate in the world. Oh, those three days! I ought sometimes to
regret them; the like have never returned.

Travelling amours are not made to last. We must separate, and
I own it was time; not that I was satiated or beginning to be so:
it engaged me every day more; but, in spite of all my mistress's
discretion, little more remained than the will; and, before we
separated, I wanted to enjoy that little more, which she allowed
as a precaution against the Montpellier girls. We flattered our
regrets by the plan of a reunion. It was determined that, as this
regimen was good for me, I should make use of it, and go pass the
winter at Bourg-Saint-Andéol, under the direction of Madame de
Larnage. I was to stay at Montpellier five or six weeks only, to
give her time to prepare things so as to prevent babble. She gave
me ample instructions on all I ought to know, on what I ought to
say, and the manner I should carry myself. In the meantime we
were to write to each other. She talked a great deal, and seriously,
on the attention to my health; exhorted me to consult men of
experience, to be extremely attentive to all they prescribed, and
undertook, however severe their prescriptions might be, to make
me execute them when with her. I believe she spoke sincerely, for
she loved me; she gave me a thousand proofs of it, more certain
than favours. She judged by my equipment I did not wallow in
opulence; though she was not herself rich, she insisted, at our separation, I should partake of her purse she brought from Grenoble

PONT DU GARD

pretty well garnished, and I had much trouble to excuse myself. I quitted her at last, with a heart full of her, and she, I thought, with a real attachment for me.

I finished my journey by beginning it again in my mind, and, for once, extremely satisfied at being in a convenient chaise to meditate, at my ease, on the pleasures I had tasted, and those which were promised me. I thought of nothing but Bourg-Saint-Andéol, and the charming hours which awaited me there. I saw nothing but Madame de Larnage, and that which surrounded her. The rest of the universe was nothing for me; even Mamma was forgot. I was employed in combining in my head every detail into which Madame de Larnage entered, to give me beforehand an idea of her dwelling, her neighbourhood, her society, of her whole method of living. She had a daughter, of whom she often spoke with extreme fondness. This daughter was more than fifteen; she was lively, charming, and of an amiable character. I had a promise of being caressed by her; I did not forget this promise, and was curious in imagining how Mlle. de Larnage would treat her Mamma's gallant. These were the subjects of my meditation from Pont-Saint-Esprit quite to Remoulin. I was told to see the Pont du Gard. I did not fail. After breakfasting on excellent figs, I took a guide, and went to see the Pont du Gard. It was the first I had seen of the works of the Romans. I expected to find a monument worthy the hands which constructed it. This once the object surpassed my expectations; it was the only time in my life. It belonged to the Romans only to produce this effect. The aspect of this simple and noble work struck me so much the more, as it is in the middle of a desert, whose silence and solitude render the object more striking, and our admiration more lively; for this pretended bridge was no more than an aqueduct. We ask ourselves what power transported these enormous stones so far from any quarry, or united the hands of so many thousand people in a place where there is not a single one? I went up the three stories of this superb edifice, which respect almost prevented me from treading on. The sound of my steps under these immense vaults made me imagine I heard the magnanimous voices of those who built them. I was lost like an insect in this immensity. While feeling my own littleness, I experienced something that elevated my soul; I said to myself with a sigh, Why am not I a Roman! I remained there several hours in a ravishing contemplation. I returned diverted and meditating, and this meditation was not favourable to Madame de Larnage. She took care to forewarn me

of the girls of Montpellier, but not of the Pont du Gard. One
cannot think of everything.

At Nîmes I went to see the Amphitheatre. It is a more magnificent building than the Pont du Gard, but made much less impression on me, whether my admiration was weakened by the
first object, or the situation of the other in the middle of a city
was less adapted to excite it. This vast and superb circus is surrounded by little dirty houses, and other houses less and dirtier
fill the Amphitheatre; so that the whole produces but an unequal
and confused effect, where regret and indignation stifle pleasure
and surprise. Since this I have seen the circus of Verona, infinitely
less as to size and beauty than that of Nîmes, but kept in order,
and preserved with all possible decency and cleanness, and which
from thence only made a much stronger and more agreeable impression on me. The French are careful of nothing, nor respect
any monument. They are all fire for undertaking, and cannot
finish or keep in order anything.

I was changed to such a point, and my sensuality, put in motion,
was so well awakened, I stopped one day at the *Pont de Lunel* to
feast myself with a company I found there. This tavern, the most
esteemed in Europe, at that time merited it. Those who kept it
knew how to make the most of its happy situation, to keep it
abundantly supplied with choice provisions. It was really curious
to find, in a lone house, in the middle of a plain, a table supplied
with fresh and sea fish, excellent game, fine wines, served with
those attentions and care you meet with at the houses of the rich
and great only, and all this for thirty-five sous. But the *Pont de
Lunel* did not long remain on this footing, and, by continually
wearing out its reputation, it at last lost it entirely.

I had forgot on my road I was ill, and recollected it only on my
arrival at Montpellier. My vapours were quite cured, but all my
other disorders remained; and though, from habit, I felt them less,
it was sufficient to believe oneself dead, to him who should be
attacked by them all at once. In fact, they were less painful than
dreadful, and caused the mind to suffer more than the body, whose
destruction they seemed to announce. This was the reason that,
diverted by lively passions, I thought no more of my situation;
but, as it was not imaginary, I felt it as soon as I was cool. I therefore thought seriously on the advice of Madame de Larnage, and
on the intention of my journey. I went and consulted the most
noted practitioners, particularly M. Fizes, and from a super-
abundance of precaution I boarded at a physician's. He was an

Irishman, named Fitz-Moris, who kept a table for a number of
students in medicine: it was very convenient for patients, as M.
Fitz-Moris contented himself with a decent price for board, and
took nothing of his boarders for his attendance as physician. He
undertook the execution of M. Fize's prescriptions, and to take
care of my health. He acquitted himself well of this employment,
as to regimen; no indigestions were heard of at his house: and
though I am not very sensible to privations of this sort, the objects
of comparison were so near, I could not help finding sometimes in
myself that M. de Torignan was a better provider than M. Fitz-
Moris. However, as we were not starved, and these youths were
quite gay, this manner of living really did me good, and prevented
my falling again into languor. I spent the morning in taking drugs,
particularly I know not what waters, I believe the waters of Vals,
and writing to Madame de Larnage; for our correspondence kept
its course, and Rousseau undertook to receive Dudding's letters.
At twelve I took a turn to the Canourgue, with a few of our young
boarders, who were all good fellows; we re-assembled, went to
dinner. After dinner an important business occupied the most of
us till the evening: this was going out of town to play the price of
the afternoon's collation at two or three games of mall. I did not
play; I had neither strength nor address; but I betted, and following, with the interest in the bet, the players and the bowls across
rugged roads, and full of stones, I used an agreeable and salutary
exercise which agreed with me very well. We took our collation
at an inn without the city. I have no occasion to say these collations were gay, but I will add they were pretty decent, though
the landlord's daughters were pretty. M. Fitz-Moris, a great
player at mall, was our president; and I will say, in opposition
to the bad reputation of the students, I found more morality and
decency among these youths, than it would be easy to find among
the same number of grown men. They were more noisy than in-
temperate, more gay than libertine; and I get up so easily to a way
of life when it is voluntary, I had desired nothing better than to
see that always last. There were several Irishmen among these
students, from whom I endeavoured to learn some words of English, by way of precaution for Bourg-Saint-Andéol; for the time
of going there approached. Madame de Larnage pressed me to it
every post, and I prepared to obey her. It is clear my physicians,
who understood nothing of my disorder, regarded it as an imaginary illness, and treated me on this footing with their drugs, their
waters and their whey. Entirely in contradiction to theologians,

physicians and philosophers admit as true only what they can explain, and make of their understanding the measure of possibilities. These gentlemen knew nothing of my disorder; therefore I had none: for how suppose that doctors do not know all? I saw they only sought to amuse and make me spend my money, and judging their substitute of Bourg-Saint-Andéol might do that as well as they, but more agreeably, I resolved to give her the preference, and left Montpellier with this sage intention.

I set off near the end of November,[1] after six weeks' or two months' residence in this city, where I left a dozen guineas without any benefit to my health or instruction, except a course of anatomy begun under M. Fitz-Moris, which I was obliged to abandon from the horrible stench of the bodies they dissected, and which it was impossible I could support.

Inwardly uneasy at the resolution I had taken, I reflected on it as I advanced towards the Pont-Saint-Esprit, which was equally the road to Bourg-Saint-Andéol and Chambéry. The remembrance of Mamma and her letters, though less frequent than those from Madame de Larnage, awakened in my heart the remorses I had stifled during my first journey. They became so violent on my return, that, balancing love with pleasure, they put me in a situation of listening to reason only. First, in the character of adventurer I was going to recommence, I might be less happy than the first time; nothing was wanting in all Bourg-Saint-Andéol, but a single person who had been in England, who knew the English, or their language, to unmask me. Madame de Larnage's family might show some ill-humours, and treat me uncivilly. Her daughter, on whom I still thought more than I ought to have done, gave me uneasiness. I dreaded becoming amorous, and this fear did more than half the business. Was I then going, as a return for the mother's kindness, to endeavour to corrupt her daughter, join the most detestable connexions, bring dissension, dishonour, scandal and hell on her house? This thought appeared horrible; I therefore took the firm resolution of combating and vanquishing this unhappy turn, should it happen to declare itself. But why expose myself to this conflict? What a miserable state to live with the mother, by whom I should be cloyed, and burn for the daughter, without daring to declare it? What necessity of seeking this state, and exposing myself to ills, affronts, remorse, for pleasures whose greatest charms I had exhausted in advance; for it is cer-

---

[1] In fact in December (1737).

tain my fancy had lost its first vivacity. The relish of pleasure still remained, but the passion was no more. With this were mixed reflections relative to my situation, my duty, and to that Mamma so kind, so generous, who, already loaded with debts, was more so by my foolish expenses, who drained herself for me, and whom I was going so basely to deceive. This reproach became so violent, it carried it at last. In approaching Saint-Esprit, I took the resolution to hurry over the Bourg-Saint-Andéol stage, and go straight on. I executed it courageously, with a few sighs, I own; but also with that inward satisfaction I tasted for the first time in my life, when I could say to myself, I deserve my own esteem; I can prefer my duty to my pleasures. This was the first real obligation I had to reading. That it was which taught me to reflect and compare. After having adopted principles so pure not long before, after those rules of wisdom and virtue I had made myself, and that I felt myself so ambitious to follow, the shame of being so little consistent with myself, of belying so soon and so openly my own maxims, got the better of pleasure: pride had, perhaps, as great a share in my resolution as virtue; but if this pride is not virtue, it produces effects so like it, the mistake is pardonable.

One of the advantages of good actions is to raise the soul and dispose it to better: for such is human weakness, one must add to the number of good actions abstinence from the evil we are tempted to commit. The moment I had taken my resolution, I became another man, or rather became that I was before, and which this hour of intoxication had caused to disappear. Full of good sentiments and good resolutions, I continued my journey in the prudent intention of expiating my fault; thinking to regulate my future conduct by the laws of virtue, to consecrate myself without reserve to the best of mothers, to promise her as much fidelity as I had attachment, and to listen to no other love than that of my duty. Alas! the sincerity of my return to prudence seemed to promise me another destiny; but mine was written and already began; and when my heart, filled with the love of right and honest things, saw nought but innocence and blessings in life, I had reached the fatal moment which was to drag after it the long string of my misfortunes.

My eagerness to get home had made me more diligent than I intended: I had written to her from Valence the day and hour of my arrival. Having gained half a day on my calculation, I stayed that time at Chaparillan, in order to arrive just at the moment I had fixed. I would taste in all its delight the pleasure of seeing her again. I chose rather to defer it a little, to add to it that of being expected. This precaution had always succeeded. I always observed my arrival distinguished by a kind of holiday: I expected no less this time, and this eagerness about me, of which I was so sensible, was worth taking care of.

I thus arrived exactly at the hour. From a great distance I kept looking to see her in the road; my heart beat more and more still as I drew near. I come in, quite out of breath; for I had left my carriage in town: I see nobody in the court, at the door, or the window; I begin to be uneasy; I dread some accident. I go in, all is quiet; some workmen were eating in the kitchen; as to the rest, no preparation. The servant appeared surprised to see me; she was ignorant of my being expected. I go up, I see her at last, this dear Mamma, so purely, so tenderly, so passionately loved; I run, I throw myself at her feet. Ah! there thou art, my little one, said she, and embraced me; hast thou had a pleasant journey? How dost thou do? This reception put me a little to the stand. I asked her if she had received my letter. She told me she had. I should have thought not, said I; and the explanation ended there. There was a young man with her. I knew him, having seen him in the house before my departure: but now he seemed fixed there; so he was. In short, I found my place filled.

This young man was from the country of Vaud; his father, whose name was Vintzenried, was keeper, or, as he styled himself, captain of the castle of Chillon. The son of the noble captain was a journeyman barber, and ran about the country in this quality, when he came to present himself to Madame de Warens, who received him well, as she did every traveller, and particularly those of her own country. He was a great, senseless fellow, well enough made, with a flat face, and mind the same, talking like the beau Léandre,[1] mixing all the style and accent of his trade with the long history of his good successes, naming only half the Marchionesses he had lain with, and pretending never to have dressed a pretty woman's head without dressing that of her husband. Vain, sottish, ignorant, insolent; at bottom the best fellow in the world. This was the substitute which was taken during my absence, and the associate offered me after my return.

Oh! if souls, disengaged from their terrestrial clog, still see from the womb of eternal light what passes among mortals, pardon, beloved and respected shade, my showing no more favour to your

---

[1] A fop; a stock Italian comic character.

faults than my own, and equally unveiling both one and the other to the reader's sight! I ought, I will speak truth, as well of you as of myself; your loss will be trifling compared to mine. Ah! how much your mild and lovely character, your inexhaustible bounty of heart, your frankness, and all your excellent virtues, outweigh your weakness, if the straying of reason only can be called so! Yours were errors, not vices; your conduct was reprehensible, but your heart was always pure. Weigh the good with the evil, and be fair; what other woman, were her secret life laid open like yours, would ever dare to compare herself with you?

The newcomer showed himself zealous, diligent, exact in all his trifling commissions, which were without number; he made himself the overseer of her workmen. As noisy as I was otherwise, he was seen and particularly heard at the plough, the haystack, the wood, the stable, the poultry. He neglected nothing but the garden, because it was too peaceable a business, and made no noise. His greatest pleasure was in loading and carting, sawing and cleaving of wood; he always had a hatchet or pickaxe in hand; you might hear him running, wedging, and bawling as loud as he could. I know not how many men's work he did, but he made as much noise as ten or twelve would have done. All this bustle imposed on poor Mamma; she thought this young man a treasure. Willing to attach him to herself, she used every means she thought would answer that end, without forgetting that she most depended on.

My heart cannot be hid, nor its constant and true feelings, particularly those which at that moment brought me back to her. What a swift, complete disorder over all my frame! Take my place and judge. In one moment I saw for ever vanish all my future promised blessings. All those pleasing thoughts so affectionately caressed disappear; and I, who from my childhood could see my existence but in hers, saw myself alone for the first time. This moment was dreadful; those which followed were always gloomy. I was still young; but the lovely sentiment of hope and enjoyment which enlivens youth, left me for ever. Thenceforward the sensible being remained but half alive. I saw nothing more before me than the dull remains of an insipid life; and if sometimes an image of hope still glanced through my thoughts, this hope was not for me; I felt that even in its possession I could not be truly happy.

I was so stupid and so full of confidence that, in spite of the familiar tone of the newcomer, which I regarded as an effect of

Mamma's easy humour, which was familiar with all, I should
not have suspected the real cause, had she not told it me herself;
but she hastened to make this acknowledgement with a frankness
capable of adding to my rage, could my heart have inclined that
way; finding, as to herself, the thing quite simple, reproaching
my negligence in the house, and alleging my frequent absence,
as if she was of a constitution in haste to fill up the void. Ah,
Mamma, said I, with a heart oppressed with anguish, what do you
dare inform me of? What a return for an affection like mine! Did
you so often save my life, but to deprive it of all it loved? It will
be my death, you will be sorry for me. She answered me, in a
tone so easy as to distract me, that I was a baby; that people did
not die of those things; that I lost nothing by that; that we should
be equally good friends, not less intimate in every sense; that her
tender attachment to me could neither decrease nor end but with
herself. She made me understand, in fine, that my rights continued the same, and that dividing them with another did not
deprive me of them.

Never did the purity, reality, the power of my feelings for her
— never did the sincerity, the honesty of my soul, make themselves better known to me than on this occasion. I fell at her feet,
I embraced her knees, pouring forth a torrent of tears. No, Mamma, said I, with emotion, I love you too well to debase you; your
possession is too dear to be divided: the regret which accompanied
its acquisition has increased with my love; no, I cannot keep it
at that price. You will always be adored by me; be always worthy
of it: it is more necessary I should honour than possess you. It is
to yourself, Mamma, I resign you; it is to the union of our minds
I sacrifice every pleasure. May I perish a thousand times, rather
than taste any which degrades her I love!

I kept this resolution with a constancy worthy, I will say, of
the sentiment which made me form it. From that moment I no
longer saw this beloved Mamma but with the eyes of a real son;
and it is to be noticed that, though my resolution was far from
having her private approbation, as I too well perceived, she never,
to make me renounce it, made use of insinuating discourses,
caresses, or any of those artful oglings women so well know to
make use of without exposing themselves, and in which they
rarely fail of success. Reduced to seeking a destiny for myself independent of her, and not being able to think of any, I soon passed
to the other extremity and sought it all in her. I sought it so perfectly, I was almost so fortunate as to forget myself. The ardent

desire of seeing her happy, at whatever price it might be, absorbed every affection: she in vain would separate her happiness from mine; I saw it mine, in spite of her.

Thus those virtues began to grow up with my misfortunes, whose seeds were in the centre of my soul, which reading had cultivated, and which to ripen waited only for the ferment of adversity. The first fruit of this disinterested disposition was to drive from my mind every sentiment of envy and hatred against him who had supplanted me. I wished, on the contrary, and sincerely wished, to attach myself to this young man, to form him, labour in his education, let him see his happiness, if possible make him worthy of it, and do, in a word, all Anet had done for me on a like occasion. But parity between the persons was wanting. With more mildness and knowledge, I had not the coolness and steadiness of Anet, nor that strength of character which imposes, and which was necessary to success. I found still less in this young man those qualities Anet found in me; docility, attachment, and gratitude, particularly my feeling the necessity I was under for his attention, and the ardent desire of rendering it useful. These things were all wanting. He whom I wanted to form, saw me only as an importunate pedant, who had nothing but chatter. On the contrary, he admired himself as a man of importance in the house, and, measuring the services he thought he rendered by the noise he made, he looked on his hatchet and pickaxe as infinitely more useful than all my old books. In some respect he was right; but he set himself up on it to give himself airs which made one die of laughter. He acted, with the peasants, the country squire; he soon did as much with me, and at last with Mamma herself. The name of Vintzenried did not appear noble enough for him: he quitted it for that of Monsieur de Courtilles; and it is by this last he has since been known at Chambéry, and at Maurienne, where he married.

In fine, so well did this illustrious personage manage his affairs, that he was everything in the house, and I nothing. As, when I had the misfortune to displease him, it was Mamma he grumbled at, not me, the fear of exposing her to his brutality rendered me docile to all he desired; and each time he cleaved wood, an occupation he fulfilled with a pride not to be equalled, I must be there, an idle and tranquil spectator of his prowess. This young fellow was not, for all that, of a bad disposition; he loved Mamma because it was impossible not to love her: he had not an aversion even to me; and when the intervals of his fury permitted us to speak to him, he sometimes listened with docility enough, frankly agreeing he was but a fool, and soon after ran, nevertheless, into new follies. He had, besides, so shallow an understanding, and inclinations so mean, it was difficult to talk reasonably to him, and almost impossible to be happy with him. To the possession of a woman full of charms, he added the relish of an old, rusty, toothless chambermaid, whose disgustful service Mamma had the patience to endure, though she made her sick. I perceived this new intrigue, and was exasperated with indignation: but I perceived another thing which more lively affected me, and which threw me into greater despair than all which had happened. It was the coolness Mamma showed me.

The privation I had imposed on myself, and which she made a show of approving, is one of those things which women never pardon, however they may appear to, not so much from the privation which results from it, as from the indifference they perceive for their possession. Take the most sensible woman, the most philosophical, the least attached to the senses, the most unpardonable crime a man, whom she has the least regard for, can commit, is, to be able to enjoy and yet to reject her. This must surely be without exception, since so natural and strong a sympathy changed her by an abstinence which had no other motive than virtue, respect, and esteem. From that time I ceased to perceive that intimacy of hearts which always had been the sweetest enjoyment of mine. She no longer mixed her heart with mine, but when she complained of her newcomer; when they agreed together, I entered little into her confidence. In fine, she chose by degrees a manner of being of which I no longer made a part. My presence still gave her pleasure, but it was not necessary: I had spent whole days without seeing her, and she would not have perceived it.

I insensibly saw I was left by myself, alone in the same house of which I before was the soul, and where, in some measure, I doubly lived. I accustomed myself by degrees to withdraw from everything that was doing, from those even who inhabited it; and to lessen the continual tearings of my heart, I either shut myself up with my books, or was weeping and lamenting in fields and woods. This life soon became insupportable. I found that the presence of the person, and the absence of the heart, of a woman I so much loved, only increased my pain, and that in ceasing to see her I should feel the separation less cruelly. I formed the intention of leaving the house. I told her so, and, far from opposing, she favoured it. She had an acquaintance at Grenoble named Madame Deybens, whose husband was acquainted with M. de Mably, grand provost of Lyons. M. Deybens proposed me the education of M. de Mably's children: I agreed, and set off for Lyons, without leaving or hardly feeling the least regret at separating, whereof, before, the thought only had brought on the anguish of death.

I had nearly the necessary knowledge of a preceptor, and thought I had the talents. During a year spent at M. de Mably's, I had time to undeceive myself. My natural mildness would have rendered me proper for this undertaking, had not passion mixed its storms. Whilst it went on well, and I saw my attention and trouble, which were not spared, succeed, I was an angel; I was a devil when things went cross. If my pupils did not understand me, I raved; and if I saw them malicious, I could have murdered them: that was not a method to make them learned or good. I had two of them; their humours were extremely different. One of eight or nine years old, named Ste. Marie, was a likely boy, of an open mind, pretty lively, unsteady, waggish, mischievous, but gaily so. The younger, named Condillac,[1] seemed almost stupid, a loiterer, and as stubborn as a mule, and could learn nothing. It may be easily guessed that, between these two, I had business enough. With patience and coolness I had perhaps succeeded; but for want of both one and the other, I did nothing useful, and my pupils turned out but poorly. I did not want assiduity, but I wanted evenness, particularly prudence. I knew to make use but of three instruments, always useless and often pernicious to children; sentiment, reasoning, and passion. Sometimes I was moved with Ste. Marie even to tears; I wanted to move him, as if the child was susceptible of a real emotion of heart: sometimes I fatigued myself in preaching to him reason, as if he could understand me; and as he sometimes held subtle argument, I took him in good earnest for reasonable, because he could argue. Little Condillac was more embarrassing, because, understanding nothing, answering nothing, being moved at nothing, and of an obstinacy proof against everything, he never triumphed so much as when he made me furious: thus he was the sage and I the child. I saw all my faults, I felt them, studied my pupils' turn, penetrated them well, and do not believe I was ever once the dupe of their subtlety; but

---

[1] Paris MS. adds: "called after his celebrated uncle." The Abbé de Condillac, a philosophical writer, was M. de Mably's brother.

what signified seeing the evil, without knowledge to apply the remedy? In penetrating everything, I prevented nothing, I succeeded in nothing; and everything I did was precisely that I ought not to have done.

I succeeded very little better for myself than for my pupils. I had been recommended by Madame Deybens to Madame de Mably. She begged her to form my manners, and give me the tone of the world: she took some pains, and would make me learn to do the honours of her house; but I did it so awkwardly, and was so ashamed, so stupid, she grew tired and left off there. That did not prevent my falling in love with her, according to custom. I did enough for her to perceive it, but never dared declare myself; she was not of a humour to make advances, so I got nothing for my sighs and oglings, of which I soon grew tired myself, perceiving them to no purpose.

I had entirely lost at Mamma's my inclination to roguery; because, everything being at my command, stealing was unnecessary: besides, the elevated principles I had formed should have rendered me superior to such baseness, and it is certain that since then I have in general been so. But it was not so much from having overcome the temptation, as from cutting up the root. I should dread stealing as in my childhood, were I subject to the same desires. I had a proof of it at M. de Mably's. Surrounded by little stealable things which I did not even look at, I took it in my head to covet some certain white wine of Arbois, very pretty, of which a few glasses now and then at table had greatly allured me. It was a little foul; I thought I understood fining wine, and boasted of it; I was entrusted with that; I fined and spoiled it, but to the eye only. It remained agreeable to the taste, and the opportunity caused me from time to time to accommodate myself with a few bottles to drink at my ease in private. Unfortunately, I could never drink without eating. But how manage to come at some bread? It was impossible to put any in reserve. To get it brought by the footman was to discover myself, and almost insult the master of the family. For me to buy it, would never do. What, a fine spark, with a sword by his side, go to the baker's for a loaf, was it feasible? At last I recollected the last shift of a great princess, to whom it was told the peasants had no bread, Why then, said she, let them eat pastry. I bought pastry. What ceremonies even to attain that! Going out alone on this errand, I ran all over the town, and passed by thirty shops before I could go into one. It was necessary there should be only one person in the shop, and that her look attracted me much, before I dared set my foot on the step of her door. But then when once I had hold of my dear bit of cake, and that, well secured in my room, I drew out my bottle from the farther end of my cupboard, what charming sips I took, snug by myself in reading a few pages of a romance! For to read whilst eating, was always my fancy, in default of a tête-à-tête. That is the substitute for the society I lack. I alternately devour a page and a piece: it is as if my book dined with me.

I never was dissolute or a sot, nor ever was drunk in my life. Thus my little thefts were not very indiscreet: they were, nevertheless, discovered; the bottles detected me. No notice was taken to me; but I had no longer the direction of the cellar. In the whole affair M. de Mably's conduct was prudent and genteel. He was very much of a gentleman, who, with an air as flinty as his employment, was of a character really mild and a heart full of goodness. He was judicious, equitable, and, that which is not expected in an officer of the Maréchaussée,[1] extremely humane too. Seeing his indulgence, I became more attached to him, which caused me to prolong my stay in his house farther than I had done without it. But at last, disgusted of an employment for which I was not proper, and a situation extremely troublesome, which had nothing agreeable for me, after a year's trial in which I spared no pains, I determined to leave my disciples, well convinced I should never attain educating them properly. M. de Mably saw all this as well as I. However, I do not believe he had ever undertaken to discharge me, had I not saved him the trouble; but this excess of condescension, in such a case, is assuredly what I do not approve.[2]

That which rendered my situation more insupportable, was the continual comparison I made with that I had left: it was the remembrance of my dear Charmettes, my garden, my trees, my fountain, my orchard, and particularly of her for whom I was created, and who gave life to the whole. Thinking of her, of our pleasures, our innocent life, I was seized with such an oppression of the heart, such a suffocation, it bereaved me of all the resolution I had taken. A hundred times I have been tempted to set out instantly on foot to return and seek her; provided I saw her once more, I had been contented to die the next moment. At last I could

---

[1] The mounted police of the pre-*gendarme* era.

[2] Rousseau's "year's trial" of his skill as a preceptor ended in May 1741. The chronology of this book, as of other parts of the *Confessions*, is much confused: the reader who seeks a guide through the maze will do well to consult the notes of M. Louis Martin-Chauffier's edition of the French text (1933).

no longer resist the tender remembrance which called me back to her, whatever the consequence might be. I said to myself, I was not sufficiently patient, sufficiently complaisant, or sufficiently caressing; that I might still be happy in so sweet a friendship, was I more assiduous than before. I lay out the finest projects in the world, I am mad till I execute them. I leave all, I renounce everything, I go, I fly, I run indoors with all the transport of my youthful age, I fall down at her feet. Ah! I had died of pleasure, had I

J.-J., ABOUT THIRTY

found in her reception, in her caresses, in fine, had I found in her heart, a quarter of that I used to find, and which I yet brought back to her.

Frightful illusions of things below! She still received me with an excellent heart, which could die only with her; but I came to seek the past which was no more, and which could not be renewed. I had scarcely been with her half an hour, when I saw my former happiness gone for ever. I found myself in the same afflicting situation I had been forced to fly, and that without being able to say it was the fault of anyone; for, at bottom, Courtilles was not ill-natured, and seemed to receive me with more pleasure than pain. But how remain a supernumerary with her to whom I had been all, and who could never cease to be my all? How live an alien in an house where I before was the son? The sight of objects which were witness to my former happiness, rendered the comparison more cruel. I had suffered less in another habitation. But to see so many sweet remembrances incessantly brought to my mind, was irritating the sense of my loss. Wasted by vain repinings, given up to the most dreadful melancholy, I returned to the course of remaining alone, except at the hour of meals. Shut up with my books, I sought for useful distractions; and seeing the imminent danger I so much formerly feared, I tortured my brain anew, to seek within myself the means of a subsistence when Mamma should have no other resource. I had brought the affairs of the house to a point of not growing worse; but all was changed since that. Her economist was a dissipator. He would shine; a good horse, a good carriage; he was fond of making a noble appearance in the eyes of the neighbours; he was continually undertaking things he knew nothing of. Her pension was eaten up beforehand, quarterly payments were mortgaged, the rent was behindhand, and debts kept their course. I foresaw the pension would soon be seized, and perhaps abolished. In fine, I looked for nought but ruin and misfortune; and the time appeared to me so nigh, I already saw all its horrors.

My dear closet was all I had to divert my melancholy. By dint of seeking remedies to ease my mind, I took it in my head to seek others against the evils I foresaw; and, returning to my old notions, I am once more building new castles in the air, to draw this poor Mamma from the cruel extremity I saw her falling into. I did not think I had learning enough, or believe I had sense enough, to shine in the commonwealth of the learned, and make a fortune that way. A new idea which presented itself inspired me with that confidence which the mediocrity of my talents denied me. I had not abandoned music in ceasing to teach it. On the contrary, I had studied its theory sufficiently to be able to think myself tolerably proficient. Reflecting on the trouble I had to understand notes, and that I had likewise in singing by book, I began to think the difficulty might proceed as much from the thing as myself, knowing besides that, in general, to learn music was for no one an easy thing. Examining the order of the signs, I found them often badly devised. I had long thought of pricking the scale in figures, to avoid tracing lines and staves whenever it was necessary to prick down the most trifling air. I was stopped by the difficulty of the octave, and by that of time and value. This former notion came once more into my brain, and I saw, on second thought, these difficulties were not insurmountable. I meditated on it with success, and arrived at pricking down all sorts of music, by means of figures, with the greatest exactness, and I may say with the greatest simplicity. From this moment I believed my fortune made, and in the ardour of dividing it with her to whom I owed everything, I dreamed of nothing but setting off for Paris, not doubting that, in presenting my project to the Academy, I should cause a revolution. I had brought a little money from Lyons; I sold my books. In a fortnight my resolution was taken and executed. In fine, filled with the magnificent ideas which inspired it, and always the same in every situation, I set off from Savoy with my system of music, as formerly I had done from Turin with my Hero-fountain.[1]

Such were the errors and faults of my youth. I have related their history with a faithfulness which gives satisfaction to my heart. If I afterwards honoured my riper years with some virtues, I should have told them with the same frankness; that was my intention. But I must stop here. Time may discover many things. Should my memory reach posterity, it may, perhaps, one day learn what I had to say. Then it will be known why I am silent.

---

[1] See page 90.

PART TWO

[There was an interval of three years between the completion of the preceding six books of the *Confessions* and the beginning of the six which follow. The first six books were published in 1782, and the English translation of them printed here was dated 1783. The second part of the work was published at Geneva in 1789, and the English version in which they are here presented appeared in 1790 with a London imprint. The second part was written at Bourgoin and in Dauphiné in the years 1769-1770.]

Foreword

THESE *pages, full of faults of every kind, and
which I have not even had time to read over, suffice to set every friend of truth upon its track, and
to give him the means of verifying it from his
own information. Unhappily, it would be difficult, nay impossible, for them to elude the vigilance of my enemies. If they fall into the hands
of an honest man, or of the friends of M. de
Choiseul, if they come to M. de Choiseul himself, I suppose the honour of my memory is not
wholly without resource. But, O heaven, protector of innocence, keep safe these last testimonies
of mine from the hands of Mesdames de Boufflers,
de Verdelin, and their friends. Hide at least from
these two Furies the memory of an unfortunate
wretch whom, while he was alive, thou hast
abandoned to them.*

J.-J. ROUSSEAU

This foreword is absent from the Paris MS.

BOOK SEVEN

Intus et in cute

After two years' silence and patience, and notwithstanding my resolutions, I again take up my pen. Reader, suspend your judgement as to the reasons which force me to such a step; of these you can be no judge until you have read my book.

My peaceful youth has been seen to pass away calmly and agreeably without any great disappointments or remarkable prosperity. This mediocrity was mostly owing to my ardent yet feeble nature, less prompt in undertaking than easy to discourage; quitting repose by violent agitations, but returning to it from lassitude and inclination, and which, placing me in the idle and tranquil state for which alone I felt I was born, at a distance from the paths of great virtues, and still farther from those of great vices, never permitted me to arrive at anything great either good or bad. What a different account shall I soon have to give of myself! Fate, which for thirty years favoured my inclinations, for thirty others has seemed to oppose them; and this continued opposition between my situation and inclinations will appear to have been the source of enormous faults, unheard of misfortunes, and every virtue except that fortitude which alone can do honour to adversity.

The history of the first part of my life was written from memory, and is consequently full of errors. As I am obliged to write the second part from memory also, the errors in it will probably be still more numerous. The agreeable remembrance of the finest portion of my years, passed with as much tranquillity as innocence, has left in my heart a thousand charming impressions which I love incessantly to call to my recollection. It will soon appear how different from these, those of the rest of my life have been. To recall them to my mind would be to renew their bitterness. Far from increasing that of my situation by these sorrowful reflections, I repel them as much as possible, and in this endeavour often succeed so well as to be unable to find them at will. This facility of forgetting my misfortunes is a consolation heaven has reserved to me in the midst of those which fate was one day to accumulate upon my head. My memory, which presents to me no objects but such as are agreeable, is the happy counterpoise of my terrified imagination, by which I foresee nothing but a cruel futurity.

All the papers I had collected to aid my recollection, and guide me in this undertaking, are no longer in my possession, nor can I ever again hope to regain them. I have but one faithful guide on which I can depend: this is the chain of the sentiments by which the succession of my existence has been marked,[1] and by these the events which have been either the cause or the effect of the manner of it. I easily forget my misfortunes, but I cannot forget my faults, and still less my virtuous sentiments. The remembrance of these is too dear to me ever to suffer them to be effaced from my mind. I may omit facts, transpose events, and fall into some errors of dates; but I cannot be deceived in what I have felt, nor in that which from sentiment I have done; and to relate this is the chief end of my present work. The real object of my confessions is to communicate an exact knowledge of what I interiorly am and have been in every situation of my life. I have promised the history of my mind, and to write it faithfully I have no need of other memories: to enter into my own heart, as I have hitherto done, will alone be sufficient.[2]

There is, however, and very happily, an interval of six or seven years, relative to which I have exact references, in a collection of letters copied from the originals in the hands of M. du Peyrou. This collection, which concludes in 1760, comprehends the whole time of my residence at the Hermitage, and my great quarrel with those who called themselves my friends; a memorable epoch of my life, and the source of all my other misfortunes. With respect to more recent original letters which may remain in my possession, and are but few in number, instead of transcribing them at the end of this collection, too voluminous to enable me to deceive the vigilance of my Arguses, I will copy them into the work wherever they appear to furnish any explanation, be this either for or against myself; for I am not under the least apprehension lest the reader should forget I make my confession, and be induced to

---

[1] In the Paris MS. this passage runs: ". . . has been marked, and whose impression is never effaced from my heart. These feelings will recall to me the events which gave rise to them well enough to enable me to flatter myself that I relate them faithfully; and if any omission be found, any transposition of facts or dates, which can only be the case with regard to indifferent matters and such as have made but little impression on me, there remain enough memorials of each fact to enable it easily to be given its place in the order of those I have noted. The real object of my confessions," etc.

[2] In the Paris MS.: ". . . the history of my mind, and this history becomes henceforth more interesting as it is the key to a tissue of events well known to all the world, which will never be easily explained without it. There is, however," etc.

believe I make my apology; but he cannot expect I shall conceal the truth when it testifies in my favour.

This second part, it is likewise to be remembered, contains nothing in common with the first, except truth; nor has any other advantage over it, but the importance of the facts; in everything else, it is inferior to the former. I wrote the first with pleasure, with satisfaction, and at my ease, at Wootton, or in the castle of Trye: everything I had to recollect was a new enjoyment. I returned to my closet with an increased pleasure, and, without constraint, gave that turn to my descriptions which most flattered my imagination.

At present my head and memory are become so weak, as to render me almost incapable of every kind of application: my present undertaking is the result of constraint, and a heart full of sorrow. I have nothing to treat of but misfortunes, treacheries, perfidies, and sad and heartrending memories. I would give the world, could I bury in the obscurity of time everything I have to say, and which, in spite of myself, I am obliged to relate. I am, at the same time, under the necessity of being mysterious and subtle, of endeavouring to impose, and of descending to things the most foreign to my nature. The ceiling under which I write has eyes; the walls of my chamber have ears. Surrounded by spies and by vigilant and malevolent inspectors, disturbed, and my attention diverted, I hastily commit to paper a few broken sentences, which I have scarcely time to read, and still less to correct. I know that, notwithstanding the barriers which are multiplied around me, my enemies are afraid truth should escape by some little opening. What means can I take to introduce it to the world? This, however, I attempt with but few hopes of success. The reader will judge whether or not such a situation furnishes the means of agreeable descriptions, or of giving them a seductive colouring! I therefore inform such as may undertake to read this work, that nothing can secure them from weariness in the prosecution of their task, unless it be the desire of becoming more fully acquainted with a man whom they already know, and a sincere love of justice and truth.

In my first part I brought down my narrative to my departure with infinite regret for Paris, leaving my heart at les Charmettes, and there building my last castle in the air, intending some day to return to the feet of Mamma, restored to herself, with the treasures I should have acquired, and depending upon my system of music as upon a certain fortune.

I made some stay at Lyons to visit my acquaintance, procure letters of recommendation to Paris, and to sell my books of geometry which I had brought with me. I was well received by all whom I knew. M. and Madame de Mably seemed pleased to see me again, and several times invited me to dinner. At their house I became acquainted with the Abbé de Mably, as I had already done with the Abbé de Condillac, both of whom were on a visit to their brother. The Abbé de Mably gave me letters to Paris; among others, one to M. de Fontenelle, and another to the Comte de Caylus. These were very agreeable acquaintances, especially the former, to whose friendship for me his death only put a period, and from whom, in our private conversations, I received advice which I ought to have more exactly followed.

I likewise saw M. Bordes, with whom I had been long acquainted, and who had frequently obliged me with the greatest cordiality and the most real pleasure. On this occasion I found him the same as ever. He it was who enabled me to sell my books; and he also gave me from himself, or got me, good recommendations to Paris. I again saw the Intendant, for whose acquaintance I was indebted to M. Bordes, and who introduced me to the Duke de Richelieu, who was then passing through Lyons. M. Pallu presented me. The Duke received me well, and invited me to come and see him at Paris; I did so several times; although this great acquaintance, of which I shall frequently have occasion to speak, was never of the most trifling utility to me.

I visited the musician David, who, in one of my former journeys, and in my distress, had rendered me service. He had either lent or given me a cap and a pair of stockings, which I have never returned, nor has he ever asked me for them, although we have since that time frequently seen each other. I, however, made him afterwards a present, something like an equivalent. I would say more upon this subject, were what I have owed in question; but I have to speak of what I have done, which, unfortunately, is far from being the same thing.

I also saw the noble and generous Perrichon, and not without feeling the effects of his accustomed munificence; for he made me the same present he had previously done to the elegant Bernard,[1] by paying for my place in the diligence. I visited the surgeon Parisot, the best and most benevolent of men; as also his beloved Godefroi, who had lived with him ten years, and whose merit

---

[1] Pierre Joseph Bernard, author of *L'Art d'aimer*.

chiefly consisted in her gentle manners and goodness of heart. It was impossible to see this woman without pleasure, or to leave her without regret; for she was approaching the crisis of a consumption of which she soon after died. Nothing better shows the inclinations of a man, than the nature of his attachment.[1] Those who had once seen the gentle Godefroi, immediately knew the good and amiable Parisot.

I was much obliged to all these good people, but I afterwards neglected them all; not from ingratitude, but from that invincible indolence which so often in me assumes its appearance. The remembrance of their services has never been effaced from my mind, nor the impression they made, from my heart: but I could more easily have proved my gratitude, than assiduously have shown them the exterior of that sentiment. Exactitude in correspondence has ever been what I never could observe; the moment I begin to relax, the shame and embarrassment of repairing my fault make me aggravate it, and I entirely desist from writing; I have, therefore, been silent, and appeared to forget them. Parisot and Perrichon took not the least notice of my negligence, and I ever found them the same. But twenty years afterwards it will be seen, in M. Bordes, to what a degree the self-love of a wit can make him carry his vengeance when he feels himself neglected.

Before I leave Lyons, I must not forget an amiable person, whom I again saw with more pleasure than ever, and who left in my heart the most tender remembrance. This was Mademoiselle Serre, of whom I have spoken in my first part; I renewed my acquaintance with her whilst I was at M. de Mably's.

Being this time more at leisure, I saw her more frequently, and she made the most sensible impressions on my heart. I had some reason to believe her own was not unfavourable to my pretensions; but she honoured me with her confidence so far as to remove from me all temptation to allure her partiality. She had no fortune, and in this respect exactly resembled myself; our situations were too similar to permit us to become united; and with the views I then had, I was far from thinking of marriage. She gave me to

---

[1] Unless he be deceived in his choice, or that she, to whom he attaches himself, changes her character by a concurrence of extraordinary causes, which is not absolutely impossible. Were this consequence to be admitted without modification, Socrates must be judged of by his wife Xantippe, and Dion by his friend Calippus, which would be the most false and iniquitous judgement ever made. However let no injurious application be here made to my wife. She is weak and more easily deceived than I at first imagined, but by her pure and excellent character she is worthy of all my esteem, and will possess it as long as I live. (*Note by Rousseau.*)

understand, that a young merchant, one M. Genève, seemed to
wish to obtain her hand. I saw him once or twice at her lodgings;
he appeared to me to be an honest man, and this was his general
character. Persuaded she would be happy with him, I was desirous
he should marry her, which he afterwards did; and that I might
not disturb their innocent love, I hastened my departure; offering
up, for the happiness of that charming woman, prayers which,
here below, were not long heard. Alas! her time was very short,
for I afterwards heard she died in the second or third year after
her marriage. My mind, during the journey, was wholly absorbed
in tender regret. I felt, and since that time, when these circumstances have been present to my recollection, have frequently
done the same, that although the sacrifices made to virtue and our
duty may sometimes be painful, we are well rewarded by the
agreeable remembrance they leave deeply engraven in our hearts.

HÔTEL DE VILLE   ÉGLISE ST. JEAN
PLACE DE GRÈVE   ARCADE ST. JEAN
PORT AU BLÉ   RUE DE MORTELLERIE

I this time saw Paris in as favourable a point of view as it had
appeared to me in an unfavourable one at my first journey; not
that my ideas of its brilliancy arose from the splendour of my
lodgings; for in consequence of an address given me by M. Bordes,

I resided at the Hotel St. Quentin, Rue des Cordiers, near the Sorbonne; a vile street, a miserable hotel, and a wretched apartment: but nevertheless a house in which several men of merit, such as Gresset, Bordes, the Abbé Mably, Condillac, and several others, of whom unfortunately I found not one, had taken up their quarters: but I there met with M. de Bonnefond, a man unacquainted with the world, lame, litigious, and who affected to be a purist. To him I owe the acquaintance of M. Roguin, at present the oldest friend I have, and by whose means I became acquainted with Diderot, of whom I shall soon have occasion to say a good deal.

I arrived at Paris in the autumn of 1741, with fifteen louis in my purse, and with my comedy of *Narcisse* and my musical project in my pocket. These composed my whole stock; consequently, I had not much time to lose before I attempted to turn the latter to some advantage. I therefore immediately thought of making use of my recommendations.

A young man who arrives at Paris, with a tolerable figure, and announces himself by his talents, is sure to be well received. This was my good fortune, which procured me some pleasures without leading to anything solid. Of all the persons to whom I was recommended, three only were useful to me. M. Damesin, a gentleman of Savoy, at that time equerry, and I believe favourite, of the Princess of Carignan; M. de Boze, secretary to the Academy of Inscriptions, and keeper of the medals of the King's cabinet; and Father Castel, a Jesuit, author of the *Clavecin oculaire*.[1]

All these recommendations, except that to M. Damesin, were given me by the Abbé de Mably.

M. Damesin provided me with that which was most needful, by means of two persons with whom he brought me acquainted. One was M. de Gasc, *président à mortier* of the parliament of Bordeaux, and who played very well upon the violin; the other, the Abbé de Léon, who then lodged in the Sorbonne, a young nobleman, extremely amiable, who died in the flower of his age, after having, for a few moments, made a figure in the world under the name of the Chevalier de Rohan. Both these gentlemen had an inclination to learn composition. In this I gave them lessons for a few months, by which means my decreasing purse received some little aid. The Abbé de Léon conceived a friendship for me, and wished me to become his secretary; but he was far from being rich, and all the salary he could offer me was eight hundred livres,

---

[1] An instrument for producing harmonious colour combinations.

which, with infinite regret, I refused; since it was insufficient to defray the expenses of my lodging, food, and clothing.

I was well received by M. de Boze. He had a thirst for knowledge, of which he possessed not a little, but was somewhat pedantic. Madame de Boze much resembled him, she was lively and affected. I sometimes dined with them, and it is impossible to be more awkward than I was in her presence. Her easy manner intimidated me, and rendered mine more remarkable. When she presented me a plate, I modestly put forward my fork to take one of the least bits of what she offered me, which made her give the plate to her servant, turning her head aside that I might not see her laugh. She had not the least suspicion that in the head of the rustic with whom she was so diverted there was some small portion of wit. M. de Boze presented me to M. de Réaumur, his friend, who came to dine with him every Friday, the day on which the academy of sciences met. He mentioned to him my project and the desire I had of having it examined by the academy. M. de Réaumur consented to make the proposal, and his offer was accepted. On the day appointed, I was introduced and presented by M. de Réaumur, and on the same day, August 22nd, 1742, I had the honour to read to the academy the memoir I had prepared for that purpose. Although this illustrious assembly might certainly well be expected to inspire me with awe, I was less intimidated on this occasion than I had been in the presence of Madame de Boze, and I got tolerably well through my reading and the answers I was obliged to give. The memoir was well received, and acquired me some compliments by which I was equally surprised and flattered, imagining that before such an assembly, whoever was not a member of it could not have common sense. The persons appointed to examine my system, were M. Mauran, M. Hellot, and M. de Fouchy, all three men of merit, but not one of them understood music, at least not enough of composition to enable them to judge of my project.

During my conferences with these gentlemen, I was convinced with no less certainty than surprise, that if men of learning have sometimes fewer prejudices than others, they more tenaciously retain those they have. However weak or false most of their objections were, and although I answered them with great timidity, and, I confess, in bad terms, yet with decisive reasons, I never once made myself understood, or gave them any explanation in the least satisfactory. I was constantly surprised at the facility with which, by the aid of a few sonorous phrases, they refuted, without having comprehended me. They had learned, I know not where, that a monk of the name of Souhaitti had formerly invented a mode of noting the gamut by ciphers: a sufficient proof that my system was not new. And that was enough; for although I had never heard of Father Souhaitti, and notwithstanding his manner of writing the seven notes of plainchant without attending to the octaves was not, under any point of view, worthy of entering into competition with my simple and commodious invention for easily noting by ciphers every possible kind of music, keys, rests, octaves, measure, time, and length of notes; things on which Souhaitti had never thought: it was, nevertheless, true that with respect to the elementary expression of the seven notes, he was the first inventor.

But besides their giving to this primitive invention more importance than was due to it, they went still farther, and, whenever they spoke of the fundamental principles of the system, talked nonsense. The greatest advantage of my scheme was to supersede transpositions and keys, so that the same piece of music was noted and transposed at will, to any desired tone, by means of the change of a single initial letter at the head of the air. These gentlemen had heard from the music masters of Paris that the method of executing by transposition was a bad one; and on this authority converted the most evident advantage of my system into an invincible objection against it, and affirmed that my mode of notation was good for vocal music, but bad for instrumental; instead of concluding, as they ought to have done, that it was good for vocal, and still better for instrumental. On their report the academy granted me a certificate full of fine compliments, amidst which it appeared that in reality it judged my system to be neither new nor useful. I did not think proper to ornament with such a paper the work entitled, *Dissertation sur la musique moderne*, by which I appealed to the public.

I had reason to remark on this occasion that, even with a narrow understanding, the sole but profound knowledge of a thing is preferable, for the purpose of judging of it, to all the lights resulting from a cultivation of the sciences, when to these a particular study of that in question has not been joined. The only solid objection to my system was that made by Rameau. I had scarcely explained it to him before he discovered its weak part. Your signs, said he, are very good, in as much as they clearly and simply determine the length of notes, exactly represent intervals, and show the simple in the double note, which the common notation does

JEAN PHILIPPE RAMEAU

not do; but they are objectionable on account of their requiring an operation of the mind, which cannot always accompany the rapidity of execution. The position of our notes, continued he, is described to the eye without the concurrence of this operation. If two notes, one very high and the other very low, be joined by a series of intermediate ones, I see at the first glance the progress from one to the other by conjoined degrees; but in your system, to perceive this series, I must necessarily run over all your ciphers one after the other; the glance of the eye is here useless. The objection appeared to me insurmountable, and I instantly assented to it. Although it be simple and striking, nothing can suggest it but great knowledge and practice of the art, and it is by no means astonishing that not one of the academicians should have thought of it. But what creates much surprise is, that these men of great learning, and who are supposed to possess so much knowledge, should so little know that each ought to confine his judge-

DENIS DIDEROT

ment to that which relates to the study with which he has been conversant.

My frequent visits to the literati appointed to examine my system and the other academicians gave me an opportunity of becoming acquainted with the most distinguished men of letters in Paris, and by this means the acquaintance that would have been the consequence of my sudden admission amongst them, which afterwards came to pass, was already established. With respect to the present moment, absorbed in my new system of music, I obstinately adhered to my intention of effecting a revolution in the art, and by that means of acquiring a kind of celebrity which, in the fine arts, is in Paris always accompanied by fortune. I shut myself in my chamber and laboured two or three months with inexpressible ardour, in forming into a work for the public eye, the memoir I had read before the academy. The difficulty was to find a bookseller to take my manuscript; and this on account of the necessary expenses for the new characters, and because book-sellers give not their money by handfuls to young authors; although to me it seemed but just my work should render me the bread I had eaten while employed in its composition.

Bonnefond introduced me to Quillau the elder, with whom I agreed to divide the profits, without reckoning the privilege, of which I paid the whole expense. Such were the future proceedings of this Quillau, that I lost the expenses of my privilege, never having received a farthing from that edition; which, probably, had but very middling success, although the Abbé Desfontaines promised to give it celebrity, and notwithstanding the other journalists had spoken of it very favourably.

The greatest obstacle to making the experiment of my system, was the fear, in case of its not being received, of losing the time necessary to learn it. To this I answered, that my notes rendered the ideas so clear, that in learning music by means of the ordinary characters, time would still be gained by beginning with mine. To prove this by experience, I taught music gratis to a young American lady, Mademoiselle Desroulins, with whom M. Roguin had brought me acquainted. In three months she read every kind of music, by means of my notation, and sung at sight better than I did myself, any piece that was not too difficult. This success was convincing, but not known; any other person would have filled the journals with the detail, but with some talents for discovering useful things, I never have possessed that of setting them off to advantage.

Thus was my airy castle again overthrown; but this time I was thirty years of age, and in Paris, where it is impossible to live for a trifle. The resolution I took upon this occasion will astonish none but those by whom the first part of these memoirs has not been read with attention. I had just made great and fruitless efforts and was in need of relaxation. Instead of sinking with despair I gave myself up quietly to my indolence and to the care of Providence; and the better to wait for its assistance with patience, I laid down a frugal plan for the slow expenditure of a few louis, which still remained in my possession, regulating the expense of my indifferent pleasures without retrenching it; going to the coffee-house but every other day, and to the theatre but twice a week. With respect to the expenses of girls of easy virtue, I had no retrenchment to make; never having in the whole course of my life applied so much as a farthing to that use, except once, of which I shall soon have occasion to speak.

The security, voluptuousness and confidence with which I gave myself up to this indolent and solitary life which I had not the means of continuing for three months, is one of the singularities of my life, and the oddities of my disposition. The extreme desire I had the public should think of me was precisely what discouraged me from showing myself; and the necessity of paying visits rendered them to such a degree insupportable, that I ceased visiting the academicians and other men of letters, with whom I had cultivated an acquaintance. Marivaux, the Abbé de Mably, and Fontenelle were almost the only persons whom I sometimes went to see. To the first I showed my comedy of *Narcisse*. He was pleased with it, and had the goodness to make in it some improvements. Diderot, younger than these, was much about my own age. He was fond of music, and knew its theory; we conversed together, and he communicated to me some of his literary projects. This soon formed betwixt us a more intimate connexion, which lasted fifteen years, and which probably would still exist were not I, unfortunately, and by his own fault, of the same profession with himself.

It would be impossible to imagine in what manner I employed this short and precious interval which still remained to me, before circumstances forced me to beg my bread: — in learning by memory passages from the poets which I had learned and forgotten a hundred times. Every morning, at ten o'clock, I went to walk in the Luxembourg with a Virgil and a Rousseau[1] in my pocket, and there, until the hour of dinner, I passed away the time in restoring to my memory a sacred ode or a bucolic, without being discouraged by forgetting, by the study of the morning, what I had learned the evening before. I recollected that after the defeat of Nicias at Syracuse, the captive Athenians obtained a livelihood by reciting the poems of Homer. The use I made of this erudition to ward off misery was to exercise my happy memory by learning all the poets by rote.

I had another expedient, not less solid, in the game of chess, to which I regularly dedicated, at Maugis's, the evenings on which I did not go to the theatre. I became acquainted there with M. de Légal, M. Husson, Philidor, and all the great chess players of the day, without making the least improvement in the game. However, I had no doubt but, in the end, I should become superior to them all, and this, in my own opinion, was a sufficient resource.

---

[1] *Cf.* note, p. 143.

The same manner of reasoning served me in every folly to which I felt myself inclined. I said to myself: whoever excels in anything is sure to acquire a distinguished reception in society. Let us therefore excel, no matter in what, I shall certainly be sought after; opportunities will present themselves, and my own merit will do the rest. This childishness was not the sophism of my reason; it was that of my indolence. Dismayed at the great and rapid efforts which would have been necessary to call forth my endeavours, I strove to flatter my idleness, and by arguments suitable to the purpose, veiled from my own eyes the shame of such a state.

I thus calmly waited for the moment when I was to be without money; and had not Father Castel, whom I sometimes went to see in my way to the coffee-house, roused me from my lethargy, I believe I should have seen myself reduced to my last farthing without the least emotion. Father Castel was a madman, but a

good man upon the whole; he was sorry to see me thus impoverish myself to no purpose. Since musicians and the learned, said he, do not sing by your scale, change the string, and apply to the women. You will perhaps succeed better with them. I have spoken of you to Madame de Bezenval; go to her from me; she is a good woman who will be glad to see the countryman of her son and husband. You will find at her house, Madame de Broglie, her daughter, who is a woman of wit. Madame Dupin is another to whom I also have mentioned you; carry her your work; she is desirous of seeing you, and will receive you well. Nothing is done in Paris without the women. They are the curves of which the wise are the asymptotes; they incessantly approach each other, but never touch.

After having from day to day delayed these very disagreeable steps, I at length took courage, and called upon Madame de Bezenval. She received me with kindness; and Madame de Broglie entering the chamber, she said to her: Daughter, this is M. Rousseau, of whom Father Castel has spoken to us. Madame de Broglie complimented me upon my work, and going to her harpsichord proved to me she had already given it some attention. Perceiving it to be about one o'clock, I prepared to take my leave. Madame de Bezenval said to me: you are at a great distance from the quarter of the town in which you reside: stay and dine here. I did not want asking a second time. A quarter of an hour afterwards, I understood, by a word, that the dinner to which she had invited me was that of her servant's hall. Madame de Bezenval was a very good kind of a woman, but of a confined understanding, and too full of her illustrious Polish nobility: she had no idea of the respect due to talents. On this occasion, likewise, she judged me by my manner rather than by my dress, which although very plain was very neat, and by no means announced a man to dine with servants. I had too long forgotten the way to the place where they ate to be inclined to take it again. Without suffering my anger to appear, I told Madame de Bezenval that an affair of a trifling nature which I had just recollected obliged me to return home, and I immediately prepared to depart. Madame de Broglie approached her mother, and whispered in her ear a few words which had their effect. Madame de Bezenval rose to prevent me from going, and said, I expect that you will do us the honour to dine *with us*. In this case I thought to show pride would be a mark of folly, and I determined to stay. The goodness of Madame de Broglie had besides made an impression upon me, and rendered her interesting in my eyes. I was very glad to dine with her, and hoped that when she knew me better, she would not regret having procured me that honour. The president de Lamoignon, very intimate in the family, dined there also. He, as well as Madame de Broglie, was a master of all the modish and fashionable small-talk jargon of Paris. Poor Jean-Jacques was unable to make a figure in this way. I had sense enough not to pretend to it, *invita Minerva*, and was silent. Happy would it have been for me, had I always possessed the same wisdom; I should not be in the abyss into which I am now fallen.

I was vexed at my own stupidity, and at being unable to justify to Madame de Broglie what she had done in my favour. After dinner I thought of my ordinary resource. I had in my pocket an epistle in verse, written to Parisot during my residence at Lyons. This fragment was not without some fire, which I increased by my manner of reading, and made them all three shed tears. Whether it was vanity, or really the truth, I thought the eyes of

Madame de Broglie seemed to say to her mother: Well, mamma, was I wrong in telling you this man was fitter to dine with us than with your women? Until then my heart had been rather burdened, but after this revenge I felt myself satisfied. Madame de Broglie, carrying her favourable opinion of me rather too far, thought I should immediately acquire fame in Paris, and become a favourite with fine ladies. To guide my inexperience she gave me the *Confessions of the Comte de . . .*[1] This book, said she, is a Mentor, of which you will stand in need in the great world. You will do well by sometimes consulting it. I kept the book upwards of twenty years, with a sentiment of gratitude to her from whose hand I had received it, although I frequently laughed at the opinion the lady seemed to have of my merit in gallantry. From the moment I had read the work, I was desirous of acquiring the friendship of the author. My inclination led me right; he is the only real friend I have ever possessed amongst men of letters.[2]

From this time I thought I might depend on the services of Madame the Baroness de Bezenval, and the Marchioness of Broglie, and that they would not long leave me without resource. In this I was not deceived. But I must now speak of my first visit to Madame Dupin, which produced more lasting consequences.

Madame Dupin was, as everyone in Paris knows, the daughter of Samuel Bernard and Madame Fontaine. There were three sisters who might be called the three graces. Madame de la Touche, who played a little prank, and went to England with the Duke of Kingston. Madame D'Arty, the mistress, and more, the friend, the only sincere friend of the Prince of Conti, an adorable woman, as well by her sweetness and the goodness of her charming character, as by her agreeable wit and incessant cheerfulness. Lastly, Madame Dupin, more beautiful than either of her sisters, and the only one who has not been reproached with some levity of conduct.

She was the reward of the hospitality of M. Dupin, to whom her mother gave her in marriage with the place of farmer general and an immense fortune, in return for the good reception he had given her in his province. When I saw her for the first time, she was still one of the finest women in Paris. She received me at her

---

[1] By Charles Pinet Duclos (1704-1772).

[2] I have so long been of the same opinion, and so perfectly convinced of its being well founded, that since my return to Paris I confided to him the manuscript of my confessions. The unsuspicious Jean-Jacques never suspected perfidy and falsehood until he had been their victim. (*Note by Rousseau.*) In place of this note the Paris MS. has: "This is what I should have always thought, if I had never returned to Paris."

toilette; her arms were uncovered, her hair dishevelled, and her combing-cloth ill arranged. This scene was new to me; it was too powerful for my poor head, I became confused, my senses wandered; in short, I was violently smitten by Madame Dupin.

My confusion was not prejudicial to me, she did not perceive it. She kindly received the book, and the author; spoke with information of my plan, sang, accompanied herself on the harpsichord, kept me to dinner, and placed me at table by her side. Less than this would have turned my brain; I became mad. She permitted me to visit her, and I used and abused the permission. I went to see her almost every day, and dined with her twice or thrice a week. I burned with inclination to speak, but never dared attempt it. Several circumstances increased my natural timidity. Permission to visit in an opulent family was a door open to fortune, and in my situation I was unwilling to run the risk of shutting it against myself. Madame Dupin, amiable as she was, was serious and unanimated; I found nothing in her manners sufficiently alluring to embolden me. Her house, at that time as brilliant as any other in Paris, was frequented by gatherings which, had they been only somewhat less numerous, would have been supreme in their kind. She was fond of seeing everyone who had claims to a marked superiority; the great, men of letters, and fine women. No person was seen in her circle but dukes, ambassadors, and blue ribands. The Princess of Rohan, the Countess of Forcalquier, Madame de Mirepoix, Madame de Brignolé, and Lady Hervey passed for her intimate friends. The Abbés de Fontenelle, de Saint Pierre, and Sallier, M. de Fourmont, M. de Bernis, M. de Buffon, and M. de Voltaire were of her circle and dinners. If her reserved manner did not attract many young people, her society inspired the greater awe, as it was composed of graver persons, and the poor Jean-Jacques had no reason to flatter himself he should be able to take a distinguished part in the midst of such superior talents. I therefore had not courage to speak; but no longer able to contain myself, I took a resolution to write. For the first two days she said not a word to me upon the subject. On the third day she returned me my letter, accompanying it with a few exhortations in a cold tone which froze my blood. I attempted to speak, but my words expired upon my lips; my sudden passion was extinguished with my hopes, and after a declaration in form I continued to live with her upon the same terms as before, without so much as speaking to her even by the language of the eyes.

I thought my folly was forgotten, but I was deceived. M. de Francueil, son to M. Dupin, and son-in-law to Madame Dupin, was much of the same age with herself and me. He had wit, a good person, and might have pretensions; this was said to be the case, and probably proceeded only from his mother-in-law's having given him an ugly wife of a mild disposition, with whom, as well as with her husband, she lived upon the best of terms. M. de Francueil was fond of talents in others, and cultivated those he possessed. Music, which he understood very well, was a means of producing a connexion between us. I frequently saw him, and he soon gained my friendship. He, however, suddenly gave me to understand that Madame Dupin thought my visits too frequent, and begged me to discontinue them. Such a compliment would have been proper when she returned my letter; but eight or ten days afterwards, and without any new cause, it appeared to me ill-timed. This rendered my situation the more singular, as M. and Madame de Francueil still continued to give me the same good reception as before.

I, however, made the intervals between my visits longer, and I should entirely have ceased calling on them, had not Madame Dupin, by another unexpected caprice, sent to desire I would for a few days take care of her son, who, changing his preceptor, remained alone during that interval. I passed eight days in such torments as nothing but the pleasure of obeying Madame Dupin could render supportable: for poor Chenonceaux had even at that time that evil bent which almost dishonoured his family, and brought about his death in the Isle of Bourbon. While I was with him, I prevented his harming himself or others; that was all; it was not an easy undertaking, and I would not have undertaken to pass eight other days like them had Madame Dupin given me herself for the recompense.

M. de Francueil conceived a friendship for me, and I studied with him. We began together a course of chemistry at Rouelle's. That I might be nearer at hand, I left my Hotel St. Quentin, and went to lodge at the Tennis Court, Rue Verdelet, which leads into the Rue Plâtrière, where M. Dupin lived. There, in consequence of a cold neglected, I contracted an inflammation of the lungs that had like to have carried me off. In my younger days I frequently suffered from inflammatory disorders, pleurisies, and especially quinsies, to which I was very subject, which I will not here enumerate, and which frequently brought me near enough to death to familiarise me with its image.

During my convalescence, I had leisure to reflect upon my situation, and to lament my timidity, weakness, and indolence; these, notwithstanding the fire with which I felt myself inflamed, left me to languish in an inactivity of mind, continually on the verge of misery. The evening preceding the day on which I was taken ill, I went to an opera by Royer; the name I have forgotten. Notwithstanding my prejudice in favour of the talents of others, which has ever made me distrustful of my own, I still thought the music feeble, and devoid of animation and invention. I sometimes had the vanity to say to myself; I think I could do better than that. But the terrible idea I had formed of the composition of an opera, and the importance I heard men of the profession affix to such an undertaking, instantly discouraged me, and made me blush at having so much as thought of it. Besides, where was I to find a person to write the words, and one who would give himself the trouble of turning the poetry to my liking? These ideas of music and the opera had possession of my mind during my illness, and in the delirium of my fever I composed songs, duets, and choruses. I am certain I composed two or three little pieces, *di prima intenzione*, perhaps worthy of the admiration of masters, could they have heard them executed. Oh, could an account be taken of the dreams of a man in a fever, what great and sublime things would sometimes proceed from his delirium!

These subjects of music and opera still engaged my attention during my convalescence, but my ideas were less energetic. After frequent meditations, which were often involuntary, I wished to deliver myself of the matter, and attempt an opera by myself alone, both words and music. This was not the first time I had undertaken so difficult a task. Whilst I was at Chambéry, I had composed an opera, entitled, *Iphis and Anaxarète*, which I had the good sense to throw into the fire. At Lyons I had composed another, entitled, *La Découverte du nouveau Monde*, which, after having read it to M. Bordes, the Abbés Mably, Trublet and others, had met the same fate, notwithstanding I had set the prologue and the first act to music, and although David, after examining the composition, had told me there were passages in it worthy of Buononcini.

Before I began the work, I took time to consider of my plan. In an heroic ballet, I proposed three different subject, in three acts, detached from each other, set to music of a different character, taking for each subject the amours of a poet. I entitled this opera *Les Muses galantes*. My first act, in music strongly characterised, was Tasso; the second, in tender harmony, Ovid; and the third, entitled Anacreon, was to partake of the gaiety of the dithyrambus. I tried my skill on the first act, and applied to it with an ardour which, for the first time, made me feel the delightful sensation produced by the creative power of composition. One evening, as I entered the Opera, feeling myself strongly incited and overpowered by my ideas, I put my money again into my pocket, returned to my apartment, locked the door, and, after having close drawn all the curtains that every ray of light might be excluded, I went to bed, abandoning myself entirely to this musical and poetical *œstrum*, and in seven or eight hours rapidly composed the greatest part of an act. I can truly say my love for the Princess of Ferrara (for I was Tasso for the moment) and my noble and lofty sentiments with respect to her unjust brother, procured me a night an hundred times more delicious than one passed in the arms of the Princess would have been. In the morning but very little of what I had done remained in my head, but this little, almost effaced by sleep and lassitude, still sufficiently evinced the energy of the pieces of which it was the scattered remains.

I, this time, did not proceed far with my undertaking, being interrupted by other affairs. Whilst I attached myself to the family of Dupin, Madame de Bezenval and Madame de Broglie, whom I sometimes continued to visit, had not forgotten me. The Count de Montaigu, captain in the guards, had just been appointed ambassador to Venice. He was an ambassador after Barjac,[1] to whom he assiduously paid his court. His brother, the Chevalier de Montaigu, *gentilhomme de la manche*[2] to the Dauphin, was acquainted with these ladies, and with the Abbé Alary of the French academy, whom I sometimes visited. Madame de Broglie, having heard the ambassador was seeking a secretary, proposed me to him. A conference was opened between us. I asked a salary of fifty guineas, a trifle for an employment which required me to make some appearance. The ambassador was unwilling to give more than a thousand livres, leaving me to make the journey at my own expense. The proposal was ridiculous. We could not agree, and M. de Francueil, who used all his efforts to prevent my departure, prevailed.

I stayed, and M. de Montaigu set out on his journey, taking with him another secretary, one M. Follau, who had been recom-

---

[1] Confidential servant of Cardinal de Fleury.

[2] "Gentleman of the cuff" — a name given to noblemen who attended on the young French princes.

mended to him by the office for foreign affairs. They no sooner
arrived at Venice than they quarrelled. Follau, perceiving he had
to do with a madman, left him there, and M. de Montaigu, having
nobody with him, except a young abbé of the name of de Binis,
who wrote under the secretary, and was unfit to succeed him, had
recourse to me. The chevalier, his brother, a man of wit, by giving
me to understand there were advantages annexed to the place of
secretary, prevailed upon me to accept the thousand livres. I was
paid twenty louis in advance for my journey, and I immediately
departed.

GENOA: ''THE LANTERN''

At Lyons I would most willingly have taken the road by Mont
Cenis, to see my poor Mamma. But I went down the Rhône, and
embarked at Toulon, as well on account of the war, and from a
motive of economy, as to obtain a passport from M. de Mirepoix,
who then commanded in Provence, and to whom I was recommended. M. de Montaigu not being able to do without me, wrote

letter after letter, desiring I would hasten my journey; this, however, an accident considerably prolonged.

It was at the time of the plague at Messina, and the English fleet had anchored there, and visited the felucca on board of which I was, and this circumstance subjected us, on our arrival at Genoa, after a long and difficult voyage, to a quarantine of one-and-twenty days.

The passengers had the choice of performing it on board or in the Lazaretto, where we were told we should find but four walls, as there had been no time to furnish it. They all chose the felucca. The insupportable heat, the closeness of the vessel, the impossibility of walking in it, and the vermin with which it swarmed, made me at all risks prefer the Lazaretto. I was therefore conducted to a large building of two stories, quite empty, in which I found neither window, bed, table, nor chair, not so much as even a joint stool or bundle of straw. My cloak, my night sack and my two trunks being brought me, I was shut in by great doors with huge locks, and remained there at full liberty to walk at my ease from chamber to chamber, and story to story; everywhere finding the same solitude and nakedness.

This, however, did not induce me to repent that I had preferred the Lazaretto to the felucca; and, like another Robinson Crusoe, I began to arrange myself for my one-and-twenty days, just as I should have done for my whole life. In the first place, I had the amusement of destroying the vermin I had caught in the felucca. As soon as I had got clear of these, by means of changing my clothes and linen, I proceeded to furnish the chamber I had chosen. I made a good mattress with my waistcoats and shirts; my napkins I converted, by sewing them together, into sheets; my robe de chambre, into a counterpane; and my cloak into a pillow. I made myself a seat with one of my trunks laid flat, and a table with the other. I took out some writing paper and an inkstand, and distributed, in the manner of a library, a dozen books which I had with me. In a word, I so well arranged my few moveables, that, except curtains and windows, I was almost as commodiously lodged in this Lazaretto, absolutely empty as it was, as I had been at the Tennis Court in the Rue Verdelet. My dinners were served with no small degree of pomp; they were escorted by two grenadiers with bayonets fixed; the staircase was my dining-room, the landing place my table, and the step served me for a seat; and as soon as my dinner was served up a little bell was rung to inform me I might sit down to table.

Between my repasts, when I did not either read or write or work at the furnishing of my apartment, I went to walk in the burying-ground of the Protestants, which served me as a court-yard. From this place I ascended to a lantern which looked into the harbour, and from which I could see the ships come in and go out. In this manner I passed fourteen days, and should have thus passed the whole time of the quarantine without the least weariness had not M. de Joinville, envoy from France, to whom I found means to send a letter, vinegared, perfumed, and half burnt, procured eight days of the time to be taken off; these I went and spent at his house, where I confess I found myself better lodged than in the Lazaretto. He was extremely civil to me. Du-pont, his secretary, was a good creature; he introduced me, as well at Genoa as in the country, to several families, the company of which I found very entertaining and agreeable; and I formed with him an acquaintance and a correspondence which we kept up for a considerable length of time. I continued my journey, very agree-ably, through Lombardy. I saw Milan, Verona, Brescia, and Padua, and at length arrived at Venice, where I was impatiently expected by the ambassador.

I found there piles of despatches, from the court and from other ambassadors, the ciphered part of which he had not been able to read, although he had all the ciphers necessary for that purpose. Never having been employed in any office, nor ever seen the cipher of a minister, I was at first apprehensive of meeting with some embarrassment; but I found nothing could be more easy, and in less than a week I had deciphered the whole, which cer-tainly was not worth the trouble; for, not to mention the little ac-tivity required in the embassy of Venice, it was not to such a man as M. de Montaigu that government would confide a negotiation of even the most trifling importance. Until my arrival he had been much embarrassed, neither knowing how to dictate nor to write legibly. I was very useful to him, of which he was sensible; and he treated me well. To this he was also induced by another motive. Since the time of M. de Froulay, his predecessor, whose head be-came deranged, the consul from France, M. Le Blond, had been charged with the affairs of the embassy, and after the arrival of M. de Montaigu, continued to manage them until he had put him into the track. M. de Montaigu, hurt at this discharge of his duty by another, although he himself was incapable of it, became dis-gusted with the consul, and as soon as I arrived deprived him of the functions of secretary to the embassy, to give them to me. They were inseparable from the title, and he told me to take it. As long as I remained with him, he never sent any person except myself under this title to the Senate, or to its Conferente,[1] and upon the whole it was natural enough he should prefer having for secretary to the embassy a man attached to him, to a consul or office clerk named by the court.

This rendered my situation very agreeable, and prevented his gentlemen, who were Italians, as well as his pages, and most of his suite, from disputing precedence with me in his house. I made an advantageous use of the authority annexed to the title he had conferred upon me, by maintaining his right of protection, that is, the freedom of his neighbourhood, against the attempts several times made to infringe it, a privilege which his Venetian officers took no care to defend. But I never permitted banditti to take refuge there, although this would have produced me advantages of which his excellency would not have disdained to partake. He thought proper, however, to claim a part of those of the secretaryship, which was called the chancery. It was in time of war, and there were many passports issued. For each of these passports a sequin was paid to the secretary who made it out and countersigned it. All my predecessors had been paid this sequin by Frenchmen and others without distinction. I thought this unjust, and although I was not a Frenchman I abolished it in favour of the French; but I so rigorously demanded my right from persons of every other nation, that the Marquis Scotti, brother to the favourite of the Queen of Spain, having asked for a passport without taking notice of the sequin, I sent to demand it; a boldness which the vindictive Italian did not forget. As soon as the new regulation I had made, relative to passports, was known, none but pretended Frenchmen, who in a gibberish the most mispronounced, called themselves Provençals, Picards, or Burgundians, came to demand them. My ear being very fine, I was not thus made a dupe, and I am almost persuaded that not a single Italian ever cheated me of my sequin, and that not one Frenchman ever paid it. I was foolish enough to tell M. de Montaigu, who was ignorant of everything that passed, what I had done. The word sequin made him open his ears, and without giving me his opinion of the abolition of that tax upon the French, he pretended I ought to account with him for the others, promising me at the same time equivalent advantages. More filled with indignation at this meanness, than concerned for

---

[1] A Venetian officer who negotiated with ambassadors on behalf of the Senate.

my own interest, I rejected his proposal. He insisted, and I grew
warm. No, Sir, I said, with some heat, Your Excellency may keep
what belongs to you, but do not take from me that which is mine;
I will not suffer you to touch a penny of the perquisites arising
from passports. Perceiving he could gain nothing by these means
he had recourse to others, and blushed not to tell me that since I
had appropriated to myself the profits of the chancery, it was but
just I should pay the expenses. I was unwilling to dispute upon
this subject, and from that time I furnished, at my own expense,
ink, paper, wax, wax-candle, tape, and even a new seal, for which
he never reimbursed me to the amount of a farthing. This, however, did not prevent my giving a small part of the produce of the
passports to the Abbé de Binis, a good creature, and who was far
from pretending to have the least right to any such thing. If he
was obliging to me, my politeness to him was an equivalent, and
we always lived together upon the best of terms.

On the first trial I made of his talents in my official functions,
I found him less troublesome than I expected he would have been,
considering he was a man without experience, in the service of an
ambassador who possessed no more than himself, and whose

ignorance and obstinacy constantly counteracted everything with which commonsense and some information inspired me for his service and that of the King. The best thing the ambassador did was to connect himself with the Marquis Mari, ambassador from Spain, an ingenious and artful man, who, had he wished so to do, might have led him by the nose, yet, on account of the union of the interests of the two crowns, he generally gave him good advice, which might have been of essential service, had not the other, by joining his own opinion, counteracted it in the execution. The only business they had to conduct in concert with each other, was to engage the Venetians to maintain their neutrality. These did not neglect to give the strongest assurances of their fidelity to their engagements at the same time that they publicly furnished ammunition to the Austrian troops, and even recruits under pretence of desertion. M. de Montaigu, who I believe wished to render himself agreeable to the republic, failed not on his part, notwithstanding my representations, to make me assure government in all my despatches, that the Venetians would never violate an article of the neutrality. The obstinacy and stupidity of this poor wretch made me write and act extravagantly: I was obliged to be the agent of his folly because he would have it so, but he sometimes rendered my employment insupportable and the functions of it almost impracticable. For example, he insisted on the greatest part of his despatches to the King, and of those to the minister, being written in cipher, although neither of them contained anything which required that precaution. I represented to him that between the Friday, the day the despatches from the Court arrived, and Saturday, on which ours were sent off, there was not sufficient time to write so much in cipher, and carry on the considerable correspondence with which I was charged for the same courier. He found an admirable expedient, which was to prepare on Thursday the answer to the despatches we were expected to receive on the next day. This appeared to him so happily imagined, that notwithstanding all I could say on the impossibility of the thing, and the absurdity of attempting its execution, I was obliged to comply during the whole time I afterwards remained with him, after having made notes of the few loose words he spoke to me in the course of the week, and of some trivial circumstances which I collected by hurrying from place to place. Provided with these materials I never once failed carrying to him on the Thursday morning a rough draft of the despatches which were to be sent off on Saturday, excepting the few additions and corrections I hastily made in answer to the letters which arrived on the Friday, and to which ours served for answer. He had another custom, diverting enough, and which made his correspondence ridiculous beyond imagination. He sent back all information to its respective source, instead of making it follow its course. To M. Amelot, he transmitted the news of the Court; to M. Maurepas, that of Paris; to M. d'Havrincourt, the news from Sweden; to M. de la Chetardie, that from Petersburg; and sometimes to each of these the news they had respectively sent to him, and which I was employed to dress up in terms different from those in which it was conveyed to us. As he read nothing of what I laid before him, except the despatches for the Court, and signed those of other ambassadors without reading them, this left me more at liberty to give what turn I thought proper to the latter, and in these therefore I made the articles of information cross each other. But it was impossible for me to do the same by despatches of importance; and I thought myself happy when M. de Montaigu did not take it into his head to cram into them an impromptu of a few lines after his manner. This obliged me to return, and hastily transcribe the whole despatch decorated with his new nonsense, and honour it with the cipher, without which he would have refused his signature. I was frequently almost tempted, for the sake of his reputation, to cipher something different from what he had written, but feeling that nothing could authorise such a deception, I left him to answer for his own folly, satisfying myself with having spoken to him with freedom, and discharged at my own peril the duties of my station.

This is what I always did with an uprightness, a zeal, and courage which merited on his part a very different recompense from that which in the end I received from him. It was time I should once be what heaven, which had endowed me with a happy disposition, what the education that had been given by the best of women, and that I had given myself, had prepared me for, and I became so. Left to my own reflections, without a friend or advice, without experience, and in a foreign country, in the service of a foreign nation, surrounded by a crowd of knaves, who, for their own interest, and to avoid the scandal of good example, endeavoured to prevail upon me to imitate them; far from yielding to their solicitations, I served France well, to which I owed nothing, and the ambassador still better, as it was right and just I should do, to the utmost of my power. Irreproachable in a post sufficiently exposed to censure, I merited and obtained the esteem of the republic, that of all the ambassadors with whom we were

in correspondence, and the affection of the French who resided
at Venice; not even excepting the consul, whom with regret I
supplanted in the functions which I knew belonged to him, and
which occasioned me more embarrassment than they afforded me
satisfaction.

M. de Montaigu, confiding without reserve to the Marquis
Mari, who did not thoroughly understand his duty, neglected it to
such a degree, that without me the French who were at Venice
would not have perceived an ambassador from their nation resided
there. Always put off without being heard when they stood in
need of his protection, they became disgusted and no longer appeared in his company or at his table, to which, indeed, he never
invited them. I frequently did from myself what it was his duty
to have done: I rendered to the French who applied to him, all the
services in my power. In any other country I should have done
more, but, on account of my employment, not being able to see
persons in place, I was often obliged to apply to the consul, and
the consul, who was settled in the country with his family, had
many persons to oblige, which prevented him from acting as he
otherwise would have done. However, perceiving him unwilling
and afraid to speak, I sometimes ventured hazardous measures,
which sometimes succeeded. I recollect one which still makes me
laugh. No person would suspect it was to me the lovers of the
theatre at Paris owe Coraline and her sister Camille: nothing,
however, can be more true. Veronese, their father, had engaged
himself with his children in the Italian company, and after having
received two thousand livres for the expenses of his journey, instead of setting out for France, quietly continued at Venice, and
accepted an engagement in the theatre of Saint Luke,[1] to which
Coraline, a child as she still was, drew great numbers of people.
The Duke de Gesvres, as first gentleman of the chamber, wrote to
the ambassador to claim the father and the daughter. M. de Montaigu, when he gave me the letter, confined his instructions to
saying, *voyez cela*, examine and pay attention to this. I went to
M. Le Blond to beg he would speak to the patrician, to whom the
theatre of Saint Luke belonged, and who, I believe, was named
Zustiniani, that he might discharge Veronese, who had engaged
in the name of the King. Le Blond, to whom the commission was
not very agreeable, executed it badly.

---

[1] I have my doubts whether or not it was not Saint Samuel; proper names
absolutely escape my memory. (*Note by Rousseau*, not in Paris MS.).

Zustiniani answered vaguely, and Veronese was not discharged. I was piqued at this. It was during the Carnival, and having taken the bahute and a mask, I set out for the Palace Zustiniani. Those who saw my gondola arrive with the livery of the ambassador, were lost in astonishment. Venice had never seen such a thing. I entered, and caused myself to be announced by the name of *Una Siora Maschera*. As soon as I was introduced I took off my mask, and told my name. The senator turned pale, and appeared stupe-

fied with surprise. Sir, said I to him in Venetian, it is with much regret I importune your excellency with this visit; but you have in your theatre of Saint Luke, a man of the name of Veronese, who is engaged in the service of the King, and whom you have been requested, but in vain, to give up: I come to claim him in the name of His Majesty. My short harangue was effectual. I had no sooner left the palace than Zustiniani ran to communicate the adventure to the state inquisitors, by whom he was severely reprehended. Veronese was discharged the same day. I sent him word that if he did not set off within a week, I would have him arrested. He did not wait for my giving him this intimation a second time.

On another occasion I relieved from difficulty solely by my own means, and almost without the assistance of any other person, the captain of a merchant-ship. This was one Captain Olivet, from Marseilles: the name of the vessel I have forgotten. His men had quarrelled with some Slavonians in the service of the republic, some violence had been committed, and the vessel was under so severe an embargo that nobody except the master was suffered to go on board, or leave it, without permission. He applied to the ambassador, who would hear nothing he had to say. He afterwards went to the consul, who told him it was not an affair of commerce, and that he could not interfere in it. Not knowing what farther steps to take, he applied to me. I told M. de Montaigu, he ought to permit me to lay before the senate a memoir on the subject. I do not recollect whether or not he consented, or that I presented the memoir; but I perfectly remember that if I did it was ineffectual, and the embargo still continuing, I took another method, which succeeded. I inserted a relation of the affair in one of our letters to M. de Maurepas, though I had much difficulty in prevailing upon M. de Montaigu to suffer the article to pass.

I knew that our despatches, although their contents were insignificant, were opened at Venice. Of this I had a proof by finding the articles they contained verbatim in the gazette, a treachery of which I had in vain attempted to prevail upon the ambassador to complain. My object in speaking of the affair in the letter was to turn the curiosity of the ministers of the republic to advantage, to inspire them with some apprehensions, and to induce the state to release the vessel: for had it been necessary to this effect to wait for an answer from the Court, the captain would have been ruined before it could have arrived. I did still more, I went alongside the vessel to make enquiries of the ship's company. I took with me the Abbé Patizel, chancellor of the consulship, who would rather have been excused, so much were these poor creatures afraid of displeasing the senate. As I could not go on board, on account of the order from the states, I remained in my gondola and there took the depositions successfully, interrogating each of the mariners, and directing my questions in such a manner as to produce answers which might be to their advantage. I wished to prevail upon Patizel to put the questions and take the depositions himself, which in fact was more his business than mine; but to this he would not consent: he never once opened his mouth, and almost refused to sign the depositions after me. This step, somewhat bold, was, however, successful, and the vessel was released long before an answer came from the minister. The captain wished to make me a present; but, without being angry with him on that account,

I tapped him on the shoulder, saying, Captain Olivet, can you imagine that he who does not receive from the French the perquisite for passports, which he found his established right, is a man likely to sell them the King's protection? He, however, insisted on giving me a dinner on board his vessel, which I accepted, and took with me the secretary to the Spanish embassy, M. Carrio, a man of wit and amiable manners, to partake of it: he has since been secretary to the Spanish embassy at Paris and chargé d'affaires. I had formed an intimate connection with him after the example of our ambassadors.

Happy should I have been, if, when in the most disinterested manner I did all the service I could, I had known how to introduce sufficient order into all these little details, that I might not have served others at my own expense. But in employments similar to that I held, in which the most trifling faults are of consequence, my whole attention was engaged in avoiding all such mistakes as might be detrimental to my service. I conducted, till the last moment, everything relative to my immediate duty, with the greatest order and exactness. Excepting a few errors which a forced precipitation made me commit in ciphering, and of which the clerks of M. Amelot once complained, neither the ambassador nor any other person had ever the least reason to reproach me with negligence in any one of my functions. This is remarkable in a man so negligent and thoughtless as I am. But my memory sometimes failed me, and I was not sufficiently careful in the private affairs with which I was charged; however, a love of justice always made me take the loss on myself, and this voluntarily, before anybody thought of complaining. I will mention but one circumstance of this nature; it relates to my departure from Venice, and I afterwards felt the effects of it in Paris.

Our cook, whose name was Rousselot, had brought from France an old note for two hundred livres, which a hairdresser, a friend of his, had received from a noble Venetian of the name of Zanetto Nani, who had had wigs of him to that amount. Rousselot brought me the note, begging I would endeavour to obtain payment of some part of it, by way of accommodation. I knew, and he knew it also, that the constant custom of noble Venetians was, when once returned to their country, never to pay the debts they had contracted abroad. When means are taken to force them to payment, the wretched creditor finds so many delays and incurs such enormous expenses, that he becomes disgusted, and concludes by giving up his debt or accepting the most trifling composition. I begged M. Le Blond to speak to Zanetto. The Venetian acknowledged the note but did not agree to payment. After a long dispute he at length promised three sequins; but when Le Blond carried him the note, even these were not ready, and it was necessary to wait. In this interval happened my quarrel with the ambassador, and I quitted his service. I had left the papers of the embassy in the greatest order, but the note of Rousselot was not to be found. M. Le Blond assured me he had given it me back. I knew him to be too honest a man to have the least doubt of the matter; but it was impossible for me to recollect what I had done with it. As Zanetto had acknowledged the debt, I desired M. Le Blond to endeavour to obtain from him the three sequins on giving him a receipt for the amount, or to prevail upon him to renew the note by way of duplicate. Zanetto, knowing the note to be lost, would not agree to either. I offered Rousselot the three sequins from my own purse, as a discharge of the debt. He refused them, and said I might settle the matter with the creditor at Paris, of whom he gave me the address. The hairdresser, having been informed of what had passed, would either have his note or the whole sum for which it was given. What, in my indignation, would I have given to have found this vexatious paper! I paid the two hundred livres, and that in my greatest distress. In this manner the loss of the note produced to the creditor the payment of the whole sum, whereas had it, unfortunately for him, been found, he would have had some difficulty in recovering even the ten crowns, which his excellency, Zanetto Nani, had promised to pay.

The talents I thought I felt in myself for my employment made me discharge the functions of it with satisfaction, and except the society of my friend de Carrio, that of the virtuous Altuna, of whom I shall soon have occasion to speak, the innocent recreations of the place Saint Mark, of the theatre, and of a few visits which we, for the most part, made together, my only pleasure was in the duties of my station. Although these were not considerable, especially with the aid of the Abbé de Binis, yet, as the correspondence was very extensive, and there was a war, I was a good deal employed. I applied to business the greatest part of every morning, and on the days previous to the departure of the courier, in the evenings, and sometimes till midnight. The rest of my time I gave to the study of the political profession I had entered upon, and in which I hoped, from my successful beginning, to be later advantageously employed. In fact, I was in favour with everyone; the ambassador himself spoke highly of my services, and never complained of anything I did for him; his dissatisfaction proceeded from my having insisted on quitting him, in consequence of the useless complaints I had frequently made on several occasions. The ambassadors and ministers of the King with whom we were in correspondence, complimented him on the merit of his secretary, in a manner by which he ought to have been flattered, but which in his poor head produced quite a contrary effect. He received one in particular relative to an affair of importance, for which he never pardoned me. This is worth explaining.

PIAZZA DI SAN MARCO

He was so incapable of bearing the least constraint, that on the Saturday, the day of the despatches for most of the courts, he could not contain himself, and wait till the business was done before he went out, and incessantly pressing me to hasten the despatches to the King and ministers, he signed them with precipitation, and immediately went I know not where, leaving most of the other letters without signing; this obliged me, when these contained nothing but news, to convert them into journals; but when affairs which related to the King were in question, it was necessary somebody should sign, and I did it. This once happened relative to some important advice we had just received from M. Vincent, chargé d'affaires of the King at Vienna. The Prince Lobkowitz was then marching to Naples, and Count Gages had just made that most memorable retreat, the finest military manœuvre of the whole century, of which Europe has not sufficiently spoken. The despatch informed us that a man, whose person M. Vincent described, had set out from Vienna, and was to pass by Venice, in his way into Abruzzi, where he was secretly to stir up the people at the approach of the Austrians.

In the absence of M. le Comte de Montaigu, who did not give himself the least concern about anything, I forwarded this advice to the Marquis de l'Hôpital, so apropos, that it is perhaps to the poor Jean-Jacques, so abused and laughed at, that the house of Bourbon owes the preservation of the kingdom of Naples.

The Marquis de l'Hôpital, when he thanked his colleague, as it was proper he should do, spoke to him of his secretary, and mentioned the service he had just rendered to the common cause. The Comte de Montaigu, who in that affair had to reproach himself with negligence, thought he perceived in the compliment paid him by M. de l'Hôpital, something like a reproach, and spoke of it to me with signs of ill humour. I had found it necessary to act in the same manner with the Count de Castellane, ambassador at Constantinople, as I had done with the Marquis de l'Hôpital, although in things of less importance. As there was no other conveyance to Constantinople than by the couriers, sent from time to time by the senate to its Bailli,[1] advice of their departure was given to the ambassador of France, that he might write by them to his colleague, if he thought proper so to do. This advice was commonly sent a day or two beforehand; but M. de Montaigu was held in so little respect, that merely for the sake of form he was sent to a couple of hours before the couriers set off. This frequently obliged me to write the despatch in his absence. M. de Castellane, in his answers, made honourable mention of me; M. de Jonville, at Genoa, did the same, and these instances of their regard and esteem became new grievances.

I acknowledge I did not neglect any opportunity of making myself known; but I never sought one improperly, and in serving well I thought I had a right to aspire to the natural return for essential services; the esteem of those capable of judging of, and rewarding them. I will not say whether or not my exactness in discharging the duties of my employment was a just subject of complaint from the ambassador, but I cannot refrain from declaring that it was the sole grievance he ever mentioned previous to our separation.

[1] Title of the Venetian ambassador in Constantinople.

His house, which he had never put upon a good footing, was constantly filled with rabble; the French were ill-treated in it, and the ascendancy was given to the Italians; of these even, the more honest part, they who had long been in the service of the embassy, were indecently discharged, his first gentleman in particular, whom he had taken from the Comte de Froulay, and who, if I remember right, was called Comte Peati, or something very like that name. The second gentleman, chosen by M. de Montaigu, was an outlawed highwayman from Mantua, called Dominic Vitali, to whom the ambassador entrusted the care of his house, and who, by means of flattery and sordid economy, obtained his confidence, and became his favourite, to the great prejudice of the few honest people he still had about him, and of the secretary who was at their head. The honest countenance of an upright man always gives inquietude to knaves. Nothing more was necessary to make Vitali conceive a hatred against me: but for this sentiment there was still another cause which rendered it more cruel. Of this I must give an account, that I may be condemned, if I am found in the wrong.

The ambassador had, according to custom, a box at each of the five theatres. Every day at dinner he named the theatre to which it was his intention to go: I chose after him, and the gentlemen disposed of the other boxes. When I went out I took the key of the box I had chosen. One day, Vitali not being in the way, I ordered the footman who attended on me, to bring me the key to a house which I named to him. Vitali, instead of sending the key, said he had disposed of it. I was the more enraged at this as the footman delivered his message in public. In the evening, Vitali wished to make me some apology, to which however I would not listen. To-morrow, sir, said I to him, you will come, at such an hour, and apologise to me in the house where I received the affront, and in the presence of the persons who were witnesses to it; or after to-morrow, whatever may be the consequence, either you or I will leave the house. This firmness intimidated him. He came to the house at the hour appointed, and made me a public apology, with a meanness worthy of himself. But he afterwards took his measures at leisure, and, at the same time that he cringed to me in public, he secretly acted in so Italian a manner that, although unable to prevail on the ambassador to give me my dismission, he laid me under the necessity of resolving to leave him.

A wretch like him, certainly, could not know me, but he knew enough of my character to make it serviceable to his purpose. He knew I was mild to an excess, and patient in bearing involuntary wrongs; but haughty and impatient when insulted with premeditated offences; loving decency and dignity in things in which these were requisite, and not more exact in requiring the respect due to myself, than attentive in rendering that which I owed to others. In this he undertook to disgust me, and in this he succeeded. He turned the house upside down, and destroyed the order and subordination I had endeavoured to establish in it. A house without a woman stands in need of rather a severe discipline to preserve that modesty which is inseparable from dignity. He soon converted ours into a place of filthy debauch and scandalous licentiousness, the haunt of knaves and debauchees. He procured for second gentleman to His Excellency, in the place of him whom he got discharged, another pimp like himself, who kept a house of ill-fame, at the Cross of Malta; and the indecency of these two rascals was equalled by nothing but their insolence. Except the bedchamber of the ambassador, which, however, was not in very good order, there was not a corner in the whole house supportable to a modest man.

As His Excellency did not sup, the gentlemen and myself had a private table, at which the Abbé de Binis and the pages also ate. In the most paltry ale-house, people are served with more cleanliness and decency, have cleaner linen, and a table better supplied. We had but one little and very filthy candle, pewter plates, and iron forks.

I could have overlooked what passed in secret, but I was deprived of my gondola. I was the only secretary to an ambassador, who was obliged to hire one or go on foot, and the livery of His Excellency no longer accompanied me, except when I went to the senate. Besides, everything which passed in the house was known in the city. All those who were in the service of the ambassador loudly exclaimed; Dominic, the only cause of all, exclaimed louder than anybody, well knowing the indecency with which we were treated was more affecting to me than to any other person. Though I was the only one in the house who said nothing of the matter abroad, I complained loudly of it to the ambassador, as well as of himself, who, secretly excited by the wretch entirely devoted to his will, daily made me suffer some new affront. Obliged to expend a good deal to keep upon a footing with those in the same situation with myself, and to make an appearance proper to my employment, I could not touch a farthing of my salary, and when I asked him for money, he spoke of his esteem for me, and his confidence, as if either of these could have filled my purse, and provided for everything.

These two banditti at length quite turned the head of their master, who naturally had not a good one, and ruined him by a continual traffic, and by bargains, of which he was the dupe, whilst they persuaded him they were greatly in his favour. They persuaded him to take upon the Brenta a palazzo, at twice the rent it was worth, and divided the surplus with the proprietor. The apartments were inlaid with mosaic, and ornamented with columns and pilasters of fine marble, in the taste of the country. M. de Montaigu had all these superbly masked by fir wainscoting; for no other reason than because at Paris apartments were thus fitted up. It was for a similar reason that he only, of all the ambassadors who were at Venice, took from his pages their swords, and from his footmen their canes. Such was the man who, perhaps from the same motive, took a dislike to me only on account of my serving him faithfully.

I patiently endured his disdain, his brutality, and ill treatment, as long as, perceiving them accompanied by ill humour, I thought they had in them no portion of hatred: but the moment I saw the design formed of depriving me of the honour I merited by my faithful services, I resolved to resign my employment. The first mark I received of his ill-will was relative to a dinner he was to give to the Duke of Modena and his family, who were at Venice, and at which he signified to me I should not be present. I answered, piqued, but not angry, that having the honour daily to dine at his table, if the Duke of Modena, when he came, required I should not appear at it, the dignity of His Excellency and of my own duty would not suffer me to consent to such a request. How, said he, passionately, my secretary, who is not even a gentleman, pretends to dine with a sovereign when my gentlemen do not! Yes, sir, replied I: the post with which Your Excellency has honoured me, as long as I discharge the functions of it, so far ennobles me that my rank is superior to that of your gentlemen, or of the persons calling themselves such; and I am admitted where they cannot appear. You cannot but know that on the day on which you shall make your public entry, I am called by etiquette, and by an immemorial custom, to follow you in a dress of ceremony, and afterwards to dine with you at the palace of Saint Mark; and I know not why a man who has a right and is to eat in public with the Doge and the senate of Venice should not eat in private with the Duke of Modena. Though this argument was unanswerable, it did not convince the ambassador: but we had no occasion to renew the dispute, as the Duke of Modena did not come to dine with him.

From that moment he did everything in his power to make things disagreeable to me; and endeavoured unjustly to deprive me of my right, by taking from me the pecuniary advantages annexed to my employment, to give them to his dear Vitali; and I am convinced that had he dared to send him to the senate, in my place, he would have done it. He commonly employed the Abbé de Binis in his closet, to write his private letters: he made use of him to write to M. de Maurepas an account of the affair of Captain Olivet, in which, far from taking the least notice of me, the only person who gave himself any concern about the matter, he deprived me of the honour of the depositions, of which he sent him a duplicate, for the purpose of attributing them to Patizel, who had not opened his mouth. He wished to mortify me, and please his favourite; but had no desire to dismiss me his service. He perceived it would be more difficult to find me a successor, than one to M. Follau, who had already made him known to the world. An Italian-speaking secretary was absolutely necessary to him, on account of the answers from the senate: one who could write all his despatches; and conduct his affairs, without his giving himself the least trouble about anything; a person who, to the merit of serving him well, could join the baseness of being the toad-eater of his gentlemen. He wished to retain, and humble, me, by keeping me far from my country, and his own, without money to return to either, and in this he would, perhaps, have succeeded, had he begun with more moderation: but Vitali, who had other views, and wished to force me to extremities, carried his point. The moment I perceived I lost all my trouble, that the ambassador imputed to me my services as so many crimes, instead of being satisfied with them; that with him I had nothing to expect, but things disagreeable at home, and injustice abroad; and that, in the general disesteem into which he was fallen, his ill offices might be prejudicial to me, without the possibility of my being served by his good ones; I took my resolution, and asked him for my dismission, leaving him sufficient time to provide himself with another secretary. Without answering yes or no, he continued to treat me in the same manner, as if nothing had been said. Perceiving things to remain in the same state, and that he took no measures to procure himself a new secretary, I wrote to his brother, and, explaining to him my motives, begged he would obtain my dismission from His Excellency, adding that whether I received it or not, I could not possibly remain with him. I waited a long time without any answer, and began to be embarrassed: but at length the ambassador received a letter from his brother, which must have remonstrated with him in very plain terms; for, although he was extremely subject to ferocious rage, I never saw him so violent as on this occasion. After torrents of insufferable reproaches, not knowing what more to say, he accused me of having sold his ciphers. I burst into a loud laughter, and asked him, in a sneering manner, if he thought there was in Venice a man who would be fool enough to give half a crown for them all. He threatened to call his servants to throw me out of the window. Until then I had been very composed; but on this threat, anger and indignation seized me in my turn. I sprang to the door, and, after having turned a button which fastened it within; No, Count, said I, returning to him with a grave step, your servants shall have nothing to do with this affair: please to let it be settled between ourselves. My action and manner instantly made him calm: fear and surprise were marked in his countenance. The moment I saw his fury abated, I bid him adieu in a very few words, and without waiting for his answer, went to the door, opened it, and passed slowly across the ante-chamber, through the midst of his people; who rose according to custom, and who, I am of opinion, would rather have lent their assistance against him than me. Without going back to my apartment, I descended the stairs, and immediately went out of the palace never more to enter it.

I hastened immediately to M. Le Blond, and related to him what had happened. Knowing the man, he was but little surprised. He kept me to dinner. This dinner, although without preparation, was splendid. All the French of consequence who were at Venice, partook of it. The ambassador had not a single person. The consul related my case to the company. The cry was general, and by no means in favour of His Excellency. He had not settled my account, nor paid me a farthing, and, being reduced to the few louis I had in my pocket, I was extremely embarrassed about my return to France. Every purse was opened to me. I took twenty sequins from that of M. Le Blond, and as many from that of M. de St. Cyr, with whom, next to M. Le Blond, I was the most intimately connected. I returned thanks to the rest; and, till my departure, went to lodge at the house of the chancellor of the consulship, to prove to the public that the nation was not an accomplice in the injustice of the ambassador.

His Excellency, furious at seeing me taken notice of in my misfortune, at the same time that, notwithstanding his being an ambassador, nobody went near his house, quite lost his senses and behaved like a madman. He forgot himself so far as to present a memoir to the senate to get me arrested. On being informed of this by the Abbé de Binis, I resolved to remain a fortnight longer, instead of setting off the next day but one, as I had intended. My conduct had been known and approved by everybody. I was universally esteemed. The senate did not deign to return an answer to the extravagant memoir of the ambassador, but sent me word by the consul I might remain in Venice as long as I thought proper, without making myself uneasy about the attempts of a madman. I continued to see my friends: I went to take leave of the ambassador from Spain, who received me well, and of the Comte de Finochietti, minister from Naples, whom I did not find at home. I wrote him a letter and received from His Excellency the most polite and obliging answer. At length I took my departure, leaving behind me, notwithstanding my embarrassments, no other debts than the two sums I had borrowed, and of which I have just spoken; and an account of fifty crowns with a shopkeeper, of the name of Morandi, which Carrio promised to pay, and which I have never reimbursed him, although we have frequently met since that time; but with respect to the two sums of money, I returned them very exactly the moment I had it in my power.

I cannot take leave of Venice without saying something of the celebrated amusements of that city, or at least of the little part of them of which I partook during my residence there. It has been seen how little in my youth I ran after the pleasures of that age, or those which are so called. My inclinations did not change at Venice, but my occupations, which moreover would have prevented this, rendered more agreeable to me the simple recreations I permitted myself. The first and most pleasing of all was the society of men of merit. MM. Le Blond, de St. Cyr, Carrio, Altuna, and a gentleman whose name I am very sorry to have forgotten, and whom I never call to my recollection without emotion; he was the man of all I ever knew whose heart most resembled my own. We were connected with two or three Englishmen of great wit and information, and, like ourselves, passionately fond of music. All these gentlemen had their wives, female friends, or mistresses: the latter were most of them women of talents, at whose apartments there were balls and concerts. There was but little play; a lively turn, talents, and the theatres rendered this

STREET IN VENICE

amusement insipid. Play is the resource of none but men whose time hangs heavy on their hands. I had brought with me from Paris the prejudice of that city against Italian music; but I had also received from nature a sensibility and niceness of distinction which prejudice cannot withstand. I soon contracted that passion for Italian music with which it inspires all those who are capable of feeling its excellence. In listening to *barcarolles*, I found I had not yet known what singing was, and I soon became so fond of the opera that, tired of babbling, eating, and playing in the boxes, when I wished to listen, I frequently withdrew from the company to another part of the theatre. There, quite alone, shut up in my box, I abandoned myself, notwithstanding the length of the representation, to the pleasure of enjoying it at ease unto the conclusion. One evening at the theatre of Saint Chrysostom, I fell into a more profound sleep than I should have done in my bed. The loud and brilliant airs did not disturb my repose. But who can explain the delicious sensations given me by the soft harmony of the angelic music, by which I was charmed from sleep; what an awaking! what ravishment! what ecstasy, when at the same instant I opened my ears and eyes! my first idea was to believe I was in paradise. The ravishing air, which I still recollect and shall never forget, began with these words:

Conservami la bella,
Che si m'accende il cor.

I was desirous of having it; I had and kept it for a long time; but it was not the same thing upon paper as in my head. The notes were the same, but the thing was different. This divine composition can never be executed but in my mind, in the same manner as it was the evening on which it awoke me from sleep.

A kind of music far superior, in my opinion, to that of operas, and which in all Italy has not its equal, nor perhaps in the whole world, is that of the *scuole*. The *scuole* are houses of charity, established for the education of young girls without fortune, to whom the republic afterwards gives a portion either in marriage or for the cloister. Amongst the talents cultivated in these young girls, music is in the first rank. Every Sunday at the church of each of the four *scuole*, during vespers, motettos or anthems with full choruses, accompanied by a great orchestra, and composed and directed by the best masters in Italy, are sung in the galleries by girls only; not one of whom is more than twenty years of age. I have not an idea of anything so voluptuous and affecting as this music: the richness of the art, the exquisite taste of the vocal part, the excellence of the voices, the justness of the execution, everything in these delightful concerts concurs to produce an impression which certainly is not the mode, but from which I am of opinion no heart is secure. Carrio and I never failed being present at these vespers at the *Mendicanti*, and we were not alone. The church was always full of the lovers of the art, and even the actors of the opera came there to form their tastes after these excellent models. What vexed me was the iron grate, which suffered nothing to escape but sounds, and concealed from me the angels of beauty of which they were worthy. I talked of nothing else. One day I spoke of it at Le Blond's: if you are so desirous, said he, to see those little girls, it will be an easy matter to satisfy your wishes. I am one of the administrators of the house, I will give you a collation with them. I did not let him rest until he had fulfilled his

promise. In entering the saloon, which contained these beauties
I so much sighed to see, I felt a trembling of love which I had
never before experienced. M. Le Blond presented to me one after
the other these celebrated female singers, of whom the names and
voices were all with which I was acquainted. Come, Sophia, —
she was horrid. Come, Cattina, — she had but one eye. Come,
Bettina, — the smallpox had entirely disfigured her person.
Scarcely one of them was without some striking defect. Le Blond
laughed at my surprise: however, two or three of them appeared
tolerable; these never sung but in the choruses: I was almost in
despair. During the collation, we endeavoured to excite them, and
they soon became enlivened; ugliness does not exclude the graces,
and I found they possessed them. I said to myself: they cannot
sing in this manner without intelligence and sensibility, they
must have both; in fine, my manner of seeing them changed to
such a degree, that I left the house almost in love with each of
these ugly figures. I had scarcely courage enough to return to
vespers. But, after having seen the girls, the danger was lessened.
I still found their singing delightful; and their voices so much
embellished their persons, that, in spite of my eyes, as long as they
sang, I obstinately continued to think them beautiful.

Music in Italy is accompanied with so trifling an expense, that
it is not worth while for such as have a taste for it to deny themselves the pleasure it affords. I hired a harpsichord, and, for half a
crown, I had at my apartment four or five symphonists, with
whom I practised once a week in executing such airs, etc., as had
given me most pleasure at the opera. I also had some symphonies
performed from my *Muses Galantes*. Whether these pleased the
performers, or the ballet master of St. John Chrysostom wished to
flatter me, he desired to have two of them; and I had afterwards
the pleasure of hearing these executed by that admirable orchestra. They were danced to by a little Bettina, pretty and amiable,
and kept by a Spaniard, M. Fagoaga, a friend of ours with whom
we often went to spend the evening. But apropos of girls of easy
virtue: it is not in Venice that a man abstains from them. Have
you nothing to confess, somebody will ask me, upon this subject?
Yes: I have something to say upon it, and I will proceed to this
confession with the same ingenuousness with which I have made
all my former ones.

I always had a distaste for girls of pleasure, and at Venice those
were all I had within my reach; most of the houses being shut
against me on account of my place. The daughters of M. Le Blond

were very amiable, but difficult of access; and I had too much
respect for the father and mother ever once to have the least
desire for them.

I should have had a much stronger inclination to a young lady
named Mademoiselle de Cataneo, daughter to the agent from the
King of Prussia, but Carrio was in love with her: there was even
between them some question of marriage. He was in easy circumstances, and I had no fortune: his salary was a hundred louis a
year, and mine amounted to no more than a thousand livres:
and besides my being unwilling to oppose a friend, I knew that
in all places, and especially at Venice, with a purse so ill furnished
as mine was, gallantry was out of the question. I had not lost the
pernicious custom of deceiving my wants. Too busily employed
forcibly to feel those proceeding from the climate, I lived about
a year in that city as chastely as I had done in Paris; and at the
end of eighteen months, I quitted it without having approached
the sex, except twice by means of the singular opportunities of
which I am going to speak.

The first was procured me by that honest gentleman, Vitali,
some time after the formal apology I obliged him to make me.
The conversation at table turned on the amusements of Venice.
These gentlemen reproached me with my indifference with regard to the most delightful of them all; at the same time extolling
the gracefulness and elegant manners of the women of easy virtue
of Venice; and adding, that they were superior to all others of the
same description in any other part of the world. Dominic said I
must make an acquaintance with the most amiable of them all; he
offered to take me to her apartments, and assured me I should
be pleased with her. I laughed at this obliging offer; and Count
Peati, a man in years and venerable, observed to me, with more
candour than I should have expected from an Italian, that he
thought me too prudent to suffer myself to be taken to such a
place by my enemy. In fact, I had no inclination or temptation to
do it: but, notwithstanding this, by an incoherence I cannot myself comprehend, I at length was prevailed upon to go, contrary
to my inclination, the sentiment of my heart, my reason, and even
my will; solely from weakness, and being ashamed to show an
appearance of the least mistrust; and besides, as the expression of
the country is, *per non parer troppo coglione*. The Padoana whom
we went to visit was pretty, she was even handsome, but her
beauty was not of that kind which pleased me. Dominic left me
with her, I sent for *Sorbetti* and asked her to sing, in about half

an hour I wished to take my leave after having put a ducat on the table; but this by a singular scruple she refused until she had deserved it, and I from as singular a folly consented to remove her doubts. I returned to the palace, so fully persuaded that I was infected that the first thing I did was to send for the surgeon to ask him for drugs. Nothing can equal the uneasiness of mind I suffered for three weeks, without its being justified by any real inconvenience or apparent sign. I could not believe it was possible to withdraw with impunity from the arms of the Padoana. The surgeon himself had the greatest difficulty in removing my apprehensions; nor could he do this by any other means than by persuading me I was formed in such a manner as not to be easily infected: and although in the experiment I exposed myself perhaps less than any other man would have done, my health in that respect never having suffered the least inconvenience is in my opinion a proof that the surgeon was right. However, this never made me imprudent, and if in fact I have received such an advantage from nature I can safely assert I have never abused it.

ALONG THE RIALTO

My second adventure, although likewise with a common girl, was of a nature very different, as well in its origin as in its effects. I have already said that Captain Olivet gave me a dinner on board his vessel, and that I took with me the secretary of the Spanish embassy. I expected a salute of cannon. The ship's company was drawn up to receive us, but not so much as a priming was burnt, at which I was mortified, on account of Carrio, whom I perceived to be rather piqued at the neglect. A salute of cannon was given on board merchant-ships, to people of less consequence than we were; I besides thought I deserved some distinguished mark of respect from the captain. I could not conceal my thoughts, because this at all times was impossible to me, and although the dinner was a very good one, and Olivet did the honours of it perfectly well, I began it in an ill-humour, eating but little, and speaking still less. At the first health, at least, I expected a volley; — nothing. Carrio, who read what passed within me, laughed at hearing me grumble like a child. Before dinner was half over I saw a gondola approach the vessel. Bless me, sir, said the captain, take care of yourself, the enemy approaches. I asked him what he meant, and he answered jocosely. The gondola made the ship's side, and I observed a gay young damsel come on board, very lightly and coquettishly dressed, and who at three steps was in the cabin, seated by my side, before I had time to perceive a cover was laid for her. She was equally charming and lively, a brunette, not more than twenty years of age. She spoke nothing but Italian, and her accent alone was sufficient to turn my head. As she ate and chattered she cast her eyes upon me; steadfastly looked at me for a moment; and then exclaimed, Good Virgin! Ah, my dear Brémond, what an age it is since I saw thee! She then threw herself into my arms, sealed her lips to mine, and pressed me almost to strangling. Her large black eyes, like those of the beauties of the east, darted fiery shafts into my heart, and although the surprise at first stupefied my senses, voluptuousness made a rapid progress within, and this to such a degree that the beautiful seducer herself was, notwithstanding the spectators, obliged to restrain my ardour, for I was intoxicated, or rather become furious. When she perceived she had made the impression she desired, she became more moderate in her caresses, but not in her vivacity, and when she thought proper to explain to us the real or false cause of all her petulance, she said I resembled M. de Brémond, director of the customs of Tuscany, to such a degree as to be mistaken for him; that she had turned this M. de Brémond's head and would do it again; that she had quitted him because he was a fool; that she took me in his place; that she would love me because it pleased her so to do, for which reason I must love her as long as it was agreeable to her, and when she thought proper to send me about my business, I must be patient as her dear Brémond had been.

What was said was done. She took possession of me as of a man who belonged to her, gave me her gloves to keep, her fan, her *cinda*, and her coif, and ordered me to go here or there, to do this or that, and I instantly obeyed her. She told me to go and send away her gondola, because she chose to make use of mine, and I immediately sent it away; she bid me to move from my place, and pray Carrio to sit down in it, because she had something to say to him; and I did as she desired. They chatted a good while together, but spoke low, and I did not interrupt them. She called me, and I approached her. Hark thee, Zanetto, said she to me, I will not be loved in the French manner: this indeed would not be well. In the first moment of lassitude, get thee gone: but stay not by the way, I caution thee. After dinner, we went to see the glass manufactory at Murano. She bought a great number of little curiosities, for which she left us to pay without the least ceremony. But she everywhere gave away little presents to a much greater amount than that of the things we had purchased. By the indifference with which she threw away her money, and let us throw away ours, I perceived she annexed to it but little value. When she insisted upon payment, I am of opinion it was more from a motive of vanity than avarice. She was flattered by the price her admirers set upon her favours.

In the evening we conducted her to her apartments. As we conversed together, I perceived a couple of pistols upon her toilette. Ah! Ah! said I, taking one of them up, this is a patch-box of a new construction: may I ask what is its use? I know you have other arms which give more fire than those upon your table. After a few pleasantries of the same kind, she said to us, with an ingenuousness which rendered her still more charming, When I am complaisant to persons whom I do not love, I make them pay for the weariness they cause me; nothing can be more just: but if I suffer their caresses, I will not bear their insults; nor miss the first who shall be wanting to me in respect.

At taking leave of her, I made another appointment for the next day. I did not make her wait. I found her *in vestito di confidenza*, in an undress, more than wanton, unknown to northern countries, and which I will not amuse myself in describing although I recollect it perfectly well. I shall only remark that her ruffles and collar were edged with silk net-work, ornamented with rose-coloured pompons. This, in my eyes, much enlivened a beautiful complexion. I afterwards found it to be the mode at Venice, and the effect is so charming that I am surprised it has never been introduced in France. I had no idea of the transports which awaited me. I have spoken of Madame de Larnage, with the transport which the remembrance of her still sometimes gives me: but how old, ugly, and cold she appeared, compared with my Zulietta! Do not attempt to form to yourself an idea of the charms and graces of this enchanting girl: you will be too far short of truth. Young virgins in cloisters are not so fresh: the beauties of the seraglio are less animated: the houris of paradise less engaging. Never was so sweet an enjoyment offered to the heart and senses of a mortal. Ah! had I at least been capable of fully tasting of it for a single moment! — I tasted of it, but without a charm. I enfeebled all its delights: I destroyed them as at will. No: nature has not made me capable of enjoyment. She has infused into my wretched head the poison of that ineffable happiness, the desire of which she first placed in my heart.

If there be a circumstance in my life, which describes my nature, it is that which I am going to relate. The forcible manner in which I at this moment recollect the object of my book, will here make me hold in contempt the false delicacy which would prevent me from fulfilling it. Whoever you may be who are desirous of knowing a man, have the courage to read the two or three following pages, and you will become fully acquainted with Jean-Jacques Rousseau.

I entered the chamber of a woman of easy virtue, as the sanctuary of love and beauty: and, in her person, I thought I saw the divinity. I should have been inclined to think that without respect and esteem it was impossible to feel anything like that which she made me experience. Scarcely had I, in her first familiarities, discovered the force of her charms and caresses, before I wished, for fear of losing the fruit of them beforehand, to gather it with all speed. Suddenly, instead of the flame which consumed me, I felt a mortal cold run through all my veins; my legs failed me; and, ready to faint away, I sat down and wept like a child.

Who would guess the cause of my tears, and what, at this moment, passed within me? I said to myself: the object in my power is the masterpiece of nature and love: her wit and person equally approach perfection: she is as good and generous, as she is amiable and beautiful. Great men and princes should be her slaves; sceptres laid at her feet. Yet she is a miserable prostitute, abandoned to the public. The captain of a merchant ship disposes of her at will: she has thrown herself into my arms, although she knows I have nothing; and my merit, with which she cannot be

acquainted, can to her be no inducement. In this there is something inconceivable. Either my heart deceives me, fascinates my
senses, and makes me the dupe of an unworthy slut, or some secret
defect, of which I am ignorant, destroys the effect of her charms,
and renders her odious in the eyes of those by whom her charms
would otherwise be disputed. I endeavoured, by an extraordinary
effort of mind, to discover this defect; but it did not so much as
strike me that the pox might possibly have some influence. The
clearness of her skin, the brilliancy of her complexion, her white
teeth, sweet breath, and the appearance of neatness about all her
person, so far removed from me this idea that, still in doubt relative to my situation after the affair of the Padoana, I rather apprehended I was not sufficiently in health for her; and I am firmly
persuaded I was not deceived in my opinion. These reflections, so
apropos, agitated me to such a degree as to make me shed tears.
Zulietta, to whom the scene was surely quite novel, was struck
speechless for a moment. But having made a turn in her chamber,
and passing before her glass, she comprehended, and my eyes confirmed her opinion, that disgust had no part in what had happened. It was not difficult for her to recover me, and dispel this
little shamefacedness. But, at the moment in which I was ready
to faint upon a bosom which for the first time seemed to suffer
the impression of the hand and lips of a man; I perceived she had
a withered nipple. I struck my forehead: I examined, and thought
I perceived this nipple was not formed like the other. I immediately began to consider how it was possible to have such a defect,
and persuaded of its proceeding from some great natural vice,
by turning this idea over and over, I was clearly convinced that,
instead of the most charming person of whom I could form to myself an idea, I had in my arms a species of monster, the refuse of
nature, of men, and of love. I carried my stupidity so far as to
speak to her of the discovery I had made. She, at first, took what I
said jocosely; and, in her frolicsome humour, did and said things
of a nature to make me die of love. But perceiving an inquietude
I could not conceal, she at length reddened, adjusted her dress,
raised herself up, and, without saying a word, went and placed
herself at the window. I attempted to place myself by her side: she
prevented me, withdrew to a sofa, rose from it the next moment,
and, fanning herself as she walked about the chamber, said to me,
in a reserved and disdainful tone of voice: Zanetto, *lascia le donne,
e studia la matematica.*[1]

---

[1] "Leave the ladies alone and study mathematics."

Before I took leave, I requested her to appoint another rendez-vous for the next day, which she postponed for three days, adding, with a satirical smile, that I must needs be in want of repose. I was very ill at ease during this interval; my heart was full of her charms and graces; I felt my extravagance, and reproached my-self with it, regretting the loss of the moments I had so ill em-ployed, and which, had I chosen, I might have rendered more agreeable than any in my whole life; waiting with the most burn-ing impatience for the moment in which I might repair the loss, and yet, notwithstanding all my reasoning upon what I had dis-covered, anxious to reconcile the perfections of this adorable girl with the indignity of her situation. I ran, I flew to her apartment at the hour appointed. I know not whether or not her ardour would have been more satisfied with this visit, her pride at least would have been flattered by it, and I already rejoiced at the idea of my convincing her, in every respect, that I knew how to repair the wrongs I had done. She spared me this justification. The gon-dolier whom I had sent to her apartment brought me for answer that she had set off, the evening before, for Florence. If I had not felt all the love I had for her person when this was in my posses-sion, I felt it in the most cruel manner on losing her. My stupid regret has never left me. Amiable and charming as she was in my eyes, I could have consoled myself for the loss of her; but this I have never been able to do relative to the contemptible idea which at her departure she must have had of me.

These are my two narratives. The eighteen months[1] I passed at Venice furnished me with no other of the same kind, except a simple prospect at most. Carrio was a gallant. Tired of visiting girls engaged to others, he took a fancy to have one to himself, and, as we were inseparable, he proposed to me an arrangement common enough at Venice, which was to keep one girl for us both. To this I consented. The question was, to find one who was safe. He was so industrious in his researches that he found out a little girl of from eleven to twelve years of age, whom her infamous mother was endeavouring to sell, and I went with Carrio to see her. The sight of the child moved me to the most lively compas-sion. She was fair, and as gentle as a lamb. Nobody would have taken her for an Italian. Living is very cheap at Venice; we gave a little money to the mother, and provided for the subsistence of her daughter. She had a voice, and to procure her some resource, we gave her a spinet, and a singing master. All these expenses did

[1] Less than a year (Sept. 1743 — Aug. 1744).

not cost us more than two sequins each a month, and we contrived to save a much greater sum in other matters; but as we were obliged to wait until she became of a riper age, this was sowing a long time before we could possibly reap. However, satisfied with passing our evenings, chatting, and innocently playing with the child, we perhaps enjoyed greater pleasure than if we had received the last favours. So true is it that men are more attached to women by a certain pleasure they have in living with them, than by any kind of libertinism. My heart became insensibly attached to little Anzoletta, but my attachment was paternal, in which the senses had so little share, that in proportion as the former increased, to have connected it with the latter would have been less possible; and I felt I should have experienced, at approaching this little creature when become nubile, the same horror with which the abominable crime of incest would have inspired me. I perceived the sentiments of Carrio take, unobserved by himself, exactly the same turn. We thus prepared for ourselves, without intending it, pleasure not less delicious, but very different from that of which he first had an idea; and I am fully persuaded that, however beautiful the poor child might have become, far from being the corruptors of her innocence, we should have been the protectors of it. The catastrophe which shortly afterwards befell me deprived me of the happiness of taking a part in this good work, and my only merit in the affair was the inclination of my heart.

I will now return to my journey.

My first intention, after leaving M. de Montaigu, was to retire to Geneva, until time and more favourable circumstances should have removed the obstacles which prevented my union with my poor Mamma; but the quarrel between me and M. de Montaigu being become public, and he having had the folly to write about it to the court, I resolved to go there to give an account of my conduct and complain of that of a madman. I communicated my intention, from Venice, to M. du Theil, charged *per interim* with foreign affairs after the death of M. Amelot. I set off as soon as my letter, and took my route through Bergamo, Como and Domodossola, and crossing the Simplon. At Sion, M. de Chaignon, chargé d'affaires from France, showed me great civility; at Geneva M. de la Closure treated me with the same polite attention. I there renewed my acquaintance with M. de Gauffecourt, from whom I had some money to receive. I had passed through Nyon without going to see my father: not that this was a matter of indifference to me, but because I was unwilling to appear before my mother-in-law after the disaster which had befallen me, certain of being condemned by her without being heard. The bookseller, Duvillard, an old friend of my father's, reproached me severely with this neglect. I gave him my reasons for it, and to repair my fault, without exposing myself to meet my mother-in-law, I took a chaise and we went together to Nyon and stopped at a public house. Duvillard went to fetch my father, who came running to embrace me. We supped together, and after passing an evening very agreeable to the wishes of my heart, I returned the next morning to Geneva, with Duvillard, for whom I have ever since retained a sentiment of gratitude in return for the service he did me on this occasion.

Lyons was a little out of my direct road, but I was determined to pass through that city in order to convince myself of a knavish trick played me by M. de Montaigu. I had sent me from Paris a little box containing a waistcoat, embroidered with gold, a few pairs of ruffles, and six pairs of white silk stockings; nothing more. Upon a proposition made me by M. de Montaigu, I ordered this box to be added to his baggage. In the apothecary's bill he offered me in payment of my salary, and which he wrote out himself, he stated the weight of this box, which he called a bale, at eleven hundred pounds, and charged me with the carriage of it at an enormous rate. By the care of M. Boy de la Tour, to whom I was recommended by M. Roguin, his uncle, it was proved from the registers of the customs of Lyons and Marseilles, that the said bale weighed no more than forty-five pounds, and had paid carriage according to that weight. I joined this authentic extract to the memoir of M. de Montaigu, and provided with these papers and others to the same effect, I returned to Paris, very impatient to make use of them. During the whole of this long journey I had little adventures; at Como, in Valais, and elsewhere. I there saw many curious things, amongst others the Borromeo islands, which are worthy of being described. But I am pressed by time, and surrounded by spies. I am obliged to write in haste, and very imperfectly, a work which requires the leisure and tranquillity I do not enjoy. If ever Providence in its goodness grants me days more calm, I shall destine them to new modelling this work, should I be able to do it, or at least to giving a supplement, of which I perceive it stands in the greatest need.[1]

---

[1] I have given up this project. (*Note by Rousseau,* not in Paris MS.).

The news of my quarrel had reached Paris before me, and on my arrival I found the people in all the offices, and the public in general, scandalised at the follies of the ambassador. Notwithstanding this, the public talk of Venice and the unanswerable proof I exhibited, I could not obtain even the shadow of justice. Far from obtaining satisfaction or reparation, I was left at the discretion of the ambassador for my salary, and this for no other reason than because, not being a Frenchman, I had no right to national protection, and that it was a private affair between him and myself. Everybody agreed I was insulted, injured, and unfortunate; that the ambassador was mad, cruel, and iniquitous, and that the whole of the affair dishonoured him for ever. But what of this! He was the ambassador, and I was nothing more than the secretary.

Order, or that which is so called, was in opposition to my obtaining justice, and of this the least shadow was not granted me. I supposed that, by loudly complaining, and by publicly treating this madman in the manner he deserved, I should at length be told to hold my tongue; this was what I wished for, and I was fully determined not to obey until I had obtained redress. But at that time there was no minister for foreign affairs. I was suffered to exclaim, nay, even encouraged to do it, and joined with; but the affair still remained in the same state, until, tired of being in the right without obtaining justice, my courage at length failed me, and I let the whole drop.

The only person by whom I was ill received, and from whom I should have least expected such an injustice, was Madame de Bezenval. Full of the prerogatives of rank and nobility, she could not conceive it was possible an ambassador could ever be in the wrong with respect to his secretary. The reception she gave me was conformable to this prejudice. I was so piqued at it that, immediately after leaving her, I wrote her perhaps one of the strongest and most violent letters that ever came from my pen, and since that time I never once returned to her house. I was better received by Father Castel; but in the midst of his jesuitical wheedling I perceived him faithfully to follow one of the great maxims of his society, which is to sacrifice the weak to the powerful. The strong conviction I felt of the justice of my cause, and my natural greatness of mind, did not suffer me patiently to endure this partiality. I ceased visiting Father Castel, and, on that account, going to the college of the Jesuits, where I knew nobody but himself. Besides, the intriguing and tyrannical spirit of his brethren, so

different from the cordiality of the good Father Hemet, gave me
such a disgust to their conversation that I have never since been
acquainted with, nor seen any one of them except Father Berthier, whom I saw twice or thrice at M. Dupin's, in conjunction
with whom he laboured with all his might at the refutation of
Montesquieu.

That I may not have to return to the subject, I will conclude
what I have to say of M. de Montaigu. I had told him in our quarrels that a secretary was not what he wanted, but an attorney's
clerk. He took the hint, and the person whom he procured to succeed me was a real attorney, who in less than a year robbed him
of twenty or thirty thousand livres. He discharged him, and sent
him to prison, dismissed his gentlemen with disgrace, and in
wretchedness, got himself everywhere into quarrels, received
affronts which a footman would not have put up with, and, after
numerous follies, was recalled, and sent from the capital. It is
very probable that among the reprimands he received at court,
his affair with me was not forgotten. At least, a little time after
his return he sent his steward to settle my account, and give me
some money. I was in want of it at that moment; my debts at
Venice, debts of honour, if ever there were any, lay heavy upon
my mind. I made use of the means which offered to discharge
them, as well as the note of Zanetto Nani. I received what was
offered me, paid all my debts, and remained as before, without
a farthing in my pocket, but relieved from a weight which had
become insupportable. From that time I never heard speak of
M. de Montaigu, until his death, with which I became acquainted
by means of the Gazette. The peace of God be with that poor man!
He was as fit for the functions of an ambassador as in my infancy
I had been for those of a lawyer. However, it was in his power to
have honourably supported himself by my services, and rapidly
to have advanced me in a career to which the Comte de Gouvon
had destined me in my youth, and of the functions of which I had
in a more advanced age rendered myself capable.

The justice and inutility of my complaints left in my mind
seeds of indignation against our foolish civil institutions, by which
the welfare of the public and real justice are always sacrificed to
I know not what appearance of order, destructive in the end of all
order, and which does nothing more than add the sanction of public authority to the oppression of the weak, and the iniquity of the
powerful. Two things prevented these seeds from putting forth
at that time as they afterwards did: one was, myself being in

question in the affair, and private interest, whence nothing great or noble ever proceeded, could not draw from my heart the divine soarings, which the most pure love only of that which is just and sublime, can produce. The other was the charm of friendship, which tempered and calmed my wrath by the ascendency of a more pleasing sentiment. I had become acquainted at Venice with a Biscayan, a friend of my friend Carrio's, and worthy of being that of every honest man. This amiable young man, born with every talent and virtue, had just made the tour of Italy to gain a taste for the fine arts, and, imagining he had nothing more to acquire, intended to return by the most direct road to his own country. I told him the arts were nothing more than a relaxation to a genius like his, fit to cultivate the sciences; and to give him a taste for these, I advised him to make a journey to Paris and reside there for six months. He took my advice and went to Paris. He was there and expected me when I arrived. His lodging was too considerable for him, and he offered me the half of it, which I instantly accepted. I found him absorbed in the study of the sublimest sciences. Nothing was above his reach. He digested everything with a prodigious rapidity. How cordially did he thank me for having procured him this food for his mind, which was tormented by a thirst after knowledge, without his being aware of it! What a treasure of light and virtue I found in the vigorous mind of this young man! I felt he was the friend I wanted. We soon became intimate. Our tastes were not the same, and we constantly disputed. Both opinionated, we never could agree about anything. Nevertheless we could not separate; and, notwithstanding our reciprocal and incessant contradiction, we neither of us wished the other to be different from what he was.

Ignacio Emanuel de Altuna was one of those rare beings which Spain only produces, and of which she produces too few for her glory. He had not the violent national passions common in his own country. The idea of vengeance could no more enter his head, than the desire of it could proceed from his heart. His mind was too great to be vindictive, and I have frequently heard him say, with the greatest coolness, that no mortal could offend him. He was gallant, without being tender. He played with women as with so many pretty children. He amused himself with the mistresses of his friends, but I never knew him to have one of his own, nor the least desire for it. The emanations from the virtue with which his heart was stored, never permitted the fire of the passions to excite sensual desires. After his travels he married, died young, and left children; and, I am as convinced as of my existence, that his wife was the first and only woman with whom he ever tasted of the pleasures of love.

Externally he was devout, like a Spaniard, but in his heart he had the piety of an angel. Except myself, he is the only man I ever saw whose principles were not intolerant. He never in his life asked any person his opinion in matters of religion. It was not of the least consequence to him whether his friend was a Jew, a Protestant, a Turk, a Bigot, or an Atheist, provided he was an honest man. Obstinate and headstrong in matters of indifference, but the moment religion was in question, even the moral part, he collected himself, was silent or simply said: *I am charged with the care of myself only.* It is astonishing so much elevation of mind should be compatible with a spirit of detail carried to minuteness. He previously divided the employment of the day by hours, quarters, and minutes; and so scrupulously adhered to this distribution, that had the clock struck whilst he was reading a phrase, he would have shut his book without finishing it. His portions of time thus laid out, were some of them set apart to studies of one kind, and others to those of another; he had some for reflection, conversation, divine service, the reading of Locke, for his rosary, for visits, music, and painting; and neither pleasure, temptation, nor complaisance, could interrupt this order: a duty he might have had to discharge was the only thing that could have done it. When he gave me the list of his distributions, that I might conform myself thereto, I first laughed, and then shed tears of admiration. He never constrained anybody nor suffered constraint: he was rather rough with people, who, from politeness, attempted to put it upon him. He was passionate without being sullen. I have often seen him warm, but never saw him really angry with any person. Nothing could be more cheerful than his temper; he knew how to pass and receive a joke : raillery was one of his distinguished talents, and with it he possessed that of pointed wit and repartee. When he was animated, he was noisy and heard at a great distance; but whilst he loudly inveighed, a smile was spread over his countenance, and in the midst of his warmth he used some diverting expression which made all his hearers break out into a loud laugh. He had no more of the Spanish complexion than of the phlegm of that country. His skin was white, his cheeks finely coloured, and his hair of a light chestnut. He was tall and well made: his body was well formed for the residence of his mind.

This wise-hearted, as well as wise-headed, man knew mankind, and was my friend: this is my only answer to such as are not so. We were so intimately united, that our intention was to pass our days together. In a few years I was to go to Ascoytia to live with him at his estate; every part of the project was arranged, the eve of his departure; nothing was left undertermined, except that which depends not upon men in the best concerted plans. Posterior events, my disasters, his marriage, and finally, his death, separated us for ever. Some men would be tempted to say, that nothing succeeds except the dark conspiracies of the wicked, and that the innocent intentions of the good are seldom or never accomplished.

I had felt the inconvenience of dependence, and took a resolution never again to expose myself to it. Having seen the projects of ambition, which circumstances had induced me to form, overturned in their birth; discouraged in the career I had so well begun, from which, however, I had just been expelled, I resolved never more to attach myself to any person, but to remain in an independent state, turning my talents to the best advantage; of these I at length began to feel the extent, and that I had hitherto had too modest an opinion of them. I again took up my opera, which I had laid aside to go to Venice; and, that I might be less interrupted after the departure of Altuna, I returned to my old hotel St. Quentin; which, in a solitary part of the town, and not far from the Luxembourg, was more proper for my purpose than the noisy Rue St. Honoré.

There the only real consolation of which Heaven suffered me to taste in my misery, and the only one which rendered it supportable, awaited me. This was not a transient acquaintance; I must enter into some detail relative to the manner in which it was made.

We had a new landlady from Orleans; she took for a needlewoman a girl from her own country, of between twenty-two and twenty-three years of age, and who, as well as the hostess, ate at our table. This girl, named Thérèse le Vasseur, was of a good family; her father was an officer in the mint of Orleans, and her mother a shopkeeper; they had many children. The functions of the mint of Orleans being suppressed, the father found himself without employment; and the mother having suffered losses, was reduced to narrow circumstances. She quitted her business and came to Paris with her husband and daughter, who, by her industry, maintained all the three.

The first time I saw this girl at table, I was struck with her modesty; and still more so with her lively, yet charming, look; which, with respect to the impression it made upon me, was never equalled. Besides M. de Bonnefond, the company was composed of several Irish priests, Gascons, and others of much the same description. Our hostess herself had not made the best possible use of her time, and I was the only person at table who spoke and behaved with decency. Allurements were thrown out to the young girl; I took her part, and the joke was then turned against me. Had I no natural inclination to the poor girl, compassion and contradiction would have produced it in me: I was always a great friend to decency in manners and conversation, especially in the fair sex. I openly declared myself her champion, and perceived she was not insensible of my attention; her looks, animated by the gratitude she dared not express by words, were for this reason still more penetrating.

She was very timid, and I was as much so as herself. The connexion, which this disposition common to both seemed to remove to a distance, was however rapidly formed. Our landlady perceiving its progress, became furious, and her brutality forwarded my affair with the young girl, who having no person in the house except myself to give her the least support, was sorry to see me go from home, and sighed for the return of her protector. The affinity our hearts bore to each other, and the similarity of our dispositions, had soon their ordinary effect. She thought she saw in me an honest man, and in this she was not deceived. I thought I perceived in her a woman of great sensibility, simple in her manners, and devoid of all coquetry: I was no more deceived in her than she in me. I began by declaring to her that I would never either abandon or marry her. Love, esteem, artless sincerity were the ministers of my triumph, and it was because her heart was tender and virtuous, that I was happy without being presuming.

The apprehensions she was under of my not finding in her that for which I sought, retarded my happiness more than every other circumstance. I perceived her disconcerted and confused before she yielded her consent, wishing to be understood and not daring to explain herself. Far from suspecting the real cause of her embarrassment, I falsely imagined it to proceed from another motive, a supposition highly insulting to her morals, and thinking she gave me to understand my health might be exposed to danger, I fell into so perplexed a state that, although it was no restraint upon me, it poisoned my happiness during several days. As we did not understand each other, our conversations upon the subject were so many enigmas more than ridiculous. She was upon the point of believing I was absolutely mad; and I on my part was as near not knowing what else to think of her. At last we came to an explanation; she confessed to me with tears the only fault of the kind of her whole life, immediately after she became nubile; the fruit of her ignorance and the address of her seducer. The moment I comprehended what she meant, I gave a shout of joy. A hymen! exclaimed I; sought for at Paris, and at twenty years of age! Ah, my Thérèse! I am happy in possessing thee, virtuous and healthy as thou art, and in not finding that for which I never sought.

At first, amusement was my only object; I perceived I had gone farther, and had given myself a companion. A little intimate connexion with this excellent girl, and a few reflections upon my situation, made me discover that, while thinking of nothing more than my pleasures, I had done a great deal towards my happiness. In the place of extinguished ambition, a lively sentiment, which had entire possession of my spirit, was necessary to me. In a word, I wanted a successor to Mamma; since I was never again to live with her, it was necessary some person should live with her pupil, and a person too in whom I might find that simplicity and docility of mind and heart which she found in me. It was, moreover, necessary the happiness of domestic life should indemnify me for the splendid career I had just renounced. When I was quite alone there was a void in my heart, which wanted nothing more than another heart to fill it up. Fate had deprived me of this, or at least in part alienated me from that for which by nature I was formed. From that moment I was alone, for there never was for me the least thing intermediate between everything and nothing. I found in Thérèse the supplement of which I stood in need; by means of her I lived as happily as I possibly could do, according to the course of events.

I first attempted to improve her mind. In this my pains were useless. Her mind is as nature formed it: it was not susceptible of cultivation. I do not blush in acknowledging she never knew how to read well, although she writes tolerably. When I went to lodge in the Rue Neuve des Petits Champs, opposite to my windows at the Hôtel de Pontchartrain, there was a sundial, on which for a whole month I used all my efforts to teach her to know the hours; yet, she scarcely knows them at present. She never could enumerate the twelve months of the year in order, and cannot distinguish one numeral from another, notwithstanding all the trouble I took in endeavouring to teach them to her. She neither knows how to count money, nor to reckon the price of anything. The word which, when she speaks, presents itself to her mind, is frequently the opposite to that of which she means to make use. I formerly made a dictionary of her phrases, to amuse Madame de Luxembourg, and her *quid pro quos* often became celebrated among those with whom I was most intimate. But this person, so confined in her intellects, and, if the world pleases, so stupid, can give excellent advice in cases of difficulty. In Switzerland, in England, and in France, in the troubles I met with, she frequently saw what I had not myself perceived; she has often given me the best advice I could possibly follow; she has rescued me from dangers into which I had blindly precipitated myself, and in the presence of great ladies, princes, and the great, her sentiments, good sense, answers, and conduct have acquired her universal esteem, and myself the most sincere congratulations on her merit.

With persons whom we love, sentiment fortifies the mind as well as the heart; and they who are thus attached, have little need of searching for ideas elsewhere.

I lived with my Thérèse as agreeably as with the finest genius in the world. Her mother, proud of having been brought up under the Marchioness of Monpipeau, attempted to be witty, wished to direct the judgement of her daughter, and by her knavish cunning, destroyed the simplicity of our intercourse.

The fatigue of this importunity made me in some degree surmount the foolish shame which prevented me from appearing with Thérèse in public; and we took short country walks, tête-à-tête, and ate of little collations, which, to me, were delicious. I perceived she loved me sincerely, and this increased my tenderness. This charming intimacy left me nothing to wish: futurity no longer gave me the least concern, or at most appeared only as the present moment prolonged: I had no other desire than that of ensuring its duration.

This attachment rendered all other dissipation superfluous and insipid to me. I never went but for the purpose of going to the apartment of Thérèse, her place of residence almost became my own. My retirement was so favourable to the work I had undertaken, that, in less than three months, my opera was entirely finished, both words and music, except a few accompaniments and fillings up which still remained to be added. This manœuvring business was very fatiguing to me. I proposed it to Philidor, offering him, at the same time, a part of the profits. He came twice, and did something to the middle parts in the act of Ovid; but he could not confine himself to an assiduous application by the allurement of advantages which were distant and uncertain. He did not come a third time, and I finished the work myself.

My opera completed, the next thing was to make something of it: this was by much the most difficult task of the two. A man living in solitude in Paris will never succeed in anything. I was on the point of making my way by means of M. de la Poplinière, to whom Gauffecourt, at my return to Geneva, had introduced me. M. de la Poplinière was the Mæcenas of Rameau; Madame de la Poplinière his very humble scholar. Rameau was said to govern in that house. Judging he would with pleasure protect the work of one of his disciples, I wished to show him what I had done. He refused to examine it; saying he could not read in score, it was too fatiguing to him. M. de la Poplinière, to obviate this difficulty, said he might hear it; and offered me to send for musicians to execute certain detached pieces. I wished for nothing better. Rameau consented with an ill grace, incessantly repeating that the composition of a man not regularly bred to the science, and who had learned music without a master, must certainly be very fine. I hastened to copy into parts five or six select passages. Ten musicians were procured, and Albert, Bérard, and Mademoiselle Bourbonnois undertook the vocal part. Rameau, the moment he heard the overture, was purposely extravagant in his eulogium, by which he intended it should be understood it could not be my composition. He showed signs of impatience at every passage: but after a counter tenor song, the air of which was noble and harmonious, with a brilliant accompaniment, he could no longer contain himself: he apostrophised me with a brutality at which everybody was shocked, maintaining that a part of what he had heard was by a man experienced in the art, and the rest by some ignorant person who did not so much as understand music. It is true my composition, unequal and without rule, was sometimes sublime, and at others insipid, as that of a person who forms himself in the art by the soarings of his own genius, unsupported by science, must necessarily be. Rameau pretended to see nothing in me but a contemptible pilferer, without talents or taste. The rest of the company, among whom I must distinguish the master of the house, were of a different opinion. M. de Richelieu, who at that time frequently visited M. and Madame de la Poplinière, heard speak of my work, and wished to hear the whole of it, with an intention, if it pleased him, to have it performed at court. The opera was executed with full choruses, and by a great orchestra, at the expense of the King, at M. de Bonneval's, intendant of the Menus.[1] Francœur directed the band. The effect was surprising: the Duke never ceased to exclaim and applaud; and, at the end of one of the choruses, in the act of Tasso, he rose and came to me, and, pressing my hand, said: M. Rousseau, this is transporting harmony. I never heard anything finer. I will get this performed at Versailles.

M. LE DUC DE RICHELIEU

Madame de la Poplinière, who was present, said not a word. Rameau, although invited, refused to come. The next day, Madame de la Poplinière received me at her toilette, very ungraciously, affected to undervalue my piece, and told me that although a little

---

[1] The officer concerned with the expenses of court entertainments.

false glitter had at first dazzled M. de Richelieu, he had recovered from his error, and she advised me not to place the least dependence upon my opera. The Duke arrived soon after, and spoke to me in quite a different language. He said very flattering things of my talents, and seemed as much disposed as ever to have my composition performed before the King. There is nothing, said he, but the act of Tasso which cannot pass at court: you must write another. Upon this single word, I shut myself up in my apartment; and, in three weeks produced, in the place of Tasso, another act, the subject of which was Hesiod inspired by the muses. In this I found the secret of introducing a part of the history of my talents, and of the jealousy with which Rameau had been pleased to honour me. There was in the new act an elevation less gigantic and better supported than that in the act of Tasso. The music was as noble and the composition better; and had the other two acts been equal to this, the whole piece would have supported a representation to advantage. But whilst I was endeavouring to give it the last finishing, another undertaking suspended the completion of that I had in my hand.

In the winter which succeeded the battle of Fontenoy, there were many galas at Versailles, and several operas performed at the theatre of the Little Stables. Among the number of the latter was the dramatic piece of Voltaire, entitled *La Princesse de Navarre*, the music by Rameau, the name of which had just been changed to that of the *Fêtes de Ramire*. This new subject required several changes to be made in the divertissements, as well in the poetry as in the music. A person capable of both was now sought after Voltaire was in Lorraine, and Rameau also; both of whom were employed on the opera of the *Temple of Glory*, and could not give their attention to this. M. de Richelieu thought of me, and sent to desire I would undertake the alterations; and, that I might the better examine what there was to do, he gave me separately the poem and the music. In the first place, I would not touch the words without the consent of the author, to whom I wrote upon the subject a very polite and respectful letter, such a one as was proper; and received from him the following answer:

December 15, 1745.

SIR,

In you two talents, which hitherto have always been separate, are united. These are two good reasons for me to esteem and to endeavour to love you. I am sorry, on your account, you should

employ these talents in a work which is so little worthy of them.
A few months ago the Duke de Richelieu commanded me to make,
absolutely in the twinkling of an eye, a little and bad sketch of a
few insipid and imperfect scenes to be adapted to divertissements
which are not of a nature to be joined with them. I obeyed with
the greatest exactness. I wrote very fast and very ill. I sent this
wretched production to M. de Richelieu, imagining he would
make no use of it, or that I should have it again to make the necessary corrections. Happily, it is in your hands, and you are at full
liberty to do with it whatever you please: I have entirely lost
sight of the thing. I doubt not but you will have corrected all the
faults which cannot but abound in so hasty a composition of such
a very simple sketch, and am persuaded you will have supplied
whatever was wanting.

I remember that, amongst other stupid inattentions, no account
is given in the scenes which connect the divertissements of the
manner in which the Grenadian princess immediately passes
from a prison to a garden or palace. As it is not a magician but a
Spanish nobleman who gives her the gala, I am of opinion nothing
should be effected by enchantment.

I beg, sir, you will examine this part, of which I have but a
confused idea.

You will likewise consider, whether or not it be necessary the
prison should be opened and the princess conveyed from it to a
fine palace, gilt and varnished, and prepared for her. I know all
this is wretched, and that it is beneath a thinking being to make
a serious affair of such trifles; but, since we must displease as little
as possible, it is necessary we should conform to reason, even in
a bad divertissement of an opera.

I depend wholly upon you and M. Ballod, and soon expect to
have the honour of returning you my thanks, and assuring you
how much I am, etc.

There is nothing surprising in the great politeness of this letter,
compared with the almost rude ones which he has since written
to me. He thought I was in great favour with Madame de Richelieu; and the courtly suppleness, which everyone knows to be
the character of this author, obliged him to be extremely polite to
a newcomer, until he became better acquainted with the measure
of the favour and patronage he enjoyed.

Authorised by M. de Voltaire, and not under the necessity of
giving myself the least concern about M. Rameau, who only en-

M. DE VOLTAIRE

deavoured to injure me, I set to work, and in two months my undertaking was finished. With respect to the poetry, it was confined to a mere trifle; I aimed at nothing more than to prevent the difference of style from being perceived, and had the vanity to think I had succeeded. The musical part was longer and more laborious. Besides my having to compose several preparatory pieces, and, amongst others, the overture, all the recitative, with which I was charged, was extremely difficult on account of the necessity there was of connecting, in a few lines, and by very rapid modulations, symphonies and choruses, in keys very different from each other; for I was determined neither to change nor transpose any of the airs, that Rameau might not accuse me of having disfigured them. I succeeded in the recitative; it was well accented, full of energy and excellent modulation. The idea of two men of superior talents, with whom I was associated, had elevated my genius, and I can assert, that in this barren and inglorious task, of which the public could have no knowledge, I was for the most part equal to my models.

The piece, in the state to which I had brought it, was rehearsed in the great theatre of the Opera. Of the three authors who had contributed to the production, I was the only one present. Voltaire was not in Paris, and Rameau either did not come, or concealed himself. The words of the first monologue were very mournful; they began with,

O Mort! viens terminer les malheurs de ma vie.

To these, suitable music was necessary. It was, however, upon this, that Madame de la Poplinière founded her censure; accusing me, with much bitterness, of having composed a funeral anthem. M. de Richelieu very judiciously began by informing himself who was the author of the poetry of this monologue; I presented him the manuscript he had sent me, which proved it was by Voltaire. In that case, said the Duke, Voltaire alone is to blame. During the rehearsal, everything I had done was disapproved by Madame de la Poplinière, and approved of by M. de Richelieu; but I had to do with too powerful an adversary. It was signified to me that several parts of my composition wanted revising, and that on this it was necessary I should consult M. Rameau; my heart was wounded by such a conclusion, instead of the eulogium I expected, and which certainly I merited, and I returned to my apartment overwhelmed with grief, exhausted with fatigue and consumed by chagrin. I was immediately taken ill, and confined to my chamber for upwards of six weeks.

Rameau, who was charged with the alterations indicated by Madame de la Poplinière, sent to ask me for the overture of my grand opera, to substitute it for that I had just composed. Happily I perceived the trick he intended to play me, and refused him the overture. As the performance was to be in five or six days, he had not time to make one, and was obliged to leave that I had prepared. It was in the Italian taste, and in a style at that time quite new in France. It gave satisfaction, and I learned from M. de Valmalette, maître d'hôtel to the King, and son-in-law to M. Mussard, my relation and friend, that the connoisseurs were highly satisfied with my work, and that the public had not distinguished it from that of Rameau. However, he and Madame de la Poplinière took measures to prevent any person from knowing I had any concern in the matter. In the books distributed to the audience, and in which the author was always named, Voltaire was the only person mentioned, and Rameau preferred the suppression of his own name to seeing it associated with mine.

As soon as I was in a situation to leave my room, I wished to wait upon M. de Richelieu, but it was too late; he had just set off for Dunkirk, where he was to command the expedition destined for Scotland. At his return, said I to myself, to authorise my idleness, it will be too late for my purpose. Not having seen him since that time, I lost the honour of my work and the emoluments it should have produced me, besides considering my time, trouble, grief, and vexation, my illness, and the money this cost me, were all at my own expense, without ever receiving the least benefit, or, rather, recompense. However, I always thought M. de Richelieu was disposed to serve me, and that he had a favourable opinion of my talents; but my misfortune, and Madame de la Poplinière, prevented the effect of his good wishes.

I could not divine the reason of the aversion this lady had to me. I had always endeavoured to make myself agreeable to her, and regularly paid her my court. Gauffecourt explained to me the causes of her dislike: the first, said he, is her friendship for Rameau, of whom she is the declared panegyrist, and who will not suffer a competitor; the next is an original sin, which loses you in her estimation, and which she will never forgive; you are a Genevese. Upon this, he told me the Abbé Hubert, who was from the same city, and the sincere friend of M. de la Poplinière, had used all his efforts to prevent him from marrying this lady, with whose character and temper he was very well acquainted; and that after the marriage, she had vowed him an implacable hatred, as well as all the Genevese. Although la Poplinière has a friendship for you, as I know is the case, do not, said he, depend upon his protection: he is still in love with his wife: she hates you, and is vindictive and artful: you will never do anything in that house. All this I took for granted.

The same Gauffecourt rendered me much about this time a service of which I stood in the greatest need. I had just lost my virtuous father, who was about sixty[1] years of age. I felt this loss less severely than I should have done at any other time, when the embarrassments of my situation had less engaged my attention. During his lifetime I had never claimed what remained of the property of my mother, and of which he received the little inter-

---

[1] Seventy-five: he died March 9, 1747.

est. His death removed all my scruples upon this subject. But the want of a legal proof of the death of my brother, created a difficulty which Gauffecourt undertook to remove, and this he effected by means of the good offices of the advocate de Lorme. As I stood in need of the little resource, and the event being doubtful, I waited for a definitive account with the greatest anxiety.

One evening, on entering my apartment, I found a letter, which I knew to contain the information I wanted, and I took it up with an impatient trembling, of which I was inwardly ashamed. What! said I, to myself, with disdain, shall Jean-Jacques thus suffer himself to be subdued by interest and curiosity? I immediately laid the letter again upon the chimney-piece. I undressed myself, want to bed with great composure, slept better than ordinary, and rose in the morning at a late hour, without thinking more of my letter. As I dressed myself, it caught my eye, I broke the seal very leisurely, and found under the envelope a bill of exchange. I felt a variety of pleasing sensations at the same time; but I can assert, upon my honour, that the most lively of them all was that proceeding from having known how to be master of myself.

I could mention twenty such circumstances in my life, but I am too much pressed for time to say everything. I sent a small part of this money to my poor Mamma; regretting, with my eyes suffused with tears, the happy time when I should have laid it all at her feet. All her letters contained evident marks of her distress. She sent me piles of receipts, and numerous secrets, with which she pretended I might make my fortune and her own. The idea of her wretchedness already affected her heart and contracted her mind. The little I sent her fell a prey to the knaves by whom she was surrounded; she received not the least advantage from anything. The idea of dividing what was necessary to my own subsistence with these wretches disgusted me, especially after the vain attempt I had made to deliver her from them, and of which I shall have occasion to speak.

Time slipped away, and with it the little money I had: we were two, or indeed, four persons; or, to speak still more correctly, seven or eight. Although Thérèse was disinterested to a degree of which there are but few examples, her mother was not so. She was no sooner a little relieved from her necessities by my cares, than she sent for her whole family to partake of the fruits of them. Her sisters, sons, daughters, granddaughters, all, except her eldest daughter, married to the director of the coaches of Angers, came to Paris. Everything I did for Thérèse her mother diverted from its original destination in favour of these people who were starving. I had not to do with an avaricious person; and, not being under the influence of an unruly passion, I was not guilty of follies. Satisfied with genteelly supporting Thérèse without luxury, and unexposed to present wants, I readily consented to let all the earnings of her industry go to the profit of her mother; and to this even I did not confine myself; but, by a fatality, by which I was pursued, whilst Mamma was a prey to the rascals about her, Thérèse was the same to her family; and I could not do anything on any side for the benefit of her to whom the succour I gave was destined. It was odd enough the youngest child of Madame le Vasseur, the only one who had not received a marriage portion from her parents, should alone provide for their subsistence; and that, after having a long time been beaten by her brothers, sisters, and even her nieces, the poor girl should be plundered by them all, without being more able to defend herself from their thefts than from their blows. One of her nieces, named Goton Leduc, was of a mild and amiable character; although spoiled by the lessons and examples of the others. As I frequently saw them together, I gave them names, which they afterwards gave to each other: I called the niece *my niece*, and the aunt *my aunt*; they both called me uncle. Hence the name of *aunt*, by which I continued to call Thérèse, and which my friends sometimes jocosely repeated.

It will be judged that in such a situation I had not a moment to lose, before I attempted to extricate myself. Imagining M. de Richelieu had forgotten me, and having no more hopes from the court, I made some attempts to get my opera brought out at Paris; but I met with difficulties which could not immediately be removed, and my situation became daily more painful. I presented my little comedy of *Narcisse* at the Italians; it was received, and I had the freedom of the theatre, which gave me much pleasure. But this was all. I could never get my piece performed, and, tired of paying my court to players, I gave myself no more trouble about them. At length, I had recourse to the last expedient which remained to me, and the only one of which I ought to have made use. While frequenting the house of M. de la Poplinière, I had neglected the family of Dupin. The two ladies, although related, were not upon good terms, and never saw each other. There was not the least intercourse between the two families, and Thiériot was the only person who visited both. He was desired to endeavour to bring me again to M. Dupin's. M. de Francueil was then studying natural history and chemistry, and collecting a cabinet. I believe he aspired to become a member of the academy of sciences; to this effect he intended to write a book, and judged I might be of use to him in the undertaking. Madame Dupin, who on her part had another work in contemplation, had much the same views with respect to me. They wished to have me in common as a kind of secretary, and this was the reason of the invitations of Thiériot.

MME. DUPIN

I required that M. de Francueil should previously employ his interest with that of Jelyotte[1] to get my work rehearsed at the opera house; to this he consented. The *Muses galantes* was several times rehearsed, first at the *Magazin*,[2] and afterwards at the great theatre. The audience was very numerous at the great rehearsal, and several parts of the composition were highly applauded. However, during this rehearsal, very ill conducted by Rebel, I felt the piece would not be received; and that, before it could appear, great alterations were necessary. I therefore withdrew it without saying

[1] A famous singer at the Opera (1713-1797).
[2] The wardrobe of the theatre.

a word, or exposing myself to a refusal: but I plainly perceived, by several indications, that the work, had it been perfect, could not have succeeded. M. de Francueil had promised me to get it rehearsed, but not that it should be received. He exactly kept his word. I thought I perceived on this occasion, as well as many others, that neither Madame Dupin nor himself were willing I should acquire a certain reputation in the world, lest, after the publication of their books, it should be supposed they had grafted their talents upon mine. Yet, as Madame Dupin always supposed those I had to be very moderate, and never employed me except it was to write what she dictated, or in researches of pure erudition, the reproach, with respect to her, would have been unjust.

This last failure of success completed my discouragement. I abandoned every prospect of fame and advancement; and, without farther troubling my head about real or imaginary talents, with which I had so little success, I dedicated my whole time and cares to procure myself and Thérèse a subsistence in the manner most pleasing to those to whom it should be agreeable to provide for it. I therefore entirely attached myself to Madame Dupin and M. de Francueil. This did not place me in a very opulent situation; for with eight or nine hundred livres a year, which I had the two first years, I had scarcely enough to provide for my primary wants; being obliged to live in their neighbourhood, a dear part of the town, in a furnished lodging, and having to pay for another lodging at the extremity of Paris, at the very top of the Rue Saint Jacques, to which, let the weather be as it would, I went almost every evening to supper. I soon got into the track of my new occupations, and conceived a taste for them. I attached myself to the study of chemistry, and attended several courses of it with M. de Francueil, at M. Rouelle's, and we began to scribble over paper upon that science, of which we scarcely possessed the elements. In 1747, we went to pass the autumn in Touraine, at the castle of Chenonceaux, a royal mansion upon the Cher, built by Henry II for Diana of Poitiers, of whom the ciphers are still seen, and which is now in the possession of M. Dupin, a farmer general. We amused ourselves very agreeably in this beautiful place, and lived very well: I became as fat there as a monk. Music was a favourite relaxation; I composed several trios full of harmony, and of which I may perhaps speak in my supplement if ever I should write one. Theatrical performances were another resource. I wrote a comedy in fifteen days, entitled *l'Engagement Téméraire*, which will be found amongst my papers; it has no other merit than that of being

lively. I composed several other little things: amongst others, a
poem entitled, *l'Allée de Sylvie*, from the name of an alley in the
park upon the bank of the Cher; and this without discontinuing
my chemical studies, or interrupting what I had to do for Madame
Dupin.

Whilst I was increasing my corpulency at Chenonceaux, that
of my poor Thérèse was augmented at Paris in another manner,
and at my return I found the work I had put upon the frame in
greater forwardness than I had expected. This, on account of my
situation, would have thrown me into the greatest embarrassment,
had not one of my messmates furnished me with the only resource
which could relieve me from it. This is one of those essential narratives which I cannot give with too much simplicity; because, in
commenting on them, I should either excuse or inculpate myself,
both of which in this place are entirely out of the question.

During the residence of Altuna at Paris, instead of going to eat
at a *Traiteur's*, he and I commonly ate in the neighbourhood,
almost opposite the Cul de Sac of the Opera, at the house of a
Madame la Selle, the wife of a tailor, who gave but very ordinary
dinners, but whose table was much frequented, on account of the
safe company which generally resorted to it; no person was received without being introduced by one of those who used the
house. The Commander de Graville, an old debauchee, with much
wit and politeness, but obscene in conversation, lodged at the
house, and brought to it a set of riotous and extravagant young
men; officers in the guards and musketeers. The Commander de
Nonant, chevalier to all the girls of the opera, was the daily oracle
which conveyed to us the news of this motley crew. M. du Plessis,
a lieutenant-colonel retired from the service, an old man of great
goodness and wisdom; and M. Ancelet,[1] an officer in the musketeers, kept the young people in a certain kind of order. The table
was also frequented by commercial people, financiers and con-
tractors, but extremely polite, and such as were distinguished

---

[1] It was to this M. Ancelet I gave a little comedy, after my own manner,
entitled *les Prisonniers de Guerre*, which I wrote after the disasters of the
French in Bavaria and Bohemia; I dared not either avow this comedy or show
it, and this for the singular reason that neither the King of France, nor the
French were ever better spoken of nor praised with more sincerity of heart
than in my piece; though written by a professed republican, I dared not declare
myself the panegyrist of a nation, whose maxims were exactly the reverse of
my own. More grieved at the misfortunes of France than the French themselves, I was afraid the public would construe into flattery and mean complaisance the marks of a sincere attachment, of which in my first part I have
mentioned the date and the cause, and which I was ashamed to show. (*Note
by Rousseau*, not in Paris MS.)

amongst those of the same profession. M. de Besse, M. de Forcade, and others whose names I have forgotten, in short, well-dressed people of every description, were seen there; except Abbés and men of the long robe, not one of whom I ever met in the house, and it was agreed not to introduce men of either of these professions. This table, sufficiently resorted to, was very cheerful without being noisy, and many of the guests were waggish, without descending to vulgarity. The old commander with all his smutty stories, with respect to the substance, never lost sight of the politeness of the old court; nor did any indecent expression, which even women would not have pardoned him, escape his lips. His manner served as a rule to every person at table; all the young men related their adventures of gallantry with equal grace and freedom, and these narratives were the more complete, as the seraglio was at the door; the entry which led to it was the same; for there was a communication between this and the shop of la Duchapt, a celebrated milliner, who at that time had several very pretty girls, with whom our young people went to chat before or after dinner. I should thus have amused myself as well as the rest, had I been less modest: I had only to go on as they did, but this I never had courage enough to do. With respect to Madame la Selle, I often went to eat at her house after the departure of Altuna. I learned a great number of amusing anecdotes, and by degrees I adopted, thank God, not the morals, but the maxims I found to be established there. Honest men injured, husbands deceived, women seduced, secret lyings-in, were the most ordinary topics, and he who had best filled the foundling hospital was always the most applauded. I caught the manners I daily had before my eyes: I formed my manner of thinking upon that I observed to be the reigning one amongst amiable, and, upon the whole, very honest people. I said to myself, since it is the custom of the country, they who live here may adopt it; this is the expedient for which I sought. I cheerfully determined upon it without the least scruple, and the only one I had to overcome was that of Thérèse, whom, with the greatest imaginable difficulty, I persuaded to adopt this only means of saving her honour. Her mother, who was moreover apprehensive of a new embarrassment by an increase of family, came to my aid, and she at length suffered herself to be prevailed upon. We made choice of a midwife, a safe and prudent woman, Mademoiselle Gouin, who lived at the *Pointe Saint-Eustache*, and when the time came, Thérèse was conducted to her lying-in at Gouin's by her mother.

I went thither several times to see her, and gave her a cipher
which I had made double upon two cards; one of them was put
into the linen of the child, and by the midwife deposited with the
infant in the office of the foundling hospital according to the customary form. The year following, a similar inconvenience was
remedied by the same expedient, excepting the cipher, which was
forgotten: no more reflection on my part, nor approbation on that
of the mother; she obeyed with trembling. All the vicissitudes
which this fatal conduct has produced in my manner of thinking,
as well as in my destiny, will be successively seen. For the present, we will confine ourselves to this first period; its cruel and
unforeseen consequences will but too frequently oblige me to
refer to it.

MME. D'EPINAY

I here mark that of my first acquaintance with Madame
d'Epinay, whose name will frequently appear in these memoirs.
She was a Mademoiselle d'Esclavelles, and had lately been married to M. d'Epinay, son to M. de Lalive de Bellegarde, a farmer
general. Her husband, like M. de Francueil, was a musician. She

understood music, and a passion for the art produced between these three persons the greatest intimacy. M. de Francueil introduced me to Madame d'Epinay, and we sometimes supped together at her house. She was amiable, had wit and talents, and was certainly a desirable acquaintance; but she had a female friend, a Mademoiselle d'Ette, who was said to have much malignancy in her disposition; she lived with the Chevalier de Valory, whose temper was far from being one of the best. I am of opinion, an acquaintance with these two persons was prejudicial to Madame d'Epinay, to whom, with a disposition which required the greatest attention from those about her, Nature had given very excellent qualities to regulate or counterbalance her extravagant pretensions. M. de Francueil inspired her with a part of the friendship he had conceived for me, and told me of the connexion between them, of which, for that reason, I would not now speak, were it not become so public as not to be concealed from M. d'Epinay himself.

M. de Francueil confided to me secrets of a very singular nature relative to this lady, of which she herself never spoke to me, nor so much as suspected my having a knowledge; for I never opened my lips to her upon the subject, nor will I ever do it to any person. The confidence of all parties had in my prudence rendered my situation very embarrassing, especially with Madame de Francueil, whose knowledge of me was sufficient to remove from her all suspicion on my account, although I was connected with her rival. I did everything I could to console this poor woman, whose husband certainly did not return the affection she had for him. I listened to these three persons separately; I kept all their secrets so faithfully that not one of the three ever drew from me those of the two others, and this without concealing from either of the women my attachment to the other. Madame de Francueil, who frequently wished to make me an agent, received refusals in form, and Madame d'Epinay, once desiring me to charge myself with a letter to M. de Francueil, received the same mortification, accompanied by a very express declaration, that if ever she wished to drive me for ever from the house, she had only a second time to make me a like proposition.

In justice to Madame d'Epinay, I must say, that far from being offended with me, she spoke of my conduct to M. de Francueil in terms of the highest approbation, and continued to receive me as well, and as politely as ever. It was thus, amidst the heartburnings of three persons to whom I was obliged to behave with the greatest circumspection, on whom I in some measure depended, and for whom I had conceived an attachment, that by conducting myself with mildness and complaisance, although accompanied with the greatest firmness, I preserved unto the last not only their friendship but their esteem and confidence. Notwithstanding my absurdities and awkwardness, Madame d'Epinay would have me make one of the party to la Chevrette, a country house near Saint Denis, belonging to M. de Bellegarde. There was a theatre, in which performances were not infrequent. I had a part given me, which I studied for six months without intermission, and in which, on the evening of the representation, I was obliged to be prompted from the beginning to the end. After this experiment no second proposal of the kind was ever made to me.

My acquaintance with Madame d'Epinay procured me that of her sister-in-law, Mademoiselle de Bellegarde, who soon afterwards became Countess of Houdetot. The first time I saw her she was upon the point of marriage; when she conversed with me a long time, with that charming familiarity which was natural to her. I thought her very amiable, but I was far from perceiving that this young person would decide the course of my life, and lead me, although innocently, into the abyss in which I still remain.

Although I have not spoken of Diderot since my return from Venice, no more than of my friend M. Roguin, I did not neglect either of them, especially the former, with whom I daily became more intimate. He had a Nanette, as well as I a Thérèse; this was between us another conformity of circumstances. But my Thérèse, as fine a woman as his Nanette, was of a mild and amiable character, which might gain and fix the affections of a worthy man; whereas Nanette was a vixen, a troublesome prater, and had no qualities in the eyes of others which in any measure compensated for her want of education. However, he married her, which was well done of him, if he had given a promise to that effect. I, for my part, not having entered into any such engagement, was not in the least haste to imitate him.

I was also connected with the Abbé de Condillac, who had acquired no more literary fame than myself, but in whom there was every appearance of his becoming what he now is. I was perhaps the first who discovered the extent of his abilities, and esteemed them as they deserved. He on his part seemed satisfied with me, and whilst, shut up in my chamber in the Rue Jean St. Denis, near the opera house, I composed my act of Hesiod, he sometimes came to dine with me in a picnic tête-à-tête. He was at that time employed on his *Essay on the Origin of Human Knowledge*, which was his first work. When this was finished, the difficulty was to find a bookseller who would take it. The booksellers of Paris are shy of every author at his beginning, and metaphysics, not much then in vogue, were no very inviting subject. I spoke to Diderot of Condillac and his work, and I afterwards brought them acquainted with each other. They were worthy of each other's esteem, and were presently on the most friendly terms. Diderot persuaded the bookseller, Durand, to take the manuscript from the Abbé, and this great metaphysician received for his first work, and almost as a favour, a hundred crowns, which perhaps he would not have obtained without my assistance. As we lived in quarters of

MLLE. DE BELLEGARDE, LATER LA COMTESSE D'HOUDETOT

the town very distant from each other, we all assembled, once a week, at the Palais Royal, and went to dine at the Hôtel du Panier Fleuri. These little weekly dinners must have been extremely pleasing to Diderot; for he who failed in almost all his appoint-

ments[1] never missed one of these. At our little meeting I formed
the plan of a periodical paper, entitled *le Persifleur*, which Diderot
and I were alternately to write. I sketched out the first sheet, and
this brought me acquainted with d'Alembert, to whom Diderot
had mentioned it. Unforeseen events frustrated our intention,
and the project was carried no farther.

These two authors had just undertaken the *Dictionnaire Ency-
clopédique*, which at first was intended to be nothing more than
a kind of translation of Chambers, something like that of the
Medical Dictionary of James, which Diderot had just finished.
Diderot was desirous I should do something in this second undertaking, and proposed to me the musical part, which I accepted.
This I executed in great haste, and consequently very ill, in the
three months he had given me, as well as all the authors who were
engaged in the work. But I was the only person in readiness at
the time prescribed. I gave him my manuscript, which I had
copied by a lackey, belonging to M. de Francueil, of the name of
Dupont, who wrote very well. I paid him ten crowns out of my
own pocket, and these have never been reimbursed me. Diderot
had promised me a retribution on the part of the booksellers, of
which he has never since spoken to me nor I to him.

This undertaking of the *Encyclopédie* was interrupted by his
imprisonment. The *Pensées Philosophiques* drew upon him some
temporary inconvenience which had no disagreeable consequences. He did not come off so easily on account of the *Lettre
sur les Aveugles*, in which there was nothing reprehensible, but
some personal attacks with which Madame Dupré de St. Maur,
and M. de Réaumur were displeased: for this he was confined in
the dungeon of Vincennes. Nothing can describe the anguish I felt
on account of the misfortune of my friend. My wretched imagination, which always sees everything in the worst light, was terri-
fied.I imagined him to be confined for the remainder of his life:
I was almost distracted with the thought. I wrote to Madame de
Pompadour, beseeching her to release him or obtain an order to
shut me up in the same dungeon. I received no answer to my
letter: this was too unreasonable to be efficacious, and I do not
flatter myself that it contributed to the alleviation which, some
time afterwards, was granted to the severities of the confinement
of poor Diderot. Had this continued for any length of time with
the same rigour, I verily believe I should have died in despair at

---

[1] Paris MS. adds: "Even those with women."

the foot of the hated dungeon. However, if my letter produced but
little effect, I did not, on account of it, attribute to myself much
merit, for I mentioned it but to very few people, and never to
Diderot himself.

BOOK EIGHT

At the end of the preceding book a pause was necessary. With
this begins the long chain of my misfortunes, deduced from their
origin.

Having lived in two of the most splendid houses in Paris, I had,
notwithstanding my candour and modesty, made some acquaintance. Amongst others at Madame Dupin's, that of the young
hereditary Prince of Saxe-Gotha, and of the Baron de Thun, his
governor: at the house of M. de la Poplinière, that of M. Segui,
friend to the Baron de Thun, and known in the literary world by
his beautiful edition of Rousseau.[1] The Baron invited M. Segui
and myself to go and pass a day or two at Fontenay-sous-Bois,[2]
where the Prince had a house. We went. As I passed Vincennes,
at the sight of the dungeon, my feelings were acute; the effect of
which the Baron perceived on my countenance. At supper the
Prince mentioned the confinement of Diderot. The Baron, to hear
what I had to say, accused the prisoner of imprudence; and I
showed not a little of the same in the impetuous manner in which
I defended him. This excess of zeal, inspired by the misfortune
which had befallen my friend, was pardoned; and the conversation immediately changed. There were present two Germans in
the service of the Prince; M. Klupffel, a man of great wit, his
chaplain, and who afterwards, having supplanted the Baron, became his governor. The other was a young man named M. Grimm,
who served him as a reader until he could obtain some place, and
whose indifferent appearance sufficiently proved the pressing
necessity he was under of immediately finding one. From this
very evening Klupffel and I began an acquaintance which soon

[1] See note, p. 143.
[2] Paris MS.: Fontenay-aux-Roses, which is correct.

led to friendship. That with the Sieur Grimm did not make quite
so rapid a progress: he made but few advances, and was far from
having that haughty presumption which prosperity afterwards
gave him. The next day at dinner, the conversation turned upon
music: he spoke well on the subject. I was transported with joy
when I learned from him he could play an accompaniment on
the harpsichord. After dinner was over music was introduced, and
we amused ourselves the rest of the afternoon on the harpsichord
of the Prince.—Thus began that friendship which, at first, was
so agreeable to me, afterwards so fatal; and of which I shall hereafter have so much to say.

At my return to Paris I learned the agreeable news that Diderot
was released from the dungeon, and that he had, on his parole,
the castle and park of Vincennes for a prison, with permission to
see his friends. How painful was it to me not to be able instantly
to fly to him! But I was detained two or three days at Madame
Dupin's by indispensable business. After ages of impatience, I flew
to the arms of my friend. Inexpressible moment! He was not alone:
d'Alembert and the treasurer of the *Sainte Chapelle* were with
him. As I entered I saw nobody but himself, I made but one step,
one cry: I riveted my face to his: I pressed him in my arms, without speaking to him, except by tears and sighs: I stifled him with
my affection and joy. The first thing he did, after quitting my
arms, was to turn himself towards the ecclesiastic, and say: You
see, sir, how much I am beloved by my friends.

My emotion was so great, that it was then impossible for me to
reflect upon this manner of turning it to advantage; but, I have
since thought that, had I been in the place of Diderot, the idea he
manifested would not have been the first that would have occurred
to me.

I found him much affected by his imprisonment. The dungeon
had made a terrible impression upon his mind, and, although he
was very agreeably situated in the castle and at liberty to walk
where he pleased in the park, which was not enclosed even by a
wall, he wanted the society of his friends to prevent him from
yielding to melancholy. As I was the person most concerned for
his sufferings, I imagined I should also be the friend, the sight of
whom would give him most consolation; on which account, notwithstanding very pressing occupations, I went every two days
at farthest, either alone, or accompanied by his wife, to pass the
afternoon with him.

The heat of the summer was this year (1749) excessive. Vincennes is two leagues from Paris. The state of my finances not permitting me to pay for hackney coaches, at two o'clock in the afternoon, I went on foot, when alone, and walked as fast as possible, that I might arrive the sooner. The trees by the side of the road, always lopped, according to the custom of the country, afforded but little shade, and, exhausted by fatigue, I frequently threw myself on the ground, being unable to proceed any farther. I thought a book in my hand might make me moderate my pace. One day I took the *Mercure de France*, and, as I walked and read, I came to the following question proposed by the academy of Dijon, for the prize of the ensuing year: *Has the progress of sciences and arts contributed to corrupt or purify morals?*

VINCENNES: THE DUNGEON

The moment I had read this, I seemed to behold another world, and became a different man. Although I have a lively remembrance of the impression it made upon me, the detail has escaped

my mind, since I communicated it to M. de Malesherbes in one
of my four letters to him. This is one of the singularities of my
memory which merits to be remarked. It serves me in proportion
to my dependence upon it; the moment I have committed to paper
that with which it was charged, it forsakes me, and I have no
sooner written a thing than I have forgotten it entirely. This singularity is the same with respect to music. Before I learned the use
of notes I knew a great number of songs; the moment I had made
a sufficient progress to sing an air set to music, I could not recollect
any one of them; and at present, I much doubt whether I should
be able entirely to go through one of those of which I was the most
fond.

All I distinctly recollect upon this occasion is, that on my arrival at Vincennes, I was in an agitation which approached a
delirium. Diderot perceived it; I told him the cause, and read to
him the prosopopoeia of Fabricius, written with a pencil under a
tree. He encouraged me to pursue my ideas, and to become a competitor for the prize. I did so, and from that moment I was ruined.
All the rest of my misfortunes during my life were the inevitable
effect of this moment of error.

My sentiments became elevated with the most inconceivable
rapidity to the level of my ideas. All my little passions were stifled
by the enthusiasm of truth, liberty, and virtue; and what is most
astonishing, this effervescence continued in my mind upwards of
four or five years, to as great a degree perhaps as it has ever done
in that of any other man. I composed the discourse in a very singular manner, and in that which I have almost always followed in
all my other works. I dedicated to it the hours of the night in which
sleep deserted me, I meditated in my bed with my eyes closed,
and in my mind turned over and over again my periods with
incredible labour and care; the moment they were finished to my
satisfaction, I deposited them in my memory, until I had an opportunity of committing them to paper; but the time of rising and
putting on my clothes made me lose everything, and when I took
up my pen, I recollected but little of what I had composed. I made
Madame le Vasseur my secretary. I had lodged her with her
daughter and husband nearer to myself; and she, to save me the
expense of a servant, came every morning to make my fire, and
do such other little things as were necessary. As soon as she arrived
I dictated to her while in bed what I had composed in the night,
and this method, which for a long time I observed, preserved me
many things I should otherwise have forgotten.

As soon as the discourse was finished, I showed it to Diderot. He was satisfied with the production, and pointed out some corrections he thought necessary to be made. However, this composition, full of force and fire, absolutely wants logic and order; of all the works I ever wrote, this is the weakest in reasoning, and the most devoid of number and harmony. With whatever talent a man may be born, the art of writing is not easily learned.

I sent off this piece without mentioning it to anybody, except, I think, to Grimm, with whom, after his going to live with the Comte de Frièse, I began to be upon the most intimate footing. His harpsichord served as a rendezvous, and I passed with him at it all the moments I had to spare, in singing Italian airs, and *barcarolles;* sometimes without intermission, from morning till night, or rather from night until morning; and when I was not to be found at Madame Dupin's, everybody concluded I was with Grimm at his apartment, the public walk, or the theatre. I left off going to the *Comédie Italienne,* of which I was free, but which he did not like, to go with him, and pay, to the *Comédie Française,* of which he was passionately fond. In short, so powerful an attraction connected me with this young man, and I became so inseparable from him, that the poor aunt herself was rather neglected, that is, I saw her less frequently; for in no moment of my life has my attachment to her been diminished.

This impossibility of dividing, in favour of my inclinations, the little time I had to myself, renewed more strongly than ever the desire I had long entertained of having but one home for Thérèse and myself; but the embarrassment of her numerous family, and especially the want of money to purchase furniture, had hitherto withheld me from accomplishing it. An opportunity to endeavour at it presented itself, and of this I took advantage. M. de Francueil, and Madame Dupin, clearly perceiving that eight or nine hundred livres a year were unequal to my wants, increased of their own accord my salary to fifty guineas; and Madame Dupin, having heard I wished to furnish myself lodgings, assisted me with some articles for that purpose. With this furniture and that Thérèse already had, we made one common stock, and having taken an apartment in the Hôtel de Languedoc, Rue de Grenelle St. Honoré, kept by very honest people, we arranged ourselves in the best manner we could, and lived there peaceably and agreeably during seven years, at the end of which I removed to go and live at the Hermitage.

Thérèse's father was a good old man, very mild in his disposi-

tion, and much afraid of his wife; for this reason he had given
her the surname of Lieutenant Criminal, which Grimm, jocosely,
afterwards transferred to the daughter. Madame le Vasseur did
not want sense, that is, address; and pretended to the politeness
and airs of the first circles; but she had a mysterious wheedling,
which to me was insupportable, gave bad advice to her daughter,
endeavoured to make her dissemble with me, and separately,
cajoled my friends at my expense, and that of each other; excepting these circumstances, she was a tolerable good mother, because
she found her account in being so, and concealed the faults of her
daughter to turn them to her own advantage. This woman, who
had so much of my care and attention, to whom I made so many
little presents, and by whom I had it extremely at heart to make
myself beloved, was, from the impossibility of my succeeding
in this wish, the only cause of the uneasiness I suffered in my
little establishment. Except the effects of this cause I enjoyed,
during these six or seven years, the most perfect domestic happiness of which human weakness is capable. The heart of my
Thérèse was that of an angel; our attachment increased with
our intimacy, and we were more and more and daily convinced
how much we were made for each other. Could our pleasures be
described, their simplicity would cause laughter. Our walks, tête-
à-tête, on the outside of the city, where I magnificently spent
eight or ten sous in each ale-house. Our little suppers at my window, seated opposite to each other upon two little chairs, placed
upon a trunk, which filled up the space of the embrasure. In this
situation the window served us as a table, we respired the fresh
air, enjoyed the prospect of the environs and the people who
passed; and, although upon the fourth story, looked down into
the street as we ate.

Who can describe, and how few can feel, the charms of these
repasts, consisting of a quartern loaf, a few cherries, a morsel of
cheese, and half a pint of wine, which we drank between us?
Friendship, confidence, intimacy, sweetness of disposition, how
delicious are your seasonings! We sometimes remained in this
situation until midnight, and never thought of the hour, unless
informed of it by the old lady. But let us quit these details which
are either insipid or laughable; I have always said and felt that
real enjoyment was not to be described.

Much about the same time I indulged in one not so delicate, and
the last of the kind with which I have to reproach myself. I have
observed that the minister Klupffel was an amiable man; my

connexions with him were almost as intimate as those I had with Grimm, and in the end became as familiar; Grimm and he sometimes ate at my apartment. These repasts, a little more than simple, were enlivened by the witty and extravagant wantonness of expression of Klupffel, and the diverting Germanicisms of Grimm, who was not yet become a purist.

J.-J., DIDEROT, BARON DE GRIMM

Sensuality did not preside at our little orgies, but joy, which was preferable, reigned in them all, and we found ourselves so well together that we knew not how to separate. Klupffel had furnished a lodging for a little girl, who, notwithstanding this, was at the service of anybody, because he could not support her entirely himself. One evening, as we were going into the coffee-house, we met him coming out to go and sup with her. We rallied him; he revenged himself gallantly, by inviting us to the same supper, and there rallying us in our turn. The poor young creature appeared to be of a good disposition, mild, and little fitted to the way of life to which an old hag she had with her, prepared her in the best manner she could. Wine and conversation enlivened us to such a degree that we forgot ourselves. The amiable Klupffel was unwilling to do the honours of his table by halves, and we all three successively took a view of the next chamber, in company with his little friend, who knew not whether she should laugh or cry. Grimm has always maintained that he never touched her; it was therefore to amuse himself with our impatience, that he remained so long in the other chamber, and if he abstained, there is not much probability of his having done so from scruple, because previous to his going to live with the Comte de Frièse, he lodged with girls of the town in the same quarter of St. Roch.

I left the Rue des Moineaux, where this girl lodged, as much ashamed as Saint Preux left the house in which he had become intoxicated, and when I wrote his story I well remembered my own. Thérèse perceived by some sign, and especially by my confusion, I had something with which I reproached myself; I relieved my mind by my free and immediate confession. I did well, for the next day Grimm came in triumph to relate to her my crime with aggravation, and since that time he has never failed maliciously to recall it to her recollection; in this he was the more culpable, since I had freely and voluntarily given him my confidence, and had a right to expect he would not make me repent of it. I never had a more convincing proof than on this occasion, of the goodness of my Thérèse's heart; she was more shocked at the behaviour of Grimm than at my infidelity, and I received nothing from her but tender reproaches, in which there was not the least appearance of anger.

The simplicity of mind of this excellent girl was equal to her goodness of heart; and this is saying everything: but one instance of it, which is present to my recollection, is worthy of being related. I had told her Klupffel was a minister, and chaplain to the Prince of Saxe-Gotha. A minister was to her so singular a man, that oddly confounding the most dissimilar ideas, she took it into her head to take Klupffel for the pope; I thought her mad the first time she told me when I came in, that the pope had called to see me. I made her explain herself, and lost not a moment in going to relate the story to Grimm and Klupffel, who amongst ourselves never lost the name of pope. We gave to the girl in the Rue des Moineaux the name of Pope Joan. Our laughter was incessant; it almost stifled us. They who in a letter which it has pleased them to attribute to me, have made me say I never laughed but twice in my life, did not know me at this period, nor in my younger days; for if they had, the idea could never have entered their heads.

The year following (1750), not thinking more of my *Discourse*, I learned it had gained the prize at Dijon. This news awakened all the ideas which had dictated it to me, gave them new animation, and completed the fermentation in my heart of that first leaven of heroism and virtue which my father, my country, and Plutarch had inspired in my infancy. Nothing now appeared great and fine in my eyes but to be free and virtuous, superior to fortune and opinion, and independent of all exterior circumstances. Although a false shame, and the fear of disapprobation at first prevented me from conducting myself according to these principles, and from suddenly quarrelling with the maxims of the age in which I lived, I from that moment took a decided resolution to do it. And of this I purposely delayed the execution, that irritated by contradiction, it might be rendered triumphant.

While I was philosophising upon the duties of man, an event happened which made me better reflect on my own. Thérèse became pregnant for the third time. Too sincere with myself, too haughty in my mind to contradict my principles by my actions, I began to examine the destination of my children, and my connexions with the mother, according to the laws of nature, justice, and reason, and those of that religion, pure, holy, and eternal, like its author, which men have polluted while they pretended to purify it, and which by their formularies, they have reduced to a religion of words, since the difficulty of prescribing impossibilities is but trifling to those by whom they are not practised.

If I deceived myself in my conclusions, nothing can be more astonishing than the security with which I depended upon them. Were I one of those men unfortunately born deaf to the voice of nature, in whom no sentiment of justice or humanity ever took the least root, this obduracy would be natural. But that warmth of heart, strong sensibility, and facility of forming attachments; the force with which they subdue me; my cruel sufferings when obliged to break them; the innate benevolence I cherish towards my fellow creatures; the ardent love I bear to great virtues, to truth and justice; the horror in which I hold evil of every kind; the impossibility of hating, of injuring, or wishing to injure anyone; the soft and lively emotion I feel at the sight of whatever is virtuous, generous, and amiable; can these meet in the same mind with the depravity, which without scruple treads under foot the most pleasing of all our duties? No, I feel, and openly declare this to be impossible. Never in his whole life could Jean-Jacques be a man without sentiment, or an unnatural father. I may have been deceived, but it is impossible I should have lost the least of my feelings. Were I to give my reasons I should say too much; since they have seduced me, they would seduce many others. I will not therefore expose those young persons by whom I may be read to the same danger. I will satisfy myself by observing, that my error was such, that in abandoning my children to public education[1] for want of the means of bringing them up myself; in destining them to become workmen and peasants, rather than adventurers and fortune hunters, I thought I acted like an honest citizen, and a good father, and considered myself as a member of the republic of Plato. Since that time the regrets of my heart have more than once told me I was deceived; but my reason was so far from giving me the same intimation, that I have frequently returned thanks to heaven for having, by this means, preserved them from the fate of their father, and that by which they were threatened the moment I should have been under the necessity of leaving them. Had I left them to Madame d'Epinay or Madame de Luxembourg, who, from friendship, generosity, or some other motive, offered to take care of them in due time, would they have been more happy, better brought up, or honester men? To this I cannot answer, but I am certain they would have been taught to hate and perhaps betray their parents: it is much better that they have never known them.

My third child was therefore carried to the foundling hospital as well as the two former, and the next two were disposed of in the same manner; for I have had five children in all. This arrangement seemed to me to be so good, reasonable, and lawful, that if I did not publicly boast of it, the motive by which I was withheld, was merely my regard for their mother; but I mentioned it to all those to whom I had declared our connexion, to Diderot, to Grimm, afterwards to Madame d'Epinay, and after another interval, to Madame de Luxembourg; and this freely and voluntarily, without being under the least necessity of doing it, having it in my power to conceal the step from all the world: for La Gouin was an honest woman, very discreet, and a person on whom I had the greatest reliance. The only one of my friends to whom it was in some measure my interest to open myself, was Thierry the physician, who had the care of my poor aunt in one of her lyings in, in which she was very ill. In a word, there was no mystery in my conduct, not only on account of my never having concealed anything from my friends, but because I never found any harm in it. Everything considered, I chose the best destination for my children, or that

---

[1] Paris MS. reads: ". . . my error was such, that at that time I looked upon my relation with Thérèse only as an honourable and decent, but free and voluntary engagement; my faithfulness to her, so long as it lasted, as an indispensable duty; and the breach of it I had once committed as a real adultery. And as for my children, in abandoning them to public education . . ."

which I thought to be such. I could have wished, and still should be glad, I had been brought up as they have been.

Whilst I was thus communicating what I had done, Madame le Vasseur did the same thing amongst her acquaintance, but with less disinterested views. I introduced her and her daughter to Madame Dupin, who from friendship to me, showed them the greatest kindness. The mother confided to her the secret of the daughter. Madame Dupin, who is generous and kind, and to whom she never told how attentive I was to her, notwithstanding my moderate resources, in providing for everything, provided on her

DIJON: PLACE DES DUCS

part for what was necessary, with a liberality which, by order of her mother, the daughter concealed from me during my residence at Paris, nor ever mentioned it until we were at the Hermitage, when she informed me of it, after having disclosed to me several secrets of her heart. I did not know Madame Dupin, who never

took the least notice to me of the matter, was so well informed:
I know not yet whether or not Madame de Chenonceaux, her
daughter-in-law, was as much in the secret: but Madame de Francueil knew the whole and could not refrain from prattling. She
spoke of it to me the following year, after I had left her house.
This induced me to write her a letter upon the subject, which will
be found in my collections, and wherein I gave such of my reasons
as I could make public, without exposing Madame le Vasseur
and her family; the most determinative of them came from that
quarter, and these I kept profoundly secret.

I can rely upon the discretion of Madame Dupin, and the friendship of Madame de Chenonceaux; I had the same dependence
upon that of Madame de Francueil, who, however, was long dead
before my secret made its way into the world. This it could never
have done except by means of the persons to whom I had entrusted it, nor did it until after my rupture with them. By this
single fact they are judged: without exculpating myself from the
blame I deserve, I prefer it to that resulting from their malignity.
My fault is great, but it was an error. I have neglected my duty,
but the desire of doing an injury never entered my heart; and the
feelings of a father were never more eloquent in favour of children whom he never saw. But betraying the confidence of friendship, violating the most sacred of all engagements, publishing
secrets confided to us, and wantonly dishonouring the friend we
have deceived, and who in detaching himself from our society still
respects us, are not faults but baseness of mind and the last degree
of heinousness.

I have promised my confession and not my justification; on
which account I shall stop here. It is my duty faithfully to relate
the truth, that of the reader to be just; more than this I shall never
require of him.

The marriage of M. de Chenonceaux rendered his mother's
house still more agreeable to me, by the wit and merit of the new
bride, a very amiable young person, who seemed to distinguish
me amongst the scribes of M. Dupin. She was the only daughter
of the Viscountess de Rochechouart, a great friend of the Comte
de Frièse, and consequently of Grimm's, who was very attentive
to her. However, it was I who introduced him to her daughter;
but their characters not suiting each other, this connexion was not
of long duration; and Grimm, who from that time aimed at what
was solid, preferred the mother, a woman of the world, to the
daughter, who wished for steady friends, such as were agreeable

to her, without troubling her head about the least intrigue or making any interest amongst the great. Madame Dupin no longer finding in Madame de Chenonceaux all the docility she expected, made her house very disagreeable to her; and Madame de Chenonceaux, having a great opinion of her own merit, and perhaps of her birth, chose rather to give up the pleasures of society, and remain almost alone in her apartment, than to submit to a yoke she was not disposed to bear. This species of exile increased my attachment to her, by that natural inclination which excites me to approach the wretched. I found her mind metaphysical and reflective, although at times a little sophistical; her conversation, which was by no means that of a young woman coming from a convent, had for me the greatest attractions; yet she was not twenty years of age. Her complexion was seducingly fair; her figure would have been majestic had she held herself more upright. Her hair, which was fair, bordering upon ash colour, and uncommonly beautiful, called to my recollection that of my poor Mamma in the flower of her age, and strongly agitated my heart. But the severe principles I had just laid down for myself, by which at all events I was determined to be guided, secured me from the danger of her and her charms. During the whole summer I passed three or four hours a day in a tête-à-tête conversation with her, teaching her arithmetic, and fatiguing her with my innumerable ciphers, without uttering a single word of gallantry, or even once glancing my eyes upon her. Five or six years later I should not have had so much wisdom or folly; but it was decreed I was never to love but once in my life, and that another person was to have the first and last sighs of my heart.

Since I had lived in the house of Madame Dupin, I had always been satisfied with my situation, without showing the least sign of a desire to improve it. The addition which, in conjunction with M. de Francueil, she had made to my salary, was entirely of their own accord. This year M. de Francueil, whose friendship for me daily increased, had it in his thoughts to place me more at ease, and in a less precarious situation. He was receiver-general of finance. M. Dudoyer, his cash-keeper, was old and rich, and wished to retire. M. de Francueil offered me this place, and to prepare myself for it, I went, during a few weeks, to M. Dudoyer, to take the necessary instructions. But whether my talents were ill suited to the employment, or that Dudoyer, who I thought wished to procure his place for another, was not in earnest in the instructions he gave me, I acquired by slow degrees, and very imperfectly,

the knowledge I was in want of, and could never understand the
nature of accounts, rendered intricate, perhaps designedly. However, without having possessed myself of the whole scope of the
business, I learned enough of the method to pursue it after a
fashion: I even entered on my new office; I kept the cash-book and
the cash; I paid and received money, took and gave receipts; and
although this business was as ill suited to my inclinations as to my
abilities, maturity of years beginning to render me sedate, I was
determined to conquer my disgust, and entirely devote myself to
my new employment. Unfortunately for me, I had no sooner
begun to proceed without difficulty, than M. de Francueil took a
little journey, during which I remained entrusted with the cash,
which, at that time, did not amount to more than from twenty-
five to thirty thousand livres. The anxiety of mind this sum of
money occasioned me, made me perceive I was very unfit to be a
cash-keeper, and I have no doubt but my uneasy situation, during
his absence, contributed to the illness with which I was seized
after his return.

I have observed in my first part that I was born in a dying state.
A defect in the bladder caused me, during my early years, to
suffer an almost continual retention of urine; and my aunt Suzon,
to whose care I was entrusted, had inconceivable difficulty in preserving me. However, she succeeded, and my robust constitution
at length got the better of all my weakness, and my health became
so well established that, except the illness from languor, of which
I have given an account, and frequent heats in the bladder, which
the least heating of the blood rendered troublesome, I arrived at
the age of thirty almost without feeling my original infirmity.
The first time this happened was upon my arrival at Venice. The
fatigue of the voyage and the extreme heat I had suffered, renewed the burnings, and gave me a pain in the loins, which
continued until the beginning of winter. After having seen the
Padoana, I thought myself near the end of my career, but I suffered not the least inconvenience. After exhausting my imagination more than my body for my Zulietta, I enjoyed better health
than ever. It was not until after the imprisonment of Diderot, that
the heat of blood, brought on by my journey to Vincennes during
the terrible heat of that summer, gave me a violent nephritic colic,
since which I have never recovered my primitive good state of
health.

At the time of which I speak, having perhaps fatigued myself
too much in the filthy work of the cursed receiver-general's office,

I fell into a worse state than ever, and remained five or six weeks in my bed in the most melancholy state imaginable. Madame Dupin sent me the celebrated Morand, who, notwithstanding his address and the delicacy of his touch, made me suffer the greatest torments, and was never able to finish probing me. He advised me to have recourse to Daran, who managed to insert his more flexible instruments; but Morand, when he gave Madame Dupin an account of the state I was in, declared to her I should not be alive in six months. This afterwards came to my ear, and made me reflect seriously on my situation and the folly of sacrificing the repose of the few days I had to live to the slavery of an employment, for which I felt nothing but disgust. Besides, how was it possible to reconcile the severe principles I had just adopted, to a situation with which they had so little relation? Should not I, the cash-keeper of a receiver-general of finances, have preached poverty and disinterestedness with a very good grace? These ideas fermented so powerfully in my mind with the fever, and were so strongly impressed, that from that time nothing could remove them; and, during my convalescence, I confirmed myself with the greatest coolness in the resolutions I had taken during my delirium. I for ever abandoned all projects of fortune and advancement. Resolved to pass in independence and poverty the little time I had to exist, I made every effort of which my mind was capable, to break the fetters of prejudice, and courageously to do everything that was right without giving myself the least concern about the judgement of others. The obstacles I had to combat, and the efforts I made to triumph over them, are inconceivable. I succeeded as much as it was possible I should, and to a greater degree than I myself had hoped for. Had I at the same time shaken off the yoke of friendship as well as that of prejudice my design would have been accomplished, perhaps the greatest, at least the most useful one to virtue, that mortal ever conceived; but whilst I despised the foolish judgements of the vulgar tribe of the self-called great and wise, I suffered myself to be influenced and led by persons who called themselves my friends. These, hurt at seeing me walk alone in a new path, while they seemed to take measures for my happiness, used all their endeavours to render me ridiculous, and that they might afterwards defame me, first strove to make me contemptible. It was less my literary fame than my personal reformation, of which I here state the period, that drew upon me their jealousy; they perhaps might have pardoned me for having distinguished myself in the art of writing; but they could never forgive my setting them, by my conduct, an example which, in their eyes, seemed to reflect on themselves. I was born for friendship; my mild and easy disposition nourished it without difficulty. As long as I lived unknown to the public I was beloved by all my private acquaintance, and I had not a single enemy. But the moment I acquired literary fame, I had no longer a friend. This was a great misfortune; but a still greater was that of being surrounded by people who called themselves my friends, and used the rights attached to that sacred name to lead me on to destruction. The succeeding part of these memoirs will explain this odious conspiracy. I here speak only of its origin, and the manner of the first intrigue will shortly appear.

In the independence in which I lived, it was, however, necessary to subsist. To this effect I thought of very simple means: which were copying music at so much a page. If any employment more solid would have fulfilled the same end I would have taken it up; but this occupation being to my taste, and the only one which, without personal attendance, could procure me daily bread, I adopted it. Thinking I had no longer need of foresight, and stifling my vanity, of cash-keeper to a financier I made myself a copyist of music. I thought I had made an advantageous choice, and of this I so little repented, that I never quitted my new profession until I was forced to do it, after taking a fixed resolution to return to it as soon as possible.

The success of my first discourse rendered the execution of this resolution more easy. As soon as it had gained the prize, Diderot undertook to get it printed. Whilst I was in my bed, he wrote me a note, informing me of the publication and effect: *It takes*, said he, *beyond all imagination; never was there an instance of a like success.*

This favour of the public, by no means solicited, and to an unknown author, gave me the first real assurance of my talents, of which, notwithstanding an internal sentiment, I had always had my doubts. I conceived the great advantage to be drawn from it in favour of the way of life I had determined to pursue; and was of opinion, that a copyist of some celebrity in the republic of letters, was not likely to want employment.

The moment my resolution was confirmed, I wrote a note to M. de Francueil, communicating to him my intentions, thanking him and Madame Dupin for all their goodness, and offering them my services in the way of my new profession. Francueil did not understand my note, and, thinking I was still in the delirium of a fever, hastened to my apartment; but he found me so determined, that all he could say to me was without the least effect. He went to Madame Dupin, and told her, and everybody he met, that I was become insane. I let him say what he pleased, and pursued the plan I had conceived. I began the change in my dress; I quitted laced clothes and white stockings; I put on a round wig, laid aside my sword, and sold my watch; saying to myself with inexpressible pleasure: Thank heaven! I shall no longer want to know the hour! M. de Francueil had the goodness to wait a considerable time before he disposed of my place. At length, perceiving me inflexibly resolved, he gave it to M. d'Alibard, formerly tutor to the young Chenonceaux, and known as a botanist by his *Flora Parisiensis.*[1]

However austere my sumptuary reform might be, I did not at first extend it to my linen, which was fine and in great quantity, the remainder of my stock when at Venice, and to which I was particularly attached. I had made it so much an object of cleanliness that it became one of luxury, which was rather expensive. Some person, however, did me the favour to deliver me from this servitude. On Christmas-eve, whilst the Governesses[2] were at vespers, and I was at the spiritual concert, the door of a garret, in which all our linen was hung up after being washed, was broken open. Everything was stolen; and, amongst other things, forty-two of my shirts, of very fine linen, and which were the principal part of my stock. By the manner in which the neighbours described a man whom they had seen come out of the hotel with several parcels whilst we were all absent, Thérèse and myself suspected her brother, whom we knew to be a worthless man. The mother strongly endeavoured to remove this suspicion, but so many circumstances concurred to prove it to be well founded, that, notwithstanding all she could say, our opinions remained still the same: I dared not make a strict search for fear of finding more than I wished to do. The brother never returned to the place where I lived, and, at length, was no more heard of by any of us. I was much grieved Thérèse and myself should be connected with such a family, and I exhorted her more than ever to shake off so dan-

---

[1] I doubt not but these circumstances are now differently related by M. de Francueil and his consorts; but I appeal to what he said of them at the time, and long afterwards, to everybody he knew, until the forming of the conspiracy, and of which men of commonsense and honour have preserved the remembrance. (*Note by Rousseau*, not in Paris MS.).

[2] A name given by Gauffecourt to Mme. le Vasseur and her daughter.

gerous a yoke. This adventure cured me of my inclination for fine linen, and since that time all I have had has been very common, and more suitable to the rest of my dress.

Having thus completed the change of that which related to my person, all my cares tended to render it solid and lasting, by striving to root out from my heart everything susceptible of receiving an impression from the judgement of men, or which, from the fear of blame, might turn me aside from anything good and reasonable in itself. In consequence of the success of my work, my resolution made some noise in the world also, and procured me employment; so that I began my new profession with great appearance of success. However, several causes prevented me from succeeding in it to the same degree I should under my other circumstances have done. In the first place, my ill state of health. The attack I had just had, brought on consequences which prevented my ever being so well as I was before; and I am of opinion, the physicians, to whose care I entrusted myself, did me as much harm as my illness. I was successively under the hands of Morand, Daran, Helvétius, Malouin, and Thierry; men able in their profession, and all of them my friends, who treated me each according to his own manner, without giving me the least relief, and weakened me considerably. The more I submitted to their direction, the yellower, thinner, and weaker I became. My imagination, which they terrified, judging of my situation by the effect of their drugs, presented to me, on this side of the tomb, nothing but continued sufferings from the gravel, stone, and retention of urine. Everything which gave relief to others, drugs, baths, and bleeding, increased my tortures. Perceiving the bougies of Daran, the only ones that had any favourable effect, and without which I thought I could no longer exist, to give me but a momentary relief, I procured a prodigious number of them at great expense, that, in case of Daran's death, I might never be at a loss. During the eight or ten years in which I made such frequent use of these, they must, with what I have left, have cost me fifty louis.

It will easily be judged, that such expensive and painful means did not permit me to work without interruption; and that a dying man is not ardently industrious in the business by which he gains his daily bread.

Literary occupations caused another interruption not less prejudicial to my daily employment. My discourse had no sooner appeared, than the defenders of letters fell upon me as if they had agreed with each other to do it. My indignation was so raised at seeing so many blockheads, who did not understand the question, attempt to decide upon it imperiously, that in my answer I gave some of them the worst of it. One M. Gautier, of Nancy, the first who fell under the lash of my pen, was very roughly treated in a letter to M. Grimm. The second was King Stanislaus himself, who did not disdain to enter the lists with me. The honour he did me, obliged me to change my manner in combating his opinion; I made use of a graver style, but not less nervous; and, without failing in respect to the author, I completely refuted his work.

STANISLAUS, KING OF POLAND

I knew a Jesuit, Father de Menou, had been concerned in it. I depended on my judgement to distinguish what was written by the Prince, from the production of the monk, and falling without mercy upon all the jesuitical phrases, I remarked, as I went along, an anachronism, which I thought could come from nobody but the priest. This composition, which, for what reason I know not, has been less spoken of than any of my other writings, is so far the only one of its kind. I seized the opportunity which offered of showing to the public in what manner an individual may defend the cause of truth even against a sovereign. It is difficult to adopt a more dignified and respectful manner than that in which I answered him. I had the happiness to have to do with an adversary to whom, without adulation, I could show every mark of the esteem, of which my heart was full; and this I did with success and a proper dignity. My friends, concerned for my safety, imagined they already saw me in the Bastille. This apprehension never once entered my head, and I was right in not being afraid. The good Prince, after reading my answer, said: *I have enough of it; I will not return to the charge.* I have, since that time, received from him different marks of esteem and benevolence, some of which I shall have occasion to speak of; and what I had written was read in France, and throughout Europe, without meeting with the least censure.

In a little time I had another adversary whom I had not expected: this was the same M. Bordes, of Lyons, who ten years before had shown me much friendship, and from whom I had received several services. I had not forgotten him, but had neglected him from idleness, and had not sent him my writings for want of an opportunity, without seeking for it, to get them conveyed to his hands. I was therefore in the wrong, and he attacked me; this, however, he did politely, and I answered in the same manner. He replied more decidedly. This produced my last answer: after which I heard no more from him upon the subject; but he became my most violent enemy, took the advantage of the time of my misfortunes, to publish against me the most indecent libels, and made a journey to London on purpose to do me an injury.

All this controversy employed me a good deal, and caused me a great loss of time in my copying, without much contributing to the progress of truth, or the good of my purse. Pissot, at that time my bookseller, gave me but little for my pamphlets, frequently nothing at all, and I never received a farthing for my first discourse. Diderot gave it him for nothing. I was obliged to wait a long time for the little he gave me, and to take it from him in the most trifling sums. Notwithstanding this, my copying went on but slowly. I had two things together upon my hands, which was the most likely means of doing them both ill.

They were very opposite to each other in their effects by the different manners of living to which they rendered me subject. The success of my first writings had given me celebrity. My new situation excited curiosity. Everybody wished to know that whimsical man who sought not the acquaintance of anyone, and whose only desire was to live free and happy in the manner he had chosen: this was sufficient to make the thing impossible to me. My apartment was continually full of people, who, under different pretences, came to take up my time. The women employed a thousand artifices to engage me to dinner. The more unpolite I was with people, the more obstinate they became. I could not refuse everybody. While I made myself a thousand enemies by my refusals, I was incessantly a slave to my complaisance, and, in whatever manner I made my engagements, I had not an hour in a day to myself.

I then perceived it was not so easy to be poor and independent, as I had imagined. I wished to live by my profession: the public would not suffer me to do it. A thousand means were thought of to indemnify me for the time I lost.[1] The next thing would have been showing myself like Punch, at so much each person. I know no dependence more cruel and degrading than this. I saw no other method of putting an end to it, than refusing all kinds of presents, great and small, let them come from whom they would. This had no other effect than to increase the number of givers, who wished to have the honour of overcoming my resistance, and to force me, in spite of myself, to be under an obligation to them. Many who would not have given me half a crown, had I asked it from them, incessantly importuned me with their offers, and, in revenge for my refusal, taxed me with arrogance and ostentation.

It will naturally be conceived, that the resolution I had taken, and the system I wished to follow, were not agreeable to Madame le Vasseur. All the disinterestedness of the daughter did not prevent her from following the directions of her mother; and the *Governesses*, as Gauffecourt called them, were not always so steady in their refusals as I was. Although many things were concealed from me, I perceived so many as were necessary to enable me to judge that I did not see all, and this tormented me, less by the accusation of connivance, which it was easy for me to foresee, than by the cruel idea of never being master in my own apartments, nor even of my own person. I prayed, conjured, and became angry, all to no purpose; the mother made me pass

---

[1] Paris MS. here adds: "Presents of every kind reached me."

for an eternal grumbler, and a man who was peevish and un-governable. She held perpetual whisperings with my friends; everything in my little family was mysterious and a secret to me; and, that I might not incessantly expose myself to noisy quarrelling, I no longer dared to take notice of what passed in it. A firmness of which I was not capable, would have been neces-sary to withdraw me from this domestic strife. I knew how to complain, but not how to act: they suffered me to say what I pleased, and continued to act as they thought proper.

This constant teasing, and the daily importunities to which I was subject, rendered the house, and my residence at Paris, dis-agreeable to me. When my indisposition permitted me to go out, and I did not suffer myself to be led by my acquaintance first to one place and then to another, I took a walk, alone, and reflected on my grand system, something of which I committed to paper, bound up between two covers, which, with a pencil, I always had in my pocket. In this manner, the unforeseen disagreeableness of a situation I had chosen entirely led me back to literature, to which I had recourse as a means of relieving my mind; and thus, in the first works I wrote, I introduced the peevishness and ill humour which were the cause of my undertaking them.

There was another circumstance which contributed not a little to this: thrown into the world in despite of myself, without having the manners of it, or being in a situation to adopt and conform myself to them, I took it into my head to adopt others of my own, to enable me to dispense with those of society. My foolish timid-ity, which I could not conquer, having for principle the fear of being wanting in the common forms, I took, by way of encourag-ing myself, a resolution to tread them under foot. I became sour and a cynic from shame, and affected to despise the politeness which I knew not how to practise. This austerity, conformable to my new principles, I must confess seemed to ennoble itself in my mind; it assumed in my eyes the form of the intrepidity of virtue, and I dare assert it to be upon this noble basis, that it supported itself longer and better than could have been expected from any-thing so contrary to my nature. Yet, notwithstanding I had the name of a misanthrope, which my exterior appearance and some happy expressions had given me in the world; it is certain I did not support the character well in private, that my friends and acquaintance led this intractable bear about like a lamb, and that confining my sarcasms to serve but general truths, I was never capable of saying an uncivil thing to any person whatsoever.

The *Devin du Village* brought me completely into vogue, and presently after there was not a man in Paris whose company was more sought after than mine. The history of this piece, which is a kind of era in my life, is joined with that of the connexions I had at that time. I must enter a little into particulars to make what is to follow the better understood.

I had a numerous acquaintance, yet no more than two friends: Diderot and Grimm. By an effect of the desire I have ever felt to unite everything that is dear to me, I was too much a friend to both not to make them shortly become so to each other. I connected them: they agreed well together, and shortly became more intimate with each other than with me. Diderot had a numerous acquaintance, but Grimm, a stranger and a newcomer, had his to procure, and with the greatest pleasure I procured him all I could. I had already given him Diderot. I afterwards brought him acquainted with Gauffecourt. I introduced him to Madame de Chenonceaux, Madame d'Epinay, and the Baron d'Holbach; with whom I had become connected almost in spite of myself. All my friends became his: this was natural: but not one of his ever became mine; which was inclining to the contrary. Whilst he yet lodged at the house of the Comte de Frièse, he frequently gave us dinners in his apartment, but I never received the least mark of friendship from the Comte de Frièse, the Comte de Schomberg, his relation, very familiar with Grimm, nor from any other person, man or woman, with whom Grimm, by their means, had any connexion. I except the Abbé Raynal, who, although his friend, gave proofs of his being mine; and, in cases of need, offered me his purse with a generosity not very common. But I knew the Abbé Raynal long before Grimm had any acquaintance with him, and had entertained a great regard for him on account of his delicate and honourable behaviour to me upon a slight occasion, which I shall never forget.

The Abbé Raynal is certainly a warm friend; of this I saw a proof, much about the time of which I speak, with respect to Grimm himself, with whom he was very intimate. Grimm, after having been sometime on a footing of friendship with Mademoiselle Fel,[1] fell violently in love with her, and wished to supplant Cahusac. The young lady piquing herself on her constancy, refused her new admirer. He took this so much to heart, that the appearances of his affliction became tragical. He suddenly fell

---

[1] Marie Féel, an opera singer.

into the strangest state imaginable. He passed days and nights in
a continued lethargy. He lay with his eyes open; and, although
his pulse continued to beat regularly, without speaking, eating,
or stirring, yet sometimes seeming to hear what was said to him,
but never answering, not even by a sign, and remaining almost
as immovable as if he had been dead, yet without agitation, pain,
or fever. The Abbé Raynal and myself watched over him; the
Abbé, more robust, and in better health than I was, by night and
I by day, without ever both being absent at one time. The Comte
de Frièse was alarmed and brought to him Senac, who, after having examined the state in which he was, said there was nothing
to apprehend, and took his leave without giving a prescription.
My fears for my friend made me carefully observe the countenance of the physician, and I perceived him smile as he went
away. However, the patient remained several days almost motion-
less, without taking anything except a few preserved cherries,
which from time to time I put upon his tongue, and which he
swallowed without difficulty. At length he, one morning, rose,
dressed himself, and returned to his usual way of life, without
either at that time or afterwards speaking to me, or to the Abbé
Raynal, at least that I know of, or to any other person of this
singular lethargy, or the care we had taken of him during the time
it lasted.

The affair made a noise, and it would really have been a wonderful circumstance had the cruelty of an opera girl made a man
die of despair. This strong passion brought Grimm into vogue; he
was soon considered as a prodigy in love, friendship, and attachments of every kind. Such an opinion made his company sought
after, and procured him a good reception in the first circles; by
which means he separated from me, with whom he was never
inclined to associate when he could do it with anybody else. I perceived him to be on the point of breaking with me entirely; for
the lively and ardent sentiments, of which he made a parade,
were those which, with less noise and pretension, I had really conceived for him. I was glad he succeeded in the world; but I did
not wish him to do this by forgetting his friend. I one day said to
him: Grimm, you neglect me, and I forgive you for it. When the
first intoxication of your success is over, and you begin to perceive
a void in your enjoyments, I hope you will return to your friend,
whom you will always find in the same sentiments: at present
do not constrain yourself, I leave you at liberty to act as you
please, and wait your leisure. He said I was right, made his ar-

rangements in consequence, and shook off all restraint, so that I saw no more of him except in company with our common friends.

Our chief rendezvous, before he was so connected with Madame d'Epinay as he afterwards became, was at the house of Baron d'Holbach. This said Baron was the son of a man who had raised himself from obscurity. His fortune was considerable, and he used it nobly, receiving at his house men of letters and merit; and, by the knowledge he himself had acquired, was very worthy of holding a place amongst them. Having been long attached to Diderot, he endeavoured to become acquainted with me by his means, even before my name was known to the world. A natural repugnancy prevented me a long time from answering his advances. One day, when he asked me the reason of my unwillingness, I told him, he was too rich. He was however resolved to carry his point, and at length succeeded. My greatest misfortune proceeded from my being unable to resist the force of marked attention. I have ever had reason to repent of having yielded to it.

Another acquaintance which, as soon as I had any pretensions to it, was converted into friendship, was that of M. Duclos. I had several years before seen him, for the first time, at la Chevrette, at the house of Madame d'Epinay, with whom he was upon very good terms. On that day we only dined together, and he returned to town in the afternoon. But we had a conversation of a few moments after dinner. Madame d'Epinay had mentioned me to him, and my opera of the *Muses Galantes*. Duclos, endowed with too great talents not to be a friend to those in whom the like were found, was prepossessed in my favour, and invited me to go and see him. Notwithstanding my former wish, increased by an acquaintance, I was withheld by my timidity and indolence, as long as I had no other passport to him than his complaisance. But encouraged by my first success, and by his eulogiums, which reached my ears, I went to see him; he returned my visit, and thus began the connexion between us, which will ever render him dear to me. By him, as well as from the testimony of my own heart, I learned that uprightness and probity may sometimes be connected with the cultivation of letters.

Many other connexions less solid, and which I shall not here particularise, were the effects of my first success, and lasted until curiosity was satisfied. I was a man so easily known, that on the next day nothing new was to be discovered in me. However, a woman, who at that time was desirous of my acquaintance, became much more solidly attached to me than any of those whose curiosity I had excited: this was the Marchioness of Créqui, niece to M. le Bailli de Froulay, ambassador to Malta, whose brother had preceded M. de Montaigu in the embassy to Venice, and whom I had gone to see at my return from that city. Madame de Créqui wrote to me; I visited her: she received me into her friendship. I sometimes dined with her. I met at her table several men of letters, amongst others M. Saurin, the author of *Spartacus*, *Barnevelt*, etc., since become my implacable enemy; for no other reason, at least that I can imagine, than my bearing the name of a man whom his father has cruelly persecuted.

It will appear that for a copyist, who ought to be employed in his business from morning to night, I had many interruptions, which rendered my days not very lucrative, and prevented me from being sufficiently attentive to what I did to do it well; for which reason, half the time I had to myself was lost in erasing errors or beginning my sheet anew. This daily importunity rendered Paris more insupportable every day, and made me ardently wish to be in the country. I several times went to pass a few days at Marcoussis, the vicar of which was known to Madame le Vasseur, and with whom we all arranged ourselves in such a manner as not to make things disagreeable to him. Grimm once went thither with us.[1] The vicar had a tolerable voice, sang well, and, although he did not read music, learned his part with great facility and precision. We passed our time in singing the trios I had composed at Chenonceaux. To these I added two or three new ones, to the words Grimm and the vicar wrote, well or ill. I cannot refrain from regretting those trios composed and sung in moments of pure joy, and which I left at Wootton with all my music. Mademoiselle Davenport has perhaps curled her hair with them; but they were worthy of being preserved, and are, for the most part, of a very good counterpoint. It was after one of these little excursions in which I had the pleasure of seeing the aunt at her ease and very cheerful, and in which my spirits were much enlivened, that I wrote to the vicar, very rapidly and very ill, an epistle in verse, which will be found amongst my papers.

I had nearer to Paris another station much to my liking with M. Mussard, my countryman, relation, and friend, who at Passy had made himself a charming retreat, where I have passed some

---

[1] Since I have neglected to relate here a trifling, but memorable adventure I had, with the said Grimm, one day, on which we were to dine at the fountain of St. Vandrille, I will let it pass; but when I thought of it afterwards, I concluded that he was brooding in his heart the conspiracy he has with so much success since carried into execution. (*Note by Rousseau*, not in Paris MS.).

CHARLES DUCLOS

very peaceful moments. M. Mussard was a jeweller, a man of
good sense, who, after having acquired a genteel fortune, and
given his only daughter in marriage to M. de Valmalette, the son
of an exchange broker, and maître d'hôtel to the King, took the
wise resolution to quit business in his declining years, and to place
an interval of repose and enjoyment between the hurry of life
and its end. The good man Mussard, a real philosopher in practice, lived without care, in a very pleasant house which he himself
had built in a very pretty garden, laid out with his own hands.
In digging the terraces of this garden he found fossil shells, and
in such great quantities that his lively imagination saw nothing
but shells in nature. He really thought the universe was composed
of shells and the remains of shells, and that the whole earth was
only the sand of these in different strata. His attention thus con-

stantly engaged with his singular discoveries, his imagination became so heated with the ideas they gave him, that, in his head,
they would soon have been converted into a system, that is, into
folly, if, happily for his reason, but unfortunately for his friends,
to whom he was dear, and to whom his house was an agreeable
asylum, a most cruel and extraordinary disease had not put an end
to his existence. A constantly increasing tumour in his stomach
prevented him from eating, long before the cause of it was discovered, and, after several years of suffering, absolutely occasioned
him to die of hunger. I can never, without the greatest affliction of
mind, call to my recollection the last moments of this worthy man,
who still received with so much pleasure, Lenieps and myself,
the only friends whom the sight of his sufferings did not separate
from him until his last hour, when he was reduced to devouring
with his eyes the repasts he had placed before us, scarcely having
the power of swallowing a few drops of weak tea, which came up
again a moment afterwards. But before these days of sorrow, how
many pleasant ones have I passed at his house, with the chosen
friends he had made himself! At the head of the list I place the
Abbé Prévôt, a very amiable man, and very sincere, whose heart
vivified his writings worthy of immortality, and who, neither in
his disposition nor in society, had the least of the melancholy
colouring he gave to his works: Procope the physician, a little
Esop, a favourite with the ladies: Boulanger, the celebrated posthumous author of *Despotisme Oriental*, and who, I am of opinion,
extended the systems of Mussard on the duration of the world.
The female part of his friends consisted of Madame Denis, niece
of Voltaire, who, at that time, was nothing more than a good kind
of woman, and pretended not to wit: Madame Vanloo, certainly
not handsome, but charming, and who sang like an angel: Madame Valmalette, herself, who sang also, and who, although very
thin, would have been very amiable had she had fewer pretensions. Such, or very nearly such, was the society of M. Mussard,
with which I should have been much pleased, had not his *con-
chyliomania* more engaged my attention; and I can say, with
great truth, that, for upwards of six months, I worked with him
in his cabinet with as much pleasure as he felt himself.

He had long insisted upon the virtue of the waters of Passy,
that they were proper in my case, and recommended me to come
to his house to drink them. To withdraw myself from the tumult
of the city, I at length consented, and went to pass eight or ten
days at Passy, which, on account of my being in the country were

of more service to me than the waters I drank during my stay there. Mussard played the violoncello, and was passionately fond of Italian music. This was the subject of a long conversation we had one evening after supper, particularly the *opere-buffe* we had both seen in Italy, and with which we were highly delighted. My sleep having forsaken me in the night, I considered in what manner it would be possible to give in France an idea of this kind of drama. The *Amours de Ragonde*[1] did not in the least resemble it. In the morning, whilst I took my walk and drank the waters, I hastily threw together a few couplets to which I adapted such airs as occurred to me at the moment. I scribbled over what I had composed, in a kind of a vaulted saloon at the end of the garden, and at tea. I could not refrain from showing the airs to Mussard, and to Mademoiselle Duvernois, his *gouvernante*, who was a very good and amiable girl. The three pieces of composition I had sketched out, were the first monologue: *J'ai perdu mon serviteur;* the air of the *Devin: L'amour croît s'il s'inquiète;* and the last duo: *A jamais, Colin, je t'engage,* etc. I was so far from thinking it worth while to continue what I had begun, that, had it not been for the applause and encouragement I received from both Mussard and Mademoiselle, I should have thrown my papers into the fire and thought no more of their contents, as I had frequently done by things of much the same merit; but I was so animated by the encomiums I received, that, in six days, my drama, excepting a few couplets, was written. The music also was so far sketched out, that all I had farther to do to it, after my return to Paris, was to compose a little of the recitative, and to add the middle parts, the whole of which I finished with so much rapidity, that in three weeks my work was ready for representation. The only thing now wanting, was the divertissement, which was not composed until a long time afterwards.

My imagination was so warmed by the composition of this work, that I had the strongest desire to hear it performed, and would have given anything to have seen and heard the whole in the manner I should have chosen; which would have been in private, like that of Lully, who is said to have had *Armide* performed for himself only. As it was not possible I should hear the performance unaccompanied by the public, I could not see the effect of my piece without getting it received at the Opera. Unfortunately it was quite a new species of composition, to which

---

[1] A comedy by Néricault-Destouches, with music by Mouret.

the ears of the public were not accustomed; and besides, the ill success of the *Muses Galantes* gave too much reason to fear for the *Devin*, if I presented it in my own name. Duclos relieved me from this difficulty, and engaged to get the piece rehearsed without mentioning the author. That I might not discover myself, I did not go to the rehearsal, and the *Petits violons*,[1] by whom it was directed, knew not who the author was until after a general plaudit had borne the testimony of the work. Everybody present was so delighted with it, that, on the next day, nothing else was spoken of in the different companies. M. de Cury, *Intendant des Menus*, who was present at the rehearsal, demanded the piece to have it performed at Court. Duclos, who knew my intentions, and thought I should be less master of my work at the Court than at Paris, refused to give it. Cury claimed it authoritatively. Duclos persisted in his refusal, and the dispute between them was carried to such a length, that one day they would have gone out from the Opera-house together, had they not been separated. M. de Cury applied to me, and I referred him to Duclos. This made it necessary to return to the latter. The Duke d'Aumont interfered; and at length Duclos thought proper to yield to authority, and the piece was given to be played at Fontainebleau.

The part to which I had been most attentive, and in which I had kept at the greatest distance from the common track, was the recitative. Mine was accented in a manner entirely new, and accompanied the utterance of the words. The directors dared not suffer this horrid innovation to pass, lest it should shock the ears of persons who never judge for themselves. Another recitative was proposed by Francueil and Jelyotte, to which I consented, but refused at the same time to have anything to do with it myself.

When everything was ready and the day of performance fixed, a proposition was made me to go to Fontainebleau, that I might at least be at the last rehearsal. I went with Mademoiselle Fel, Grimm, and I think the Abbé Raynal, in one of the stages to the Court. The rehearsal was tolerable: I was more satisfied with it than I expected to have been. The orchestra was numerous, composed of the orchestras of the Opera and the King's band. Jelyotte played *Colin*, Mademoiselle Fel, *Colette*, Cuvillier the *Devin:* the choruses were those of the Opera. I said but little: Jelyotte had prepared everything: I was unwilling either to approve of, or censure what he had done; and, notwithstanding I had assumed

---

[1] Rebel and Francœur, who, when they were very young, went together from house to house playing on the violin, were so called. (*Note by Rousseau.*)

the air of an old Roman, I was, in the midst of so many people, as
bashful as a schoolboy.

The next morning, the day of performance, I went to breakfast
at the coffee-house *du grand commun,* where I found a great number of people. The rehearsal of the preceding evening, and the
difficulty of getting into the theatre, were the subjects of conversation. An officer present said he entered with the greatest ease,
gave a long account of what had passed, described the author, and
related what he had said and done: but what astonished me most
in this long narrative, given with as much assurance as simplicity,
was that it did not contain a syllable of truth. It was clear to me,
that he who spoke so positively of the rehearsal, had not been at it,
because, without knowing him, he had before his eyes that author
whom he said he had seen and examined so minutely. However,
what was still more singular in this scene, was its effect upon me.
The officer was a man rather in years; he had nothing of the
appearance of a coxcomb; his features appeared to announce a
man of merit; and his cross of Saint Louis an officer of long standing. He interested me, notwithstanding his impudence. Whilst
he uttered his lies, I blushed, looked down, and was upon thorns;
I, for some time, endeavoured within myself to find the means of
believing him to be in an involuntary error. At length, trembling
lest some person should know me, and by this means confound
him, I hastily drank my chocolate without saying a word, and,
holding down my head as I passed before him, got out of the
coffee-house as soon as possible, whilst the company were making
their remarks upon the relation that had been given. I was no

sooner in the street, than I felt I was in a perspiration, and had anybody known and named me before I left the room, I am certain all the shame and embarrassment of a guilty person would have appeared in my countenance, proceeding from what I felt the poor man would have had to have suffered had his lie been discovered.

I am come to one of the critical moments of my life, in which it is difficult to do anything more than to relate, because it is almost impossible that even narrative should not carry with it the marks of censure or apology. I will however endeavour to relate how and upon what motives I acted, without adding either approbation or censure.

MME. DE POMPADOUR

I was on that day[1] in the same careless undress as usual; with a long beard, and a wig badly combed. Considering this want of decency as an act of courage, I entered the theatre wherein the King, Queen, the Royal Family, and the whole Court were to enter immediately after. I was conducted to a box by M. de Cury, and which belonged to him. It was very spacious, upon the stage, and opposite to a lesser but more elevated one in which the King sat with Madame de Pompadour. As I was surrounded by women, and the only man in front of the box, I had no doubt of my having

[1] Oct. 18, 1752.

been placed there purposely to be exposed to view. As soon as the theatre was lighted up, finding I was in the midst of people all extremely well dressed, I began to be less at my ease, and asked myself if I was in my place? whether or not I was properly dressed? After a few minutes of inquietude: yes, replied I, with an intrepidity which perhaps proceeded more from the impossibility of retracting, than the force of all my reasoning, I am in my place, because I am going to see my own piece performed, to which I have been invited, for which reason only I am come here; and after all, no person has a greater right than I have to reap the fruit of my labour and talents. I am dressed as usual, neither better nor worse; and if I once begin to subject myself to public opinion in any respect, I shall shortly become a slave to it in everything. To be always consistent with myself, I ought not to blush, in any place whatever, at being dressed in a manner suitable to the state I have chosen. My exterior appearance is simple, but neither dirty nor slovenly; nor is a beard either of these in itself, because it is given us by nature, and, according to time, place, and custom, is sometimes an ornament. People think I am ridiculous, nay even absurd; but what signifies this to me? I ought to know how to bear censure and ridicule, provided I do not deserve them. After this little soliloquy, I became so firm that, had it been necessary, I could have been intrepid. But whether it was the effect of the presence of a master, or the natural disposition of those about me, I perceived nothing but what was civil and obliging in the curiosity of which I was the object. This so much affected me, that I began again to be uneasy for myself, and the fate of my piece; fearing I should efface the favourable prejudices which seemed to lead to nothing but applause. I was armed against raillery; but so far overcome by the flattering and obliging treatment I had not expected, that I trembled like a child when the performance was begun.

I had soon sufficient reason to be encouraged. The piece was very ill played with respect to the actors, but the musical part was well sung and executed. During the first scene, which was really of a delightful simplicity, I heard in the boxes a murmur of surprise and applause, which, relative to pieces of the same kind, had never yet happened. The fermentation was soon increased to such a degree as to be perceptible through the whole audience, and of which, to speak after the manner of Montesquieu, the effect was augmented by itself. In the scene between the two good little folks, this effect was complete. There is no clapping of hands before the King, therefore everything was heard, which was advantageous to the author and the piece. I heard about me a whispering of women, who appeared as beautiful as angels. They said to each other in a low voice: This is charming: That is ravishing: There is not a sound which does not go to the heart. The pleasure of giving this emotion to so many amiable persons, moved me to tears; and these I could not contain in the first duo, when I remarked that I was not the only person who wept. I collected myself for a moment, on recollecting the concert of M. de Treytorens. This reminiscence had the effect of the slave who held the crown over the head of the general who triumphed, but my reflection was short, and I soon abandoned myself without interruption to the pleasure of enjoying my success. However, I am certain the voluptuousness of the sex was more predominant than the vanity of the author, and had none but men been present, I certainly should not have had the incessant desire I felt of catching on my lips the delicious tears I had caused to flow. I have known pieces excite more lively admiration, but I never saw so complete, delightful, and affecting an intoxication of the senses reign, during a whole representation, especially at Court, and at a first performance. They who saw this must recollect it, for it has never yet been equalled.

The same evening the Duke d'Aumont sent to desire me to be at the palace the next day at eleven o'clock, when he would present me to the King. M. de Cury, who delivered me the message, added that he thought a pension was intended, and that His Majesty wished to announce it to me himself. Will it be believed that the night of so brilliant a day was for me a night of anguish and perplexity? My first idea, after that of being presented, was that of my frequently wanting to retire; this had made me suffer very considerably at the theatre, and might torment me the next day when I should be in the gallery, or at the King's apartment, amongst all the great, waiting for the passing by of His Majesty. My infirmity was the principal cause which prevented me from mixing in polite companies, and enjoying the conversation of the fair. The idea alone of the situation in which this want might place me, was sufficient to produce it to such a degree as to make me faint away, short of a scandal to which, in my opinion, death was much preferable. None but persons who are acquainted with this situation can judge of the horror, which being exposed to the risk of it inspires.

I then supposed myself before the King, presented to His Maj-

esty, who deigned to stop and speak to me. In this situation, justness of expression and presence of mind were peculiarly necessary
in answering. Would my timidity, which disconcerts me in presence of any stranger whatever, have been shaken off in presence
of the King of France; or would it have suffered me instantly to
make choice of proper expressions? I wished, without laying aside
the austere manner I had adopted, to show myself sensible of the
honour done me by so great a monarch, and in a handsome and
merited eulogium to convey some great and useful truth. I could
not prepare a suitable answer without exactly knowing what His
Majesty was to say to me; and had this been the case, I was certain that, in his presence, I should not recollect a word of what
I had previously meditated. What, said I, will become of me in
this moment, and before the whole Court, if in my confusion any
of my stupid expressions should escape me? This danger alarmed
and terrified me. I trembled to such a degree that at all events I
was determined not to expose myself to it.

I lost, it is true, the pension, which in some measure was offered
me; but I at the same time exempted myself from the yoke it
would have imposed. Adieu, truth, liberty and courage! How
should I afterwards have dared to speak of disinterestedness and
independence? Had I received the pension I must either have
become a flatterer or remained silent; and moreover, who would
have insured to me the payment of it? What steps should I have
been under the necessity of taking! How many people must I
have solicited! I should have had more trouble and anxious cares
in preserving than in doing without it. Therefore, I thought I
acted according to my principles by refusing, and sacrificing appearances to reality. I communicated my resolution to Grimm,
who said nothing against it. To others I alleged my ill state of
health, and left the Court in the morning.

My departure made some noise, and was generally condemned.
My reasons could not be known to everybody; it was therefore
easy to accuse me of foolish pride, and thus not irritate the jealousy
of such as felt they would not have acted as I had done. The next
day Jelyotte wrote me a note, in which he stated the success of
my piece, and the pleasure it had afforded the King. All day long,
said he, His Majesty sings with the worst voice in his kingdom:
J'ai perdu mon serviteur: J'ai perdu tout mon bonheur. He likewise added, that in a fortnight the *Devin* was to be performed a
second time; which confirmed in the eyes of the public the complete success of the first.

LOUIS XV

Two days afterwards, about nine o'clock in the evening, as I was going to sup with Madame d'Epinay, I perceived a hackney-coach pass by the door. Somebody within made a sign to me to approach. I did so, and got into it, and found the person to be Diderot. He spoke of the pension with more warmth than, upon such a subject, I should have expected from a philosopher. He did not blame me for having been unwilling to be presented to the King, but severely reproached me with my indifference about the pension. He observed that although on my own account I might be disinterested, I ought not to be so on that of Madame le Vasseur, and her daughter; that it was my duty to seize every means of providing for their subsistence; and that as, after all, it could not be said I had refused the pension, he maintained I ought, since the King seemed disposed to grant it me, to solicit and obtain it by one means or other. Although I was obliged to him for his good wishes, I could not relish his maxims, which produced a warm dispute, the first I ever had with him. All our disputes were of this kind, he prescribing to me what he pretended I ought to do, and I defending myself because I was of a different opinion.

It was late when we parted. I would have taken him to supper at Madame d'Epinay's, but he refused to go; and, notwithstanding all the efforts which at different times the desire of uniting those I love induced me to make, to prevail upon him to see her, even that of conducting her to his door which he kept shut against us, he constantly refused to do it, and never spoke of her but with the utmost contempt. It was not until after I had quarrelled with them both that they became acquainted, and that he began to speak honourably of her.

From this time Diderot and Grimm seemed to have undertaken to alienate from me the Governesses, by giving them to understand that if they were not in easy circumstances the fault was my own, and that they would never be so with me. They endeavoured to prevail on them to leave me, promising them the privilege for retailing salt, a snuff shop, and I know not what other advantages by means of the influence of Madame d'Epinay. They likewise wished to gain over Duclos and d'Holbach, but the former constantly refused their proposals. I had at the time some intimation of what was going forward, but I was not fully acquainted with the whole until long afterwards; and I had frequently reason to lament the effects of the blind and indiscreet zeal of my friends, who, in my ill state of health striving to reduce me to the most melancholy solitude, endeavoured, as they imagined, to render me happy by the means most proper to make me miserable.

In the carnival following, in 1753, the *Devin* was performed at Paris, and in this interval I had sufficient time to compose the overture and divertissement. This divertissement, such as it stands engraved, was to be in action from the beginning to the end, and in a continual subject, which in my opinion afforded very agreeable representations. But when I proposed this idea at the Opera-house, nobody would so much as hearken to me, and I was obliged to tack together music and dances in the usual manner: on this account the divertissement, although full of charming ideas, which do not diminish the beauty of the scenes, succeeded but very middlingly. I suppressed the recitative of Jelyotte, and substituted my own, such as I had first composed it, and as it is now engraved; and this recitative, a little after the French manner, I confess, drawled out, instead of being pronounced by the actors, far from shocking the ears of any person, equally succeeded with the airs, and seemed in the judgement of the public to possess as much musical merit. I dedicated my piece to Duclos, who had given it his protection, and declared it should be my only dedication. I had however, with his consent, written a second; but he must have thought himself more honoured by the exception, than if I had not written a dedication to any person.

I could relate many anecdotes concerning this piece, but things of greater importance prevent me from entering into a detail of them at present. I shall perhaps resume the subject in a supplement. There is however one which I cannot omit, as it relates to the greater part of what is to follow. I one day examined the music of d'Holbach, in his closet. After having looked over many different kinds, he said, showing me a collection of pieces for the harpsichord: These were composed for me; they are full of taste and harmony, and unknown to everybody but myself. You ought to make a selection from them for your divertissement. Having in my head more subjects of airs and symphonies than I could make use of, I was not the least anxious to have any of his. However, he pressed me so much, that, from a motive of complaisance, I chose a pastoral which I abridged and converted into a trio, for the entry of the companions of Colette. Some months afterwards, and whilst the *Devin* still continued to be performed, going into Grimm's, I found several people about his harpsichord, whence he hastily rose on my arrival. As I accidentally looked towards his music stand, I there saw the same collection of the Baron d'Holbach, opened precisely at the piece he had prevailed upon me to take, assuring me at the same time that it should never go out of his hands. Some time afterwards, I again saw the collection open on the harpsichord of M. d'Epinay, one day when he gave a little concert. Neither Grimm nor anybody else ever spoke to me of the air, and my reason for mentioning it here is because some time afterwards a rumour was spread that I was not the author of the *Devin*. As I never made a great progress in the practical part, I am persuaded that had it not been for my *Dictionary of Music*, it would in the end have been said I did not understand composition.[1]

Some time before the *Devin du Village* was performed, a com-

---

[1] I little suspected this would be said of me, notwithstanding my *Dictionary*. (*Note by Rousseau*, not in Paris MS.).

pany of Italian buffoons had arrived at Paris, and were ordered
to perform at the Opera-house, without the effect they would produce there being foreseen. Although they were detestable, and
the orchestra, at that time very ignorant, mutilated at will the
pieces they gave, they did the French opera an injury that will
never be repaired. The comparison of these two kinds of music,
heard the same evening in the same theatre, opened the ears of
the French; nobody could endure their languid music after the
marked and lively accents of Italian composition; and the moment
the buffoons had done, everybody went away. The managers were

obliged to change the order of representation, and let the performance of the buffoons be the last. *Eglé*, *Pygmalion* and *Le
Sylphe* were successively given: nothing could bear the comparison. The *Devin du Village* was the only piece that did, and this
was still relished after *la Serva Padrona*. When I composed my
interlude, my head was filled with those pieces, and they gave
me the first idea of it: I was, however, far from imagining they
would one day be passed in review by the side of my composition.
Had I been a plagiarist, how many pilferings would then have
been manifest, and what care would have been taken to point
them out to the public! But I had done nothing of the kind. All
attempts to discover any such things were fruitless: nothing was
found in my music which led to the recollection of that of any
other person; and my whole composition, compared with the pretended original, was found to be as new as the musical characters

I had invented. Had Mondonville or Rameau undergone the same ordeal, they would have lost much of their substance.

The buffoons acquired Italian music very warm partisans. All Paris was divided into two parties, the violence of which was greater than if an affair of state or religion had been in question. One of them, the more powerful and numerous, composed of the great, of men of fortune, and the ladies, supported French music; the other, more lively and haughty, and fuller of enthusiasm, was composed of real connoisseurs, and men of talents and genius. This little group assembled at the Opera-house, under the box belonging to the Queen. The other party filled up the rest of the pit and the theatre; but the heads were mostly assembled under the box of His Majesty. Hence the party names of *Coin du Roi*, *Coin de la Reine*, then in great celebrity. The dispute, as it became more animated, produced several pamphlets. The King's corner aimed at pleasantry; it was laughed at by the *Petit Prophète*. It attempted to reason: the *Lettre sur la Musique française* refuted its reasoning. These two little productions, the former of which was by Grimm, the other by myself, are the only ones which have outlived the quarrel; all the rest are long since forgotten.

But the *Petit Prophète*, which, notwithstanding all I could say, was for a long time attributed to me, was considered as a pleasantry, and did not produce the least inconvenience to the author: whereas the *Lettre sur la Musique* was taken seriously, and incensed against me the whole nation, which thought itself offended by this attack on its music. The description of the incredible effect of this pamphlet would be worthy of the pen of Tacitus. The great quarrel between the parliament and the clergy was then at its height. The parliament had just been exiled; the fermentation was general; everything announced an approaching insurrection. The pamphlet appeared: from that moment every other quarrel was forgotten; the perilous state of French music was the only thing by which the attention of the public was engaged, and the only insurrection was against myself. This was so general that it has never since been totally calmed. At Court, the Bastile or banishment was absolutely determined on, and a *lettre de cachet* would have been issued had not M. de Voyer set forth in the most forcible manner that such a step would be ridiculous. Were I to say this pamphlet probably prevented a revolution, the reader would imagine I was in a dream. It is, however, a fact, the truth of which all Paris can attest, it being no more than fifteen years since the date of this singular fact.

Although no attempts were made on my liberty, I suffered numerous insults; and even my life was in danger. The musicians of the Opera orchestra humanely resolved to murder me as I went out of the theatre. Of this I received information; but the only effect it produced on me was to make me more assiduously attend the Opera; and I did not learn, until a considerable time afterwards, that M. Ancelet, officer in the musketeers, and who had a friendship for me, had prevented the effect of this conspiracy by giving me an escort, which, unknown to myself, accompanied me until I was out of danger. The direction of the Opera-house had just been given to the city. The first exploit performed by the Prévôt des Marchands, was to take from me my freedom of the theatre, and this in the most uncivil manner possible. Admission was publicly refused me on my presenting myself, so that I was obliged to take a ticket that I might not that evening have the mortification to return as I had come. This injustice was the more shameful, as the only price I had set on my piece when I gave it to the managers was a perpetual freedom of the house; for although this was a right common to every author, and which I enjoyed under a double title, I expressly stipulated for it in presence of M. Duclos. It is true, the treasurer brought me fifty louis, for which I had not asked; but, besides the smallness of the sum, compared with that which, according to the rules established in such cases, was due to me, this payment had nothing in common with the right of entry formally granted, and which was entirely independent of it. There was in this behaviour such a complication of iniquity and brutality, that the public, notwithstanding its animosity against me, which was then at its highest, was universally shocked at it, and many persons who insulted me the preceding evening, the next day exclaimed in the open theatre, that it was shameful thus to deprive an author of his right of entry; and particularly one who had so well deserved it, and was entitled to claim it for himself and another person. So true is the Italian proverb: *Ogn'un ama la giustizia in cosa d'altrui.*

In this situation the only thing I had to do was to demand my work, since the price I had agreed to receive for it was refused me. For this purpose I wrote to M. d'Argenson, who had the department of the Opera. I likewise enclosed to him a memoir which was unanswerable; but this, as well as my letter, was ineffectual, and I received no answer to either. The silence of that unjust man hurt me extremely, and did not contribute to increase the very moderate good opinion I always had of his character and abilities.

It was in this manner the managers kept my piece while they deprived me of that for which I had given it them. From the weak to the strong, such an act would be a theft: from the strong to the weak, it is nothing more than an appropriation of property, without a right.

With respect to the pecuniary advantages of the work, although it did not produce me a fourth part of the sum it would have done to any other person, they were considerable enough to enable me to subsist several years, and to make amends for the ill success of copying, which went on but very slowly. I received a hundred louis from the King; fifty from Madame de Pompadour, for the performance at Bellevue, where she herself played the part of Colin; fifty from the Opera; and five hundred livres from Pissot, for the engraving: so that this interlude, which cost me no more than five or six weeks' application, produced, notwithstanding the ill treatment I received from the managers and my stupidity at Court, almost as much money as my *Emile*, which had cost me twenty years' meditation, and three years' labour. But I paid dearly for the pecuniary ease I received from the piece, by the infinite vexations it brought upon me. It was the germ of the secret jealousies which did not appear until a long time afterwards. After its success I did not remark, either in Grimm, Diderot, or any of the men of letters, with whom I was acquainted, the same cordiality and frankness, nor that pleasure in seeing me, I had previously experienced. The moment I appeared at the Baron's the conversation was no longer general; the company divided into small parties; whispered into each other's ears; and I remained alone, without knowing to whom to address myself. I endured for a long time this mortifying neglect; and, perceiving that Madame d'Holbach, who was mild and amiable, still received me well, I bore with the vulgarity of her husband as long as it was possible. But he one day attacked me without reason or pretence, and with such brutality, in presence of Diderot, who said not a word, and Margency, who since that time has often told me how much he admired the moderation and mildness of my answers, that, at length, driven from his house by this unworthy treatment, I took leave with a resolution never to enter again. This did not however prevent me from speaking honourably of him and his house, whilst he continually expressed himself relative to me in the most insulting terms, calling me that *petit cuistre:* the little college pedant, or servitor in a college; without, however, being able to charge me with having done either to himself or any person to whom he was attached the most trifling injury. In this manner he verified my fears and predictions. I am of opinion my pretended friends would have pardoned me for having written books, and even excellent ones, because this merit was not foreign to themselves; but that they could not forgive my writing an opera, nor the brilliant success it had; because there was not one amongst them capable of the same, nor in a situation to aspire to like honours. Duclos, the only person superior to jealousy, seemed to become more attached to me: he introduced me to Mademoiselle Quinault, in whose house I received a polite attention, and civility to as great an extreme, as I had found a want of it in that of M. d'Holbach.

Whilst the performance of the *Devin du Village* was continued at the Opera-house, the author of it was also concerned, though not so happily, with the *Comédie Française*. Not having, during seven or eight years, been able to get my *Narcisse* performed at the Italian theatre, I had, by the bad performance in French of the actors, become disgusted with that theatre, and should rather have had my piece received at the French theatre than by them. I mentioned this to La Noue, the comedian, with whom I had become acquainted, and who, as everybody knows, was a man of merit, and an author. He was pleased with the piece, and promised to get it performed without suffering the name of the author to be known; and, in the meantime procured me the freedom of the theatre, which was extremely agreeable to me, for I always preferred it to the two others. The piece was favourably received,[1] and without the author's name being mentioned; but I have reason to believe it was known to the actors, actresses and many other persons. Mesdemoiselles Gaussin and Grandval played the amorous parts; and although the whole performance was, in my opinion, injudicious, the piece could not be said to be absolutely ill played. The indulgence of the public, for which I felt much gratitude, surprised me; the audience had the patience to listen to it from the beginning to the end, and to permit a second representation without showing the least sign of disapprobation. For my part, I was so wearied with the first, that I could not hold out to the end; and the moment I left the theatre, I went into the *Café de Procope*, where I found Boissy, and others of my acquaintance, who had probably been as much fatigued as myself. I there boldly uttered my *Peccavi*, and humbly or haughtily avowed myself the author of the piece, judging it as everybody else had done. This

[1] It was given on Dec. 18, 1752.

public avowal of an author of a piece which had not succeeded, was much admired, and was by no means painful to myself. My self-love was flattered by the courage with which I made it: and I am of opinion that, on this occasion, there was more pride in speaking, than there would have been foolish shame in being silent. However, as it was certain the piece, although insipid in the performance, would bear to be read, I had it printed; and in the preface, which is one of the best things I ever wrote, I began to make my principles more public than I had before done.

I soon had an opportunity to explain them entirely in a work of the greatest importance: for it was, I think, this year, 1753, that the Programme of the Academy of Dijon upon the *Origin of the Inequality of Mankind* made its appearance. Struck with the great question, I was surprised the Academy had dared to propose it: but since it had shown sufficient courage to do it, I thought I might venture to treat it, and immediately undertook the discussion.

That I might consider this grand subject more at my ease, I went to St. Germain for seven or eight days with Thérèse, our hostess, who was a good kind of woman, and one of her friends. I consider this walk as one of the most agreeable ones I ever took. The weather was very fine. These good women took upon themselves all the cares and expense. Thérèse amused herself with them; and I, free from all domestic concerns, diverted myself, without restraint, at the hours of dinner and supper. All the rest of the day wandering in the forest, I sought for and found there the image of the primitive ages of which I boldly traced the history. I confounded the pitiful lies of men; I dared to unveil their nature; to follow the progress of time, and the things by which it has been disfigured; and comparing the man of art with the natural man, to show them, in their pretended improvement, the real source of all their misery. My mind, elevated by these contemplations, ascended to the Divinity, and thence, seeing my fellow creatures follow, in the blind track of their prejudices, that of their errors, crimes, and misfortunes, I cried out to them, in a feeble voice, which they could not hear: Madmen who continually complain of Nature! know that all your evils proceed from yourselves!

From these meditations resulted the *Discourse on Inequality*, a work more to the taste of Diderot than any of my other writings, and in which his advice was of the greatest service to me.[1] It was,

---

[1] At the time I wrote this I had not the least suspicion of the grand conspir-

however, understood but by few readers in all Europe, and not
one of these would ever speak of it. I had written it to become a
competitor for the prize, and sent it away fully persuaded it would
not obtain it; well convinced it was not for productions of this
nature that the prizes of academies were founded.

This excursion and this occupation enlivened my spirits and
was of service to my health. Several years before, tormented by
my disorder, I had entirely given myself up to the care of physicians, who, without alleviating my sufferings, exhausted my
strength and destroyed my constitution. At my return from St.
Germain, I found myself stronger and perceived my health to be
improved. I followed this indication, and determined to cure myself, or die without the aid of physicians and medicine. I bade
them for ever adieu, and lived from day to day, keeping close,
when I found myself indisposed, and going abroad the moment
I had sufficient strength to do it. The manner of living in Paris
amidst people of pretensions was so little to my liking; the cabals
of men of letters, their shameful quarrels, their little candour in
their writings, and the air of importance they gave themselves in
the world were so odious to me; I found so little mildness, openness of heart, and frankness in the intercourse even of my friends;
that, disgusted with this life of tumult, I began ardently to wish
to reside in the country, and not perceiving that my occupations
permitted me to do it, I went to pass there all the time I had to
spare. For several months I went after dinner to walk alone in
the Bois de Boulogne, meditating on subjects for future works, and
not returning until evening.

Gauffecourt, with whom I was at that time extremely intimate,
being on account of his employment obliged to go to Geneva, proposed to me the journey, to which I consented. The state of my
health was such as to require the cares of the Governess; it was
therefore decided she should accompany us, and that her mother
should remain in the house. After thus having made our arrangements, we set off all three together on the first of June, 1754.

This was the period when, at the age of forty-two, I for the first

---

acy of Diderot and Grimm, otherwise I should easily have discovered how
much the former abused my confidence, by giving to my writings that severity
and melancholy which were not to be found in them, the moment he ceased
to direct me. The passage of the philosopher, who argues with himself, and
stops his ears against the complaints of a man in distress, is after his manner;
and he gave me others still more extraordinary, which I could never resolve to
make use of. But, attributing this melancholy to that he had acquired in the
dungeon of Vincennes, and of which there is a very sufficient dose in his *Clair-
val*, I never once suspected the least unfriendly dealing. (*Note by Rousseau.*)

time in my life felt a diminution of my natural confidence, to which I had abandoned myself without reserve or inconvenience. We had a private carriage in which with the same horses we travelled very slowly. I frequently got out and walked. We had scarcely performed half our journey when Thérèse showed the greatest uneasiness at being left in the carriage with Gauffecourt; and when, notwithstanding her remonstrances, I would get out as usual, she insisted upon doing the same, and walking with me. I chid her for this caprice, and so strongly opposed it, that at length she found herself obliged to declare to me the cause whence it proceeded. I thought I was in a dream; my astonishment was beyond expression, when I learned that my friend M. de Gauffecourt, upwards of sixty years of age, crippled by the gout, impotent and exhausted by pleasures, had, since our departure, incessantly endeavoured to corrupt a person who belonged to his friend, and was no longer young nor handsome, by the most base and shameful means, such as presenting to her a purse, attempting to inflame her imagination by the reading of an abominable book, and by the sight of infamous figures, with which it was filled. Thérèse, full of indignation, once threw his scandalous book out of the carriage; and I learned that on the first evening of our journey, a violent headache having obliged me to retire before supper, he had employed the whole time of this tête-à-tête in actions more worthy of a satyr or goat than a man of worth and honour, to whom I had entrusted my companion and myself. What astonishment and grief of heart for me! I, who until then had believed friendship to be inseparable from every amiable and noble sentiment which constitutes all its charm, for the first time in my life found myself under the necessity of connecting it with disdain, and of withdrawing my confidence and esteem from a man for whom I had an affection, and by whom I imagined myself beloved! The wretch concealed from me his turpitude; and that I might not expose Thérèse, I was obliged to conceal from him my contempt, and secretly to harbour in my heart such sentiments as were foreign to its nature. Sweet and sacred illusion of friendship! Gauffecourt first took the veil from before my eyes. What cruel hands have since that time prevented it from again being drawn over them!

At Lyons I quitted Gauffecourt to take the road to Savoy, being unable to be so near Mamma without seeing her. I saw her—Good God, in what a situation! How contemptible! What remained to her of primitive virtue? Was it the same Madame de Warens, formerly so gay and lively, to whom the vicar of Pontverre had given me recommendations? How my heart was wounded! The only resource I saw for her was to quit the country. I earnestly but vainly repeated the invitation I had several times given her in my letters to come and live peacefully with me, assuring her I would dedicate the rest of my life, and that of Thérèse, to render hers happy. Attached to her pension, from which, although it was regularly paid, she had not for a long time received the least advantage, my offers were lost upon her. I again gave her a trifling part of the contents of my purse, much less than I ought to have done, and considerably less than I should have offered her had not I been certain of its not being the least service to herself. During my residence at Geneva, she made a journey into Chablais, and came to see me at Grange-canal. She was in want of money to continue her journey: what I had in my pocket was insufficient to this purpose, but an hour afterwards I sent it her by Thérèse. Poor Mamma! I must relate this proof of the goodness of her heart. A little diamond ring was the last jewel she had left. She took it from her finger to put it upon that of Thérèse, who instantly replaced it upon that whence it had been taken, kissing the generous hand which she bathed with her tears. Ah! this was the proper moment to discharge my debt! I should have abandoned everything to follow her, attach myself to her till her last hour, and share her fate, let it be what it would. I did nothing of the kind. My attention was engaged by another attachment, and I perceived the attachment I had to her was abated by the slender hopes there were of rendering it useful to her. I sighed after her, but I did not follow her. Of all the remorse I ever felt this was the strongest and most lasting. I merited thereby the terrible chastisement with which I have since that time incessantly been overwhelmed: may this have expiated my ingratitude! Of this I appear guilty in my conduct, but my heart has been too much distressed by what I did, ever to have been that of an ungrateful man.

Before my departure from Paris I had sketched out the dedication of my *Discourse on the Inequality of Mankind*. I finished it at Chambéry, and dated it from that place, thinking that, to avoid all chicane, it was better not to date it either from France or Geneva. The moment I arrived in that city I abandoned myself to the republican enthusiasm which had brought me to it. This was augmented by the reception I there met with. Kindly treated by persons of every description, I entirely gave myself up to a patriotic zeal, and mortified at being excluded from the rights of a

J.-J. SITS FOR LA TOUR

citizen by the profession of a religion different from that of my
forefathers, I resolved openly to return to the latter. I thought,
the gospel being the same for every Christian, and the only difference in religious opinions the result of the explanations given
by men to that which they did not understand, it was the exclu-
sive right of the sovereign power in every country to fix the mode
of worship, and these unintelligible opinions; and that consequently it was the duty of a citizen to admit the one, and conform
to the other in the manner prescribed by the law. The conversation of the Encyclopedists, far from staggering my faith, gave it
new strength by my natural aversion to disputes and party. The
study of man and the universe had everywhere shown me the
final causes and the wisdom by which they were directed. The
reading of the Bible, and especially that of the New Testament,
to which I had for several years past applied myself, had given
me a sovereign contempt for the base and stupid interpretations
given to the words of Jesus Christ by persons the least worthy of
understanding His divine doctrine. In a word, philosophy, while
it attached me to the essential part of religion, had detached
me from the trash of the little formularies with which men had
rendered it obscure. Judging that for a reasonable man there
were not two ways of being a Christian, I was also of opinion
that in each country everything relative to form and discipline
was within the jurisdiction of the laws. From this principle, so

sound, social, and pacific, and which has brought upon me such cruel persecutions, it followed that, if I wished to be a citizen of Geneva, I must become a Protestant, and conform to the mode of worship established in my country. This I resolved upon; I moreover put myself under the instructions of the pastor of the parish in which I lived, which was without the city. All I desired was not to be made to appear at the consistory. However, the ecclesiastical edict was expressly to that effect; but it was agreed upon to dispense with it in my favour, and a commission of five or six members was named to receive my profession of faith. Unfortunately the minister Perdriau, a mild and an amiable man, for whom I had a friendship, took it into his head to tell me the members were rejoiced at the thought of hearing me speak in the little assembly. This expectation alarmed me to such a degree that having night and day during three weeks studied a little discourse I had prepared, I was so confused when I ought to have pronounced it that I could not utter a single word, and during the conference I had the appearance of the most stupid schoolboy. The persons deputed spoke for me, and I answered *yes* and *no*, like a blockhead; I was afterwards admitted to the communion, and reinstated in my rights as a citizen. I was enrolled as such in the list of guards, paid by none but citizens and burgesses, and I attended at a council-general extraordinary to receive the oath from the syndic Mussard. I was so impressed with the kindness shown me on this occasion by the council and the consistory, and by the great civility and obliging behaviour of the magistrates, ministers and citizens, that, pressed by the worthy de Luc, who was incessant in his persuasions, and still more so by my own inclination, I did not think of going back to Paris for any other purpose than to break up housekeeping, settle my little affairs, find a situation for M. and Madame le Vasseur, or provide for their subsistence, and then return with Thérèse to Geneva, there to settle for the rest of my days.

After taking this resolution, I suspended all serious affairs the better to enjoy the company of my friends until the time of my departure. Of all the amusements of which I partook, that with which I was most pleased, was sailing round the lake in a boat, with de Luc the elder, his daughter-in-law, his two sons, and my Thérèse. We gave seven days to this excursion in the finest weather possible. I preserved a lively remembrance of the situations which struck me at the other extremity of the lake, and of which I, some years afterwards, gave a description in my *Nouvelle Héloïse*.

The principal connexions I made at Geneva, besides the de Lucs, of whom I have spoken, were the young minister Vernes, with whom I had already been acquainted at Paris, and of whom I then formed a better opinion than he afterwards merited; M. Perdriau, then a country pastor, now professor of Belles Lettres, whose mild and agreeable society will ever make me regret the loss of it, although he has since thought proper to detach himself from me; M. Jalabert, at that time professor of natural philosophy, since become counsellor and syndic, to whom I read my *Discourse upon Inequality* (but not the dedication), with which he seemed to be delighted; the professor Lullin, with whom I maintained a correspondence until his death, and who gave me a commission to purchase books for the library; the professor Vernet, who, like most other people, turned his back upon me after I had given him proofs of attachment and confidence of which he ought to have been sensible, if a theologian can be affected by anything; Chappuis, clerk and successor to Gauffecourt, whom he wished to supplant, and who, soon afterwards, was himself supplanted; Marcet de Mezières, an old friend of my father's, who had also shown himself to be mine: after having well deserved of his country, he became a dramatic author; and aspiring to be of the Council of two hundred, changed his principles, and, before he died, became ridiculous. But he from whom I expected most was Moultou,[1] a very promising young man by his talents and his brilliant imagination, whom I have always loved, although his conduct with respect to me was frequently equivocal, and notwithstanding his being connected with my most cruel enemies; whom I cannot but look upon as destined to become one day the defender of my memory and the avenger of his friend.

In the midst of these dissipations, I neither lost the taste for my solitary excursions, nor the habit of them; I frequently made long ones upon the banks of the lake, during which my mind, accustomed to reflection, did not remain idle. I digested the plan already formed of my *Political Institutions*, of which I shall shortly have to speak; I meditated a *History of the Valais;* the plan of a tragedy in prose, the subject of which, nothing less than Lucretia, did not deprive me of the hope of succeeding, although I dared again to exhibit that unfortunate heroine, when she could no longer be suffered upon any French stage. I at that time tried

---

[1] Paris MS. reads: ". . . the younger Moultou, who was received into the ministry while I was at Geneva, though he afterwards forsook it; a very promising . . ."

my abilities with Tacitus, and translated the first book of his history, which will be found amongst my papers.

After a residence of four months at Geneva, I returned in the month of October to Paris; and avoided passing through Lyons that I might not again have to travel with Gauffecourt. As the arrangements I had made did not require my being at Geneva until the spring following, I returned, during the winter, to my habits and occupations; the principal of the latter was examining the proof sheets of my *Discourse on the Inequality of Mankind*, which I had procured to be printed in Holland, by the bookseller Rey, with whom I had just become acquainted at Geneva. This work was dedicated to the Republic; but as the dedication might be unpleasing to the Council, I wished to wait until it had taken its effect at Geneva before I returned thither. This effect was not favourable to me; and the dedication, which the most pure patriotism had dictated, only created me enemies in the Council, and inspired even many of the burgesses with jealousy. M. Chouet, at that time first syndic, wrote me a polite but very cold letter, which will be found amongst my papers. I received from private persons, amongst others from de Luc and de Jalabert, a few compliments, and these were all. I did not perceive that a single Genevese was pleased with the hearty zeal found in the work. This indifference shocked all those by whom it was remarked. I remember that dining one day at Clichy, at Madame Dupin's, with Crommelin, resident from the republic, and M. de Miran, the latter openly declared the Council owed me a present and public honours for this work, and that it would dishonour itself if it failed in either. Crommelin, who was a black and mischievous little man, dared not reply in my presence, but he made a frightful grimace, which, however, forced a smile from Madame Dupin. The only advantage this work procured me, besides that resulting from the satisfaction of my own heart, was the title of citizen given me by my friends, afterwards by the public after their example, and which I afterwards lost by having too well merited it.

This ill success would not however have prevented my retiring to Geneva, had not more powerful motives tended to the same effect. M. d'Epinay, wishing to add a wing which was wanting to the château of la Chevrette was at an immense expense in completing it. Going one day with Madame d'Epinay to see the building, we continued our walk a quarter of a league further to the reservoir of the waters of the park which joined the forest of Montmorency, and where there was a handsome kitchen garden,

with a little lodge, much out of repair, called the Hermitage. This
solitary and very agreeable place had struck me when I saw it for
the first time before my journey to Geneva. I had exclaimed in
my transport: Ah, madam, what a delightful habitation! This
asylum was purposely prepared for me. Madame d'Epinay did
not pay much attention to what I said; but at this second journey
I was quite surprised to find, instead of the old decayed building,
a little house almost entirely new, well laid out, and very habitable
for a little family of three persons. Madame d'Epinay had caused
this to be done in silence, and at a very small expense, by detaching a few materials and some of the workmen from the castle. She
now said to me, on remarking my surprise: My dear, here behold
your asylum: it is you who have chosen it; friendship offers it to
you. I hope this will remove from you the cruel idea of separating
from me. I do not think I was ever in my life more strongly or
more deliciously affected. I bathed with tears the beneficent hand
of my friend; and if I were not conquered from that very instant
even, I was extremely staggered. Madame d'Epinay, who would
not be denied, became so pressing, employed so many means, so
many people to circumvent me, proceeding even so far as to gain
over Madame le Vasseur and her daughter, that at length she triumphed over all my resolutions. Renouncing the idea of residing
in my own country, I resolved, I promised, to inhabit the Hermitage; and, whilst the building was drying, Madame d'Epinay
took care to prepare furniture, so that everything was ready the
following spring.

One thing which greatly aided me in determining, was the
residence Voltaire had chosen near Geneva; I easily comprehended this man would cause a revolution there, and that I should
find in my country the tone, the airs, the manners which drove
me from Paris; that I should be under the necessity of incessantly
struggling hard, and have no other alternative than that of being
an unsupportable pedant, a poltroon, or a bad citizen. The letter
Voltaire wrote me on my last work, induced me to insinuate my
fears in my answer; and the effect this produced confirmed them.
From that moment I considered Geneva as lost, and I was not
deceived. I perhaps ought to have met the storm, had I thought
myself capable of resisting it. But what could I have done alone,
timid and speaking badly, against a man, arrogant, opulent, supported by the credit of the great, eloquent, and already the idol
of the women and young men? I was afraid of uselessly exposing
myself to danger. I listened to nothing but my peaceful disposi-

tion, to my love of repose, which, if it then deceived me, still continues to deceive me on the same subject. By retiring to Geneva I should have avoided great misfortunes; but I have my doubts whether, with all my ardent and patriotic zeal, I should have been able to effect anything great and useful for my country.

Tronchin, who about the same time went to reside at Geneva, came afterwards to Paris to play the buffoon, and brought with him treasures. At his arrival he came to see me, with the Chevalier de Jaucourt. Madame d'Epinay had a strong desire to consult him in private, but this it was not easy to do. She addressed herself to me, and I engaged Tronchin to go and see her. Thus under my auspices they began a connexion, which was afterwards increased at my expense. Such has ever been my destiny: the moment I had united two friends who were separately mine, they never failed to combine against me. Although, in the conspiracy then formed by the Tronchins to enslave their country, they must all have borne me a mortal hatred, the doctor still continued friendly to me: he even wrote me a letter after his return to Geneva, to propose to me the place of honorary librarian. But I had taken my resolution, and the offer did not tempt me to depart from it.

About this time I again visited M. d'Holbach. My visit was occasioned by the death of his wife, which, as well as that of Madame de Francueil, happened whilst I was at Geneva. Diderot, when he communicated to me these melancholy events, spoke of the deep affliction of the husband. His grief affected my heart. I myself was keenly grieved for the loss of that excellent woman, and wrote to M. d'Holbach a letter of condolence. I forgot all the wrongs he had done me, and at my return from Geneva, and after he had made the tour of France with Grimm and other friends to alleviate his affliction, I went to see him, and continued my visits until my departure for the Hermitage. As soon as it was known in his society that Madame d'Epinay, whom he had not yet seen, was preparing me a habitation there, innumerable sarcasms, founded upon the want I must feel of the flattery and amusements of the city, and the supposition of my not being able to support the solitude for a fortnight, were uttered against me. Feeling within myself how I stood affected, I left him and his friends to say what they pleased, and pursued my intention. M. d'Holbach rendered me some services[1] in finding a place for the old le Vas-

[1] This is an instance of the treachery of my memory. A long time after I had written what I have stated above, I learned, in conversing with my wife, that it was not M. d'Holbach but M. de Chenonceaux, then one of the administra-

seur, who was over eighty years of age, and a burden to his wife
from which she begged me to relieve her. He was put into a house
of charity, where almost as soon as he arrived, age and the grief
of finding himself removed from his family sent him to the grave.
His wife and all his children, except Thérèse, did not much regret
his loss. But she, who loved him tenderly, has ever since been in-
consolable, and never forgiven herself for having suffered him,
at so advanced an age, to end his days in any other house than her
own.

Much about the same time I received a visit I little expected,
although it was from a very old acquaintance. My friend Venture, accompanied by another man, came upon me one morning
by surprise. What a change did I discover in his person! Instead of
his former gracefulness, he appeared sottish and vulgar, which
made me extremely reserved with him. My eyes deceived me, or
either debauchery had stupefied his mind, or all his first splendour
was the effect of his youth which was past. I saw him almost with
indifference, and we parted rather coolly. But when he was gone,
the remembrance of our former connexion so strongly called to
my recollection that of my younger days, so charmingly, so prudently dedicated to that angelic woman who was not much less
changed than himself; the little anecdotes of that happy time, the
romantic day of Toune passed with so much innocence and enjoyment between those two charming girls, from whom a kiss of the
hand was the only favour, and which, notwithstanding its being
so trifling, had left me such lively, affecting, and lasting regrets;
and the ravishing delirium of a young heart, which I had then
felt in all its force, and of which I thought the season for ever past
for me: the tender remembrance of these delightful circumstances
made me shed tears over my faded youth and its transports for
ever lost to me. Ah! how many tears should I have shed over their
tardy and fatal return, had I foreseen the evils I had yet to suffer
from them!

Before I left Paris, I enjoyed, during the winter which preceded
my retreat, a pleasure after my own heart, and of which I tasted
in all its purity. Palissot, academician of Nancy, known by a few
dramatic compositions, had just had one of them performed at
Lunéville before the King of Poland. He perhaps thought to make

---

tors of the Hôtel Dieu, who procured this place for her father. I had so totally
forgotten the circumstance, and the idea of M. d'Holbach's having done it was
so strong in my mind, that I would have sworn it had been he. (*Note by
Rousseau.*)

his court by representing in his piece a man who had dared to enter into a literary dispute with the King. Stanislaus, who was generous, and did not like satire, was filled with indignation at the author's daring to be personal in his presence. The Comte de Tressan, by order of the Prince, wrote to M. d'Alembert, as well as to myself, to inform me that it was the intention of His Majesty to have Palissot expelled his academy. My answer was a strong solicitation in favour of Palissot, begging M. de Tressan to intercede with the King in his behalf. His pardon was granted, and M. de Tressan, when he communicated to me the information in the name of the monarch, added that the whole of what had passed should be inserted in the register of the academy. I replied that this was less granting a pardon than perpetuating a punishment. At length, after repeated solicitations, I obtained a promise that nothing relative to the affair should be inserted in the register, and that no public trace should remain of it. The promise was accompanied, as well on the part of the King as on that of M. de Tressan, with assurances of esteem and respect with which I was extremely flattered; and I felt on this occasion that the esteem of men who are themselves worthy of it, produces in the mind a sentiment infinitely more noble and pleasing than that of vanity. I have transcribed into my collection the letters of M. de Tressan, with my answers to them; and the original of the former will be found amongst my other papers.

I am perfectly aware that if ever these memoirs become public, I here perpetuate the remembrance of a fact of which I would wish to efface every trace; but I transmit many others as much against my inclination. The grand object of my undertaking, constantly before my eyes, and the indispensable duty of fulfilling it to its utmost extent, will not permit me to be turned aside by trifling considerations, which would lead me from my purpose. In my strange and unparalleled situation I owe too much to truth to be farther than this indebted to any person whatever. They who wish to know me well must be acquainted with me in every point of view, in every relative situation, both good and bad. My confessions are necessarily connected with those of many other people: I write both with the same frankness in everything that relates to that which has befallen me; and am not obliged to spare any person more than myself, although it is my wish to do it. I am determined always to be just and true, to say of others all the good I can, never speaking of evil except when it relates to my own conduct, and there is a necessity for my so doing. Who, in the situation in which the world has placed me, has a right to require more at my hands? My confessions are not intended to appear during my lifetime, nor that of those whom they may disagreeably affect. Were I master of my own destiny, and that of the book I am now writing, it should never be made public until long after my death and theirs. But the efforts which the dread of truth obliges my powerful enemies to make to destroy every trace of it, render it necessary for me to do everything which the strictest right, and the most severe justice, will permit, to preserve what I have written. Were the remembrance of me to be lost at my dissolution, rather than expose any person alive, I would, without a murmur, suffer an unjust and momentary reproach. But since my name is to live,[1] it is my duty to endeavour to transmit with it to posterity the remembrance of the unfortunate man by whom it was borne, such as he really was, and not such as his unjust enemies incessantly endeavour to describe him.

BOOK NINE

My impatience to inhabit the Hermitage not permitting me to wait until the return of fine weather, the moment my lodging was prepared I hastened to take possession of it, to the great amusement of the Holbachian coterie, which publicly predicted I should not be able to support solitude for three months, and that I should unsuccessfully return to Paris, and live there as they did. For my part, having, for fifteen years, been out of my element, and finding myself upon the eve of returning to it, I paid no attention to their pleasantries. Since, contrary to my inclinations, I had again entered the world, I had incessantly regretted my dear Charmettes, and the agreeable life I led there. I felt a natural inclination to retirement and the country; it was impossible for me to live happily elsewhere. At Venice, in a train of public affairs, in the dignity of a kind of representation, in the pride of the projects of advancement; at Paris, in the vortex of the great world, in

---

[1] Paris MS. adds: "And pass to Posterity."

the luxury of suppers, in the brilliancy of spectacles, in the rays of splendour; my groves, rivulets, and solitary walks, constantly presented themselves to my recollection, interrupted my thoughts, rendering me melancholy, and made me sigh with desire. All the labour to which I had subjected myself, every project of ambition which by fits had animated my ardour, all had for object this happy country retirement, which I now thought near at hand. Without having acquired a genteel independence, which I had judged to be the only means of accomplishing my views, I imagined myself, in my particular situation, to be able to do without it, and that I could obtain the same end by a means quite opposite. I had no regular income; but I possessed some talents, and had acquired a name. My wants were few, and I was laborious when I chose to be so. My idleness was less that of an indolent man, than that of an independent one who applies to business when it pleases him. My profession of a copyist of music was neither splendid nor lucrative, but it was certain. The world gave me credit for the courage I had shown in making choice of it. I might depend upon having sufficient employment to enable me to live. Two thousand livres, which remained of the produce of the *Devin du Village*, and my other writings, were a sum which kept me from being straitened, and several works I had upon the stocks promised me, without extorting money from the booksellers, supplies sufficient to enable me to work at my ease without exhausting myself, even by turning to advantage the leisure of my walks. My little family, consisting of three persons, all of whom were usefully employed, was not expensive to support. Finally, from my resources, proportioned to my wants and desires, I might reasonably expect a happy and permanent existence, in that manner of life which my inclination had induced me to adopt.

I might have taken the interested side of the question, and, instead of subjecting my pen to copying, entirely devoted it to works which, from the elevation to which I had soared, might have enabled me to live in the midst of abundance, nay even of opulence, had I been the least disposed to join the manœuvres of an author to the care of publishing a good book. But I felt that writing for bread would soon have extinguished my genius, and destroyed my talents, which were less in my pen than in my heart, and solely proceeded from an elevated and noble manner of thinking, by which alone they could be cherished and preserved. Nothing vigorous or great can come from a pen totally venal. Necessity, nay even avarice, perhaps, would have made me write rather rapidly than well. If the desire of success had not led me into cabals, it might have made me endeavour to publish fewer true and useful works than those which might be pleasing to the multitude; and instead of a distinguished author, which I might possibly become, I should have been nothing more than a scribbler. No: I have always felt that the profession of letters was illustrious in proportion as it was less a trade. It is too difficult to think nobly when we think for a livelihood. To be able, to dare even to speak great truths, an author must be independent of success. I gave my books to the public with a certainty of having written for the general good of mankind, without giving myself the least concern about what was to follow. If the work was thrown aside, so much the worse for such as did not choose to profit by it. Their approbation was not necessary to enable me to live, my profession was sufficient to maintain me had not my works had a sale, for which reason alone they all sold.

It was on the ninth of April, 1756, that I left cities, never to reside in them again: for I do not call a residence the few short stays I afterwards made in Paris, London, or other cities, always on the wing, or contrary to my inclinations. Madame d'Epinay came and took us all three in her coach; her farmer carted away my little baggage, and I was put into possession the same day. I found my little retreat simply furnished, but neatly and with some taste. The hand which had lent its aid in this furnishing, rendered it inestimable in my eyes, and I thought it charming to be the guest of my female friend in a house I had made choice of, and which she had caused to be built purposely for me.

Although the weather was cold, and the ground lightly covered with snow, the earth began to vegetate: violets and primroses already made their appearance, the trees began to bud, and the evening of my arrival was distinguished by the first song of the nightingale, which was heard, almost under my window, in a wood adjoining to the house. After a light sleep, forgetting when I awoke my change of abode, I still thought myself in the Rue de Grenelle, when, suddenly, this warbling made me give a start, and I exclaimed in my transport: At length, all my wishes are accomplished! The first thing I did was to abandon myself to the impression of the rural objects with which I was surrounded. Instead of beginning to set things in order in my new habitation, I began by doing it for my walks, and there was not a path, a copse, a grove, nor a corner in the environs of my place of residence that I did not visit the next day. The more I examined this charming retreat, the more I found it to my wishes. This solitary, rather than savage, spot transported me in idea to the end of the world. It had striking beauties which are but seldom found near cities, and never, if suddenly transported thither, could any person have imagined himself within four leagues of Paris.

After abandoning myself for a few days to this rural delirium, I began to arrange my papers, and regulate my occupations. I set apart, as I had always done, my mornings to copying, and my afternoons to walking, provided with my little paper book and a pencil, for never having been able to write and think at my ease except *sub divo*,[1] I had no inclination to depart from this method, and I was persuaded the forest of Montmorency, which was almost at my door, would in future be my closet and study. I had several works begun: these I cast my eye over. My mind was indeed fertile in great projects, but in the noise of the city the execution of them had gone on but slowly. I proposed to myself to use more diligence when I should be less interrupted. I am of opinion, I had sufficiently fulfilled this intention; and for a man frequently ill, often at la Chevrette, at Epinay, at Eaubonne, at the castle of Montmorency, at other times interrupted by the indolent and curious, and always employed half the day in copying, if what I produced, during the six years I passed at the Hermitage, and at Montmorency, be considered, I am persuaded it will appear, that if, in this interval, I lost my time, it was not in idleness.

Of the different works I had upon the stocks, that I had longest resolved in my mind, which was most to my taste, at which I wished to work all my life, and which, in my opinion, was to confirm the reputation I had acquired, was my *Institutions Politiques*. I had, fourteen years before, when at Venice, where I had an opportunity of remarking the defects of that government so much boasted of, conceived the first idea of them. Since that time my views had become much more extended by the historical study of morality. I had perceived everything to be radically connected with politics, and that, upon whatever principles these were founded, a people would never be more than that which the nature of the government made them; therefore the great question of the best government possible appeared to me to be reduced to this: What is the nature of a government the properest to form the most virtuous and enlightened, the wisest and best people, taking the last epithet in its most extensive meaning? I thought

---

[1] In the open air.

this question was much if not quite of the same nature with that which follows: What government is that which by its nature always maintains itself nearest to the laws (or least deviates from the laws)? Hence, what is the law? and a series of questions of similar importance. I perceived all this led to great truths, useful to the happiness of mankind, but more especially to that of my country, wherein, in the journey I had just made to it, I had not found notions of law and liberty either sufficiently just or clear. I had thought this indirect manner of communicating these to my fellow citizens would be least mortifying to their pride, and might obtain me forgiveness for having seen a little farther than themselves.

Although I had already laboured five or six years at the work, the progress I had made in it was not considerable. Writings of this kind require meditation, leisure, and tranquillity. I had besides written the *Institutions Politiques,* as the expression is, *en bonne fortune,* and had not communicated my project to any person, not even to Diderot. I was afraid it would be thought too daring for the age and country in which I wrote, and that the fears of my friends would restrain me from carrying it into execution.[1] I did not yet know if it would be finished in time and in such a manner as to appear before my decease. I wished fearlessly to give to my subject everything it required; fully persuaded that not being of a satirical turn, and never wishing to be personal, I should in equity always be judged irreprehensible. I undoubtedly wished fully to enjoy the right of thinking which I had by birth; but still respecting the government under which I lived, without ever disobeying its laws, and very attentive not to violate the rights of persons, I would not from fear renounce its advantages.

I confess even that, as a stranger, and living in France, I found my situation very favourable in daring to speak the truth; well knowing that continuing, as I was determined to do, not to print anything in the kingdom without permission, I was not obliged to give to any person in it an account of my maxims nor of their publication elsewhere. I should have been less independent even at Geneva, where, in whatever place my books might have been

[1] It was more especially the wise severity of Duclos which inspired me with this fear; as for Diderot, I know not by what means all my conferences with him tended to make me more satirical than my natural disposition inclined me to be. This prevented me from consulting him upon an undertaking, in which I wished to introduce nothing but the force of reasoning without the least appearance of ill humour or partiality. The manner of this work may be judged of by that of the *Contrat Social* which is taken from it. (*Note by Rousseau.*)

printed, the magistrate had a right to criticise their contents. This consideration had greatly contributed to make me yield to the solicitations of Madame d'Epinay, and abandon the project of fixing my residence at Geneva. I felt, as I have remarked in my *Emile*, that unless an author be a man of intrigue, when he wishes to render his works really useful to his native land, he must compose them in some other.

What made me find my situation still more happy, was my being persuaded that the government of France would, perhaps without looking upon me with a very favourable eye, make it a point to protect me, or at least not to disturb my tranquillity. It appeared to me a stroke of simple, yet dexterous policy, to make a merit of tolerating that which there was no means of preventing; since had I been driven from France, which was all government had the right to do, my work would still have been written, and, perhaps, with less reserve; whereas if I were left undisturbed, the author remained to answer for what he wrote, and a prejudice, general throughout all Europe, would be destroyed by acquiring the reputation of observing a proper respect for the rights of persons.

They who, by the event, shall judge I was deceived, may perhaps be deceived in their turn. In the storm which has since broken over my head, my books served as a pretence, but it was against my person that every shaft was directed. My persecutors gave themselves but little concern about the author, but they wished to ruin Jean-Jacques; and the greatest evil they found in my writings was the honour they might possibly do me. Let us not encroach upon the future. I do not know that this mystery, which is still one to me, will hereafter be cleared up to my readers; but had my avowed principles been of a nature to bring upon me the treatment I received, I should sooner have become their victim, since the work in which these principles are manifested with most courage, not to call it audacity, seemed to have had its effect previous to my retreat to the Hermitage, without I will not only say my having received the least censure, but without any steps having been taken to prevent the publication of it in France, where it was sold as publicly as in Holland. The *Nouvelle Héloïse* afterwards appeared with the same facility, I dare add with the same applause; and, what seems incredible, the profession of faith of this Héloïse at the point of death, is exactly similar to that of the Savoyard Vicar. Every strong idea in the *Social Contract* had been before published in the *Discourse on Inequality*; and every bold opinion in *Emile* previously found in *Julie*. This unrestrained freedom did not excite the least murmur against the first two works; therefore it was not that which gave cause to it against the latter.

Another undertaking much of the same kind, but of which the project was more recent, then engaged my attention: this was the extract of the works of the Abbé de Saint Pierre,[1] of which, having been led away by the thread of my narrative, I have not hitherto been able to speak. The idea was suggested to me after my return from Geneva, by the Abbé Mably, not immediately from himself, but by the interposition of Madame Dupin, who had some interest in engaging me to adopt it. She was one of three or four pretty women of Paris, of whom the Abbé de Saint Pierre had been the spoiled child, and although she had not decidedly had the preference, she had at least partaken of it with Madame d'Aiguillon. She preserved for the memory of the good man a respect and an affection which did honour to them both; and her self-love would have been flattered by seeing the still-born works of her friend brought to life by her secretary. These works contained excellent things, but so badly told that the reading of them was almost insupportable; and it is astonishing the Abbé de Saint Pierre, who looked upon his readers as schoolboys, should nevertheless have spoken to them as men, by the little care he took to induce them to give him a hearing. It was for this purpose that the work was proposed to me as useful in itself and very proper for a man laborious in manœuvre, but idle as an author, who, finding the trouble of thinking very fatiguing, preferred, in things which pleased him, throwing a light upon and extending the ideas of others, to producing any himself. Besides, not being confined to the function of a translator, I was at liberty sometimes to think for myself; and I had it in my power to give such a form to my work, that many important truths would pass in it under the name of the Abbé de Saint Pierre, much more safely than under mine. The undertaking also was not trifling: the business was nothing less than to read and meditate twenty-three volumes, diffuse, confused, full of long narrations and periods, repetitions, and false or little views, from amongst which it was necessary to select some few that were great and useful and sufficiently encouraging to enable me to support the painful labour. I frequently wished to have given it up, and should have done so could I have

---

[1] 1658-1743: author of a *Projet de paix universelle entre les potentats d'Europe* (Utrecht, 1713), a kind of draft scheme for a League of Nations.

got it off my hands with a good grace; but when I received the manuscripts of the Abbé, which were given me by his nephew, the Comte de Saint Pierre, on the solicitation of Saint Lambert, I had in some measure engaged to make use of them, which I must either have done or have given them back. It was with the former intention I had taken the manuscripts to the Hermitage, and this was the first work to which I proposed to dedicate my leisure hours.

I had likewise in my own mind projected a third, the idea of which I owed to the observations I had made upon myself, and I felt the more disposed to undertake this work, as I had reason to hope I could make it a truly useful one, and, perhaps, the most so of any that could be offered to the world, were the execution equal to the plan I had laid down. It has been remarked that most men are in the course of their lives frequently unlike themselves, and seem to be transformed into others very different from what they were. It was not to establish a thing so generally known that I wished to write a book; I had a newer and more important object. This was to search for the causes of these variations, and, by confining my observations to those which depend on ourselves, to demonstrate in what manner it might be possible to direct them, in order to render us better and more certain of our dispositions. For it is undoubtedly more painful to an honest man to resist desires already formed, and which it is his duty to subdue, than to prevent, change, or modify the same desires in their source, were he capable of tracing them to it. A man under temptation resists once because he has strength of mind, he yields another time because this is overcome; had he been the same as before, he would again have triumphed.

By examining within myself, and searching in others what could be the cause of these different manners of being, I discovered that, in a great measure, they depended on the anterior impression of external objects; and that, continually modified by our senses and organs, we, without knowing it, bore in our ideas, sentiments, and even actions, the effect of these modifications. The striking and numerous observations I had collected were beyond all manner of dispute, and by their natural principles seemed proper to furnish an exterior regimen, which, varied according to circumstances, might place and support the mind in the state most favourable to virtue. From how many mistakes would reason be preserved, how many vices would be stifled in their birth, were it possible to force animal economy to favour moral order, which it so frequently disturbs! Climates, seasons, sounds, colours, light, darkness, the elements, aliments, noise, silence, motion, rest, all act on the animal machine, and consequently on the mind; all offer us a thousand means, almost certain of directing in their origin the sentiments by which we suffer ourselves to be governed. Such was the fundamental idea of which I had already made a sketch upon paper, and whence I hoped for an effect the more certain, in favour of persons well disposed, who, sincerely loving virtue, were afraid of their own weakness, as it appeared to me easy to make of it a book as agreeable to read as it was to compose. I have, however, applied myself but very little to this work, the title of which was to have been *Morale Sensitive, ou le Matérialisme du Sage*. Interruptions, the cause of which will soon appear, prevented me from continuing it, and the fate of the sketch, which is more connected with my own than it may appear to be, will hereafter be seen.

Besides this, I had for some time meditated a system of education, of which Madame de Chenonceaux, alarmed for her son by that of her husband, had desired me to consider. The authority of friendship placed this object, although less in itself to my taste, nearer to my heart than any other. On which account this subject, of all those of which I have just spoken, is the only one I carried to its utmost extent. The end I proposed to myself in treating of it should, I think, have procured the author a better fate. But I will not here anticipate this melancholy subject. I shall have too much reason to speak of it in the course of my work.

These different objects offered me subjects of meditation for my walks: for, as I believe I have already observed, I am unable to reflect when I am not walking: the moment I stop, I think no more, and as soon as I am again in motion, my head resumes its workings. I had, however, provided myself with a work for the closet upon rainy days. This was my *Dictionary of Music*, which my scattered, mutilated, and unshapen materials made it necessary to rewrite almost entirely. I had with me some books necessary to this purpose; I had spent two months in making extracts from others, which I had borrowed from the King's library, whence I was permitted to take several to the Hermitage. I was thus provided with materials for composing in my apartment when the weather did not permit me to go out, and my copying fatigued me. This arrangement was so convenient that I made it turn to advantage as well at the Hermitage as at Montmorency, and afterwards even at Motiers, where I completed the work whilst I was engaged in others, and constantly found a change of occupation to be a real relaxation.

During a considerable time I exactly followed the distribution I had prescribed myself, and found it very agreeable; but as soon as the fine weather brought Madame d'Epinay more frequently to Epinay, or to la Chevrette, I found that attentions, in the first instance natural to me, but which I had not considered in my scheme, considerably deranged my projects. I have already observed that Madame d'Epinay had many amiable qualities: she sincerely loved her friends; served them with zeal; and, not sparing for them either time or pains, certainly deserved on their part every attention in return. I had hitherto discharged this duty, without considering it as one; but at length I found I had given myself a chain of which nothing but friendship prevented me from feeling the weight, and this was still aggravated by my dislike to numerous societies. Madame d'Epinay took advantage of these circumstances to make me a proposition seemingly agreeable to me, but which was more so to herself: this was to let me know when she was alone, or had but little company. I consented without perceiving to what a degree I engaged myself. The consequence was that I no longer visited her at my own hour but at hers, and that I never was certain of being master of myself for a day together. This constraint considerably diminished the pleasure I had in going to see her. I found the liberty she had so frequently promised was given me upon no other condition than that of my never enjoying it; and once or twice when I wished to do this there were so many messages, notes, and alarms relative to my health, that I perceived I could have no excuse but being confined to my bed for not immediately running to her upon the first intimation. It was necessary I should submit to this yoke, and I did it, even more voluntarily than could be expected from so great an enemy to dependence: the sincere attachment I had to Madame d'Epinay preventing me in a great measure from feeling the inconvenience with which it was accompanied. She, on her part, filled up, well or ill, the void which the absence of her usual circle left in her amusements. This for her was but a slender supplement, although preferable to absolute solitude, which she could not support. She had the means of doing it much more at her ease after she began with literature, and at all events to write novels, letters, comedies, tales, and other trash of the same kind. But she was not so much amused in writing these as in reading them; and she never scribbled over two or three pages at one sitting, without being previously assured of having, at least, two or three benevolent auditors at the end of so much labour. I seldom had the honour of being one of the chosen few except by means of another. When alone, I was, for the most part, considered as a cipher in everything; and this not only in the company of Madame d'Epinay, but in that of M. d'Holbach, and in every place where Grimm gave the *ton*. This nullity was very convenient to me, except in a tête-à-tête, when I knew not what countenance to put on, not daring to speak of literature, of which it was not for me to say a word; nor of gallantry, being too timid; and fearing, more than death, the ridiculousness of an old gallant; besides that, I never had such an idea when in the company of Madame d'Epinay, and that it perhaps would never have occurred to me, had I passed my whole life with her: not that her person was in the least disagreeable to me; on the contrary, I loved her perhaps too much as a friend to do it as a lover. I felt a pleasure in seeing and speaking to her. Her conversation, although agreeable enough in a mixed company, was uninteresting in private; mine, not more elegant or entertaining than her own, was no great amusement to her. Ashamed of being long silent, I endeavoured to enliven our tête-à-tête, and, although this frequently fatigued me, I never was disgusted with it. I was happy to show her little attentions, and give her little fraternal kisses, which seemed not to be more sensual to herself; these were all. She was very thin, very pale, and had a bosom which resembled the back of my hand. This defect alone would have been sufficient to moderate my most ardent desires; my heart and senses never could distinguish a woman in a person who had no breasts; and besides other causes, useless to mention, always made me forget the sex of this lady.

Having resolved to conform to a constraint which was necessary, I immediately and voluntarily entered upon it, and, for the first year at least, found it less burdensome than I could have expected. Madame d'Epinay, who commonly passed almost all the summer in the country, continued there but a part of this; whether she was more detained by her affairs at Paris, or that the absence of Grimm rendered the residence of la Chevrette less agreeable to her, I know not. I took the advantage of the intervals of her absence, or when the company with her was numerous, to enjoy my solitude with my good Thérèse and her mother, in such a manner as to taste all its charms. Although I had for several years past been frequently in the country, I seldom had enjoyed much of its pleasures; and these excursions, always made in com-

pany with people who considered themselves as persons of consequence, and rendered insipid by constraint, served to increase in
me that natural desire I had for rustic pleasures. The want of
these was the more sensible to me, as I had the image of them
immediately before my eyes. I was so tired of saloons, fountains,

J.-J. WITH MME. D'EPINAY

groves, partners, and of the more fatiguing persons by whom they
were shown; so exhausted with pamphlets, harpsichords, wool-
winding, making knots, stupid *bons mots*, insipid affectation, pitiful story-tellers, and great suppers; that when I gave a side-glance
at a poor simple hawthorn bush, a hedge, a barn, or a meadow;
when, in passing through a hamlet, I scented a good chervil
omelette, and heard, at a distance, the burden of the rustic song
of the goatherds; I wished all rouge, furbelows, and amber at the
devil, and envying the dinner of the good housewife, and the wine
of her own vineyard, I heartily wished to give a slap of the chops
to Monsieur le Chef and Monsieur le Maître, who made me dine
at the hour of supper, and sup when I should have been asleep,
but especially to Messieurs the lackeys, who devoured with their
eyes the morsels I put into my mouth, and upon pain of dying
with thirst, sold me the adulterated wine of their masters, ten

times dearer than that of a better quality would have cost me at a public house.

At length I was settled in my own home, in an agreeable and solitary asylum, at liberty to pass there the rest of my days, in that peaceful, equal, and independent life for which I felt myself born. Before I relate the effect this situation, so new to me, had upon my heart, it is proper I should recapitulate its secret affections, that the reader may better follow in their causes the progress of these new modifications.

I have always considered the day on which I was united to Thérèse as that which fixed my moral existence. An attachment was necessary for me, since that which should have been sufficient to my heart had been so cruelly broken. The thirst after happiness is never extinguished in the heart of man. Mamma was advancing into years, and dishonoured herself. I had proofs that she could never more be happy here below; it, therefore, remained to me to seek my own happiness, having lost all hopes of partaking of hers. I was some time irresolute, and fluctuated from one idea to another, and from project to project. My journey to Venice would have thrown me into public life, had the man with whom, almost against my inclination, I was connected there had common sense. I was easily discouraged, especially in undertakings of length and difficulty. The ill success of this disgusted me with every other; and, according to my old maxim, considering distant objects as deceitful allurements, I resolved in future to provide for immediate wants, seeing nothing in life which could tempt me to make extraordinary efforts.

It was precisely at this time that we became acquainted. The mild character of the good Thérèse seemed so fitted to my own, that I united myself to her with an attachment which neither time nor injuries have been able to impair, and which has constantly been increased by everything by which it might have been expected to be diminished. The force of this sentiment will hereafter appear when I come to speak of the wounds she has given my heart in the height of my misery, without my ever having, until this moment, once uttered a word of complaint to any person whatever.

When it shall be known, that after having done everything, braved everything, not to separate from her; that after passing with her twenty-five years in despite of fate and men; I have, in my old age, made her my wife, without the least expectation or solicitation on her part, or promise or engagement on mine, the world will think that love bordering upon madness, having from the first moment turned my head, led me by degrees to the last act of extravagance; and this will no longer appear doubtful when the strong and particular reasons which should for ever have prevented me from taking such a step are made known. What, therefore, will the reader think when I shall have told him, with all the truth he has ever found in me, that, from the first moment in which I saw her, until that wherein I write, I have never felt the least love for her, that I never desired to possess her more than I did to possess Madame de Warens, and that the physical wants which were satisfied with her person were, for me, solely those of the sex, and by no means proceeding from the individual? He will think, that being of a constitution different from that of other men, I was incapable of love, since this was not one of the sentiments which attached me to women the most dear to my heart. Patience, O my dear reader! the fatal moment approaches in which you will be but too much undeceived.

I fall into repetitions; I know it; and these are necessary. The first of my wants, the greatest, strongest, and most insatiable, was wholly in my heart; the want of an intimate connexion, and as intimate as it could possibly be: for this reason especially, a woman was more necessary to me than a man, a female rather than a male friend. This singular want was such, that the closest corporal union was not sufficient: two souls would have been necessary to me in the same body, without which I always felt a void. I thought I was upon the point of filling it up for ever. This young person, amiable by a thousand excellent qualities, and at that time, by her form, without the shadow of art or coquetry, would have confined within herself my whole existence, could hers, as I had hoped it would, have totally been confined to me. I had nothing to fear from men; I am certain of being the only man she ever really loved, and her moderate passions seldom wanted another, not even after I ceased in this respect to be one to her. I had no family; she had one; and this family, composed of individuals whose dispositions were so different from hers, was never such that I could make it my own. This was the first cause of my unhappiness. What would I not have given to have been the child of her mother! I did everything in my power to become so, but could never succeed. I in vain attempted to unite all our interests: this was impossible. She always created herself one different from mine, contrary to it, and to that even of her daughter, which already was no longer separated from it. She, her other children, and grandchildren, became so many leeches, and the least evil these did to Thérèse was robbing her. The poor girl, accustomed to submit, even to her nieces, suffered herself to be pilfered from and governed without saying a word; and I perceived with grief that by exhausting my purse, and giving her advice, I did nothing that could be of any real advantage to her. I endeavoured to detach her from her mother; but she constantly resisted such a proposal. I could not but respect her resistance, and esteemed her the more for it; but her refusal was not on this account less to the prejudice of us both. Abandoned to her mother and the rest of her family, she was more their companion than mine, and rather at their command, than mistress of herself. Their avarice was less ruinous than their advice was pernicious to her; in fact, if, on account of the love she had for me, added to her good natural disposition, she was not quite their slave, she was enough so to prevent in a great measure the effect of the good maxims I endeavoured to instil into her; and, notwithstanding all my efforts, to prevent our being united.

Thus was it, that notwithstanding a sincere and reciprocal attachment, in which I had lavished all the tenderness of my heart, the void in that heart was never completely filled. Children, by whom this effect should have been produced, were brought into the world, but these only made things worse. I trembled at the thought of entrusting them to a family ill brought up, to be still worse educated. The risk of the education of the Foundling Hospital was much less. This reason for the resolution I took, much stronger than all those I stated in my letter to Madame de Francueil, was, however, the only one with which I dared not make her acquainted. I chose rather to appear less excusable than expose to reproach the family of the person I loved. But by the conduct of her wretched brother, notwithstanding all that can be said in his defence, it will be judged whether or not I ought to have exposed my children to an education similar to his.

Not having it in my power to taste in all its plenitude the charms of that intimate connexion, of which I felt the want, I sought for substitutes, which did not fill up the void, yet they made it less sensible. Not having a friend entirely devoted to me, I wanted others, whose impulse should have overcome my indolence; for this reason I cultivated and strengthened my connexions with Diderot and the Abbé de Condillac, formed with Grimm a new one still more intimate, till at length, by the unfortunate discourse, of which I have related some particulars, I unexpectedly found myself thrown back into a literary circle which I thought I had quitted for ever.

My first steps conducted me by a new path to another intellectual world, the simple and noble economy of which I cannot contemplate without enthusiasm. I reflected so much upon the subject that I soon saw nothing but error and folly in the doctrine of our sages, and oppression and misery in our social order. In the illusion of my foolish pride, I thought myself capable of destroying all imposture; and thinking that, to make myself listened to, it was necessary my conduct should agree with my principles, I adopted the singular manner of life which I have not been permitted to continue, the example of which my pretended friends have never forgiven me, which at first made me ridiculous, and would at length have rendered me respectable, had it been possible for me to persevere.

Until then I had been good; from that moment I became virtuous, or at least infatuated with virtue. This infatuation had begun in my head, but afterwards passed into my heart. The most noble pride there took root amongst the ruins of extirpated vanity. I affected nothing: I became what I appeared to be, and during four years at least, whilst this effervescence continued at its greatest height, there is nothing great and good that can enter the heart of man, of which I was not capable between heaven and myself. Hence flowed my sudden eloquence, hence, in my first writings, that fire really celestial, which consumed me, and whence during forty years not a single spark had escaped, because it was not yet lighted up.

I was really transformed; my friends and acquaintance scarcely knew me. I was no longer that timid, and rather bashful than modest man, who neither dared to present himself, nor utter a word; whom a single pleasantry disconcerted, and whose face was covered with a blush the moment his eyes met those of a woman. I became bold, haughty, intrepid, with a confidence the more firm, as it was simple, and resided in my soul rather than in my manner. The contempt with which my profound meditations had inspired me for the manners, maxims, and prejudices of the age in which I lived, rendered me proof against the raillery of those by whom they were possessed, and I crushed their little pleasantries with a sentence as I would have crushed an insect with my fingers. What a change! All Paris repeated the severe and acute sarcasms of the same man, who, two years before, and ten years afterwards, knew not how to find what he had to say, nor the word he ought to employ. Let the situation in the world the most contrary to my natural disposition be sought after, and this will be found. Let one of the short moments of my life in which I became another man, and ceased to be myself, be recollected; this also will be found in the time of which I speak; but, instead of continuing only six days, or six weeks, it lasted almost six years, and would perhaps still continue, but for the particular circumstances which caused it to cease, and restored me to nature, above which I had wished to soar.

The beginning of this change took place as soon as I had quitted Paris, and the sight of the vices of that city no longer kept up the indignation with which it had inspired me. I no sooner had lost sight of men than I ceased to despise them, and once removed from those who designed me evil, my hatred against them no longer existed. My heart, little fitted for hatred, pitied their misery, and even their wickedness. This situation, more pleasing but less sublime, soon allayed the ardent enthusiasm by which I had so long been transported; and I insensibly, almost to myself even, again became fearful, complaisant, and timid; in a word, the same Jean-Jacques I before had been.

Had this revolution gone no farther than restoring me to myself, all would have been well; but unfortunately it rapidly carried me away to the other extreme. From that moment my mind in agitation passed the line of repose, and its oscillations, continually renewed, have never permitted it to remain there. I must enter into some detail of this second revolution; terrible and fatal era, of a fate unparalleled amongst mortals.

We were but three persons in our retirement; it was therefore natural our intimacy should be increased by leisure and solitude. This was the case between Thérèse and myself. We passed in conversations in the shade, the most charming and delightful hours, more so than any I had hitherto enjoyed. She seemed to taste of this sweet intercourse more than I had until then observed her to do; she opened her heart, and communicated to me, relative to her mother and family, things she had had resolution enough to conceal for a great length of time. Both had received from Madame Dupin numerous presents, made them on my account, and mostly for me, but which the cunning old woman, to prevent my being angry, had appropriated to her own use, and that of her other children, without suffering Thérèse to have the least share, strongly forbidding her to say a word to me of the matter: an order the poor girl had obeyed with an incredible exactness.

But another thing which surprised me more than this had done, was the discovery that besides the private conversations Diderot and Grimm had frequently had with both to endeavour to detach them from me, in which, by means of the resistance of Thérèse, they had not been able to succeed, they had afterwards had frequent conferences with the mother, the subject of which was a secret to the daughter. However, she knew little presents had been made, and that there were mysterious goings backward and forward, the motive of which was entirely unknown to her. When we left Paris, Madame le Vasseur had long been in the habit of going to see Grimm twice or thrice a month, and continuing with him for hours together in conversation so secret that Grimm's servant was always sent out of the room.

I judged this motive to be of the same nature with the project into which they had attempted to make the daughter enter, by promising to procure her and her mother, by means of Madame d'Epinay, a salt hucksterer's licence, or a snuff-shop; and, in a word, by tempting them with the allurements of gain. They had been told that, as I was not in a situation to do anything for them, I could not, on their account, do anything for myself. As in all this I saw nothing but good intentions, I was not absolutely displeased with them for it. The mystery was the only thing which gave me pain, especially on the part of the old woman who, moreover, daily became more parasitical and flattering towards me. This, however, did not prevent her from reproaching her daughter in private with telling me everything and loving me too much, observing to her, she was a fool and would at length be made a dupe.

This woman possessed, to a supreme degree, the art of multiplying the presents made her, by concealing from one what she received from another, and from me what she received from all. I could have pardoned her avarice, but it was impossible I should forgive her dissimulation. What could she have to conceal from me whose happiness she knew principally consisted in that of herself and her daughter? What I had done for the daughter I had done for myself, but the services I had rendered the mother, merited on her part some acknowledgement. She ought, at least, to have thought herself obliged for them to her daughter, and to have loved me for the sake of her by whom I was already beloved. I had raised her from the lowest state of wretchedness; she received from my hands the means of subsistence, and was indebted to me for her acquaintance with the persons from whom she found means to reap considerable benefit. Thérèse had long supported

her by her industry, and now maintained her with my bread. She
owed everything to this daughter, for whom she had done nothing, and her other children, to whom she had given marriage portions, and on whose account she had ruined herself, far from giving her the least aid, devoured her subsistence and mine. I thought
that in such a situation she ought to consider me as her only friend
and most sure protector, and that, far from making of my own
affairs a secret to me, and conspiring against me in my house, it
was her duty faithfully to acquaint me with everything in which
I was interested, when this came to her knowledge before it did
to mine. In what light, therefore, could I consider her false and
mysterious conduct? What could I think of the sentiments with
which she endeavoured to inspire her daughter? What monstrous
ingratitude was hers, to endeavour to instil it into her from whom
I expected my greatest consolation?

These reflections at length alienated my affections from this
woman, and to such a degree, that I could no longer look upon
her but with contempt. I nevertheless continued to treat with
respect the mother of the friend of my bosom, and in everything
to show her almost the reverence of a son: but I must confess I
could not remain long with her without pain, and that I never
knew how to bear constraint.

This is another short moment of my life, in which I approached
near to happiness without being able to attain it, and this by no
fault of my own. Had the mother been of a good disposition we all
three should have been happy to the end of our days; the longest
liver only would have been to be pitied. Instead of which, the
reader will see the course things took, and judge whether or not
it was in my power to change it.

Madame le Vasseur, who perceived I had got more full possession of the heart of Thérèse, and that she had lost ground with her,
endeavoured to regain it; and instead of striving to restore herself
to my good opinion by the mediation of her daughter, attempted
to alienate her affections from me. One of the means she employed
was to call her family to her aid. I had begged Thérèse not to invite any of her relations to the Hermitage, and she had promised
me she would not. These were sent for in my absence, without
consulting her, and she was afterwards prevailed upon to promise
not to say anything of the matter. After the first step was taken
all the rest were easy. When once we make a secret of anything
to the person we love, we soon make but little scruple of doing it
in everything. The moment I was at la Chevrette, the Hermitage

was full of people who sufficiently amused themselves. A mother has always great power over a daughter of a mild disposition; yet notwithstanding all the old woman could do, she was never able to prevail upon Thérèse to enter into her views, nor to persuade her to join in the league against me. For her part, she resolved upon doing it for ever; and seeing on one side her daughter and myself, who were in a situation to live, and that was all; on the other, Diderot, Grimm, d'Holbach and Madame d'Epinay, who promised great things, and gave some little ones, she could not conceive it was possible to be in the wrong with the wife of a farmer-general and a Baron. Had I been more clear-sighted, I should from this moment have perceived I nourished a serpent in my bosom. But my blind confidence, which nothing had yet diminished, was such that I could not imagine she wished to injure the person she ought to love. Though I saw numerous conspiracies formed on every side, all I complained of was the tyranny of persons who called themselves my friends, and who, as it seemed, would force me to be happy in the manner they should point out, and not in that I had chosen for myself.

Although Thérèse refused to join in the confederacy with her mother, she still kept her secret. For this her motive was commendable, although I will not determine whether she did well or ill. Two women, who have secrets between them, love to prattle together; this attracted them towards each other, and Thérèse, by dividing herself, sometimes let me feel I was alone; for I could no longer consider as a society that which we all three formed.

I now felt the neglect I had been guilty of, during the first years of our connexion, in not taking advantage of the docility with which her love inspired her, to improve her talents and give her knowledge, which, by more closely connecting us in our retirement, would agreeably have filled up her time and my own, without once suffering us to perceive the length of a private conversation. Not that this was ever exhausted between us, or that she seemed disgusted with our walks; but we had not a sufficient number of ideas, common to both, to make ourselves a great store, and we could not incessantly talk of our future projects, which were confined to those of enjoying the pleasures of life. The objects around us inspired me with reflections beyond the reach of her comprehension. An attachment of twelve years' standing had no longer need of words: we were too well acquainted with each other to have any new knowledge to acquire in that respect. The resource of puns, jests, gossiping and scandal was all that remained.

In solitude especially is it, that the advantage of living with a person who knows how to think is particularly felt. I wanted not this resource to amuse myself with her; but she would have stood in need of it to have always found amusement with me. The worst of all was our being obliged to hold our conversations when we could; her mother, who was become importunate, obliged me to watch for opportunities to do it. I was under constraint in my own house: this is saying everything; the air of love was prejudicial to good friendship. We had an intimate intercourse without living in intimacy.

The moment I thought I perceived that Thérèse sometimes sought for a pretext to elude the walks I proposed to her, I ceased to invite her to accompany me, without being displeased with her for not finding in them so much amusement as I did. Pleasure is not a thing which depends upon the will. I was sure of her heart, and the possession of this was all I desired. As long as my pleasures were hers, I tasted of them with her; when this ceased to be the case I preferred her contentment to my own.

In this manner it was that, half deceived in my expectation, leading a life after my own heart, in a residence I had chosen, with a person who was dear to me, I at length found myself almost alone. What I still wanted prevented me from enjoying what I had. With respect to happiness and enjoyment, everything or nothing was what was necessary to me. The reason of these observations will hereafter appear. At present I return to the thread of my narrative.

I imagined that I possessed treasures in the manuscripts given me by the Comte de Saint Pierre. On examination I found they were little more than the collection of the printed works of his uncle, with notes and corrections by his own hand, and a few other trifling fragments which had not yet been published. I confirmed myself by these moral writings in the idea I had received from some of his letters, shown me by Madame de Créqui, that he had more sense and ingenuity than at first I had imagined; but after a careful examination of his political works, I discerned nothing but superficial notions, and projects that were useful but impracticable, in consequence of the idea from which the author never could depart, that men conducted themselves by their sagacity rather than by their passions. The high opinion he had of the knowledge of the moderns had made him adopt this false principle of improved reason, the basis of all the institutions he proposed, and the source of his political sophisms. This extraordinary man, an honour to the age in which he lived, and to the human species, and perhaps the only person, since the creation of mankind, whose sole passion was that of reason, wandered in all his systems from error to error, by attempting to make men like himself, instead of taking them as they were, are, and will continue to be. He laboured for imaginary beings, while he thought himself employed for the benefit of his contemporaries.

All these things considered, I was rather embarrassed as to the form I should give to my work. To suffer the author's visions to pass was doing nothing useful; fully to refute them would have been unpolite, as the care of revising and publishing his manuscripts, which I had accepted, and even requested, had been entrusted to me; this trust had imposed on me the obligation of treating the author honourably. I at length concluded upon that which to me appeared the most decent, judicious, and useful. This was to give separately my own ideas and those of the author, and, for this purpose, to enter into his views, to set them in a new light, to amplify, extend them, and spare nothing which might contribute to present them in all their excellence.

My work therefore was to be composed of two parts absolutely distinct: one, to explain, in the manner I have just mentioned, the different projects of the author; in the other, which was not to appear until the first had had its effect, I should have given my opinion upon these projects, which I confess might sometimes have exposed them to the fate of the sonnet of the *Misanthrope*. At the head of the whole was to have been the life of the author. For this I had collected some good materials, and which I flattered myself I should not spoil in making use of them. I had been a little acquainted with the Abbé de Saint Pierre, in his old age, and the veneration I had for his memory warranted to me, upon the whole, the Comte would not be dissatisfied with the manner in which I should have treated his relation.

I made my first essay on the *Perpetual Peace*, the greatest and most elaborate of all the works which composed the collection; and before I abandoned myself to my reflections I had the courage to read everything the Abbé had written upon this fine subject, without once suffering myself to be digusted either by his slowness or repetitions. The public has seen the extract, on which account I have nothing to say upon the subject. My opinion of it has not been printed, nor do I know that it ever will; however, it was written at the same time the extract was made. From this I passed to the *Polysynodie*, or Plurality of Councils; a work written under the Regent to favour the administration he had chosen, and which caused the Abbé de Saint Pierre to be expelled the Academy, on account of some remarks unfavourable to the preceding administration, and with which the Duchess of Maine and the Cardinal de Polignac were displeased. I completed this work as I did the former, with an extract and remarks; but I stopped here without intending to continue the undertaking which I ought never to have begun.

The reflection which induced me to give it up naturally presents itself, and it was astonishing I had not made it sooner. Most of the writings of the Abbé de Saint Pierre were either observations, or contained observations, on some parts of the government of France, and several of these were of so free a nature that it was happy for him he had made them with impunity. But in the offices of all the ministers of state the Abbé de Saint Pierre had ever been considered as a kind of preacher rather than a real politician, and he was suffered to say what he pleased, because it appeared that nobody listened to him. Had I procured him readers the case would have been different. He was a Frenchman, and I was not one; and by repeating his censures, although in his own name, I exposed myself to be asked, rather rudely, but without injustice, what it was with which I meddled. Happily before I proceeded any farther, I perceived the hold I was about to give government against me, and I immediately withdrew. I knew that living alone in the midst of men more powerful than myself, I never could by any means whatever be sheltered from the injury they chose to do me. There was but one thing which depended upon my own efforts: this was, to observe such a line of conduct that whenever they chose to make me feel the weight of authority they could not do it without being unjust. The maxim which induced me to decline proceeding with the works of the Abbé de Saint Pierre, has frequently made me give up projects I had much more at heart. People who are always ready to construe adversity into a crime,[1] would be much surprised were they to know the pains I have taken, that, during my misfortunes, it might never with truth be said of me, *Thou hast deserved them.*

After having given up the manuscript, I remained some time without determining upon the work which should succeed it, and this interval of inactivity was destructive, by permitting me to turn my reflections on myself, for want of another object to en-

---

[1] Paris MS. adds: "and who judge of my conduct from my misfortunes."

gage my attention. I had no project for the future which could
amuse my imagination. It was not even possible to form any, as
my situation was precisely that in which all my desires were
united. I had not another to conceive, and yet there was a void in
my heart. This state was the more cruel, as I saw no other that
was to be preferred to it. I had fixed my most tender affections
upon a person who made me a return of her own. I lived with her
without constraint, and, so to speak, at discretion. Notwithstanding this, a secret grief of mind never quitted me for a moment,
either when she was present or absent. In possessing Thérèse, I
felt that I still lacked her; and the sole idea of my not being everything to her had such an effect upon my mind that she was next
to nothing to me.

I had friends of both sexes, to whom I was attached by the purest friendship and most perfect esteem; I depended upon a real
return on their part, and a doubt of their sincerity never entered
my mind; yet this friendship was more tormenting than agreeable to me, by their obstinate perseverance, and even by their
affectation, in opposing my taste, inclinations, and manner of
living; and this to such a degree, that the moment I seemed to
desire a thing which interested myself only, and depended not
upon them, they immediately joined their efforts to oblige me to
renounce it. This continued desire to control me in all my wishes,
the more unjust, as I did not so much as make myself acquainted
with theirs, became so cruelly oppressive, that I never received
one of their letters without feeling a certain terror as I opened it,
which was but too well justified by the contents. I thought being
treated like a child by persons younger than myself, and who, of
themselves, stood in great need of the advice they so prodigally
bestowed upon me, was too much: love me, said I to them, as I
love you, but, in every other respect, let my affairs be as indifferent to you, as yours are to me: this is all I ask. If they granted me
one of these two requests, it was not the latter.

I had a retired residence in a charming solitude, was master in
my own house, and could live in it in the manner I thought proper,
without being controlled by any person. This habitation imposed
on me duties agreeable to discharge, but which were indispensable. My liberty was precarious. In a greater state of subjection
than a person at the command of another, it was my duty to be so
by inclination. When I arose in the morning, I never could say to
myself: I will employ this day as I think proper. And moreover,
besides my being subject to obey the call of Madame d'Epinay, I

was exposed to the still more disagreeable importunities of the public and chance comers. The distance I was at from Paris did not prevent crowds of idlers, not knowing how to spend their time, from daily breaking in upon me, and, without the least scruple, freely disposing of mine. When I least expected visitors I was unmercifully assailed by them, and I seldom made a plan for the agreeable employment of the day that was not counteracted by the arrival of some stranger.

In short, finding no real enjoyment in the midst of the pleasures I had been most desirous to obtain, I, by sudden mental transitions returned in imagination to the serene days of my youth, and sometimes exclaimed with a sigh: Ah! this is not les Charmettes!

The recollection of the different periods of my life led me to reflect upon that at which I was arrived, and I found I was already on the decline, a prey to painful disorders, and imagined I was approaching the end of my days without having tasted, in all its plenitude, scarcely any one of the pleasures after which my heart had so much thirsted, or having given scope to the lively sentiments I felt it had in reserve. I had not favoured even that intoxicating voluptuousness with which my mind was richly stored, and which, for want of an object, was always compressed, and never exhaled but by sighs.

How was it possible that, with a mind naturally expansive, I, with whom to live was to love, should not hitherto have found a friend entirely devoted to me; a real friend: I who felt myself so capable of being such a friend to another? How can it be accounted for that, with such warm affections, and a heart wholly made up of love, I had not once at least felt its flame for a determinate object? Tormented by the want of loving, without ever having been able to satisfy it, I perceived myself approaching the eve of old age, and hastening on to death without having lived.

These melancholy but affecting reflections led me to others which, although accompanied with regret, were not wholly unsatisfactory. I thought something I had not yet received was still due to me from destiny. To what end was I born with exquisite faculties? To suffer them to remain unemployed? The sentiment of conscious merit, which made me consider myself as suffering injustice, was some kind of reparation, and caused me to shed tears which with pleasure I suffered to flow.

These were my meditations during the finest season of the year, in the month of June, in cool shades, to the song of the nightingale, and the warbling of brooks. Everything concurred in plunging me into that too seducing state of indolence for which I was born, but from which my austere manners, proceeding from a long effervescence, should for ever have delivered me. I unfortunately recollected the dinner of the Château de Toune, and my meeting with the two charming girls in the same season, in places much resembling that in which I then was. The remembrance of these circumstances, which the innocence that accompanied them rendered to me still more dear, brought several others of the same nature to my recollection. I presently saw myself surrounded by all the objects which, in my youth, had given me emotion. Mademoiselle Galley, Mademoiselle de Graffenried, Mademoiselle de Breil, Madame Basile, Madame de Larnage, my pretty scholars, and even the bewitching Zulietta, whom my heart could not forget. I found myself in the midst of a seraglio of houris of my old acquaintance, for whom the most lively inclination was not new to me. My blood became inflamed, my head turned, notwithstanding my hair was almost grey, and the grave citizen of Geneva, the austere Jean-Jacques, at forty-five years of age, again became the fond shepherd. The intoxication with which my mind was seized, although sudden and extravagant, was so strong and lasting, that, to enable me to recover from it, nothing less than the unforeseen and terrible crisis it brought on was necessary.

This intoxication, to whatever degree it was carried, went not so far as to make me forget my age and situation, to flatter me that I could still inspire love, nor to make me attempt to communicate the devouring but sterile flame by which, ever since my youth, I had felt my heart in vain consumed. For this I did not hope; I did not even desire it. I knew the season of love was past; I knew too well in what contempt the ridiculous pretensions of superannuated gallants were held, ever to add one to the number, and I was not a man to become an impudent coxcomb in the decline of life, after having been so little such during the flower of my age. Besides, as a friend to peace, I should have been apprehensive of domestic dissensions; and I too sincerely loved Thérèse to expose her to the mortification of seeing me entertain for others more lively sentiments than those with which she inspired me for herself.

What step did I take upon this occasion? My reader will already have guessed it, if he has taken the trouble to pay the least attention to my narrative. The impossibility of attaining real beings threw me into the regions of chimera, and seeing nothing in ex-

istence worthy of my delirium, I sought food for it in the ideal
world, which my imagination quickly peopled with beings after
my own heart. This resource never came more apropos, nor was
it ever so fertile. In my continual ecstasy I intoxicated my mind
with the most delicious sentiments that ever entered the heart of
man. Entirely forgetting the human species, I formed to myself
societies of perfect beings, whose virtues were as celestial as their
beauty, tender and faithful friends, such as I never found here
below. I became so fond of soaring in the empyrean, in the midst
of the charming objects with which I was surrounded, that I thus
passed hours and days without perceiving it; and, losing the remembrance of all other things, I scarcely had eaten a morsel in
haste before I was impatient to make my escape and run to regain
my groves. When, ready to depart for the enchanted world, I saw
arrive wretched mortals who came to detain me upon earth, I
could neither conceal nor moderate my vexation; and, no longer
master of myself, I gave them so uncivil a reception, that it might
justly be termed brutal. This tended to confirm my reputation as
a misanthrope, from the very cause which, could the world have
read my heart, should have acquired me one of a nature directly
opposite.

In the midst of my exaltation, I was pulled down like a paper
kite, and restored to my proper place by means of a smart attack
of my disorder. I recurred to the only means that had before given
me relief, namely bougies, and this made a truce with my angelic
amours; for besides that it seldom happens that a man is amorous
when he suffers, my imagination, which is animated in the
country and beneath the shade of trees, languishes and becomes
extinguished in a chamber, and under the joists of a ceiling. I
frequently regretted that there existed no Dryads; it would certainly have been amongst those that I should have fixed my
attachment.

Other domestic broils came at the same time to increase my
chagrin. Madame le Vasseur, while making me the finest compliments in the world, alienated from me her daughter as much as
she possibly could. I received letters from my late neighbourhood,
informing me, that the good old lady had secretly contracted several debts in the name of Thérèse, to whom these had become
known, but of which she had never mentioned to me a word. The
debts to be paid hurt me much less than the secret that had been
made of them. How could she, for whom I had never had a secret,
have one for me? Is it possible to dissimulate with persons whom

we love? The Holbachian coterie, who found I never made a journey to Paris, began seriously to be afraid I was happy and satisfied in the country, and madman enough to continue there. Hence the cabals by which attempts were made to recall me indirectly to the city. Diderot, who did not immediately wish to show himself, began by detaching from me Deleyre, whom I had brought acquainted with him, and who received and transmitted to me the impressions Diderot chose to give without suspecting to what end they were directed.

Everything seemed to concur in withdrawing me from my charming and mad reverie. I was not recovered from the late attack I had had when I received the copy of the poem on the destruction of Lisbon, which I imagined to be sent to me by the author. This made it necessary I should write to him and speak of his composition. I did so, and my letter was a long time afterwards printed without my consent, as I shall hereafter have occasion to remark.

Struck by seeing this poor man, overwhelmed, if I may so speak, with prosperity and honour, bitterly exclaiming against the miseries of this life, and always finding everything wrong; I formed the mad project of making him turn his attention to himself, and of proving to him that everything was right. Voltaire, while he appeared to believe in God, never really believed in anything but the devil; since his pretended deity is a malicious being, who, according to him, has no pleasure but in evil. The glaring absurdity of this doctrine is particularly disgusting from a man enjoying the greatest prosperity; who, from the bosom of happiness, endeavours, by the frightful and cruel image of all the calamities from which he is exempt, to reduce his fellow creatures to despair. I, who had a better right than he to calculate and weigh all the evils of human life, impartially examined them, and proved to him that of all possible evils there was not one to be attributed to Providence, and which had not its source rather in the abusive use man made of his faculties than in nature. I treated him, in this letter, with the greatest respect and delicacy possible. Yet, knowing his self-love to be extremely irritable, I did not send the letter immediately to himself, but to Doctor Tronchin, his physician and friend, with full power either to give it him or destroy it, as he should find most suitable. He gave it. Voltaire informed me in a few lines that being ill, having likewise the care of a sick person, he postponed his answer until some future day, and said not a word upon the subject. Tronchin, when he sent me the letter, enclosed in it another, in which he expressed but very little esteem for the person from whom he received it.

I have never published, nor even shown, either of these two letters, not liking to make a parade of such little triumphs; but the originals are in my collections. Since that time Voltaire has published the answer he promised me, but which I never received. This is the novel of *Candide*, of which I cannot speak because I have not read it.

All these interruptions ought to have cured me of my fantastic amours, and they were perhaps the means offered me by heaven to prevent their destructive consequences; but my evil genius prevailed, and I had scarcely begun to go out before my heart, my head, and my feet returned to the same paths. I say the same in certain respects; for my ideas, rather less exalted, remained this time upon earth, but yet were busied in making so exquisite a choice of all that was to be found there amiable of every kind, that it was not much less chimerical than the imaginary world I had abandoned.

I figured to myself love and friendship, the two idols of my heart, under the most ravishing images. I amused myself in adorning them with all the charms of the sex I had always adored. I imagined two female friends rather than two of my own sex, because, although the example be more rare, it is also more amiable. I endowed them with characters different, but analogous, with two faces, not perfectly beautiful, but according to my taste, and animated with benevolence and sensibility. I made one brown and the other fair, one lively and the other languishing, one wise and the other weak, but of so amiable a weakness that it seemed to add a charm to virtue. I gave to one of the two a lover, of whom the other was the tender friend, and even something more, but I did not admit their rivalry, quarrels, or jealousy; because every painful sentiment is painful to me to imagine, and I was unwilling to tarnish this delightful picture by anything which was degrading to nature. Smitten with my two charming models, I drew my own portrait in the lover and the friend, as much as it was possible to do it; but I made him young and amiable, giving him, at the same time, the virtues and defects which I felt in myself.

That I might place my characters in a residence proper for them, I successively passed in review the most beautiful places I had seen in my travels. But I found no grove sufficiently delightful, no landscape that pleased me. The valleys of Thessaly would have satisfied me had I but once had a sight of them; but my imagination, fatigued with invention, wished for some real place which might serve it as a point to rest upon, and create in me an illusion with respect to the real existence of the inhabitants I intended to place there. I thought a good while upon the Borromean islands,[1] the delightful prospect of which had transported me, but I found in them too much art and ornament for my lovers. I however wanted a lake, and I concluded by making choice of that about which my heart has never ceased to wander. I fixed myself upon that part of the banks of this lake where my wishes have long since placed my residence in the imaginary happiness to which fate has confined me. The native place of my poor Mamma had still for me a charm. The contrast of the situations, the richness and variety of the sites, the magnificence, the majesty of the whole, which ravishes the senses, affects the heart, and elevates the mind, determined me to give it the preference, and I placed my young pupils at Vevey. This is what I imagined at the first sketch; the rest was not added until afterwards.

I for a long time confined myself to this vague plan, because it was sufficient to fill my imagination with agreeable objects, and my heart with sentiments in which it delighted. These fictions, by frequently presenting themselves, at length gained a consistence and took in my mind a determined form. I then had an inclination to express upon paper some of the situations fancy presented to me, and, recollecting everything I had felt during my youth, thus, in some measure, gave scope to that desire of loving, which I had never been able to satisfy, and by which I felt myself consumed.

I first wrote a few unconnected letters, and when I afterwards wished to give them connexion, I frequently found a difficulty in doing it. What is scarcely credible, although most strictly true, is my having written the two first parts almost wholly in this manner, without having any plan formed, and not foreseeing I should one day be tempted to make it a regular work. For this reason the two parts, afterwards formed of materials not prepared for the places in which they are disposed, are full of wordy padding not found in others.

In the midst of my reveries I had a visit from Madame d'Houdetot, the first she had ever made me, but which unfortunately was not the last, as will hereafter appear. The Comtesse d'Houdetot

---

[1] Islands in Lago Maggiore.

was the daughter of the late M. de Bellegarde, a farmer-general, sister to M. d'Epinay, and Messieurs de Lalive and de la Briche, both of whom have since been introductors to ambassadors. I have spoken of the acquaintance I made with her before she was married; since that event I had not seen her, except at the fêtes of la Chevrette, with Madame d'Epinay, her sister-in-law. Having frequently passed several days with her, both at la Chevrette and Epinay, I always thought her amiable, and that she seemed to be my well-wisher. She was fond of walking with me; we were both good walkers, and the conversation between us was inexhaustible. However, I never went to see her in Paris, although she had several times requested and solicited me to do it. Her connexions with M. de St. Lambert, with whom I began to be intimate, rendered her more interesting to me, and it was to bring me some account of that friend who was, I believe, then at Mahon, that she came to see me at the Hermitage.

This visit had something of the appearance of the beginning of a romance. She lost her way. Her coachman, quitting the road, which turned, attempted to cross straight over from the mill of Clairvaux to the Hermitage: her carriage stuck in a quagmire in the bottom of the valley, and she got out and walked the rest of the road. Her delicate shoes were soon worn through; she sank into the dirt, her servants had the greatest difficulty in extricating her; and she at length arrived at the Hermitage in boots, making the place resound with her laughter, in which I most heartily joined. She was obliged to change everything. Thérèse provided her with what was necessary, and I prevailed upon her to forget her dignity and partake of a rustic collation, with which she seemed highly satisfied. It was late, and her stay was short; but the interview was so mirthful that it pleased her, and she seemed disposed to return. She did not however put this project into execution until the next year: but, alas! the delay was not favourable to me in anything.

I passed the autumn in an employment no person would suspect me of undertaking: this was guarding the fruit of M. d'Epinay. The Hermitage was the reservoir of the waters of the park of la Chevrette: there was a garden walled round and planted with wall-fruit and other trees which produced M. d'Epinay more fruit than his kitchen garden at la Chevrette, although three-fourths of it were stolen from him. That I might not be a guest entirely useless, I took upon myself the direction of the garden and the inspection of the conduct of the gardener. Everything went on well until the fruit season, but as this became ripe, I observed that it disappeared without knowing in what manner it was disposed of. The gardener assured me it was the dormice which ate it all. I destroyed a great number of these animals, notwithstanding which the fruit still diminished. I watched the gardener's motions so narrowly, that I found he was the great dormouse. He lodged at Montmorency, whence he came in the night with his wife and children to take away the fruit he had concealed in the day-time, and which he sold in the market at Paris as publicly as if he had brought it from a garden of his own. This wretch, whom I loaded with kindness, whose children were clothed by Thérèse, and whose father, who was a beggar, I almost supported, robbed us with as much ease as effrontery, not one of the three being sufficiently vigilant to prevent him; and in one night he emptied my cellar, where next day I found nothing. Whilst he seemed to address himself to me only, I suffered everything, but being desirous of giving an account of the fruit, I was obliged to declare by whom a great part of it had been stolen. Madame d'Epinay desired me to pay and discharge him and look out for another: I did so. As this rascal rambled about the Hermitage in the night, armed with a thick club staff with an iron ferrule, and accompanied by other villains like himself, to relieve the Governesses, whom the man greatly terrified, from their fears, I made his successor sleep in the house with us; and this not being sufficient to remove their apprehensions, I sent to ask Madame d'Epinay for a musket, which I kept in the chamber of the gardener, with a charge not to make use of it except an attempt was made to break open the door or scale the walls of the garden, and to fire nothing but powder, meaning only to frighten the thieves. This was certainly the least precaution a man indisposed could take for the common safety of himself and his family, having to pass the winter in the midst of a wood, alone with two timid women. I also procured a little dog to serve as a sentinel. Deleyre coming to see me about this time, I related to him my situation, and we laughed together at my military apparatus. At his return to Paris he wished to amuse Diderot with the story, and by this means the group around Holbach learned that I was seriously resolved to pass the winter at the Hermitage. This perseverance, of which they had not imagined me to be capable, disconcerted them, and, until they could think of some other means of making my residence disagreeable to me, they sent back, by means of Diderot, the same Deleyre, who, though at first he had thought my precautions quite natural, now pretended to discover that they were inconsistent with my principles,[1] and styled them more than ridiculous in his letters, in which he overwhelmed me with pleasantries sufficiently bitter and satirical to offend me had I been the least disposed to take offence. But at that time being full of tender and affectionate sentiments, and not susceptible of any other, I perceived in his biting sarcasms nothing more than a jest, and believed him only jocose when others would have thought him mad.[2]

By my care and vigilance I guarded the garden so well, that, although there had been but little fruit that year, the produce was triple that of the preceding years: it is true, I spared no pains to preserve it, and I went so far as to escort what I sent to la Chevrette and to Epinay, and to carry baskets of it myself. The aunt and I carried one of these, I remember, which was so heavy that, ready to succumb beneath the weight, we were obliged to rest at every dozen steps, and when we arrived with it we were quite wet with perspiration.

As soon as the bad season began to confine me to the house, I wished to return to my indoor amusements, but this I found impossible. I had everywhere the two charming female friends before my eyes, their friend, everything by which they were surrounded, the country they inhabited, and the objects created or embellished for them by my imagination. I was no longer by myself for a moment, my delirium never left me. After many useless efforts to banish all these fictions from my mind, they at length seduced me, and my future endeavours were confined to giving them order and coherence, for the purpose of converting them into a species of novel.

What embarrassed me most was, that I had contradicted myself so openly and fully. After the severe principles I had just so publicly asserted, after the austere maxims I had so loudly preached, and my violent invectives against effeminate books, which breathed nothing but softness and love, could anything be less expected or more extraordinary, than to see me, with my own hand, write my name in the list of authors of those books I had so

---

[1] I wonder now at my stupidity in not seeing, when I wrote these words, that the spite with which the Holbachians saw me go to stay in the country was principally concerned with Madame le Vasseur, in that they no longer had her in their power to be of use to them in their systems of imposture by helping them with definite times and places. This idea, which came to me so late, perfectly explains their strange conduct, which is not to be understood on any other supposition. (*Note by Rousseau*, not in Geneva MS.)

[2] Paris MS. adds here: "Thus those who spoke of it had their trouble for nothing on this occasion, and I passed my winter no less tranquilly."

severely censured? I felt this incoherence in all its extent, I reproached myself with it, I blushed at it and was vexed; but all this could not bring me back to reason. Completely overcome, I was at all risks obliged to submit, and to resolve to brave the *what will the world say of it?* except only deliberating afterwards whether or not I should show my work, for I did not yet suppose I should ever determine to publish it.

J.-J., ABOUT FORTY-FIVE

This resolution taken, I entirely abandoned myself to my reveries, and, by frequently revolving these in my mind, formed with them the kind of plan of which the execution has been seen. This was certainly the greatest advantage that could be drawn from my follies; the love of good, which has never once been effaced from my heart, turned them towards useful objects, the moral of which might have produced its good effects. My voluptuous descriptions would have lost all their graces, had they been devoid of the colouring of innocence.

A weak girl is an object of pity, whom love may render interesting, and who frequently is not therefore the less amiable; but who can see without indignation the manners of the age, and what is more disgusting than the pride of an unchaste wife, who, openly treading under foot every duty, pretends that her husband ought to be grateful for her unwillingness to suffer herself to be taken in the fact? Perfect beings are not in nature, and their examples are not near enough to us. But whoever says that the description of a young person born with good dispositions, and a heart equally tender and virtuous, who suffers herself when a girl to be overcome by love, and when a woman, has resolution enough to conquer in her turn, and become virtuous again, is upon the whole scandalous and useless, is a liar and a hypocrite; hearken not to him.

Besides this object of morality and conjugal chastity which is radically connected with all social order, I had in view one more secret in behalf of concord and public peace, a greater, and perhaps more important object in itself, at least for that moment. The storm brought on by the *Encyclopédie*, far from being appeased, was at this time at its height. The two parties, exasperated against each other to the last degree of fury, soon resembled enraged wolves, set on for their mutual destruction, rather than Christians and philosophers, who had a reciprocal wish to enlighten and convince each other, and lead their brethren to the way of truth. Perhaps nothing more was wanting to each party than a few turbulent chiefs, who possessed a little power, to make this quarrel terminate in a civil war; and God only knows what a civil war of religion founded on each side upon the most cruel intolerance would have produced. Naturally an enemy to all spirit of party, I had freely spoken severe truths to each, to which they had not listened. I thought of another expedient, which, in my simplicity, appeared to be admirable: this was to abate their reciprocal hatred by destroying their prejudices, and showing to each party the virtue and merit which in the other was worthy of public esteem and respect. This project, little remarkable for its wisdom, which supposed sincerity in mankind, and whereby I fell into the error with which I reproached the Abbé de Saint Pierre, had the success that was to be expected from it; it drew together and united the parties for no other purpose than that of crushing the author. Until experience made me discover my folly, I gave my attention to it with a zeal worthy of the motive by which I was inspired; and I imagined the two characters of Wolmar and Julia, in an ecstasy which made me hope to render them both amiable, and, what is still more, by means of each other.

Satisfied with having made a rough sketch of my plan, I returned to the situations in detail, which I had marked out; and from the arrangement I gave them resulted the two first parts of the *Julie*, which I finished during the winter with inexpressible pleasure, procuring gilt paper to receive a fair copy of them, azure and silver powder to dry the writing, and blue narrow ribbon to tack my sheets together; in a word, I thought nothing sufficiently elegant and delicate for my two charming girls; of whom, like another Pygmalion,[1] I became madly enamoured. Every evening, by the fireside, I read the two parts to the Governesses. The daughter, without saying a word, was, like myself, moved to tenderness, and we mingled our sighs; her mother, finding there were no compliments, understood nothing of the matter, remained unmoved, and at the intervals when I was silent, always repeated: *Sir, that is very fine.*

Madame d'Epinay, uneasy at my being alone, in winter, in a solitary house, in the midst of woods, often sent to inquire after my health. I never had such real proofs of her friendship for me, to which mine never more fully answered. It would be wrong in me were not I, amongst these proofs, to make special mention of her portrait, which she sent me, at the same time requesting instructions from me in what manner she might have mine, painted by La Tour, and which had been shown at the Salon. I ought equally to speak of another proof of her attention to me, which, although it be laughable, is a feature in the history of my character, on account of the impression received from it. One day when it froze to an extreme degree, in opening a packet she had sent me of several things I had desired her to purchase for me, I found a little under-petticoat of English flannel, which she told me she had worn, and desired I would make of it an under-waistcoat. The tone of her note was charming, frank and caressing. This care, more than friendly, appeared to me so tender, and as if she had stripped herself to clothe me, that in my emotion I repeatedly kissed, shedding tears at the same time, both the note and the petticoat.

Thérèse thought me mad. It is singular that of all the marks of friendship Madame d'Epinay ever showed me, this touched me the most, and that even since our rupture I have never recollected it without being very sensibly affected. I for a long time preserved her little note, and this would still have been in my possession had it not shared the fate of my other notes received at the same period.

Although my disorder then gave me but little respite in winter, and that a part of the interval I was reduced to the use of bougies,

---

[1] Paris MS. adds: "despite my already greying beard."

this was still upon the whole the season which since my residence
in France I had passed with most pleasure and tranquillity. During four or five months, whilst the bad weather sheltered me from
the interruptions of importunate visits, I tasted to a greater degree
than I had ever yet or have since done, of that equal simple and
independent life, the enjoyment of which still made it more desirable to me; without any other company than the two Governesses
in reality, and the two female cousins in idea. It was then especially that I daily congratulated myself upon the resolution
I had had the good sense to take, unmindful of the clamours of
my friends, who were vexed at seeing me delivered from their
tyranny; and when I heard of the attempt of a madman,[1] when
Deleyre and Madame d'Epinay spoke to me in their letters of the
trouble and agitation which reigned in Paris, how thankful was
I to heaven for having placed me at a distance from all such
spectacles of horror and guilt. These would have continued and
increased the bilious humour which the sight of public disorders
had given me; whilst seeing nothing around me in my retirement
but gay and pleasing objects, my heart was wholly abandoned to
sentiments which were amiable.

I remark here with pleasure the course of the last peaceful
moments that were left me. The spring succeeding to this winter,
which had been so calm, developed the germ of the misfortunes
I have yet to describe; in the tissue of which, a like interval,
wherein I had leisure to respire, will not be found.

I think however, I recollect, that during this interval of peace,
and in the bosom of my solitude, I was not quite undisturbed by
the Holbachians. Diderot stirred me up some strife, and I am
much deceived if it was not in the course of this winter that the
Fils Naturel, of which I shall soon have occasion to speak, made
its appearance. Independently of the causes yet to be spoken of,
I have left me but few papers relative to that period, and even
those which I have been able to preserve are not very exact with
respect to dates. Diderot never dated his letters. Madame d'Epinay
and Madame d'Houdetot seldom dated theirs, except by the day
of the week, and Deleyre mostly confined himself to the same rule.
When I was desirous of putting their letters in order I was obliged
to supply what was wanting by guessing at dates, so uncertain
that I cannot depend upon them. Unable therefore to fix with
certainty the beginning of these quarrels, I prefer relating in one
subsequent article everything I can recollect concerning them.

[1] Damiens' attempt on Louis XV.

The return of spring had increased my amorous delirium, and in my melancholy occasioned by the excess of my transports, I had composed for the last parts of *Julie*, several letters wherein evident marks of the rapture in which I wrote them are found. Amongst others I may quote those from the Elysée, and the excursion upon the lake, which, if my memory does not deceive me, are at the end of the fourth part. Whoever, in reading these two letters, does not feel his heart soften and melt into the tenderness by which they were dictated, ought to lay down the book: nature has refused him the means of judging of sentiment.

Precisely at the same time, I received a second unforeseen visit from Madame d'Houdetot in the absence of her husband, who was captain of the Gendarmerie, and of her lover, who also was in the service. She had come to Eaubonne, in the middle of the valley of Montmorency, where she had taken a pretty house; from thence she made a new excursion to the Hermitage. She came on horseback, and dressed in men's clothes. Although I am not very fond of this kind of masquerade, I was struck with the romantic appearance she made, and, for once, it was with love. As this was the first and only time in all my life, the consequences of which will for ever render it terrible to my remembrance, I must take the permission to enter into some particulars on the subject.

The Countess d'Houdetot was nearly thirty years of age, and not handsome; her face was marked with the smallpox, her complexion coarse; she was short-sighted, and her eyes were rather round; but she had with all this an air of youth, and her lively yet gentle face was attractive. She had a mass of fine long black hair, which hung down in natural curls below her waist; her figure was agreeable, and she was at once both awkward and graceful in her motions; her wit was natural and pleasing; to this, gaiety, heedlessness, and ingenuity were perfectly suited; she abounded in charming sallies, after which she so little sought, that they sometimes escaped her lips in spite of herself. She possessed several agreeable talents, played the harpsichord, danced well, and wrote pleasing poetry. Her character was angelic; this was founded upon a sweetness of mind, and, except prudence and fortitude, contained in it every virtue. She was besides so much to be depended upon in all intercourse, so faithful in society, that even her enemies were not under the necessity of concealing from her their secrets. I mean by her enemies the men, or rather the women, by whom she was not beloved, for as to herself she had not a heart capable of hatred, and I am of opinion this conformity with mine

greatly contributed towards inspiring me with a passion for her.
In the confidence of the most intimate friendship, I never heard
her speak ill of persons who were absent, nor even of her sister-in-
law. She could neither conceal her thoughts from any one, nor
disguise any of her sentiments, and I am persuaded she spoke of
her lover to her husband, as she spoke of him to her friends and
acquaintance, and to everybody without distinction of persons.

MME. D'HOUDETOT

What proved, beyond all manner of doubt, the purity and sincerity of her nature was that, subject to very extraordinary ab-
sences of mind, and the most laughable thoughtlessness, she was
often guilty of some very imprudent ones with respect to herself,
but never in the least offensive to any person whatsoever.

She had been married very young and against her inclinations
to the Comte d'Houdetot, a man of fashion, and a good officer; but
a man who loved play and chicane, who was not very amiable,

and whom she never loved. She found in M. de Saint Lambert all the merit of her husband, with more agreeable qualities of mind, joined with wit, virtue and talents. If anything in the manners of the age can be pardoned, it is an attachment which duration renders more pure, to which its effects do honour, and which becomes cemented by reciprocal esteem.

It was a little from inclination, as I am disposed to think, but much more to please St. Lambert, that she came to see me. He had requested her to do it; and there was reason to believe the friendship which began to be established between us, would render this society agreeable to all three. She knew I was acquainted with their connexion, and as she could speak to me of him without restraint, it was natural she should find my conversation agreeable. She came; I saw her; I was intoxicated with love without an object; this intoxication fascinated my eyes, the object fixed itself upon her. I saw my Julie in Madame d'Houdetot, and I soon saw nothing but Madame d'Houdetot, but with all the perfections with which I had just adorned the idol of my heart. To complete my delirium she spoke to me of St. Lambert with all the fondness of a passionate lover. — Contagious force of love! while listening to her, and perceiving myself near her, I was seized with a delicious trembling which I had never before experienced when near to any person whatsoever. She spoke, and I felt myself affected; I thought I was nothing more than interested by her sentiments, when I perceived I possessed those which were similar: I drank deeply of the empoisoned cup, of which I yet tasted nothing more than the sweetness. Finally, imperceptibly to us both, she inspired me for herself with all she expressed for her lover. Alas! it was very late in life, and cruel was it to consume with a passion not less violent than unfortunate for a woman whose heart was already in the possession of another.

Notwithstanding the extraordinary emotions I had felt when near to her, I did not at first perceive what had happened to me; it was not until after her departure that, wishing to think of Julie, I was struck with surprise at being unable to think of anything but Madame d'Houdetot. Then was it that my eyes were opened: I felt my misfortune, and lamented what had happened, but I did not foresee the consequences.

I hesitated a long time on the manner in which I should conduct myself towards her, as if real love left behind it sufficient reason to deliberate and act accordingly. I had not yet determined upon this when she unexpectedly returned and found me unprovided. I was, by this time, perfectly acquainted with my situation. Shame, the companion of evil, rendered me dumb, and made me tremble in her presence; I neither dared to open my mouth nor raise my eyes; I was in an inexpressible confusion which it was impossible she should not perceive. I resolved to confess to her my troubled state of mind, and left her to guess the cause whence it proceeded: this was telling it her in terms sufficiently clear.

Had I been young and amiable, and Madame d'Houdetot afterwards weak, I should here blame her conduct; but this was not the case, and I am obliged to applaud and admire it. The resolution she took was equally prudent and generous. She could not suddenly break with me without giving her reasons for it to St. Lambert, who himself had desired her to come and see me; this would have exposed two friends to a rupture, and perhaps a public one which she wished to avoid. She had for me esteem and good wishes; she pitied my folly without encouraging it, and endeavoured to restore me to reason. She was glad to preserve to her lover and herself a friend, for whom she had some respect; and she spoke of nothing with more pleasure than the intimate and agreeable society we might form between us three the moment I should become reasonable. She did not always confine herself to these friendly exhortations, and, in case of need, did not spare me more severe reproaches that I had richly deserved.

I spared myself still less: the moment I was alone, I began to recover; I was more calm after my declaration; love known to the person by whom it is inspired, becomes more supportable. The forcible manner in which I reproached myself with mine ought to have cured me of it had the thing been possible. What powerful motives did I call to my aid to stifle it! My morals, sentiments, and principles; the shame, the treachery, and crime, of abusing what was confided to friendship, and the ridiculousness of burning, at my age, with the most extravagant passion for an object whose heart was pre-engaged, and who could neither make me a return nor leave me the least hope; moreover with a passion which, far from having anything to gain by constancy, daily became less sufferable.

Who would imagine that the last consideration, which ought to have added weight to all the others, was that whereby I eluded them? What scruple, thought I, ought I to make of a folly prejudicial to nobody but myself? Am I then a young man of whom Madame d'Houdetot ought to be afraid? Would not it be said, by my presumptuous remorse, that, by my gallantry, manner, and dress, I was going to seduce her? Poor Jean-Jacques, love on at thy ease, in all safety of conscience, and be not afraid that thy sighs will be prejudicial to St. Lambert.

It has been seen that I never was a coxcomb, not even in my youth. The manner of thinking, of which I have spoken, was according to my turn of mind, it flattered my passion; this was sufficient to induce me to abandon myself to it without reserve, and to laugh even at the impertinent scruple I thought I had made from vanity, rather than from reason. This is a great lesson for virtuous minds, that vice never attacks openly: it finds means to surprise them by masking itself with sophisms, and not unfrequently with a virtue.

Guilty without remorse, I soon became so without measure; and I entreat it may be observed in what manner my passion followed my nature, at length to plunge me into the abyss. In the first place, it assumed an air of humility to encourage me; and to render me intrepid, it carried this humility even to mistrust. Madame d'Houdetot, incessantly putting me in mind of my duty, without once for a single moment flattering my folly, treated me with the greatest mildness, and remained with me upon the footing of the most tender friendship. This friendship would, I protest, have satisfied my wishes, had I thought it sincere; but finding it too strong to be real, I took it into my head that love, so ill suited to my age and appearance, had rendered me contemptible in the eyes of Madame d'Houdetot; that this young mad creature only wished to divert herself with me and my superannuated passion; that she had communicated this to St. Lambert; and that the indignation caused by my breach of friendship having made her lover enter into her views, they were agreed to turn my head, and then to laugh at me. This folly, which at twenty-six years of age had made me guilty of some extravagant behaviour to Madame de Larnage, whom I did not know, would have been pardonable in me at forty-five with Madame d'Houdetot had not I known that she and her lover were two persons of too much uprightness to indulge themselves in such a barbarous amusement.

Madame d'Houdetot continued her visits, which I delayed not to return. She, as well as myself, was fond of walking, and we took long walks in an enchanting country. Satisfied with loving and daring to say I loved, I should have been in the most agreeable situation had not my extravagance spoiled all the charm of it. She, at first, could not comprehend the foolish pettishness with which I received her attentions; but my heart, incapable of concealing what passes in it, did not long leave her ignorant of my suspicions; she endeavoured to laugh at them, but this expedient did not succeed; transports of rage would have been the consequence, and she changed her tone. Her compassionate gentleness was invincible: she made me reproaches which penetrated my heart; she expressed an inquietude at my unjust fears, of which I took advantage. I required proofs of her being in earnest. She perceived there was no other means of relieving me from my apprehensions. I became pressing: the step was delicate. It is astonishing, and perhaps without example, that a woman having suffered herself to be brought to hesitate, should have got herself off so well. She refused me nothing the most tender friendship could grant; yet she granted me nothing that rendered her unfaithful, and I had the mortification to see that the disorder into which her most trifling favours had thrown all my senses, had not the least effect upon hers.

I have somewhere said that nothing should be granted to the senses when we wish to refuse them anything. To prove how false this maxim was relative to Madame d'Houdetot, and how far she was right to depend upon her own strength of mind, it would be necessary to enter into the detail of our long and frequent conversations, and follow them, in all their liveliness, during the four months we passed together in an intimacy almost without example between two friends of different sexes, who contain themselves within the bounds which we never exceeded. Ah! if I had lived so long without feeling the power of real love, my heart and senses abundantly paid the arrears. What therefore are the transports we feel with the object of our affections by whom we are beloved, since the passion of which my idol did not partake inspired such as I felt!

But I am wrong in saying Madame d'Houdetot did not partake of the passion of love; that I felt was in some measure shared; love was equal on both sides, but not reciprocal. We were both intoxicated with the passion, she for her lover, and I for herself; our sighs and delicious tears were mingled together. Tender confidants of the secrets of each other, there was so great a similarity in our sentiments that it was impossible that they should not find some common point of union. In the midst of this delicious intoxication, she never forgot herself for a moment, and I solemnly protest that, if ever, led away by my senses, I have attempted to render her unfaithful, I was never really desirous of succeeding. The vehemence itself of my passion contained it within bounds.

The duty of self-denial had elevated my mind. The lustre of every virtue adorned in my eyes the idol of my heart: to have soiled their divine image would have been to destroy it. I might have committed the crime; it has been a hundred times committed in my heart; but, to dishonour my Sophie! Ah, was this ever possible? No: I have told her a hundred times it was not. Had I had it in my power to satisfy my desires, had she consented to commit herself to my discretion, I should, except in a few minutes of delirium, have refused to be happy at the price of her honour. I loved her too well to wish to possess her.

The distance from the Hermitage to Eaubonne is almost a league; in my frequent excursions to it I have sometimes slept there. One evening after having supped tête-à-tête, we went for a walk in the garden by a fine moonlight. At the bottom of the garden is a considerable copse, through which we passed in our way to a pretty grove ornamented with a cascade of which I had given her the idea, and she had procured it to be executed accordingly.

Eternal remembrance of innocence and enjoyment! It was in this grove that, seated by her side upon a seat of turf under an acacia in full bloom, I found for the emotions of my heart a language worthy of them. It was the first and only time of my life; but I was sublime, if everything amiable and seducing with which the most tender and ardent love can inspire the heart of man, can be so called. What intoxicating tears did I shed upon her knees! how many did I make her shed involuntarily! At length in an involuntary transport, she exclaimed: No, never was man so amiable, nor ever was there one who loved like you! But your friend St. Lambert hears us, and my heart is incapable of loving twice. I exhausted myself with sighs: I embraced her — what an embrace! But this was all. She had lived alone for the last six months, that is, absent from her husband and lover; I had seen her almost every day during three months, and love seldom failed to make a third. We had supped tête-à-tête, we were alone in a grove by moonlight, and after two hours of the most lively and tender conversation, she left this grove at midnight, and the arms of her lover, as morally and physically pure as she had entered it. Reader, weigh all these circumstances; I will add nothing more.

Do not however imagine that in this situation my passions left me as undisturbed, as I was with Thérèse and Mamma. I have already observed I was this time inspired not only with love, but with love in all its energy and fury. I will not describe either the agitations, tremblings, palpitations, convulsive emotions, nor

faintings of the heart, I continually experienced; these may be
judged of by the effect her image alone made upon me. I have
observed the distance from the Hermitage to Eaubonne was considerable; I went by the hills of Andilly, which are delightful.
I mused, as I walked, on her whom I was going to see, the charming reception she would give me, and upon the kiss which awaited
me at my arrival. This single kiss, this pernicious embrace, even
before I received it, enflamed my blood to such a degree as to
affect my head; my eyes were dazzled, my knees trembled, and
were unable to support me; and I was obliged to stop and sit down;
my whole frame was in inconceivable disorder, and I was upon
the point of fainting. Knowing the danger, I endeavoured, at
setting out, to divert my attention from the object, and think of
something else. I had not proceeded twenty steps before the same
recollections, and all that was the consequence of them, assailed
me in such a manner that it was impossible to avoid them, and in
spite of all my efforts I do not believe I ever made this little excursion alone with impunity. I arrived at Eaubonne weak, exhausted,
and scarcely able to support myself. The moment I saw her everything was repaired; all I felt in her presence was the importunity
of an inexhaustible and useless ardour. Upon the road to Eaubonne
there was a pleasant terrace, called Mount Olympus, at which we
sometimes met. I arrived first, it was proper I should wait for her;
but how dear this waiting cost me! To divert my attention I endeavoured to write with my pencil letters which I could have
written with the purest drops of my blood; I never could finish
one which was legible. When she found a note in the niche upon
which we had agreed, all she learned from the contents was the
deplorable state in which I was when I wrote it. This state and
its continuation, during three months of irritation and self-denial,
so exhausted me that I was several years before I recovered from
it, and at the end of these it left me an ailment which I shall carry
with me, or which will carry me, to the grave. Such was the sole
amorous enjoyment of a man of the most combustible constitution,
but who was, at the same time, perhaps one of the most timid
mortals nature ever produced. Such were the last happy days I
can reckon upon earth; at the end of these began the long train
of evils, in which there will be found but little interruption.

It has been seen that, during the whole course of my life, my
heart, as transparent as crystal, has never been capable of concealing for the space of a moment, any sentiment in the least
lively, which had taken refuge in it. It will therefore be judged

whether or not it was possible for me long to conceal my affection for Madame d'Houdetot. Our intimacy struck the eyes of everybody, we did not make of it either a secret or a mystery. It was not of a nature to require any such precaution, and as Madame d'Houdetot had for me the most tender friendship with which she did not reproach herself, and I for her an esteem with the justice of which nobody is better acquainted than myself; she, frank, absent, heedless; I, true, awkward, haughty, impatient, and choleric; we exposed ourselves more in deceitful security than we should have done had we been culpable. We both went to la Chevrette; we sometimes met there even by appointment. We lived there according to our accustomed manner; walking together every day, talking of our amours, our duties, our friend, and our innocent projects; all this in the park opposite the apartment of Madame d'Epinay, under her windows, whence incessantly examining us, and thinking herself braved, she by her eyes filled her heart with rage and indignation.

Women have the art of concealing their anger, especially when it is great. Madame d'Epinay, violent but deliberate, possessed this art to an eminent degree. She feigned not to see or suspect anything, and at the same time that she doubled toward me her cares, attention, and allurements, she affected to load her sister-in-law with incivilities and marks of disdain, which she, seemingly, wished to communicate to me. It will be easily imagined she did not succeed: but I was on the rack. Torn by opposite passions, at the same time that I was sensible of her caresses, I could scarcely contain my anger when I saw her wanting in good manners to Madame d'Houdetot. The angelic sweetness of this lady made her endure everything without a complaint, or even without being offended.

She was in fact so absent, and always so little attentive to these things, that half the time she did not perceive them.

I was so taken up with my passion, that, seeing nothing but Sophie (one of the names of Madame d'Houdetot), I did not perceive that I was becoming the laughing-stock of the whole house, and all those who came to it. The Baron d'Holbach, who never, as I had heard of, had been at le Chevrette, was one of the latter. Had I at that time been as mistrustful as I am since become, I should strongly have suspected Madame d'Epinay to have contrived this journey to give the Baron the amusing spectacle of the Amorous Citizen. But I was then so stupid that I saw not that even which was glaring to everybody. My stupidity did not, however, prevent me from finding in the Baron a more jovial and satisfied appearance than the ordinary. Instead of looking upon me with his usual moroseness, he said to me a hundred jocose things without my knowing what he meant. Surprise was painted in my countenance, but I answered not a word: Madame d'Epinay shook her sides with laughing; I knew not what possessed them. As nothing yet passed the bounds of pleasantry, the best thing I could have done, had I been in the secret, would have been to have humoured the joke. It is true, I perceived amid the rallying gaiety of the Baron, that his eyes sparkled with a malicious joy, which would have given me pain had I then remarked it to the degree it has since occurred to my recollection.

PAUL HENRI THIRY, BARON D'HOLBACH

One day when I went to see Madame d'Houdetot at Eaubonne, after her return from one of her journeys to Paris, I found her melancholy, and observed that she had been weeping. I was obliged to put a restraint on myself, because Madame de Blainville, sister to her husband, was present; but the moment I found an opportunity, I expressed to her my uneasiness. Ah! said she, with a sigh, I am much afraid your follies will cost me the repose of the rest of my days. St. Lambert has been informed of what has passed, and has informed me of it. He does me justice, but he is vexed; and what is still worse, he conceals from me a part of his vexation. Fortunately I have not concealed from him anything relative to our connexion, which was formed under his auspices. My letters, like my heart, were full of yourself; I made him acquainted with everything, except your extravagant passion, of which I hoped to cure you, and which, without speaking of it to me, I see he imputes to me as a crime. Somebody has done us ill offices: I have been injured, but what does this signify? either let us entirely break with each other, or do you be what you ought to be. I will not in future have anything to conceal from my lover.

This was the first moment in which I was sensible of the shame of feeling myself humbled by the sentiment of my fault, in presence of a young woman whose just reproaches I received, and to whom I ought to have been a Mentor. The indignation I felt against myself, would, perhaps, have been sufficient to overcome my weakness, had not the tender passion inspired in me by the victim of it again softened my heart. Alas! was this a moment to harden it when it was overflowed by the tears which penetrated it in every part? This tenderness was soon changed into rage against the vile informers, who had seen nothing but the evil of a criminal but involuntary sentiment, without believing or even imagining the sincere uprightness of heart by which it was counteracted. We did not remain long in doubt about the hand by which the blow was directed.

We both knew that Madame d'Epinay corresponded with St. Lambert. This was not the first storm she had raised up against Madame d'Houdetot, from whom she had made a thousand efforts to detach her lover, the success of some of which made the consequences to be dreaded. Besides, Grimm who, I think, had accompanied M. de Castries to the army, was in Westphalia as well as St. Lambert; they sometimes visited. Grimm had made some attempts on Madame d'Houdetot which had not succeeded, and, being extremely piqued, suddenly discontinued his visits to her. Let it be judged with what calmness, modest as he is known to be, he supposed she preferred to him a man older than himself, and of whom, since he had frequented the great, he had never spoken but as of a person he protected.

My suspicions of Madame d'Epinay were changed into a certainty the moment I heard what had passed in my own house. When I was at la Chevrette, Thérèse frequently came there, either to bring me letters or pay me that attention which my ill state of health rendered necessary. Madame d'Epinay had asked her if

Madame d'Houdetot and I did not write to each other. Upon her answering in the affirmative, Madame d'Epinay pressed her to give her the letters of Madame d'Houdetot, assuring her she would re-seal them in such a manner as it should never be known. Thérèse, without showing how much she was shocked at the proposition, and without even putting me upon my guard, did nothing more than seal the letters she brought me more carefully; a lucky precaution, for Madame d'Epinay had her watched when she arrived, and waiting for her in the passage, several times carried her audaciousness so far as to examine her tucker. She did more even than this: having one day invited herself with M. de Margency to dinner at the Hermitage, for the first time since I had resided there, she seized the moment I was walking with Margency, to go into my closet with the mother and daughter, and to press them to show her the letters of Madame d'Houdetot. Had the mother known where the letters were, they would have been given to her; but, fortunately, the daughter was the only person who was in the secret, and denied my having preserved any one of them. A virtuous, faithful, and generous falsehood; whilst truth would have been a perfidy. Madame d'Epinay, perceiving Thérèse was not to be seduced, endeavoured to irritate her by jealousy, reproaching her with her easy temper and blindness. How is it possible, said she to her, you cannot perceive there is a criminal intercourse between them? If besides what strikes your eyes you stand in need of other proofs, lend your assistance to obtain that which may furnish them: you say he tears the letters from Madame d'Houdetot, as soon as he has read them. Well; carefully gather up the pieces and give them to me; I will take upon myself to put them together. Such were the lessons my friend gave to the partner of my bed.

Thérèse had the discretion to conceal from me, for a considerable time, all these attempts; but, perceiving how much I was perplexed, she thought herself obliged to inform me of everything, to the end that, knowing with whom I had to do, I might take my measures to avoid the treachery preparing for me. My rage and indignation are not to be described. Instead of dissembling with Madame d'Epinay, according to her own example, and making use of counter-plots, I abandoned myself without reserve to the natural impetuosity of my temper; and with my accustomed inconsiderateness, came to an open rupture. My imprudence will be judged of by the following letters, which sufficiently show the manner of proceeding of both parties on this occasion.

NOTE FROM MADAME D'EPINAY

'Why, my dear friend, do not I see you? You make me uneasy. You have so often promised me to do nothing but go and come between this place and the Hermitage! In this I have left you at liberty; and you have suffered a week to pass without coming. Had not I been told you were well I should have imagined the contrary. I expected you either the day before yesterday, or yesterday, but found myself disappointed. My God, what is the matter with you? You have no business, nor can you have any uneasiness; for, had this been the case, I flatter myself you would have come and communicated it to me. You are, therefore, ill! relieve me, I beseech you, speedily from my fears. Adieu, my dear friend: let this adieu produce me a good morning from you.'

ANSWER

'I cannot yet say anything to you. I wait to be better informed, and this I shall be sooner or later. In the meantime be persuaded that innocence accused will find a defender sufficiently powerful to cause some repentance in the slanderers, be they who they may.'

SECOND NOTE FROM THE SAME

'Do you know that your letter frightens me? What does it mean? I have read it more than twenty-five times. In truth I do not understand what it means. All I can perceive is, that you are uneasy and tormented, and that you wait until you are no longer so before you speak to me upon the subject. Is this, my dear friend, what we agreed upon? What then is become of that friendship and confidence, and by what means have I lost them? Is it with me or for me that you are angry? However this may be, come to me this evening, I conjure you: remember you promised me no longer than a week ago to let nothing remain upon your mind, but immediately to communicate to me whatever might make it uneasy. My dear friend, I live in that confidence —— There —— I have just read your letter again; I do not understand the contents better, but they make me tremble. You seem to be cruelly agitated. I could wish to calm your mind, but as I am ignorant of the cause whence your uneasiness arises, I know not what to say, except that I am as wretched as yourself, and shall remain so until we meet. If you are not here this evening at six o'clock, I set off to-morrow for the Hermitage let the weather be how it will, and in whatever state of health I may be; for I can no longer support the inquietude I now feel. Good-day, my dear friend; at all risks I take the liberty to tell you, without knowing whether or not you are in need of such advice, to endeavour to take care, and to stop the progress uneasiness makes in solitude. A fly becomes a monster. I have frequently experienced it.'

ANSWER

'I can neither come to see you nor receive your visit so long as my present inquietude continues. The confidence of which you speak no longer exists, and it will not be easy for you to recover it. I see nothing more in your present anxiety than the desire of drawing from the confessions of others some advantage agreeable to your views; and my heart, so ready to pour its overflowings into another which opens itself to receive them, is shut against trick and cunning. I distinguish your ordinary address in the difficulty you find in understanding my note. Do you think me dupe enough to believe you have not comprehended what it meant? No: but I shall know how to overcome your subtleties by my frankness. I will explain myself more clearly that you may understand me still less.

'Two lovers closely united and worthy of each other's love are dear to me; I expect you will not know who I mean unless I name them. I presume attempts have been made to disunite them, and that I have been made use of to inspire one of the two with jealousy. The choice was not judicious, but it appeared convenient to the purposes of malice, and of this malice it is you whom I suspect to be guilty. I hope this becomes more clear.

'Thus the woman whom I most esteem would, with my knowledge, have been loaded with the infamy of dividing her heart and person between two lovers, and I with that of being one of these wretches. If I knew that, for a single moment in your life, you ever had thought this, either of her or myself, I should hate you until my last hour. But it is with having said, and not with having thought it, that I charge you. In this case, I cannot comprehend which of the three you wished to injure; but, if you love peace of mind, tremble lest you should have succeeded. I have not concealed either from you or her all the ill I think of certain connexions, but I wish these to end by a means as virtuous as their cause, and that an illegitimate love may be changed into an eternal friendship. Should I, who never do ill to any person, be the innocent means of doing it to my friends? No, I should never forgive you; I should become your irreconcilable enemy. Your secrets are all I should respect; for I will never be a man without honour.

'I do not apprehend my present perplexity will continue a long time. I shall soon know whether or not I am deceived. I shall then perhaps have great injuries to repair, which I will do with as much cheerfulness as that with which the most agreeable act of my life has been accompanied. But do you know in what manner I will make amends for my faults during the short space of time I have to remain near to you? By doing what nobody but myself would do; by telling you freely what the world thinks of you, and the breaches you have to repair in your reputation. Notwithstanding all the pretended friends by whom you are surrounded, the moment you see me depart, you may bid adieu to truth; you will no longer find any person who will tell it you.'

THIRD LETTER FROM THE SAME

'I did not understand your letter of this morning: this I told you because it was the case. I understand that of this evening; do not imagine I shall ever return an answer to it, I am too anxious to forget what it contains; and although you excite my pity, I am not proof against the bitterness with which it has filled my mind. I! descend to trick and cunning with you! I! accused of the blackest of all infamies! Adieu, I regret your having the —— adieu. I know not what I say —— adieu: I shall be very anxious to forgive you. You will come when you please; you will be better received than your suspicions deserve. All I have to desire of you is not to trouble yourself about my reputation. The opinion of the world concerning me is of but little importance in my esteem. My conduct is good, and this is sufficient for me. Besides I am ignorant of what has happened to the two persons who are as dear to me as they are to you.'

This last letter extricated me from a terrible embarrassment and threw me into another of almost the same magnitude. Although these letters and answers were sent and returned the same day with an extreme rapidity, the interval had been sufficient to place another between my transports of rage, and to give me time to reflect of the enormity of my imprudence. Madame d'Houdetot had not recommended to me anything so much as to remain quiet, to leave her the care of extricating herself, and to avoid, especially at that moment, all noise and rupture; and I, by the most open and atrocious insults, took the properest means

of carrying rage to its greatest height in the heart of a woman who
was already but too well disposed to it. I now could naturally
expect nothing from her but an answer so haughty, disdainful,
and expressive of contempt, that I could not, without the utmost
meanness, do otherwise than immediately quit her house. Happily she, more adroit than I was furious, avoided, by the manner
of her answer, reducing me to that extremity. But it was necessary either to quit or immediately go and see her; the alternative
was inevitable. I resolved on the latter, though I foresaw how
much I must be embarrassed in the explanation. For how was I
to get through it without exposing either Madame d'Houdetot or
Thérèse? and woe to her whom I should have named! There was
nothing that the vengeance of an implacable and an intriguing
woman did not make me fear for the person who should be the
object of it. It was to prevent this misfortune that in my letter
I had spoken of nothing but suspicions, that I might not be under
the necessity of producing my proofs. This, it is true, rendered
my transports less excusable, no simple suspicions being sufficient
to authorize me to treat a woman, and especially a friend, in the
manner I had treated Madame d'Epinay. But here begins the
noble task I worthily fulfilled of expiating my faults and secret
weaknesses by charging myself with such of the former as I was
incapable of committing, and which I never did commit.

I had not to bear the attack I had expected, and fear was the
greatest evil I received from it. At my approach, Madame d'Epinay threw her arms about my neck, bursting into tears. This
unexpected reception, and by an old friend, extremely affected
me: I also shed many tears. I said to her a few words which had
not much meaning; she uttered others with still less, and everything ended here. Supper was served; we sat down to table, where,
in expectation of the explanation I imagined to be deferred until
supper was over, I made a very poor figure; for I am so overpowered by the most trifling inquietude of mind that I cannot
conceal it from persons the least clear-sighted. My embarrassed
appearance must have given her courage, yet she did not risk anything upon that foundation. There was no more explanation after
than before supper; none took place on the next day, and our little
tête-à-tête conversations consisted of indifferent things, or some
complimentary words on my part, by which, while I informed
her I could not say more relative to my suspicions, I asserted with
the greatest truth, that, if they were ill-founded, my whole life
should be employed in repairing the injustice. She did not show

the least curiosity to know precisely what they were, nor for what reason I had formed them, and all our peace-making consisted, on her part as well as on mine, in the embrace at our first meeting. Since Madame d'Epinay was the only person offended, at least in form, I thought it was not for me to strive to bring about an explanation for which she herself did not seem anxious, and I returned as I had come; continuing, besides, to live with her upon the same footing as before, I soon almost entirely forgot the quarrel, and foolishly believed she had done the same, because she seemed not to remember what had passed.

This, as it will soon appear, was not the only vexation caused me by weakness; but I had others not less disagreeable, which I had not brought upon myself. The only cause of these was a desire of forcing me from my solitude,[1] by means of tormenting me. These originated from Diderot and the d'Holbach group. Since I had resided at the Hermitage, Diderot incessantly harassed me, either himself or by means of Deleyre, and I soon perceived from the pleasantries of the latter upon my ramblings in the groves, with what pleasure he had travestied the hermit into the gallant shepherd. But this was not the question in my quarrels with Diderot; the causes of these were more serious. After the publication of the *Fils Naturel*, he had sent me a copy of it, which I had read with the interest and attention I ever bestowed on the works of a friend. In reading the kind of poetic dialogue annexed to it, I was surprised and rather grieved to find in it, amongst several things, disobliging but supportable, against men in solitude, this bitter and severe sentence without the least softening: *Only the wicked man is alone.* This sentence is equivocal, and seems to present a double meaning; the one true, the other false; since it is impossible that a man who is determined to remain alone can do the least harm to anybody, and consequently he cannot be wicked. The sentence in itself therefore required an interpretation; the more so from an author who, when he sent it to the press, had a friend retired from the world. It appeared to me shocking and uncivil, either to have forgotten that solitary friend, or, in remembering him, not to have made from the general maxim the honourable and just exception which he owed not only to his friend, but to so many respectable sages, who, in all

---

[1] That is, to take from it the old woman who was wanted in the conspiracy. It is astonishing that, during this long quarrel, my stupid confidence prevented me from comprehending that it was not I but she whom they wanted at Paris. (*Note by Rousseau*, not in Paris MS.)

ages, have sought for peace and tranquillity in retirement, and of
whom, for the first time since the creation of the world, a writer
took it into his head indiscriminately with a single stroke of the
pen to make so many villains.

I had great affection and the most sincere esteem for Diderot,
and fully depended upon his having the same sentiments for me.
But tired with his indefatigable obstinacy in continually opposing my inclinations, taste, and manner of living, and everything
which related to no person but myself; shocked at seeing a man
younger than I was wish, at all events, to govern me like a child;
disgusted with his facility in promising, and his negligence in performing; weary of so many appointments given by himself and
capriciously broken, while new ones were again given only to be
again broken; displeased at uselessly waiting for him three or four
times a month on the days he had assigned, and in dining alone
at night after having gone to Saint Denis to meet him, and waited
the whole day for his coming; my heart was already full of these
multiplied injuries. This last appeared to me still more serious,
and gave me infinite pain. I wrote to complain of it, but in so mild
and tender a manner that I moistened my paper with my tears,
and my letter was sufficiently affecting to have drawn others from
himself. It would be impossible to guess his answer on this subject; it was literally as follows: I am glad my work has pleased
and affected you. You are not of my opinion relative to hermits.
Say as much good of them as you please, you will be the only one
in the world of whom I shall think well: even on this there would
be much to say were it impossible to speak to you without giving
you offence. A woman eighty years of age! etc. A phrase of a
letter from the son of Madame d'Epinay, which, if I know you
well, must have given you much pain, has been mentioned to me.

The two last expressions of this letter want explanation.

Soon after I went to reside at the Hermitage, Madame le Vasseur seemed dissatisfied with her situation, and to think the habitation too retired. Having heard she had expressed her dislike to
the place, I offered to send her back to Paris, if that were more
agreeable to her; to pay her lodging, and to have the same care
taken of her as if she had remained with me. She rejected my
offer, assured me she was very well satisfied with the Hermitage,
and that the country air was of service to her. This was evident,
for, if I may so speak, she seemed to become young again, and
enjoyed better health than at Paris. Her daughter told me her
mother would, on the whole, have been very sorry to quit the

Hermitage, which was really a delightful abode, being fond of the little amusements of the garden and the care of the fruit, of which she had the handling, but that she had said what she had been desired to say, to induce me to return to Paris.

Failing in this attempt, they endeavoured to obtain by scruple the effect which complaisance had not produced, and construed into a crime my keeping the old woman at a distance from the succours of which, at her age, she might be in need. They did not recollect that she, and many other old people, whose lives were prolonged by the air of the country, might obtain these succours at Montmorency, near to which I lived; as if there were no old people except in Paris, and that it was impossible for them to live in any other place. Madame le Vasseur, who ate a great deal, and with extreme voracity, was subject to overflowings of bile and to strong diarrhœas, which lasted several days, and served her instead of clysters. At Paris she neither did nor took anything for them, but left nature to itself. She observed the same rule at the Hermitage, knowing it was the best thing she could do. No matter, since there were not in the country either physicians or apothecaries, keeping her there must, no doubt, be with the desire of putting an end to her existence, although she was in perfect health. Diderot should have determined at what age, under pain of being punished for homicide, it is no longer permitted to let old people remain out of Paris.

This was one of the two atrocious accusations from which he did not except me in his remark, that none but the wicked were alone; and the meaning of his pathetic exclamation, with the *et cetera*, which he had benignantly added: *A woman of eighty years of age,*[1] *etc.*

I thought the best answer that could be given to this reproach would be from Madame le Vasseur herself. I desired her to write freely and naturally her sentiments to Madame d'Epinay. To relieve her from all constraint, I would not even see her letter, and I showed her one that I am going to transcribe. I wrote it to Madame d'Epinay, upon the subject of an answer I wished to return to a letter still more severe from Diderot, and which she had prevented me from sending.

'*Thursday.*

'My good friend: Madame le Vasseur is to write to you: I have desired her to tell you sincerely what she thinks. To remove from

---

[1] Mme. le Vasseur was 69 at this time.

her all constraint, I have intimated to her that I will not see what she writes, and I beg of you not to communicate to me any part of the contents of her letter.

'I will not send my letter, because you do not choose I should; but, feeling myself grievously offended, it would be baseness and falsehood, of either of which it is impossible for me to be guilty, to acknowledge myself in the wrong. Holy writ commands him to whom a blow is given, to turn the other cheek, but not to ask pardon. Do you remember the man in the comedy who exclaims, while he is giving another blows with his staff? This is the part of a philosopher!

'Do not flatter yourself that he will be prevented from coming by the bad weather we now have. His rage will give him the time and strength which friendship refuses him, and it will be the first time in his life he ever came upon the day appointed.

'He will neglect nothing to come and repeat to me verbally the injuries with which he loads me in his letters; I will endure them all with patience. He will return to Paris to be ill again; and, according to custom, I shall be a very hateful man. What is to be done? Endure it all.

'But do you not admire the wisdom of the man who would come to take me to Saint Denis in a hackney coach to dine there, bring me home in a hackney coach, and whose finances, eight days afterwards, oblige him to come to the Hermitage on foot? It is not absolutely impossible, to speak his own language, that this should be the style of sincerity. But were this the case, strange changes in his fortune must have happened in the course of a week.

'I join in your affliction for the illness of madame, your mother, but you will perceive your grief is not equal to mine. We suffer less by seeing the persons we love ill, than when they are unjust and cruel.

'Adieu, my good friend, I shall never again mention to you this unhappy affair. You speak of going to Paris with an unconcern which, at any other time, would give me pleasure.'

I wrote to Diderot, telling him what I had done relative to Madame le Vasseur, upon the proposal of Madame d'Epinay herself; and Madame le Vasseur having, as it may be imagined, chosen to remain at the Hermitage, where she enjoyed a good state of health, always had company, and lived very agreeably, Diderot, not knowing what else to attribute to me as a crime, construed my precaution into one, and discovered another in Madame le Vasseur continuing to reside at the Hermitage, although this was by her own choice; and though her going to Paris had depended, and still did, upon herself, where she would continue to receive the same succours from me as I gave her in my house.

This is the explanation of the first reproach in the letter of Diderot. That of the second is in the letter which follows: 'The learned man (a name given in a joke by Grimm to the son of Madame d'Epinay) must have informed you there were upon the rampart twenty poor persons who were dying with cold and hunger, and waiting for the farthing you customarily gave them. This is a specimen of our little babbling . . . And if you heard the rest it would amuse you perhaps.'

My answer to this terrible argument, of which Diderot seemed so proud, was in the following words:

'I think I answered the *learned man,* that is, the son of a farmer-general, that I did not pity the poor whom he had seen upon the rampart, waiting for my farthing; that he had apparently amply made it up to them; that I appointed him my substitute, that the poor of Paris would have no reason to complain of the exchange; and that I should not easily find so good a one for the poor of Montmorency, who were in much greater need of assistance. Here is a good and respectable old man, who, after having worked hard all his lifetime, no longer being able to continue his labours, is in his old days dying with hunger. My conscience is more satisfied with the two sous I give him every Monday, than with the hundred farthings I should have distributed amongst all the beggars on the rampart. You are pleasant men, you philosophers, while you consider the inhabitants of cities as the only persons whom you ought to befriend. It is in the country men learn how to love and serve humanity; all they learn in cities is to despise it.'

Such were the singular scruples on which a man of sense had the folly to attribute to me as a crime my retiring from Paris, and pretended to prove to me by my own example, it was not possible to live out of the capital without becoming a bad man. I cannot at present conceive how I could be guilty of the folly of answering him, and of suffering myself to be angry instead of laughing in his face. However, the decisions of Madame d'Epinay, and the clamours of the Holbach set, had so far operated in her favour, that I was generally thought to be in the wrong; and that

Madame d'Houdetot herself, very partial to Diderot, insisted upon my going to see him at Paris, and making all the advances towards an accommodation, which, full and sincere as it was on my part, was not of long duration. The victorious argument, by which she subdued my heart, was that at that moment Diderot was in distress. Besides the storm excited against the *Encyclopédie*, he had then another violent one to make head against, relative to his piece, which, notwithstanding the short history he had printed at the head of it, he was accused of having entirely taken from Goldoni. Diderot, more wounded by criticisms than Voltaire, was overwhelmed by them. Madame de Graffigny had been malicious enough to spread a report that I had broken with him on this account. I thought it would be just and generous publicly to prove the contrary, and I went to pass two days, not only with him, but at his lodgings. This, since I had taken up my abode at the Hermitage, was my second journey to Paris. I had made the first to run to poor Gauffecourt, who had had a stroke of apoplexy, from which he has never perfectly recovered: I did not quit the side of his pillow until he was so far restored as to have no farther need of my assistance.

Diderot received me well. How many wrongs are effaced by the embraces of a friend! after these, what resentment can remain in the heart? We came to but little explanation. There is no need for reciprocal invectives. The only thing necessary is to know how to forget them. There had been no underhand proceedings, none at least that had come to my knowledge: the case was not the same with Madame d'Epinay. He showed me the plan of the *Père de Famille*. This, said I to him, is the best defence of the *Fils Naturel*. Be silent, give your attention to this piece, and then throw it at the head of your enemies as the only answer you think proper to make them. He did so, and was satisfied with what he had done. I had six months before sent him the first two parts of my *Julie* to have his opinion upon them. He had not yet read the work over. We read a part of it together. He found this *feuillet*, that was his term, by which he meant loaded with words and redundancies. I myself had already perceived it; but it was the babbling of the fever: I have never been able to correct it. The last parts are not the same. The fourth especially, and the sixth, are masterpieces of diction.

The day after my arrival, he would absolutely take me to sup with M. d'Holbach. We were far from agreeing upon this point; for I wished even to get rid of the bargain for the manuscript on chemistry, for which I was engaged to be obliged to that man. Diderot carried all before him. He swore d'Holbach loved me with all his heart, said I must forgive him his manner, which was the same to everybody, and more disagreeable to his friends than to others. He observed to me that refusing the produce of this manuscript, after having accepted it two years before, was an affront to the donor which he had not deserved, and that my refusal might be misinterpreted into a secret reproach, for having waited so long to conclude the bargain. I see, added he, d'Holbach every day, and know better than you do the nature of his disposition. Had you reason to be dissatisfied with him, do you think your friend capable of advising you to do a mean thing? In short, with my accustomed weakness, I suffered myself to be prevailed upon, and we went to sup with the Baron, who received me as he usually had done. But his wife received me coldly and almost uncivilly. I saw nothing in her which resembled the amiable Caroline, who, when a maid, expressed for me so many good wishes. I thought I had already long perceived that since Grimm had frequented the house of d'Aine, I had not met there so friendly a reception.

Whilst I was at Paris, St. Lambert arrived there from the army. As I was not acquainted with his arrival, I did not see him until after my return to the country, first at la Chevrette, and afterwards at the Hermitage; to which he came with Madame d'Houdetot, and invited himself to dinner with me. It may be judged whether or not I received him with pleasure! But I felt one still greater at seeing the good understanding between my guests. Satisfied with not having disturbed their happiness, I myself was happy in being a witness to it, and I can safely assert that, during the whole of my mad passion, and especially at the moment of which I speak, had it been in my power to take from him Madame d'Houdetot I would not have done it, nor should I have so much as been tempted to undertake it. I found her so amiable in her passion for St. Lambert, that I could scarcely imagine she would have been as much so had she loved me instead of him; and without wishing to disturb their union, all I had really desired of her in my madness was to permit herself to be loved. Finally, however violent my passion may have been for this lady, I found it as agreeable to be the confidant as the object of her amours, and I never for a moment considered her lover as a rival but always as my friend. It will be said this was not love: be it so, but it was something more.

As for St. Lambert, he behaved like an honest and a judicious man: as I was the only person culpable, so was I the only one who was punished: and this was with the greatest indulgence. He treated me severely, but in a friendly manner, and I perceived I had lost something in his esteem, but not the least part of his friendship. For this I consoled myself, knowing it would be much more easy to me to recover one than the other, and that he had too much sense to confound an involuntary and passing weakness with a vice of character. If even I were in fault in all that had passed, I was but very little so. Had I first sought after his mistress? Had not he himself sent her to me? Did not she come in search of me? Could I avoid receiving her? What could I do? They themselves had done the evil, and I was the person on whom it fell. In my situation he would have done as much as I did, and perhaps worse: for, however estimable and faithful Madame d'Houdetot might be, she was still a woman; her lover was absent; opportunities were frequent; temptations strong; and it would have been very difficult for her always to have defended herself with the same success against a more enterprising man. We certainly had done a great deal in our situation, in placing boundaries beyond which we never permitted ourselves to pass.

Although at the bottom of my heart I found evidence sufficiently honourable in my favour, so many appearances were against me, that the invincible shame always predominant in me, gave me in his presence the appearance of guilt, and of this he took advantage for the purpose of humbling me: a single circumstance will describe this reciprocal situation. I read to him, after dinner, the letter I had written the preceding year to Voltaire, and of which St. Lambert had heard speak. Whilst I was reading he fell asleep, and I, lately so haughty, at present so foolish, dared not stop, and continued to read whilst he continued to snore. Such were my indignities and such his revenge; but his generosity never permitted him to exercise them, except between ourselves.

After his return to the army, I found Madame d'Houdetot greatly changed in her manner with me. At this I was as much surprised as if it had not been what I ought to have expected; it affected me more than it ought to have done, and did me considerable harm. It seemed that everything from which I expected a cure, still plunged deeper into my heart the dart, which I, at length, broke rather than drew out.

I was quite determined to conquer myself, and leave no means untried to change my foolish passion into a pure and lasting friendship. For this purpose I had formed the finest projects in the world; for the execution of which the concurrence of Madame d'Houdetot was necessary. When I wished to speak to her I found her absent and embarrassed; I perceived I was no longer agreeable to her, and that something had passed, which she would not communicate to me, and which I have never yet known. This change, and the impossibility of knowing the reason of it, grieved me to the heart. She asked me for her letters; these I returned her with a fidelity of which she did me the insult to doubt for a moment.

This doubt was another wound given to my heart, with which she must have been so well acquainted. She did me justice, but not immediately: I understood that an examination of the packet I had sent her, made her perceive her error: I saw she reproached herself with it, by which I was the gainer of something. She could not take back her letters without returning me mine. She told me she had burnt them: of this I dared to doubt in my turn, and I confess I doubt of it at this moment. No, such letters as mine to

FRANÇOIS DE ST. LAMBERT

her were, are never thrown into the fire. Those of *Julie* have
been found ardent. Heavens! what would have been said of these?
No, no, she, who can inspire a like passion, will never have the
courage to burn the proofs of it. But I am not afraid of her having
made a bad use of them: of this I do not think her capable; and
besides, I had taken proper measures to prevent it. The foolish,
but strong, apprehension of raillery, had made me begin this
correspondence in a manner to secure my letters from all communication. I carried the familiarity I permitted myself with her in
my intoxication so far as to speak of her in the singular number:
but what *theeing* and *thouing!* she certainly could not be offended
with it. Yet she several times complained, but this was always
useless: her complaints had no other effect than that of awakening
my fears, and I besides could not suffer myself to lose ground. If
these letters be not yet destroyed, and should they ever be made
public, the world will see in what manner I have loved.

The grief caused me by the coldness of Madame d'Houdetot,
and the certainty of not having merited it, made me take the
singular resolution to complain of it to St. Lambert himself. While
waiting the effect of the letter I wrote to him, I sought dissipations
to which I ought sooner to have had recourse. Fêtes were given at
la Chevrette, for which I composed music. The pleasure of honouring myself in the eyes of Madame d'Houdetot by a talent she
loved, warmed my imagination, and another object still contributed to give it animation; this was the desire the author of
the *Devin du Village* had of showing he understood music; for
I had perceived some persons had, for a considerable time past,
endeavoured to render this doubtful, at least with respect to composition. My beginning at Paris, the ordeal through which I had
several times passed there, both at the house of M. Dupin and
that of M. de la Poplinière; the quantity of music I had composed
during fourteen years in the midst of the most celebrated masters
and before their eyes: — finally, the opera of the *Muses Galantes*,
and that even of the *Devin;* a motet I had composed for Mademoiselle Fel, and which she had sung at the spiritual concert; the
frequent conferences I had had upon this fine art with the first
composers, all seemed to prevent or dissipate a doubt of such a
nature. This, however, existed even at la Chevrette, and in the
mind of M. d'Epinay himself. Without appearing to observe it,
I undertook to compose him a motet for the dedication of the
chapel of la Chevrette, and I begged him to make choice of the
words. He directed de Linant, the tutor to his son, to furnish me

with these. De Linant gave me words proper to the subject, and, in a week after I had received them, the motet was finished. This time, spite was my Apollo, and never did better music come from my hand. The words began with: *Ecce sedes hic tonantis.*[1] The grandeur of the opening is suitable to the words, and the rest of the motet is so elegantly harmonious that every one was struck with it. I had composed it for a great orchestra. D'Epinay procured the best performers. Madame Bruna, an Italian singer, sung the motet, and was well accompanied. The composition succeeded so well that it was afterwards performed at the spiritual concert, where, in spite of secret cabals, and notwithstanding it was badly executed, it was twice generally applauded. I gave, for the birthday of M. d'Epinay, the idea of a kind of piece, half dramatic and half pantomimical, which Madame d'Epinay composed, of which I also composed the music. Grimm, on his arrival, heard speak of my musical success. An hour afterwards, not a word more was said upon the subject; but there no longer remained a doubt, not at least that I know of, of my knowledge of composition.

Grimm was scarcely arrived at la Chevrette, where I already did not much amuse myself, before he made it insupportable to me by airs I never before saw in any person, and of which I had no idea. The evening before he came, I was dislodged from the chamber of favour, contiguous to that of Madame d'Epinay: it was prepared for Grimm, and, instead of it, I was put into another further off. In this manner, said I laughingly to Madame d'Epinay, newcomers displace those which are established. She seemed embarrassed. I was better acquainted the same evening with the reason for the change, in learning that between her chamber and that I had quitted there was a private door which she had thought it needless to show me. Her intercourse with Grimm was not a secret either in her own house or to the public, not even to her husband; yet, far from confessing it to me, the confidant of secrets more important to her, and which she was sure would be faithfully kept, she constantly denied it in the strongest manner. I comprehended this reserve proceeded from Grimm, who, though entrusted with all my secrets, did not choose I should be so with any of his.

However prejudiced I was in favour of this man by my former sentiments, which were not extinguished, and by the real merit

---

[1] I have since learned these were by Santeuil, and that M. de Linant had without scruple appropriated them to himself. (*Note by Rousseau*, not in Paris MS.)

he had, all was not proof against the cares he took to destroy it.
He received me like the Comte de Tuffière;[1] he scarcely deigned to
return my salute; he never once spoke to me, and prevented my
speaking to him, by not making me any answer; he everywhere
passed first, and took the first place without ever paying me the
least attention. All this would have been supportable had he not
accompanied it with a shocking affectation, which may be judged
of by one example taken from a hundred. One evening, Madame
d'Epinay, finding herself a little indisposed, ordered something for
her supper to be carried into her chamber, and went upstairs to
sup by the side of her fire. She asked me to go up with her, which
I did. Grimm came afterwards. The little table was already placed,
and there were but two covers. Supper was served: Madame
d'Epinay took her place on one side of the fire, Grimm took an
armchair, seated himself at the other, opened his napkin, and
prepared himself for eating without speaking to me a single word.
Madame d'Epinay blushed at his behaviour, and, to induce him
to repair his rudeness, offered me her place. He said nothing, nor
did he ever look at me. Not being able to approach the fire, I
walked about the chamber until a cover was brought. Indisposed
as I was, elder than himself, longer acquainted in the house than
he had been, the person who had introduced him there, and to
whom, as favourite of the lady, he ought to have done the honours
of it, he suffered me to sup at the end of the table, at a distance
from the fire, without showing me the least civility. His whole
behaviour to me corresponded with this example of it. He did not
treat me precisely as his inferior, but he looked upon me as a
cipher. I could scarcely recognise the same Grimm, who, at the
house of the Prince de Saxe-Gotha, thought himself honoured
when I cast my eyes upon him. I had still more difficulty in reconciling this profound silence and insulting haughtiness with the
tender friendship he professed for me to those whom he knew to
be my real friends. It is true the only proof he gave of it was pitying my wretched fortune, of which I did not complain; compas-
sionating my sad fate, with which I was satisfied; and lamenting
to see me obstinately refuse the benevolent services he said he
wished to render me. Thus was it he artfully made the world
admire his affectionate generosity, blame my ungrateful misan-
thropy, and insensibly accustom people to imagine there was
nothing more between a protector like him and a wretch like my-

---

[1] A character in Destouches' comedy *Le Glorieux*.

self, than a connexion founded upon benefactions on one part, and obligations on the other, without once thinking of a friendship between equals. For my part, I have vainly sought to discover in what I was under an obligation to this new protector. I had lent him money, he had never lent me any; I had attended him in his illness, he scarcely came to see me in mine; I had given him all my friends, he never had given me any of his; I had said everything I could in his favour, he — if ever he has spoken of me, it has been less publicly and in another manner. He has never either rendered or offered me the least service of any kind. How, therefore, was he my Mæcenas? In what manner was I protected by him? This was incomprehensible to me, and still remains so.

It is true he was more or less arrogant with everybody, but I was the only person with whom he was brutally so. I remember St. Lambert once ready to throw a plate at his head, upon his, in some measure, giving him the lie at table by vulgarly saying: *that is not true.* With his naturally imperious manner he had the self-sufficiency of an upstart, and became ridiculous by being extravagantly impertinent. An intercourse with the great had so far intoxicated him that he gave himself airs which none but the contemptible part of them ever assume. He never called his lackey but by *Eh!* as if amongst the number of his servants my lord had not known which was in waiting. When he sent him to buy anything, he threw the money upon the ground instead of putting it into his hand. In short, entirely forgetting he was a man, he treated him with such shocking contempt, and so cruel a disdain in everything, that the poor lad, a very good creature whom Madame d'Epinay had recommended, quitted his service without any other complaint than that of the impossibility of enduring such treatment. This was the La Fleur of this new Glorieux.

As foppish as he was vain, with his great dim eyes and ungainly figure, he yet had pretensions with women, and after his farce with Mademoiselle Fel, he was taken by many of them for a man of much feeling. This had made him fashionable, and given him a taste for female neatness; he began to act the beau; his toilet became a business of much consequence; everyone knew he used paint, and I, who did not believe it, began to do so, not only from the change in his countenance, and from finding boxes on his dressing-table, but because, coming one morning into his room, I found him cleaning his nails with a small brush made expressly for the purpose; a task which he unblushingly continued in my presence. I judged that a man who spent two hours every morn-

ing in brushing his nails might well spend a few moments in filling his wrinkles with paint. The good Gauffecourt, who was not
a fool, had wittily named him Tyran le Blanc.

FRIEDRICH MELCHIOR, BARON DE GRIMM

All these things were nothing more than ridiculous, but, quite
opposite to my character, they contributed to render his suspicious
to me. I could easily imagine that a man whose head was so much
deranged could not have a heart well placed. He piqued himself
upon nothing so much as upon sensibility of mind and lively feeling. How could this agree with defects which are peculiar to little
minds? How can the continued overflowings of a susceptible heart
suffer it to be incessantly employed in so many little cares relative
to the person? He who feels his heart inflamed with this celestial
fire strives to diffuse it, and wishes to show what he internally is.
He would wish to place his heart in his countenance, and thinks
not of other paint for his cheeks.

I remember the summary of his morality which Madame
d'Epinay had mentioned to me and adopted. This consisted in one
single article: that the sole duty of man is to follow all the inclina-

tions of his heart. This morality, when I heard it mentioned, gave me great matter of reflection, although I at first considered it solely as a play of wit. But I soon perceived this principle was really the rule of his conduct, and of which I afterwards had, at my own expense, but too many convincing proofs. It is the interior doctrine Diderot has so frequently intimated to me, but which I never heard him explain.

I remembered having several years before been frequently told that Grimm was false, that he had nothing more than the appearance of sentiment, and particularly that he did not love me. I recollected several little anecdotes which I had heard of him by M. de Francueil and Madame de Chenonceaux, neither of whom esteemed him, and to whom he must have been known, as Madame de Chenonceaux was daughter to Madame de Rochechouart, the intimate friend of the late Comte de Frièse, and that of M. de Francueil, at that time very intimate with the Vicomte de Polignac, had lived a good deal at the *Palais Royal* precisely when Grimm began to introduce himself there. All Paris heard of his despair after the death of the Comte de Frièse. It was necessary to support the reputation he had acquired after the rigours of Mademoiselle Fel, and of which I, more than any other person, should have seen the imposture, had I been less blind. He was obliged to be dragged to the Hotel de Castries, where he worthily played his part, abandoned to the most mortal affliction. There he every morning went into the garden to weep at his ease, holding before his eyes his handkerchief moistened with tears, as long as he was in sight of the hotel, but at the turning of a certain alley, people, of whom he little thought, saw him instantly put his handkerchief into his pocket and take out of it a book. This observation, which was repeatedly made, soon became public in Paris, and was almost as soon forgotten. I myself had forgotten it; a circumstance in which I was concerned brought it to my recollection. I was at the point of death in my bed, in the Rue de Grenelle. Grimm was in the country; he came one morning, quite out of breath, to see me, saying he had arrived in town that very instant; and a moment afterwards I learned he had arrived the evening before, and had been seen at the theatre.

I heard many things of the same kind; but an observation, which I was surprised not to have made sooner, struck me more than everything else. I had given to Grimm all my friends without exception, they were all become his. I was so inseparable from him, that I should have had some difficulty in continuing to visit

at a house where he was not received. Madame de Créqui was
the only person who refused to admit him into her company, and
whom, for that reason, I had seldom since seen. Grimm, on his
part, made himself other friends, as well by his own means, as by
those of the Comte de Frièse. Of all these, not one of them ever
became my friend: he never said a word to induce me even to
become acquainted with them, and not one of those I sometimes
met at his apartments, even showed me the least goodwill; the
Comte de Frièse, in whose house he lived, and with whom it consequently would have been agreeable to me to form some connexion, not excepted, nor the Comte de Schomberg, his relation,
with whom Grimm was still more intimate.

Add to this, my own friends, whom I made his, and who were
all tenderly attached to me before his acquaintance, were no
longer so the moment it was made. He never gave me one of his;
I gave him all mine, and these he has taken from me. If these be
the effects of friendship, what are those of enmity?

Diderot, himself, told me several times at the beginning that
Grimm, in whom I had so much confidence, was not my friend.
He changed his language afterwards, the moment he was no
longer so himself.

The manner in which I had disposed of my children wanted
not the concurrence of any person. Yet I informed several of my
friends of it, solely to make it known to them, and that I might
not in their eyes appear better than I was. These friends were
three in number; Diderot, Grimm, and Madame d'Epinay. Duclos, the most worthy of my confidence, was the only real friend
whom I did not inform of it. He, nevertheless, knew what I had
done. By whom? This I know not. It is not very probable the perfidy came from Madame d'Epinay, who knew that by following
her example, had I been capable of doing it, I had in my power
the means of a cruel revenge. It remains therefore between Grimm
and Diderot, then so much united, especially against me, and it is
probable this crime was common to them both. I would lay a
wager that Duclos, to whom I never told my secret, and who consequently was at liberty to make what use he pleased of his information, is the only person who has not spoken of it again.

Grimm and Diderot, in their project to take from me the Governesses, had used the greatest efforts to make Duclos enter into
their views; but this he refused to do with disdain. It was not until
some time afterwards that I learned from him what had passed
between them on the subject; but I learned at the time from

Thérèse enough to perceive there was some secret design, and that they wished to dispose of me, if not against my own consent, at least without my knowledge, or had an intention of making these two persons serve as instruments of some project they had in view. This was far from upright conduct. The opposition of Duclos is a convincing proof of it. They who think proper may believe it to be friendship.

This pretended friendship was as fatal to me at home as it was abroad. The long and frequent conversations with Madame le Vasseur, for several years past, had made a sensible change in this woman's behaviour to me, and the change was far from being in my favour.

What was the subject of these singular conversations? Why such a profound mystery? Was the conversation of that old woman agreeable enough to take her into favour, and of sufficient importance to make of it so great a secret? During the three or four years these colloquies had, from time to time, been continued, they had appeared to me ridiculous; but when I thought of them again, they began to astonish me. This astonishment would have been carried to inquietude had I then known what the old creature was preparing for me.

Notwithstanding the pretended zeal for my welfare of which Grimm made such a public boast, difficult to reconcile with the airs he gave himself when we were together, I heard nothing of him from any quarter the least to my advantage, and his feigned commiseration tended less to do me service than to render me contemptible. He deprived me as much as he possibly could of the resource I found in the employment I had chosen, by decrying me as a bad copyist. I confess he spoke the truth; but, in this case, it was not for him to do it. He proved himself in earnest by employing another copyist, and prevailing upon everybody he could, by whom I was engaged, to do the same. His intention might have been supposed to be that of reducing me to a dependence upon him and his credit for a subsistence, and to cut off the latter until I was brought to that degree of distress.

All things considered, my reason imposed silence upon my former prejudice, which still pleaded in his favour. I judged his character to be at least suspicious, and with respect to his friendship I positively decided it to be false. I then resolved to see him no more, and informed Madame d'Epinay of the resolution I had taken, supporting it with several unanswerable facts, but which I have now forgotten.

She strongly combated my resolution without knowing how to reply to the reasons on which it was founded. She had not till then concerted with him; but the next day, instead of explaining herself verbally, she, with great address, gave me a letter they had drawn up together, and by which, without entering into a detail of facts, she justified him by his concentrated character, attributed to me as a crime my having suspected him of perfidy towards his friend, and exhorted me to come to an accommodation with him. This letter staggered me. In a conversation we afterwards had together and in which I found her better prepared than she had been the first time, I suffered myself to be quite prevailed upon, and was inclined to believe I might have judged erroneously. In this case I thought I really had done a friend a very serious injury, which it was my duty to repair. In short, as I had already done several times with Diderot, and the Baron d'Holbach, half from inclination, and half from weakness, I made all the advances I had a right to require; I went to M. Grimm, like another Georges Dandin, to make him my apologies for the offence he had given me; still in the false persuasion, which, in the course of my life, has made me guilty of a thousand meannesses to my pretended friends, that there is no hatred which may not be disarmed by mildness and proper behaviour; whereas, on the contrary, the hatred of the wicked becomes still more envenomed by the impossibility of finding anything to found it upon, and the sentiment of their own injustice is another cause of offence against the person who is the object of it. I have, without going farther than my own history, a strong proof of this maxim in Grimm, and in Tronchin, both become my implacable enemies from inclination, pleasure, and fancy, without having been able to charge me with having done either of them the most trifling injury,[1] and whose rage, like that of tigers, becomes daily more fierce by the facility of satiating it.

I expected that Grimm, confused by my condescension and advances, would receive me with open arms, and the most tender friendship. He received me as a Roman Emperor would have done, and with a haughtiness I never saw in any person but himself. I was by no means prepared for such a reception. When, in the embarrassment of the part I had to act, and which was so un-

---

[1] I did not give the surname of *Jongleur* to the latter until a long time after his enmity had been declared, and the bloody persecutions he brought upon me at Geneva and elsewhere. I soon suppressed the name the moment I perceived I was entirely his victim. Mean vengeance is unworthy of my heart, and hatred never takes the least root in it. (*Note by Rousseau*, not in Paris MS.)

worthy of me, I had, in a few words and with a timid air, fulfilled the object which had brought me to him; before he received me into favour, he pronounced, with a deal of majesty, an harangue he had prepared, and which contained a long enumeration of his rare virtues, and especially those connected with friendship. He laid great stress upon a thing which at first struck me a good deal: this was his having always preserved the same friends. Whilst he was yet speaking, I said to myself, it would be cruel for me to be the only exception to this rule. He returned to the subject so frequently, and with such affectation, that I thought, if in this he followed nothing but the sentiments of his heart, he would be less struck with the maxim, and that he made of it an art useful to his views by procuring the means of accomplishing them. Until then I had been in the same situation; I had preserved all my first friends, those even from my tenderest infancy, without having lost one of them except by death, and yet I had never before made the reflection: it was not a maxim I prescribed myself. Since, therefore, the advantage was common to both, why did he boast of it in preference, if he had not previously intended to deprive me of the merit? He afterwards endeavoured to humble me by proofs of the preference our common friends gave him over me. With this I was as well acquainted as himself; the question was, by what means he had obtained it? whether it was by merit or address? by exalting himself, or endeavouring to abase me? At last, when he had placed between us all the distance that could add to the value of the favour he was about to confer, he granted me the kiss of peace, in a slight embrace which resembled the *accolade* which the King gives to new-made knights. I was stupefied with surprise: I knew not what to say; not a word could I utter. This whole scene had the appearance of the reprimand a preceptor gives to his pupil while he graciously spares inflicting the rod. I never think of it without perceiving to what a degree judgements, founded upon appearances to which the vulgar give so much weight, are deceitful, and how frequently audaciousness and pride are found in the guilty, and shame and embarrassment in the innocent.

We were reconciled: this was a relief to my heart, which every kind of quarrel fills with anguish. It will naturally be supposed that a like reconciliation changed nothing in his manners; all it effected was to deprive me of the right of complaining of them. For this reason I took a resolution to endure everything, and for the future to say not a word.

So many successive vexations overwhelmed me to such a degree as to leave me but little power over my mind. Receiving no answer from St. Lambert, neglected by Madame d'Houdetot, and no longer daring to open my heart to any person, I began to be afraid that by making friendship my idol, I should sacrifice my whole life to chimeras. After putting all those with whom I had been acquainted to the test, there remained but two who had preserved my esteem, and in whom my heart could confide: Duclos, of whom since my retreat to the Hermitage I had lost sight, and St. Lambert. I thought the only means of repairing the wrongs I had done the latter, was to open myself to him without reserve, and I resolved to confess to him everything by which his mistress should not be exposed. I have no doubt but this was another snare of my passion, to keep me nearer to her person; but I should certainly have had no reserve with her lover, entirely submitting to his direction, and carrying sincerity as far as it was possible to do it. I was upon the point of writing to him a second letter, to which I was certain he would have returned an answer, when I learned the melancholy cause of his silence relative to the first. He had been unable to support until the end the fatigues of the campaign. Madame d'Epinay informed me he had had an attack of the palsy, and Madame d'Houdetot, ill from affliction, and unable to write to me straightway, wrote me two or three days afterwards from Paris, where she then was, that he was going to Aix-la-Chapelle to take the benefit of the waters. I will not say this melancholy circumstance affected me as it did her; but I am of opinion my grief of heart was as painful as her tears. The pain of knowing him to be in such a state, increased by the fear lest inquietude should have contributed to occasion it, affected me more than anything that had yet happened, and I felt most cruelly a want of fortitude which in my estimation was necessary to enable me to support so many misfortunes. Happily this generous friend did not long leave me so overwhelmed with affliction; he did not forget me, notwithstanding his attack; and I soon learned from himself that I had ill judged his sentiments, and been too much alarmed for his situation.

It is now time I should come to the grand revolution of my destiny, to the catastrophe which has divided my life into two parts so different from each other, and, from a very trifling cause, produced such terrible effects.

One day, little thinking of what was to happen, Madame d'Epinay sent for me to la Chevrette. The moment I saw her I perceived in her eyes and whole countenance an appearance of uneasiness, which struck me the more, as this was not customary, nobody knowing better than she did how to govern her features and their movements. My friend, said she to me, I am immediately going to set off for Geneva; my chest is in a bad state, and my health so deranged that I must go and consult Tronchin. I was the more astonished at this resolution so suddenly taken, and at the beginning of the bad season of the year, as thirty-six hours before she had not, when I left her, so much as thought of it. I asked her whom she would take with her. She said, her son and M. de Linant; and afterwards carelessly added, and you, my dear, will not you go also? As I did not think she spoke seriously, knowing that at that season of the year I was scarcely in a situation to go out of my chamber, I joked upon the utility of the company of one sick person to another. She herself had not seemed to make the proposition seriously, and here the matter dropped. The rest of our conversation ran upon the necessary preparations for her journey, about which she immediately gave orders, being determined to set off within a fortnight.

I had no need of much penetration to realise that this journey had a secret motive which had not been mentioned to me. This secret, which was a secret to me alone in the house, was disclosed the next day by Thérèse, to whom Tessier, the steward, who knew it from the maidservant, revealed it. Although I do not owe it to Madame d'Epinay to keep this secret, since I have it not from her, it is too much attached to those I have from her to be separated from them; so I will be silent on this point. But these secrets, which have never escaped, nor will escape, either my lips or my pen, were known by too many people for them to have been hidden from all those who surrounded Madame d'Epinay.

Knowing the real purpose of this journey, I should have realised the secret movement of the hand of an enemy, in the attempt to make me Madame d'Epinay's chaperon; but she had so little insisted on it, that I determined not to look upon the attempt as serious, and I only laughed at the fine appearance I should have made, had I been so foolish as to take it upon myself. Moreover, she gained much by my refusal, for in the end she prevailed upon her husband to accompany her.

A few days afterwards, I received from Diderot the note I am going to transcribe. This note, simply doubled up, so that the contents were easily read, was addressed to me at Madame d'Epinay's, via M. de Linant, tutor to the son and confidant to the mother.

NOTE FROM DIDEROT

'I am naturally disposed to love you, and am born to give you trouble. I am informed Madame d'Epinay is going to Geneva, and do not hear you are to accompany her. My friend, you are satisfied with Madame d'Epinay, you must go with her; if dissatisfied you ought still less to hesitate. Do you find the weight of the obligations you are under to her uneasy to you? This is an opportunity of discharging a part of them, and relieving your mind. Do you ever expect another opportunity like the present one, of giving her proofs of your gratitude? She is going to a country where she will be quite a stranger. She is ill, and will stand in need of amusement and dissipation. The winter season too! Consider, my friend. Your ill state of health may be a much greater objection than I think it is; but are you now more indisposed than you were a month ago, or than you will be at the beginning of spring? Will you three months hence be in a situation to perform the journey more at your ease than at present? For my part I cannot but observe to you that were I unable to bear the shaking of the carriage I would take my staff and follow her. Have you no fears lest your conduct should be misinterpreted? You will be suspected of ingratitude or of a secret motive. I will know that, let you do as you will, you will have in your favour the testimony of your conscience, but will this alone be sufficient, and is it permitted to neglect to a certain degree that which is necessary to acquire the approbation of others? What I now write, my good friend, is to acquit myself of what I think I owe to us both. Should my letter displease you, throw it into the fire, and let it be as if it had never been written. I salute, love, and embrace you.'

Although trembling, and almost blind with rage whilst I read this epistle, and hardly able to finish it, I remarked the address with which Diderot affected a milder and more polite language than he had done in his former ones, wherein he never went farther than my dear without ever deigning to add the name of friend. I easily discovered the second-hand means by which the letter was conveyed to me; the superscription, manner, and form awkwardly betrayed the manœuvre; for we commonly wrote to each other by post, or the messenger of Montmorency, and this was the first and only time he sent me his letter by any other conveyance.

As soon as the first transports of my indignation permitted me to write, I, with great precipitation, wrote him the following answer, which I immediately carried from the Hermitage, where I then was, to la Chevrette, to show it to Madame d'Epinay, to whom in my blind rage, I read the contents, as well as the letter from Diderot.

'You cannot, my dear friend, either know the magnitude of the obligations I am under to Madame d'Epinay, to what a degree I am bound by them, whether or not she really needs me and is desirous of my accompanying her on this journey; whether this is possible; or the reasons I may have for my non-compliance. I have no objection to discuss all these points with you; but you will in the meantime confess that prescribing to me so positively what I ought to do, without first enabling yourself to judge of the matter, is, my dear philosopher, acting very inconsiderately. What is still worse, I perceive the opinion you give comes not from yourself. Besides my being but little disposed to suffer myself to be led by the nose under your name by any third or fourth person, I observe in this second-hand advice, certain underhand dealing, which ill agrees with your candour, and from which you will, on your account as well as mine, do well in future to abstain.

'You are afraid my conduct should be misinterpreted; but I defy a heart like yours to think ill of mine. Others would perhaps speak better of me if I resembled them more. God preserve me from gaining their approbation! Let the vile and wicked watch over my conduct and misinterpret my actions, Rousseau is not a man to be afraid of them, nor is Diderot to be prevailed upon to hearken to what they say.

'If I am displeased with your letter, you wish me to throw it into the fire, and pay no attention to the contents. Do you imagine that anything coming from you can be forgotten in such a manner? You hold, my dear friend, my tears as cheap in the pain you give me, as you do my life and health, in the cares you exhort me to take. Could you but break yourself of this, your friendship would be more pleasing to me, and I should be less to be pitied.'

On entering the chamber of Madame d'Epinay, I found Grimm with her, with which I was highly delighted. I read to them, in a loud and clear voice, the two letters, with an intrepidity of which I should not have thought myself capable, and concluded with a few observations not in the least derogatory to it. At this unexpected audacity in a man generally timid, they were struck dumb with surprise, abashed, unable to say a word in reply; I perceived that arrogant man look down upon the ground, not daring to meet my eyes, which sparkled with indignation; but in the bottom of his heart he from that instant resolved upon my destruction, and, with Madame d'Epinay, I am certain concerted measures to that effect before they separated.

It was much about this time that I at length received, by Madame d'Houdetot, the answer from St. Lambert, dated from Wolfenbuttel, a few days after the accident that had happened to him, to my letter which had been long delayed upon the road. This answer gave me the consolation of which I then stood so much in need; it was full of assurances of esteem and friendship, and these gave me strength and courage to deserve them. From that moment I did my duty, but had St. Lambert been less reasonable, generous, and honest, I was inevitably lost.

The weather became bad, and people began to quit the country. Madame d'Houdetot informed me of the day on which she intended to come and bid adieu to the valley, and gave me a rendezvous at Eaubonne. This happened to be the same day on which Madame d'Epinay left la Chevrette, to go to Paris for the purpose of completing the preparations for her journey. Fortunately she set off in the morning, and I had still time enough, on leaving her, to go and dine with her sister-in-law. I had the letter from St. Lambert in my pocket, and read it over several times as I walked along. This letter served me as a shield against my weakness. I made and kept to the resolution of seeing nothing in Madame d'Houdetot but my friend and the mistress of St. Lambert; and I passed with her a tête-à-tête of four or five hours in a most delicious calm, infinitely preferable, even with respect to enjoyment, to the paroxysms of a burning fever, which always, until that moment, I had had when in her presence. As she too well knew my heart not to be changed, she was sensible of the efforts I made to conquer myself, and esteemed me the more for them, and I had the pleasure of perceiving that her friendship for me was not extinguished. She announced to me the approaching return of St. Lambert, who, although well enough recovered from his attack, was unable to bear the fatigues of war, and was quitting the service to come and live in peace with her. We formed the charming project of an intimate connexion between us three, and had reason to hope it would be lasting, since it was founded upon every sentiment by which honest and susceptible hearts could be united; and we had moreover amongst us all the knowledge and talents necessary to be sufficient to ourselves, without the aid of any foreign supplement. Alas! in abandoning myself to the hope of so agreeable a life, I little suspected that which awaited me.

We afterwards spoke of my situation with Madame d'Epinay. I showed her the letter from Diderot, with my answer to it; I related to her everything that had passed upon the subject, and declared to her my resolution of quitting the Hermitage. This she vehemently opposed, and by reasons all-powerful over my heart. She expressed to me how much she could have wished I had been of the party to Geneva, foreseeing she should inevitably be considered as having caused the refusal, which the letter of Diderot seemed previously to announce. However, as she was acquainted with my reasons as well as I was myself, she did not insist upon this point, but conjured me to avoid coming to an open rupture let it cost me what mortification it would, and to palliate my refusal by reasons sufficiently plausible, to put away all unjust suspicions of her having been the cause of it. I told her the task she imposed on me was not easy; but that, resolved to expiate my faults at the expense even of my reputation, I would give the preference to hers in everything that honour permitted me to suffer. It will soon be seen whether or not I fulfilled this engagement.

THE HERMITAGE

My unhappy passion was so far from having lost any part of its force that I never in my life loved my Sophie so ardently and tenderly as on that day. But such was the impression made upon me by the letter of St. Lambert, the sentiment of my duty, and the horror in which I held perfidy, that during the whole time of the interview, my senses left me in peace, and I was not so much as tempted to kiss her hand. At parting she embraced me before her servants. This embrace, so different from those I had sometimes stolen from her under the foliage, proved I was become master of myself; and I am almost certain that had my mind, undisturbed, had time to acquire more firmness, three months would have cured me radically.

Here end my personal connexions with Madame d'Houdetot; connexions of which each has been able to judge by appearances according to the dispositions of his own heart, but in which the passion inspired in me by that amiable woman, the most lively passion perhaps man ever felt, will be honourable in our own eyes by the rare and painful sacrifices we both made to duty, honour, love, and friendship. We each had too high an opinion of the other, easily to suffer ourselves to do anything derogatory to our dignity. We must have been unworthy of all esteem, had we not set a proper value upon one like this, and the energy of our sentiments which might have rendered us culpable, was that which prevented us from becoming so.

Thus after a long friendship for one of these women, and the strongest affection for the other, I bade them both adieu the same day, to one never to see her more, to the other to see her again but twice, upon occasions of which I shall hereafter speak.

After their departure, I found myself much embarrassed to fulfil so many pressing and contradictory duties, the consequences of my imprudence; had I been in my natural situation after the proposition and refusal of the journey to Geneva, I had only to remain quiet, and everything was as it should be. But I had foolishly made of it an affair which could not remain in the state it was, and an explanation was absolutely necessary, unless I quitted the Hermitage, which I had just promised Madame d'Houdetot not to do, at least for the present. Moreover, she had required me to make known the reasons for my refusal to my pretended friends that it might not be imputed to her. Yet I could not state the true reason without doing an outrage to Madame d'Epinay, who certainly had a right to my gratitude for what she had done for me. Everything well considered, I found myself reduced to the severe but indispensable necessity of failing in respect, either to Madame d'Epinay, Madame d'Houdetot, or to myself; and it was the last I resolved to make my victim. This I did without hesitation, openly and fully, and with so much generosity as to make the act worthy of expiating the faults which had reduced me to such an extremity. This sacrifice, taken advantage of by my enemies, and which they, perhaps, expected, has ruined my reputation, and, by their assiduity, deprived me of the esteem of the public; but it has restored to me my own, and given me consolation in my misfortune. This, as it will hereafter appear, is not the last time I made such a sacrifice, nor that advantages were taken of it to do me an injury.

Grimm was the only person who appeared to have taken no part in the affair, and it was to him I determined to address myself. I wrote him a long letter, in which I set forth the ridiculousness of considering it as my duty to accompany Madame d'Epinay to Geneva, the inutility of the measure, and the embarrassment even it would have caused her, besides the inconvenience to myself. I could not resist the temptation of letting him perceive in this letter how fully I was informed in what manner things were arranged, and that to me it appeared singular I should be expected to undertake the journey whilst he himself dispensed with it, and that his name was never mentioned. This letter, wherein, on account of my not being able clearly to state my reasons, I was often obliged to wander from the point, would have rendered me culpable in the eyes of the public, but it was a model of reservedness and discretion for people who, like Grimm, were fully acquainted with the things I forbore to mention, and which justified my conduct.

I did not even hesitate to raise another prejudice against myself, in attributing the advice of Diderot to my other friends. This I did to insinuate that Madame d'Houdetot had been in the same opinion, as she really was, and in not mentioning that, upon the reasons I gave her, she thought differently. I could not better remove the suspicions of her having connived at my proceedings than by appearing dissatisfied with her behaviour.

This letter was concluded by an act of confidence which would have had an effect upon any other man; for, in desiring Grimm to weigh my reasons and afterwards to give me his opinion, I informed him that, let this be what it would, I should act accordingly, and such was my intention had he even thought I ought to set off; for M. d'Epinay having appointed himself the conductor of his wife, my going with them would then have had a different appearance; whereas it was I who, in the first place, was asked to take upon me that employment, and he was out of the question until after my refusal.

The answer from Grimm was slow in coming: it was singular enough, on which account I will here transcribe it.

'The departure of Madame d'Epinay is postponed: her son is
ill, and it is necessary to wait until his health is re-established.
I will consider the contents of your letter. Remain quiet at your
Hermitage. I will send you my opinion as soon as this shall be
necessary. As she will certainly not set off for some days, there is
no immediate occasion for it. In the meantime you may, if you
think proper, make her your offers, although this to me seems a
matter of indifference. For, knowing your situation as well as you
do yourself, I doubt not of her returning to your offers such an
answer as she ought to do, and all the advantage which, in my
opinion, can result from this, will be your having it in your power
to say to those by whom you may be importuned, that your not
being of the travelling party was not for want of having made
your offers to that effect. Moreover I do not see why you will
absolutely have it that the philosopher is the speaking-trumpet of
all the world, nor because he is of opinion you ought to go, why
you should imagine all your friends think as he does. If you write
to Madame d'Epinay her answer will be yours to all your friends,
since you have it so much at heart to give them all an answer.
Adieu. I embrace Madame le Vasseur and the *Criminal*.'[1]

Struck with astonishment at reading this letter, I vainly endeavoured to find out what it meant, and could not. How! instead
of answering me with simplicity, he took time to consider of what
I had written, as if the time he had already taken was not sufficient! He intimates even the state of suspense in which he wishes
to keep me, as if a profound problem was to be resolved, or that
it was of importance to his views to deprive me of every means of
comprehending his intentions until the moment he should think
proper to make them known. What therefore did he mean by
these precautions, delays, and mysteries? Was this how to reply
to a confidence? Was this manner of acting consistent with honour
and uprightness? I vainly sought for some favourable interpretation of his conduct; it was impossible to find one. Whatever his
design might be, were this inimical to me, his situation facilitated
the execution of it, without its being possible for me in mine to
oppose the least obstacle. In favour in the house of a great Prince,
having an extensive acquaintance, and giving the tone to our
common circles of which he was the oracle, he had it in his power,

---

[1] M. le Vasseur, whose wife governed him rather rudely, called her the
Criminal Lieutenant. Grimm in a joke gave the same name to the daughter,
and by way of abridgement was pleased to retrench the second word. (*Note by
Rousseau*.)

with his usual address, to dispose everything in his favour; and I, alone in my Hermitage, far removed from all society, without the benefit of advice, and having no communication with the world, had nothing to do but to remain in peace. All I did was to write to Madame d'Epinay upon the illness of her son, as polite a letter as could be written, but in which I did not fall into the snare of offering to accompany her to Geneva.

After waiting for a long time in the most cruel uncertainty, into which that barbarous man had plunged me, I learned, at the expiration of eight or ten days, that Madame d'Epinay was set off, and received from him a second letter. It contained not more than seven or eight lines which I did not entirely read. —— It was a rupture, but in such terms as the most infernal hatred only can dictate, and these became unmeaning by the excessive degree of acrimony with which he wished to charge them. He forbade me his presence as he would have forbidden me his estates. All that was wanting to his letter, to make it laughable, was to be read over with coolness. Without taking a copy of it or reading the whole of the contents I returned it him immediately, accompanied by the following note:

'I refused to admit the force of the just reasons I had of suspicion: I now, when it is too late, am become sufficiently acquainted with your character.

'This then is the letter upon which you took time to meditate: I return it to you, it is not for me. You may show mine to the whole world and hate me openly; this on your part will be a falsehood the less.'

My telling he might show my preceding letter related to an article in his by which his profound address throughout the whole affair will be judged of.

I have observed that my letter might inculpate me in the eyes of persons unacquainted with the particulars of what had passed. This he was delighted to discover; but how was he to take advantage of it without exposing himself? By showing the letter he ran the risk of being reproached with abusing the confidence of his friend.

To relieve himself from this embarrassment he resolved to break with me in the most violent manner possible, and to set forth in his letter the favour he did me in not showing mine. He was certain that in my indignation and anger I should refuse his feigned discretion, and permit me to show my letter to everybody; and this was what he wished for, and everything turned out as he had expected it would. He sent my letter all over Paris, with his own commentaries upon it, which however were not so successful as he had expected them to be. It was not judged that the permission he had extorted to make my letter public exempted him from the blame of having so lightly taken me at my word to do me an injury. People continually asked what personal complaints he had against me to authorise so violent a hatred. Finally, it was thought that if my behaviour had been such as to authorise him to break with me, friendship, although extinguished, had rights which he ought to have respected. But unfortunately the inhabitants of Paris are frivolous; remarks of the moment are soon forgotten; the absent and unfortunate are neglected; the man who prospers secures favour by his presence, the intriguing and malicious support each other, renew their vile efforts, and the effects of these, incessantly succeeding each other, efface everything by which they were preceded.

Thus, after having so long deceived me, this man threw aside his mask; convinced that, in the state to which he had brought things, he no longer stood in need of it. Relieved from the fear of being unjust towards the wretch, I left him to his reflections and thought no more of him. A week afterwards I received an answer from Madame d'Epinay, dated from Geneva. I understood from the manner of her letter, in which, for the first time in her life, she put on airs of state with me, that both, depending but little upon the success of their measures, and considering me as a man inevitably lost, their intentions were to give themselves the pleasure of completing my destruction.

In fact, my situation was deplorable. I perceived all my friends withdrew themselves from me without my knowing how or why. Diderot, who boasted of the continuation of his attachment, and his alone, and who, for three months past, had promised me a visit, did not come. The winter began to make its appearance, and brought with it my habitual disorders. My constitution, although vigorous, had been unequal to the combat of so many opposite passions. I was so exhausted that I had neither strength nor courage sufficient to resist the most trifling indisposition. Had my engagements, and the continued remonstrances of Diderot and Madame d'Houdetot, then permitted me to quit the Hermitage, I knew not where to go, nor in what manner to drag myself along. I remained stupid and immovable, unable to act or think. The idea alone of a step to take, a letter to write, or a word to say, made me tremble. I could not however do otherwise than reply to the letter of Madame d'Epinay without acknowledging myself to be worthy of the treatment with which she and her friend overwhelmed me. I determined upon notifying to her my sentiments and resolutions, not doubting a moment that from humanity, generosity, propriety, and the good manner of thinking I imagined I had observed in her, notwithstanding her bad one, she would immediately subscribe to them. My letter was as follows:

'*The Hermitage, 23d Nov. 1757.*

'Were it possible to die of grief I should not now be alive. But I have at length made up my mind. Friendship, madam, is extinguished between us, but that which no longer exists still has its rights, and I respect them. I have not forgotten your goodness to me, and you may, on my part, expect as much gratitude as it is possible to have towards a person I no longer can love. All farther explanation would be useless. I have in my favour my own conscience, and I refer you to yours.

'I wished to quit the Hermitage, and I ought to have done it. My friends pretend I must stay there until spring; and since my friends desire it, I will remain there until that season, if you will consent to my stay.'

After writing and despatching this letter, all I thought of was remaining quiet at the Hermitage and taking care of my health; of endeavouring to recover my strength, and taking measures to remove in the spring without noise or making the rupture public. But these were not the intentions either of Grimm or Madame d'Epinay, as it will presently appear.

A few days afterwards, I had the pleasure of receiving from Diderot the visit he had so frequently promised, and in which he had as constantly failed. He could not have come more opportunely: he was my oldest friend; almost the only one who remained to me; the pleasure I felt in seeing him, as things were circumstanced, may easily be imagined. My heart was full, and I disclosed it to him. I explained to him several facts which either had not come to his knowledge, or had been disguised or supposed. I informed him, as far as I could do it with propriety, of all that had passed. I did not affect to conceal from him that with which he was but too well acquainted, that a passion, equally unreasonable and unfortunate, had been the cause of my destruction; but

I never acknowledged that Madame d'Houdetot had been made acquainted with it, or at least that I had declared it to her. I mentioned to him the unworthy manœuvres of Madame d'Epinay to intercept the innocent letters her sister-in-law wrote to me. I was determined he should hear the particulars from the mouth of the persons whom she had attempted to seduce. Thérèse related them with great precision; but what was my astonishment when the mother came to speak, and I heard her declare and maintain that nothing of this had come to her knowledge? These were her words, from which she would never depart. Not four days before she herself had recited to me all the particulars Thérèse had just stated, and, in presence of my friend, she contradicted me to my face. This, to me, was decisive, and I then clearly saw my imprudence in having so long a time kept such a woman near me. I made no use of invective; I scarcely deigned to speak to her a few words of contempt. I felt what I owed to the daughter, whose steadfast uprightness was a perfect contrast to the base manœuvres of the mother. But from that instant my resolution was taken relative to the old woman, and I waited for nothing but the moment to put it into execution.

This presented itself sooner than I expected. On the 10th of December, I received from Madame d'Epinay the following answer to my preceding letter:

'*Geneva, 1st December, 1757.*

'After having for several years given you every possible mark of friendship and interest, all I can now do is to pity you. You are very unhappy. I wish your conscience may be as calm as mine. This may be necessary to the repose of your whole life.

'Since you are determined to quit the Hermitage, and are persuaded that you ought to do it, I am astonished that your friends have prevailed upon you to stay there. For my part, I never consult mine upon my duty, and I have nothing farther to say to you upon your own.'

Such an unforeseen dismission, and so fully pronounced, left me not a moment to hesitate. It was necessary to quit immediately, let the weather and my health be in what state they might, although I were to sleep in the woods and upon the snow, with which the ground was then covered, and in defiance of everything Madame d'Houdetot might say; for I was willing to do everything to please her except rendering myself infamous.

I never had been so embarrassed in my whole life as I then was; but my resolution was taken, and I swore, let what would happen, not to sleep at the Hermitage on the night of that day week. I began to prepare for sending away my effects, resolving to leave them in the open field rather than not give up the key in the course of the week: for I was determined everything should be done before a letter could be written to Geneva, and an answer to it received. I never felt myself so inspired with courage: I had recovered all my strength. Honour and indignation, upon which Madame d'Epinay had not calculated, contributed to restore me to vigour. Fortune aided my audacity. M. Mathas, procurator fiscal to Prince de Condé, heard of my embarrassment. He sent to offer me a little house he had in his garden of Mont Louis, at Montmorency. I accepted it with eagerness and gratitude. The bargain was soon concluded: I immediately sent to purchase a little furniture to add to that we already had, so that Thérèse and I could sleep. My effects I had carted away with a deal of trouble, and at a great expense: notwithstanding the ice and snow my removal was completed in a couple of days, and, on the fifteenth of December, I gave up the keys of the Hermitage, after having paid the wages of the gardener, not being able to pay my rent.

With respect to Madame le Vasseur, I told her we must part; her daughter attempted to make me renounce my resolution, but I was inflexible. I sent her off to Paris in the carriage of the messenger with all the furniture and effects she and her daughter had in common. I gave her some money, and engaged to pay her lodging with her children or elsewhere, to provide for her subsistence as much as it should be possible for me to do it, and never to let her want bread as long as I should have it myself.

Finally, two days after my arrival at Mont Louis, I wrote to Madame d'Epinay the following letter:

'*Montmorency, 17th December, 1757.*

'Nothing, madam, is so natural and necessary as to leave your house the moment you no longer approve of my remaining there. Upon your refusing your consent to my passing the rest of the winter at the Hermitage, I quitted it on the fifteenth of December. My destiny was to enter it in spite of myself and to leave it the same. I thank you for the residence you prevailed upon me to make there, and I would thank you still more had I paid for it less dear. You are right in believing me unhappy; nobody upon earth knows better than yourself to what a degree I must be so. If being deceived in the choice of our friends be a misfortune, it is another not less cruel to recover from so pleasing an error.

'*P. S.* Your gardener is paid up to January 1st.'[1]

Such is the faithful narration of my residence at the Hermitage, and of the reasons which obliged me to leave it. I am glad to conclude the recital, and it was necessary to continue it with the greatest exactness: this epoch of my life having had upon the rest of it an influence which will extend to my latest remembrance.

BOOK TEN

THE extraordinary degree of strength a momentary effervescence had given me to quit the Hermitage, left me the moment I was out of it. I was scarcely established in my new habitation before sharp and frequent attacks of retention were accompanied by a new complaint; that of a rupture which I had for some time, without knowing that I had it. I soon was reduced to the most cruel state. The physician Thierry, my old friend, came to see me, and made me acquainted with my situation. The sight of probes, bougies, bandages, all the apparatus of the infirmities of advancing years assembled around me, made me severely feel that when the body is no longer young, the heart is not so with impunity. The fine season did not restore me, and I passed the whole year 1758 in a state of languor, which made me think I was almost at the end of my career. I saw, with a kind of impatience, the closing scene approach. Recovered from the chimeras of friendship, and detached from everything which had rendered life desirable to me, I saw nothing more in it that could make it agreeable; all I perceived was wretchedness and misery, which prevented me from enjoying myself. I sighed after the moment when I was to be free and escape from my enemies. But I must follow the order of events.

My retreat to Montmorency seemed to disconcert Madame d'Epinay; probably she did not expect it. My melancholy situa-

---

[1] The Paris MS. omits the postscript.

tion, the severity of the season, the general dereliction of me by
my friends, all made her and Grimm believe, that by driving me
to the last extremity, they should oblige me to implore mercy, and
thus, by vile meanness, render myself contemptible, to be suffered
to remain in an asylum which honour commanded me to leave.
I left it so suddenly that they had not time to prevent the step from
being taken, and they were reduced to the alternative of double
or quit, to endeavour to ruin me entirely, or to prevail upon me
to return. Grimm chose the former, but I am of opinion Madame
d'Epinay would have preferred the latter, and this from her
answer to my last letter, in which she seemed to have laid aside
the airs she had given herself in the preceding ones, and to give an
opening to an accommodation. The long delay of this answer, for
which she made me wait a whole month, sufficiently indicates the
difficulty she found in giving it a proper turn, and the delibera-
tions by which it was preceded. She could not make any farther
advances without exposing herself; but after her former letters,
and my sudden retreat from her house, it is impossible not to be
struck with the care she takes in this letter not to suffer an offensive expression to escape her. I will copy it at length to enable my
reader to judge of what she wrote.

'*Geneva, January 17th, 1758.*

'Sir, I did not receive your letter of the 17th of December until
yesterday. It was sent me in a box filled with different things,
and which has been all this time upon the road. I shall answer
only the postscript; as for the letter, I do not fully understand it,
and if we were able to make mutual explanations, I would gladly
put down all that has passed to a misunderstanding. I return to
the postscript. You may recollect, sir, that we agreed the wages
of the gardener of the Hermitage should pass through your hands,
the better to make him feel that he depended upon you, and to
avoid the ridiculous and indecent scenes which happened in the
time of his predecessor. As a proof of this, the first quarters of his
wages were given to you, and a few days before my departure,
we agreed I should reimburse you what you had advanced. I know
that of this you, at first, made some difficulty; but I had desired
you to make these advances; it was natural I should acquit myself
towards you, and this we concluded upon. Cahouet informs me
that you refused to receive the money. There is certainly some
mistake in the matter. I have given orders that it may again be
offered to you, and I see no reason for your wishing to pay my

gardener, notwithstanding our agreements, and beyond the term even of your inhabiting the Hermitage. I expect therefore, sir, that recollecting everything I have the honour to state, you will not refuse to be reimbursed for the sums you have been pleased to advance for me.'

After what had passed, not having the least confidence in Madame d'Epinay, I was unwilling to renew my connexion with her; I returned no answer to this letter, and there our correspondence ended. Perceiving I had taken my resolution, she took hers; and, entering into all the views of Grimm and the Holbach fraternity, she united her efforts with theirs to accomplish my destruction. Whilst they manœuvred at Paris, she did the same at Geneva. Grimm, who afterwards went to her there, completed what she had begun. Tronchin, whom they had no difficulty in gaining over, seconded them powerfully, and became the most violent of my persecutors, without having against me, any more than Grimm had, the least subject of complaint. They all three spread in silence at Geneva that of which the effects were seen there four years afterwards.

They had more trouble at Paris where I was better known to the citizens, whose hearts, less disposed to hatred, less easily received its impressions. The better to direct their blow, they began by giving out that it was I who had left them. Thence, still feigning to be my friends, they dexterously spread their malignant accusations by complaining of the injustice of their friend. Their auditors, thus thrown off their guard, listened more attentively to what was said of me, and were more ready to blame my conduct. The secret accusations of perfidy and ingratitude were made with greater precaution, and by that means with greater effect. I knew they imputed to me the most atrocious crimes without being able to learn in what these consisted. All I could infer from public rumour was that this was founded upon the four following capital offences: my retiring to the country; my passion for Madame d'Houdetot; my refusing to accompany Madame d'Epinay to Geneva; and my leaving the Hermitage. If to these they added other griefs, they took their measures so well, that it has been perfectly impossible for me to learn the subject of them.

It is therefore at this period that I think I may fix the establishment of a system, since adopted by those by whom my fate has been determined, and which has made such a rapid and successful progress as will seem miraculous to persons who know not with what facility everything which favours the malignity of men is established. I will endeavour to explain in a few words what to me appeared visible in this profound and obscure system.

With a name already distinguished and known throughout all Europe, I had still preserved my primitive simplicity. My mortal aversion to all party, faction, and cabal, had kept me free and independent, without any other chain than the attachments of my heart. Alone, a stranger, without family or fortune, and unconnected with everything except my principles and duties, I intrepidly followed the paths of uprightness, never flattering or favouring any person at the expense of truth and justice. Besides, having lived for two years past in solitude, without observing the course of events, I was unconnected with the affairs of the world, and not informed of what passed nor desirous of being acquainted with it. I lived four leagues from Paris, as much separated from that capital by my negligence, as I should have been in the island of Tinian[1] by the sea.

Grimm, Diderot and d'Holbach were on the contrary in the centre of the vortex, lived in the great world, and divided amongst them almost all the spheres of it. The great, wits, men of letters, men of the long robe, and women, all listened to them when they chose to act in concert. The advantage three men in this situation united must have over a fourth in mine, cannot but already appear. It is true Diderot and d'Holbach were incapable, at least I think so, of forming black conspiracies; one of them was not base enough,[2] nor the other sufficiently able; but it was for this reason that the party was more united. Grimm alone formed his plan in his mind, and discovered no more of it than was necessary to induce his associates to concur in the execution. The ascendency he had gained over them made this quite easy, and the effect of the whole answered to the superiority of his talents.

It was with these, which were of a superior kind, that, perceiving the advantage he might acquire from our respective situations, he conceived the project of overturning my reputation, and, without exposing himself, of giving me one of a nature quite opposite, beginning by raising up about me an edifice of obscurity which it was impossible for me to penetrate, and by that means throw a light upon his manœuvres and unmask him.

---

[1] One of the Ladrones.

[2] I confess that since I wrote this book, everything that I have been able to glimpse through the mysteries which surround me makes me fear that I did not know Diderot. (*Note by Rousseau*, in the Paris MS. only.)

This enterprise was difficult, because it was necessary to palliate the iniquity in the eyes of those of whose assistance he stood in need. He had honest men to deceive, to alienate from me the good opinion of everybody, and to deprive me of all my friends, great and small. What say I? He had to cut off all communication with me, that not a single word of truth might reach my ears. Had a single man of generosity come and said to me: you assume the appearance of virtue, yet this is the manner in which you are treated, and these the circumstances by which you are judged: what have you to say? — truth would have triumphed and Grimm have been undone. Of this he was fully convinced: but he had examined his own heart and estimated men according to their merit. I am sorry, for the honour of humanity, that he judged with so much truth.

In these dark and crooked paths his steps, to be the more sure, were necessarily slow. He has for twelve[1] years pursued his plan, and the most difficult part of the execution of it is still to come; this is to deceive the public entirely. He is afraid of this public and dares not lay his conspiracy open.[2] But he has found the easy means of accompanying it with power, and this power has the disposal of me. Thus supported, he advances with less danger. The agents of power generally piquing themselves but little on uprightness, and still less on candour, he has no longer the indiscretion of any honest man to fear. His safety is in my being enveloped in an impenetrable obscurity, and in concealing from me his conspiracy, well knowing that with whatever art he may have formed it, I could, by a single glance of the eye, discover the whole. His great address consists in appearing to favour whilst he defames me, and in giving to his perfidy an air of generosity.

I felt the first effects of this system by the secret accusations of the d'Holbach party without its being possible for me to know in what the accusations consisted, or to form a probable conjecture as to the nature of them. Deleyre informed me in his letters that heinous things were attributed to me. Diderot more mysteriously told me the same thing, and when I came to an explanation with both, the whole was reduced to the heads of accusation of which I have already spoken. I perceived a gradual increase of coolness

---

[1] Paris MS., ten.

[2] Since this was written he has made the dangerous step with the fullest and most inconceivable success. I am of opinion it was Tronchin who inspired him with courage, and supplied him with the means. (*Note by Rousseau*, not in Paris MS.)

in the letters from Madame d'Houdetot. This I could not attribute to St. Lambert; he continued to write to me with the same friendship and came to see me after his return. It was also impossible to think myself the cause of it, as we had separated well satisfied with each other, and nothing since that time had happened on my part, except my departure from the Hermitage, of which she herself felt the necessity. Therefore not knowing whence this coolness, which she refused to acknowledge, although my heart was not to be deceived, could proceed, I was uneasy upon every account. I knew she greatly favoured her sister-in-law and Grimm, in consequence of their connexions with St. Lambert; and I was afraid of their machinations. This agitation opened my wounds, and rendered my correspondence so disagreeable as quite to disgust her with it. I saw, as at a distance, a thousand cruel circumstances, without discovering anything distinctly. I was in a situation the most insupportable to a man whose imagination is easily heated. Had I been quite retired from the world, and knowing nothing of the matter, I should have become more calm; but my heart still clung to attachments by means of which my enemies had great advantages over me; and the feeble rays which penetrated my asylum, conveyed to me nothing more than a knowledge of the blackness of the mysteries which were concealed from my eyes.

I should have sunk, I have not a doubt of it, under these torments, too cruel and insupportable to my open disposition, which, by the impossibility of concealing my sentiments, makes me fear everything from those concealed from me, if fortunately objects sufficiently interesting to my heart to divert it from others with which, in spite of myself, my imagination was filled, had not presented themselves. In the last visit Diderot paid me at the Hermitage, he had spoken of the article *Geneva*, which d'Alembert had inserted in the *Encyclopédie;* he had informed me that this article, concerted with people of the first consideration, had for object the establishment of a theatre at Geneva, that measures had been taken accordingly, and that the establishment would soon take place. As Diderot seemed to think all this very proper, and did not doubt of the success of the measure; and as I had besides to speak to him upon too many other subjects to touch upon that article, I made him no answer; but scandalised at these preparatives to corruption and licentiousness in my country, I waited with impatience for the volume of the *Encyclopédie*, in which the article was inserted, to see whether or not it would be possible to give an answer which might ward off the blow. I received the volume soon after my establishment at Mont Louis, and found the article to be written with much art and address, and worthy of the pen whence it proceeded. This however did not abate my desire to answer it, and notwithstanding the dejection of spirits I then laboured under, my griefs and pains, the severity of the season, and the inconvenience of my new abode in which I had not yet had time to arrange myself, I set to work with a zeal which surmounted every obstacle.

In a severe winter, in the month of February, and in the situation I have described, I went every day, morning and evening, to pass a couple of hours in an open alcove which was at the bottom of the garden in which my habitation stood. This alcove, which terminated an alley in a terrace, looked upon the valley and the pond of Montmorency, and presented to me, as the closing point of a prospect, the plain but respectable castle of St. Gratien, the retreat of the virtuous Catinat. It was in this place, then, exposed to freezing cold, that, without being sheltered from the wind and snow, and having no other fire than that in my heart, I composed, in the space of three weeks, my *Letter to d'Alembert on Theatres*. It was in this, for my *Julie* was not then half written, that I first found charms in philosophical labour. Until then virtuous indignation had been a substitute to Apollo; tenderness and a gentleness of mind now became so. The injustice I had only been witness to had irritated me, that of which I became the object rendered me melancholy; and this melancholy without bitterness was that of a heart too tender and affectionate, and which, deceived by those in whom it had confided, was obliged to remain concentred. Full of that which had lately befallen me, and still affected by so many violent emotions, my heart added the sentiment of its sufferings to the ideas with which a meditation on my subject had inspired me: what I wrote bore evident marks of this mixture. Without perceiving it, I described the situation I was then in, and gave portraits of Grimm, Madame d'Epinay, Madame d'Houdetot, St. Lambert and myself. What delicious tears did I shed as I wrote! Alas! in these descriptions there are proofs but too evident that love, the fatal love of which I made such efforts to cure myself, still remained in my heart. With all this there was a certain sentiment of tenderness relative to myself: I thought I was dying, and imagined I bade the public my last adieu. Far from fearing death, I joyfully saw it approach; but I felt some regret at leaving my fellow-creatures without their

having perceived my real merit, and being convinced how much
I should have deserved their love had they known me better. These
are the secret causes of the singular manner in which this work,
so opposite to that of the work by which it was preceded,[1] is
written.

I corrected and copied the letter, and was preparing to print it
when, after a long silence, I received one from Madame d'Houdetot which brought upon me a new affliction more painful than any
I had yet suffered. She informed me that my passion for her was

JEAN D'ALEMBERT

known to all Paris, that I had spoken of it to persons who had
made it public, that this rumour having reached the ears of her
lover had nearly cost him his life; that at last he did her justice,

---

[1] *Discours sur l'Inégalité.* (*Note by Rousseau.*)

and peace was restored between them; but on his account, as well
as on hers, and for the sake of her reputation, she thought it her
duty to break off all correspondence with me, at the same time
assuring me that she and her friend would never cease to be
interested in my welfare, that they would defend me to the public,
and that she herself would from time to time send to enquire
after me.

And thou also, Diderot, exclaimed I! unworthy friend! ——
I could not, however, yet resolve to condemn him. My weakness
was known to others who might have spoken of it. I wished to
doubt —— but this was soon out of my power. St. Lambert shortly
after performed an action worthy of himself. Knowing my manner of thinking, he judged of the state in which I must be; betrayed by one part of my friends, and forsaken by the other. He
came to see me. The first time he had not many moments to spare.
He came again. Unfortunately, not expecting him, I was not at
home. Thérèse had with him a conversation of upwards of two
hours, in which they informed each other of facts of great importance to us all. The surprise with which I learned that nobody
doubted of my having lived with Madame d'Epinay, as Grimm
then did, cannot be equalled, except by that of St. Lambert, when
he was convinced that the rumour was false. He, to the great dissatisfaction of the lady, was in the same situation with myself,
and the enlightenment resulting from the conversation removed
from me all regret on account of my having broken with her for
ever. Relative to Madame d'Houdetot, he mentioned several circumstances with which neither Thérèse nor Madame d'Houdetot
herself was acquainted; these were known to me only in the first
instance, and I had never mentioned them, except to Diderot,
under the seal of friendship; and it was to St. Lambert himself
to whom he had chosen to communicate them. This last step was
sufficient to determine them. I resolved to break with Diderot for
ever, and this without farther deliberation, except on the manner
of doing it; for I had perceived secret ruptures turned to my prejudice, because they left the mask of friendship in possession of my
most cruel enemies.

The rules of good breeding, established in the world on this
head, seem to have been dictated by a spirit of treachery and
falsehood. To appear the friend of a man when in reality we are
no longer so, is to reserve to ourselves the means of doing him an
injury by surprising honest men into an error. I recollected that
when the illustrious Montesquieu broke with Father de Tourne-

mine, he immediately made it quite clear, and said to everybody: Listen neither to Father Tournemine nor myself, when we speak of each other, for we are no longer friends. This open and generous proceeding was universally applauded. I resolved to follow the example with Diderot; but what method was I to take to publish the rupture authentically from my retreat, and yet without scandal? I concluded on inserting, in the form of a note, in my work, a passage from the Book of Ecclesiasticus,[1] which declared the rupture and even the subject of it, in terms sufficiently clear to such as were acquainted with the previous circumstances, but could signify nothing to the rest of the world. I determined not to speak in my work of the friend whom I renounced, except with the honour always due to extinguished friendship. The whole may be seen in the work itself.

There is nothing in this world but time and misfortune, and every act of courage seems to be a crime in adversity. For that which had been admired in Montesquieu, I received only blame and reproach. As soon as my work was printed, and I had copies of it, I sent one to St. Lambert, who, the evening before, had written to me in his own name and that of Madame d'Houdetot, a note expressive of the most tender friendship. The following is the letter he wrote to me when he returned the copy I had sent him.

'*Eaubonne, 10th October, 1758.*

'Indeed, sir, I cannot accept the present you have just made me. In that part of your preface where, relative to Diderot, you quote a passage from Ecclesiastes (he mistakes, it is from Ecclesiasticus) the book dropped from my hand. In the conversations we had together in the summer, you seemed to be persuaded Diderot was not guilty of the pretended indiscretions you had imputed to him. You may, for aught I know to the contrary, have reason to complain of him, but this does not give you a right to insult him publicly. You are not unacquainted with the nature of the persecutions he suffers, and you join the voice of an old friend to that of envy. I cannot refrain from telling you, sir, how much this heinous act of yours has shocked me. I am not acquainted with Diderot, but I honour him, and I have a lively sense of the pain you give to a man, whom, at least not in my hearing, you have never reproached with anything more than a trifling weakness. You and I, sir, differ too much in our principles ever to be agreeable to each

---

[1] Ecclus. xxii, 26-27 (Vulgate).

other. Forget that I exist; this you will easily do. I have never
done to men either good or evil of a nature to be long remembered.
I promise you, sir, to forget your person, and to remember nothing relative to you but your talents.'

This letter filled me with indignation and affliction; and, in the
excess of my pangs, feeling my pride wounded, I answered him
by the following note:

'*Montmorency, 11th October, 1758.*

'Sir, While reading your letter, I did you the honour to be surprised at it, and had the weakness to suffer it to affect me; but I
find it unworthy of an answer.

'I will no longer continue the copies of Madame d'Houdetot.
If it be not agreeable to her to keep that she has, she may send it
me back and I will return her money. If she keeps it, she must
still send for the rest of her paper and the money; and at the same
time I beg she will return me the prospectus which she has in her
possession. Adieu, sir.'

Courage under misfortunes irritates the hearts of cowards, but
it is pleasing to generous minds. This note seemed to make St.
Lambert reflect with himself, and to regret his having been so
violent; but, too haughty in his turn to make open advances, he
seized, and perhaps prepared, the opportunity of palliating what
he had done. A fortnight afterwards I received from Madame
d'Epinay the following letter:

'*Thursday, 26th.*

'Sir, I received the book you had the goodness to send me, and
which I have read with much pleasure. I have always experienced
the same sentiment in reading all the works which have come
from your pen. Receive my thanks for the whole. I should have
returned you these in person had my affairs permitted me to
remain any time in your neighbourhood; but I was not this year
long at la Chevrette. M. and Madame Dupin will come there on
Sunday to dinner. I expect M. de St. Lambert, M. de Francueil,
and Madame d'Houdetot will be of the party; you will do me
much pleasure by making one also. All the persons who are to
dine with me, desire, and will, as well as myself, be delighted to
pass with you a part of the day. I have the honour to be with the
most perfect consideration, etc.'

This letter made my heart beat violently. After having for a year past been the subject of conversation of all Paris, the idea of presenting myself as a spectacle before Madame d'Houdetot made me tremble, and I had much difficulty to find sufficient courage to support that ceremony. Yet as she and St. Lambert were desirous of it, and Madame d'Epinay spoke in the name of her guests without naming one whom I should not be glad to see, I did not think I should expose myself by accepting a dinner to which I was in some degree invited by all the persons who with myself were to partake of it. I therefore promised to go: on Sunday the weather was bad, and Madame d'Epinay sent me her carriage.

My arrival caused a sensation. I never met a better reception. An observer would have thought the whole company felt how much I stood in need of encouragement. None but French hearts are susceptible of this kind of delicacy. However, I found more people than I had expected to see: amongst others the Comte d'Houdetot, whom I did not know, and his sister Madame de Blainville, without whose company I should have been as well pleased. She had the year before come several times to Eaubonne, and her sister-in-law had left her, in our solitary walks, to wait until she thought proper to suffer her to join us. She had harboured a resentment against me, which during this dinner she gratified at her ease. The presence of the Comte d'Houdetot and St. Lambert did not give me the laugh on my side, and it may be judged that a man embarrassed in the most common conversations was not very brilliant in that which then had place. I never suffered so much, appeared so awkward, nor received more unexpected mortifications. As soon as we had risen from table, I withdrew from that shrew; I had the pleasure of seeing St. Lambert and Madame d'Houdetot approach me, and we conversed together a part of the afternoon, upon things very indifferent, it is true, but with the same familiarity as before my involuntary error. This friendly attention was not lost upon my heart, and could St. Lambert have read what passed there, he certainly would have been satisfied with it. I can safely assert that although on my arrival the presence of Madame d'Houdetot gave me the most violent palpitations, on returning from the house I scarcely thought of her; my mind was entirely taken up with St. Lambert.

Notwithstanding the malignant sarcasms of Madame de Blainville, the dinner was of great service to me, and I congratulated myself upon not having refused the invitation. I not only discovered that the intrigues of Grimm and the Holbachians had not deprived me of my old acquaintance,[1] but, what flattered me still more, that Madame d'Houdetot and St. Lambert were less changed than I had imagined, and I at length understood that his keeping her at a distance from me proceeded more from jealousy than disesteem. This was a consolation to me, and calmed my mind. Certain of not being an object of contempt in the eyes of persons whom I esteemed, I worked upon my own heart with greater courage and success. If I did not quite extinguish in it a guilty and

JEAN FRANÇOIS MARMONTEL

an unhappy passion, I at least so well regulated the remains of it that they have never since that moment led me into the most trifling error. The copies of Madame d'Houdetot, which she prevailed upon me to take again, and my works, which I continued

---

[1] Such in the simplicity of my heart was my opinion when I wrote these confessions. (*Note by Rousseau*, not in Paris MS.)

to send her as soon as they appeared, produced me from her from time to time a few notes and messages, indifferent but obliging. She did still more, as will hereafter appear, and the reciprocal conduct of her lover and myself, after our intercourse had ceased, may serve as an example of the manner in which persons of honour separate when it is no longer agreeable to them to associate with each other.

Another advantage this dinner procured me was its being spoken of in Paris, where it served as a refutation of the rumour spread by my enemies, that I had quarrelled with every person who partook of it, and especially with M. d'Epinay. When I left the Hermitage I had written him a very polite letter of thanks, to which he answered not less politely, and mutual civilities had continued, as well between us as between me and M. de Lalive, his brother, who even came to see me at Montmorency, and sent me some of his engravings. Excepting the two sisters-in-law of Madame d'Houdetot, I have never been upon bad terms with any person of the family.

My *Letter to d'Alembert* had great success. All my works had been very well received, but this was more favourable to me. It taught the public to guard against the insinuations of the Holbach group. When I went to the Hermitage, this group predicted with its usual sufficiency, that I should not remain there three months. When I had stayed there twenty months, and was obliged to leave it, I still fixed my residence in the country. The Holbachians insisted this was from a motive of pure obstinacy, and that I was weary even to death of my retirement; but that, eaten up with pride, I chose rather to become a victim to my stubbornness than to recover from it and return to Paris. The *Letter to d'Alembert* breathed a gentleness of mind which everyone perceived not affected. Had I been dissatisfied with my retreat, my style and manner would have borne evident marks of my ill humour. This reigned in all the works I had written at Paris; but in the first I wrote in the country not the least appearance of it was to be found. To persons who knew how to distinguish, this remark was decisive. They perceived I was returned to my element.

Yet the same work, notwithstanding all the mildness it breathed, made me, by a mistake of my own and my usual ill luck, another enemy amongst men of letters. I had become acquainted with Marmontel at the house of M. de la Poplinière, and this acquaintance had been continued at that of the Baron. Marmontel at that time wrote the *Mercure de France*. As I had too much pride to send my works to the authors of periodical publications, and wishing to send him this without his imagining it was on that ground, or being desirous he should speak of it in the *Mercure*, I wrote upon the book that it was not for the author of the *Mercure*, but for M. Marmontel. I thought I paid him a very fine compliment; he mistook it for a cruel offence, and became my irreconcilable enemy. He wrote against the *Letter*, with politeness it is true, but with a bitterness easily perceivable, and since that time has never lost an opportunity of injuring me in society, and of indirectly ill-treating me in his works. Such difficulty is there in managing the irritable self-love of men of letters, and so careful ought every person to be not to leave anything equivocal in the compliments they pay them.

Having nothing more to disturb me, I took advantage of my leisure and independence to continue my literary pursuits with more coherence. I this winter finished my *Julie*, and sent it to Rey, who had it printed the year following. I was however interrupted in my projects by a circumstance sufficiently disagreeable. I heard new preparations were making at the Opera-house to give the *Devin du Village*. Enraged at seeing these people arrogantly dispose of my property, I again took up the memoir I had sent to M. d'Argenson, to which no answer had been returned, and having made some trifling alterations in it, I sent the manuscript by M. Sellon, resident from Geneva, and a letter with which he was pleased to charge himself, to the Comte de St. Florentin, who had succeeded M. d'Argenson in the Opera department. M. de Florentin promised an answer, but made none. Duclos, to whom I communicated what I had done, mentioned it to the *petits violons*, who offered to restore me, not my Opera, but my freedom of the theatre, which I was no longer in a situation to enjoy. Perceiving I had not from any quarter the least justice to expect, I gave up the affair; and the directors of the Opera, without either answering or listening to my reasons, have continued to dispose as of their own property, and to turn to their profit, the *Devin du Village*, which incontestably belongs to nobody but myself.[1]

Since I had shaken off the yoke of my tyrants, I led a life sufficiently agreeable and peaceful; deprived of the charm of too strong attachments, I was delivered from the weight of their chains. Disgusted with the friends who pretended to be my protectors, and wished absolutely to dispose of me at will, and in

---

[1] It now belongs to them by virtue of a new agreement recently made to that effect. (*Note by Rousseau*, not in Paris MS.)

spite of myself to subject me to their pretended good services, I resolved in future to have no other connexions than those of simple benevolence. These, without the least constraint upon liberty, constitute the pleasure of society, of which equality is the basis. I had of them as many as were necessary to enable me to taste of the charms of liberty without being subject to the dependence of it; and as soon as I had made an experiment of this manner of life, I felt it was the most proper to my age, to end my days in peace, far removed from the agitations, quarrels, and cavillings, in which I had just been half submerged.

During my residence at the Hermitage, and after my settlement at Montmorency, I had made in the neighbourhood some agreeable acquaintances, which did not subject me to any inconvenience. The principal of these was young Loyseau de Mauléon, who, then beginning to plead at the bar, did not yet know what rank he would one day hold there. I for my part was not in the least doubt about the matter. I soon pointed out to him the illustrious career in the midst of which he is now seen, and predicted that, if he laid down to himself rigid rules for the choice of causes, and never became the defender of anything but virtue and justice, his genius, elevated by this sublime sentiment, would be equal to that of the greatest orators. He followed my advice, and now feels the good effects of it. His defence of M. de Portes is worthy of Demosthenes. He came every year within a quarter of a league of the Hermitage to pass the vacation at St. Brice, in the fief of Mauléon, belonging to his mother, and where the great Bossuet had formerly lodged. This is a fief, of which a like succession of proprietors would render nobility difficult to support.

I had also for a neighbour in the same village of St. Brice, the bookseller Guérin, a man of wit, learning, of an amiable disposition, and one of the first in his profession. He brought me acquainted with Jean Néaulme, bookseller of Amsterdam, his friend and correspondent, who afterwards printed *Emile*.

I had another acquaintance still nearer than St. Brice; this was M. Maltor, vicar of Groslay, a man better adapted for the functions of a statesman and a minister than for those of the vicar of a village, and to whom a diocese at least would have been given to govern if talents decided the disposal of places. He had been secretary to the Comte du Luc, and was formerly intimately acquainted with Jean Baptiste Rousseau. Holding in as much esteem the memory of that illustrious exile, as he held the villainous Saurin in horror, he possessed curious anecdotes of both,

which Ségui had not inserted in the life, still in manuscript, of
the former, and he assured me that the Comte du Luc, far from
ever having had reason to complain of his conduct, had until his
last moment preserved for him the warmest friendship. M. Maltor, to whom M. de Vintimille gave this pleasant retreat after the
death of his protector, had formerly been employed in many affairs of which, although far advanced in years, he still preserved
a distinct remembrance, and reasoned upon them tolerably well.
His conversation, equally amusing and instructive, had nothing
in it resembling that of a village pastor; he joined the manners
of a man of the world to the knowledge of one who passes his life
in study. He, of all my permanent neighbours, was the person
whose society was the most agreeable to me, and whom I regretted
most to leave.

I was also acquainted at Montmorency with several Fathers of
the Oratory, and amongst others Father Berthier, professor of
natural philosophy; to whom, notwithstanding some little tinc-
ture of pedantry, I became attached on account of a certain air of
cordial good nature which I observed in him. I had however some
difficulty to reconcile this great simplicity with the desire and the
art he had of everywhere thrusting himself into the company of
the great, as well as that of the women, devotees, and philosophers.
He knew how to accommodate himself to everything. I was greatly pleased with the man, and spoke of my satisfaction to all my
other acquaintance. Apparently what I said of him came to his
ear. He one day thanked me sneeringly for having thought him a
good-natured man. I observed something in his forced smile
which, in my eyes, totally changed his physiognomy, and which
has since frequently occurred to my mind. I cannot better compare this little smile than to that of Panurge purchasing the sheep
of Dindenaut. Our acquaintance had begun a little time after my
arrival at the Hermitage, to which place he frequently came to
see me. I was already settled at Montmorency when he left it to
go and reside in Paris. He often saw Madame le Vasseur there.
One day, when I least expected anything of the kind, he wrote to
me in behalf of that woman, informing me that Grimm offered
to maintain her, and to ask my permission to accept the offer. This
I understood consisted in a pension of three hundred livres, and
that Madame le Vasseur was to come and live at Deuil, between
la Chevrette and Montmorency. I will not say what impression
the application made on me. It would have been less surprising
had Grimm had ten thousand livres a year, or any relation more

easy to comprehend with that woman, and had not such a crime been made of my taking her to the country, where, as if she had become younger, he was now pleased to think of placing her. I perceived the good old lady had no other reason for asking my permission, which she might easily have done without, had I refused it, but the fear of losing what I already gave her, should I think ill of the step she took. Although this charity appeared to be very extraordinary, it did not strike me so much then as afterwards. But had I known even everything I have since discovered, I would still as readily have given my consent as I did and was obliged to do, unless I had exceeded the offer of M. Grimm. Father Berthier thenceforward cured me a little of my opinion of his good nature and cordiality with which I had so unthinkingly charged him.

This same Father Berthier was acquainted with two men who, for what reason I know not, sought to become so with me; there was little similarity between their taste and mine. They were children of Melchisedec, of whom neither the country nor the family was known, no more than, in all probability, the real name. They were Jansenists, and passed for priests in disguise, perhaps on account of their ridiculous manner of wearing long swords, to which they appeared to have been fastened. The prodigious mystery in all their proceedings gave them the appearance of the heads of a party, and I never had the least doubt of their being the authors of the *Gazette Ecclésiastique*. The one, tall, smooth-tongued, and sharping, was named Ferrand; the other, short, squat, a sneerer, and punctilious, was a M. Minard. They called each other cousin. They lodged at Paris with d'Alembert, in the house of his nurse, named Madame Rousseau, and had taken at Montmorency a little apartment to pass the summers there. They did everything for themselves, and had neither a servant nor runner; each had his turn weekly to purchase provisions, do the business of the kitchen, and sweep the house. They managed tolerably well, and we sometimes ate with each other. I know not for what reason they gave themselves any concern about me: for my part, my only motive for beginning an acquaintance with them was their playing at chess, and to make a poor little party I suffered four hours' fatigue. As they thrust themselves into all companies, and wished to intermeddle in everything, Thérèse called them *the gossips*, and by this name they were long known at Montmorency.

Such, with my host M. Mathas, who was a good man, were

my principal country acquaintance. I still had a sufficient number at Paris to live there agreeably whenever I chose it, out of the sphere of men of letters, amongst whom Duclos was the only friend I reckoned; for Deleyre was still too young, and although, after having been a witness to the manœuvres of the philosophical tribe against me, he had withdrawn from it, at least I thought so; I could not yet forget the facility with which he made himself the mouthpiece of all the people of that description.

In the first place I had my old and respectable friend Roguin. This was a good old-fashioned friend for whom I was not indebted to my writings but to myself, and whom for that reason I have always preserved. I had the good Lenieps, my countryman, and his daughter, then alive, Madame Lambert. I had a young Genevese, named Coindet, a good creature, careful, officious, zealous, but ignorant, forward, greedy, and presumptuous, who came to see me soon after I had gone to reside at the Hermitage, and, without any other introducer than himself, had made his way into my good graces. He had a taste for drawing, and was acquainted with artists. He was of service to me relative to the engravings of *Julie;* he undertook the direction of the drawings and the plates, and acquitted himself well of the commission.

I had free access to the house of M. Dupin, which, less brilliant than in the young days of Madame Dupin, was still, by the merit of the heads of the family and the choice of company which assembled there, one of the best houses in Paris. As I had not preferred anybody to them, and had separated myself from their society only to live free and independent, they had always received me in a friendly manner, and I was always certain of being well received by Madame Dupin. I might even have counted her amongst my country neighbours after their establishment at Clichy, to which place I sometimes went to pass a day or two, and where I should have been more frequently had Madame Dupin and Madame de Chenonceaux been upon better terms. But the difficulty of dividing my time in the same house between two women whose manner of thinking was unfavourable to each other, made Clichy disagreeable. Attached to Madame de Chenonceaux in a more equal and familiar friendship, I had the pleasure of seeing her more at my ease at Deuil, where, at a trifling distance from me, she had taken a small house, and even at my own habitation, where she often came to see me.

I had likewise for a friend Madame de Créqui, who, become a devotee, no longer received d'Alembert, Marmontel, nor a single

man of letters, except I believe, the Abbé Trublet, half a hypocrite, of whom she was weary. I, whose acquaintance she had
sought, neither lost her good wishes nor intercourse. She sent me
as presents young fat pullets from Le Mans, and her intention
was to come and see me the year following, had not a journey,
upon which Madame de Luxembourg determined, prevented her.
I here owe her a place apart; she will always hold a distinguished
one in my remembrance.

In this list I should also place a man whom, except Roguin,
I ought to have mentioned as the first upon it: my old friend and
brother politician de Carrio, formerly titular secretary to the
embassy from Spain at Venice, afterwards in Sweden, where he
was chargé d'affaires, and at length really secretary to the embassy from Spain at Paris. He came and surprised me at Montmorency when I least expected him. He was decorated with the
ensigns of a Spanish order, the name of which I have forgotten,
with a fine cross in jewellery. He had been obliged, in his proofs
of nobility, to add a letter to his name, and bore that of the Chevalier de Carrion. I found him still the same man, possessing the
same excellent heart, and his mind daily improving and becoming
more and more amiable. We should have renewed our former
intimacy had not Coindet interposed according to custom, taken
advantage of the distance I was at from town to insinuate himself
into my place, and, in my name, into his confidence, and supplant
me by the excess of his zeal to render me services.

The remembrance of Carrion makes me recollect one of my
country neighbours, of whom I should be inexcusable not to
speak, as I have to make confession of an unpardonable neglect
of which I was guilty towards him: this was the honest M. Le
Blond who had done me a service at Venice, and, having made an
excursion to France with his family, had taken a house in the
country, at La Briche, not far from Montmorency.[1] As soon as
I heard he was my neighbour, I, in the joy of my heart, and
making it more a pleasure than a duty, went to pay him a visit.
I set off upon this errand the next day. I was met by people who
were coming to see me, and with whom I was obliged to return.
Two days afterwards I set off again for the same purpose: he had
dined at Paris with all his family. A third time he was at home:
I heard the voice of women, and saw, at the door, a coach which

[1] When I wrote this, full of my old blind confidence, I was far from suspecting the real motive and the effect of this journey to Paris. (Note by Rousseau,
not in Paris MS.)

alarmed me. I wished to see him, at least for the first time, quite at my ease, that we might talk over what had passed during our former connexion. In fine I so often postponed my visit from day to day, that the shame of discharging a like duty so late prevented me from doing it at all; after having dared to wait so long, I no longer dared to present myself. This negligence, at which M. Le Blond could not but be justly offended, gave, relative to him, the appearance of ingratitude to my indolence, and yet I felt my heart so little culpable that, had it been in my power to do M. Le Blond the least service, even unknown to himself, I am certain he would not have found me idle. But indolence, negligence, and delay, in little duties to be fulfilled, have been more prejudicial to me than great vices. My greatest faults have been omissions: I have seldom done what I ought not to have done, and unfortunately it has still more rarely happened that I have done what I ought.

Since I am now upon the subject of my Venetian acquaintance, I must not forget one, which I still preserved for a considerable time after my intercourse with the rest had ceased. This was M. de Jonville, who had continued after his return from Genoa to show me much friendship. He was fond of seeing me, and of conversing with me upon the affairs of Italy, and the follies of M. de Montaigu, of whom he of himself knew many anecdotes by means of his acquaintance in the office for foreign affairs in which he was much connected. I had also the pleasure of seeing at his house my old comrade Dupont, who had purchased a place in the province of which he was, and whose affairs brought him sometimes to Paris. M. de Jonville became by degrees so desirous of seeing me, that he in some measure laid me under constraint; and although our places of residence were at a great distance from each other, we had a friendly quarrel when I let a week pass without going to dine with him. When he went to Jonville he was always desirous of my accompanying him; but having once been there to pass a week, which seemed very long, I had not the least desire to return. M. de Jonville was certainly an honest man, and even amiable in certain respects, but his understanding was beneath mediocrity; he was handsome, rather fond of his person, and tolerably fatiguing. He had one of the most singular collections perhaps in the world, to which he gave much of his attention, and endeavoured to acquire it that of his friends, to whom it sometimes afforded less amusement than it did to himself. This was a very complete collection of songs of the Court and Paris, for upwards of fifty years past, in which many anecdotes were to be found that would have been sought for in vain elsewhere. These are memoirs for the history of France, which would scarcely be thought of in any other country.

One day, whilst we were still upon the very best terms, he received me so coldly, and in a manner so different from that which was customary to him, that after having given him an opportunity to explain, and even having begged him to do it, I left his house with a resolution, in which I have persevered, never to return to it again; for I am seldom seen where I have been once ill received, and in this case there was no Diderot who pleaded for M. de Jonville. I vainly endeavoured to discover what I had done to offend him; I could not recollect a circumstance at which he could possibly have taken offence. I was certain of never having spoken of him, or his, in any other than in the most honourable manner; for I was sincerely attached to him, and besides my having nothing but favourable things to say of him, my most inviolable maxim has been that of never speaking but in an honourable manner of the houses I frequented.

At length, by continually ruminating, I formed the following conjecture: the last time we had seen each other, I had supped with him at the apartment of some girls of his acquaintance, in company with two or three clerks in the office of foreign affairs, very amiable men, and who had neither the manner nor the appearance of libertines; and, on my part, I can assert that the whole evening passed in making melancholy reflections on the wretched fate of the creatures with whom we were. I did not pay anything, as M. de Jonville gave the supper, nor did I make the girls the least present, because I gave them not the opportunity I had done to the Padoana of establishing a claim to the trifle I might have offered. We all came away together, cheerfully and upon very good terms. Without having made a second visit to the girls, I went three or four days afterwards to dine with M. de Jonville, whom I had not seen during that interval, and who gave me the reception of which I have spoken. Unable to suppose any other cause for it than some misunderstanding relative to the supper, and perceiving he had no inclination to explain, I resolved to visit him no longer, but I still continued to send him my works: he frequently sent me his compliments, and, one evening, meeting him in the green room of the French theatre, he obligingly reproached me with not having called to see him, which, however, did not induce me to depart from my resolution. Therefore this affair had rather the appearance of a coolness than a rupture.

However, not having heard nor seen him since that time, it would have been too late, after an absence of several years, to renew my acquaintance with him. It is for this reason M. de Jonville is not named in my list, although I had for a considerable time frequented his house.

I will not swell my catalogue with the names of many other persons with whom I was or had become less intimate, although I sometimes saw them in the country either at my own house or that of some neighbour, such for instance as the Abbés de Condillac and de Mably, M. de Mairan, de Lalive, de Boisgelou, Watelet, Ancelet and others. I will also pass lightly over that of M. de Margency, gentleman in ordinary of the King, an ancient member of the Holbach group, which he had quitted as well as myself, and the old friend of Madame d'Epinay from whom he had separated as I had done; I likewise consider that of M. Desmahis his friend, the celebrated but short-lived author of the comedy of the *Impertinent*, of much the same importance. The first was my neighbour in the country, his estate at Margency being near to Montmorency. We were old acquaintance, but the neighbourhood and a certain conformity of experience connected us still more. The last died soon afterwards. He had merit and even wit, but he was in some degree the original of his comedy, and a little of a coxcomb with women, by whom he was not much regretted.

I cannot, however, omit taking notice of a new correspondence I entered into at this period, which has had too much influence over the rest of my life not to make it necessary for me to mark its origin. The person in question is M. de Lamoignon de Malesherbes, First President of the *Cour des aides*, then censor of books, which office he exercised with equal intelligence and mildness to the great satisfaction of men of letters. I had not once been to see him at Paris; yet I had never received from him any other than the most obliging condescensions relative to the censorship, and I knew that he had more than once very severely reprimanded persons who had written against me. I had new proofs of his goodness upon the subject of the printing of *Julie*. The proofs of so great a work being very expensive from Amsterdam by post, he, to whom all letters were free, permitted these to be addressed to him, and sent them to me under the countersign of the Chancellor his father. When the work was printed, he did not permit the sale of it in the kingdom until, contrary to my wishes, an edition had been sold for my benefit. As the profit of this would on my part have been a theft committed upon Rey, to whom I had sold the manuscript, I not only refused to accept the present intended me, without his consent, which he very generously gave, but insisted upon dividing with him the hundred pistoles the amount of it, but of which he would not receive anything. For these hundred pistoles I had the mortification, against which M. de Malesherbes had not guarded me, of seeing my work horridly mutilated, and the sale of the good edition stopped until the bad one was entirely disposed of.

I have always considered M. de Malesherbes as a man whose uprightness was proof against every temptation. Nothing that has happened has ever made me doubt for a moment of his probity; but, as weak as he is polite, he sometimes injures those he wishes to serve by the excess of his zeal to preserve them from evil. He not only retrenched a hundred pages in the edition of Paris, but he made another retrenchment which no person but the author could permit himself to do in the copy of the good edition he sent to Madame de Pompadour. It is somewhere said in that work that the wife of a coal-heaver is more respectable than the mistress of a Prince. This phrase had occurred to me in the warmth of composition without any application. In reading over the work I perceived it would be applied, yet in consequence of the very imprudent maxim I had adopted of not suppressing anything on account of the applications which might be made, when my conscience bore witness to me that I had not made them at the time I wrote, I determined not to expunge the phrase, and contented myself with substituting the word *Prince* for *King*, which I had first written. This softening did not seem sufficient to M. de Malesherbes; he retrenched the whole expression in a new sheet which he had printed on purpose and stuck in between the other with as much exactness as possible in the copy of Madame de Pompadour. She was not ignorant of this manœuvre. Some good-natured people took the trouble to inform her of it. For my part it was not until a long time afterwards, and when I began to feel the consequences of it, that the matter came to my knowledge.

Is not this the origin of the concealed but implacable hatred of another lady, who was in a like situation, without my knowing it or even being acquainted with her person when I wrote the passage? When the book was published the acquaintance was made, and I was very uneasy. I mentioned this to the Chevalier de Lorenzy, who laughed at me, and said the lady was so little offended that she had not even taken notice of the matter. I believed him, perhaps rather too lightly, and made myself easy when there was much reason for my being otherwise.

At the beginning of the winter I received an additional mark of the goodness of M. de Malesherbes, of which I was very sensible, although I did not think proper to take advantage of it. A place was vacant in the *Journal des Savants*. Margency wrote to me, proposing to me the place as from himself. But I easily perceived from the manner of the letter, that he was dictated to and authorised; he afterwards told me he had been desired to make me the offer. The occupations of this place were but trifling. All I should have had to do would have been to make two extracts a month, from the books brought to me for that purpose, without being under the necessity of going once to Paris, nor even to pay the magistrate a visit of thanks. By this employment I should have entered a society of men of letters of the first merit; MM. de Mairan, Clairaut, de Guignes and the Abbé Barthélemy, with the first two of whom I had already made an acquaintance, and that of the two others was very desirable. In fine, for this trifling employment, the duties of which I might so commodiously have discharged, there was a salary of eight hundred livres. I was for a few hours undecided, and this only from a fear of making Margency angry and displeasing M. de Malesherbes. But at length the insupportable constraint of not having it in my power to work when I thought proper and to be commanded by time; and moreover the certainty of badly performing the functions with which I was to charge myself, prevailed over everything, and determined me to refuse a place for which I was unfit. I knew that my whole talent consisted in a certain warmth of mind with respect to the subjects of which I had to treat, and that nothing but the love of that which was great, beautiful and sublime could animate my genius. What would the subjects of the extracts I should have had to make from books, or even the book themselves, have signified to me? My indifference about them would have frozen my pen, and stupefied my mind. People thought I could make a trade of writing, as most of the other men of letters did, instead of which I never could write but from the warmth of imagination.

This certainly was not necessary for the *Journal des Savants*. I therefore wrote to Margency a letter of thanks in the politest terms possible, and so well explained to him my reasons, that it was not possible that either he or M. de Malesherbes could imagine there was pride or ill humour in my refusal. They both approved of it without receiving me less politely, and the secret was so well kept that it was never known to the public.

The proposition did not come in a favourable moment. I had some time before this formed the project of entirely quitting literature, and especially the trade of an author. I had been disgusted with men of letters by everything that had lately befallen me, and had learned from experience that it was impossible to proceed in the same track without having some connexions with them. I was not much less dissatisfied with men of the world, and in general with the mixed life I had lately led, half to myself, and half devoted to societies for which I was unfit. I felt more than ever, and by constant experience, that every unequal association is disadvantageous to the weaker person. Living with opulent people, and in a situation different from that I had chosen, without keeping a house as they did, I was obliged to imitate them in many things, and little expenses which were nothing for their fortunes, were for me not less ruinous than indispensable. Another man in the country-house of a friend, is served by his own servant, as well at table as in his chamber; he sends him to seek for everything he wants; having nothing directly to do with the servants of the house, not even seeing them, he gives them what he pleases, and when he thinks proper; but I, alone, and without servant, was at the mercy of the servants of the house, of whom it was necessary to gain the good graces that I might not have too much to suffer, and being treated as the equal of their master, I was obliged to treat them accordingly, and better than another would have done, because in fact I stood in greater need of their services. This, where there are but few domestics, may be complied with; but in the houses I frequented there were a great number, all very arrogant, rascally, and concerned for their own interests, which the knaves so well understood that they knew how to make me want the services of them all successively. The women of Paris, who have so much wit, have no just idea of this inconvenience, and in their zeal to economise my purse, they ruined me. If I supped in town, at any considerable distance from my lodgings, instead of permitting me to send for a hackney-coach, the mistress of the house ordered her horses to be put to, and sent me home in her carriage; she was very glad to save me the twenty-four sous for the fiacre, but never thought of the half-crown I gave to her coachman and footman. If a lady wrote to me from Paris to the Hermitage or to Montmorency, she regretted the four sous the postage of the letter would have cost me, and sent

it by one of her servants, who came sweating on foot, and to whom
I gave a dinner and half a crown, which he certainly had well
earned. If she proposed to me to pass with her a week or a fortnight at her country-house, she still said to herself, it will be a
saving to the poor man; during that time his eating will cost him
nothing. She never recollected that I was the whole time idle,
that the expenses of my family, my rent, linen, and clothes were
still going on, that I paid my barber double, that it cost me more
being in her house than in my own, and although I confined my
little largesses to the houses in which I customarily lived, that
these were still ruinous to me. I am certain I have paid upwards
of twenty-five crowns in the house of Madame d'Houdetot, at
Eaubonne, where I never slept more than four or five times, and
upwards of a thousand livres as well at Epinay as at la Chevrette,
during the five or six years I was most assiduous there. These
expenses are inevitable to a man like me, who knows not how to
provide anything for himself, or make shift for himself, and cannot support the sight of a lackey who grumbles, and serves him
with a sour look. With Madame Dupin even, where I was one of
the family, and in whose house I rendered many services to the
servants, I never received theirs but for my money. In course of
time it was necessary to renounce these little liberalities which
my situation no longer permitted me to bestow, and I felt still
more severely the inconvenience of associating with people in a
situation different from my own.

Had this manner of life been to my taste, I should have been
consoled for a heavy expense, which I dedicated to my pleasures;
but to ruin myself at the same time that I fatigued my mind, was
insupportable, and I had so felt the weight of this that, profiting
by the interval of liberty I then had, I was determined to perpetuate it, and entirely to renounce great companies, the composition
of books, and all literary concerns, and for the remainder of my
days to confine myself to the narrow and peaceful sphere in which
I felt I was born to move.

The produce of the *Letter to d'Alembert*, and of the *Nouvelle
Héloïse*, had a little improved the state of my finances, which had
been considerably exhausted at the Hermitage. I had now about
a thousand crowns in my purse. The *Emile*, to which, after I had
finished *Héloïse*, I had given great application, was in forwardness, and the produce of this could not be less than the sum of
which I was already in possession. I intended to place this money
in such a manner as to produce me a little annual income, which,

with my copying, might be sufficient to my wants without writing any more. I had two other works upon the stocks. The first of these was my *Institutions Politiques*. I examined the state of this work, and found it required several years' labour. I had not courage enough to continue it, and to wait until it was finished before I carried my intentions into execution. Therefore, laying the book aside, I determined to take from it all I could, and to burn the rest; and continuing this with zeal without interrupting *Emile*, I finished in less than two years the *Contrat Social*.

The *Dictionary of Music* now remained. This was mechanical, and might be taken up at any time; the object of it was entirely pecuniary; I reserved to myself the liberty of laying it aside, or of finishing it at my ease, according as my other resources collected should render this necessary or superfluous. With respect to the *Morale Sensitive*, of which I had made nothing more than a sketch, I entirely gave it up.

As my last project, if I found I could entirely do without copying, was that of removing from Paris, where the affluence of my visitors rendered my housekeeping expensive, and deprived me of the time I should have turned to advantage to provide for it; to prevent in my retirement the state of lassitude, into which an author is said to fall when he has laid down his pen, I reserved to myself an occupation which might fill up the void in my solitude without tempting me to print anything more in my lifetime. I know not for what reason Rey had long tormented me to write the memoirs of my life. Although these were not until that time very interesting as to the facts, I felt they might become so by the candour with which I was capable of giving them, and I determined to make of these the only work of the kind, by an unexampled veracity, that, for once at least, the world might see a man such as he internally was. I had always laughed at the false ingenuousness of Montaigne, who, feigning to confess his faults, takes great care not to give himself any, except such as are amiable; whilst I, who have ever thought, and still think myself, considering everything, the best of men, felt there is no human being, however pure he may be, who does not internally conceal some odious vice. I knew I was described to the public very different from what I really was, and so opposite, that notwithstanding my faults, all of which I was determined to relate, I could not but be a gainer by showing myself in my proper colours. This, besides, not being to be done without setting forth others also in theirs, and the work for the same reason not being of a nature to appear during my lifetime, and that of several other persons, I was the more encouraged to make my confession, at which I should never have to blush before any person. I therefore resolved to dedicate my leisure to the execution of this undertaking, and immediately began to collect such letters and papers as might guide or assist my memory, greatly regretting the loss of all I had burned, mislaid, and destroyed.

The project of absolute retirement, one of the most reasonable I had ever formed, was strongly impressed upon my mind, and for the execution of it I was already taking measures, when heaven, which prepared me a different destiny, plunged me into another vortex.

Montmorency, the ancient and fine patrimony of the illustrious family of that name, was taken from it by confiscation. It passed by the sister of Duke Henry to the house of Condé, which has changed the name of Montmorency to that of Enghien, and the duchy has no other castle than an old tower, where the archives are kept, and to which the vassals come to do homage. But at Montmorency, or Enghien, there is a private house, built by Croisat, called *le pauvre*, which having the magnificence of the most superb chateaux, deserves and bears the name of a castle. The majestic appearance of this noble edifice, the terrace on which it is built, the view from it, not equalled perhaps in any country; the spacious saloon, painted by the hand of a master; the garden planted by the celebrated Le Nôtre; all combined form a whole strikingly majestic, in which there is still a simplicity that enforces admiration. The Maréchal Duke de Luxembourg, who then inhabited this house, came every year into the neighbourhood where formerly his ancestors were the masters, to pass, in two parts, five or six weeks as a private inhabitant, but with a splendour which did not degenerate from the ancient lustre of his family. On the first journey he made to it after my residing at Montmorency, he and his lady sent to me a valet de chambre, with their compliments, inviting me to sup with them as often as it should be agreeable to me; and at each time of their coming they never failed to reiterate the same compliments and invitation. This called to my recollection Madame de Bezenval, sending me to dine in the servants'-hall. Times were changed; but I was still the same man. I did not choose to be sent to dine in the servants'-hall, and was but little desirous of appearing at the table of the great. I should have been much better pleased had they left me as I was without caressing me and rendering me ridiculous. I answered politely and respectfully to M. and Madame de Luxembourg, but I did not accept their offers, and my indisposition and timidity, with my embarrassment in speaking, making me tremble at the idea alone of appearing in an assembly of people of the Court, I did not even go to the castle to pay a visit of thanks, although I sufficiently comprehended this was all they desired, and that their eager politeness was rather a matter of curiosity than benevolence.

However, advances were still made, and even became more pressing. The Countess de Boufflers, who was very intimate with the lady of the Maréchal, having come to Montmorency, sent to inquire after my health, and to beg I would go and see her. I returned her a proper answer, but did not stir from my house. At the journey of Easter, the year following, 1759, the Chevalier de Lorenzy, who belonged to the Court of the Prince of Conti, and was intimate with Madame de Luxembourg, came several times to see me, and we became acquainted; he pressed me to go to the castle, but I refused to comply. At length, one afternoon, when I least expected anything of the kind, I saw, coming up to the house, the Maréchal de Luxembourg, followed by five or six persons. There was now no longer any means of defence, and I could not, without being arrogant and unmannerly, do otherwise than return this visit, and make my court to Madame la Maréchale, from whom the Marshal had been the bearer of the most obliging compliments to me. Thus, under unfortunate auspices, began the connexions from which I could no longer preserve myself, although a too well founded foresight made me afraid of them until they were made.

I was excessively afraid of Madame de Luxembourg. I knew she was amiable. I had seen her several times at the theatre, and with Madame Dupin, ten or twelve years before, when she was Duchess of Boufflers and in the bloom of her beauty. But she was said to be malignant, and this in a woman of her rank made me tremble. I had scarcely seen her before I was subjugated. I thought her charming, with that charm proof against time and which had the most powerful action upon my heart. I expected to find her conversation satirical and full of pleasantries and points. It was not so: it was much better. The conversation of Madame de Luxembourg is not remarkably full of wit; it has no sallies nor even finesse; it is exquisitely delicate, never striking but always pleasing. Her flattery is the more intoxicating as it is natural; it seems to escape her involuntarily, and her heart to overflow because it is too full. I thought I perceived, on my first visit, that notwith-

standing my awkward manner and embarrassed expression, I was
not displeasing to her. All the women of the Court know how to
persuade us of this when they please, whether it be true or not,
but they do not all, like Madame de Luxembourg, possess the art
of rendering that persuasion so agreeable that we are no longer
disposed ever to have a doubt remaining. From the first day my
confidence in her would have been as full as it soon afterwards
became, had not the Duchess of Montmorency, her daughter-in-
law, young, giddy, and malicious, also taken it into her head to
attack me, and in the midst of the eulogiums of her mamma, and
feigned allurements on her own account, made me suspect I was
only considered by them as a subject of ridicule.

It would perhaps have been difficult to relieve me from this fear
with these two ladies, had not the extreme goodness of the Maréchal confirmed me that theirs was real. Nothing is more surprising, considering my timidity, than the promptitude with which
I took him at his word as to the footing of equality to which he
would absolutely reduce himself with me, except it be that with
which he took me at mine with respect to the absolute independence in which I was determined to live. Both persuaded I had
reason to be content with my situation, and that I was unwilling
to change it, neither he nor Madame de Luxembourg seemed to
think a moment of my purse or fortune: although I can have no
doubt of the tender concern they had for me, they never proposed
to me a place nor offered me their interest, except it were once,
when Madame de Luxembourg seemed to wish me to become a
member of the French Academy. I alleged my religion; this she
told me was no obstacle, or if it was one she engaged to remove it.
I answered that however great the honour of becoming a member
of so illustrious a body might be, having refused M. de Tressan,
and, in some measure, the King of Poland, to become a member
of the academy of Nancy, I could not with propriety enter into
any other. Madame de Luxembourg did not insist, and nothing
more was said upon the subject. This simplicity of intercourse
with persons of such rank, and who had the power of doing any
thing in my favour, M. de Luxembourg being and highly deserving to be the particular friend of the King, affords a singular contrast with the continual cares, equally importunate and officious,
of the friends and protectors from whom I had just separated, and
who endeavoured less to serve me than to render me contemptible.

When the Maréchal came to see me at Mont Louis, I was uneasy at receiving him and his retinue in my only chamber; not

MME. LA DUCHESSE DE LUXEMBOURG

because I was obliged to make them all sit down in the midst of my dirty plates and broken pots, but on account of the state of the floor, which was rotten and falling to ruin, and I was afraid the weight of his attendants would entirely sink it. Less concerned on account of my own danger than for that to which the affability of the Maréchal exposed him, I hastened to remove him from it by conducting him, notwithstanding the coldness of the weather, to my alcove, which was quite open to the air, and had no chimney. When he was there I told him my reason for having brought him to it: he told it to his lady, and they both pressed me to accept, until the floor was repaired, a lodging at the castle; or, if I preferred it, in a separate edifice called the Petit Château, which was in the middle of the park. This delightful abode deserves to be spoken of.

The park or garden of Montmorency is not a plain like that of la Chevrette. It is uneven, mountainous, raised by little hills and valleys of which the able artist has taken advantage and thereby varied his groves, ornaments, waters, and points of view, and, if I may so speak, multiplied by art and genius a space in itself rather narrow. This park is terminated at the top by a terrace and the castle: at bottom it forms a narrow passage which opens and becomes wider towards the valley, the angle of which is filled up with a large piece of water. Between the orangery, which is in this widening, and the piece of water, the banks of which are agreeably decorated, stands the Petit Château of which I have spoken. This edifice, and the ground about it, formerly belonged to the celebrated Le Brun, who amused himself in building and decorating it in the exquisite taste of architectural ornaments which that great painter had formed to himself. The Château has since been rebuilt, but still according to the plan and design of its first master. It is little and simple, but elegant. As it stands in a hollow between the orangery and the large piece of water, and consequently is liable to be damp, it is open in the middle of a peristyle between two rows of columns, by which means the air circulating throughout the whole edifice keeps it dry notwithstanding its unfavourable situation. When the building is seen from the opposite elevation, which shows it in perspective, it appears absolutely surrounded with water, and we imagine we have before our eyes an enchanted island, or the most beautiful of the three Borromean Islands called *Isola bella* in Lago Maggiore.

In this solitary edifice I was offered the choice of four complete apartments it contains, besides the ground floor, consisting of a dancing room, billiard room, and a kitchen. I chose the smallest over the kitchen, which also I had with it. It was charmingly neat, with blue and white furniture. In this profound and delicious solitude, in the midst of woods and waters, the singing of birds of every kind, and the perfume of orange flowers, I composed, in a continual ecstasy, the fifth book of the *Emile*, the colouring of which I owed in a great measure to the lively impression I received from the place I inhabited.

With what eagerness did I run every morning at sunrise to respire the perfumed air in the peristyle! What excellent coffee I took there tête-à-tête with my Thérèse! My cat and dog were our company. This retinue alone would have been sufficient for me during my whole life, in which I should not have had one weary moment. I was there in a terrestrial paradise; I lived in innocence and tasted of happiness.

At the journey of July, M. and Madame de Luxembourg showed me so much attention and were so extremely kind that, lodged in their house, and overwhelmed with their goodness, I could not do less than make them a proper return in assiduous respect near their persons. I scarcely quitted them: I went in the morning to pay my court to Madame la Maréchale; after dinner I walked with the Maréchal; but did not sup at the castle on account of the numerous guests, and because they supped too late for me. Thus far everything was as it should be, and no harm would have been done could I have remained at this point. But I have never known how to preserve a medium in my attachments, and simply fulfil the duties of society. I have ever been everything or nothing: I was soon everything; and receiving the most polite attention from persons of the highest rank, I passed the proper bounds, and conceived for them a friendship not permitted except among equals. Of these I had all the familiarity in my manners, whilst they still preserved in theirs the same politeness to which they had accustomed me. Yet I was never quite at my ease with Madame de Luxembourg. Although I was not quite relieved from my fears relative to her character, I apprehended less danger from it than from her wit. It was by this especially that she impressed me with awe. I knew she was difficult as to conversation, and she had a right to be so. I knew women, especially those of her rank, would absolutely be amused, that it was better to offend than to weary them, and I judged by her commentaries upon what the people who went away had said, what she must think of my blunders. I thought of a supplement to spare me with her the embarrassment of speaking: this was reading. She had heard of my *Julie*, and knew it was in the press; she expressed a desire to see the work; I offered to read it to her, and she accepted my offer. I went to her every morning at ten o'clock: M. de Luxembourg was present, and the door was shut. I read by the side of her bed, and so well proportioned my readings that there would have been sufficient for the whole time she had to stay, had they even not been interrupted.[1] The success of this expedient surpassed my expectation. Madame de Luxembourg took a great liking to *Julie* and the author; she spoke of nothing but me, thought of

---

[1] The loss of a great battle, which much afflicted the King, obliged M. de Luxembourg precipitately to return to Court. (*Note by Rousseau.*)

nothing else, said civil things to me from morning till night, and
embraced me ten times a day. She insisted on my always having
my place by her side at table, and when any great lords wished to
take it she told them it was mine, and made them sit down somewhere else. The impression these charming manners made upon
me, who was subjugated by the least mark of affection, may easily
be judged of. I became really attached to her in proportion to the
attachment she showed me. All my fear in perceiving this infatuation, and feeling the want of agreeableness in myself to support
it, was, that it would be changed into disgust; and unfortunately
this fear was but too well founded.

There must have been a natural opposition between her turn
of mind and mine, since, independently of the numerous stupid
things which at every instant escaped me in conversation, and
even in my letters, and when I was upon the best terms with her,
there were certain other things with which she was displeased
without my being able to imagine the reason. I will quote one
instance from amongst twenty. She knew I was writing for
Madame d'Houdetot a copy of the *Héloïse* at so much a page. She
was desirous to have one on the same footing. This I promised her,
and thereby making her one of my customers, I wrote her a polite
letter upon the subject; at least such was my intention. Her answer, which was as follows, stupefied me with surprise.

'*Versailles, Tuesday.*

'I am ravished, I am satisfied: your letter has given me infinite
pleasure, and I take the earliest moment to acquaint you with,
and thank you for it.

'These are the exact words of your letter: *Although you are a
very good customer, I have some pain in receiving your money:
according to regular order I ought to pay for the pleasure I should
have in working for you.* I will say nothing more on the subject.
I have to complain of your not speaking of your state of health:
nothing interests me more. I love you with all my heart; and be
assured that I write this to you in a very melancholy mood, for
I should have much pleasure in telling it you myself. M. de
Luxembourg loves and embraces you with all his heart.'

On receiving the letter I hastened to answer it, reserving to
myself more fully to examine the matter, protesting against all
disobliging interpretation, and after having given several days to
this examination with an inquietude which may easily be con-

ceived, and still without being able to discover in what I could
have erred, what follows was my final answer on the subject.

'*Montmorency, 8th December, 1759.*

'Since my last letter I have examined a hundred and a hundred
times the passage in question. I have considered it in its proper
and natural meaning, as well as in every other which may be
given to it, and I confess to you, madam, that I know not whether
it be I who owe to you excuses or you from whom they are due
to me.'

It is now ten years since these letters were written. I have since
that time frequently thought of the subject of them; and such is
still my stupidity that I have hitherto been unable to discover
what in the passage, quoted from my letter, she could find offensive, or even displeasing.

IN THE ORANGERIE

I must here mention, relative to the manuscript copy of *Héloïse*
Madame de Luxembourg wished to have, in what manner I
thought to give it some marked advantage which should distin-

guish it from all others. I had written separately the adventures
of Lord Edward, and had long been undetermined whether I
should insert them wholly, or in extracts, in the work in which
they seemed to be wanting. I at length determined to retrench
them entirely, because, not being in the manner of the rest, they
would have spoiled the interesting simplicity, which was its principal merit. I had still a stronger reason when I came to know
Madame de Luxembourg. There was in these adventures a Roman
marchioness, of a bad character, some parts of which, without
being applicable, might have been applied to her, by those to
whom she was not particularly known. I was therefore highly
pleased with the determination to which I had come, and resolved
to abide by it. But in my ardent desire to enrich her copy with
something which was not in any other, what should I fall upon
but these unfortunate adventures, and I concluded on making an
extract from them to add to the work; a project dictated by madness, of which the extravagance is inexplicable, except by the
blind fatality which led me on to destruction.

Quos vult perdere Jupiter dementat.

I was stupid enough to make this extract with the greatest care
and pains, and to send it her as the finest thing in the world; it is
true, I at the same time informed her the original was burned,
which was really the case, that the extract was for her alone and
would never be seen, except by herself, unless she chose to show
it; which, far from proving to her my prudence and discretion,
as it was my intention to do, clearly intimated what I thought of
the applications by which she might be offended. My stupidity
was such, that I had no doubt of her being delighted with what
I had done. She did not make me the compliments upon it which I
expected, and, to my great surprise, never once mentioned the
paper I had sent her. I was so satisfied with myself, that it was not
until a long time afterwards, I judged, from other indications, of
the effect it had produced.

I had still, in favour of her manuscript, another idea more
reasonable, but which, by more distant effects, has not been much
less prejudicial to me; so much does everything concur with the
work of destiny, when that hurries on a man to misfortune. I
thought of ornamenting the manuscript with the originals of the
engravings of the *Julie*, which were of the same size. I asked
Coindet for these engravings, which belonged to me by every
kind of title, and the more so as I had given him the produce of

the plates, which had a considerable sale. Coindet is as cunning as I am the contrary. By frequently asking him for the engravings he came to the knowledge of the use I intended to make of them. He then, under pretence of adding some new ornament, still kept them from me, and at length presented them himself.

Ego versiculos feci, tulit alter honores.[1]

This gave him an introduction upon a certain footing to the Hôtel de Luxembourg. After my establishment at the Petit Château he came rather frequently to see me, and always in the morning, especially when M. and Madame de Luxembourg were at Montmorency. Therefore that I might pass the day with him, I did not go to the castle. Reproaches were made me on account of my absence; I told the reason of them. I was desired to bring with me M. Coindet; I did so. This was what he had sought after. Therefore, thanks to the excessive goodness M. and Madame de Luxembourg had for me, a clerk to M. Théluson, who was sometimes pleased to give him his table when he had nobody else to dine with him, was suddenly at that of a Marshal of France, with Princes, Duchesses, and persons of the highest rank at Court. I shall never forget that, one day being obliged to return early to Paris, the Maréchal said, after dinner, to the company, Let us take a walk upon the road to St. Denis, and we will accompany M. Coindet. This was too much for the poor man; his head was quite turned. For my part my heart was so affected that I could not say a word. I followed the company, weeping like a child, and having the strongest desire to kiss the foot of the good Maréchal; but the continuation of the history of the manuscript has made me anticipate. I will go a little back, and, as far as my memory will permit, mark each event in its proper order.

As soon as the little house of Mont Louis was ready, I had it neatly and simply furnished, and again established myself there. I could not break through the resolution I had made on quitting the Hermitage, of always having my apartment to myself; but I found a difficulty in resolving to quit the Petit Château. I kept the key of it, and being delighted with the charming breakfasts of the peristyle, frequently went to the castle to sleep, and stayed three or four days as at a country house. I was at that time perhaps better and more agreeably lodged than any private individual in Europe. My host, M. Mathas, one of the best men in the world,

---

[1] Vergil: "I made the verses, but another took the honour."

had left me the absolute direction of the repairs at Mont Louis,
and insisted upon my disposing of his workmen without his in-
terference. I therefore found the means of making of a single
chamber upon the first story, a complete set of apartments, consisting of a chamber, antechamber, and a water closet. Upon the
ground floor were the kitchen and the chamber of Thérèse. The
alcove served me for a closet by means of a glazed partition and a
chimney I had made there. After my return to this habitation,
I amused myself in decorating the terrace, which was already
shaded by two rows of linden trees; I added two others to make a
summer-house, and placed in it a table and stone benches; I surrounded it with lilac, syringa, and woodbines, and had a beautiful border of flowers parallel with the two rows of trees. This
terrace, more elevated than that of the castle, from which the
view was at least as fine, and where I had tamed a great number
of birds, was my drawing room, in which I received M. and
Madame de Luxembourg, the Duke of Villeroy, the Prince of
Tingry, the Marquis of Armentières, the Duchess of Montmorency, the Duchess of Boufflers, the Countess of Valentinois, the
Countess of Boufflers, and others persons of the first rank; who,
from the castle, disdained not to make, over a very fatiguing
mountain, the pilgrimage of Mont Louis. I owed all these visits
to the favour of M. and Madame de Luxembourg; this I felt, and
my heart on that account did them all due homage. It was with
the same sentiment that I once said to M. de Luxembourg, embracing him: Ah! Monsieur le Maréchal, I hated the great before
I knew you, and I have hated them still more since you have
shown me with what ease they might acquire universal respect.

Further than this, I defy any person with whom I was then
acquainted, to say I was ever dazzled for an instant with splendour, or that the vapour of the incense I received ever affected my
head; that I was less uniform in my manner, less plain in my
dress, less easy of access to people of the lowest rank, less familiar
with neighbours, or less ready to render service to every person
when I had it in my power so to do, without ever once being discouraged by the numerous and frequently unreasonable importunities with which I was incessantly assailed. Although my heart
led me to the castle of Montmorency, by my sincere attachment
to those by whom it was inhabited, it by the same means drew me
back to the neighbourhood of it, there to taste the sweets of the
equal and simple life, in which my only happiness consisted.
Thérèse had contracted a friendship with the daughter of one of

my neighbours, a mason of the name of Pilleu; I did the same with
the father, and after having dined at the castle, not without some
constraint, to please Madame de Luxembourg, with what eagerness did I return in the evening to sup with the good man Pilleu
and his family, sometimes at his own house and at others at mine!

Besides my two lodgings in the country, I soon had a third at
the Hôtel de Luxembourg, the proprietors of which pressed me so
much to go sometimes and see them there that I consented, notwithstanding my aversion to Paris, where, since my retiring to
the Hermitage, I had been but twice, upon the two occasions of
which I have spoken. I did not go there except on the days agreed
upon, solely to supper, and the next morning I returned to the
country. I entered and came out by the garden which faces the
boulevard, so that I could, with the greatest truth, say I had not
set my foot upon the stones of Paris.

In the midst of this transient prosperity, a catastrophe, which
was to be the conclusion of it, was preparing at a distance. A short
time after my return to Mont Louis, I made there, and as it was
customary, against my inclination, a new acquaintance, which
makes another era in my private history. Whether this be favourable or unfavourable, the reader will hereafter be able to judge.
The person with whom I became acquainted, was the Marchioness
of Verdelin, my neighbour, whose husband had just bought a
country-house at Soisy, near Montmorency. Mademoiselle d'Ars,
daughter to the Comte d'Ars, a man of fashion but poor, had
married M. de Verdelin, old, ugly, deaf, uncouth, brutal, jealous,
with gashes in his face, and blind of one eye, but, upon the whole,
a good man when properly managed, and in possession of a fortune of from fifteen to twenty thousand livres a year, to which
fortune she was married. This charming object, swearing, roaring, scolding, storming, and making his wife cry all day long,
ended by doing whatever she thought proper, and this to set her
in a rage, because she knew how to persuade him that it was he
who would, and she who would not have it so. M. de Margency,
of whom I have spoken, was the friend of Madame, and became
that of Monsieur. He had, a few years before, let them his castle
of Margency, near Eaubonne and Andilly, and they resided there
precisely at the time of my passion for Madame d'Houdetot.
Madame d'Houdetot and Madame de Verdelin became acquainted
with each other by means of Madame d'Aubeterre their common
friend; and as the garden of Margency was in the road by which
Madame d'Houdetot went to Mont Olympe, her favourite walk,

Madame de Verdelin gave her a key that she might pass through
it. By means of this key I crossed it several times with her; but
I did not like unexpected meetings, and when Madame de Verdelin was by chance upon our way I left them together without
speaking to her, and went on before. This want of gallantry must
have made on her an impression unfavourable to me. Yet when
she was at Soisy she was anxious to have my company. She came
several times to see me at Mont Louis without finding me at home,
and perceiving I did not return her visit, took it into her head, as
a means of forcing me to do it, to send me pots of flowers for my
terrace. I was under the necessity of going to thank her; this was
all she wanted, and we thus became acquainted.

This connexion, like every other I formed, or was led into contrary to my inclination, began rather boisterously. There never
reigned in it a real calm. The turn of mind of Madame de Verdelin was too opposite to mine. Malignant expressions and pointed
sarcasms came from her with so much simplicity, that a continual
attention too fatiguing for me was necessary to perceive she was
turning into ridicule the person to whom she spoke. One trivial
circumstance which occurs to my recollection will be sufficient to
give an idea of her manner. Her brother had just obtained the
command of a frigate cruising against the English. I spoke of the
manner of fitting out this frigate without diminishing its swift-
ness of sailing. Yes, replied she, in the most natural tone of voice,
no more cannon are taken than are necessary for fighting. I seldom have heard her speak well of any of her absent friends without letting slip something to their prejudice. What she did not see
with an evil eye she looked upon with one of ridicule, and her
friend Margency was not excepted. What I found most insupportable in her was the perpetual constraint proceeding from her
little messages, presents, and billets, to which it was a labour for
me to answer, and I had continual embarrassments either in
thanking or refusing. However, by frequently seeing this lady
I became attached to her. She had her troubles as well as I had
mine. Reciprocal confidence rendered our conversations interesting. Nothing so cordially attaches two persons as the satisfaction
of weeping together. We sought the company of each other for
our reciprocal consolation, and the want of this has frequently
made me pass over many things. I had been so severe in my frankness with her, that after having sometimes shown so little esteem
for her character, a great deal was necessary to be able to believe
she could sincerely forgive me. The following letter is a specimen

of the epistles I sometimes wrote to her, and it is to be remarked that she never once in any of her answers to them seemed to be in the least degree piqued.

'*Montmorency, 5th November, 1760.*

'You tell me, madam, you have not well explained yourself, in order to make me understand I have explained myself ill. You speak of your pretended stupidity for the purpose of making me feel my own. You boast of being nothing more than a good kind of woman, as if you were afraid to be taken at your word, and you make me apologies to tell me I owe them to you. Yes, madam, I know it; it is I who am a fool, a good kind of man; and, if it be possible, worse than all this; it is I who make a bad choice of my expressions in the opinion of a fine French lady, who pays as much attention to words, and speaks as well as you do. But consider that I take them in the common meaning of the language, without knowing or troubling my head about the polite acceptations in which they are taken in the virtuous societies of Paris. If my expressions are sometimes equivocal, I endeavour by my conduct to determine their meaning, etc.'

The rest of the letter is much the same. Consider her reply, which is among my papers, and judge of the unbelievable moderation of feeling of a woman who had no greater resentment at such a letter than that reply manifests, and of which she showed me no token.

Coindet, enterprising, bold even to effrontery, and who was upon the watch after all my friends, soon introduced himself in my name to the house of Madame de Verdelin, and, unknown to me, shortly became there more familiar than myself. This Coindet was an extraordinary man. He presented himself in my name in the houses of all my acquaintance, gained a footing in them, and ate there without ceremony. Transported with zeal to do me service, he never mentioned my name without his eyes being suffused with tears; but, when he came to see me, he kept the most profound silence on the subject of all these connexions, and on everything in which he knew I must be interested. Instead of telling me what he had heard, said, or seen, relative to my affairs, he waited for my speaking to him, and even interrogated me. He never knew anything of what passed in Paris, except that which I told him: finally, although everybody spoke to me of him, he never once spoke to me of any person; he was secret and mysterious with his friend only; but I will for the present leave Coindet and Madame de Verdelin, and return to them at a proper time.

Some time after my return to Mont Louis, La Tour, the painter, came there to see me, and brought with him my portrait in crayons, which a few years before he had exhibited at the Salon. He wished to give me this portrait, which I did not choose to accept. But Madame d'Epinay, who had given me hers, and would have this, had prevailed on me to ask him for it. He had taken some time to retouch the features. In the interval happened my rupture with Madame d'Epinay; I returned her her portrait; and giving her mine being no longer in question, I put it into my chamber, in the Petit Château. M. de Luxembourg saw it there, and found it a good one; I offered it him, he accepted it, and I sent it to the castle. He and his lady comprehended I should be very glad to have theirs. They had them taken in miniature by a very skilful hand, set in a box of rock crystal, mounted with gold, and in a very handsome manner, with which I was delighted, made me a present of both. Madame de Luxembourg would never consent that her portrait should be on the upper part of the box. She had reproached me several times with loving M. de Luxembourg better than I did her; I had not denied it, because it was true. By this manner of placing her portrait she showed very politely, but very clearly, she had not forgotten the preference.

Much about this time I was guilty of a folly which did not contribute to preserve to me her good graces. Although I had no knowledge of M. de Silhouette,[1] and was not much disposed to like him, I had a great opinion of his administration. When he began to let his hand fall rather heavily upon financiers, I perceived he did not begin his operation in a favourable moment, but he had my warmest wishes for his success; and as soon as I heard he was displaced I wrote to him, in my intrepid heedless manner, the following letter, which I certainly do not undertake to justify.

'*Montmorency, 2d December, 1759.*

'Vouchsafe, sir, to receive the homage of a solitary man, who is not known to you, but who esteems you for your talents, respects you for your administration, and who did you the honour to believe you would not long remain in it. Unable to save the state, except at the expense of the capital by which it has been ruined, you have braved the clamours of the gainers of money. When I

---

[1] Controller-General of Finance in 1759.

saw you crush these wretches, I envied you your place; and at seeing you quit it without departing from your system, I admire you. Be satisfied with yourself, sir; the step you have taken will leave you an honour you will long enjoy without a competitor. The malediction of knaves is the glory of an honest man.'

Madame de Luxembourg, who knew I had written this letter, spoke to me of it when she came into the country at Easter; I showed it to her, and she was desirous of a copy; this I gave her, but when I did it I did not know she was one of those money-gainers who were interested in under-farms, and had displaced M. de Silhouette. By my numerous follies any person would have imagined I wilfully endeavoured to bring on myself the hatred of an amiable woman who had power, and to whom, in truth, I daily became more attached, and was far from wishing to occasion her displeasure, although by my awkward manner of proceeding, I did everything proper for that purpose. I think it superfluous to remark here, that it is to her the story of the opiate of M. Tronchin, of which I have spoken in the first part of my memoirs, relates; the other lady was Madame de Mirepoix. They have never mentioned to me the circumstance, nor has either of them, in the least, seemed to have preserved a remembrance of it; but to presume that Madame de Luxembourg can possibly have forgotten it appears to me very difficult, and would still remain so, even were the subsequent events entirely unknown. For my part, I fell into a deceitful security relative to the effects of my stupid mistakes, by the internal evidence of my not having taken any step with an intention to offend; as if a woman could ever forgive what I had done, although she might be certain the will had not the least part in the matter.

Although she seemed not to see or feel anything, and that I did not immediately find either her warmth of friendship diminished or the least change in her manner, the continuation and even increase of a too well founded foreboding made me incessantly tremble, lest disgust should succeed to infatuation. Was it possible for me to expect in a lady of such high rank, a constancy proof against my want of address to support it? I was unable even to conceal from her this secret foreboding, which made me uneasy and rendered me still more disagreeable. This will be judged of by the following letter, which contains a very singular prediction.

N.B. *This letter, without date in my rough copy, was written in October, 1760, at latest.*

'. . . How cruel is your goodness! Why disturb the peace of a solitary mortal who had renounced the pleasures of life that he might no longer suffer the fatigues of them? I have passed my days in vainly searching for solid attachments. I have not been able to form any in the ranks to which I was equal; is it in yours that I ought to seek for them? Neither ambition nor interest can tempt me; I am not vain, and but little fearful; I can resist everything except caresses. Why do you both attack me by a weakness which I must overcome, because in the distance by which we are separated, the overflowings of susceptible hearts cannot bring mine near to you? Will gratitude be sufficient for a heart which knows not two manners of bestowing its affections, and feels itself incapable of everything except friendship? Of friendship, Madame la Maréchale! Ah! there is my misfortune! It is good in you and the Maréchal to make use of this expression; but I am mad when I take you at your word. You must amuse yourselves and I become attached; and the end of this prepares for me new regrets. How do I hate all your titles, and pity you on account of your being obliged to bear them! You seem to me to be so worthy of tasting the charms of private life! Why do not you reside at Clarens? I would go there in search of happiness; but the castle of Montmorency, and the Hôtel de Luxembourg! Is it in these places Jean-Jacques ought to be seen? Is it there a friend to equality ought to carry the affections of a sensible heart, and who, thus paying the esteem in which he is held, thinks he returns as much as he receives? You are good and susceptible also; this I know and have seen; I am sorry I was not sooner convinced of it; but in the rank you hold, in your manner of living, nothing can make a lasting impression; a succession of new objects efface each other so that not one of them remains. You will forget me, madam, after having made it impossible for me to imitate you. You have done a great deal to render me unhappy, to be inexcusable.'

I joined with her the Maréchal, to render the compliment less severe: for, I was moreover so sure of him, that I never had a doubt in my mind of the continuation of his friendship. Nothing that intimidated me in Madame la Maréchale, ever, for a moment, extended to him. I never have had the least mistrust relative to his character, which I knew to be feeble but constant. I no more feared a coldness on his part than I expected from him an heroic attachment. The simplicity and familiarity of our manners with each other, proved how far dependence was reciprocal. We were both always right: I shall ever honour and hold dear the memory of this worthy man, and, notwithstanding everything that was done to detach him from me, I am as certain of his having died my friend as if I had been present in his last moments.

At the second journey to Montmorency, in the year 1760, the reading of *Julie* being finished, I had recourse to that of *Emile*, to support myself in the good graces of Madame de Luxembourg; but this, whether the subject was less to her taste, or that so much reading at length fatigued her, did not succeed so well. However, as she reproached me with suffering myself to be the dupe of booksellers, she wished me to leave to her care the printing the work, that I might reap from it a greater advantage. I consented to her doing it, on the express condition of its not being printed in France, on which we had a long dispute; I affirming that it was impossible to obtain, and even imprudent to solicit a tacit permission; and being unwilling to permit the impression upon any other terms in the kingdom; she, that the censor could not make the least difficulty, according to the system government had adopted. She found means to make M. de Malesherbes enter into her views. He wrote to me on the subject a long letter with his own hand, to prove the *Profession of Faith of the Savoyard Vicar* to be a composition which must everywhere gain the approbation of its readers and that of the Court, as things were then circumstanced. I was surprised to see this magistrate, always so prudent, become so smooth in the business. As the printing of a book he approved was by that alone legal, I had no longer any objection to make to that of the work. Yet, by an extraordinary scruple, I still required it should be printed in Holland, and by the bookseller Néaulme, whom, not satisfied with indicating him, I informed of my wishes, consenting the edition should be brought out for the profit of a French bookseller, and that as soon as it was ready it should be sold at Paris, or wherever else it might be thought proper, provided I had no manner of concern with this. This is exactly what was agreed upon between Madame de Luxembourg and myself, after which I gave her my manuscript.

Madame de Luxembourg was this time accompanied by her granddaughter Mademoiselle de Boufflers, now Duchess of Lauzun. Her name was Amelia. She was a charming girl. She really had a maiden beauty, mildness, and timidity. Nothing could be more lovely than her person, nothing more chaste and tender than the sentiments she inspired. She was, besides, still a child under eleven years of age. Madame de Luxembourg, who thought her

too timid, used every endeavour to animate her. She permitted me
several times to give her a kiss, which I did with my usual awkwardness. Instead of saying flattering things to her, as any other
person would have done, I remained silent and disconcerted, and
I know not which of the two, the little girl or myself, was most
ashamed. I met her one day alone in the staircase of the Petit
Château. She had been to see Thérèse, with whom her governess
still was. Not knowing what else to say, I proposed to her a kiss,
which, in the innocence of her heart, she did not refuse; having
in the morning received one from me by order of her grandmother
and in her presence. The next day, while reading *Emile* by the
side of the bed of Madame de Luxembourg, I came to a passage in
which I justly censure that which I had done the preceding evening. She thought the reflection extremely just, and said some
very sensible things upon the subject which made me blush. How
was I enraged at my incredible stupidity, which has frequently
given me the appearance of guilt when I was nothing more than
a fool and embarrassed! a stupidity, which in a man known to be
endowed with some wit, is considered as a false excuse. I can
safely swear that in this kiss, as well as in the others, the heart
and thoughts of Mademoiselle Amelia were not more pure than
my own, and that if I could have avoided meeting her I should
have done it; not that I had not great pleasure in seeing her, but
from the embarrassment of not finding a word proper to say.
Whence comes it that even a child can intimidate a man, whom
the power of kings has never inspired with fear? What is to be
done? How, without presence of mind, am I to act? If I strive to
speak to the persons I meet, I certainly say some stupid thing to
them: if I remain silent, I am a misanthrope, an unsociable animal, a bear. Total imbecility would have been more favourable
to me; but the talents which I have failed to improve in the world
have become the instruments of my destruction and of that of the
talents I possessed.

At the latter end of this journey, Madame de Luxembourg did
a good action in which I had some share. Diderot having very
imprudently offended the Princess of Robeck, daughter of M. de
Luxembourg, Palissot, whom she protected, took up the quarrel
and revenged her by the comedy of *The Philosophers*, in which
I was ridiculed, and Diderot very roughly handled. The author
treated me with more gentleness, less, I am of opinion, on account
of the obligation he was under to me, than for the fear of displeasing the father of his protectress, by whom he knew I was

beloved. The bookseller Duchesne, with whom I was not at that time acquainted, sent me the comedy when it was printed, and this I suspect was by the order of Palissot, who, perhaps, thought I should have a pleasure in seeing a man with whom I was no longer connected defamed. He was greatly deceived. When I broke with Diderot, whom I thought less ill-natured than weak and indiscreet, I still always preserved for his person an attachment, an esteem even, and a respect for our ancient friendship, which I know was for a long time as sincere on his part as on mine. The case was quite different with Grimm; a man false by nature, who never loved me, who is not even capable of friendship, and a person who, from gaiety of heart, without the least subject of complaint, and solely to satisfy his gloomy jealousy, became, under the mask of friendship, my most cruel calumniator. This man is to me a cipher; the other will always be my old friend. My very bowels yearned at the sight of this odious piece: the reading of it was insupportable to me, and, without going through the whole, I returned the copy to Duchesne with the following letter.

'*Montmorency, 21st May, 1760.*

'In casting my eye over the piece you sent me, I trembled at seeing myself well spoken of in it. I do not accept the horrid present. I am persuaded that in sending it me, you did not intend an insult; but you do not know, or have forgotten, that I have the honour to be the friend of a respectable man, who is shamefully defamed and calumniated in this libel.'

Duchesne showed the letter.[1] Diderot, upon whom it ought to have had an effect quite contrary, was vexed at it. His pride could not forgive me the superiority of a generous action, and I was informed his wife everywhere inveighed against me with a bitterness with which I was not in the least affected, as I knew she was known to everybody to be a noisy babbler.

Diderot in his turn found an avenger in the Abbé Morellet, who wrote against Palissot a little work, imitated from the *Petit Prophète*, and entitled *The Vision*. In this production he very imprudently offended Madame de Robeck, whose friends got him sent to the Bastile; though she, not naturally vindictive, and at that time in a dying state, I am certain had nothing to do in the affair.

---

[1] For the preceding sentence, Paris MS. reads: "This letter was made public."

THE BASTILE

D'Alembert, who was very intimately connected with Morellet, wrote me a letter, desiring I would beg of Madame de Luxembourg to solicit his liberty, promising her in return encomiums in the *Encyclopédie;*[1] my answer to his letter was as follows:

'I did not wait the receipt of your letter before I expressed to Madame de Luxembourg the pain the confinement of the Abbé Morellet gave me. She knows my concern, and shall be made acquainted with yours, and her knowing that the Abbé is a man of merit will be sufficient to make her interest herself in his behalf. However, although she and the Maréchal honour me with a benevolence which is my greatest consolation, and that the name of your friend be to them a recommendation in favour of the Abbé Morellet, I know not how far, on this occasion, it may be proper for them to employ the credit attached to the rank they hold, and the consideration due to their persons. I am not even convinced that the vengeance in question relates to the Princess of Robeck so much as you seem to imagine; and were this even the case, we must not suppose that the pleasure of vengeance belongs to philosophers exclusively, and that when they choose to become women, women will become philosophers.

'I will communicate to you whatever Madame de Luxembourg

---

[1] This letter, with several others, disappeared at the Hôtel de Luxembourg, while my papers were deposited there. (*Note by Rousseau*, not in Paris MS.)

may say to me after having shown her your letter. In the meantime, I think I know her well enough to assure you that, should
she have the pleasure of contributing to the enlargement of the
Abbé Morellet, she will not accept the tribute of acknowledgement you promise her in the *Encyclopédie*, although she might
think herself honoured by it, because she does not do good in the
expectation of praise, but from the dictates of her heart.'

I made every effort to excite the zeal and commiseration of
Madame de Luxembourg in favour of the poor captive, and succeeded to my wishes. She went to Versailles on purpose to speak
to M. le Comte de St. Florentin, and this journey shortened the
residence at Montmorency, which the Maréchal was obliged to
quit at the same time to go to Rouen, whither the King sent him as
governor of Normandy on account of the motions of the parliament, which government wished to keep within bounds. Madame
de Luxembourg wrote me the following letter the day after her
departure.

'Versailles, Wednesday.

'M de Luxembourg set off yesterday morning at six o'clock.
I do not yet know that I shall follow him. I wait until he writes
to me, as he is not yet certain of the stay it will be necessary for
him to make. I have seen M. de St. Florentin, who is as favourably
disposed as possible towards the Abbé Morellet; but he finds some
obstacles to his wishes, which however he is in hopes of removing
the first time he has to do business with the King, which will be
next week. I have also desired as a favour that he might not be
exiled, because this was intended: he was to be sent to Nancy.
This, sir, is what I have been able to obtain; but I promise you
I will not let M. de St. Florentin rest until the affair is terminated
in the manner you desire. Let me now express to you how sorry
I am on account of my being obliged to leave you so soon, of which
I flatter myself you have not the least doubt. I love you with all
my heart, and shall do so for my whole life.'

A few days afterwards I received the following note from
d'Alembert which gave me real joy.

'August 1st.

'Thanks to your cares, my dear philosopher, the Abbé has left
the Bastile, and his imprisonment will have no other consequence.
He is setting off for the country, and, as well as myself, returns
you a thousand thanks and compliments. *Vale et me ama.'*

The Abbé also wrote to me a few days afterwards a letter of thanks which did not, in my opinion, seem to breathe a certain effusion of the heart, and in which he seemed in some measure to extenuate the service I had rendered him. Some time afterwards, I found that he and d'Alembert had, to a certain degree, I will not say supplanted, but succeeded me in the good graces of Madame de Luxembourg, and that I had lost with her all they had gained. However I am far from suspecting the Abbé Morellet of having contributed to my disgrace: I have too much esteem for him to harbour any such suspicion. With respect to d'Alembert, I shall at present leave him out of the question, and hereafter say of him what may seem necessary.

I had, at the same time, another affair which occasioned the last letter I wrote to Voltaire; a letter against which he vehemently exclaimed, as an abominable insult, although he never showed it to any person. I will here supply the want of that which he refused to do.

The Abbé Trublet, with whom I had a slight acquaintance, but whom I had but seldom seen, wrote to me on the 13th of June, 1760, informing me that M. Formey, his friend and correspondent, had printed, in his Journal, my letter to Voltaire upon the disaster at Lisbon. The Abbé wished to know how the letter came to be printed, and, in his jesuitical manner, asked me my opinion, without giving me his own, on the necessity of reprinting it. As I most sovereignly hate this kind of artifice and stratagem, I returned such thanks as were proper, but in a manner so reserved as to make him feel it, although this did not prevent him from wheedling me in two or three other letters until he had gathered all he wished to know.

I clearly understood that, notwithstanding all Trublet could say, Formey had not found the letter printed, and that the first impression of it came from himself. I knew him to be an impudent pilferer, who, without ceremony, made himself a revenue by the works of others, although he had not yet had the incredible effrontery to take from a book already published the name of the author, to put his own in the place of it, and to sell the book for his own profit.[1] But by what means had this manuscript fallen into his hands? That was a question not difficult to resolve, but by which I had the weakness to be embarrassed. Although Voltaire was excessively honoured by the letter, as in fact, notwithstanding his

---

[1] In this manner he afterwards appropriated to himself *Emile*. (*Note by Rousseau*, not in Paris MS.)

rude proceedings, he would have a right to complain had I had it printed without his consent, I resolved to write to him upon the subject. The second letter was as follows, to which he returned no answer, and, giving greater scope to his brutality, he feigned to be irritated to fury.

M. DE VOLTAIRE

'*Montmorency, 17th June, 1760.*

'I did not think, sir, I should ever have occasion to correspond with you. But learning the letter I wrote to you, in 1756, has been printed at Berlin, I owe you an account of my conduct in that respect, and will fulfil this duty with truth and simplicity.

'The letter having really been addressed to you was not intended to be printed. I communicated the contents of it, on certain conditions, to three persons to whom the rights of friendship did not permit me to refuse anything of the kind, and whom the

same rights still less permitted to abuse my confidence by betraying their promise. These persons are Madame de Chenonceaux,
daughter-in-law to Madame Dupin, the Comtesse d'Houdetot,
and a German of the name of Grimm. Madame de Chenonceaux
was desirous the letter should be printed, and asked my consent.
I told her that depended on yours. This was asked of you, which
you refused, and the matter dropped.

'However, the Abbé Trublet, with whom I have not the least
connexion, has just written to me, from a motive of the most
polite attention, that having received the papers of a Journal of
M. Formey he found in them this same letter, with an advertisement, dated on the 23d of October 1759, in which the editor states,
that he had a few weeks before found it in the shops of the booksellers of Berlin, and as it is one of those loose sheets which shortly
disappear, he thought proper to give it a place in his Journal.

'This, sir, is all I know of the matter. It is very certain the letter
had not until lately been heard of at Paris. It is also as certain that
the copy, either in manuscript or print, fallen into the hands of
M. Formey, could never have reached them except by your means,
which is not probable, or of those of one of the three persons I have
mentioned. Finally it is well known the two ladies are incapable
of such a perfidy. I cannot, in my retirement, learn more relative
to the affair. You have a correspondence by means of which you
may, if you think it worth your trouble, go back to the source and
verify the fact.

'In the same letter the Abbé Trublet informs me that he keeps
the paper in reserve, and will not lend it without my consent,
which most assuredly I will not give. But it is possible this copy
may not be the only one in Paris. I wish, sir, the letter may not
be printed there, and I will do all in my power to prevent this
from happening; but if I cannot succeed, and that, timely perceiving it, I can have the preference, I will not then hesitate to have
it immediately printed. This to me appears just and natural.

'With respect to your answer to the same letter, it has not been
communicated to anyone, and you may be assured it shall not
be printed without your consent, which I certainly shall not be
indiscreet enough to ask of you, well knowing that what one man
writes to another is not written to the public. But should you
choose to write one you would wish to have published, and address
it to me, I promise you faithfully to add it to my letter and not to
make to it a single word of reply.

'I love you not, sir; you have done me, your disciple and enthusiastic admirer, injuries that might have caused me the most exquisite pain. You have ruined Geneva, in return for the asylum it has afforded you; you have alienated from me my fellow citizens, in return for the eulogiums I made of you amongst them; it is you who render to me the residence of my own country insupportable; it is you who will oblige me to die in a foreign land, deprived of all the consolations usually administered to a dying person; and cause me, instead of receiving funeral rites, to be thrown to the dogs, whilst all the honours man can expect will accompany you in my country. Finally, I hate you because you have been desirous I should; but I hate you as a man more worthy of loving you had you chosen it. Of all the sentiments with which my heart was penetrated for you, admiration, which cannot be refused your fine genius, and a partiality to your writings, are those you have not effaced. If I can honour nothing in you except your talents, the fault is not mine. I shall never be wanting in the respect due to them, nor in that which this respect requires. Adieu, Sir.'

In the midst of these little literary cavillings, which still fortified my resolution, I received the greatest honour letters ever acquired me, and of which I was the most sensible, in the two visits the Prince of Conti deigned to make to me, one at the Petit Château and the other at Mont Louis. He chose the time for both these when Madame de Luxembourg was not at Montmorency, in order to render it more manifest that he came there solely on my account. I have never had a doubt of my owing the first condescensions of this Prince to Madame de Luxembourg and Madame de Boufflers; but I am of opinion I owe to his own sentiments and to myself those with which he has since that time continually honoured me.[1]

My apartment at Mont Louis being small, and the situation of the alcove charming, I conducted the Prince to it, where to complete the condescension he was pleased to show me, he chose I should have the honour of playing with him a game at chess. I knew he beat the Chevalier de Lorenzy, who played better than I did. However, notwithstanding the signs and grimaces of the Chevalier and the spectators, which I feigned not to see, I won the two games we played. When they were ended, I said to him in a

---

[1] Remark the perseverance of this blind and stupid confidence in the midst of all the treatment which should soonest have undeceived me. It continued until my return to Paris in 1770. (*Note by Rousseau*, not in Paris MS.)

respectful but very grave manner; My lord, I honour your serene
highness too much not to beat you always at chess. This great
Prince, who had real wit, sense, and knowledge, and so was worthy
not to be treated with mean adulation, felt in fact, at least I think
so, that I was the only person present who treated him like a man,
and I have every reason to believe he was not displeased with me
for it.

Had this even been the case, I would not have reproached myself with having been unwilling to deceive him in anything, and
I certainly cannot do it with having in my heart made an ill return for his goodness, but solely with having sometimes done it
with an ill grace, whilst he himself accompanied with infinite
gracefulness the manner in which he showed me the marks of it.
A few days afterwards he ordered a hamper of game to be sent
me, which I received as I ought. This, in a little time, was succeeded by another, and one of his game-keepers wrote me, by
order of his highness, that the game it contained had been shot by
the Prince himself. I received this second hamper, but I wrote to
Madame de Boufflers that I would not receive a third. This letter
was generally blamed, and deservedly so. Refusing to accept presents of game from a prince of the blood, who moreover sends it
in so polite a manner, is less the delicacy of a haughty man, who
wishes to preserve his independence, than the rusticity of a clown,
who does not know himself. I have never read this letter in my
collection without blushing and reproaching myself for having
written it. But I have not undertaken my Confessions with an
intention of concealing my faults, and that of which I have just
spoken is too shocking in my own eyes to suffer me to pass it
over in silence.

If I were not guilty of the offence of becoming his rival, I was
very near doing it; for Madame de Boufflers was still his mistress,
and I knew nothing of the matter. She came rather frequently to
see me with the Chevalier de Lorenzy. She was yet young and
beautiful, affected Roman wit, and my mind was always romantic, which was much of the same nature. I was near being laid
hold of; I believe she perceived it; the Chevalier saw it also, at
least he spoke to me upon the subject, and in a manner not discouraging. But I was this time reasonable, and at the age of fifty
it was time I should be so. Full of the doctrine I had just preached
to greybeards in my *Letter to d'Alembert*, I should have been
ashamed of not profiting by it myself; besides, coming to the
knowledge of that of which I had been ignorant, I must have been

mad to have carried my pretensions so far as to expose myself to such a high competition. Finally, ill cured perhaps of my passion for Madame d'Houdetot, I felt nothing could replace her in my heart, and I bade adieu to love for the rest of my life. I have this moment just withstood the dangerous allurements of a young woman who had her views, a dangerous allure, and very disturbing eyes; but if she feigned to forget my twelve lustres I remem-

LOUIS FRANÇOIS DE BOURBON, PRINCE DE CONTI

ber them. After having thus withdrawn myself from danger, I am no longer afraid of a fall, and I answer for myself for the rest of my days.

Madame de Boufflers, perceiving the emotion she caused in me, might also observe I had triumphed over it. I am neither mad nor vain enough to believe I was at my age capable of inspiring her with the same feelings; but from certain words which she let drop to Thérèse, I thought I had inspired her with a curiosity; if this be the case and that she has not forgiven me the disappointment she met with, it must be confessed I was born to be the victim of my weakness, since triumphant love was so prejudicial to me, and love triumphed over not less so.

Here finishes the collection of letters which has served me as a guide in the two last books. My steps will in future be directed by memory only; but this is of such a nature, relative to the period to which I am now come, and the strong impression of objects has remained so perfectly upon my mind, that, lost in the immense sea of my misfortunes, I cannot forget the detail of my first shipwreck, although the consequences present to me but a confused remembrance. I therefore shall be able to proceed in the succeeding book with sufficient confidence. If I go farther it will be groping in the dark,

BOOK ELEVEN

ALTHOUGH the *Julie*, which for a long time had been in the press, had not yet, at the end of the year 1760, appeared, the work already began to make a great noise. Madame de Luxembourg had spoken of it at Court, Madame d'Houdetot at Paris. The latter had obtained from me permission for St. Lambert to read the manuscript to the King of Poland, who had been delighted with it. Duclos, to whom I had also given the perusal of the work, had spoken of it at the Academy. All Paris was impatient to see the novel; the booksellers' shops in the Rue Saint Jacques and the Palais Royal were beset with people, who came to enquire when it was to be published. It was at length brought out, and the success it had, answered, contrary to custom, to the impatience with which it had been expected. The Dauphiness, who was one of the first who read it, spoke of it to M. de Luxembourg as a ravishing performance. The opinions of men of letters differed from each other, but in those of every other class approbation was general, especially with the women, who became so intoxicated with the book and the author, that there was not one in high life with whom I might not have succeeded had I undertaken to do it. Of this I have such proofs as I will not commit to paper, and which, without the aid of experience, authorise my opinion. It is singular, that the book should have succeeded better in France than in the rest of Europe, although the French, both men and women, are severely treated in it. Contrary to my expectation, it was least successful in Switzerland, and most so in Paris. Do friendship, love, and virtue reign in this capital more than elsewhere? Certainly not, but there reigns in it an exquisite sensibility which transports the heart to their image, and makes us cherish in others the pure, tender, and virtuous sentiments we no longer possess. Corruption is everywhere the same; virtue and morality no longer exist in Europe; but if the least love of them still remains, it is in Paris that this will be found.[1]

In the midst of so many prejudices and feigned passions, the real sentiments of nature are not to be distinguished from others, unless we well know to analyse the human heart. A very nice discrimination, not to be acquired except by the education of the world, is necessary to feel the finesses of the heart, if I dare use the expression, with which this work abounds. I do not hesitate to place the fourth part of it upon an equality with *The Princess of Cleves:* nor to assert that had these two works been read nowhere but in the provinces, their merit would never have been discovered. It must not, therefore, be considered as a matter of astonishment, that the greatest success of my work was at Court. It abounds with lively but veiled touches of the pencil, which could not but give pleasure there, because the persons who frequent it are more accustomed than others to discover them. A distinction must, however, be made. The work is by no means proper for the species of men of wit who have nothing but cunning, who possess no other kind of discernment than that which penetrates evil, and see nothing where good only is to be found. If, for instance, the *Julie* had been published in a certain country I have in mind, I am convinced it must not have been read through by a single person, and the work would have been stifled in its birth.

I have collected most of the letters written to me on the subject of this publication, and deposited them, tied up together, in the hands of Madame de Nadaillac. Should this collection ever be given to the world, very singular things will be seen, and an opposition of opinion, which shows what it is to have to do with the public. The thing least kept in view, and which will ever distinguish it from every other work, is the simplicity of the subject and the continuation of the interest, which, confined to three persons, is kept up throughout six volumes, without episode, romantic adventure, or anything malicious either in the persons or actions. Diderot complimented Richardson on the prodigious

[1] I wrote this in 1769. (*Note by Rousseau*, not in Paris MS.)

variety of his portraits and the multiplicity of his persons. In fact, Richardson has the merit of having well characterised them all; but with respect to their number, he has that in common with the most insipid writers of novels, who attempt to make up for the sterility of their ideas by multiplying persons and adventures. It is easy to awaken the attention by incessantly presenting unheard-of adventures and new faces, which pass before the imagination as the figures of a magic lantern do before the eye; but to keep up that attention to the same objects, and without the aid of the wonderful, is certainly more difficult; and if, everything equal, the simplicity of the subject adds to the beauty of the work, the novels of Richardson, superior in so many other respects, cannot in this be compared to mine. I know it is already forgotten, and the cause of its being so; but it will be taken up again.

All my fear was that, by an extreme simplicity, the narrative would be fatiguing, and that it was not sufficiently interesting to engage the attention throughout the whole. I was relieved from this apprehension by a circumstance which alone was more flattering to my pride than all the compliments made me upon the work.

It appeared at the beginning of the carnival; a hawker carried it to the Princess of Talmont,[1] on the evening of a ball night at the Opera. After supper, the Princess dressed herself for the ball, and, until the hour of going there, took up the new novel. At midnight she ordered the horses to be put to the carriage, and continued to read. The servant returned to tell her the horses were put to; she made no answer. Her people, perceiving she forgot herself, came to tell her it was two o'clock. There is yet no hurry, replied the Princess, still reading on. Some time afterwards, her watch having stopped, she rang to know the hour. She was told it was four o'clock. That being the case, said she, it is too late to go to the ball; let the horses be taken off. She undressed herself, and passed the rest of the night in reading.

Ever since I came to the knowledge of this circumstance, I have had a constant desire to see the lady, not only to know from herself whether or not what I have related be exactly true; but because I have always thought it impossible to be interested in so lively a manner in *Héloïse*, without having that sixth and moral sense with which so few hearts are endowed, and without which no person whatever can understand the sentiments of mine.

---

[1] It was not she, but some other lady, whose name I do not know. (*Note by Rousseau.*)

What rendered the women so favorable to me was, their being persuaded that I had written my own history, and was myself the hero of the romance. This opinion was so firmly established, that Madame de Polignac wrote to Madame de Verdelin, begging she would prevail upon me to show her the portrait of Julie. Everybody thought it was impossible so strongly to express sentiments without having felt them, or thus to describe the transports of love, unless immediately from the feelings of the heart. This was true, and I certainly wrote the novel during the time my imagination was inflamed to ecstasy; but they who thought real objects necessary to this effect were deceived, and far from conceiving to what a degree I can at will produce it for imaginary beings. Without Madame d'Houdetot, and the recollection of a few circumstances in my youth, the amours I have felt and described would have been only with fairy nymphs. I was unwilling either to confirm or destroy an error which was advantageous to me. The reader may see, in the preface in dialogue, which I had printed separately, in what manner I left the public in suspense. Rigorous people say, I ought to have explicitly declared the truth. For my part, I see no reason for this, nor anything that could force me to it, and am of opinion there would have been more folly than candour in the declaration without necessity.

Much about the same time the *Paix Perpétuelle* made its appearance; of this I had the year before given the manuscript to a certain M. de Bastide, the author of a journal called *Le Monde*, into which he would at all events cram all my manuscripts. He was known to M. Duclos, and came in his name, to beg I would help him to fill the *Monde*. He had heard speak of *Julie*, and would have me put this into his journal; he was also desirous of making the same use of *Emile*; he would have asked me for the *Social Contract*, for the same purpose, had he suspected it to be written. At length fatigued with his importunities, I resolved upon letting him have the *Paix Perpétuelle*, which I gave him for twelve louis. Our arrangement was, that he should print it in his Journal; but as soon as he became the proprietor of the manuscript, he thought proper to print it separately, with a few retrenchments, which the censor required him to make. What would have happened had I joined to the work my opinion of it, which fortunately I did not communicate to M. de Bastide, nor was it comprehended in our agreement? This remains still in manuscript amongst my papers. If ever it be made public, the world will see how much the pleasantries and self-sufficient manner of M. de Voltaire on the subject must have made me, who was so well acquainted with the short-sightedness of this poor man in political matters, of which he took it into his head to speak, shake my sides with laughter.

MONTMORENCY: MONT LOUIS

In the midst of my success with the women and the public, I felt I lost ground at the Hôtel de Luxembourg; not with the Maréchal, whose goodness to me seemed daily to increase, but with his lady. Since I had had nothing more to read to her, the door of her apartment was not so frequently open to me, and during her stay at Montmorency, although I regularly presented myself, I seldom saw her except at table. My place even there was not distinctly marked out as usual. As she no longer offered me that by her side, and spoke to me but seldom, not having on my part much to say to her, I was as well satisfied with another where I was more at my ease, especially in the evening; for I mechanically contracted the habit of placing myself nearer and nearer to the Maréchal.

A propos of the evening; I recollect having said I did not sup at the castle, and this was true at the beginning of my acquaintance there; but as M. de Luxembourg did not dine, nor even sit down to table, it happened that I was for several months, and already very familiar in the family, without ever having eaten with him. This he had the goodness to remark, upon which I determined to sup there from time to time, when the company was not numerous; I did so, and found the suppers very agreeable, as the dinners were taken almost out of doors, and unceremoniously; whereas the former were long, everybody remaining seated with pleasure after a long walk; and very good and agreeable, because M. de Luxembourg loved good eating, and the honours of them were done in a charming manner by Madame la Maréchal. Without this explanation it would be difficult to understand the end of a letter from M. de Luxembourg, in which he says he recollects our walk with the greatest of pleasure; especially, adds he, when in the evening we entered the court, and did not find there the traces of carriages. The rake being every morning drawn over the gravel to efface the marks left by the coach wheels, I judged by the number of ruts of that of the persons who had arrived in the afternoon.

This year 1761 completed the heavy losses this good man had suffered since I had the honour of being known to him; as if it had been ordained that the evils prepared for me by destiny should begin by the man to whom I was most attached, and who was the most worthy of esteem. The first year he lost his sister, the Duchess of Villeroy; the second, his daughter, the Princess of Robeck; the third, he lost in the Duke of Montmorency, his only son; and in the Comte de Luxembourg, his grandson, the two last supporters of the branch of which he was, and of his name. He supported all these losses with apparent courage, but his heart incessantly bled in secret during the rest of his life, and his health was for ever after upon the decline. The unexpected and tragical death of his son must have afflicted him the more, as it happened immediately after the King had granted him for this child, and given him in promise for his grandson, the reversion of the commission he himself then held of captain of the *Gardes du Corps*. He had the mortification to see the last, a most promising young man, perish by degrees, from the blind confidence of the mother in the physician, who giving the unhappy youth medicines for food, suffered him to die of inanition. Alas! had my advice been taken, the grandfather and the grandson would both still have been alive. What did not I say and write to the Maréchal, what remonstrances did I not make to Madame de Montmorency, upon the more than severe regimen, which, upon the faith of physicians, she made her son observe! Madame de Luxembourg, who thought as I did, would not usurp the authority of the mother; M. de Luxembourg, a man of a mild and easy character, did not like to contradict her. Madame de Montmorency had in Bordeu a confidence to which her son at length became a victim. How delighted was the poor creature when he could obtain permission to come to Mont Louis with Madame de Boufflers, to ask Thérèse for some victuals for his famished stomach! How did I secretly deplore the miseries of greatness in seeing this only heir to an immense fortune, a great name, and so many dignified titles, devour with the greediness of a beggar a wretched morsel of bread! At length, notwithstanding all I could say and do, the physician triumphed, and the child died of hunger.

The same confidence in quacks, which lost the grandson, hastened the dissolution of the grandfather, and to this he added the pusillanimity of wishing to dissimulate the infirmities of age. M. de Luxembourg had at intervals a pain in the great toe; he was seized with it at Montmorency, which deprived him of sleep, and brought on a slight fever. I had courage enough to pronounce the word gout. Madame de Luxembourg gave me a reprimand. The surgeon, valet de chambre of the Maréchal,[1] maintained it was not the gout, and dressed the suffering part with healing balsam. Unfortunately the pain subsided, and when it returned the same remedy was had recourse to. The constitution of the Maréchal was weakened, and his disorder increased, as did his remedies in the same proportion. Madame de Luxembourg, who at length perceived the primary disorder to be the gout, objected to the dangerous manner of treating it. Things were afterwards concealed from her, and M. de Luxembourg in a few years lost his life in consequence of his obstinate adherence to what he imagined to be a method of cure. But let me not anticipate misfortune: how many others have I to relate before I come to this!

It is singular with what fatality everything I could say and do seemed of a nature to displease Madame de Luxembourg, even when I had it most at heart to preserve her benevolence. The repeated afflictions which fell upon M. de Luxembourg still attached me to him the more, and consequently to Madame de Luxembourg; for they always seemed to me to be so sincerely united, that the sentiments in favour of the one necessarily extended to the other. The Maréchal grew old. His assiduity at Court, the cares this brought on, continually hunting, fatigue, and especially that of the service during the quarter he was in waiting, required the vigour of a young man, and I did not perceive anything that could support his in that course of life; since, besides, after his death, his dignities were to be dispersed and his name extinct, it was by no means necessary for him to continue in a laborious life of which the principal object had been to dispose the Prince favourably to his children. One day when we three were together, and he complained of the fatigues of the Court, as a man who had been discouraged by his losses, I took the liberty to speak of retire-

---

[1] Paris MS. adds: "Whose name was Marlane."

ment, and to give him the advice Cyneas gave to Pyrrhus. He sighed and returned no positive answer. But the moment Madame de Luxembourg found me alone, she reprimanded me severely for what I had said, at which she seemed to be alarmed. She made a remark of which I so strongly felt the justness that I determined never again to touch upon the subject: this was that the long habit of living at Court made that life necessary, that it was become a matter of amusement for M. de Luxembourg, and that the retirement I proposed to him would be less a relaxation from care than an exile, in which inactivity, weariness and melancholy would soon put an end to his existence. Although she must have perceived I was convinced, and ought to have relied upon the promise I made her, and which I faithfully kept, she still seemed to doubt of it; and I recollect that the conversations I afterwards had with the Maréchal were less frequent and almost always interrupted.

Whilst my stupidity and awkwardness injured me in her opinion, persons, whom she frequently saw and most loved, were far from being disposed to aid me in gaining what I had lost. The Abbé de Boufflers especially, a young man, as lofty as it was possible for a man to be, never seemed well disposed towards me; and besides his being the only person of the society of Madame de Luxembourg who never showed me the least attention, I thought I perceived I lost something with her every time he came to the castle. It is true that without his wishing this to be the case, his presence alone was sufficient to produce the effect: so much did his graceful and elegant manner render still more dull my stupid *spropositi*.[1] During the two first years he seldom came to Montmorency, and by the indulgence of Madame de Luxembourg I had tolerably supported myself, but as soon as his visits began to be regular, I was irretrievably lost. I wished to take refuge under his wing, and gain his friendship; but the same awkwardness which made it necessary I should please him, prevented me from succeeding in the attempt I made to do it, and what I did with that intention entirely lost me with Madame de Luxembourg, without being of the least service to me with the Abbé. With his understanding he might have succeeded in anything, but the impossibility of applying himself, and his turn for dissipation, prevented his acquiring a perfect knowledge of any subject. His talents are however various, and this is sufficient for the circles in which he wishes to distinguish himself. He writes light poetry and fashion-

---

[1] Blunders.

able letters, strums on the cithern, and pretends to draw with crayons. He took it into his head to attempt the portrait of Madame de Luxembourg: the sketch he produced was horrid. She said it did not in the least resemble her, and this was true. The traitorous Abbé consulted me, and I like a fool and a liar said there was a likeness. I wished to flatter the Abbé, but I did not please the lady, who noted down what I said, and the Abbé, having obtained what he wanted, laughed at me in his turn. I perceived by the ill success of this my late beginning the necessity of never making another attempt to flatter *invita Minerva*.

My talent was that of telling men useful but severe truths with energy and courage; to this it was necessary to confine myself. Not only I was not born to flatter, but I knew not how to commend. The awkwardness of the manner in which I have sometimes bestowed eulogium has done me more harm than the severity of my censure. Of this I have to adduce one terrible instance, the consequences of which have not only fixed my fate for the rest of my life, but will perhaps decide on my reputation throughout all posterity.

During the residence of M. de Luxembourg at Montmorency, M. de Choiseul sometimes came to supper at the castle. He arrived there one day after I had left it. My name was mentioned, and M. de Luxembourg related to him what had happened at Venice between me and M. de Montaigu. M. de Choiseul said it was a pity I had quitted that track, and that if I chose to enter it again he would most willingly give me employment. M. de Luxembourg told me what had passed. Of this I was the more sensible as I was not accustomed to be spoiled by ministers, and had I been in a better state of health it is not certain that in spite of my resolutions I should not have been guilty of a new folly. Ambition never had power over my mind except during the short intervals in which every other passion left me at liberty; but one of these intervals would have been sufficient to determine me. This good intention of M. de Choiseul gained him my attachment and increased the esteem which, in consequence of some operations in his administration, I had conceived for his talents; and the Family Compact[1] in particular had appeared to me to evince a statesman of the first order. He moreover gaining ground in my estimation by the little respect I entertained for his predecessors, not excepting Madame de Pompadour, whom I considered as a species of prime

---

[1] The Franco-Spanish treaty of 1761.

minister, and when it was reported that one of these two would expel the other, I thought I offered up prayers for the honour of France when I wished that M. de Choiseul might triumph. I had always felt an antipathy to Madame de Pompadour, even before her preferment, when I had seen her with Madame de Poplinière when her name was still Madame d'Etioles. I was afterwards dissatisfied with her silence on the subject of Diderot, and with her proceedings relative to myself, as well on the subject of the *Fêtes de Ramire* and the *Muses galantes*, as on that of the *Devin du Village*, which had not in any manner produced me advantages proportioned to its success; and on all occasions I had found her but little disposed to serve me. This however did not prevent the Chevalier de Lorenzy from proposing to me to write something in praise of that lady, insinuating that I might acquire some advantage by it. The proposition excited my indignation, the more as I perceived it did not come from himself, knowing that, passive as he was, he thought and acted according to the impulsion he received. I am so little accustomed to constraint that it was impossible for me to conceal from him my disdain, nor from anybody the moderate opinion I had of the favourite; this I am sure she knew, and thus my own interest was added to my natural inclination in the prayers I made for M. de Choiseul. Having a great esteem for his talents, which were all I knew of him, full of gratitude for his kind intentions, and moreover unacquainted in my retirement with his taste and manner of living, I already considered him as the avenger of the public and myself; and being at that time writing the conclusion of my *Social Contract*, I stated in it, in a single passage, what I thought of preceding ministers, and of him by whom they began to be eclipsed. On this occasion I acted contrary to my most constant maxim; and besides, I did not recollect that, in bestowing praise and strongly censuring in the same article, without naming the persons, the language must be so appropriated to those to whom it is applicable, that the most ticklish pride cannot find in it the least thing equivocal. I was in this respect in such an impudent security, that I never once thought it was possible anyone should make a false application. It will soon appear whether or not I was right.

One of my misfortunes was always to be connected with some female author. This I thought I might avoid amongst the great. I was deceived; it still pursued me. Madame de Luxembourg was not, however, at least that I know of, attacked with the mania of writing; but Madame la Comtesse de Boufflers was. She wrote a tragedy in prose, which, in the first place, was read, handed about and highly spoken of in the society of the Prince of Conti; and upon which, not satisfied with the encomiums she received, she would also consult me for the purpose of having mine. This she obtained, but with that moderation which the work deserved. She, besides, had with it the information I thought it my duty to give her, that her piece, entitled *L'Esclave généreux*, greatly resembled the English tragedy of *Oroonoko*, but little known in France, although translated into the French language. Madame de Boufflers thanked me for the remark, but, however, assured me there was not the least resemblance between her piece and the other. I never spoke of the plagiarism except to herself, and I did it to discharge a duty she had imposed on me; but this has not since prevented me from frequently recollecting the consequences of the sincerity of Gil Blas to the preaching bishop.

Besides the Abbé de Boufflers, by whom I was not beloved, and Madame de Boufflers, in whose opinion I was guilty of that which neither women nor authors ever pardon, the other friends of Madame de Luxembourg never seemed much disposed to become mine, particularly the President Hénault, who, enrolled amongst authors, was not exempt from their weaknesses; also Madame du Deffand and Mademoiselle de Lespinasse, both intimate with Voltaire and friends of d'Alembert, with whom the latter at length lived; however upon an honourable footing, for it cannot be understood I mean otherwise. I first began to interest myself for Madame du Deffand, whom the loss of her eyes made an object of commiseration in mine; but her manner of living, so contrary to my own that her hour of going to bed was almost mine for rising; her unbounded passion for low wit, the importance she gave to every kind of printed trash, either complimentary or abusive, the despotism and transports of her oracles, her excessive admiration or dislike of everything which did not permit her to speak upon any subject without convulsions, her inconceivable prejudices, invincible obstinacy, and the enthusiasm of folly to which this carried her in her passionate judgements; all disgusted me and diminished the attention I wished to pay her. I neglected her and she perceived it; this was enough to set her in a rage; and, although I was sufficiently aware how much a woman of her character was to be feared, I preferred exposing myself to the scourge of her hatred rather than to that of her friendship.

My having so few friends in the society of Madame de Luxembourg would not have been in the least dangerous had I had no enemies in her family. Of these I had but one, who, in my present situation, is as powerful as a hundred. It certainly was not the Duke de Villeroy, her brother; for he not only came to see me, but had several times invited me to Villeroy; and as I had answered to the invitation with all possible politeness and respect, he had taken my vague manner of doing it as a consent, and arranged with M. and Madame de Luxembourg a journey of a fortnight, in which it was proposed to me to make one of the party. As the cares my health then required did not permit me to go from home without risk, I prayed M. de Luxembourg to have the goodness to make my apologies. His answer proves this was done with all possible ease, and M. de Villeroy still continued to show me his usual marks of goodness. His nephew and heir, the young Marquis of Villeroy, had not for me the same benevolence, nor had I for him the respect I had for his uncle. His hair-brained manner rendered him insupportable to me, and my coldness drew upon me his aversion. He insultingly attacked me one evening at table, and I had the worst of it, because I am a fool, without presence of mind; and because anger, instead of rendering my wit more poignant, deprives me of the little I have. I had a dog which had been given me when he was quite young, soon after my arrival at the Hermitage, and which I called *Duke*. This dog, not handsome, but rare of his kind, of which I had made my companion and friend, a title he certainly merited much more than most of the persons by whom it was taken, became in great request at the castle of Montmorency, for his good-nature and fondness and the attachment we had to each other; but from a foolish pusillanimity I had changed his name to *Turk*, as if there were not many dogs called *Marquis*, without giving the least offence to any marquis whatsoever. The Marquis of Villeroy, who knew of this change of name, attacked me in such a manner that I was obliged openly at table to relate what I had done. Whatever there might be offensive in the name of Duke, it was not in my having given, but in my having taken it away. The worst of all was, there were several dukes present; amongst others M. de Luxembourg, and his son; and the Marquis of Villeroy, who was one day to have, and now has that title, enjoyed in the most cruel manner the embarrassment into which he had thrown me, and the effect it had produced. I was told the next day his aunt had severely reprimanded him, and it may be judged whether or not, supposing her to have been serious, this put me upon better terms with him.

To enable me to support his enmity I had no person, neither

at the Hôtel de Luxembourg nor at the Temple, except the Chevalier de Lorenzy, who professed himself my friend; but he was
more that of d'Alembert, under whose protection he passed with
women for a great geometrician. He was moreover the cicisbeo,
or rather the complaisant chevalier of the Countess of Boufflers,
a great friend also to d'Alembert, and the Chevalier de Lorenzy
was the most passive instrument in her hands. Thus, far from
having in the world any counterbalance to my ineptitude, to keep
me in the good graces of Madame de Luxembourg, everybody who
approached her seemed to concur in injuring me in her opinion.
Yet, besides *Emile*, with which she charged herself, she gave me
at the same time another mark of her benevolence, which made
me imagine that, although wearied with my conversation, she
preserved and would still preserve for me the friendship she had
so many times promised me for life.

As soon as I thought I could depend upon this, I began to ease
my heart, by confessing to her all my faults, having made it an
inviolable maxim to show myself to my friends such as I really
was, neither better nor worse. I had declared to her my connexion
with Thérèse, and everything that had resulted from it, without
concealing the manner in which I had disposed of my children.
She had received my confessions favourably, and even too much
so, since she spared me the censures I so much merited; and what
made the greatest impression upon me was her goodness to
Thérèse, making her little presents, sending for her, and begging
her to come and see her, receiving her with caresses, and often
embracing her in public. This poor girl was in transports of joy
and gratitude, of which I certainly partook; the friendship M. and
Madame de Luxembourg showed me in their condescensions to
Thérèse affected me much more than if they had been made
immediately to myself.

Things remained in this state for a considerable time; but at
length Madame de Luxembourg carried her goodness so far as to
have a desire to take one of my children from the hospital. She
knew I had put a cipher into the swaddling clothes of the eldest;
she asked me for the counterpart of the cipher, and I gave it her.
In this research she employed La Roche, her valet de chambre,
and confidential servant, who made vain enquiries, but found
nothing, although after only about twelve or fourteen years, had
the register of the Foundling Hospital been in order, or the search
properly made, the original cipher ought to have been found.
However this may be, I was less sorry for his want of success than

I should have been had I from time to time continued to see the child from his birth until that moment. If by the aid of the indications given, some child had been presented as my own, the doubt of its being so in fact, and the fear of having one thus substituted for it, would have contracted my affections, and I should not have tasted of the charm of the real sentiment of nature. This during infancy stands in need of being supported by habit. The long absence of a child whom the father has seen but for an instant, weakens, and at length annihilates paternal or maternal sentiment, and parents will never love a child sent to nurse, like that which is brought up under their eyes. This reflection may extenuate my faults in their effects, but it must aggravate them in their source.

It may not perhaps be useless to remark that by the means of Thérèse, the same La Roche became acquainted with Madame le Vasseur, whom Grimm still kept at Deuil, near la Chevrette, and not far from Montmorency.

After my departure it was by means of La Roche that I continued to send this woman the money I have constantly sent her at stated times, and I am of opinion he often carried her presents from Madame de Luxembourg; therefore she certainly was not to be pitied, although she constantly complained. With respect to Grimm, as I am not fond of speaking of persons whom I ought to hate, I never mentioned his name to Madame de Luxembourg, except when I could not avoid it: but she frequently made him the subject of conversation, without telling me what she thought of the man, or letting me discover whether or not he was of her acquaintance. Reserve with people I love and who are open with me, being contrary to my nature, especially in things relating to themselves, I have since that time frequently thought of that of Madame de Luxembourg, but never except when other events rendered the reflection natural.

Having waited a long time without hearing speak of *Emile*, after I had given it to Madame de Luxembourg, I at last heard the agreement was made at Paris, with the bookseller Duchesne, and by him with Néaulme, of Amsterdam. Madame de Luxembourg sent me the original, and the duplicate of my agreement with Duchesne, that I might sign them. I discovered the writing to be by the same hand as that of the letters of M. de Malesherbes, which he himself did not write. The certainty that my agreement was made by the consent, and under the eye of that magistrate, made me sign without hesitation. Duchesne gave me for the manuscript six thousand livres, half in specie, and one or two hundred copies. After having signed the two parts, I sent them both to Madame de Luxembourg, according to her desire; she gave one to Duchesne, and insteading of returning the other, kept it herself, so that I never saw it afterwards.

My acquaintance with M. and Madame de Luxembourg, though it diverted me a little from my plan of retirement, did not make me entirely renounce it. Even at the time in which I was most in favour with Madame de Luxembourg, I always felt that nothing but my sincere attachment to the Maréchal and herself could render to me supportable the people with whom they were connected, and all the difficulty I had was in conciliating this attachment with a manner of life more agreeable to my inclination, and less contrary to my health, which constraint and late suppers continually deranged, notwithstanding all the care taken to prevent it; for in this, as in everything else, attention was carried as far as possible: thus, for instance, every evening after supper the Maréchal, who went early to bed, never failed, notwithstanding everything that could be said to the contrary, to make me withdraw at the same time. It was not until some little time before my catastrophe that, for what reason I know not, he ceased to pay me that attention.

Before I perceived the coolness of Madame de Luxembourg, I was desirous, that I might not expose myself to it, to execute my old project; but not having the means to that effect, I was obliged to wait for the conclusion of the agreement for *Emile*, and in the meantime I finished the *Social Contract* and sent it to Rey, fixing the price of the manuscript at a thousand livres, which he paid me.

I ought not perhaps to omit a trifling circumstance relative to this manuscript. I gave it, well sealed up, to Duvoisin, a minister in the pays de Vaud, and chaplain at the Hôtel de Hollande, who sometimes came to see me, and took upon himself to send the packet to Rey, with whom he was connected. The manuscript, written in a small letter, was but very trifling, and did not fill his pocket. Yet, in passing the barrier, the packet fell, I know not by what means, into the hands of the clerk, who opened and examined it, and afterwards returned it to him, when he had reclaimed it in the name of the ambassador. This gave him an opportunity of reading it himself, which he ingenuously wrote me he had done, speaking highly of the work, without suffering a word of criticism or censure to escape him, undoubtedly reserving to himself to become the avenger of Christianity as soon as the work should appear. He resealed the packet, and sent it to Rey. Such is the substance of his narrative, in the letter in which he gave an account of the affair, and is all I ever knew of the matter.

Besides these two books and my *Dictionary of Music*, at which I still did something as opportunity offered, I had some other works of less importance ready to make their appearance, and which I proposed to publish either separately or in my general collection, should I ever undertake it. The principal of these works, most of which are still in manuscript in the hands of du Peyrou, was an *Essay on the Origin of Languages*, which I had read to M. de Malesherbes and the Chevalier de Lorenzy, who spoke favourably of it. I expected all these productions together would produce me a neat capital, after paying all expenses, of from eight to ten thousand livres, which I intended to place in annuities for my life and that of Thérèse; after which our design, as I have already mentioned, was to go and live together in the midst of some province, without farther troubling the public about me, or myself with any other project than that of peacefully ending my days, and still continuing to do in my neighbourhood all the good in my power, and to write at leisure the memoirs which I meditated.

Such was my intention, and the execution of it was facilitated by an act of generosity in Rey, upon which I cannot be silent. This bookseller, of whom so many unfavourable things were told me in Paris, is notwithstanding the only one with whom I have always had reason to be satisfied.[1] It is true we frequently disagreed as to the execution of my works; he was heedless, and I was choleric; but in matters of interest which related to them, although I never made with him an agreement in form, I always found in him great exactness and probity. He is also the only person of his profession who frankly confessed to me he gained largely by my means; and he frequently, when he offered me a part of his fortune, told me I was the author of it all. Not finding the means of exercising his gratitude immediately upon myself, he wished at least to give me proofs of it in the person of my *Governess*, upon whom he settled an annuity of three hundred livres, expressing in the deed that it was in acknowledgement for the advantages I had procured him. This he did between himself and me, without ostentation, pretension, or noise, and had not I spoken of it to everybody, not a single person would ever have known

---

[1] When I wrote this, I was far from imagining or conceiving the frauds I have since discovered in the printed version of my writings, and which he has had to admit. (*Note by Rousseau*, not in Paris MS.)

anything of the matter. I was so pleased with this action that I became attached to Rey, and conceived for him a real friendship. Some time afterwards he desired I would become godfather to one of his children; I consented, and a part of my regret in the situation to which I am reduced, is my being deprived of the means of rendering in future my attachment to my god-daughter useful to her and her parents. Why am I, who am so sensible of the modest generosity of this bookseller, so little so of the noisy eagerness of many persons of the highest rank, who pompously fill the world with accounts of the services they say they wished to render me, but the good effects of which I never felt? Is it their fault or mine? Are they nothing more than vain; is my insensibility purely ingratitude? Intelligent reader, weigh and determine; for my part I say no more.

This pension was a great resource to Thérèse, and a considerable alleviation to me, although I was far from receiving from it a direct advantage, any more than from the presents that were made her. She herself has always disposed of everything. When I kept her money I gave her a faithful account of it, without ever applying any part of the deposit to our common expenses, not even when she was richer than myself. *What is mine is ours*, said I to her; *and what is thine is thine*. I never departed from this maxim, which I have often repeated to her. They who have had the baseness to accuse me of receiving by her hands that which I refused to take with mine, undoubtedly judged of my heart by their own, and knew but little of me. I would willingly eat with her the bread she should have earned, but not that she should have had given her. For a proof of this I appeal to herself, both now and hereafter, when, according to the course of nature, she shall have survived me. Unfortunately she understands but little of economy in any respect, and is besides careless and extravagant, not from vanity nor gluttony, but solely from negligence. No creature is perfect here below, and since her excellent qualities must be accompanied with some defects, I prefer these to vices; although her defects are perhaps more prejudicial to us both. The efforts I have made, as formerly I did for Mamma, to accumulate something in advance which might some day be to her a never-failing resource, are not to be conceived; but my cares were always ineffectual. Neither of these women ever called themselves to an account, and, notwithstanding all my efforts, everything I acquired was dissipated as fast as it came. Notwithstanding the great simplicity of Thérèse's dress, the pension from Rey has never been sufficient to buy her clothes, and I have every year been under the necessity of adding something to it for that purpose. We are neither of us born to be rich, and this I certainly do not reckon amongst our misfortunes.

The *Social Contract* was soon printed. This was not the case with *Emile*, for the publication of which I waited to go into the retirement I meditated. Duchesne, from time to time, sent me specimens of printing to choose from; when I had made my choice, instead of beginning he sent me others. When, at length, we were fully determined on the size and letter, and several sheets were already printed off; on some trifling alteration I made in a proof, he began the whole again, and at the end of six months we were in less forwardness than on the first day. During all these experiments I clearly perceived the work was printing in France as well as in Holland, and that two editions of it were preparing at the same time. What could I do? The manuscript was no longer mine. Far from having anything to do with the edition in France, I was always against it; but since at length this was preparing in spite of all opposition, and was to serve as a model to the other, it was necessary I should cast my eyes over it, and examine the proofs, that my work might not be mutilated. It was besides printed so much by the consent of the magistrate, that it was he who, in some measure, directed the undertaking; he likewise wrote to me frequently, and once came to see me and converse on the subject upon an occasion of which I am going to speak.

Whilst Duchesne crept like a snail, Néaulme, whom he withheld, scarcely moved at all. The sheets were not regularly sent him as they were printed. He thought there was some trick in the manœuvre of Duchesne, that is of Guy who acted for him; and perceiving the terms of the agreement to be departed from, he wrote me letter after letter full of complaints, and it was less possible for me to remove the subject of them than that of those I myself had to make. His friend Guérin, who at that time came frequently to see me, never ceased speaking to me about the work, but always with the greatest reserve. He knew and he did not know that it was printing in France, and that the magistrate had a hand in it. In expressing his concern for my embarrassment, he seemed to accuse me of imprudence without ever saying in what this consisted; he incessantly equivocated, and seemed to speak for no other purpose than to hear what I had to say. I thought myself so secure that I laughed at his mystery and circumspection as at a habit he had contracted with ministers and magistrates,

whose offices he much frequented. Certain of having conformed
to every rule with the work, and strongly persuaded that I had not
only the consent and protection of the magistrate, but that the
book merited and had obtained the favour of the minister, I congratulated myself upon my courage in doing good, and laughed
at my pusillanimous friends who seemed uneasy on my account.
Duclos was one of these, and I confess my confidence in his understanding and uprightness might have alarmed me, had I had less
in the utility of the work, and in the probity of those by whom it
was patronised. He came from the house of M. Baille to see me
whilst *Emile* was in the press; he spoke to me concerning it: I read
to him the *Profession of Faith of the Savoyard Vicar*, to which he
listened attentively and, as it seemed to me, with pleasure. When
I had finished, he said: What! citizen, this is a part of a work now
printing at Paris? Yes, answered I, and it ought to be printed at
the Louvre by order of the King. I confess it, replied he, but pray
do not mention to anybody your having read to me this fragment.

CHRÉTIEN GUILLAUME DE MALESHERBES

This striking manner of expressing himself surprised without
alarming me. I knew Duclos was intimate with M. de Malesher-

bes, and I could not conceive how it was possible he should think so differently from him upon the same subject.

I had lived at Montmorency for the last four years without ever having had there one day of good health. Although the air is excellent the water is bad, and this may possibly be one of the causes which contributed to increase my habitual complaints. Towards the end of the autumn of 1761, I fell quite ill, and passed the whole winter in suffering almost without intermission. The physical ill, augmented by a thousand inquietudes, rendered these terrible. For some time past, my mind had been disturbed by melancholy forebodings without my knowing to what these directly tended. I received anonymous letters of an extraordinary nature, and others, that were signed, much of the same import. I received one from a Counsellor of the Parliament of Paris, who, dissatisfied with the present constitution of things, and foreseeing nothing but disagreeable events, consulted me upon the choice of an asylum at Geneva, or in Switzerland, to retire to with his family. Another was brought me from M. de ——, *Président à mortier* of the Parliament of ——, who proposed to me to draw up for this Parliament, which was then at variance with the Court, memoirs and remonstrances, and offering to furnish me with all the documents and materials necessary to that purpose.

When I suffer I am subject to ill humour. This was the case when I received these letters, and my answers to them, in which I flatly refused everything that was asked of me, bore strong marks of the effect they had upon my mind. I do not, however, reproach myself with this refusal, as the letters might be so many snares laid by my enemies,[1] and what was required of me was contrary to the principles from which I was less willing than ever to swerve. But having it in my power to refuse with politeness, I did it with brutality, and in this consists my error.

The two letters, of which I have just spoken, will be found amongst my papers. The letters from the Counsellor did not absolutely surprise me, because I agreed with him in opinion, and with many others, that the declining constitution of France threatened an approaching destruction. The disasters of an unsuccessful war,[2] all of which proceeded from a fault in the government; the incredible confusion of the finances; the perpetual drawings upon

---

[1] I knew for instance the President de —— to be connected with the Encyclopedists and the Holbachians. (*Note by Rousseau.*)

[2] The Seven Years' War (1756-1763).

the treasury by the administration, which was then divided between two or three ministers, amongst whom reigned nothing but discord, and who, to counteract the operations of each other, let the kingdom go to ruin; the discontent of the people, and of every other rank of subjects; the obstinacy of a woman who, constantly sacrificing her judgement, if she indeed possessed any, to her inclinations, kept almost always from public employments persons the most capable of discharging the duties of them, to place in them such as pleased her best; everything concurred in justifying the foresight of the Counsellor, that of the public, and my own. This made me several times consider whether or not I myself should seek an asylum out of the kingdom before it was torn by the dissension by which it seemed to be threatened; but relieved from my fears by my insignificance, and the peacefulness of my disposition, I thought that in the state of solitude in which I was determined to live, no public commotion could reach me. I was sorry only that, in this state of things, M. de Luxembourg should accept commissions which tended to injure him in the opinion of the persons of the place of which he was governor. I could have wished he had prepared himself there a retreat in case the great machine had fallen to pieces, which seemed much to be apprehended; and it still appears to me beyond a doubt, that if the reins of government had not fallen into a single hand, the French monarchy would now be at the last gasp.

Whilst my situation became worse, the printing of *Emile* went on more slowly, and was at length suspended without my being able to learn the reason why; Guy did not deign to answer my letter of enquiry, and I could obtain no information from any person of what was going forward, M. de Malesherbes being then in the country. A misfortune, whatever it be, never makes me uneasy provided I know in what it consists; but it is my nature to be afraid of darkness, I tremble at the appearance of it; mystery always gives me inquietude, it is too opposite to my natural disposition in which there is an openness bordering on imprudence. The sight of the most hideous monster would, I am of opinion, alarm me but little; but if by night I saw a figure in a white sheet I should be afraid of it. My imagination, wrought upon by this long silence, was now employed in creating phantoms. I tormented myself the more in endeavouring to discover the impediment to the printing of my last and best production, as I had the publication of it much at heart; and, as I always carried everything to an extreme, I imagined that I perceived in the suspension the suppression of the work. Yet being unable to discover either the cause or manner of it, I remained in the most cruel state of suspense. I wrote letter after letter to Guy, to M. de Malesherbes, and to Madame de Luxembourg, and not receiving answers, at least when I expected them, my head became so affected that I was not far from a delirium. I unfortunately heard that Father Griffet, a Jesuit, had spoken of *Emile*, and repeated from it some passages. My imagination instantly unveiled to me the mystery of iniquity; I saw the whole progress of it as clearly as if it had been revealed to me. I figured to myself that the Jesuits, furious on account of the contemptible manner in which I had spoken of colleges, were in possession of my work; that it was they who delayed the publication; that informed by their friend Guérin of my situation, and foreseeing my approaching dissolution, of which I myself had no manner of doubt, they wished to delay the appearance of the work until after that event, with an intention to curtail and mutilate it, and, in favour to their own views, to attribute to me sentiments not my own. The number of facts and circumstances which occurred to my mind, in confirmation of this silly supposition, and gave it an appearance of truth, nay more, supported it by evidence and demonstration, is astonishing.

I knew Guérin to be entirely in the interest of the Jesuits. I attributed to them all the friendly advances he had made me; I was persuaded he had, by their entreaties, pressed me to engage with Néaulme, who had given them the first sheets of my work; that they had afterwards found means to stop the printing of it by Duchesne, and perhaps to get possession of the manuscript to make such alterations in it as they should think proper, that after my death they might publish it disguised in their own manner. I had always perceived, notwithstanding the wheedling of Father Berthier, that the Jesuits did not like me, not only as an Encyclopedist, but because all my principles were more in opposition to their maxims and influence than the incredulity of my colleagues, since atheistical and devout fanaticism, approaching each other by their common enmity to toleration, may become united; a proof of which is seen in China, and in the cabal against myself; whereas religion, both reasonable and moral, taking away all human power over the conscience, deprives those who assume that power of every resource. I knew the Counsellor was a great friend to the Jesuits, and I had my fears lest the son, intimidated by the father, should find himself under the necessity of abandoning the work he had protected. I besides imagined that I perceived this to be the case in the chicanery employed against me relative to the two first volumes, in which cancel-pages were required for reasons of which I could not feel the force; whilst the two other volumes were known to contain things of such a nature as, had the censor objected to them in the manner he did to the passages he thought exceptionable in the others, would have required their being entirely written over again. I also understood, and M. de Malesherbes himself told me of it, that the Abbé de Grave, whom he had charged with the inspection of this edition, was another partisan of the Jesuits. I saw nothing but Jesuits everywhere, without considering that, upon the point of being suppressed, and wholly taken up in making their defence, they had something which interested them much more than the cavillings relative to a work in which they were not in question. I am wrong, however, in saying this did not occur to me; for I really thought of it, and M. de Malesherbes took care to make the observation to me the moment he heard of my extravagant suspicions. But by another of those absurdities of a man who, from the bosom of obscurity, will absolutely judge of the secret of great affairs, with which he is totally unacquainted, I never could bring myself to believe the Jesuits were in danger, and I considered the rumour of their suppression as an artful manœuvre of their own to deceive their adversaries. Their past successes, which had been uninterrupted, gave me so terrible an idea of their power, that I already was grieved at the overthrow of the Parliament. I knew M. de Choiseul had prosecuted his studies under the Jesuits, that Madame de Pompadour was not upon bad terms with them, and that their league with favourites and ministers had constantly appeared advantageous to both, against their common enemies. The Court seemed to remain neuter, and, persuaded as I was that should the Society receive a severe check it would not come from the Parliament, which would not be strong enough to procure it, I saw in the inaction of government the ground of their confidence and the omen of their triumph.

In fine, perceiving in the rumours of the day nothing more than art and dissimulation on their part, and thinking they, in their state of security, had time to watch over all their interests, I had not the least doubt of their shortly crushing Jansenism, the Parliament, and the Encyclopedists, with every other association which should not submit to their yoke; and that if they ever suffered my work to appear, this would not happen until it should be so transformed as to favour their pretensions, and thus make use of my name the better to deceive my readers.

I felt my health and strength decline; and such was the horror with which my mind was filled, at the idea of dishonour to my memory in the work most worthy of myself, that I am surprised so many extravagant ideas did not occasion a speedy end to my existence. I never was so much afraid of death as at this time, and had I died with the apprehensions I then had upon my mind, I should have died in despair. At present, although I perceive no obstacle to the execution of the blackest and most dreadful conspiracy ever formed against the memory of a man, I shall die much more in peace, certain of leaving in my writings a testimony in my favour, which sooner or later will triumph over the calumnies of mankind.

M. de Malesherbes, who discovered the agitation of my mind, and to whom I acknowledged it, used such endeavours to restore me to tranquillity as proved his excessive goodness of heart. Madame de Luxembourg aided him in his good work, and several times went to Duchesne to know in what state the edition was. At length the impression was again begun, and the progress of it became more rapid without my ever knowing for what reason it had been suspended. M. de Malesherbes took the trouble to come to Montmorency to calm my mind; in this he succeeded, and the full confidence I had in his uprightness having overcome the derangement of my poor head, gave efficacy to the endeavours he made to restore it. After what he had seen of my anguish and delirium, it was natural he should think I was to be pitied; and he really commiserated my situation. The expressions, incessantly repeated, of the philosophical cabal by which he was surrounded, occurred to his memory. When I went to live at the Hermitage, they, as I have already remarked, said I should not remain there long. When they saw I persevered, they charged me with obstinacy and pride, proceeding from a want of courage to retract, and insisted that my life was there a burden to me; in short, that I was very wretched. M. de Malesherbes believed this really to be the case, and wrote to me upon the subject. This error in a man for whom I had so much esteem gave me some pain, and I wrote to him four letters successively, in which I stated the real motives of my conduct, and made him fully acquainted with my taste, inclination, and character, and with the most interior sentiments of my heart. These letters, written hastily, almost without taking pen from paper, and which I neither copied, corrected, nor even read, are perhaps the only things I ever wrote with facility, which in the midst of my sufferings and extreme despondency, was, I think, astonishing. I sighed, as I felt myself declining, at the thought of leaving in the minds of honest men an opinion of me so far from truth; and by the sketch hastily given in my four letters, I endeavoured, in some measure, to provide a substitute for the memoirs I had proposed to write. These letters pleased M. de Malesherbes, who showed them in Paris, and are, besides, a kind of summary of what I here give in detail, and, on this account, merit preservation. The copy I begged of them some years afterward, will be found amongst my papers.

The only thing which continued to give me pain, in the idea of my approaching dissolution, was my not having a man of letters for a friend, to whom I could confide my papers, that after my death he might make a proper choice of such as were worthy of publication. After my journey to Geneva, I conceived a friendship for Moultou; this young man pleased me, and I could have wished him to receive my last breath. I expressed to him this desire, and am of opinion he would readily have complied with it, had not his affairs and family prevented him from so doing. Deprived of this consolation, I still wished to give him a mark of my confidence by sending him the *Profession of Faith of the Savoyard Vicar* before it was published. He was pleased with the work, but did not in his answer seem so fully to expect from it the effect of which I had but little doubt. He wished to receive from me some fragment which I had not given to anybody else. I sent him the *Funeral Oration on the late Duke of Orleans;* this I had written for the Abbé Darty, who had not pronounced it, because, contrary to his expectation, another person was appointed to perform the ceremony.

The printing of *Emile*, after having been again taken in hand, was continued and completed without much difficulty; and I remarked this singularity, that after the cancel-pages, so much insisted upon in the two first volumes, the two last were passed over without any objection, and their contents did not delay the publication for a moment. I had, however, some uneasiness which I must not pass over in silence. After having been afraid of the Jesuits, I began to fear the Jansenists and philosophers. An enemy to party, faction, and cabal, I never expected the least good of persons concerned in them. The *Gossips* had quitted their old abode, and taken up their residence by the side of me, so that in their chamber, everything said in mine, and upon the terrace, was distinctly heard; and from their garden it would have been easy to scale the low wall by which it was separated from my alcove. This was become my study; my table there was covered with proof-sheets of *Emile* and the *Social Contract*, and stitching these sheets as they were sent to me, I had all my volumes a long time before they were published. My negligence and the confidence I had in M. Mathas, in whose garden I was shut up, frequently made me forget to lock the door at night, and in the morning I several times found it wide open: this, however, would not have given me the least inquietude had not I thought my papers seemed to have been deranged. After having several times made the same remark, I became more careful, and locked the door. The lock was a bad one, and the key turned in it no more than half round. As I became more attentive, I found my papers in a much greater confusion than they were when I left everything open. At length I missed one of my volumes for a day and two nights, without knowing what was become of it until the morning of the third day, when I again found it upon the table. I never suspected either M. Mathas or his nephew, M. Dumoulin, knowing myself to be beloved by both, and my confidence in them was unbounded. That I had in the *Gossips* began to diminish. Although they were Jansenists, I knew them to have some connexion with d'Alembert, and moreover they all three lodged in the same house.

This gave me some uneasiness, and put me more upon my guard. I removed my papers from the alcove to my chamber, and dropped my acquaintance with these people, having learned they had shown in several houses the first volume of *Emile*, which I had been imprudent enough to lend them. Although they continued until my departure to be my neighbours, I never, after my first suspicions, had the least communication with them.

The *Social Contract* appeared a month or two before *Emile*. Rey, whom I had desired never secretly to introduce into France any of my books, applied to the magistrate for leave to send this book by Rouen, to which place he sent his package by sea. He received no answer, and his bales, after remaining at Rouen several months, were returned to him, but not until an attempt had been made to confiscate them; this, probably, would have been done had not he made a great clamour. Several persons, whose curiosity the work had excited, sent to Amsterdam for copies, which were circulated without being much noticed. Mauléon, who had heard of this, and had, I believe, seen the work, spoke to me on the subject with an air of mystery which surprised me, and would likewise have made me uneasy, if, certain of having conformed to every rule and having no reproach to make against myself, I had not, by virtue of my grand maxim, kept my mind calm. I moreover had no doubt but M. de Choiseul, already well disposed towards me, and sensible of the eulogium of his administration, which my esteem for him had induced me to make in the work, would support me on this occasion against the malevolence of Madame de Pompadour.

I certainly had then as much reason as ever to hope for the goodness of M. de Luxembourg, and even for his assistance in case of need; for he never at any time had given me more frequent or more pointed marks of his friendship. At the journey of Easter, my melancholy state no longer permitting me to go to the castle, he never suffered a day to pass without coming to see me, and, at length, perceiving my sufferings to be incessant, he prevailed upon me to determine to see Friar Côme.[1] He immediately sent for him, came with him, and had the courage, uncommon and meritorious in a man of his rank, to remain with me during the operation, which was cruel and tedious. However, there was nothing for it but for me to be sounded; but I had never been able to endure this, even from Morand, who tried it several times, and always without success. Friar Côme, who had an unequalled skill and lightness of hand, managed at last to introduce a very small hollow sound, after having made me suffer greatly for more than two hours, during which I was obliged to hold in my cries, for fear of wounding the tender feelings of the good Maréchal. Upon the first examination, Côme thought he found a great stone, and told me so; at the second, he could not find it again. After having made a third attempt with so much care and circumspection that I thought the time long, he declared there was no stone, but that the prostate gland was schirrous and considerably thickened. He found the bladder large and in good condition, and he besides added, that I had a great deal to suffer, and should live a long time. Should the second prediction be as fully accomplished as the first, my sufferings are far from being at an end.

It was thus I learned, after having been so many years treated for disorders which I never had, that my incurable disease, without being mortal, would last as long as myself. My imagination, repressed by this information, no longer presented to me in per-

---

[1] The name in religion of Jean Baseilhac, a Cistercian, renowned as an authority on diseases of the bladder.

spective a cruel death in the agonies of the stone. I ceased to fear that the end of a bougie, which had a long time ago broken off in the urethra, might have become the kernel of a stone.

Delivered from imaginary evils, more cruel to me than those which were real, I more patiently suffered the latter. It is certain I have since suffered less from my disorder than I had done before, and every time I recollect that I owe this alleviation to M. de Luxembourg, his memory becomes more dear to me.

Restored, as I may say, to life, and more than ever occupied with the plan according to which I was determined to pass the rest of my days, all the obstacle to the immediate execution of my design was the publication of *Emile*. I thought of Touraine where I had already been and which pleased me much, as well on account of the mildness of the climate, as on that of the character of the inhabitants.

La terra molle e lieta e dilettosa
Simili a se gl' habitator produce.[1]

I had already spoken of my project to M. de Luxembourg, who endeavoured to dissuade me from it; I mentioned it to him a second time as a thing resolved upon. He then offered me the castle of Merlou, fifteen leagues from Paris, as an asylum which might be agreeable to me, and where he and Madame de Luxembourg would have a real pleasure in seeing me settled. The proposition made a pleasing impression on my mind. But the first thing necessary was to see the place, and we agreed upon a day when the Maréchal was to send his valet de chambre with a carriage to take me to it. On the day appointed, I was much indisposed; the journey was postponed, and different circumstances prevented me from ever making it. I have since learned the estate of Merlou did not belong to the Maréchal but to his lady, on which account I was the less sorry I had not gone to live there.

Emile was at length given to the public, without my having heard farther of cancels or difficulties. Previous to the publication, the Maréchal asked me for all the letters M. de Malesherbes had written to me on the subject of the work. My great confidence in both, and the perfect security in which I felt myself, prevented me from reflecting upon this extraordinary and even alarming request. I returned all the letters, excepting one or two which, from inattention, were left between the leaves of a book. A little

---

[1] Tasso: "The pleasant, fruitful and delightsome land brings forth inhabitants like to itself."

time before this, M. de Malesherbes told me he should withdraw the letters I had written to Duchesne during my alarm relative to the Jesuits, and, it must be confessed, these letters did no great honour to my reason. But in my answer I assured him I would not in anything pass for being better than I was, and that he might leave the letters where they were. I know not what he resolved upon.

The publication of this work was not succeeded by the applause which had followed that of all my other writings. No work was ever more highly spoken of in private, nor had any literary production ever had less public approbation. What was said and written to me upon the subject by persons most capable of judging, confirmed me in my opinion that it was the best, as well as the most important of all the works I had produced. But everything favourable was said with an air of the most extraordinary mystery, as if there had been a necessity of keeping it a secret. Madame de Boufflers, who wrote to me that the author of the work merited a statue, and the homage of mankind, at the end of her letter desired it might be returned to her. D'Alembert, who in his note said the work gave me a decided superiority, and ought to place me at the head of men of letters, did not sign what he wrote, although he had signed every note I had before received from him. Duclos, a sure friend, a man of veracity, but circumspect, although he had a good opinion of the work, avoided mentioning it in his letters to me. La Condamine fell upon the *Profession of Faith*, and wandered from the subject. Clairaut confined himself in his letter to the same part; but he was not afraid of expressing to me the emotion which the reading of it had caused in him, and in the most direct terms wrote to me that it had warmed his old imagination: of all those to whom I had sent my book, he was the only person who spoke aloud freely, to all the world, what he thought of it.

Mathas, to whom also I had given a copy before the publication, lent it to M. de Blaire, counsellor in the Parliament, and father of the Intendant of Strasbourg. M. de Blaire had a country house at St. Gratien, and Mathas, his old acquaintance, sometimes went to see him there. He made him read the *Emile* before it was published. When he returned it to him, M. de Blaire expressed himself in the following terms, which were repeated to me the same day: 'M. Mathas, this is a very fine work, but it will in a short time be spoken of more than, for the author, might be wished.' I laughed at the prediction, and saw in it nothing more than the importance of a man of the robe, who treats everything with an air of mystery. All the alarming observations repeated to me made no more impression upon my mind, and, far from foreseeing the catastrophe so near at hand, certain of the utility and excellence of my work, and that I had in every respect conformed to established rules; convinced, as I thought I was, that I should be supported by all the credit of Madame de Luxembourg, and the favour of the ministry, I was satisfied with myself for the resolution I had taken to retire in the midst of my triumphs, and when I had just crushed those by whom I was envied.

One thing alone in the publication of the work alarmed me, less on account of my safety than for the unburdening of my mind. At the Hermitage, and at Montmorency, I had seen with indignation the vexations which the jealous care of the pleasures of princes cause to be exercised upon wretched peasants, forced to suffer the havoc made by game in their fields, without daring to take any other measure to prevent this devastation than that of making a noise, forced to pass the night amongst their beans and peas, with drums, kettles, and bells, to keep off the wild boars. As I had been a witness to the barbarous cruelty with which the Comte de Charolais treated those poor people, I had towards the end of *Emile* exclaimed against it. This was another infraction of my maxims, which has not remained unpunished. I was informed that the people of the Prince of Conti were but little less severe upon his estates; I trembled lest that Prince, for whom I was penetrated with respect and gratitude, should take to his own account what shocked humanity had made me say on that of his uncle, and feel himself offended. Yet, as my conscience fully acquitted me upon this article, I made myself easy, and by so doing acted wisely: at least I have not heard this great Prince took notice of the passage, which besides was written long before I had the honour of being known to him.

A few days either before or after the publication of my work, for I do not exactly recollect the time, there appeared another work upon the same subject, taken verbatim from my first volume, except a few stupid things which were joined to the extract. The book bore the name of a Genevese, one Balexert, and according to the title-page, had gained the prize in the academy of Harlem. I easily imagined the academy and the prize to be newly founded, the better to conceal the plagiarism from the eyes of the public; but I farther perceived there was some prior intrigue which I could not unravel; either by the lending of my manu-

script, without which the theft could not have been committed, or
for the purpose of forging the story of the pretended prize, to
which it was necessary to give some foundation. It was not until
several years afterwards, that by a word which escaped d'Ivernois,
I penetrated the mystery, and discovered those by whom Balexert
had been brought forward.

The low murmurings which precede a storm began to be heard,
and men of some penetration clearly saw there was something
gathering, relative to me and my book, which would shortly break
over my head. For my part, my stupidity was such, that, far from
foreseeing my misfortune, I did not suspect even the cause of it
after I had felt its effect. It was artfully given out that, while
treating the Jesuits with severity, no indulgence could be shown
to books nor the authors of them in which religion was attacked.
I was reproached with having put my name to *Emile*, as if I had
not put it to all my other works, of which nothing was said. Government seemed to fear it should be obliged to take some steps
with regret, but which circumstances rendered necessary, on account of my imprudence. Rumours to this effect reached my ears,
but gave me not much uneasiness; it never even came into my
head, that there could be the least thing in the whole affair which
related to me personally, so perfectly irreproachable and well
supported did I think myself; having besides conformed to every
ministerial regulation, I did not apprehend Madame de Luxembourg would leave me in difficulties for an error which, if it existed, proceeded entirely from herself. But knowing the manner
of proceeding in like cases, and that it was customary to punish
booksellers while authors were favoured, I had some uneasiness
on the account of poor Duchesne, whom I saw exposed to danger,
should M. de Malesherbes abandon him.

My tranquillity still continued. Rumours increased and soon
changed their nature. The public, and especially the Parliament,
seemed irritated by my composure. In a few days the ferment
became terrible, and the object of the menaces being changed,
these were immediately addressed to me. The parliamentarians
were heard to declare that burning books was of no effect, the
authors also should be burned with them: not a word was said of
the booksellers. The first time these expressions, more worthy of
an inquisitor of Goa than of a senator, were related to me, I had
no doubt of their coming from the Holbachians with an intention
to alarm me, and drive me from France. I laughed at their puerile
manœuvre, and said, mockingly, that they would, had they known

the real state of things, have thought of some other means of inspiring me with fear; but the rumour at length became such that I perceived the matter was serious. M. and Madame de Luxembourg had this year come to Montmorency in the month of June, which, for their second journey, was more early than common. I heard but little there of my new books, notwithstanding the noise they made at Paris; neither the Maréchal nor his lady said a single word to me on the subject. However, one morning when M. de Luxembourg and I were alone together he asked me if, in the *Social Contract*, I had spoken ill of M. de Choiseul. I! said I, retreating a few steps with surprise; no, I swear to you I have not; but on the contrary I have made on him, and with a pen not given to praise, the finest eulogium a minister ever received. I then showed him the passage. And in *Emile?* replied he. Not a word, said I: there is not in it a single word which relates to him. Ah! said he, with more vivacity than was common to him, you should have taken the same care in the other book, or have expressed yourself more clearly! I thought, replied I, what I wrote could not be misconstrued; my esteem for him was such as to make me extremely cautious not to be equivocal.

He was again going to speak; I perceived him ready to open his mind: he stopped short, and held his tongue. Wretched policy of a courtier, which in the best of hearts subjugates friendship itself!

This conversation, although short, explained to me my situation, at least in certain respects, and gave me to understand that it was indeed against myself the anger of the administration was raised. The unheard-of fatality, which turned to my prejudice all the good I did and wrote, afflicted my heart. Yet, feeling myself shielded in this affair by Madame de Luxembourg and M. de Malesherbes, I did not perceive in what my persecutors could deprive me of their protection. However I, from that moment, was convinced equity and justice were no longer in question, and that no pains would be spared in examining whether or not I was culpable. The storm became still more menacing. Néaulme himself expressed to me, in the excess of his babbling, how much he repented having had anything to do in the business, and his certainty of the fate with which the book and the author were threatened. One thing however alleviated my fears: Madame de Luxembourg was so calm, satisfied, and cheerful, that I concluded she must necessarily be certain of the sufficiency of her credit, especially as she did not seem to have the least apprehension on my account; moreover she said not to me a word either of consolation

or apology, and saw the turn the affair took with as much unconcern as if she had nothing to do with it, or anything else that
related to me. What surprised me most was her silence; I thought
she should have said something on the subject. Madame de Boufflers seemed rather uneasy. She appeared agitated, strained herself a good deal, assuring me the Prince of Conti was taking great
pains to ward off the blow about to be directed against my person,
and which she attributed to the nature of present circumstances,
in which it was of importance to the Parliament not to leave the
Jesuits an opening whereby they might bring an accusation
against it as being indifferent with respect to religion. She did
not however seem to depend much either upon the success of her
own efforts or even those of the Prince. Her conversations, more
alarming than consolatory, all tended to persuade me to leave the
kingdom and go to England, where she offered me an introduction to many of her friends, amongst others one to the celebrated
Hume, with whom she had long been on a footing of intimate
friendship. Seeing me still unshaken, she had recourse to other
arguments more capable of disturbing my tranquillity. She intimated that, in case I was arrested and interrogated, I should be
under the necessity of naming Madame de Luxembourg, and that
her friendship for me required, on my part, such precautions as
were necessary to prevent her being exposed. My answer was,
that should what she seemed to apprehend come to pass, she need
not be alarmed; that I should do nothing by which the lady she
mentioned might become a sufferer. She said such a resolution
was more easily taken than adhered to; and in this she was right,
especially with respect to me, determined as I always have been
neither to perjure myself nor lie before judges, whatever danger
there might be in speaking the truth.

Perceiving this observation had made some impression upon
my mind, without however inducing me to resolve upon flight,
she spoke of the Bastile for a few weeks, as a means of placing me
beyond the reach of the jurisdiction of the Parliament, which
has nothing to do with prisoners of State. I had no objection to
this singular favour, provided it were not solicited in my name.
As she never spoke of it a second time, I afterwards thought her
proposition was made to sound me, and that the party did not
think proper to have recourse to an expedient which put an end
to everything.

A few days afterwards the Maréchal received from the Curé
de Deuil, the friend of Grimm and Madame d'Epinay, a letter

informing him, as from good authority, the Parliament was to proceed against me with the greatest severity, and that on such a day, which he mentioned, an order was to be given to arrest me. I imagined this was fabricated by the Holbachians; I knew the Parliament to be very attentive to forms, and that, on this occasion, to begin by arresting me, before it was juridically known I avowed myself the author of the book, was violating them all. I observed to Madame de Boufflers that none but persons accused of crimes which tend to endanger the public safety were, on a single information, ordered to be arrested lest they should escape punishment. But when government wishes to punish a crime like mine, which merits honour and recompense, the proceedings are directed against the book, and the author is as much as possible left out of the question.

Upon this she made some subtle distinction, which I have forgotten, to prove that ordering me to be arrested instead of summoning me to be heard, was a matter of favour. The next day I received a letter from Guy, who informed me that having in the morning been with the Attorney-General, he had seen in his office the rough draft of a requisition against *Emile* and the author. Guy, it is to be remembered, was the partner of Duchesne, who had printed the work, and, without apprehensions on his own account, charitably gave this information to the author. The credit I gave to him may be judged of. It was, no doubt, a very probable story, that a bookseller, admitted to an audience by the Attorney-General, should read at ease scattered rough drafts in the office of that magistrate! Madame de Boufflers and others confirmed what he had said. By the absurdities which were incessantly rung in my ears, I was almost tempted to believe everybody I heard speak had lost their senses.

Clearly perceiving there was some mystery, which no one thought proper to explain to me, I patiently waited the event, depending upon my integrity and innocence, thinking myself happy, let the persecution which awaited me be what it would, to be called to the honour of suffering in the cause of truth. Far from being afraid and concealing myself, I went every day to the castle, and in the afternoon took my usual walk. On the eighth of June, the evening before the order was concluded on, I walked in company with two professors of the Oratory, Father Alamanni and Father Mandard. We carried to Les Champeaux a little collation, which we ate with keen appetite. We had forgotten to bring glasses, and supplied the want of them by stalks of rye, through which we sucked up the wine from the bottle, piquing ourselves upon the choice of large tubes to vie with each other in pumping up what we drank. I never was more cheerful in my life.

I have related in what manner I lost my sleep during my youth. I had since that time contracted a habit of reading every night in my bed, until I found my eyes begin to grow heavy. I then extinguished my wax taper and endeavoured to slumber for a few moments, which were in general very short. The book I commonly read at night was the Bible, which, in this manner, I read five or six times from the beginning to the end. This evening, finding myself less disposed to sleep than ordinary, I continued my reading beyond the usual hour, and read the whole book, which finishes at the Levite of Ephraim, the book of Judges,[1] if I mistake not, for since that time I have never once seen it. This history affected me exceedingly and, in a kind of dream, my imagination still ran on it, when suddenly I was roused from my stupor by a noise and light. Thérèse, carrying a candle, lighted M. La Roche, who perceiving me hastily raise myself up, said: Do not be alarmed; I come from Madame de Luxembourg, who, in her letter, encloses you another from the Prince of Conti. In fact, in the letter of Madame de Luxembourg I found another, which an express from the Prince had brought her, stating that, notwithstanding all his efforts, it was determined to proceed against me with the utmost rigour. The ferment, said he, is extreme; nothing can ward off the blow; the Court requires it, and the Parliament will absolutely proceed; at seven o'clock in the morning an order will be made to arrest him, and persons will immediately be sent to execute it. I have obtained a promise that he shall not be pursued if he makes his escape; but if he persists in exposing himself to be taken this will immediately happen. La Roche conjured me in behalf of Madame de Luxembourg to rise and go and speak to her. It was two o'clock, and she had just retired to bed. She expects you, added he, and will not go to sleep without speaking to you. I dressed myself in haste and ran to her.

She appeared to be agitated; this was for the first time. Her distress affected me. In this moment of surprise and in the night, I myself was not free from emotion; but on seeing her I forgot my own situation, and thought of nothing but the melancholy part she would have to act should I suffer myself to be arrested; for feeling I had sufficient courage strictly to adhere to truth, although

---

[1] Judges 19-21.

I might be certain of its being prejudicial or even destructive to me, I was convinced I had not presence of mind, address, nor perhaps firmness enough, not to expose her should I be closely pressed. This determined me to sacrifice my reputation to her tranquillity, and to do for her on this occasion that which nothing could have prevailed upon me to do for myself. The moment I had come to this resolution, I declared it, wishing not to diminish the magnitude of the sacrifice by giving her the least trouble to obtain it. I am sure she could not mistake my motive, although she said not a word which proved to me she was sensible of it. I was so much shocked at her indifference, that I, for a moment, thought of retracting; but the Maréchal came in, and Madame de Boufflers arrived from Paris a few moments afterwards. They did what Madame de Luxembourg ought to have done. I suffered myself to be flattered; I was ashamed to retract; and the only thing that remained to be determined upon, was the place of my retreat and the time of my departure. M. de Luxembourg proposed to me to remain incognito a few days at the castle, that we might deliberate at leisure, and take such measures as should seem most proper; to this I would not consent, no more than to the proposal to go secretly to the Temple. I was determined to set off the same day rather than remain concealed in any place whatever.

Knowing I had secret and powerful enemies in the kingdom, I thought, notwithstanding my attachment to France, I ought to quit it, the better to ensure my future tranquillity. My first intention was to retire to Geneva; but a moment of reflection was sufficient to dissuade me from committing that act of folly. I knew the ministry of France, more powerful at Geneva than at Paris, would not leave me more at peace in one of these cities than in the other, were a resolution taken to torment me. I was also convinced the *Discourse upon Inequality* had excited against me in the Council a hatred the more dangerous as the Council dared not make it manifest. I had also learned, that when the *Nouvelle Héloïse* appeared, the same Council had immediately forbidden the sale of that work, upon the solicitation of doctor Tronchin; but perceiving the example not to be imitated, not even in Paris, the members were ashamed of what they had done, and withdrew the prohibition. I had no doubt but, finding in the present case a more favourable opportunity, they would be very careful to take advantage of it. Notwithstanding exterior appearances, I knew there reigned against me in the heart of every Genevese a secret jealousy, which, in the first favourable moment, would publicly show itself. Nevertheless, the love of my country called me to it, and could I have flattered myself I should there have lived in peace, I should not have hesitated; but neither honour nor reason permitting me to take refuge as a fugitive in a place of which I was a citizen, I resolved to approach it only, and to wait in Switzerland until something relative to me should be determined upon in Geneva. This state of uncertainty did not, as it will soon appear, continue long.

Madame de Boufflers highly disapproved this resolution, and renewed her efforts to induce me to go to England, but all she could say was of no effect; I have never loved England nor the English, and the eloquence of Madame de Boufflers, far from conquering my repugnancy, seemed to increase it without my knowing why.

Determined to set off the same day, I was from the morning inaccessible to everybody, and La Roche, whom I sent to fetch my papers, would not tell even Thérèse whether or not I was gone. Since I had determined to write one day my own memoirs, I had collected a great number of letters and other papers, so that he was obliged to return several times. A part of these papers, already selected, were laid aside, and I employed the morning sorting the rest, that I might take with me such only as were necessary and destroy what remained. M. de Luxembourg was kind enough to assist me in this business, which we could not finish during the morning, and I had not time to burn a single paper. The Maréchal offered to take upon himself to sort what I should leave behind me, and throw into the fire every sheet that he found useless, without trusting to any person whomsoever, and to send me those of which he should make choice. I accepted his offer, very glad to be delivered from that care, that I might pass the few hours I had to remain with persons so dear to me, from whom I was going to separate for ever. He took the key of the chamber in which I left these papers; and, at my earnest solicitation, sent for my poor aunt, who, not knowing what was become of me, or what was to become of herself, and in momentary expectation of the arrival of the officers of justice, without knowing how to act or what to answer them, was miserable to an extreme. La Roche accompanied her to the castle in silence; she thought I was already far from Montmorency: on perceiving me, she made the place resound with her cries, and threw herself into my arms. O, friendship! affinity of sentiment, habit, and intimacy!

In this pleasing, yet cruel moment, the remembrance of so

many days of happiness, tenderness, and peace passed together, augmented the grief of a first separation after a union of seventeen years, during which we had scarcely lost sight of each other for a single day.

The Maréchal, who saw this embrace, could not withhold his tears. He withdrew. Thérèse determined never more to leave me out of her sight. I made her feel the inconvenience of accompanying me at that moment, and the necessity of her remaining to take care of my effects and collect my money. When an order is made to arrest a man, it is customary to seize his papers and put a seal upon his effects, or to make an inventory of them and appoint a guardian to whose care they are entrusted. It was necessary Thérèse should remain to observe what passed and get everything settled in the most advantageous manner possible. I promised her she should shortly come to me; the Maréchal confirmed my promise; but I did not choose to tell her to what place I was going, that, in case of her being interrogated by the persons who came to take me into custody, she might with truth plead ignorance upon that head. In embracing her the moment before we separated I felt within me a most extraordinary emotion, and I said to her with an agitation which, alas! was but too prophetic: My dear girl, you must arm yourself with courage. You have partaken of my prosperity; it now remains to you, since you have chosen it, to partake of my misery. Expect nothing in future but insult and calamity in following me. The destiny begun for me by this melancholy day will pursue me until my latest hour.

I had now nothing to think of but my departure. The officers were to arrive at ten o'clock. It was four in the afternoon when I set off, and they were not yet come. It was determined I should take post. I had no carriage. The Maréchal made me a present of a cabriolet, and lent me horses and a postilion this first stage, where, in consequence of the measures he had taken, I had no difficulty in procuring others.

As I had not dined at table, nor made any appearance in the castle, the ladies came to bid me adieu in the entresol where I had passed the day. Madame de Luxembourg embraced me several times with a melancholy air; but I did not in these embraces feel the pressing I had done in those she had lavished upon me two or three years before. Madame de Boufflers also embraced me, and said to me many civil things. An embrace which surprised me more than all the rest had done was one from Madame de Mirepoix, for she also was at the castle. Madame la Maréchale de

Mirepoix is a person extremely cold, decent, and reserved, and did not, at least as she appeared to me, seem quite exempt from the natural haughtiness of the house of Lorraine. She had never shown me much attention. Whether, flattered by an honour I had not expected, I endeavoured to enhance the value of it; or that there really was in the embrace a little of that commiseration natural to generous hearts, I found in her manner and look something energetical which penetrated me. I have since that time frequently thought that, acquainted with my destiny, she could not refrain from a momentary concern for my fate.

The Maréchal did not open his mouth; he was as pale as death. He would absolutely accompany me to the carriage which waited at the watering place. We crossed the garden without uttering a single word. I had a key of the park with which I opened the gate, and, instead of putting it again into my pocket, I held it out to the Maréchal without saying a word. He took it with a vivacity which surprised me, and which has since frequently intruded itself upon my thoughts. I have not in my whole life had a more bitter moment than that of this separation. Our embrace was long and silent: we both felt this was our last adieu.

Between La Barre and Montmorency I met, in a hired carriage, four men in black who saluted me smiling. According to what Thérèse has since told me of the officers of justice, the hour of their arrival, and their manner of behaviour, I have no doubt that they were the persons I met, especially as the order to arrest me, instead of being made out at seven o'clock, as I had been told it would, had not been given till noon. I had to go through Paris. A person in a cabriolet is not much concealed. I saw several persons in the streets who saluted me with an air of familiarity, but I did not know one of them. The same evening I changed my route to pass Villeroy. At Lyons the couriers were conducted to the commandant. This might have been embarrassing to a man unwilling either to lie or change his name. I went with a letter from Madame de Luxembourg to beg M. de Villeroy would spare me this disagreeable ceremony. M. de Villeroy gave me a letter of which I made no use, because I did not go through Lyons. This letter still remains sealed up amongst my papers. The Duke pressed me to sleep at Villeroy, but I preferred returning to the high road, which I did, and travelled two more stages the same evening.

My carriage was inconvenient and uncomfortable, and I was too much indisposed to go far in a day. My appearance besides was not sufficiently distinguished for me to be well served, and in

France post-horses feel the whip in proportion to the favourable opinion the postilion has of his temporary master. By paying the guides generously I thought I should make up for my shabby appearance: this was still worse. They took me for a worthless fellow who was carrying orders, and travelling post for the first time in my life. From that moment I had nothing but worn-out hacks, and I became the sport of the postilions. I ended as I should have begun, by being patient, holding my tongue, and suffering myself to be driven as my conductors thought proper.

I had sufficient matter of reflection to prevent me from being weary on the road, employing myself in the recollection of that which had just happened: but this was neither my turn of mind nor the inclination of my heart. The facility with which I forget past evils, however recent they may be, is astonishing. The remembrance of them becomes feeble, and, sooner or later, effaced, in the inverse proportion to the greater degree of fear with which the approach of them inspires me. My cruel imagination, incessantly tormented by the apprehension of evils still at a distance, diverts my memory, and prevents me from recollecting those which are past. Caution is needless after the evil has happened, and it is time lost to give it a thought. I, in some measure, put a period to my misfortunes before they happen: the more I have suffered at their approach the greater is the facility with which I forget them; whilst, on the contrary, incessantly recollecting my past happiness, I, if I may so speak, enjoy it a second time at pleasure. It is to this happy disposition I am indebted for an exemption from that ill humour which ferments in a vindictive mind, by the continual remembrance of injuries received, and torments it with all the evil it wishes to do its enemy. Naturally choleric, I have felt all the force of anger, which in the first moments has sometimes been carried to fury, but a desire of vengeance never took root within me. I think too little of the offence to give myself much trouble about the offender. I think of the injury I have received from him only on account of that he may do me a second time, but were I certain he would never do me another, the first would be instantly forgotten. Pardon of offences is continually preached to us; it is no doubt an excellent virtue, but it is not one which I use. I know not whether or not my heart would be capable of overcoming its hatred, for it never yet felt that passion, and I give myself too little concern about my enemies to have the merit of pardoning them. I will not say to what a degree, in order to torment me, they torment themselves. I am at their mercy, they have unbounded power, and make of it what use they please. There is but one thing beyond their power, and in which I set them at defiance: which is in tormenting themselves about me, to force me to give myself the least trouble about them.

The day after my departure I had so perfectly forgotten what had passed, the Parliament, Madame de Pompadour, M. de Choiseul, Grimm, and d'Alembert, with their conspiracies and accomplices, that, had not it been for the necessary precautions during the journey, I should have thought no more of them. The remembrance of one thing which supplied the place of all these was what I had read the evening before my departure. I recollected also the *Idylles* of Gessner, which his translator Hubner had sent me a little time before. These two ideas occurred to me so strongly, and were connected in such a manner in my mind, that I was determined to endeavour to unite them by treating, after the manner of Gessner, the subject of the *Levite of Ephraim*. His pastoral and simple style appeared to me but little fitted to so horrid a subject, and it was not to be presumed the situation I was then in would furnish me with such ideas as would enliven it. However I attempted the thing, solely to amuse myself in my cabriolet, and without the least hope of success. I had no sooner begun than I was astonished at the liveliness of my ideas, and the facility with which I expressed them. In three days I composed the first three cantos of the little poem which I finished afterwards at Motiers, and I am certain of not having done anything in my life in which there is a more tender mildness of manners, a greater brilliancy of colouring, more simple delineations, greater exactness of proportion, or more antique simplicity in general, notwithstanding the horror of the subject which in itself is abominable, so that besides every other merit I had still that of a difficulty conquered. If the *Levite of Ephraim* be not the best of my works, it will ever be that most esteemed. I have never read, nor shall I ever read it again without feeling interiorly the applause of a heart without acrimony, which, far from being embittered by misfortunes, is susceptible of consolation in the midst of them, and finds within itself a resource by which they are counterbalanced. Assemble the great philosophers, so superior in their books to adversity which they have never suffered, place them in a situation similar to mine, and, in the first moments of the indignation of their injured honour, give them a like work to compose, and it will be seen in what manner they will acquit themselves of the task.

When I set off from Montmorency to go into Switzerland, I had resolved to stop at Yverdun, at the house of my old friend Roguin, who had several years before retired to that place, and had invited me to go and see him. I was told Lyons was not the direct road, for which reason I avoided going through it. But I was obliged to pass through Besançon, a fortified town and consequently subject to the same inconvenience. I took it into my head to turn about and go to Salins, under the pretence of going to see M. de Miran, the nephew of M. Dupin, who had an employment at the salt-works, and formerly had given me many invitations to his house. The expedient succeeded: M. de Miran was not in the way, and, happily, not being obliged to stop, I continued my journey without being spoken to by anybody.

BERNE

The moment I was within the territory of Berne, I ordered the postilion to stop; I got out of my carriage, prostrated myself, kissed the ground and exclaimed in a transport of joy: Heaven, the protector of virtue, be praised, I touch the land of liberty! Thus, blind and unsuspecting in my hopes, have I ever been passionately attached to that which was to make me unhappy. The man thought me mad. I got into the carriage, and a few hours afterwards I had the pure and lively satisfaction of feeling myself pressed within the arms of the respectable Roguin. Ah!

let me breathe for a moment with this worthy host! It is necessary I should gain strength and courage before I proceed farther.
I shall soon find that in my way which will give employment to
them both.

It is not without reason that I have been diffuse in the recital
of all the circumstances I have been able to recollect. Although
they may seem uninteresting, yet, when once the thread of the
conspiracy is got hold of, they may throw some light upon the
progress of it; and, for instance, without giving the first idea of the
problem I am going to propose, they afford some aid in resolving it.

Suppose that, for the execution of the conspiracy of which I was
the object, my absence was absolutely necessary, everything tend-
ing to that effect could not have happened otherwise than it did;
but if, without suffering myself to be alarmed by the nocturnal
embassy of Madame de Luxembourg, I had continued to hold out
as I had begun, and, instead of remaining at the castle, had returned to my bed and quietly slept until morning, should I have
equally had an order of arrest made out against me? This is a
great question upon which the solution of many others depends,
and for that examination of it, the hour of the comminatory decree
of arrest, and that of the real decree may be remarked to advantage. A rude but sensible example of the importance of the least
detail in the exposition of facts, of which the secret causes are
sought for to discover them by induction.

BOOK TWELVE

Here begins the work of darkness, in which I have for the
last eight years been enveloped, though it has not by any means
been possible for me to penetrate the dreadful obscurity. In the
abyss of evil into which I am plunged, I feel the blows reach me,
and their immediate instrument, without perceiving the hand by
which they are directed, or the means it employs. Shame and
misfortune seem of themselves to fall upon me without its inter-
vention. When in the affliction of my heart I suffer a groan to
escape me, I have the appearance of a man who complains with-

out reason, and the authors of my ruin have the inconceivable art of rendering the public, unknown to itself, or without its perceiving the effects of it, accomplice in their conspiracy. Therefore in my narrative of circumstances relative to myself, of the treatment I have received, and all that has happened to me, I shall not be able to indicate the hand by which the whole has been directed, nor assign the causes while I state the effect. The primitive causes are all given in the three[1] preceding books; and everything in which I am interested, and all the secret motives pointed out. But it is impossible for me to explain, even by conjecture, that in which the different causes are combined to operate the strange events of my life. If amongst my readers are any generous enough to wish to examine the mystery to the bottom, and discover the truth, let them carefully read over a second time the three preceding books, and go back from intrigue to intrigue, and from agent to agent, until they come to the first mover of all. I know where their researches will terminate; but in the meantime I lose myself in the crooked and obscure subterranean path through which their steps must be directed.

During my stay at Yverdun, I became acquainted with all the family of my friend Roguin, and amongst others with his niece, Madame Boy de la Tour, and her daughters, whose father, as I think I have already observed, I formerly knew at Lyons. She was at Yverdun, upon a visit to her uncle and his sisters; her eldest daughter, about fifteen years of age, delighted me by her fine understanding and excellent disposition. I conceived the most tender friendship for the mother and the daughter. The latter was destined by M. Roguin to the colonel, his nephew, a man already verging towards the decline of life, and who showed me marks of great esteem and affection; but although the heart of the uncle was set upon this marriage, which was much wished for by the nephew also, and I was greatly desirous to promote the satisfaction of both, the great disproportion of age, and the extreme repugnance of the young lady made me join with the mother in postponing the ceremony; and the affair was at length broken off. The colonel has since married Mademoiselle Dillan, his relation, beautiful, and amiable as my heart could wish, and who has made him the happiest of husbands and fathers. However, M. Roguin has not yet forgotten my opposition to his wishes on that occasion. My consolation is in the certainty of having discharged to him, and his family, the duty of the most pure friendship,

[1] Paris MS., two.

which does not always consist in being agreeable, but in advising for the best.

I did not remain long in doubt about the reception which awaited me at Geneva, had I chosen to return to that city. My book was burned there, and on the 18th of June, nine days after an order to arrest me had been given at Paris, another to the same effect was determined upon by the Republic. So many incredible absurdities were stated in this second decree, in which the Ecclesiastical Edict was formally violated, that I refused to believe the first accounts I heard of it, and when these were well confirmed, I trembled lest so manifest an infraction of every law, beginning with that of common sense, should create the greatest confusion in the city. I was, however, relieved from my fears; everything remained quiet. If there was any rumour amongst the populace it was unfavourable to me, and I was publicly treated by all the gossips and pedants like a scholar threatened with a flogging for not having said his catechism.

These two decrees were the signal for the cry of malediction, raised against me with unexampled fury in every part of Europe. All the gazettes, journals, and pamphlets rang the alarm bell. The French especially, that mild, generous, and polished people, who so much pique themselves upon their attention and proper condescension to the unfortunate, instantly forgetting their favourite virtues, signalised themselves by the number and violence of the outrages with which, while each seemed to strive who should afflict me most, they overwhelmed me. I was impious, an atheist, a madman, a wild beast, a wolf. The continuator of the *Journal de Trévoux* was guilty of a piece of extravagance in attacking my pretended lycanthropy, which was no mean proof of his own. A stranger would have thought an author in Paris was afraid of incurring the animadversion of the police, by publishing a work of any kind without cramming into it some insult to me. I sought in vain the cause of this unanimous animosity, and was almost tempted to believe the world was gone mad. What! said I to myself, the editor of the *Perpetual Peace*, spread discord; the author of the *Confession of the Savoyard Vicar*, impious; the writer of the *Nouvelle Héloïse*, a wolf; the author of *Emile*, a madman! Gracious God! what then should I have been had I published the Treatise *De l'Esprit*, or any similar work? And yet in the storm raised against the author[1] of that book, the public, far from joining in the cry of his persecutors, revenged him of them by eulogy.

[1] Montesquieu.

Let his book and mine, the receptions the two books met with, and the treatment of the two authors in the different countries of Europe, be compared; and for the difference, let causes, satisfactory to a man of sense, be found, and I will ask no more.

I found the residence of Yverdun so agreeable that I resolved to yield to the solicitations of M. Roguin and his family, who were desirous of keeping me there. M. de Moiry de Gingins, bailiff of that city, encouraged me by his goodness to remain within his jurisdiction. The colonel pressed me so much to accept for my habitation a little pavilion he had in his house between the court and garden, that I complied with his request, and he immediately furnished it with everything necessary for my little household establishment.

The banneret Roguin, one of the persons who showed me the most assiduous attention, did not leave me for an instant during the whole day. I was much flattered by his civilities, but they sometimes importuned me. The day on which I was to take possession of my new habitation was already fixed, and I had written to Thérèse to come to me, when suddenly I learnt that a storm was raised against me in Berne, which was attributed to the devotees, but I have never been able to learn the cause of it. The senate, excited against me, without my knowing by whom, did not seem disposed to suffer me to remain undisturbed in my retreat. The moment the bailiff was informed of the new fermentation, he wrote in my favour to several of the members of the government, reproaching them with their blind intolerance, and telling them it was shameful to refuse to a man of merit, under oppression, the asylum which so many banditti found in their states. Sensible people were of opinion the warmth of his reproaches had rather embittered than softened the minds of the magistrates. However this may be, neither his influence nor eloquence could ward off the blow. Having received an intimation of the order he was to signify to me, he gave me a previous communication of it; and that I might not wait its arrival, I resolved to set off the next day. The difficulty was to know where to go to, finding myself shut out from Geneva and all France, and foreseeing that in this affair each state would be anxious to imitate its neighbour.

Madame Boy de la Tour proposed to me to go and reside in an uninhabited, but completely furnished house, which belonged to her son, in the village of Motiers, in the Val de Travers, in the county of Neuchâtel. I had only a mountain to cross to arrive at it. The offer came the more opportunely, as in the states of the

King of Prussia I should naturally be sheltered from any persecution, at least religion could not serve as a pretext for it. But a
secret difficulty, improper for me at that moment to divulge, had
in it that which was very sufficient to make me hesitate. The innate love of justice, to which my heart was constantly subject,
added to my secret inclination to France, had inspired me with an
aversion to the King of Prussia, who, by his maxims and conduct,
seemed to tread under foot all respect for natural law and every
duty of humanity. Amongst the framed engravings, with which
I had decorated my alcove at Montmorency, was a portrait of this
Prince, and under it a distich, the last line of which was as follows:

Il pense en philosophe, et se conduit en roi.

The verse, which from any other pen would have been a fine
eulogium, from mine had an unequivocal meaning, and too clearly
explained the verse by which it was preceded.[1] The distich had
been read by everybody who came to see me, and my visitors
were numerous. The Chevalier de Lorenzy had even written it
down to give it to d'Alembert, and I had no doubt but d'Alembert
had taken care to make my court with it to the Prince. I had also
aggravated this first fault by a passage in *Emile*, where, under the
name of Adrastus, King of the Daunians, it was clearly seen whom
I had in view, and the remark had not escaped critics, because
Madame de Boufflers had several times mentioned the subject to
me. I was, therefore, certain of being inscribed in red ink in the
registers of the King of Prussia, and besides, supposing His Majesty to have the principles I had dared to attribute to him, he, for
that reason, could not but be displeased with my writings and
their author; for everybody knows the worthless part of mankind
and tyrants have never failed to conceive the most mortal hatred
against me, solely on reading my works, without being acquainted
with my person.

However, I had presumption enough to depend upon his mercy,
and was far from thinking I ran much risk. I knew none but weak
men were slaves to the base passions, and that these had but little
power over strong minds, such as I had always thought his to be.
According to his art of reigning, I thought he could not but show
himself magnanimous on this occasion, and that being so in fact
was not above his character. I thought a mean and easy vengeance
would not for a moment counterbalance his love of glory, and
putting myself in his place, his taking advantage of circumstances

---

[1] Which was: "La gloire, l'intérêt, voilà son Dieu, sa loi."

to overwhelm with the weight of his generosity a man who had dared to think ill of him, did not appear to me impossible. I therefore went to settle at Motiers, with a confidence of which I imagined he would feel all the value, and said to myself: When Jean-Jacques rises to the elevation of Coriolanus, will Frederick sink below the General of the Volsci?

Colonel Roguin insisted on crossing the mountain with me, and installing me at Motiers. A sister-in-law to Madame Boy de la Tour, named Madame Girardier, to whom the house in which I was going to live was very convenient, did not see me arrive there with pleasure; however, she with a good grace put me in possession of my lodging, and I ate with her until Thérèse came, and my little establishment was formed.

Perceiving at my departure from Montmorency I should in future be a fugitive upon the earth, I hesitated about permitting her to come to me and partake of the wandering life to which I saw myself condemned. I felt the nature of our relation to each other was about to change after this catastrophe, and that what until then had on my part been favour and friendship, would in future become so on hers. If her attachment was proof against my misfortunes, to this I knew she must become a victim, and that her grief would add to my pain. Should my disgrace weaken her affections, she would make me consider her constancy as a sacrifice, and instead of feeling the pleasure I had in dividing with her my last morsel of bread, she would see nothing but her own merit in following me wherever I was driven by fate.

I must say everything; I have never concealed the vices either of my poor Mamma or myself; I cannot be more favourable to Thérèse, and whatever pleasure I may have in doing honour to a person who is dear to me, I will not disguise the truth, although it may discover in her an error, if an involuntary change of the affections of the heart be one. I had long perceived hers to grow cooler towards me, and that she was no longer for me what she had been in our younger days. Of this I was the more sensible, as for her I was what I had always been. I fell into the same inconvenience as that of which I had felt the effect with Mamma, and this effect was the same now I was with Thérèse. Let us not seek for perfection, which nature never produces; it would be the same thing with any other woman. The manner in which I had disposed of my children, however reasonable it had appeared to me, had not always left my heart at ease. While writing my *Treatise on Education*, I felt I had neglected duties with which it was not possible to dispense. Remorse at length became so strong that it almost forced from me a public confession of my fault at the beginning of my *Emile*, and the passage is so clear, that it is astonishing any person should, after reading it, have had the courage to reproach me with my error. My situation was however still the same, or something worse, by the animosity of my enemies, who sought only to find me in a fault. I feared a relapse, and unwilling to run the risk, I preferred abstinence to exposing Thérèse to yet another similar mortification. I had besides remarked that a connexion with women was sensibly prejudicial to my health;[1] this double reason made me form resolutions to which I had sometimes but badly kept, but for the last three or four years I had more constantly adhered to them. It was in this interval I had remarked Thérèse's coolness; she had the same attachment to me from duty, but not the least from love. Our intercourse naturally became less agreeable, and I imagined that, certain of the continuation of my cares wherever she might be, she would choose to stay at Paris rather than to wander with me. Yet she had given such signs of grief at our parting, had required of me such positive promises that we should meet again, and, since my departure, had expressed to the Prince de Conti and M. de Luxembourg so strong a desire of it, that, far from having the courage to speak to her of separation, I scarcely had enough to think of it myself; and after having felt in my heart how impossible it was for me to do without her, all I thought of afterwards was to recall her to me as soon as possible. I wrote to her to this effect, and she came. It was scarcely two months since I had quitted her; but it was our first separation after a union of so many years. We had both of us felt it most cruelly. What emotion in our first embrace! O how delightful are the tears of tenderness and joy! How does my heart drink them up! Why have not I had reason to shed them more frequently?

On my arrival at Motiers I had written to Lord Keith, marshal of Scotland, and governor of Neuchâtel, informing him of my retreat into the states of his Prussian Majesty, and requesting of him his protection. He answered me with his well-known generosity, and in the manner I had expected from him. He invited me to his house. I went with M. Martinet, lord of the manor of Val de Travers, who was in great favour with His Excellency. The venerable appearance of this illustrious and virtuous Scotchman

---

[1] Paris MS. adds: "the vice corresponding to it, of which I had never been able fully to cure myself, seemed less hurtful to me."

powerfully affected my heart, and from that instant began between him and me the strong attachment, which on my part still remains the same, and would be so on his, had not the traitors, who have deprived me of all the consolation of life, taken advantage of my absence to deceive his old age and depreciate me in his esteem.

George Keith, hereditary Marshal of Scotland, and brother to the famous General Keith, who lived gloriously and died in the bed of honour, had quitted his country at a very early age, and was proscribed on account of his attachment to the house of Stuart. With that house, however, he soon became disgusted by the unjust and tyrannical spirit he remarked in it, and which was always the ruling character of the Stuart family. He lived a long time in Spain, the climate of which pleased him exceedingly, and at length attached himself, as his brother had done, to the service of the King of Prussia, who knew men and gave them the recep-

FREDERICK THE GREAT

tion they merited. His Majesty received a great return for his
reception, in the services rendered him by Marshal Keith, and by
what was infinitely more precious, the sincere friendship of his
Lordship. The great mind of this worthy man, haughty and republican, could stoop to no other yoke than that of friendship,
but to this it was so obedient, that with very different maxims, he
saw nothing but Frederick the moment he became attached to
him. The King charged the Marshal with affairs of importance,
sent him to Paris, to Spain, and at length, seeing he was already
advanced in years, let him retire with the government of Neuchâtel, and the delightful employment of passing there the remainder of his life in rendering the inhabitants happy.

The people of Neuchâtel, whose manners are trivial, know not
how to distinguish solid merit, and suppose wit to consist in long
discourses. When they saw a sedate man of simple manners appear amongst them, they mistook his simplicity for haughtiness,
his candour for rusticity, his laconicism for stupidity, and rejected his benevolent cares, because, wishing to be useful, and not
being a sycophant, he knew not how to flatter people he did not
esteem. In the ridiculous affair of the minister Petitpierre, who
was displaced by his colleagues, for having been unwilling they
should he eternally damned, my Lord, opposing the usurpations
of the ministers, saw the whole country of which he took the part,
rise up against him, and when I arrived there, the stupid murmur
had not entirely subsided. He passed for a man influenced by the
prejudices with which he was inspired by others, and of all the
imputations brought against him this was perhaps the least devoid of truth. My first sentiment on seeing this venerable old man,
was that of tender commiseration, on account of his extreme lean-
ness of body, years having already left him little else but skin and
bone; but when I raised my eyes to his animated, open, and noble
countenance, I felt a respect, mingled with confidence, which
absorbed every other sentiment. He answered the very short compliment I made him when first I came into his presence by speaking of something else, as if I had already been a week in his house.
He did not bid us sit down. The stupid châtelain, the lord of the
manor, remained standing. For my part, I at first sight saw in the
fine and piercing eye of his lordship something so conciliating
that, feeling myself entirely at ease, I, without ceremony, took
my seat by his side upon the sofa. By the familiarity of his manner
I immediately perceived the liberty I took gave him pleasure, and
that he said to himself: This is not a Neuchâtelois.

Singular effect of the similarity of characters! at an age when the heart loses its natural warmth, that of this good old man grew warm by his attachment to me to a degree which surprised everybody. He came to see me at Motiers under the pretence of quail shooting, and stayed there two days without touching a gun. We conceived such a friendship, for that is the only word for it, for each other that we knew not how to live separate: the castle of Colombier, where he passed the summer, was six leagues from Motiers; I went there at least once a fortnight, and made a stay of twenty-four hours, and then returned like a pilgrim with my heart full of affection for my host. The emotion I had formerly experienced in my journeys from the Hermitage to Eaubonne, was certainly very different, but it was not more pleasing than that with which I approached Colombier.

What tears of tenderness have I shed when on the road to it, while thinking of the paternal goodness, amiable virtues, and charming philosophy of this respectable old man! I called him father, and he called me son. These affectionate names give, in some measure, an idea of the attachment by which we were united, but by no means that of the want we felt of each other, nor of our continual desire to be together. He would absolutely give me an apartment at the castle of Colombier, and for a long time pressed me to take up my residence in that in which I lodged during my visits. I at length told him I was more free and at my ease in my own house, and that I had rather continue until the end of my life to come and see him. He approved of my candour, and never afterwards spoke to me upon the subject. O my good lord! O my worthy father! How is my heart still moved when I think of your goodness! Ah, barbarous wretches! how deeply did they wound me when they deprived me of your friendship! But no, great man, you are and will ever be the same for me, who am always the same. You have been deceived, but you are not changed.

My Lord Maréchal is not without faults; he is a man of wisdom, but he is still a man. With the greatest penetration, the nicest discrimination, and the most profound knowledge of men, he sometimes suffers himself to be deceived and never recovers from his error. His temper is very singular and foreign to the general turn of mind. He seems to forget the people he sees every day, and thinks of them in a moment when they least expect it; his attention seems ill-timed; his presents are dictated by caprice and not by propriety. He gives or sends in an instant whatever comes into

his head, be the value of it great or small. A young Genevese,
desirous of entering into the service of Prussia, made a personal
application to him; his lordship, instead of giving him a letter,
gave him a little bag of peas, which he desired him to carry to the
King. On receiving this singular recommendation his Majesty
immediately gave a commission to the bearer of it. These elevated
geniuses have between themselves a language which the vulgar
will never understand. The whimsical manner of my Lord Maréchal, something like the caprice of a fine woman, rendered him
still more interesting to me. I was certain, and afterwards had
proofs, that it had not the least influence over his sentiments, nor
did it affect the cares prescribed by friendship on serious occasions. Yet in his manner of obliging there is the same singularity
as in his manners in general. Of this I will give one instance relative to a matter of no great importance. The journey from Motiers
to Colombier being too long for me to perform in one day, I commonly divided it by setting off after dinner and sleeping at Brot,
which is half way. The landlord of the house where I stopped,
named Sandoz, having to solicit at Berlin a favour of importance
to him, begged I would request his Excellency to ask it in his
behalf. Most willingly, said I, and took him with me. I left him
in the antechamber, and mentioned the matter to his Lordship,
who returned me no answer. After passing with him the whole
morning, I saw, as I crossed the hall to go to dinner, poor Sandoz,
who was fatigued to death with waiting. Thinking the Governor
had forgotten what I had said to him, I again spoke of the business
before we sat down to table; but still received no answer. I thought
this manner of making me feel I was importunate rather severe,
and, pitying the poor man in waiting, held my tongue. On my
return the next day I was much surprised at the thanks he returned me for the welcome and the good dinner his Excellency
had given him after receiving his paper. Three weeks afterwards
his Lordship sent him the rescript he had solicited, dispatched by
the minister, and signed by the King, and this without having said
a word either to myself or Sandoz concerning the business, about
which I thought he did not choose to give himself the least concern.

I could wish incessantly to speak of George Keith; from him
proceeds my recollection of the last happy moments I have enjoyed; the rest of my life, since our separation, has been passed
in affliction and grief of heart. The remembrance of this is so
melancholy and confused, that it is impossible for me to observe
the least order in what I write, so that in future I shall be under

the necessity of stating facts without giving them a regular arrangement.

I was soon relieved from my inquietude arising from the uncertainty of my asylum, by the answer from his Majesty to the Lord Marshal, in whom, as it will readily be believed, I had found an able advocate. The King not only approved of what he had done, but desired him, for I must relate everything, to give me twelve louis. The good old man, rather embarrassed by the commission, and not knowing how to execute it properly, endeavoured to soften the insult by transforming the money into provisions, and writing to me that he had received orders to furnish me with wood and coal to begin my little establishment: he moreover added, and perhaps from himself, that his Majesty would willingly build me a little house, such a one as I should choose to have, provided I would fix upon the ground. I was extremely sensible of the kindness of the last offer, which made me forget the weakness of the other. Without accepting either, I considered Frederick as my benefactor and protector, and became so sincerely attached to him, that from that moment I interested myself as much in his glory as until then I had thought his successes unjust. At the peace he made soon after, I expressed my joy by an illumination in very good taste: it was a string of garlands, with which I decorated the house I inhabited, and in which, it is true, I had the vindictive haughtiness to spend almost as much money as he had wished to give me. The peace ratified, I thought, as he was at the highest pinnacle of military and political fame, he would think of acquiring that of another nature, by re-animating his states, encouraging in them commerce and agriculture, creating a new soil, covering it with a new people, maintaining peace among his neighbours, and becoming the arbitrator, after having been the terror, of Europe. He was in a situation to sheath his sword without danger, certain that no sovereign would oblige him again to draw it. Perceiving he did not disarm, I was afraid he would profit but little by the advantages he had gained, and be great by halves. I dared to write to him upon the subject, and with a familiarity of a nature to please men of his character, conveying to him the sacred voice of truth, which but few kings are worthy to hear. The liberty I took was a secret between him and myself. I did not communicate it even to the Lord Marshal, to whom I sent my letter to the King sealed up. His Lordship forwarded my despatch without asking what it contained. His Majesty returned me no answer, and the Marshal soon going after to Berlin, the King told him he had re-

ceived from me a scolding. By this I understood my letter had
been ill received, and that the frankness of my zeal had been mistaken for the rusticity of a pedant. In fact, this might possibly be
the case; perhaps I did not say what was necessary, nor in the
manner proper to the occasion. All I can answer for is the sentiment which induced me to take up my pen.

Shortly after my establishment at Motiers-Travers, having
every possible assurance I should be suffered to remain there in
peace, I took the Armenian habit. This was not the first time I
had thought of doing it. I had several times in my life had the
same intention, particularly at Montmorency, where the frequent
use of probes often obliging me to keep my chamber, made me
more clearly perceive the advantages of a long robe. The convenience of an Armenian tailor, who frequently came to see a
relation he had at Montmorency, almost tempted me to determine
on taking this new dress, troubling myself but little about what
the world would say of it. Yet, before I concluded upon the matter, I wished to take the opinion of Madame de Luxembourg, who
immediately advised me to follow my inclination. I therefore procured a little Armenian wardrobe, but on account of the storm
raised against me, I was induced to postpone making use of it
until I should enjoy greater tranquillity, and it was not until
some months afterwards that, forced by new attacks of my disorder to use probes again, I thought I could properly, and without
the least risk, put on my new dress at Motiers, especially after
having consulted the pastor of the place, who told me I might

wear it even in the church without indecency. I then adopted the waistcoat, caftan, fur bonnet, and girdle; and after having, in this dress, attended divine service, I saw no impropriety in going in it to visit His Lordship. His Excellency, on seeing me clothed in this manner, made me no other compliment than to say *Salamaleki*,[1] after which nothing more was said upon the subject, and I wore nothing else but my new dress.

Having quite abandoned literature, all I now thought of was leading a quiet life, and one as agreeable as I could make it. When alone, I have never felt weariness of mind, not even in complete inaction; my imagination, filling up every void, was sufficient to keep up my attention. The inactive babbling of a private circle, where, seated opposite to each other, they who speak move nothing but the tongue, is the only thing I have ever been unable to support. When walking and rambling about, there is some satisfaction in conversation; the feet and eyes do something; but to stay with one's arms folded speaking of the weather, of the biting of flies, or what is still worse, complimenting each other, is to me an insupportable torment. That I might not live like a savage, I took it into my head to learn to make laces. Like the women I carried my cushion with me when I went to make visits, or sat down to work at my door, and chatted with passers-by. This made me the better support the emptiness of babbling, and enabled me to pass my time with my female neighbours without weariness. Several of these were very amiable and not devoid of wit. One in particular, Isabella d'Ivernois, daughter of the attorney-general of Neuchâtel, I found so estimable as to induce me to enter with her into terms of particular friendship, from which she derived some advantage by the useful advice I gave her, and the services she received from me on occasions of importance, so that now a worthy and virtuous mother of a family, she is perhaps indebted to me for her reason, her husband, her life, her happiness. On my part, I received from her soft consolation, particularly during a melancholy winter, throughout the whole of which, when my sufferings were most cruel, she came to pass with Thérèse and me long evenings, which she made very short to us by her agreeable conversation, and our mutual openness of heart. She called me papa, and I called her daughter, and these names, which we still give to each other, will, I hope, continue to be as dear to her as they are to me. That my laces might be of some utility, I gave

---

[1] The Mohammedan salutation, *Salaam aleiki.*

them to my young female friends at their marriage, upon condition of their suckling their children; Isabella's eldest sister had one upon these terms, and well deserved it by her observance of them: Isabella herself also received another, which, by intention, she has as fully merited; but she has not been happy enough to be able to pursue her inclination. When I sent the laces to the two sisters, I wrote each of them a letter; the first has been shown about in the world; the second had not the same celebrity: friendship proceeds with less noise.

Amongst the connexions I made in my neighbourhood, of which I will not enter into a detail, I must mention that with Colonel Pury, who had a house upon the mountain where he came to pass the summer. I was not anxious to become acquainted with him, because I knew he was upon bad terms at Court, and with the Lord Marshal, whom he did not visit. Yet, as he came to see me, and showed me much attention, I was under the necessity of returning his visit; this was repeated, and we sometimes dined with each other. At his house I became acquainted with M. du Peyrou, and was afterwards too intimately connected with him to pass his name over in silence.

M. du Peyrou was an American, son to a commandant of Surinam, whose successor, M. le Chambrier, of Neuchâtel, married his widow. Left a widow a second time, she came with her son to live in the country of her second husband.

Du Peyrou, an only son, very rich, and tenderly beloved by his mother, had been carefully brought up, and his education was not lost upon him. He had acquired much half-knowledge, a taste for the arts, and piqued himself upon his having cultivated his rational faculty: his Dutch, cold, and philosophical appearance, yellow complexion, and silent and close disposition, favoured this opinion. Although young, he was already deaf and gouty. This rendered his motions deliberate and very grave, and although he was fond of disputing, sometimes even at some length, he in general spoke but little because his hearing was bad. I was struck with his exterior, and said to myself, This is a thinker, a man of wisdom, such a one as anybody would be happy to have for a friend. He frequently addressed himself to me without ever paying the least compliment, and this strengthened the favourable opinion I had already formed of him. He said but little to me of myself or my books, and still less of himself; he was not destitute of ideas, and what he said was just. This justness and equality attracted my regard. He had neither the elevation of mind, nor the discrimination of the Lord Marshal, but he had all his simplicity; this was still representing him in something. I did not become infatuated with him, but he acquired my attachment from esteem; and by degrees this esteem led to friendship, and I totally forgot with him the objection I made to the Baron Holbach: that he was too rich, and I think I was wrong. I have learnt to doubt whether a man in possession of a great fortune, whoever he be, can with sincerity love my principles and their author.

For a long time I saw but little of du Peyrou, because I did not go to Neuchâtel, and he came but once a year to the mountain of Colonel Pury. Why did not I go to Neuchâtel? This proceeded from a childishness upon which I must not be silent.

Although protected by the King of Prussia and the Lord Marshal, while I avoided persecution in my asylum, I did not avoid the murmurs of the public, of municipal magistrates and ministers. After what had happened in France it became fashionable to insult me; these people would have been afraid to seem to disapprove of what my persecutors had done by not imitating them. The *classe* of Neuchâtel, that is, the body of ministers of that city, gave the impulse, by endeavouring to move the council of state against me. This attempt not having succeeded, the ministers addressed themselves to the municipal magistrate, who immediately prohibited my book, treating me on all occasions with but little civility, and saying, that had I wished to reside in the city I should not have been suffered to do it. They filled their *Mercury* with absurdities, and the most stupid hypocrisy, which, although it made every man of sense laugh, excited and animated the people against me. This, however, did not prevent them from setting forth that I ought to be very grateful for their extreme favour in permitting me to live at Motiers, where they had no authority: they would willingly have measured me air by the pint, provided I had paid for it a dear price. They would have it that I was obliged to them for the protection the King granted me in spite of the efforts they incessantly made to deprive me of it. Finally, failing of success, after having done me all the injury they could, and defamed me to the utmost of their power, they made a merit of their impotence, by boasting of their goodness in suffering me to stay in their country. I ought to have laughed at their vain efforts, but I was foolish enough to be vexed at them, and had the weakness to be unwilling to go to Neuchâtel, to which I yielded for almost two years, as if it was not doing too much honour to such wretches, to pay attention to their proceedings, which, good or bad, could not be imputed to them, because they never act but from a foreign impulse. Besides, minds without sense or knowledge, whose objects of esteem are influence, power, and money, are far from imagining even that some respect is due to talents, and that it is dishonourable to injure and insult them.

A certain mayor of a village, who for sundry malversations had been deprived of his office, said to the lieutenant of Val de Travers, the husband of Isabella: *I am told this Rousseau has great wit; bring him to me that I may see whether he has or not.* The disapprobation of a man who takes such a tone[1] ought certainly to have no effect upon those on whom it falls.

After the treatment I had received at Paris, Geneva, Berne, and even at Neuchâtel, I expected no favour from the pastor of this place. I had however been recommended to him by Madame Boy de la Tour, and he had given me a good reception; but in that country, where every newcomer is indiscriminately flattered, civilities signify but little. Yet, after my solemn union with the reformed church, and living in a Protestant country, I could not, without failing in my engagements, as well as in the duty of a citizen, neglect the public profession of the religion into which I had entered: I therefore attended divine service. On the other hand, had I gone to the Holy Table, I was afraid of exposing myself to a refusal, and it was by no means probable, that after the tumult excited at Geneva by the Council, and at Neuchâtel by the *classe*, he would without difficulty administer to me the sacrament in his church. The time of communion approaching, I wrote to M. de Montmollin, the minister, to prove to him my desire of communicating and declaring myself heartily united to the Protestant church; I also told him, in order to avoid disputing upon articles of faith, that I did not wish for any particular explanation of the point of doctrine. After taking these steps, I made myself easy, not doubting but M. de Montmollin would refuse to admit me without the preliminary discussion to which I refused to consent, and that in this manner everything would be at an end without any fault of mine. I was deceived: when I least expected anything of the kind, M. de Montmollin came to declare to me, not only that he admitted me to the communion under the clause which I had proposed, but that he and the elders thought themselves much honoured by my being one of their flock. I never in my whole life felt greater surprise, or received more consolation.

---

[1] Paris MS. reads: "With whom one takes such a tone."

Living always alone and unconnected appeared to me a melancholy destiny, especially in adversity. In the midst of so many proscriptions and persecutions I found it extremely agreeable to be able to say to myself; I am at least amongst my brethren; and I went to the communion with an emotion of heart, and my eyes suffused with tears of tenderness, which perhaps were the most agreeable preparation to Him to whose table I was drawing near.

Some time afterwards His Lordship sent me a letter from Madame de Boufflers, which he had received, at least I presumed so, by means of d'Alembert, who was acquainted with the Maréchal. In this letter, the first that lady had written to me after my departure from Montmorency, she rebuked me severely for having written to M. de Montmollin, and especially for having communicated. I the less understood what she meant by her reproof, as after my journey to Geneva, I had constantly declared myself a Protestant, and had gone publicly to the Hôtel de Hollande,[1] without incurring the least censure from anybody. It appeared to me diverting enough, that Madame de Boufflers should wish to direct my conscience in matters of religion. However, as I had no doubt of the purity of her intention, though I could not understand it, I was not offended by this singular sally, and I answered her without anger, stating to her my reason.

Calumnies in print were still industriously circulated, and their benign authors reproached the different powers with treating me too mildly. This concerted howling, the actors wherein continued to work in secret, was of a sinister and terrifying nature. For my part I let them say what they pleased, without giving myself the least concern about the matter. I was told there was a censure from the Sorbonne, but this I could not believe. What could the Sorbonne have to do in the matter? Did the doctors wish to know to a certainty I was not a Catholic? Everybody already knew I was not one. Were they desirous of proving I was not a good Calvinist? Of what consequence was this to them? It was taking upon themselves a singular care, and becoming the substitutes of our ministers. Before I saw this publication I thought it was distributed in the name of the Sorbonne, by way of mockery: and when I had read it I was convinced this was the case. But when at length there was not a doubt of its authenticity all I could bring myself to believe was, that the learned doctors would have been better placed in a mad-house than they were in the college.

---

[1] A Calvinist meeting-place.

I was more affected by another publication, because it came from a man for whom I always had an esteem, and whose constancy I admired, though I pitied his blindness. I mean the mandatory letter against me by the Archbishop of Paris. I thought to return an answer to it was a duty I owed myself. This I felt I could do without derogating from my dignity; the case was something similar to that of the King of Poland. I have always detested brutal disputes, after the manner of Voltaire. I never combat but with dignity, and before I deign to defend myself I must be certain that he by whom I am attacked will not dishonour my retort. I had no doubt that this letter was fabricated by the Jesuits, and although they were at that time in distress, I discovered in it their old principle of crushing the wretched. I was therefore at liberty to follow my ancient maxim, by honouring the titulary author, and refuting the work, which I think I did completely.

I found my residence at Motiers very agreeable, and nothing was wanting to determine me to end my days there, but a certainty of the means of subsistence. Living is dear in that neighbourhood, and all my old projects had been overturned by the dissolution of my household arrangements at Montmorency, the establishment of others, the sale or scattering of my furniture, and the expenses incurred since my departure. The little capital which remained to me daily diminished. Two or three years were sufficient to consume the remainder without my having the means of renewing it, except by again engaging in literary pursuits: a pernicious profession which I had already abandoned.

Persuaded that everything which concerned me would soon change, and that the public, recovered from its frenzy, would make my persecutors blush, all my endeavours tended to prolong my resources until this happy revolution should take place, after which I should more at my ease choose a resource from among those which might offer themselves. To this effect I took up my *Dictionary of Music*, which ten years' labour had so far advanced as to leave nothing wanting to it but the last corrections. My books, which I had lately received, enabled me to finish this work; my papers, sent me by the same conveyance, furnished me with the means of beginning my memoirs, to which I was determined to give my whole attention. I began by transcribing the letters into a book, by which my memory might be guided in the order of facts and time. I had already selected those I intended to keep for this purpose, and for ten years the series was not interrupted. However, in preparing them for copying I found an interruption at which I was surprised. This was for almost six months, from October 1756 to March following. I perfectly recollected having put into my selection a number of letters from Diderot, Deleyre, Madame d'Epinay, Madame de Chenonceaux, etc., which filled up the void and were missing. What was become of them? Had any persons laid their hands upon my papers whilst they remained for some months in the Hôtel de Luxembourg? This was not conceivable, and I had seen M. de Luxembourg take the key of the chamber in which I had deposited them. Many letters from different ladies, and all those from Diderot, were without date, on which account I had been under the necessity of dating them from memory and uncertainly before they could be put in order, and thinking I might have committed errors, I again looked over all those without date, or in which I had supplied it, for the purpose of seeing whether or not I could find those which ought to fill up the void. This experiment did not succeed. I perceived the vacancy to be real, and that the letters had certainly been taken away. By whom and for what purpose? This was what I could not comprehend. These letters, written prior to my great quarrels, and at the time of my first enthusiasm in the composition of *Julie*, could not be interesting to any person. They contained nothing more than cavillings by Diderot, jeerings from Deleyre, assurances of friendship from Madame de Chenonceaux, and even Madame d'Epinay, with whom I was then upon the best of terms. To whom were these letters of consequence? To what use were they to be put? It was not until seven years afterwards that I suspected the terrible object of the theft.

The deficiency being no longer doubtful, I looked over my rough drafts to see whether or not it was the only one. I found several, which on account of the badness of my memory, made me suppose others in the multitude of my papers. Those I remarked were that of the draft of the *Morale Sensitive*, and the extract of the *Adventures of Lord Edward*. The last, I confess, made me suspect Madame de Luxembourg. La Roche, her valet de chambre, had sent me the papers, and I could think of nobody but herself to whom this fragment could be of consequence; but what concern could the other give her, any more than the rest of the letters missing, with which, even with evil intentions, nothing to my prejudice could be done, unless they were falsified? As for the Maréchal, with whose real friendship for me, and invariable integrity, I was perfectly acquainted, I never could suspect him for a moment. I could not even continue to suspect Madame de Luxembourg.

The most reasonable supposition, after long tormenting my mind
in endeavouring to discover the author of the theft, was that which
imputed it to d'Alembert, who having thrust himself into the
company of Madame de Luxembourg, might have found means
to turn over these papers, and take from amongst them such manuscripts and letters as he might have thought proper, either for the
purpose of endeavouring to embroil me with the writer of them,
or to appropriate those he should find useful to his own private
purposes. I imagined that, deceived by the title of *Morale Sensitive*, he might have supposed it to be the plan of a real treatise upon
materialism, with which he would have armed himself against me
in a manner easy to be imagined. Certain that he would soon be
undeceived by reading the sketch, and determined to quit all
literary pursuits, these larcenies gave me but little concern. They
besides were not the first the same hand had committed[1] upon
me without my having complained of these pilferings. In a very
little time I thought no more of the trick that had been played me,
than if nothing had happened, and began to collect the materials
I had left for the purpose of undertaking my projected confessions.

I had long thought the company of ministers, or at least the
citizens and burgesses of Geneva, would remonstrate against the
infraction of the edict in the decree made against me. Everything
remained quiet, at least to all exterior appearances; for discontent
was general, and ready, on the first opportunity, openly to manifest itself. My friends, or persons calling themselves such, wrote
letter after letter exhorting me to come and put myself at their
head, assuring me of public reparation from the Council. The
fear of the disturbance and troubles which might be caused by my
presence, prevented me from acquiescing with their desires, and,
faithful to the oath I had formerly made, never to take the least
part in any civil dissension in my country, I chose rather to let
the offence remain as it was, and banish myself for ever from the
country, than to return to it by means which were violent and
dangerous. It is true, I expected the burgesses would make legal
and peaceful remonstrances against an infraction in which their
interests were deeply concerned; but no such steps were taken.
They who conducted the body of citizens sought less the real re-

[1] I had found in his *Eléments de Musique* several things taken from what I
had written for the *Encyclopédie*, and which were given to him several years
before the publication of his *Eléments*. I know not what he may have had to
do with a book entitled *Dictionnaire des Beaux Arts* but I found in it articles
transcribed word for word from mine, and this long before the same articles
were printed in the *Encyclopédie*. (*Note by Rousseau*.)

dress of grievances than an opportunity to render themselves necessary. They caballed but were silent, and suffered me to be bespattered by the gossips and hypocrites set on to render me odious in the eyes of the populace, and pass upon them their boistering for a zeal in favour of religion.

After having, during a whole year, vainly expected that someone would remonstrate against an illegal proceeding, and seeing myself abandoned by my fellow-citizens, I determined to renounce my ungrateful country in which I never had lived, from which I had not received either advantage or service, and by which, in return for the honour I had endeavoured to do it, I saw myself so unworthily treated by unanimous consent, since they, who should have spoken, had remained silent. I therefore wrote to the first syndic for that year, to M. Favre, if I remember right, a letter in which I solemnly gave up my freedom of the city of Geneva, carefully observing in it, however, that decency and moderation, from which I have never departed in the acts of haughtiness which, in my misfortunes, the cruelty of my enemies has frequently forced from me.

This step at last opened the eyes of the citizens, who feeling they had neglected their own interests by abandoning my defence, took my part when it was too late. They had griefs of their own which they joined to mine, and made these the subject of several well reasoned representations, which they strengthened and extended, as the severe and disheartening refusal of the Council, supported by the ministry of France, made them more clearly perceive the project formed to impose on them a yoke. These altercations produced several pamphlets which were undecisive, until that appeared entitled *Lettres écrites de la Campagne*, a work written in favour of the Council, with infinite art, and by which the remonstrating party, reduced to silence, was crushed for a time. This production, a lasting monument of the rare talents of its author, came from the attorney-general Tronchin, a man of wit and an enlightened understanding, well versed in the laws and government of the republic. *Siluit terra.*

The remonstrators, recovered from their first overthrow, undertook to give an answer, and in time produced one which brought them off tolerably well. But they all looked to me, as the only person capable of combating a like adversary with hopes of success. I confess I was of their opinion, and excited by my former fellow-citizens, who thought it was my duty to aid them with my pen, as I had been the cause of their embarrassment, I undertook to refute the *Lettres écrites de la Campagne*, and parodied the title of them by that of *Lettres écrites de la Montagne, which I gave to* mine. I wrote this answer so secretly, that, at a meeting I had at Thonon with the chiefs of the malcontents to talk of their affairs, and where they showed me a sketch of their answer, I said not a word of mine, which was quite ready, fearing obstacles might arise relative to the impression of it, should the magistrates or my enemies hear of what I had done. This work was, however, known in France before the publication; but government chose rather to let it appear, than to suffer me to guess at the means by which my secret had been discovered. Concerning this I will state what I know, which is but trifling: what I have conjectured shall remain with myself.

I received, at Motiers, almost as many visits as at the Hermitage and Montmorency; but these, for the most part, were of a different kind. They who had formerly come to see me, were people who, having taste, talents, and principles, something similar to mine, alleged them as the causes of their visits, and introduced subjects on which I could converse. At Motiers, the case was different, especially with the visitors who came from France. They were officers, or other persons who had no taste for literature, nor had many of them read my works, although, according to their own accounts, they had travelled thirty, forty, sixty, and a hundred leagues to come and see me, and admire the illustrious man, the very celebrated, the great man, etc. For from the time of my settling at Motiers, I received the most impudent flattery, from which the esteem of those with whom I associated had formerly sheltered me. As but few of my new visitors deigned to tell me who or what they were, and as they had neither read nor cast their eye over my works, nor had their researches and mine been directed to the same objects, I knew not what to speak to them upon: I waited for what they had to say, because it was for them to know and tell me the purpose of their visit. It will naturally be imagined this did not produce conversations very interesting to me, although they, perhaps, were so to my visitors, according to the information they might wish to acquire: for as I was without suspicion, I answered, without reserve, to every question they thought proper to ask me, and they commonly went away as well informed as myself, of the particulars of my situation.

I was, for example, visited in this manner by M. de Feins, equerry to the Queen, and captain of cavalry in the Queen's regiment, who had the patience to pass several days at Motiers, and to follow me on foot even to la Ferrière, leading his horse by the bridle, without having with me any point of union, except our acquaintance with Mademoiselle Fel, and that we both played at *bilboquet*.[1]

Before and after this I had received another visit much more extraordinary. Two men arrived on foot, each leading a mule loaded with his little baggage, lodging at the inn, taking care of their mules themselves, and asking to see me. By the equipage of these muleteers they were taken for smugglers, and the news that smugglers were come to see me was instantly spread. Their manner of addressing me sufficiently showed they were persons of another description; but without being smugglers they might be adventurers, and this doubt kept me for some time on my guard. They soon removed my apprehensions. One was M. de Montauban, who had the title of Comte de la Tour-du-Pin, gentleman of Dauphiny; the other M. Dastier, of Carpentras, an old officer, who had his cross of St. Louis in his pocket, because he could not display it. These gentlemen, both very amiable, were men of sense; their conversation was pleasant and interesting, and their manner of travelling, so much to my own taste, and but little like that of French gentlemen, in that measure, gained them my attachment, which an intercourse with them served to improve. Our acquaintance did not end with the visit; it is still kept up, and they have since been several times to see me, not on foot, that was very well for the first time; but the more I have seen of these gentlemen, the less similarity have I found between their taste and mine; I have not discovered their maxims to be such as I have ever observed, that my writings are familiar to them, or that there is any real sympathy between them and myself. What therefore did they want with me? Why came they to see me with such an equipage? Why stay for several days? Why repeat their visit? Why were they so desirous of having me for their host? I did not at the time propose to myself these questions; but they have sometimes occurred to me since.

Won by their advances, my heart abandoned itself without reserve, especially to M. Dastier, with whose open countenance I was more particularly pleased. I even corresponded with him, and when I determined to print the *Letters from the Mountain*, I thought of addressing myself to him, to deceive those by whom my packet was waited for upon the road to Holland. He had

---

[1] A kind of cup and ball.

spoken to me a good deal, and perhaps purposely, upon the liberty
of the press at Avignon; he offered me his services should I have
anything to print there: I took advantage of the offer, and sent
him successively by the post my first sheets. After having kept
these for some time, he sent them back to me because, said he,
no bookseller dared to undertake them, and I was obliged to have
recourse to Rey, taking care only to send my papers one after the
other, and not to part with those which succeeded until I had advice of the reception of those already sent. Before the work was
published, I found it had been seen in the offices of the ministers,
and d'Escherny of Neuchâtel spoke to me of the book entitled,
Homme de la Montagne, which d'Holbach had told him was by
me. I assured him, and it was true, that I had never written a
book which bore that title. When the *Lettres* appeared he became
furious, and accused me of falsehood, although I had told him
truth. By this means I was certain my manuscript had been read;
as I could not doubt of the fidelity of Rey, the most rational conjecture seemed to be, that my packets had been opened at the
post-house.

Another acquaintance I made much about the same time, but
which was begun by letters, was that with M. Laliaud of Nîmes,
who wrote to me from Paris, begging I would send him my profile
in silhouette; he said he was in want of it for my bust in marble,
which Le Moine was making for him to be placed in his library.
If this was a pretence invented to deceive me, it fully succeeded. I
imagined that a man who wished to have my bust in marble in his
library, had his head full of my works, consequently of my principles, and that he loved me because his mind was in unison with
mine. It was natural this idea should seduce me. I have since seen
M. Laliaud. I found him very ready to render me many trifling
services, and to concern himself in my little affairs, but I have
my doubts of his having, in the few books he ever read, fallen
upon any one of those I have written. I do not know that he has a
library, or that such a thing is of any use to him; and for the bust,
he had a bad figure in plaster, by Le Moine, from which has been
engraved a hideous portrait that goes about in my name, as if it
bore to me some resemblance.

The only Frenchman who seemed to come to see me on account
of my sentiments, and his taste for my works, was a young officer
of the regiment of Limousin, named Séguier de St. Brisson. He
made a figure in Paris, where he still, perhaps, distinguishes himself, by his pleasing talents and his wit. He came once to Mont-

morency, the winter which preceded my catastrophe. I was pleased with his vivacity. He afterwards wrote to me at Motiers, and whether he wished to flatter me, or that his head was really turned with *Emile*, he informed me he was about to quit the service to live independently, and had begun to learn the trade of a carpenter. He had an elder brother, a captain in the same regiment, the favourite of the mother, who, a devotee to excess, and directed by I know not what hypocrite of an abbé, did not treat the youngest son well, accusing him of irreligion, and what was still worse, of the unpardonable crime of being connected with me. These were the grievances, on account of which he was determined to break with his mother, and adopt the manner of life of which I have just spoken, all to play the part of the young *Emile*.

Alarmed at this petulance, I immediately wrote to him, endeavouring to make him change his resolution, and my exhortations were as strong as I could make them. They had their effect. He returned to his duty, to his mother, and took back the resignation he had given to the colonel, who had been prudent enough to make no use of it, that the young man might have time to reflect upon what he had done. St. Brisson, cured of these follies, was guilty of another less alarming, but, to me, not less disagreeable than the rest: he became an author. He successively published two or three pamphlets which announced a man not devoid of talents, but I have not to reproach myself with having encouraged him by my praises to continue to write.

Some time afterwards he came to see me, and we made together a pilgrimage to the island of St. Pierre. During this journey I found him different from what I saw of him at Montmorency. He had, in his manner, something affected, which at first did not much disgust me, although I have since thought of it often. He once visited me at the hôtel de St. Simon, as I passed through Paris on my way to England. I learned there what he had not told me, that he lived in the great world, and often visited Madame de Luxembourg. Whilst I was at Trye, I never heard from him, nor did he so much as make enquiry after me, by means of his relation Mademoiselle Séguier, my neighbour. This lady never seemed favourably disposed towards me. In a word the infatuation of M. de St. Brisson ended suddenly, like the connexion of M. de Feins: but this man owed me nothing, and the former was under obligations to me, unless the follies I prevented him from committing were nothing more than affectation; which might very possibly be the case.

I had visits from Geneva also. The Delucs, father and son, successively chose me for their attendant in sickness. The father was taken ill on the road, the son was already sick when he left Geneva; they both came to my house. Ministers, relations, hypocrites, and persons of every description came from Geneva and Switzerland, not like those from France, to laugh at and admire me, but to rebuke and catechise me. The only person amongst them who gave me pleasure was Moultou, who passed with me three or four days, and whom I wished to retain much longer; the most persevering of all, the most obstinate, and who conquered me by importunity, was one M. d'Ivernois, a merchant at Geneva, a French refugee, and related to the attorney-general of Neuchâtel. This man came from Geneva to Motiers twice a year, on purpose to see me, remained with me several days together from morning to night, accompanied me in my walks, brought me a thousand little presents, insinuated himself in spite of me into my confidence, and intermeddled in all my affairs, notwithstanding there was not between him and myself the least similarity of ideas, inclination, sentiment, or knowledge. I do not believe he ever read a book of any kind throughout, or that he knows upon what subject mine are written. When I began to herborise, he followed me in my botanical rambles, without taste for that amusement, or having anything to say to me, or I to him. He had the patience to pass with me tête-à-tête three whole days in a public house at Goumoins, whence by wearying him, and making him feel how much he wearied me, I was in hopes of driving him. I could not, however, shake his incredible perseverance, nor by any means discover the motive of it.

Amongst these connexions, made and continued by force, I must not omit the only one that was agreeable to me, and in which my heart was really interested: this was that I had with a young Hungarian who came to live at Neuchâtel, and from that place to Motiers, a few months after I had taken up my residence there. He was called by the people of the country, the Baron de Sauttern, by which name he had been recommended from Zurich. He was tall, well made, had an agreeable countenance, and mild and social qualities. He told everybody, and gave me also to understand, that he came to Neuchâtel for no other purpose than that of forming his youth to virtue, by his intercourse with me. His physiognomy, manner, and behaviour, seemed well suited to his conversation, and I should have thought I failed in one of the greatest duties had I turned my back upon a young man in whom I perceived nothing but what was amiable, and who sought my acquaintance from so respectable a motive. My heart knows not how to connect itself by halves. He soon acquired my friendship, and all my confidence, and we were presently inseparable. He accompanied me in all my walks, and became fond of them. I took him to the Maréchal, who received him with the utmost kindness. As he was yet unable to explain himself in French, he spoke and wrote to me in Latin, I answered in French, and this mingling of the two languages did not make our conversations either less smooth or lively. He spoke of his family, his affairs, his adventures, and of the Court of Vienna, with the domestic details of which he seemed well acquainted. In fine, during nearly two years which we passed in the greatest intimacy, I found in him a mildness of character proof against everything, manners not only polite but elegant, great neatness of person, and extreme decency in his conversation, in a word, all the marks of a man born and educated a gentleman, and which rendered him, in my eyes, too estimable not to make him dear to me.

At the time we were upon the most intimate and friendly terms, d'Ivernois wrote to me from Geneva, putting me upon my guard against the young Hungarian who had taken up his residence in my neighbourhood; telling me he was a spy whom the minister of France had appointed to watch my proceedings. This information was of a nature to alarm me the more, as in that country everybody advised me to guard against the machinations of persons who were employed to keep an eye upon my actions, and to entice me into France for the purpose of betraying me.

To shut the mouths, once for all, of these foolish advisers, I proposed to Sauttern, without giving him the least intimation of the information I had received, a journey on foot to Pontarlier, to which he consented. As soon as we arrived there I put the letter from d'Ivernois into his hands, and after giving him an ardent embrace, I said: Sauttern has no need of a proof of my confidence in him, but it is necessary I should prove to the public that I know in whom to place it. This embrace was accompanied with a pleasure which persecutors can neither feel themselves, nor take away from the oppressed.

I will never believe Sauttern was a spy, nor that he betrayed me; but I was deceived by him. When I opened to him my heart without reserve, he constantly kept his own shut, and abused me by lies. He invented I know not what kind of story, to prove to me his presence was necessary in his own country. I exhorted him to return to it as soon as possible. He set off, and when I thought he was in Hungary, I learned he was at Strasbourg. This was not the first time he had been there. He had caused some disorder in a family in that city; and the husband, knowing I received him in my house, wrote to me. I used every effort to bring the young woman back to the paths of virtue, and Sauttern to his duty. When I thought they were perfectly detached from each other, they renewed their acquaintance, and the husband had the complaisance to receive the young man at his house; from that moment I had nothing more to say. I found the pretended baron had imposed upon me by a great number of lies. His name was not Sauttern, but Sauttersheim. With respect to the title of baron, given him in Switzerland, I could not reproach him with the impropriety, because he had never taken it; but I have not a doubt of his being a gentleman, and the Marshal, who knew mankind, and had been in Hungary, always considered and treated him as such.

He had no sooner left my neighbourhood, than the girl at the inn where he ate, at Motiers, declared herself with child by him. She was so dirty a creature, and Sauttern, generally esteemed in the country for his conduct and purity of morals, piqued himself so much upon cleanliness, that everybody was shocked at this impudent pretension. The most amiable women of the country, who had vainly displayed to him their charms, were furious: I myself was almost choked with indignation. I used every effort to get the tongue of this impudent woman stopped, offering to pay all expenses, and to give security for Sauttersheim. I wrote to him in the fullest persuasion, not only that this pregnancy could not relate to him, but that it was feigned, and the whole a machination of his enemies and mine: I wished him to return and confound the strumpet, and those by whom she was dictated to. The pusillanimity of his answer surprised me. He wrote to the pastor of the parish to which the creature belonged, and endeavoured to stifle the matter. Perceiving this, I concerned myself no more about it, but I was astonished that a man who could stoop so low should have been sufficiently master of himself to deceive me by his reserve in the closest familiarity.

From Strasbourg, Sauttersheim went to seek his fortune in Paris, and found there nothing but misery. He wrote to me, acknowledging his error. My compassion was excited by the recollection of our former friendship, and I sent him a sum of money. The year following, as I passed through Paris, I saw him much in the same situation; but he was the intimate friend of M. de

Laliaud, and I could not learn by what means he had formed this acquaintance, or whether it was recent or of long standing. Two years afterwards Sauttersheim returned to Strasbourg, whence he wrote to me, and where he died. This, in a few words, is the history of our connexion, and what I know of his adventures; but while I mourn the fate of the unhappy young man, I still, and ever shall, believe he was the son of people of distinction, and that the impropriety of his conduct was the effect of the situation to which he was reduced.

Such were the connexions and acquaintance I acquired at Motiers. How many of these would have been necessary to compensate the cruel losses I suffered at the same time!

The first of these was that of M. de Luxembourg,[1] who, after having been long tormented by the physicians, at length became their victim, by being treated for the gout, which they would not acknowledge him to have, as for a disorder they thought they could cure.

According to what La Roche, the confidential servant of Madame de Luxembourg, wrote to me relative to what had happened, it is by this cruel and memorable example that the miseries of greatness are to be deplored.

The loss of this good nobleman afflicted me the more, as he was the only real friend I had in France, and the mildness of his character was such as to make me quite forget his rank, and attach myself to him as my equal. Our connexion was not broken off on account of my having quitted the kingdom; he continued to write to me as usual. I nevertheless thought I perceived that absence, or my misfortune, had cooled his affection for me. It is difficult to a courtier to preserve the same attachment to a person whom he knows to be in disgrace with courts. I moreover suspected the great ascendancy Madame de Luxembourg had over his mind, had been unfavourable to me, and that she had taken advantage of our separation to injure me in his esteem. For her part, notwithstanding a few affected marks of regard, which daily became less frequent, she less concealed the change in her friendship. She wrote to me four or five times into Switzerland, after which she never wrote to me again, and nothing but my prejudice, confidence, and blindness, could have prevented my discovering in her something more than a coolness towards me.

Guy, the bookseller, partner with Duchesne, who, after I had

---

[1] Who died May 18, 1764.

left Montmorency, frequently went to the Hôtel de Luxembourg, wrote to me that my name was in the will of the Maréchal. There was nothing in this either incredible or extraordinary, on which account I had no doubt of the truth of the information. I deliberated within myself whether or not I should receive the legacy. Everything well considered, I determined to accept it, whatever it might be, and to do that honour to the memory of an honest man, who, in a rank in which friendship is seldom found, had had a real one for me. I had not this duty to fulfil. I heard no more of the legacy, whether it were true or false; and in truth I should have felt some pain in offending against one of the great maxims of my system of morality, in profiting by anything at the death of a person whom I had once held dear. During the last illness of our friend Mussard, Lenieps proposed to me to take advantage of the grateful sense he expressed for our cares, to insinuate to him dispositions in our favour. Ah! my dear Lenieps, said I, let us not pollute by interested ideas the sad but sacred duties we discharge towards our dying friend. I hope my name will never be found in the testament of any person, at least not in that of a friend. It was about this time my Lord Marshal spoke to me of his, of what he intended to do in it for me, and that I made him the answer of which I have spoken in the first part of my memoirs.

My second loss, still more afflicting and irreparable, was that of the best of women and mothers,[1] who, already weighed down with years, and overburdened with infirmities and misery, quitted this vale of tears for the abode of the blessed, where the amiable remembrance of the good we have done here below is the eternal reward of our benevolence. Go, gentle and beneficent shade, to those of Fénelon, Bernex, Catinat, and others who, in a more humble state, have, like them, opened their hearts to true charity; go and taste of the fruit of your own benevolence, and prepare for your son the place he hopes to fill by your side. Happy in your misfortunes that heaven, in putting to them a period, has spared you the cruel spectacle of his! Fearing lest I should fill her heart with sorrow by the recital of my first disasters, I had not written to her since my arrival in Switzerland; but I wrote to M. de Conzié, to enquire after her situation, and it was from him I learned she had ceased to alleviate the sufferings of the afflicted, and that her own were at an end. I myself shall not suffer long; but if I thought I should not see her again in the life to come, my feeble imagina-

---

[1] Mme. de Warens died at Chambéry, July 29, 1762.

tion would less delight in the idea of the perfect happiness which
I there hope to enjoy.

GEORGE KEITH

My third and last loss, for since that time I have not had a friend
to lose, was that of the Lord Marshal. He did not die, but, tired of
serving the ungrateful, he left Neuchâtel, and I have never seen
him since. He still lives, and will, I hope, survive me; he is alive,
and thanks to him, all my attachments on earth are not destroyed.
There is one man still worthy of my friendship; for the real value
of this consists more in what we feel than in that which we inspire; but I have lost the pleasure I enjoyed in his, and can rank
him in the number of those only whom I love, but with whom I
am no longer connected. He went to England to receive the pardon of the King, and acquire the possession of his property which
formerly had been confiscated. We did not separate without an
intention of again being united, the idea of which seemed to give
him as much pleasure as I received from it. He determined to
reside at Keith Hall, near Aberdeen, and I was to join him as soon
as he was settled there: but this project was too flattering to my
hopes to give me any of its success. He did not remain in Scotland.
The affectionate solicitations of the King of Prussia induced him

to return to Berlin,[1] and the reason of my not going to him there
will presently appear.

Before his departure, foreseeing the storm which my enemies
began to raise against me, he, of his own accord, sent me letters
of naturalization, which seemed to be a certain means of preventing me from being driven from the country. The community of
Convet, in Val de Travers, followed the example of the Governor,
and gave me letters of *communion*, gratis as were the first. Thus,
in every respect become a citizen, I was sheltered from legal ex-
pulsion, even by the Prince; but it has never been by legitimate
means that the man who, of all others, has ever shown the greatest
respect for the laws, has been persecuted.

I do not think I ought to enumerate, amongst the number of my
losses at this time, that of the Abbé de Mably. Having lived some
time at the house of his brother, I had been acquainted with the
Abbé, but not very intimately, and I have reason to believe the
nature of his sentiments with respect to me changed after I acquired a greater celebrity than he already had. But the first time
I discovered his insincerity was immediately after the publication
of the *Letters from the Mountain*. A letter attributed to him,
addressed to Madame Saladin, was handed about in Geneva, in
which he spoke of this work as the seditious clamour of a furious
demagogue. The esteem I had for the Abbé de Mably, and my
great opinion of his understanding, did not for a moment permit
me to believe this extravagant letter was written by him. I acted
in this business with my usual candour. I sent him a copy of the
letter, informing him he was said to be the author of it. He returned me no answer. This silence astonished me: but what was my
surprise when, by a letter I received from Madame de Chenonceaux, I learned the Abbé was really the author of that which was
attributed to him, and found himself greatly embarrassed by mine.
For even supposing for a moment that what he stated was true,
how could he justify so public an attack, wantonly made, without
obligation or necessity, for the sole purpose of overwhelming, in
the midst of his greatest misfortunes, a man to whom he had
shown himself a well-wisher, and who had not done anything that
could excite his enmity? In a short time afterwards the *Dialogues
of Phocion*, in which I perceived nothing but a compilation, without shame or restraint, from my writings, made their appearance.
In reading this book I perceived the author had made up his mind

[1] Where he died May 25, 1778.

in regard to me, and that in future I must number him among my most bitter enemies. I do not believe he has ever pardoned me for the *Social Contract*, far superior to his abilities, or the *Perpetual Peace;* and I am, besides, of opinion the desire he expressed that I should make an extract from the Abbé de St. Pierre proceeded from a supposition in him that I should not acquit myself of it so well.

The farther I advance in my narrative, the less order I feel myself capable of observing. The agitation of the rest of my life has deranged in my ideas the succession of events. These are too numerous, confused and disagreeable to be recited in due order. The only strong impression they have left upon my mind is that of the horrid mystery by which the cause of them is concealed, and of the deplorable state to which they have reduced me. My narrative will in future be irregular, and according to the ideas which, without order, may occur to my recollection: I remember that about the time to which I refer, full of the idea of my confessions, I very imprudently spoke of them to everybody, never imagining it could be the wish or interest, much less within the power of any person whatsoever to throw an obstacle in the way of this undertaking, and had I suspected it, even this would not have rendered me more discreet, as from the nature of my disposition it is totally impossible for me to conceal either my thoughts or feelings The knowledge of this enterprise was, as far as I can judge, the real cause of the storm that was raised to drive me from Switzerland, and deliver me into the hands of those by whom I might be prevented from executing it.

I had another project in contemplation which was not looked upon with a more favourable eye by those who were afraid of the first: this was a general edition of my works. I thought this edition of them necessary to ascertain what books, among those to which my name was affixed, were really written by me, and to furnish the public with the means of distinguishing them from the writings falsely attributed to me by my enemies, to bring me to dishonour and contempt. This was besides a simple and an honourable means of ensuring to myself a livelihood, and the only one that remained to me. As I had renounced the profession of an author, my memoirs not being of a nature to appear during my lifetime; and as I no longer gained a farthing in any manner whatsoever, and constantly lived at a certain expense; I saw the end of my resources in that of the produce of the last things I had written. This reason had induced me to hasten the finishing of my

Dictionary of Music, which still was incomplete. I had received for it a hundred louis, and a life annuity of a hundred crowns; but a hundred louis could not last long in the hands of a man who annually expended upwards of sixty, and a hundred crowns a year was but a trifling sum to one upon whom parasites and beggarly visitors lighted like a swarm of flies.

A company of merchants from Neuchâtel came to undertake the general edition, and a printer or bookseller of the name of Reguillat, from Lyons, thrust himself, I know not by what means, amongst them to direct it. The agreement was made upon reasonable terms, and sufficient to accomplish my object. I had, in print and manuscript, matter for six volumes in quarto. I moreover agreed to give my assistance in bringing out the edition. The merchants were, on their part, to pay me a thousand crowns down, and to assign me an annuity of sixteen hundred livres for life.

The agreement was concluded but not signed, when the *Letters from the Mountain* appeared. The terrible explosion caused by this infernal work, and its abominable author, terrified the company, and the undertaking was at an end. I would compare the effect of this last production to that of the *Letter on French Music*, had not that letter, while it brought upon me hatred, and exposed me to danger, acquired me at least respect and esteem. But after the appearance of the last work, it was matter of astonishment at Geneva and Versailles, that such a monster as the author of it should be suffered to exist. The Little Council, excited by the French Resident and directed by the attorney-general, made a declaration against my work, by which, in the most severe terms, it was declared to be unworthy of being burned by the hands of the hangman, adding, with an address which bordered upon the burlesque, there was no possibility of even speaking of or answering it without dishonour. I would here transcribe the curious piece of composition, but unfortunately I have it not by me, and do not remember a word of it. I ardently wish some of my readers, animated by the zeal of truth and equity, would read over the *Letters from the Mountain:* they will, I dare hope, feel the stoical moderation which reigns throughout the whole, after cruel outrages, with which the author was loaded. But unable to answer the abuse, because no part of it could be called by that name, nor to the reasons because these were unanswerable, my enemies pretended to appear too much enraged to reply: and it is true, if they took the invincible arguments it contains for abuse, they must have felt themselves abused indeed.

The remonstrating party, far from complaining of the odious declaration, acted according to the spirit of it, and instead of making a trophy of the *Letters from the Mountain*, which they veiled to make them serve as a shield, were pusillanimous enough not to do justice or honour to that work, written to defend them, and at their own solicitation. They did not either quote or mention the letters, although they tacitly drew from them all their arguments, and by exactly following the advice with which they conclude, made them the sole cause of their safety and triumph. They had imposed on me this duty: I had fulfilled it, and unto the end had served their cause and the country. I begged of them to abandon me, and in their quarrels to think of nobody but themselves. They took me at my word, and I concerned myself no more about their affairs, further than constantly to exhort them to peace, not doubting, should they continue to be obstinate, of their being crushed by France. This however did not happen. I know the reason why it did not, but this is not the place to explain what I mean.

The effect produced at Neuchâtel by the *Letters from the Mountain* was at first very mild. I sent a copy of them to M. Montmollin, who received it favorably, and read it without making any objection. He was ill as well as myself; as soon as he recovered he came in a friendly manner to see me, and conversed on general subjects. A rumour was however begun; the book was burned I know not

where. From Geneva, Berne, and perhaps from Versailles, the effervescence quickly passed to Neuchâtel, and especially to Val de Travers, where, before even the ministers had taken any apparent steps, an attempt was secretly made to stir up the people. I ought, I dare assert, to have been beloved by the people of that country, as I have been in every country in which I have lived, giving alms in abundance, not leaving about me an indigent person without assistance, never refusing to do any service in my power, and which was consistent with justice, making myself perhaps too familiar with everybody, and avoiding, as far as it was possible for me to do it, all distinction which might excite the least jealousy. This, however, did not prevent the populace, secretly stirred up against me by I know not whom, from being by degrees irritated against me, even to fury, nor from publicly insulting me not only in the country and upon the roads, but in the street. Those to whom I had rendered the greatest services became most irritated against me, and even people who still continued to receive my benefactions, not daring to appear, excited others, and seemed to wish thus to be revenged of me for their humiliation in being obliged to me. Montmollin seemed to pay no attention to what was passing, and did not yet come forward. But as the time of communion approached, he came to advise me not to present myself at the Holy Table, assuring me, however, he was not my enemy, and that he would leave me undisturbed. I found this compliment whimsical enough; it brought to my recollection the letter from Madame de Boufflers, and I could not conceive to whom it could be a matter of such importance whether I communicated or not. Considering this condescension on my part as an act of cowardice, and moreover, being unwilling to give to the people a new pretence under which they might charge me with impiety, I refused the request of the minister, and he went away dissatisfied, giving me to understand I should repent of my obstinacy.

He could not of his own authority forbid me the communion: that of the Consistory, by which I had been admitted to it, was necessary, and as long as there was no objection from that body I might present myself without the fear of being refused. Montmollin procured from the *Classe* a commission to summon me to the Consistory, there to give an account of the articles of my faith, and to excommunicate me should I refuse to comply. This excommunication could not be pronounced without the aid of the Consistory also, and a majority of the voices. But the peasants, who, under the appellation of elders, composed this assembly, presided

over and governed by their minister, might naturally be expected
to adopt his opinion, especially in matters of theology which they
still less understood than he did. I was therefore summoned, and
I resolved to appear.

What a happy circumstance and triumph would this have been
to me could I have spoken, and had I, if I may so speak, had my
pen in my mouth! With what superiority, with what facility even,
should I have overthrown this poor minister in the midst of his
six peasants! The thirst after power having made the Protestant
clergy forget all the principles of the reformation, all I had to do
to recall these to their recollection and reduce them to silence,
was to make comments upon my first *Letters from the Mountain*,
upon which they had the folly to animadvert.

My text was ready, I had only to enlarge on it, and my adversary was confounded. I should not have been weak enough to
remain on the defensive; it was easy to me to become an assailant
without his even perceiving it, or being able to shelter himself
from my attack. The contemptible priests of the *Classe*, equally
careless and ignorant, had of themselves placed me in the most
favourable situation I could desire to crush them at pleasure. But
what of this? It was necessary I should speak without hesitation,
and find ideas, turns of expression, and words at will, preserving
a presence of mind, and keeping myself collected, without once
suffering even a momentary confusion. For what could I hope,
feeling, as I did, my want of aptitude to express myself with ease?
I had been reduced to the most mortifying silence at Geneva, before an assembly which was favourable to me, and previously
resolved to approve of everything I should say. Here, on the contrary, I had to do with a caviller who, substituting cunning for
knowledge, would spread for me a hundred snares before I could
perceive one of them, and was resolutely determined to catch
me in an error let the consequence be what it would. The more
I examined the situation in which I stood, the greater danger I
perceived myself exposed to, and feeling the impossibility of successfully withdrawing from it, I thought of another expedient.
I meditated a discourse which I intended to pronounce before the
Consistory, to exempt myself from the necessity of answering.
The thing was easy. I wrote the discourse and began to learn it
by memory, with an inconceivable ardour. Thérèse laughed at
hearing me mutter and incessantly repeat the same phrases, while
endeavouring to cram them into my head. I hoped, at length, to
remember what I had written: I knew the Châtelain, as an officer

attached to the service of the Prince, would be present at the Consistory, and that notwithstanding the manœuvres and bottles of Montmollin, most of the elders were well disposed towards me. I had, moreover, in my favour, reason, truth, and justice, with the protection of the King, the authority of the Council of State, and the good wishes of every real patriot, to whom the establishment of this inquisition was threatening. In fine, everything contributed to encourage me.

On the eve of the day appointed, I had my discourse by rote, and recited it without missing a word. I had it in my head all night: in the morning I had forgotten it. I hesitated at every word, thought myself before the assembly, became confused, stammered, and lost my presence of mind. In fine, when the time to make my appearance was almost at hand, my courage totally failed me. I remained at home and wrote to the Consistory, hastily stating my reasons, and pleaded my disorder, which really, in the state to which apprehension had reduced me, would scarcely have permitted me to stay out the whole sitting.

The minister, embarrassed by my letter, adjourned the Consistory. In the interval, he, of himself, and by his creatures, made a thousand efforts to seduce those of the elders, who, following the dictates of their consciences, rather than those they received from him, did not vote according to his wishes, or those of the *Classe*. Whatever power his arguments drawn from his cellar might have over this kind of people, he could not gain one of them, more than the two or three who were already devoted to his will, and who were called his *âmes damnées*. The officer of the Prince, and Colonel Pury, who, in this affair, acted with great zeal, kept the rest to their duty, and when Montmollin wished to proceed to excommunication, his Consistory, by a majority of voices, flatly refused to authorise him to do it. Thus reduced to the last expedient, that of stirring up the people against me, he, his colleagues, and other persons, set about it openly, and were so successful, that notwithstanding the strong and frequent rescripts of the King, and the orders of the Council of State, I was at length obliged to quit the country, that I might not expose the officer of the King to be himself assassinated while he protected me.

The recollection of the whole of this affair is so confused, that it is impossible for me to arrange or connect the circumstances of it. I can only give them singly and isolated, as they come into my mind. I remember a kind of negotiation had been entered into with the *Classe*, in which Montmollin was the mediator. He feigned to believe it was feared I should, by my writings, disturb the peace of the country, in which case the liberty I had of writing would be blamed. He had given me to understand that if I consented to lay down my pen, what was past would be forgotten. I had already entered into this engagement with myself, and did not hesitate in doing it with the *Classe*, but conditionally and solely in matters of religion. He found means to have a duplicate of the agreement, upon some change necessary to be made in it; the condition having been rejected by the *Classe*, I demanded back the writing, which was returned to me, but he kept the duplicate, pretending it was lost. After this, the people, openly excited by the ministers, laughed at the rescripts of the King, and the orders of the Council of State, and shook off all restraint. I was declaimed against from the pulpit, called Antichrist, and pursued in the country like a mad wolf. My Armenian dress discovered me to the populace; of this I felt the cruel inconvenience, but to quit it in such circumstances appeared to me an act of cowardice. I could not prevail upon myself to do it, and I quietly walked through the country with my caftan and fur bonnet in the midst of the hootings of the dregs of the people, and sometimes through a shower of stones. Several times as I passed before houses, I heard those by whom they were inhabited call out: Bring me my gun, that I may fire at him. As I did not on this account hasten my pace, my calmness increased their fury, but they never went farther than threats, at least with respect to firearms.

During all this fermentation I received from two circumstances the most sensible pleasure. The first was my having it in my power to prove my gratitude by means of the Lord Marshal. The honest part of the inhabitants of Neuchâtel, full of indignation at the treatment I received, and the manœuvres of which I was the victim, held the ministers in execration, clearly perceiving they were obedient to a foreign impulse, and the vile agents of people who, in making them act, kept themselves concealed; they were moreover afraid my case would have dangerous consequences, and be made a precedent for the purpose of establishing a real inquisition.

The magistrates, and especially M. Meuron, who had succeeded M. d'Ivernois in the office of attorney-general, made every effort to defend me. Colonel Pury, although a private individual, did more, and succeeded better. It was the colonel who found means to make Montmollin submit in his Consistory, by keeping the elders to their duty. He had credit, and employed it to stop the sedition; but he had nothing more than the authority of the laws, and the aid of justice and reason, to oppose to that of money and wine: the combat was unequal, and in this point Montmollin was triumphant. However, thankful for his zeal and cares, I wished to have it in my power to make him a return of good offices, and in some measure discharge a part of the obligations I was under to him. I knew he was very desirous of being named a counsellor of state; but having displeased the Court by his conduct in the affair of the minister Petitpierre, he was in disgrace with the Prince and governor. I however undertook, at all risks, to write to the Lord Marshal in his favour: I went so far as even to men-

DAVID HUME

tion the employment of which he was desirous, and my application was so well received that, contrary to the expectations of his most ardent well-wishers, it was almost instantly conferred upon him by the King. In this manner fate, which has constantly raised me to too great an elevation, or plunged me into an abyss of adversity, continued to toss me from one extreme to another, and whilst the populace covered me with mud I made a counsellor of state.

The other pleasing circumstance was a visit I received from

Madame de Verdelin with her daughter, with whom she had been at the baths of Bourbonne, whence she came to Motiers and stayed with me two or three days. By her attention and cares, she at length conquered my long repugnance; and my heart, won by her endearing manner, made her a return of all the friendship of which she had long given me proofs. This journey made me extremely sensible of her kindness: my situation rendered the consolations of friendship highly necessary to support me under my sufferings. I was afraid she would be too much affected by the insults I received from the populace, and could have wished to conceal them from her that her feelings might not be hurt, but this was impossible; and although her presence was some check upon the insolent populace in our walks, she saw enough of their brutality to enable her to judge of what passed when I was alone. During the short residence she made at Motiers, I began to be attacked at night in my habitation. One morning her chambermaid found my window blocked up with stones, which had been thrown at it during the night. A very heavy bench placed in the street, by the side of the house, and strongly fastened down, was taken up and reared against the door in such a manner as, had it not been perceived from the window, to have knocked down the first person who should have opened the door to go out. Madame de Verdelin was acquainted with everything that passed; for, besides what she herself was witness to, her confidential servant went into many houses in the village, spoke to everybody, and was seen in conversation with Montmollin. She did not, however, seem to pay the least attention to that which happened to me, nor even mentioned Montmollin or any other person, and answered in a few words to what I said to her of him. Persuaded that a residence in England would be more agreeable to me than any other, she frequently spoke of Mr. Hume, who was then at Paris, of his friendship for me, and the desire he had of being of service to me in his own country. It is time I should say something of Hume.

He had acquired a great reputation in France, particularly amongst the Encyclopedists, by his essays on commerce and politics, and in the last place by his *History of the House of Stuart*, the only one of his writings of which I had read a part, in the translation of the Abbé Prévost. For want of being acquainted with his other works, I was persuaded, according to what I heard of him, that Mr. Hume joined a very republican mind to the English paradoxes in favour of luxury. In this opinion I considered his whole apology of Charles I as a prodigy of impartiality, and

I had as great an idea of his virtue as of his genius. The desire of being acquainted with this great man, and of obtaining his friendship, had greatly strengthened the temptation I felt to go to England, induced by the solicitations of Madame de Boufflers, the intimate friend of Hume. After my arrival in Switzerland, I received from him, by means of this lady, a letter extremely flattering; in which, to the highest encomiums on my genius, he subjoined a pressing invitation to induce me to go to England, and the offer of all his interest, and that of his friends, to make my residence there agreeable. I found in the country to which I had retired, the Lord Marshal, the countryman and friend of Hume, who confirmed my good opinion of him, and from whom I learned a literary anecdote, which did him great honour in the opinion of His Lordship and had the same effect in mine. Wallace, who had written against Hume upon the subject of the population of the ancients, was absent whilst his work was in the press. Hume took upon himself to examine the proofs, and to do the needful to the edition. This manner of acting was according to my own way of thinking. I had thus sold at six sous a piece, the copies of a song written against myself. I was, therefore, strongly prejudiced in favour of Hume, when Madame de Verdelin came and mentioned the lively friendship he expressed for me, and his anxiety to do me the honours of England; such was her expression. She pressed me a good deal to take advantage of this zeal and write to him. As I had not naturally an inclination to England, and did not intend to go there until the last extremity, I refused to write or make any promise; but I left her at liberty to do whatever she should think necessary to keep Mr. Hume favourably disposed towards me. When she went from Motiers, she left me in the persuasion, by everything she had said to me of that illustrious man, that he was my friend, and she herself still more his.

After her departure, Montmollin carried on his manœuvres with more vigour, and the populace threw off all restraint. Yet I still continued to walk quietly amidst the hootings of the vulgar; and a taste for botany, which I had begun to contract with Doctor d'Ivernois, making my rambling more amusing, I went through the country herbalising, without being affected by the clamours of this scum of the earth, whose fury was but augmented by my calmness. What affected me most was, seeing the families of my friends,[1] or of persons who gave themselves that name, openly

---

[1] This fatality had begun with my residence at Yverdun: the banneret Roguin dying a year or two after my departure from that city, the old papa

join the league of my persecutors; such as the d'Ivernois, without excepting even the father and brother of my Isabella, Boy de la Tour, a relation to the friend in whose house I lodged, and Madame Girardier, her sister-in-law. This Peter Boy was such a brute, so stupid, and behaved so uncouthly, that, to prevent my mind from being disturbed, I took the liberty to ridicule him; and, after the manner of the *Petit Prophète*, I wrote a pamphlet of a few pages entitled, *La Vision de Pierre de la Montagne dit le Voyant*, in which I found means to be diverting enough on the miracles which then served as the great pretext for my persecution. Du Peyrou had this scrap printed at Geneva, but its success in the country was but moderate; the Neuchâtelois, with all their wit, taste but weakly Attic salt or pleasantry when these are a little refined. I took somewhat more care over another writing of the same period, of which the manuscript is among my papers, and whose subject I must here declare.

In the midst of decrees and persecutions, the Genevese had distinguished themselves by setting up a hue and cry with all their might, and my friend Vernes amongst others, with a true theological generosity, chose that moment precisely, to publish against me letters in which he pretended to prove I was not a Christian. These letters, written with an air of self-sufficiency, were not the better for it, although it was positively said the naturalist Bonnet had given them some correction: for this man, although a materialist, has an intolerant orthodoxy the moment I am in question. There certainly was nothing in this work which could tempt me to answer it; but having an opportunity of saying a few words upon it in my *Letters from the Mountain*, I inserted in them a short note sufficiently expressive of disdain to render Vernes furious. He filled Geneva with his furious exclamations, and d'Ivernois wrote me word he had quite lost his senses. Some time afterwards appeared an anonymous sheet, which instead of ink seemed to be written with the water of the Phlegethon. In this letter I was accused of having exposed my children in the streets, of taking about with me a soldier's trull, of being worn out with

---

Roguin had the candour to inform me with grief, as he said, that in the papers of his relation, proofs had been found of his having been concerned in the conspiracy formed to expel me from Yverdun and the state of Berne. This clearly proved the conspiracy not to be, as some persons pretended to believe, an affair of bigotry; since the banneret, far from being a devotee, carried materialism and incredulity to intolerance and fanaticism. Besides, nobody at Yverdun had shown me more constant attention, nor had so prodigally bestowed upon me praises and flattery as this banneret. He faithfully followed the favourite plan of my persecutors. (*Note by Rousseau*, not in Paris MS.)

debaucheries, eaten up with pox, and other fine things of a like
nature. It was not difficult for me to discover the author. My first
idea on reading this libel, was to reduce to its real value everything the world calls fame and reputation amongst men; seeing
thus a man who was never in a brothel in his life, and whose greatest defect was his being as timid and shy as a virgin, treated as a
frequenter of places of that description; and in finding myself
charged with being rotten with the pox, I, who not only never had
the least taint of any such disorder, but, according to the faculty,
was so constructed as to make it almost impossible for me to contract it. Everything well considered, I thought I could not better
refute this libel than by having it printed in the city in which I
had longest resided, and with this intention I sent it to Duchesne
to print it just as it was, with an advertisement in which I named
M. Vernes, and a few short notes by way of explanation. Not
satisfied with printing it only, I sent copies to several persons, and
amongst others one copy to the Prince Louis of Wirtemberg, who
had made me polite advances, and with whom I was in correspondence. The Prince, du Peyrou, and others, seemed to have
their doubts about the author of the libel, and blamed me for
having named Vernes upon so slight a foundation. Their remarks
produced in me some scruples, and I wrote to Duchesne to suppress the paper. Guy wrote to me he had suppressed it; this may
or may not be the case; I have been deceived by him on so many
occasions that there would be nothing extraordinary in my being
so on this, and, at the time of which I speak, I was so enveloped in
profound darkness that it was impossible for me to come at any
kind of truth.

M. Vernes bore the imputation with a moderation more than
astonishing in a man who was supposed not to have deserved it,
and after the fury with which he was seized on former occasions.
He wrote me two or three letters in very guarded terms with a
view, as it appeared to me, to endeavour by my answers to discover how far I was certain of his being the author of the paper,
and whether or not I had any proofs against him. I wrote him two
short answers, severe in the sense, but politely expressed, and with
which he was not displeased. To his third letter, perceiving he
wished to form with me a kind of correspondence, I returned no
answer, and he got d'Ivernois to speak to me. Madame Cramer
wrote to du Peyrou, telling him she was certain the libel was not
by Vernes. This however did not make me change my opinion.
But as it was possible I might be deceived, and that if I were, I

owed Vernes an explicit reparation, I sent him word by d'Ivernois I would make him such a one as he should think proper, provided he would name to me the real author of the libel, or at least prove that he himself was not so. I went farther: feeling that, after all, were he not culpable, I had no right to call upon him for proofs of any kind, I stated, in a memoir of considerable length, the reasons whence I had inferred my conclusion, and determined to submit them to the judgement of an arbitrator, against whom Vernes could not except. But few people would guess the arbitrator of whom I made choice; the Council of Geneva.[1] I declared at the end of the memoir, that if, after having examined it, and made such enquiries as should seem necessary, the Council pronounced M. Vernes not to be the author of the libel, from that moment I should be fully persuaded he was not, and would immediately go and throw myself at his feet, and ask his pardon until I had obtained it. I can say with the greatest truth that my ardent zeal for equity, the uprightness and generosity of my heart, and my confidence in the love of justice innate in every mind, never appeared more fully and perceptibly than in this wise and touching memoir, in which I took, without hesitating, my most implacable enemies for arbitrators between a calumniator and myself. I read to du Peyrou what I had written: he advised me to suppress it, and I did so. He wished me to wait for the proofs Vernes promised, and I am still waiting for them; he thought it best I should in the meantime be silent, and I held my tongue, and shall do so the rest of my life, censured as I am for having brought against Vernes a heavy imputation, false and unsupported by proof, although I am still fully persuaded, nay, as convinced as I am of my existence, that he is the author of the libel. My memoir is in the hands of du Peyrou. Should it ever be published, my reasons will be found in it, and the heart of Jean-Jacques, with which my contemporaries would not be acquainted, will I hope be known.

I have now to proceed to my catastrophe at Motiers, and to my departure from Val de Travers, after a residence of two years and a half, and an eight months' suffering with unshaken constancy of the most unworthy treatment. It is impossible for me clearly to recollect the circumstances of this disagreeable period, but a detail of them will be found in a publication to that effect by du Peyrou, of which I shall hereafter have occasion to speak.

After the departure of Madame de Verdelin the fermentation

---

[1] The last four words, necessary to the sense, but omitted by the Geneva MS., are supplied from that of Paris.

increased, and, notwithstanding the reiterated rescripts of the King, the frequent orders of the council of state, and the cares of the châtelain and magistrates of the place, the people, seriously considering me as Antichrist, and perceiving all their clamours to be of no effect, seemed at length determined to proceed to violence; stones were already thrown after me in the roads, but I was however in general at too great a distance to receive any harm from them. At last, in the night of the fair of Motiers, which is in the beginning of September,[1] I was attacked in my habitation in such a manner as to endanger the lives of everybody in the house.

At midnight I heard a great noise in the gallery which ran along the back part of the house. A shower of stones thrown against the window and the door which opened to the gallery, fell into it with so much noise and violence, that my dog, which usually slept there, and had began to bark, ceased from fright, and ran into a corner gnawing and scratching the planks to endeavour to make his escape. I immediately rose, and was preparing to go from my chamber into the kitchen, when a stone thrown by a vigorous arm crossed the latter, after having broken the window, forced open the door of my chamber, and fell at my feet, so that had I been a moment sooner upon the floor I should have had the stone against my stomach. I judged the noise had been made to bring me to the door, and the stone thrown to receive me as I went out. I ran into the kitchen, where I found Thérèse, who also had risen, and was tremblingly making her way to me as fast as she could. We placed ourselves against a wall out of the direction of the window to avoid the stones, and deliberate upon what was best to be done; for going out to call assistance was the certain means of getting ourselves knocked on the head. Fortunately the maid-servant of an old man who lodged under me was waked by the noise, and got up and ran to call the châtelain, whose house was next to mine. He jumped from his bed, put on his robe de chambre, and instantly came to me with the guard, which, on account of the fair, went the round that night, and was just at hand. The châtelain was so alarmed at the sight of the effects of what had happened that he turned pale, and on seeing the stones in the gallery, exclaimed, Good God! here is a quarry! On examining below stairs, the door of a little court was found to have been forced, and there was an appearance of an attempt having been made to get into

---

[1] This attack — which some allege to have been "staged" by Thérèse — took place on the night of Sept. 6, 1765.

the house by the gallery. On enquiring the reason why the guard had neither prevented nor perceived the disturbance, it came out that the guards of Motiers had insisted upon doing duty that night out of their turn, although it was the turn of those of another village.

The next day the châtelain sent his report to the council of state, which two days afterwards sent an order to enquire into the affair, to promise a reward and secrecy to those who should impeach such as were guilty, and in the meantime to place, at the expense of the Prince, guards about my house, and that of the châtelain, which joined to it. The day after the disturbance, Colo-

nel Pury, the attorney-general Meuron, the châtelain Martinet, the Receiver Guyenet, the treasurer d'Ivernois and his father, in a word, every person of consequence in the country, came to see me, and united their solicitations to persuade me to yield to the storm, and leave, at least for a time, a parish in which I could no longer live in safety nor with honour. I perceived even that the châtelain was frightened at the fury of the people, and apprehending it might extend to himself, would be glad to see me depart as soon as possible, that he might no longer have the trouble of protecting me there, and be able to quit the parish himself, which he did after my departure. I therefore yielded to their solicitations, and this with but little pain, for the hatred of the people so afflicted my heart that I was no longer able to support it.

I had a choice of places to retire to. After Madame de Verdelin returned to Paris, she had, in several letters, mentioned a Mr. Walpole, whom she called My Lord, who, having a strong desire to serve me, proposed to me an asylum at one of his country houses, of the situation of which she gave me the most agreeable description; entering, relative to lodging and subsistence, into a detail which proved she and Lord Walpole had held particular consultations upon the project. My Lord Marshal had always advised me to go to England or Scotland, and in case of my determining upon the latter, offered me there an asylum. But he offered me another at Potsdam, near to his person, and which tempted me more than all the rest. He had just communicated to me what the King had said to him upon my going there, which was a kind of invitation to me from that monarch, and the Duchess of Saxe-Gotha depended so much upon my taking the journey that she wrote to me, desiring I would go to see her in my way to the Court of Prussia, and stay some time before I proceeded farther; but I was so attached to Switzerland that I could not resolve to quit it so long as it was possible for me to live there, and I seized this opportunity to execute a project of which I had for several months conceived the idea, and of which I have deferred speaking that I might not interrupt my narrative.

This project consisted in going to reside in the island of Saint-Pierre, an estate belonging to the hospital of Berne, in the middle of the lake of Bienne. In a pedestrian pilgrimage I had made the preceding year with du Peyrou we had visited this isle, with which I was so much delighted, that I had since that time incessantly thought of the means of making it my place of residence. The greatest obstacle to my wishes arose from the property of the island being vested in the people of Berne, who three years before had driven me from amongst them; and, besides the mortification of returning to live with people who had given me so unfavourable a reception, I had reason to fear they would leave me no more at peace in the island than they had done at Yverdun. I had consulted the Lord Marshal upon the subject, who, thinking as I did that the people of Berne would be glad to see me banished to the island, and to keep me there as a hostage for the works I might be tempted to write, had sounded their dispositions by means of one M. Sturler, his old neighbour at Colombier. M. Sturler addressed himself to the chiefs of the state, and, according to their answer, assured the Marshal the Bernois, sorry for their past behaviour, wished nothing more than to see me settled in the island of Saint-

Pierre, and to leave me there at peace. As an additional precaution, before I determined to reside there, I desired Colonel Chaillet to make new enquiries. He confirmed what I had already heard, and the Receiver of the island having obtained from his superiors permission to lodge me in it, I thought I might without danger go to his house, with the tacit consent of the sovereign and the proprietors; for I could not expect the people of Berne would openly acknowledge the injustice they had done me, and thus act contrary to the most inviolable maxim of all sovereigns.

The island of Saint-Pierre, called at Neuchâtel the island of La Motte, in the middle of the lake of Bienne, is about half a league in circumference; but in this little space all the chief productions necessary to subsistence are found. The island has fields, meadows, orchards, woods, and vineyards, and all these, favoured by variegated and mountainous situations, form a distribution the more agreeable, as the parts, not being discovered all at once, are seen successively to advantage, and make the island appear greater than it really is. A very elevated terrace forms the western part of it, and commands Gleresse and La Bonneville. This terrace is planted with trees which form a long alley, interrupted in the middle by a great saloon, in which, during the vintage, the people from the neighbouring shores assemble on Sundays and divert themselves. There is but one house in the whole island, but that is very spacious and convenient, inhabited by the Receiver, and situated in a hollow by which it is sheltered from the winds.

Five or six hundred paces to the south of the island of Saint-Pierre, is another island considerably less than the former, wild and uncultivated, which appears to have been detached from the greater isle by storms: its gravelly soil produces nothing but willows and persicaria, but there is in it a high hill well covered with greensward and very pleasant. The form of the lake is an almost regular oval. The banks, less rich than those of the lakes of Geneva and Neuchâtel, form a beautiful decoration, especially towards the western part, which is well peopled, and edged with vineyards at the foot of a chain of mountains, something like those of Côte-Rôtie, but which produce not such excellent wine. The bailiwick of Saint-Jean, La Bonneville, Bienne, and Nidau lies in a line from the south to the north, at the extremity of the lake, the whole interspersed with very agreeable villages.

Such was the asylum I had prepared for myself, and to which I was determined to retire after quitting Val de Travers.[1] This

1 It may perhaps be necessary to remark that I left there an enemy in M. du

choice was so agreeable to my peaceful inclinations, and my solitary and indolent disposition, that I consider it as one of the pleasing reveries, of which I am most passionately fond. I thought I should in that island be more separated from men, more sheltered from their outrages, and sooner forgotten by mankind; in a word, more abandoned to the delightful pleasures of inaction and a contemplative life. I could have wished to have been confined in it in such a manner as to have had no more intercourse with mortals, and I certainly took every measure I could imagine to relieve me from the necessity of troubling my head about them.

The great question was that of subsistence, and by the dearness of provisions, and the difficulty of carriage, this is expensive in the island; the inhabitants are besides at the mercy of the Receiver. This difficulty was removed by an arrangement which du Peyrou made with me, in becoming a substitute for the company which had undertaken and abandoned my general edition. I gave him all the materials necessary, and made the proper arrangement and distribution. To the engagement between us I added that of giving him the memoirs of my life, and made him the general depositary of all my papers, under the express condition of making no use of them until after my death, having it at heart quietly to end my days without doing anything which should again bring me back to the recollection of the public. The life annuity he undertook to pay me was sufficient to my subsistence. My Lord Marshal having recovered all his property, had offered me twelve hundred livres a year, only half of which I accepted. He wished to send me the principal, but this I refused on account of the difficulty of placing it. He then sent the amount to du Peyrou, in whose hands it remained, and who pays me the annuity according to the terms agreed upon with His Lordship. Adding therefore to the result of my agreement with du Peyrou, the annuity of the Marshal, two-thirds of which were reversible to Thérèse after my death, and the annuity of three hundred livres from Duchesne, I was assured of a genteel subsistence for myself, and after me for Thérèse, to whom I left seven hundred livres a year, from the annuities paid me by Rey and the Lord Marshal; I had therefore no longer to fear a want of bread for her or myself. But it was ordained that honour should oblige me to reject all those resources

Terreaux, mayor of Verrières, not much esteemed in the country, but who has a brother, said to be an honest man, in the office of M. de St. Florentin. The mayor had been to see him some time before my adventure. Little remarks of this kind, though of no consequence in themselves, may lead to the discovery of many underhand dealings. (*Note by Rousseau.*)

which fortune and my labours placed within my reach, and that I should die as poor as I had lived. It will be seen whether or not, without reducing myself to the last degree of infamy, I could abide by the engagements which care has always been taken to render ignominious, by depriving me of every other resource to force me to consent to my own dishonour. How was it possible anybody could doubt of the choice I should make in such an alternative? Others have judged of my heart by their own.

My mind at ease relative to subsistence, I was without care upon every other subject. Although I left in the world the field open to my enemies, there remained in the noble enthusiasm by which my writings were dictated, and in the constant uniformity of my principles, an evidence of the uprightness of my heart, which answered to that deducible from my conduct in favour of my natural disposition. I had no need of any other defence against my calumniators. They might under my name describe another man, but it was impossible they should deceive such as were unwilling to be imposed upon. I could have given them my whole life to animadvert upon, with a certainty, notwithstanding all my faults and weaknesses, and my want of aptitude to support the lightest yoke, of their finding me in every situation a just and good man, without bitterness, hatred, or jealousy, ready to acknowledge my errors, and still more prompt to forget the injuries I received from others; seeking all my happiness in love, friendship, and affection, and in everything carrying my sincerity even to imprudence and the most incredible disinterestedness.

I therefore in some measure took leave of the age in which I lived and my contemporaries, and bade adieu to the world, with an intention to confine myself for the rest of my days to that island; such was my resolution, and it was there I hoped to execute the great project of the indolent life to which I had until then uselessly consecrated the little activity with which heaven had endowed me. The island was going to become for me that of Papimanie, that happy country where the inhabitants sleep.

Où l'on fait plus, où l'on fait nulle chose.[1]

This *more* was everything for me, for I never much regretted sleep; indolence is sufficient to my happiness, and provided I do nothing, I had rather dream waking than asleep. Being past the age of romantic projects, and having been more stunned than

---

[1] Quoted from La Fontaine, *Le Diable de Papefiguière.*

flattered by the trumpet of fame, my only hope was that of living at ease, and constantly at leisure. This is the life of the blessed in the world to come, and for the rest of mine here below I made it my supreme happiness.

They who reproach me with so many contradictions, will not fail here to add another to the number. I have observed the indolence of great companies made them insupportable to me, and I am now seeking solitude for the sole purpose of abandoning myself to inaction. This, however, is my disposition; if there be in it

a contradiction, it proceeds from nature and not from me; but there is so little that it is precisely on that account that I am always consistent. The indolence of company is burdensome because it is forced. That of solitude is charming because it is free, and depends upon the will. In company I suffer cruelly by inaction because this is of necessity, I must there remain nailed to my chair, or stand upright like a picket, without stirring hand or foot, not daring to run, jump, sing, exclaim, nor gesticulate when I please, not allowed even to dream, suffering at the same time the fatigue of inaction and all the torment of constraint; obliged to pay attention to every foolish thing uttered, and to all the idle compliments paid, and constantly wear out my Minerva that I may not fail to introduce in my turn my jest or my lie. And this is called idleness! It is the labour of the galley-slave.

The indolence I love is not that of a lazy fellow who sits with his arms across in total inaction, and thinks no more than he acts, but that of a child which is incessantly in motion doing nothing, and that of a dotard who wanders while his limbs are at rest. I love to amuse myself with trifles, by beginning a hundred things and never finishing one of them, by going and coming as I take either into my head, by changing my project at every instant, by following a fly through all its windings, in wishing to overturn a rock to see what is under it, by undertaking with ardour the work of ten years, and abandoning it without regret at the end of ten minutes; finally, in musing from morning until night without order or coherence, and in following in everything the caprice of the moment.

Botany, such as I have always considered it, and of which after my own manner I began to become passionately fond, was precisely an idle study, proper to fill up the void of my leisure, without leaving room for the delirium of imagination or the weariness of total inaction. Carelessly wandering in the woods and the country, mechanically gathering here a flower and there a branch; eating my morsel almost by chance, observing a thousand and a thousand times the same things, and always with the same interest, because I always forgot them, were to me the means of passing an eternity without a weary moment. However elegant, admirable, and variegated the structure of plants may be, it does not strike an ignorant eye sufficiently to fix the attention. The constant analogy, with, at the same time, the prodigious variety which reigns in their conformation, gives pleasure to those only who have already some idea of the vegetable system. Others at the sight of these treasures of nature feel nothing more than a stupid and monotonous admiration. They see nothing in detail because they know not for what to look, nor do they perceive the whole, having no idea of the chain of connexion and combinations which overwhelms with its wonders the mind of the observer. I was arrived at that happy point of knowledge, and my want of memory was such as constantly to keep me there, that I knew little enough to make the whole new to me, and yet everything that was necessary to make me sensible of the beauties of all the parts. The different soils into which the island, although little, was divided, offered a sufficient variety of plants, for the study and amusement of my whole life. I was determined not to leave a blade of grass without analysing it, and I began already to take measures for compiling, with an immense collection of curious observations, the *Flora Petrinsularis.*

I sent for Thérèse, who brought with her my books and effects. We boarded with the Receiver of the island. His wife had sisters at Nidau, who by turns came to see her, and were company for Thérèse. I here made the experiment of the agreeable life which I could have wished to continue to the end of my days, and the pleasure I found in it only served to make me feel to a greater degree the bitterness of that by which it was shortly to be succeeded.

I have ever been passionately fond of water, and the sight of it throws me into a delightful reverie, although frequently without a determinate object. Immediately after I rose from my bed I never failed, if the weather was fine, to run to the terrace to respire the fresh and salubrious air of the morning, and glide my eye over the horizon of the lake, bounded by banks and mountains ravishing to the view. I know no homage more worthy of the Divinity than the silent admiration excited by the contemplation of His works, and which is not exteriorly expressed. I can easily comprehend the reason why the inhabitants of great cities, who see nothing but walls, streets, and crimes, have but little faith; but not whence it happens that people in the country, and especially such as live in solitude, can possibly be without it. How comes it to pass these do not a hundred times a day elevate their minds in ecstasy to the author of the wonders which strike their senses? For my part, it is especially at rising, wearied by a want of sleep, that long habit inclines me to this elevation which imposes not the fatigue of thinking. But to this effect my eyes must be struck with the ravishing beauties of nature. In my chamber I pray less frequently, and not so fervently; but at the view of a fine landscape I feel myself moved, but by what I am unable to tell. I have somewhere read of a wise bishop who in a visit to his diocese found an old woman whose only prayer consisted in the single interjection Oh! Good mother, said he to her, continue to pray in this manner; your prayer is better than ours. This better prayer is mine also.

After breakfast, I hastened, with a frown on my brow, to write a few pitiful letters, longing ardently for the moment after which I should have no more to write. I busied myself for a few minutes about my books and papers, to unpack and arrange them, rather than to read what they contained; and this arrangement, which to me became the work of Penelope, gave me the pleasure of musing for a while. I then grew weary and quitted my books to spend the three or four hours which remained to me of the morning in the study of botany, and especially of the system of Linnæus, of which I became so passionately fond, that, after having felt how useless my attachment to it was, I could not entirely shake it off. This great observer is, in my opinion, the only one who, with Ludwig, has hitherto considered botany as a naturalist and a philosopher; but he has too much studied it in herbals and gardens, and not sufficiently in nature herself. For my part, whose garden was always the whole island, the moment I wanted to make or verify an observation, I ran into the woods or meadows with my book under my arm, and there laid myself upon the ground near the plant in question, to examine it at my ease as it stood. This method was of great service to me in gaining a knowledge of vegetables in their natural state, before they had been cultivated and changed in their nature by the hands of men. Fagon, first physician to Louis XIV, who named and perfectly knew all the plants in the royal garden, is said to have been so ignorant in the country as not to know how to distinguish the same plants. I am precisely the contrary. I know something of the work of nature, but nothing of that of the gardener.

I gave every afternoon totally up to my indolent and careless disposition, and to following without regularity the impulse of the moment. When the weather was calm I frequently went, immediately after I rose from dinner, and alone got into a little boat. The Receiver had taught me to row with one oar; I rowed out into the middle of the lake. The moment I withdrew from the bank, I felt a secret joy which almost made me leap, and of which it is impossible for me to tell or even comprehend the cause, if it were not a secret congratulation on my being out of reach of the wicked. I afterwards rowed alone about the lake, sometimes approaching the opposite bank, but never touching at it. I often let my boat float at the mercy of the wind and water, abandoning myself to reveries without object, and which by their stupidity were not the less agreeable. I sometimes exclaimed, O nature! O my mother! I am here under thy guardianship alone; here is no deceitful and cunning mortal to interfere between thee and me. In this manner I withdrew half a league from land; I could have wished the lake had been the ocean. However, to please my poor dog, who was not so fond as I was of such a long stay on the water, I commonly followed one constant course; this was going to land

at the little island, where I walked an hour or two, or laid myself
down on the grass at the summit of the hill, there to satiate myself
with the pleasure of admiring the lake and its environs, to examine and dissect all the herbs within my reach, and, like another
Robinson Crusoe, build myself an imaginary place of residence in
the island. I became very much attached to this eminence. When
I brought Thérèse, with the wife of the Receiver and her sisters, to
walk there, how proud was I to be their pilot and guide! We took
there rabbits to stock it. This was another source of pleasure to
Jean-Jacques. These animals rendered the island still more interesting to me. I afterwards went to it more frequently, and with
greater pleasure, to observe the progress of the new inhabitants.

To these amusements I added one which recalled to my recollection the delightful life I led at les Charmettes, and to which the
season particularly invited me. This was assisting in the rustic
labours of gathering of roots and fruits, of which Thérèse and I
made it a pleasure to partake, with the wife of the Receiver and
his family. I remember a Bernois, one M. Kirkebergher, coming
to see me, found me perched upon a tree with a sack fastened to
my waist, and already so full of apples that I could not stir from
the branch on which I stood. I was not sorry to be caught in this
and similar situations. I hoped the people of Berne, witnesses to
the employment of my leisure, would no longer think of disturbing my tranquillity, but leave me at peace in my solitude. I should
have preferred being confined there by their desire than by my
own; this would have rendered the continuation of my repose
more certain.

This is another declaration upon which I am certain in advance
of the incredulity of many of my readers, who obstinately continue to judge of me by themselves, although they cannot but have
seen, in the course of my life, a thousand internal affections, which
bore no resemblance to any of theirs. But what is still more extraordinary is, that while they refuse me every sentiment, good or
indifferent, which they have not, they are constantly ready to
attribute to me such bad ones as cannot enter the heart of man;
they then find it easy to set me in opposition to nature, and to
make of me such a monster as cannot in reality exist. Nothing absurd appears to them incredible the moment it has a tendency to
blacken me, and nothing in the least extraordinary seems to them
possible if it tends to do me honour.

But notwithstanding what they may think or say, I will still
continue faithfully to state what J.-J. Rousseau was, did, and

thought; without explaining or justifying the singularity of his sentiments and ideas, or endeavouring to discover whether or not others have thought as he did. I became so delighted with the island of Saint-Pierre, and my residence there was so agreeable to me, that, by concentring all my desires within it, I formed the wish that I might stay there to the end of my life. The visits I had to return in the neighbourhood, the journeys I should be under the necessity of making to Neuchâtel, Bienne, Yverdun, and Nidau, already fatigued my imagination. A day passed out of the island seemed to me a loss of so much happiness, and to go beyond the bounds of the lake was to go out of my element. Past experiences had besides rendered me apprehensive. The satisfaction alone I received from anything whatever was sufficient to make me fear the loss of it, and the ardent desire I had to end my days in that island, was inseparable from the apprehension of being obliged to leave it. I had contracted a habit of going in the evening to sit upon the sandy shore, especially when the lake was agitated. I felt a singular pleasure in seeing the waves break at my feet. I formed of them in my imagination the image of the tumult of the world contrasted with the peace of my habitation, and this pleasing idea sometimes softened me even to tears. The repose I enjoyed with ecstasy was disturbed by nothing but the fear of being deprived of it, but this inquietude was accompanied with some bitterness. I felt my situation so precarious as not to dare to depend upon its continuance. Ah! how willingly, said I to myself, would I renounce the liberty of quitting this place, for which I have no desire, for the assurance of always remaining in it. Instead of being permitted to stay here by favour, why am I not detained by force! They who suffer me to remain may in a moment drive me away, and can I hope my persecutors, seeing me happy, will leave me here to continue to be so? Permitting me to live in the island is but a trifling favour, I could wish to be condemned to do it, and constrained to remain here that I may not be obliged to go elsewhere. I cast an envious eye upon the happy Micheli Ducrêt, who, quiet in the castle of Arberg, had only to determine to be happy to become so. In fine, by abandoning myself to these reflections and the alarming apprehensions of new storms always ready to break over my head, I came to desire, with an incredible ardour, that instead of merely suffering me to reside in the island, the Bernois would give it me for a perpetual prison; and I can assert that had it depended upon me to get myself condemned to this, I would most joyfully have done it, preferring a thousand times the necessity of passing my life there to the danger of being driven to another place.

This fear did not long remain vain. When I least expected what was to happen, I received a letter from the bailiff of Nidau, within whose jurisdiction the island of Saint-Pierre was; by his letter he announced to me from Their Excellencies, an order to quit the island and their states. I thought myself in a dream. Nothing could be less natural, reasonable, or foreseen than such an order: for I had considered my apprehensions rather as the result of inquietude in a man whose imagination was disturbed by his misfortunes, than as proceeding from a foresight which could have the least foundation. The measures I had taken to ensure myself the tacit consent of the sovereign, the tranquillity with which I had been left to make my establishment, the visits of several people from Berne, and that of the bailiff himself, who had shown me much friendship and attention, and the rigour of the season, in which it was barbarous to expel a man who was sickly and infirm, all these circumstances made me and many people believe there was some mistake in the order, and that ill-disposed people had purposely chosen the time of the vintage, and the vacation of the senate, hastily to do me an injury.

Had I yielded to the first impulse of my indignation I should immediately have departed. But to what place was I to go? What was to become of me at the beginning of the winter, without object, preparation, guide, or carriage? Not to leave my papers and effects at the mercy of the first comer, time was necessary to make proper arrangements, and it was not stated in the order whether or not this would be granted me. The continuance of misfortune began to weigh down my courage. For the first time in my life I felt my natural haughtiness stoop to the yoke of necessity, and, notwithstanding the murmurs of my heart, I was obliged to demean myself by asking for a delay. I applied to M. de Graffenried, who had sent me the order, for an explanation of it. His letter, conceived in the strongest terms of disapprobation of the step that had been taken, assured me that it was with the greatest regret he communicated to me the nature of it, and the expressions of grief and esteem it contained seemed so many gentle invitations to open to him my heart: I did so: I had no doubt but my letter would open the eyes of my persecutors to their barbarity, and that if so cruel an order was not revoked, at least a reasonable delay, perhaps the whole winter, to make the necessary preparations for my retreat, and to choose a place of abode, would be granted me.

Whilst I waited for an answer, I reflected upon my situation, and deliberated upon the steps I had to take. I perceived so many difficulties on all sides, the vexation I had suffered had so strongly affected me, and my health was then in such a bad state, that I was quite overcome, and the effect of my discouragement was to deprive me of the little resource which remained in my mind, by which I might, as well as it was possible to do it, have withdrawn myself from my melancholy situation. In whatever asylum I should take refuge, it appeared impossible to avoid either of the two means made use of to expel me. One of these was to stir up against me the populace by secret manœuvres; and the other to drive me away by open force, without giving a reason for so doing. I could not therefore depend upon a safe retreat, unless I went in search of it farther than my strength and the season

seemed likely to permit. These circumstances again bringing to my recollection the ideas which had lately occurred to me, I would have desired and proposed to my persecutors to condemn me to perpetual imprisonment, rather than oblige me incessantly to wander upon the earth, by successively expelling me from the asylums of which I should make choice. Two days after my first letter to M. de Graffenried, I wrote him a second, desiring he would state what I had proposed to Their Excellencies. The answer from Berne to both was an order, conceived in the most formal and severe terms, to go out of the island, and leave every territory mediate and immediate of the republic, within the space of twenty-four hours, and never to enter them again under the most grievous penalties.

This was a terrible moment. I have since that time felt greater anguish, but never have I been more embarrassed. What afflicted me most was being forced to abandon the project which had made me desirous to pass the winter in the island. It is now time I should relate the fatal anecdote which completed my disasters, and involved in my ruin an unfortunate people whose rising virtues already promised to equal one day those of Rome and Sparta.

I had spoken of Corsicans in the *Social Contract* as a new people, the only nation in Europe not too worn out for legislation, and had expressed the great hope there was of such a people, if it were fortunate enough to have a wise legislator. My work was read by some of the Corsicans, who were sensible of the honourable manner in which I had spoken of them, and the necessity under which they found themselves of endeavouring to establish their republic, made their chiefs think of asking me for my ideas upon the subject. M. Buttafuoco, of one of the first families in the country, and captain in France in the Royal Italian Regiment, wrote to me to that effect, and sent me several papers for which I had asked to make myself acquainted with the history of the nation and the state of the country. M. Paoli, also, wrote to me several times, and although I felt such an undertaking to be superior to my abilities, I thought I could not refuse to give my assistance in so great and noble a work, the moment I should have acquired all the necessary information. It was to this effect I answered both these gentlemen, and the correspondence lasted until my departure.

Precisely at the same time, I heard that France was sending troops to Corsica, and that she had entered into a treaty with the Genoese. This treaty and sending of troops gave me uneasiness, and without imagining I had any farther relation with the business I thought it impossible, and the attempt ridiculous, to labour at an undertaking which required such undisturbed tranquillity as the political institution of a people in the moment when perhaps they were upon the point of being subjugated. I did not conceal my fears from M. Buttafuoco, who rather relieved me from them by the assurance that, were there in the treaty things contrary to the liberty of his country, a good citizen like himself would not remain as he did in the service of France. In fact, his zeal for the legislation of the Corsicans, and his close connexion with M. Paoli, could not leave a doubt on my mind respecting him; and when I heard he made frequent journeys to Versailles and Fontainebleau, and had relations with M. de Choiseul, all I concluded from the whole was, that with respect to the real intentions of France, he had assurances which he gave me to understand, but concerning which he did not choose openly to explain himself by letter.

This removed a part of my apprehensions. Yet, as I could not comprehend the meaning of the transportation of troops from France, nor reasonably suppose they were sent to Corsica to protect the liberty of the inhabitants, which they of themselves were very well able to defend against the Genoese, I could neither make myself perfectly easy, nor seriously undertake the plan of the proposed legislation, until I had solid proofs that the whole was serious, and that the parties meant not to trifle with me. I much wished for an interview with M. Buttafuoco, as that was certainly the best means of coming at the explanation I wished. Of this he gave me hopes, and I waited for it with the greatest impatience. I know not whether he really intended me any interview or not; but had this even been the case, my misfortunes would have prevented me from profiting by it.

The more I considered the proposed undertaking, and the farther I advanced in the examination of the papers I had in my hands, the greater I found the necessity of studying, in the country, the people for whom institutions were to be made, the soil they inhabited, and all the relative circumstances by which it was necessary to appropriate to them that institution. I daily perceived more clearly the impossibility of acquiring at a distance all the information necessary to guide me. This I wrote to M. Buttafuoco, and he felt it as I did. Although I did not form the precise resolution of going to Corsica, I considered a good deal of the means necessary to make that voyage. I mentioned it to M. Dastier, who, having formerly served in the island under M. de

Maillebois, was necessarily acquainted with it. He used every effort to dissuade me from this intention, and I confess the frightful description he gave me of the Corsicans and their country, considerably abated the desire I had of going to live amongst them.

But when the persecutions of Motiers made me think of quitting Switzerland, this desire was again strengthened by the hope of at length finding amongst these islanders the repose refused me in every other place. One thing only alarmed me, which was my unfitness for the active life to which I was going to be condemned, and the aversion I had always had to it. My disposition, proper for meditating at leisure and in solitude, was not so for speaking and acting, and treating of affairs with men. Nature which had endowed me with the first talent had refused me the last. Yet I felt that without taking a direct and active part in public affairs, I should, as soon as I was in Corsica, be under the necessity of yielding to the desires of the people, and of frequently conferring with the chiefs. The object even of the voyage required that, instead of seeking retirement, I should, in the heart of the country, endeavour to gain the information of which I stood in need. It was certain I should no longer be master of my own time, and that, in spite of myself, precipitated into a vortex in which I was not born to move, I should there lead a life contrary to my inclination and never appear but to disadvantage. I foresaw that, ill suporting by my presence the opinion my books might have given the Corsicans of my capacity, I should lose my reputation amongst them, and, as much to their prejudice as to my own, be deprived of the confidence they had in me, without which, however, I could not successfully produce the work they expected from me. I was certain that, by thus going out of my sphere, I should become useless to the inhabitants, and render myself unhappy.

Tormented, beaten by storms from every quarter, and for several years past fatigued by journeys and persecution, I strongly felt a want of the repose of which my barbarous enemies wantonly deprived me; I sighed more than ever after that amiable indolence, that soft tranquillity of body and mind, which I had so much desired, and to which, recovered from the chimeras of love and friendship, my heart confined its supreme felicity. I viewed with terror the work I was about to undertake; the tumultuous life into which I was to enter made me tremble, and if the grandeur, beauty, and utility of the object animated my courage, the impossibility of conquering so many difficulties entirely deprived me of it. Twenty years of profound meditation in solitude would have been less painful to me than an active life of six months in the midst of men and public affairs, with a certainty of not succeeding in my undertaking.

I thought of an expedient which seemed proper to obviate every difficulty. Pursued by the underhand dealings of my secret persecutors to every place in which I took refuge, and seeing no other except Corsica where I could in my old days hope for the repose I had until then been everywhere deprived of, I resolved to go there with the directions of M. Buttafuoco as soon as this was possible, but to live there in tranquillity; renouncing, in appearance, everything relative to legislation, and in some measure to make my hosts a return for their hospitality, to confine myself to writing in the country the history of the Corsicans, with a reserve in my own mind of the intention of secretly acquiring the necessary information to become more useful to them should I see a probability of success. In this manner, by not entering into an engagement, I hoped to be enabled better to meditate in secret and more at my ease, a plan which might be useful to their purpose, and this without much breaking in upon my dearly beloved solitude, or submitting to a kind of life which I had ever found insupportable and for which I had no talent.

But the journey was not, in my situation, a thing so easy to get over. According to what M. Dastier had told me of Corsica, I could not expect to find there the most simple conveniences of life, except such as I should take with me: linen, clothes, plate, kitchen furniture, paper, and books, all must be conveyed thither. To get there myself with my Governess, I had the Alps to cross, and in a journey of two hundred leagues to drag after me all my baggage; I had also to pass through the states of several sovereigns, and, according to the example set by all Europe, I had, after what had befallen me, naturally to expect to find obstacles in every quarter, and that each sovereign would think he did himself honour by overwhelming me with some new insult, and violating in my person all the rights of persons and humanity. The immense expense, fatigue, and risk of such a journey made a previous consideration of them, and weighing every difficulty, the first step necessary. The idea of being alone, and, at my age, without resource, far removed from all my acquaintance, and at the mercy of these barbarous and ferocious people, such as M. Dastier had described them to me, was sufficient to make me deliberate before I resolved to expose myself to such dangers. I ardently wished for the interview for which M. Buttafuoco had given me reason to hope, and I waited the result of it to guide me in my determination.

Whilst I thus hesitated, came on the persecutions of Motiers, which obliged me to retire. I was not prepared for a long journey, especially to Corsica. I expected to hear from Buttafuoco; I took refuge in the island of Saint-Pierre, whence I was driven at the beginning of winter, as I have already stated. The Alps, covered with snow, then rendered my emigration impracticable, especially with the precipitation prescribed me. It is true, the extravagant severity of a like order rendered the execution of it almost impossible; for, in the midst of that concentred solitude, surrounded by water, and having but twenty-four hours after receiving the order to prepare for my departure, and find a boat and carriages to get out of the island and the territory, had I had wings, I should scarcely have been able to pay obedience to it. This I wrote to the bailiff of Nidau, in answer to his letter, and hastened to take my departure from this country of iniquity. In this manner was I obliged to abandon my favorite project, for which reason, not having in my oppression been able to prevail upon my persecutors to dispose of me otherwise, I determined, in consequence of the invitation of my Lord Marshal, upon a journey to Berlin, leaving Thérèse to pass the winter in the island of Saint-Pierre, with my books and effects, and depositing my papers in the hands of M. du Peyrou. I used so much diligence that next morning I left the island, and arrived at Bienne before noon. An accident which I cannot pass over in silence, had here like to have put an end to my journey.

As soon as the news of my having received an order to quit my asylum was circulated, I received a great number of visits from the neighbourhood, and especially from the Bernois, who came with the most detestable falsehood to flatter and soothe me, protesting that my persecutors had seized the moment of the vacation of the Senate to obtain and send me the order, which, said they, had excited the indignation of the Two Hundred. Some of these comforters came from the city of Bienne, a little free state within that of Berne, and amongst others a young man of the name of Wildremet, whose family was of the first rank, and had the greatest credit in that little city. Wildremet strongly solicited me in the name of his fellow citizens to choose my retreat amongst them, assuring me that they were anxiously desirous of it, and that they would think it an honour and their duty to make me forget the persecutions I had suffered; that with them I had nothing to fear from the influence of the Bernois, that Bienne was a free city, governed by its own laws, and that the citizens were unanimously resolved not to hearken to any solicitation which should be unfavourable to me.

Wildremet, perceiving all he could say to be ineffectual, brought to his aid several other persons, as well from Bienne and the environs as from Berne even, and amongst others the same Kirkebergher of whom I have spoken, who after my retreat to Switzerland had sought me out, and by his talents and principles had interested me in his favour. But I received much less expected and more weighty solicitation from M. Barthès, secretary to the embassy from France, who came with Wildremet to see me, exhorted me to accept his invitation, and surprised me by the lively and tender concern he seemed to feel for my situation. I did not know M. Barthès; however I perceived in what he said the warmth and zeal of friendship, and that he had it at heart to persuade me to fix my residence at Bienne. He made the most pompous eulogy of the city and its inhabitants, with whom he showed himself so intimately connected as to call them several times in my presence his patrons and fathers.

This from Barthès bewildered me in my conjectures. I had always suspected M. de Choiseul to be the secret author of all the persecutions I suffered in Switzerland. The conduct of the French resident at Geneva, and that of the ambassador at Soleure but too much confirmed my suspicion; I perceived the secret influence of France in everything that happened to me at Berne, Geneva, and Neuchâtel, and I did not think I had any powerful enemy in that kingdom, except the Duke de Choiseul. What therefore could I think of the visit of Barthès, and the tender concern he showed for my welfare? My misfortunes had not yet destroyed the confidence natural to my heart, and I had still to learn from experience to discern ambushes under the appearance of friendship. I sought with surprise the reason of the benevolence of M. Barthès; I was not weak enough to believe he had acted from himself; there was in his manner something public, affected even, which declared a concealed intention, and I was far from having found in any of these little subaltern agents that generous intrepidity which, in a similar employment, had often caused a ferment in my own heart.

I had formerly known something of the Chevalier Beauteville, at the castle of Montmorency; he had shown me marks of esteem: since his appointment to the embassy he had given me proofs of his not having entirely forgotten me, accompanied with an invitation to go and see him at Soleure. Though I did not accept this invitation, I was extremely sensible of his civility, not having been accustomed to be treated with such kindness by people in place. I presumed M. de Beauteville, obliged to follow his instructions in what related to the affairs of Geneva, yet, pitying me under my misfortunes, had by his private cares, prepared for me the asylum of Bienne, that I might live there in peace under his auspices. I was properly sensible of his attention, but without wishing to profit by it, and quite determined upon the journey to Berlin, I sighed after the moment in which I was to see my Lord Marshal, persuaded I should in future find real repose and lasting happiness nowhere but near his person.

On my departure from the island, Kirkebergher accompanied me to Bienne. I found Wildremet and other Biennois, who by the waterside waited my getting out of the boat. We all dined together at the inn, and on my arrival there my first care was to provide a chaise, being determined to set off the next morning. Whilst we were at dinner, these gentlemen repeated their solicitations to prevail upon me to stay with them, and this with such warmth and obliging protestations, that, notwithstanding all my resolutions, my heart, which has never been able to resist friendly attentions, received an impression by theirs: the moment they perceived I was shaken they redoubled their efforts with so much effect that I was at length overcome, and consented to remain at Bienne, at least until the spring.

Wildremet immediately set about providing me with a lodging, and boasted, as of a fortunate discovery, of a dirty little chamber in the back of a house, on the third story, looking into a courtyard, where I had for a view the display of the stinking skins of a dresser of chamois leather. My host was a little man of a mean appearance, and a good deal of a rascal: the next day after I went to his house, I heard he was a debauchee, a gamester, and in bad credit in the neighbourhood. He had neither wife, children, nor servant, and, shut up in my solitary chamber, I was, in the midst of the most agreeable country in the world, lodged in a manner to make me die of melancholy in the course of a few days. What affected me most was, that notwithstanding what I had heard of the anxious wish of the inhabitants to receive me amongst them, I had not perceived, as I passed through the streets, anything polite towards me in their manners, or obliging in their looks. I was however determined to remain there, when I learned, saw, and felt, the very day after, that there was in the city a terrible ferment, of which I was the cause. Several persons hastened obligingly to inform me that on the next day I was to receive an order, conceived in the most severe terms, immediately to quit the state, that is the city. I had nobody in whom I could confide: all those who had detained me were dispersed. Wildremet had disappeared, I heard no more of Barthès, and it did not appear that his recommendations had brought me into great favour with those whom he had styled his patrons and fathers. One, M. de Vau-Travers, a Bernois, who had an agreeable house not far from the city, offered it me for my asylum, hoping, as he said, that I might there avoid being stoned. The advantages of this offer were not sufficiently flattering to tempt me to prolong my stay with these hospitable people.

Yet, having lost three days by the delay, I had greatly exceeded the twenty-four hours the Bernois had given me to quit their states, and, knowing their severity, I was not without apprehensions as to the manner in which they would suffer me to cross them, when the bailiff of Nidau came opportunely and relieved me from my embarrassment. As he had highly disapproved of the violent proceedings of their Excellencies, he thought, in his generosity, he owed me some public proof of his taking no part in them, and had the courage to leave his bailiwick to come and pay me a visit at Bienne. He did me this favour the evening before my departure, and far from coming incognito he affected ceremony, coming *in fiocchi*[1] in his coach with his secretary, and brought me a passport in his own name, that I might cross the state of Berne at my ease, and without fear of molestation. I was more flattered by the visit than by the passport, and should have been as sensible of the merit of it, had it had for object any other person whatsoever. Nothing makes a greater impression upon my heart than a well-timed act of courage in favour of the weak, unjustly oppressed.

At length, after having with difficulty procured a chaise, I next morning left this barbarous country, before the arrival of the deputation with which I was to be honoured, and even before I had seen Thérèse, to whom I had written to come to me, when I thought I should remain at Bienne, and whom I had scarcely time to countermand by a short letter, informing her of my new disaster.[2] In the third part of my memoirs, if ever I am able to

---

[1] "In full regimentals."

[2] The Paris MS. omits all from "I used so much diligence" (p. 631) to this point.

write them, I shall state in what manner, thinking to set off for Berlin, I really took my departure for England, and the means by which the two ladies who wished to dispose of my person, after having by their manœuvres driven me from Switzerland, where I was not sufficiently in their power, at last delivered me into the hands of their friend.

I added what follows on reading my memoirs to M. and Madame the Countess of Egmont, the Prince Pignatelli, the Marchioness of Mesme, and the Marquis of Juigné.

I have written the truth: if any person has heard of things contrary to those I have just stated, were they a thousand times proved, he has heard calumny and falsehood; and if he refuses thoroughly to examine and compare them with me whilst I am alive, he is not a friend either to justice or truth. For my part, I openly and without the least fear, declare, that whoever, even without having read my works, shall have examined with his own eyes my disposition, character, manners, inclinations, pleasures, and habits, and pronounce me a dishonest man, is himself one who deserves a gibbet.

Thus I concluded, and every person was silent. Madame d'Egmont was the only person who seemed affected: she visibly trembled, but soon recovered herself, and was silent like the rest of the company. Such were the fruits of my reading and declaration.